OGRAPHY.

Geo. Aikman Sculp.

The Treasury

OF THE

ENCYCLOPÆDIA BRITANNICA

This euphoric frontispiece from the 3rd edition (1788–1797) seems to suggest what riches the library (and, inferentially, the Britannica*) might unlock: learned disputations, all the arts and sciences, Adam and Eve disporting chastely among the beasts of the field, and, floating high above it all, perhaps the intrepid editor of the 2nd edition, James "Balloon" Tytler.*

The Treasury

OF THE

ENCYCLOPÆDIA BRITANNICA

More than two centuries of facts, curiosities, and discoveries from the most distinguished reference work of all time

GENERAL EDITOR

Clifton Fadiman

CONTRIBUTING EDITORS

BRUCE L. FELKNOR

ROBERT McHENRY

VIKING

VIKING
Published by the Penguin Group
Viking Penguin, a division of Penguin Books USA Inc.,
375 Hudson Street, New York, New York 10014, U.S.A.
Penguin Books Ltd, 27 Wrights Lane, London W8 5TZ, England
Penguin Books Australia Ltd, Ringwood, Victoria, Australia
Penguin Books Canada Ltd, 10 Alcorn Avenue, Suite 300,
Toronto, Ontario, Canada M4V 3B2
Penguin Books (N.Z.) Ltd, 182–190 Wairau Road,
Auckland 10, New Zealand

Penguin Books Ltd, Registered Offices:
Harmondsworth, Middlesex, England

First published in 1992 by Viking Penguin,
a division of Penguin Books USA Inc.

1 3 5 7 9 10 8 6 4 2

The endpapers reproduce the plate "Physical Geography"
from *Britannica*'s seventh edition (1830–42).

LIBRARY OF CONGRESS CATALOGING IN PUBLICATION DATA
The Treasury of the Encyclopædia Britannica: more than two centuries of facts, curiosities, and discoveries from the most distinguished reference work of all time/ compiled by Clifton Fadiman.
p. cm.
Includes index.
ISBN 0 670 83568 4
I. Fadiman, Clifton, 1904– . II. Encyclopaedia Britannica.
AC5.T74 1992
031—dc20 92-54069

Printed in the United States of America
Set in Bembo · Designed by Francesca Belanger

CONTENTS

Appendix

A NOTE FROM THE CHAIRMAN

One day in 1768, two gentlemen of Edinburgh, an engraver, Andrew Bell, and a printer, Colin Macfarquhar, engaged a local editor, William Smellie, and set in motion a train of events that profoundly affected the world of learning for well over two centuries.

To do so, they had first to round up a society of Edinburgh gentlemen who would agree to buy a series of pamphlets they proposed to issue every several weeks; at length, these pamphlets would be bound into the volumes of a new encyclopedia to be called *Britannica*.

One of the many surprises awaiting these optimists was that it would take them three years to complete the task. One may wonder what goals drove these original publishers, what fueled their bustling zeal to seek out subscribers and pay out money for paper and ink and editorial labors.

Their editor, William Smellie, answered the question for them all in his preface to what became the first edition of *Encyclopædia Britannica:* Utility, and the diffusion of knowledge—these were the goals, which "ought to be the principal intention of every publication."

After Macfarquhar died, Bell remained the principal proprietor of the encyclopedia, continuing to enlarge and improve it until his death in 1809, while the fourth edition was in press. His successor, Archibald Constable, having devised a grand plan for a landmark supplement to the 4th, 5th, and 6th editions, pressed forward with it even though it sapped his own fortune.

And so this great tradition continued through the years, the succession of publishers and editors breaking new ground, ever building the stature of the work and jealously guarding its integrity.

When Bell, Macfarquhar, and Smellie embarked on their magnificent venture in 1768, they were already conscious that a legacy could unfold, outliving them and passing on to succeeding generations. It was the awareness of this potential that helped direct their efforts.

Certainly for the publishers of *Britannica* in our own time, diligent stewardship of the tradition is of great, perhaps dominant, importance. That tradition may perhaps be summarized as ensuring the encyclopedia's authority, accuracy, comprehensiveness, and, as today's editors sometimes put it, presenting every respectable side of issues and theories still in dispute.

Responsible stewardship of the *Britannica* tradition demands far more than a mere preening over ancient laurels. It demands—and it receives—informed and continually inquiring attention to those original objectives of utility and diffusion, even as the sum of human knowledge multiplies ever faster.

That onrush of knowledge was already accelerating when the first edition began to appear. Indeed, it surely contributed to the decision of Bell and Macfarquhar to create a new encyclopedia. The samplings contained in this volume make it a kind of snapshot album of the *Britannica* tradition as it arose, evolved, and was refined, and as it is carried on to this day.

Stewardship over such a tradition carries immense responsibilities, but it also has its rewards. One of these is the pleasure of access to the memorable writings of those wise men and women, ancient and modern, who have made the *Encyclopædia Britannica* what it is.

And the principal intention of this publication is to share that pleasure with you.

—Robert P. Gwinn

PREFACE

Every great library must be a collection of obsolete information, offering us much that no longer passes for knowledge, leaving us to choose. But a great encyclopedia must do more. It must help by showing us the state of knowledge in our time, culling knowledge from ignorance, myth, and superstition. When an owner of the current *Encyclopædia Britannica* turns to it for the authoritative, up-to-date answer to any question, he may not realize that he is participating in a great human adventure of discovery. This quest for knowledge has gone on relentlessly—often with painful consequences—ever since Eve persuaded Adam to eat of the Apple. *Britannica* has led this quest in the English-speaking world and elsewhere for more than two centuries. This *Britannica* treasury allows us to join in the adventures, the misadventures, the suspense, and the drama of that quest.

Behind the scenes at *Britannica* the quest has been going on with the collaboration of the thousands of staff members during these centuries, with the assistance of the best minds and noblest spirits of the age—and at the greatest cost ever for such an adventure. By letting us share these efforts and sample the stages in man's most recent search for knowledge, this book is an adventure in self-discovery. We can have an encyclopedia-eye view of what Western mankind has been up to, and what it thought it knew.

From its beginning in 1768, *Britannica* was committed to the progress of knowledge, but every discovery of new knowledge is also a new discovery of our former ignorance—and so a reminder of how ephemeral may be our present "knowledge." To read these articles is not merely amusing. Of course it is chastening, but it can also be encouraging, reassuring us of the progress of knowledge.

We rejoice in this progress. Yet additions to our knowledge require a painful adjustment. Adding to what we know subtracts from what we thought we knew. "Facts" become myths. "There is a strong shadow," Goethe observed, "where there is much light." The stronger the light of new knowledge, the wider and deeper the shadows on old facts and fancies. During the past two centuries, every new edition of *Britannica*, with new realms of knowledge—in chemistry, physics, anatomy, physiology, economics, anthropology, history, psychology—has revealed vast areas of error and ignorance in earlier editions.

Britannica's quest for authenticity has left us a dividend that is shared in this treasury. For the authentic, originating voices of one generation become the voices of history to the next. Which has made the corpus of *Britannica* editions an unsung and vivid archive of modern history. Earlier editions of *Britannica* have brought us the Reverend Thomas Malthus on population growth, Sir Walter Scott on chivalry, Marie Curie on the discovery of radium, Sigmund Freud on psychoanalysis, George Bernard Shaw on socialism, Irene Castle on ballroom dancing, Lawrence of Arabia on guerrilla warfare, Albert Einstein on space-time, Orville Wright on his brother, Wilbur, Gene Tunney on boxing, and Leon Trotsky on Lenin.

When Thomas Henry Huxley, the great champion of Darwinian theories of evolution, was asked to write on the subject, he was reluctant. "Don't see how it is practicable to do justice to it with the time at my disposal," he wrote the editor, "though I should really like to do it and am at my wit's end to think of anybody else who can be trusted with it." We are not merely acquiring knowledge, we are witnessing history and hearing the authentic voices.

The survey of obsolete "knowledge" that this treasury offers us should temper our complacency at the wondrous state of knowledge in our time. May not later editions of *Britannica* prove our knowledge no less illusory and just as entertaining to future readers as the earliest editions of *Britannica* are to us? All this justifies *Britannica*'s enlightened policy of aiming to present what Robert Gwinn calls "every respectable side" of issues still in dispute. Just as the certitudes of one age become myths to the learned of the next, so controversies also become obsolete or are transformed. The naval architecture of Noah's Ark has ceased to be debated. The alchemical aspiration to make base elements into gold was dissolved by the chemists' discoveries of the "elements" described in nineteenth-century editions, only to be revived anew by the atomic discoveries that followed.

The adventure of self-discovery on which this treasury takes us can bring cheer to us and future generations. We are inoculated with a wholesome suspicion of the knowledge brought us by Aristotle, Ptolemy—and even Copernicus, Newton, and Einstein. But the works of art reported and recounted here—the great creations of architecture, painting, sculpture, literature, and music—do not obsolesce. Instead, as *Britannica* has repeatedly reminded us, they somehow enrich one another. Literature and the arts have the uncanny quality, portrayed here in bold relief, of enriching human life without in the least subtracting from our earlier inheritance. The realms of the arts, surveyed in *Britannica*, in our scientific age allow us to transcend the ephemeral lives of the sciences.

Despite all else, the quest and the adventure continue. That is the enduring import of this treasury and the accumulated editions of *Britannica*. Nowhere is there a more vivid witness to our determination to fulfill our humanity, our refusal to abdicate the quest to know. However attractive may be the bound volumes of our *Britannica,* or however conveniently compact the latest disks, the essential mission of *Britannica* remains not the product but the process. Not a neat catalogue of what we think we know, but a catalytic reminder that we somehow know less than we think we know, and can always know more. This treasury can carry us along in *Britannica*'s knowledge-enterprise of more than two centuries, and help us find delight in the quest.

—Daniel J. Boorstin
Librarian of Congress Emeritus

INTRODUCTION

1. Brown Studies

For one thing, the very idea of an encyclopedia is crazy. Even if condensed, how can all that we know (What is "all"? Who are "we"? What is "to know"?) be funneled into a set of books bound in brown buckram? Absurd. Yet, echoing Tertullian (v. 11, p. 652),* I must believe: It is certain because it is impossible. There stands *Britannica* on my shelves: 32 weighable volumes, 32,000 turnable pages, 44 million legible words, 19,000 visible illustrations. It looks real. Indeed, it comes with our favorite sign of reality: $. Excluding printing expenses, the current 15th edition, published in 1974, cost $32 million to produce. The 1985 redesign and revision cost another $24 million. The whole phenomenon is as irrefutable as it is fantastic.

An encyclopedia is often singled out as evidence of the powers of the rational mind. But merely to contemplate my set evokes irrational musings. For example, there's the thrill of mere ownership, as unreasonable as it is human. The Hollywood super-rich superstar, viewing his Jackson Pollock, feels a legitimate pleasure quite apart from the esthetic value of his purchase. It's *there*, ready for him in the event that he should decide to learn how to enjoy it. With my *Britannica* I feel an identical complacence. Though I know I shall die relatively uneducated, the key to erudition is always available. Like

* Unless otherwise indicated, all volume and page references in this introduction are to the 15th edition, 1988 printing.

the Jackson Pollock, the set is somehow supportive. Doubtless snobbery and other questionable factors are lurking somewhere. Let them lurk. The vibration of ownership cannot be denied.

These staid tomes are a fetish in 32 volumes, alive with magical forces. I summon up a genie from a lamp labeled Index. Lo! He is ready to deliver 180,000 entries and 419,000 references, from " . . . & Company," a novel by Jean-Richard Bloch, to "Zwyny, Wojciech Adalbert," a Polish musician associated, however unspellably, with Chopin. Such power is eerie. Aristotle (v. 14, p. 59), perhaps the first to envision the notion of an encyclopedia, would have given his right arm to possess it.

But how substantial is this magic? If I could read and retain the set's whole content, would I emerge from the logothon a wiser, perhaps even a better, man? Aldous Huxley could have told us: He's rumored to have read the *Britannica* from *A* to *Z*. I suppose its top editors must have survived the same ordeal. Philip Goetz (editor-in-chief, 1979–1991) once told me that, if challenged, he could deliver a two-minute lecture on hundreds of subjects. It was the third minute, he said, that would do him in. As the encyclopedist Frank Moore Colby (v. 3, p. 443) once put it, "One learns little more about a man from the feats of his memory than from the feats of his alimentary canal."*

I have heard of several others who claim to have read *Britannica*'s every word. But I find this unsettling rather than impressive. There is something compulsive about wanting to know everything. Mental omniphagy (panophagy?) is linked less to intellectual curiosity than to a trust in the preternatural: the encyclopedia as mantra. Are not polymaths candidates for the couch? There is something to be said for a reasonable amount of ignorance. Omniscience and progress make poor yoke-fellows. I greatly admire John Stuart Mill (v. 24, p. 100), who by the age of eight had read all of Herodotus (v. 5, p. 881) —in Greek. But I wouldn't vote for him for president. However, we shouldn't

* Colby wrote "Trials of an Encyclopedist," possibly the best, certainly the funniest, essay ever written on this subject. You can find it in *Reading I've Liked,* a collection assembled by the present writer.

fly to the opposite extreme. Ignorance is not in itself a sufficient qualification, even for the vice-presidency.

Occasionally, awed by *Britannica*'s Himalayan bulk, people ask me whether the editor-in-chief is a monster of erudition. I have already suggested that this is not so. Editors are first-rate executives, triply armed: They know where to go for authoritative information; they know how to organize that information; and they have an unshakable passion for knowledge.

Digression: I have been acquainted with six *Britannica* top editors, of whom four, despite what they have been through, are still extant. They are or were highly intelligent and well-informed, but not more so than thousands of others quite incapable of holding down their jobs. Because the work they do will never receive recognition from either our government or the public, I herewith list these six benefactors: Walter Yust, Harry S. Ashmore, Sir William Haley, Warren E. Preece, Philip W. Goetz, and the present incumbent, Robert McHenry. The book you hold in your hands owes much to them, as it does to their eighteen equally unsung predecessors.

Back to my brown studies: Reflecting on what these editors and their colleagues and contributors have created—an institution eight years older than the United States—I am struck by its multifunctionality. The *Britannica* may be used as furniture. It may be used to settle a bet. It may also be used to get a passable general education at about 2 percent of the cost of four years at a good college, though it doesn't supply the right contacts. It's probably most frequently used by high-school students faced with research and writing assignments. The academy, of course, finds it indispensable. Professional writers like me employ it as a device to make us appear more learned and authoritative than we actually are. Like Paul (v. 25, p. 456), it is made all things to all men.

First and foremost, like its cousin the dictionary, it is a tool, one no less extraordinary than the internal combustion engine (v. 3, p. 507) or the digital computer (v. 16, p. 638). It comes out of our thirst for order. The block of Carrara marble is a whirling chaos of atoms (v. 14, p. 329). Using an impalpable tool called genius plus two palpable ones called mallet and chisel, Michelangelo (v. 24, p. 55) shaped this chaos into something called "David." The current

Britannica, faced with the far more daunting chaos called knowledge, cuts it up into ten parts★ and, using various editorial devices, makes that knowledge available to the reader who otherwise would not know how to go about acquiring it. Give me a place to stand and I will move the Earth, said an apocryphal Archimedes (v. 13, p. 930). *Britannica* supplies us with a platform from which we can exert leverage on the world of learning.

That last sentence is a bit too full of pomp and circumstance. Most of us refer to the encyclopedia to confirm a fact (as I did five seconds ago to check Archimedes's reputed words) or to get reliable, condensed information about a specific subject. Perfectly normal behavior.

But I have still another use for it. Chaos, no less than order, has its charms, and the aleatory helps keep us human. St. Augustine (v. 14, p. 387) had one of the most orderly minds in the history of Christianity. But, as the familiar story tells us, his real conversion to order came about by chance. In his garden in Milan he heard a child's voice saying *"tolle, lege"* ("take up and read"). He opened his New Testament at a random page and found the text that shaped his life.

With less world-shaking results, I do the same with the *Britannica,* merely to sharpen my sense of the fortuitous, the unexpectable. Let's try it. Eyes closed, I select a volume, turn to a chance page, place my finger on it, open my eyes, and discover that "in 1969, the Swiss-born psychiatrist Elisabeth Kübler-Ross conceptualized five stages in facing one's terminal illness: denial, anger, bargaining, depression, and acceptance." As I am almost eighty-eight, I find this quite interesting.

Try again. This time I open at "Technology." I learn that "despite the immense achievements of technology by 1900, the following decades witnessed more advance over a wide range of human activities than the whole of previously recorded history." Well, in a vague way I guess I knew that, but it's a good thing to have this vastly important fact enunciated with such brisk authority. It settles the mind.

★ Matter and Energy, the Earth, Life on Earth, Human Life, Human Society, Art, Technology, Religion, the History of Mankind, and the Branches of Knowledge.

Last stab: This one throws up "*ectropion,* sagging of the lower eyelid away from the eyeball." At first I see no reason to be grateful for this information. But, as I read through the brief article, I become aware that some of the symptoms listed resemble those my younger brother suffers from. At least I now know enough to sympathize with him a little more intelligently than before.

Each of these three Augustinian gestures has, if only to the tiniest degree, spoken to my human condition. Surprising.

Such exploitation of the desultory, the haphazard, may even evoke in us the rare emotion we call awe. To sense the wondrous miscellaneity of creation we need only (but with eyes, ears, and mind wide open) walk down a crowded street, or thread a wood in summer, or with a microscope explore the life pullulating in a cubic foot of fertile earth. These are the best ways. But there is another, shaped for lazier moods: the encyclopedic riffle.

Turning the pages of any single volume, idly, mindlessly, with no wish to learn a thing, can sometimes awaken in us Miranda's thrill, the fresh wonder poets are said to possess by nature but that visits us common folk only occasionally, when we fall in love or gaze at our newborn child.

In my hand I hold Otter-Réthimnon. What an extraordinary multiverse of objects, ideas, institutions, people, and places it contains, made neighbors by an odd invention, the alphabet: Papuan languages, Pappus of Alexandria, Perugia, Phaulkon-Tachard conspiracy, polychaete hypothesis, Portsmouth, John Cowper Powys, pozzolana, property tax, pump, puma, Quebec, Srinivasa Ramanujan, the Reformation, Jean de Reszke . . . Suddenly this world is richer than it seemed three minutes ago. (I can no longer keep it from you: Réthimnon is a town in Crete, pop. [1981] 17,736.)

Such sortilegious excursions do not always produce something I want to know, but they quicken in me what is worth preserving: a constant alertness to the depth of my ignorance. My *Britannica* has an ethical, a didactic dimension. It warns me to take it easy on my lively impulse to think well of myself. My trade—that of a writer and judge of other writers—is a show-off trade, akin to acting. It does not encourage modesty, much less humility. But *Britannica* does, and I am grateful.

Thus it is salutary to know that there exist enormous areas of knowledge with which I am totally, completely unacquainted but which, through the medium of an open book, become an open book. One of these days I mean to be an expert on Reptiles (v. 26, pp. 735–764). Or maybe I don't mean to. Still, the mere contemplation of the world of possibility lends wings to the spirit.

But it is equally salutary to keep in mind—and I have tried to do so in putting this book together—that *Britannica* is a fallible creation. Each edition reflects its era and the capacities of its readers, and these change. More to the point, in our time (less so in the eighteenth and early nineteenth centuries) it must inevitably reflect the mental level of the academicians who, for the most part, create its text. Robert Maynard Hutchins (v. 6, p. 174), chairman of the Board of Editors, 1943–1974, would constantly and quietly remind us that *Britannica*'s level could never rise higher at any given time than the condition of the higher learning of its era. Should that decay, should it cease to be informed by the most objective ideals, the set would faithfully mirror such retrogression. Should we descend into another Dark Age, *Britannica* will become an index of that darkness. The advance of knowledge, much less that of wisdom, is not inevitable but rather a function of history, of the total behavior of men and women.

These days we hear much talk of a declining confidence in the wisdom of our species. Whether or not such gloom is justified, there is no harm in seizing upon anything that will bolster our confidence. An encyclopedia is a small bolster. Other animals, such as the bees, may possess a language, and it is not entirely certain that dolphins do not exchange ideas of some sort. But we seem to be the only animals genetically equipped to incessantly investigate the universe, including ourselves, and then to set down our findings in some more or less permanent form. We store for the future, and in our immense warehouse the device called an encyclopedia occupies its own tiny niche.

As grateful user of the *Britannica,* as one of its employees, and as general editor of this celebratory collection, I have tried to keep in mind the noble phrases fashioned by Diderot (v. 4, p. 79) to describe his own great *Encyclopédie:* "In fact, the purpose of an encyclopaedia is to assemble the knowledge scattered over the surface of the earth; to explain its general system to the men with whom we live, and to transmit it to the men who will come after us; in order that the labours of centuries past may not be useless for the centuries to come; that our descendants, by becoming better instructed, may as a consequence be more virtuous and happier, and that we may not die without having deserved well of the human race."

2. *Origins*

An aeon or two ago I worked for *The New Yorker* when Harold Ross (see E. B. White's essay in Part II of this volume) was running it. Office folklore had it that no staff member had been properly blooded until Ross had offered him the job of managing editor. We got the impression that the boss made this proposition regularly to any number of bewildered scriveners, as well as to miscellaneous nonstaffers he might chance to encounter during the course of a busy day.

Similarly, over the last few decades no *Britannica* editor had any respect for himself until he had come up with a scheme for a *Britannica* anthology. Our enthusiasm for re-inventing the wheel never flagged. The present volume, therefore, is merely the last avatar in a series of projects, all concerned to rescue from its vasty deep *Britannica*'s best and brightest.

Though they did not achieve publication, two of these projects assumed concrete form.

One was the work of Robert McHenry, now general editor. Many years ago he selected, sometimes condensed, and headnoted a large number of outstanding articles, some of considerable length. Arranged chronologically, these were drawn from editions appearing from 1813 (when contributors were first identified) up to and including the 14th edition of 1929.

Bruce Felknor, retired at the time but previously *Britannica*'s executive editor and also director of its *Yearbook,* then tried his hand at the job. His organizing principle differed from Mr. McHenry's. Though he inevitably adopted (and sometimes abridged) some of the latter's excellent choices, his aim was to show systematically how a constantly changing *Britannica* had reflected the development and progress of human knowledge since 1768. Drawing upon all fifteen editions, he organized his material in eleven categories, a scheme suggested by the ten-part "Circle of Learning" with which owners of the current edition are familiar. His assemblage of extracts, many brief, was given coherence by headnotes and linking commentary. The result was a vast work, of high historical interest, but perhaps a bit daunting to the general reader.

The publishers of this volume invited me to construct still another anthology that would make use of Mr. Felknor's impressive research and also, as it turned out, Mr. McHenry's. This would, they hoped, illustrate the ways in which *Britannica* had over the centuries dealt with the world of knowledge and also offer examples of the best writing that had appeared in its pages from its inception to the present day.

I have relied so heavily on the labors of Messrs. McHenry and Felknor that it is quite proper to list their names on the title page as contributing editors. Where I have used their headnotes, their initials are affixed. For all unsigned headnotes, I am accountable.

In a few cases I have also stolen from a kind of keepsake anthology published more or less for fun in 1963 by the *Britannica*'s London office. Now a collector's item, it brought together in brief compass some hundred-odd excerpts from the 1st through the 8th edition. They were chosen mainly for their oddity, their capacity to amuse the present-day reader. I have retained a few, reminding all of us that two hundred years from now a fair proportion of the current edition will also seem quaint.

For all other selections, as well as the organization of this book, the contributing editors are not to be blamed. For some decades I have worked for the *Britannica,* familiarized myself with its history, and, naturally enough, found myself recalling favorite articles. The reader will find many such in the pages that follow.

3. About This Book

In his preface to *Britannica*'s first edition the editor, William Smellie, wrote: "Utility ought to be the principal intention of every publication. Wherever this intention does not plainly appear, neither the books nor their authors have the smallest claim to the approbation of mankind."

Mr. Smellie, of course, was referring only to books of reference. Succeeding editors did not have enough iron in their souls to adhere to his stern, utilitarian standard. In general, a more flexible, even idealistic view has come to prevail.

In 1943 *Britannica* began its association with the University of Chicago. Since then its preliminary pages have reproduced the University's motto: "Let knowledge grow from more to more and thus be human life enriched." The heading of this present volume's Part I appropriates the motto's first three words: "Let Knowledge Grow." Drawing on every edition of the set and on the labors of Messrs. Felknor and McHenry, Part I reproduces about 200 extracts, arranged under ten convenient rubrics. These, we hope, will suggest (for they can do no more) the impact of the growth of knowledge on the editors, from William Smellie, described as "a veteran of wit, genius, and bawdry," to the present incumbents, whose modesty would preclude a comparison with Mr. Smellie on any of these three counts.

They are intended to reflect not only the growth of knowledge but also the comparatively minor matter of the evolution of *Britannica* itself. The first edition (1768–1771), published in three volumes, bore as its subtitle "A Dictionary of Arts and Sciences." Though the edition was far more than a dictionary, the word points to its limitations. One is, for instance, brought up short by the terseness of some entries: "BITCH, the female of the dog kind."

The second editor was more adaptable. He even included biographies, which Mr. Smellie rejected as undignified, and enlarged the geographical articles to encompass history. And so the expansion has continued. The current edition, thirty-two volumes in all, can truly claim that in its pages the world of knowledge is as systematically and comprehensively covered as the limitations of space and the weaknesses of human intelligence allow.

This development has been accompanied by changes in style and mood. While current practice favors neutrality, a certain intrusion of mere temperament marks earlier editions. The 8th edition (1852–1860) carried a highly technical article, "Telescope," by the great English astronomer Sir John Herschel (1792–1871), successor to his greater father, Sir William Herschel (1738–1822). Discussing "the durable casting of a speculum," Sir John cites a certain Dr. Macculloch who recommended "quick cooling to the fixing point . . . but without a word as to the mode of accomplishing it." This was not sufficient, and so he appends a footnote: "In all other respects his paper is a wonderful example of what a multitude of words can do towards obliterating meaning."

Perhaps the advance toward scholarly objectivity can be suggested by reproducing two dedications. The first example is a passage from the editor's dedication to the King, printed in the Supplement to the 3rd edition (1801):

> . . . THE *French* Encyclopédie *has been accused, and justly accused, of having disseminated, far and wide, the seeds of Anarchy and Atheism. If the* ENCYCLOPÆDIA BRITANNICA *shall, in any degree, counteract the tendency of that pestiferous Work, even these two Volumes will not be wholly unworthy of Your* MAJESTY'S *Patronage; and the Approbation of my* SOVEREIGN, *added to the consciousness of my own upright intentions, will, to me, be an ample reward for the many years of labour which I have employed on them, and on the Volumes to which they are Supplementary. I am,*
>
> *SIR,*
>
> YOUR MAJESTY'S
>
> *Most faithful Subject,*
>
> *And most devoted Servant,*
>
> *GEORGE GLEIG.*

And here, almost forbidding in its chastity, is the dedication in the 1988 printing of the current 15th edition:

Dedicated by permission to
RONALD W. REAGAN
PRESIDENT OF THE UNITED STATES OF AMERICA
and
HER MAJESTY QUEEN ELIZABETH II

That same George III to whom the first dedication is addressed, reading the article "Midwifery" in the first edition—partially reproduced in this volume—ordered it torn out. (Only 6 of the 3,000 sets sold survive complete). *Britannica* today is not hampered by such accesses of moral feeling.

Many of the bits and pieces in Part I are wonderfully quaint, appealing to the antiquarian hidden in many of us. Others inevitably mirror the defective knowledge of their period. Yet none departs from the spirit that animated the "Society of Gentlemen" who organized the first edition. Throughout its career *Britannica* has tried to answer questions of fact. But, despite Mr. Smellie's passion for utility, it has also tried, in constantly differing ways, to organize and present facts so that they may be an instrument of education. Part I, we hope, may give some hint of how, over more than two centuries, *Britannica,* sometimes eccentrically, has pursued these two aims.

The second aim, that of education, is more fully illuminated in Part II, "Best Foot Forward." Mr. Smellie boasted that he had done his job with scissors and paste pot, coolly borrowing much of his material from already published books and articles. By the time of the 3rd edition this fiscally conservative policy was changed to include freshly written, important articles by authorities. In the Supplement to the 4th, 5th and 6th editions, these authorities were first identified. The great 11th edition used outstanding contributors whose style and temper enabled them to address a new audience of intelligent but not necessarily scholarly readers.

An encyclopedia cannot be a work of art. Much of its material must be workaday, produced by quiet scholars who do not pretend to be masters of prose. Nevertheless, the evolution of *Britannica* reflects a growing dependence on first-rate writers who can use the language with power as well as authority. Part II selects some of the finest pieces produced over the years, from Sir Walter Scott to Sigmund Freud. I suppose they are what the nineteenth century called "gems," continuing to shine and glow irrespective of their date of composition.

It is no accident that this section should feature many names that are, as our current jargon has it, world-class: Curie, Einstein, a brace of Huxleys, Malthus, Toynbee, Russell, Shaw, Trotsky. While Part II may be read for pleasure as well as instruction, its underlying purpose is to demonstrate that, given the proper vehicle and opportunity, such intellects of the very highest order can fruitfully communicate with the curious, intelligent, but not elitist reader. The force of this simple democratic idea would have been lost on Mr. Smellie, whose clientele was restricted to a small group of the genteelly educated, including many clergymen. That it is now commonplace is a measure of the evolution of knowledge and also of political sanity.

Ever since the famous 11th edition, the editors have become increasingly aware that, given a first-rate writer, it is often advisable to give him a loose rein. Detachment and objectivity, while important, must sometimes be qualified by the writer's personality, the direction of his mind toward originality of thought and expression. In Part II, Burgess on the novel, Chesterton on Dickens, Nemerov on poetry, Koestler on wit and humor—each gives "the facts." But each also puts his best foot forward, adding stimulating views of his own, clothed in prose of idiosyncratic warmth and energy. Such contributions break the mold of traditional encyclopedic writing and make some claim to be works of art.

A word about the Appendix. We felt that many readers of this book might well be interested in encyclopedias in general. Hence the Appendix's first item, which reproduces the relevant material from the 15th edition's article "Encyclopedias and Dictionaries." It is the joint product of the late Robert L. Collison (author of *Encyclopaedias: Their History Throughout the Ages*) and Warren E. Preece (*Britannica* editor 1964, editor-in-chief 1965–1967, general editor 1968–1973, and editor 1973–1975).

The Appendix's second item requires a little explanation. Up to the time of the 11th edition (1910–1911) *Britannica* was sold on the installment plan, being issued serially in fascicles, pamphlets, or half volumes. I have never quite understood how buyers adapted themselves to this fits-and-starts mode of presentation, but apparently they did.

I have retrieved from the dim past a humorous piece by Eugene Field that I chuckled over when I was nine years old. "The Cyclopeedy," published just over a century ago, evokes for us, with homespun, old-fashioned good humor, the tribulations of a typical installment-plan purchaser of a few generations ago. Do not be put off by the dialect. Think of it, as our politically correct would put it, merely as another language.

Assembling pieces from an encyclopedia, while an interesting task, is not one that evokes outbursts of hilarity in the editor. Perhaps it is the need for comic relief that accounts for the appearance in these pages of "The Cyclopeedy."

4. *Acknowledgments*

I have already referred to the vital assistance of the two contributing editors. The very conception of this book also owes much to the pioneering efforts of Carl Bakal, public affairs consultant to *Encyclopædia Britannica* and the author of a detailed proposal whose influence may be found in these pages. Another valuable scheme for an anthology was drawn up by Warren Preece; several of his choices reappear here.

I also acknowledge with gratitude the aid given me by the following: *Britannica*'s editorial librarian, Terry Miller; Cynthia Wilkins, who did much of the photocopying from crumbling older editions; Helen L. Carlock, supervisor of the Correspondence and Research Department; Mortimer J. Adler, chairman of the Board of Editors; Harry Ashmore, one-time editor-in-chief; Al Silverman and Dawn Drzal of Viking-Penguin; and especially my assistant Anne Marcus, whose judgment and careful attention to detail have been invaluable.

—*Clifton Fadiman*

PART ONE

Let Knowledge Grow

CHAPTER ONE

Sound Mind and Healthy Body

First Things First

Encyclopedists in every age have paid careful attention to the nourishment of the body, mind, and soul. First the body. This extract comes from the Supplement to the 4th, 5th, and 6th editions (1815–1824). (B.L.F.)

FOOD

Our observations upon this subject may be conveniently arranged as relating to the *Selection, Preservation,* and *Preparation* of the various substances which are commonly used for Food.

Selection

Animal matters in general are safe articles of food. In regard to the higher classes, the mammalia and birds, this is universally true of those in a state of health. A few exceptions occur among the fishes, depending either upon the constitution of certain persons, who are injuriously affected by substances generally alimentary, or upon some singularity in the nature of the individual fish by which it becomes poisonous, although the species is generally nutritious and wholesome. As we descend still lower in the scale, these exceptions occur more frequently, and more species are absolutely and universally unwholesome, or furnish poisons hurtful to every constitution. In the vegetable kingdom, the alimentary vegetables form but a small proportion of the whole, and almost an equal number are absolutely poisonous, or at least injurious, except when given in small quantities, to counteract some existing disease.

Although quadrupeds, without exception, furnish articles which may be safely used as food, their flesh differs much in palatibility, and probably in its nutritious qualities. There is also no part of this class of animals that may not be, and indeed is not occasionally used as food, although the flesh, or voluntary muscles upon the limbs, trunk, and head, is by far the most considerable and important. The heart, the largest of the involuntary muscles, is also commonly eaten; and the brain, and spinal marrow or pith; all the glands, the kidneys, liver, udder, and sweetbread; the compound internal organs, the lungs, stomach, and intestines, the uterus, placenta, and even the contents of the stomach, the fat and marrow of the bones; the blood and skin are all nutritious, and some of them highly prized, and even the bones themselves can be made to furnish much wholesome nutriment. Also the milk of all quadrupeds is alimentary, and generally agreeable. . . .

To understand the theory of cookery, we must attend to the action of heat upon the various constituents of alimentary substances, as applied directly and indirectly through the medium of some fluid. In the former way, as exemplified in the processes of roasting and broiling, the chief constituents of animal substances undergo the following changes—the fibrine is corrugated, the albumen coagulated, the gelatine and osmazome rendered more soluble in water, the fat liquified, and the water evaporated. If the heat exceed a certain degree, the surface becomes first brown, and then scorched. In consequence of these changes, the muscular fibre becomes opaque, shorter, firmer, and drier; the tendons less opaque, softer, and gluey; the fat is either melted out, or rendered semitransparent. . . .

Vegetable substances are most commonly boiled or baked; or if apparently fried or roasted, there is always much water present, which prevents the greater action of the fire from penetrating below the surface. The universal effect of cookery upon vegetable substances, is to dissolve in the water some of their constituents, such as the mucilage and starch, and to render those that are not properly soluble, as the gluten and fibre, softer and more pulpy.

We cannot pretend to enter into the details of the various processes, nor explain the many precautions requisite to ensure success. For practical receipts we recommend *L'Art de Cuisinier,* par A. Beauvilliers; *A New System of Domestic Cookery,* by a Lady; and, lastly and chiefly, *Apicius Redivivus, or the Cook's Oracle,* in which, along with the plainest directions, there is more of the philosophy, and, if we may so speak, of the literature of *gastronomie,* than in any work we have seen.

A Strange Assemblage

Today's Britannica *offers no recipes. It cannot compete with Julia Child. But, as we have noted, earlier editors felt the* Britannica *to be not only an instrument of general information but also a manual of practical instruction. The 3rd edition (1788–1797) entry on "Olio," for example, is virtually nothing but recipe. It assumes that the reader's household boasts a vast number of ill-paid servants ready and willing to put together the thirty-seven ingredients required to make it.*

OLIO, or oglio, a savoury dish, or food, composed of a great variety of ingredients; chiefly found at Spanish tables.

The forms of olios are various. To give a notion of the strange assemblage, we shall here add one from an approved author.

Take rump of beef, neats tongues boiled and dried, and Bologna sausages; boil them together, and, after boiling two hours, add mutton, pork, venison, and bacon, cut in bits; as also turnips, carrots, onions, and cabbage, borage, endive, marigolds, sorrel, and spinach; then spices, as saffron, cloves, mace, nutmeg, &c. This done, in another pot put a turkey or goose, with capons, pheasants, wigeons, and ducks, partridges, teals, and stock-doves, snipes, quails, and larks, and boil them in water and salt. In a third vessel, prepare a sauce of white wine, strong broth, butter, bottoms of artichokes, and chestnuts, with cauliflowers, bread, marrow, yolks of eggs, mace, and saffron. Lastly, dish the olio, by first laying out the beef and veal, then the venison, mutton, tongues, and sausages, and the roots over all; then the largest fowls, then the smallest, and lastly pour on the sauce.

Cheese

Britannica*'s usefulness two hundred years ago knew no bounds. If you wanted to know how to prepare "Brawn," the pickled flesh of a boar, it told you. Under "Bread" you found a lengthy paragraph telling you how to prepare six large loaves in the style followed in Debrecen, Hungary. Along with other surprising information, the 4th edition (1801–1809) teaches us that cheese is useful as fish bait.*

CHEESE, a sort of food prepared of curdled milk purged from the serum or whey, and afterwards dried for use.

Cheese differs in quality according as it is made from new or skimmed milk, from the curd which separates spontaneously upon standing, or that which is more speedily produced by the addition of runnet. Cream also affords a kind of cheese, but quite fat and butyraceous, and which does not keep long. Analyzed chemically, cheese appears to partake much more of an animal nature than butter, or the milk from which it was made. It is insoluble in every liquor except spirit of nitre, and caustic alkaline ley. Shaved thin, and properly treated with hot water, it forms a very strong cement if mixed with quicklime. When prepared with the hot water, it is recommended in the Swedish Memoirs to be used by anglers as a bait; it may be made into any form, is not softened by the cold water, and the fishes are fond of it.—As a food, physicians condemn the too free use of cheese. When new, it is extremely difficult of digestion: when old, it becomes acrid and hot; and, from Dr Percival's experiments, is evidently of a septic nature. It is a common opinion that old cheese digests every thing, yet is left undigested itself; but this is without any solid foundation. Cheese made from the milk of sheep digests sooner than that from the milk of cows, but is less nourishing; that from the milk of goats digests sooner than either, but is also the least nourishing. In general it is a kind of food fit only for the laborious, or those whose organs of digestion are strong.

Blithe Spirits

The Supplement to the 4th, 5th, and 6th editions (1815–1824) contained a long article on "Distillation," a subject of peculiar interest to the Scotsmen who at that time edited Britannica. *It was written by Charles McKenzie, Esq., a fellow of the Royal Society and no glad sufferer of legislative folly or inferior whiskey. Here are some of his remarks on Dutch gin and whiskey.*

OF THE MODE OF MANUFACTURING OTHER KINDS OF SPIRITS

In this chapter we shall merely make a few very short observations on the processes followed by the distillers in other countries.

1. Dutch Geneva

The Dutch have long been famous for the manufacture of an excellent kind of spirits, known in Scotland by the name of *Gin,* in England by the name of *Hollands,* and sometimes by the name of *Geneva.* We have been told, that the manufacture of it originated in the city of Geneva; and that this was the origin of the name Geneva, still applied to it in commerce. But we have no means of determining how far this statement may be depended on. We have not seen in print any accurate account of the mode of making Geneva, practised by the Dutch. But the following account may, we believe, be relied on. We are indebted for it to a friend, who, about forty years ago, went over to Holland, on purpose to make himself acquainted with the process. His object was to establish a similar manufactory in Scotland. But the severe laws, by which the Scotch distillers were soon after bound, put it out of his power to execute his plan. . . .

Every person acquainted with the flavour of Hollands and Lowland whisky, must admit that the former is greatly superior to the latter. Indeed, the flavour of Hollands is equal to that of malt whisky. . . .

We suspect that another reason [for the superiority] of the Dutch spirit over the Scotch, is the small quantity of yeast employed by the manufacturers of Hollands. The vast quantity of porter yeast used by the Scotch distillers, often in a state almost approaching to putrefaction, cannot but have an injurious effect upon the flavour of their spirits, and has undoubtedly contributed to the superior reputation of Highland over Lowland whisky. For the Highland distillers (especially the smugglers) have not the means of procuring yeast from London. Of course, their wash is less perfectly fermented; but the flavour of their spirits is much more agreeable. We think, indeed, that the flavour communicated by the yeast to Scotch Lowland whisky may be distinctly perceived, and on that account are disposed to suspect that the flavour of the spirits always suffers in proportion as the fermentation is brought nearer a state of perfection. Any person who should find out a method of fermenting wort without the necessity of employing such quantities of porter yeast as the distillers use, would undoubtedly prodigiously improve the flavour of the spirits manufactured by the Scotch distillers. If government were to make such an alteration in the laws, as would enable the distiller to employ a greater proportion of malt without any material increase of expence, the object might be considered as accomplished. In the present state of the manufactures of Great Britain, it would be impossible to confer a greater favour on the country, than a thorough revisal of the excise laws, under the auspices of a set of individuals, at once intimately acquainted with the most improved state of chemical science, and with the most liberal principles of political economy. Every thing that improves the quality, and diminishes the price of our manufactures, is of more value to the country than our legislators seem to be aware of.

Medicine

The 1st edition (1768–1771), at the beginning of its 113-page article on the subject of "Medicine," said that it "is generally defined to be, The art of preserving health when present, and of restoring it when lost." Some of the terms we recognize today meant quite different things in the eighteenth century. For example, "hypochondriac passion" literally meant acute distress of the upper abdomen. (B.L.F.)

The hypochondriac passion is a spasmodico-flatulent affection of the stomach and intestines, arising from an inversion or perversion of their peristaltic motion, and by a consent of parts, throwing the whole nervous system into irregular motions, and disturbing the whole animal oeconomy.

This disease is attended with such a train of symptoms, that it is a difficult task to enumerate them all; for there is no function or part of the body, that is not soon or late a sufferer by its tyranny. It begins with tensions and windy inflations of the stomach and intestines, especially under the spurious ribs of the left hypochondrium, in which a pretty hard tumour may sometimes be perceived. . . .

As to the prognostics, if the disease be recent and left to itself, it is rather troublesome than dangerous; but if it be inveterate, and not skilfully treated, or a bad regimen is followed, it is attended with more grievous symptoms, producing obstructions and ichirri of the viscera, a cachexy, a dropsy, an hectic, a convulsive asthma, an incurable melancholy or madness, a fatal polypus, etc. But if it is caused by a suppression of the menses, or bleeding piles, the restoring the flux is the cure of the disease.

Midwifery

When Britannica *first appeared (1768–1771), knowledge of the human body and its healthy functioning was quite erratic. Anatomy was understood in great detail, physiology in part, hygiene hardly, and antisepsis in medicine and surgery not at all. Definitions and classification of diseases by our standards were at the least exotic and often absurd. Marvelously, the prescribed cures sometimes worked. The early* Britannica*s did much to disseminate existing knowledge throughout the British Isles and the colonies. For the 1st edition's instruction of midwives, the editor, William Smellie, relied heavily on the work of his older and distantly related namesake, the obstetrician William Smellie, the first man to teach and practice obstetrics on a scientific basis. Numerous and explicit illustrations were engraved by the copublisher, Andrew Bell. There is a tradition that either the monarch George III or his court chamberlain was so incensed by the detailed illustrations of the birth process that he ordered all loyal subjects to rip out and destroy the offending plates. (B.L.F.)*

MIDWIFERY is the art of assisting nature in bringing forth a perfect foetus, or child, from the womb of the mother.

The knowledge of this art depends greatly on an intimate acquaintance with the anatomy of the parts of generation in women, both internal and external. But, as those have already been fully described under the article ANATOMY, we must refer

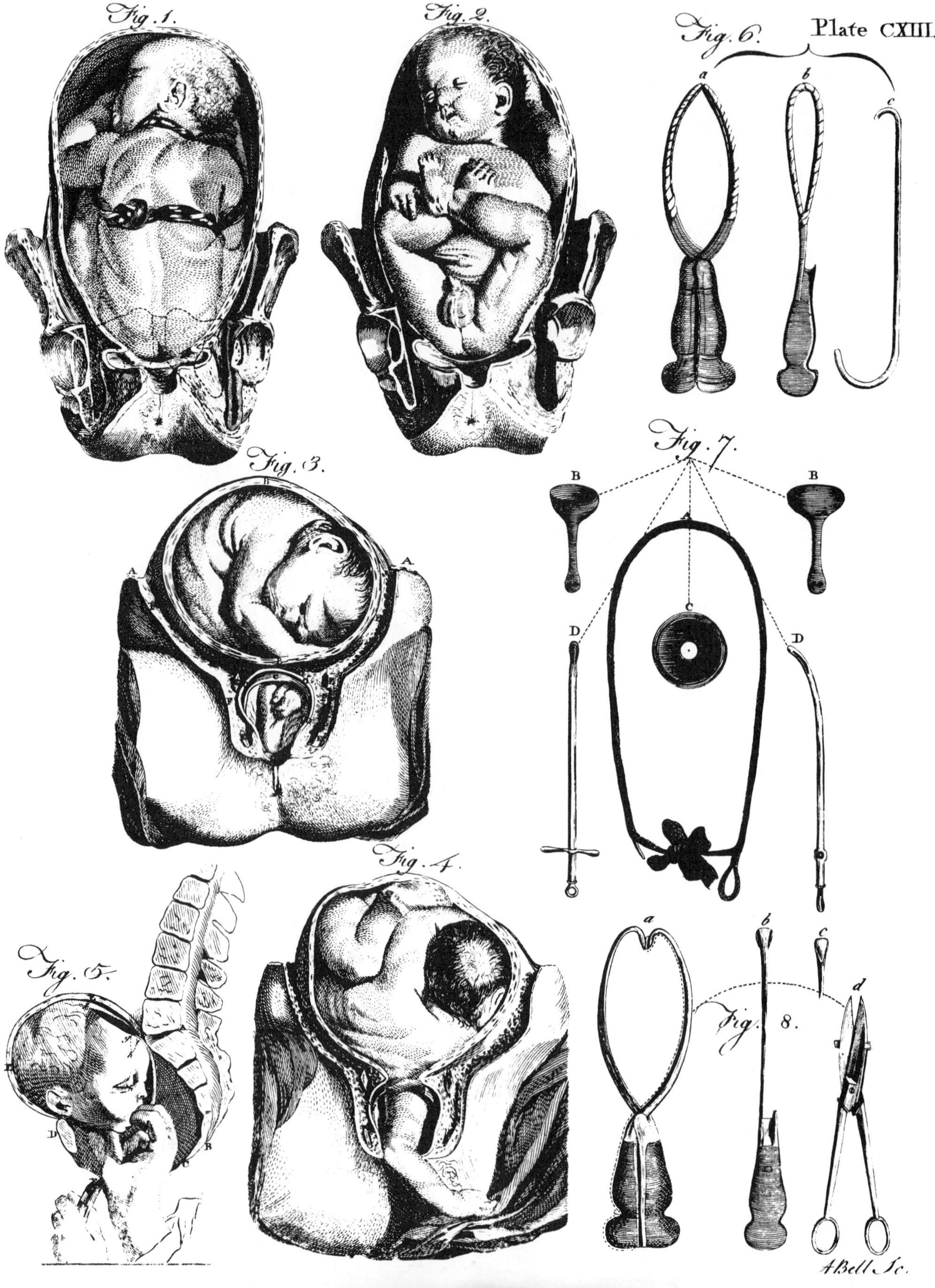
Fig. 1.
Fig. 2.
Fig. 6.
a
b
c
Fig. 3.
B
A
A
Fig. 7.
B
B
A
C
D
D
Fig. 4.
Fig. 5.
a
b
c
d
Fig. 8.
A Bell Sc.

Plate CXIII

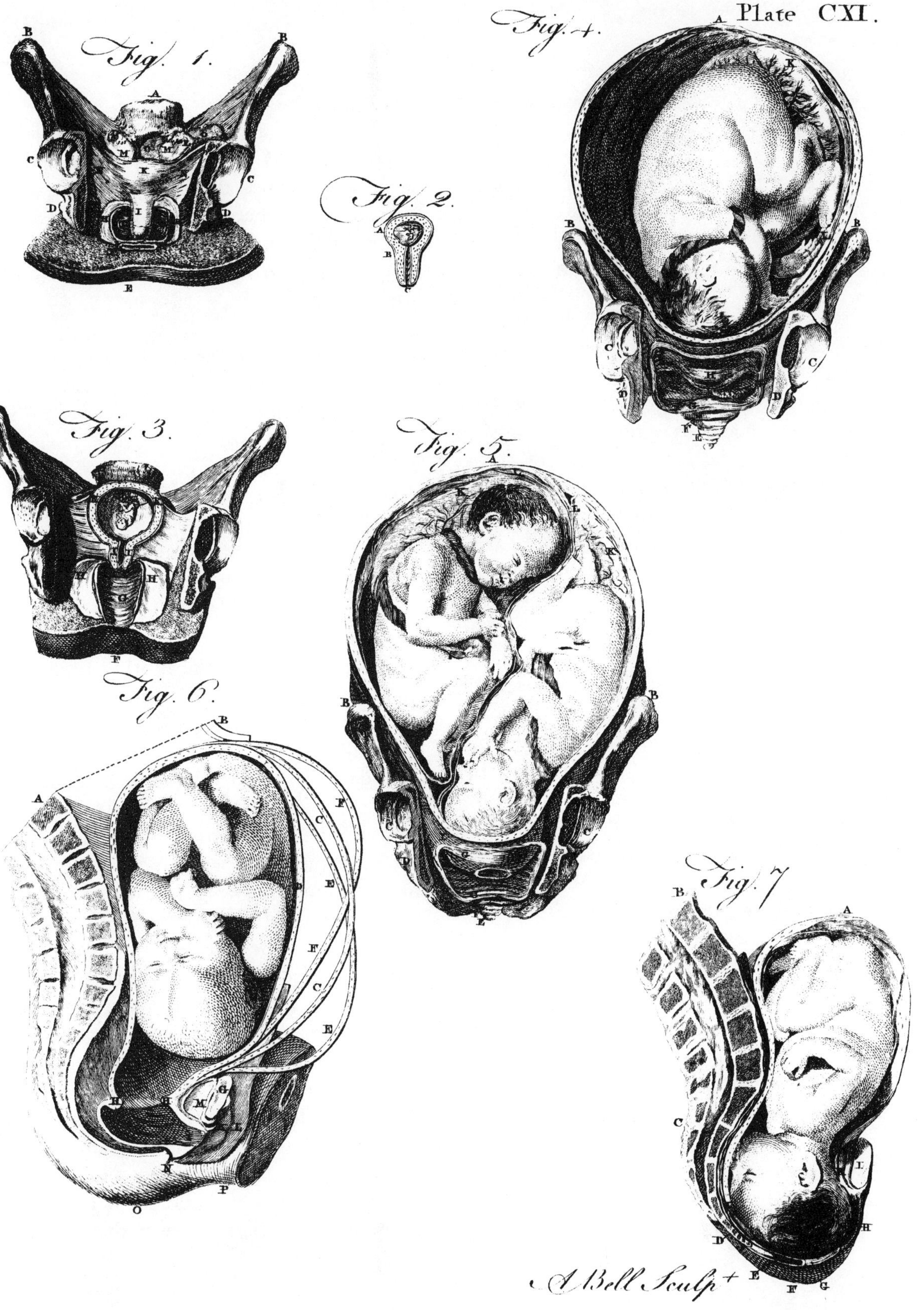

Plate CXI.
Fig. 1.
Fig. 2.
Fig. 3.
Fig. 4.
Fig. 5.
Fig. 6.
Fig. 7
A Bell Sculp.t

to the different parts of that science upon which the knowledge of midwifery depends.

Of the Increase of the Uterus After Conception

It is supposed, that the ovum swims in a fluid, which it absorbs so as to increase gradually in magnitude, till it comes in contact with all the inner surface of the fundus uteri; and this being distended in proportion to the augmentation of its contents, the upper part of the neck begins also to be stretched.

About the third month of gestation, the ovum in bigness equals a goose egg; and then nearly one fourth of the neck, at its upper part, is distended equal with the fundus. At the fifth month, the fundus is increased to a much greater magnitude, and rises upwards to the middle space betwixt the upper part of the pubes and the navel; and at that period, one half of the neck is extended. At the seventh month, the fundus reaches as high as the navel; at the eighth month, it is advanced midway between the navel and *serebiculus cerdis;* and in the ninth month, is raised quite up to this last mentioned part, the neck of the womb being then altogether distended.

Smallpox

Perhaps nothing more dramatically illustrates the progress of medicine than the long and finally successful effort to stamp out smallpox. It is often supposed that Edward Jenner (1749–1823), in discovering an effective vaccine against the lethal disease, also invented inoculation. Not so: The idea had been around since early in the eighteenth century and probably much longer. The 2nd edition (1778–1783) has a brief item:

INOCULATION, in medicine, the art of transplanting the small-pox from one person to another, by impregnating the blood of the sound person with the variolous matter from a pustule taken from the other.

Dangerous though the practice was, it was widely essayed, and it often worked. Then came the breakthrough that soon would make it virtually foolproof. Here is "Inoculation" from the Supplement to the 4th, 5th, and 6th editions (1813–1824). (B.L.F.)

On the 14th of May 1796, Edward Jenner, a physician in Berkeley, near Gloucester, first applied to the arm of a healthy boy of eight years, by means of two superficial incisions, the morbid fluid secreted by a sore on the hand of a dairymaid, who had contracted Cow-pock from the udders of her master's cows. The seventh day after the operation he had uneasiness in the arm-pit; on the ninth, became chill, had headache, lost appetite, was otherwise indisposed, and spent a restless night; but the following day, was free from complaint. Of the appearances of the local sore, we have no particular information, but that it resembled a bluish pustule, was surrounded by an erysipelatous or red circle, and afterwards formed scabs and eschars without producing other inconvenience. The object of this operation, which was chiefly experimental, was to ascertain the degree of immunity from smallpox contagion thus obtained; and on the 1st of July, therefore, variolous matter was inserted by inoculation, but without being attended with the usual disease; and when this was repeated some months after, the same effect was observed. Further inquiry was prevented, in consequence of the disease disappearing till the spring of 1798, when it once more made its appearance among the dairies of Gloucestershire. On the 16th of March, a child of five and a half years was inoculated with matter taken from the teat of an infected cow. On the 6th day after the operation, he was unwell, and vomited; but on the 8th appeared to be in his usual health. The progress of the local vesicle was similar to that of the former case, except in the absence of the livid or bluish tint observed. On the 28th of March, the disease was transferred from the arm of this patient to that of William Pead, a boy of eight, with the usual appearances, and especially the red circle, quite similar to that which is observed after variolous inoculation. To this redness Dr Jenner first applied the term *areola*. From the fluid produced in this case, several patients, both young and adult, were infected, and in all, the phenomena appear to have been pretty uniform; or, at least, with deviations so trifling, that they do not require particular notice. From the previous conclusions derived from persons who had been affected with cow-pox, and who resisted the variolous action, it might be presumed to be unnecessary to try how far those who had been artificially subjected to cow-pock could resist small-pox. To render his conclusions more certain, however, Dr Jenner tried it without effect on his first vaccinated patient; and with the second and last cases, his nephew was equally unsuccessful.

Such were the first trials of the effect of vaccine fluid on the human subject; and so far as they were carried by Dr Jenner, the results appeared to warrant the main conclusion, that the process of vaccination renders the human body unsusceptible of being acted on by the infection of small-pox. We must not omit to remark, however, that the *Inquiry* of Dr Jenner shows that he had formed, in the year 1798, no very distinct idea of the nature and phenomena of the vaccine disease, or, at most, that he imagined it to be identical with small-pox. It is evident, that, in his early researches, Dr Jenner believed that the origin of small-pox could be traced to the heel of the horse; and that though cow-pox was a disease transmitted from the horse, and modified by the system of the cow, it was *specially* identical with, or allied to *variola,* and differed in variety only. On this principle, he applied to it the denomination of *variolae vaccinae;* and it is obvious that he was confirmed in this opinion by observing, that a person who had suffered the vaccine disease is not liable to be affected with small-pox contagion.

Many of Jenner's colleagues scoffed at his reports, and controversy raged. Misunderstandings and misinformation and careless experimental efforts to discredit the cowpox vaccine abounded, leading the Britannica*'s great Supplement to the 4th, 5th, and 6th editions to a ringing endorsement near the conclusion of its eleven-page article "Vaccination." (B.L.F.)*

It is in its power of diminishing the mortality of small-pox, therefore, that the superiority of vaccination consists; and it is on this strong ground only, that its partisans and true friends should defend its general adoption. Let the governors of charitable institutions, the guardians of the poor, the parents of families, and the public at large, be convinced of the facts which we have now stated, and the inferences derived from them, and it cannot be doubted that the practice of vaccination, instead of being opposed, or apprehended as a source of new and disastrous maladies, or ridiculed as a useless and inefficient ceremony, will be dispassionately estimated, and raised to that rank among the benefits of science, to which its happy effects unquestionably entitle it. It is surely superfluous to show the duty incumbent on all ranks to extend vaccination as widely as possible, if for no other reason than to preserve the lives of their relatives during the prevalence of epidemic small-pox,—and to say that, in proportion as vaccination is general, the infection of small-pox must be gradually limited and confined, until it is almost entirely expelled from the habitations of men. There cannot be a doubt, that every variolous epidemic, especially in large cities, is developed much more readily in consequence of the practice of variolous inoculation, or suffering children to be exposed to the infection of natural small-pox; and it is equally certain, that where vaccination is general, the introduction of variolous infection is either difficult, or when introduced, it is disarmed of its gigantic strength.

The Groin

If modern editors are perhaps a bit too austere, their predecessors tended to be all too human. The writer of the subjoined (from the 3rd edition, 1788–1797) is only mildly interested in conveying facts.

GROIN, that part of the belly next the thigh.—In the Philosophical Transactions we have an account of a remarkable case, where a peg of wood was extracted from the groin of a young woman of 21, after it had remained 16 years in the stomach and intestines, having been accidentally swallowed when she was about five years of age.

Anorexia and Bulimia

We think of anorexia (we call it anorexia nervosa) and bulimia as characteristic of our Age of Anxiety, often associating these diseases with young middle- or upper-class women. But they have a long history. Bulimia is as ancient as the vomitoria of classical Rome. The treatment for bulimia suggested in the 3rd edition (1788–1797) seems of doubtful efficacy, but even today therapy remains a baffling problem, as reference to Britannica*'s current edition will show.*

ANOREXIA

WANT OF APPETITE

The anorexia is symptomatic of many diseases, but seldom appears as a primary affection; and it is very generally overcome only by the removal of the affection on which it depends.

BULIMIA

INSATIABLE HUNGER, OR CANINE APPETITE

This disease is commonly owing to some fault in the stomach, by which the aliments are thrown out too soon; and unless the person be indulged in his desire for eating, he frequently falls into fainting fits. Sometimes it is attended with such a state of the stomach, that the aliment is rejected by vomit almost immediately after being swallowed; after which the appetite for food returns as violent as ever. But there are many circumstances which seem to render it probable that it more frequently arises from a morbid condition of the secreted fluid poured into the stomach, by means of which the aliment is dissolved. When the activity of this fluid is morbidly increased, it will both produce too sudden a solution of the solid aliment, and likewise operate as a powerful and peculiar stimulus to the stomach, giving an uneasy sensation, similar to that which takes place in natural hunger. Such things are proper for the cure as may enable the stomach to perform its office: chalybeates and other tonics will generally be proper. In some, brandy drunk in a morning has been useful; and frequent smoking tobacco has relieved others. Oil, fat meat, pork, opiates, and in short every thing which in a sound person would be most apt to pall the appetite, may also be used as temporary expedients, but cannot be expected to perform a cure. In some, the pylorus has been found too large; in which case the disease must have been incurable.

Embalming and Cremation

When medical intervention failed, some of the skills of the apothecary and the surgeon were needed to prepare the body for burial or other disposal. Early editions dealt with these preparations in vivid detail. "Embalming" is from the 1st edition (1768–1771), "Cremation" from the 3rd (1788–1797). (B.L.F.)

EMBALMING is the opening a dead body, taking out the intestines, and filling the place with odoriferous and desiccative drugs and spices, to prevent its putrifying. The Egyptians excelled all other nations in the art of preserving bodies from corruption; for some that they have embalmed upwards of two thousand years ago, remain whole to this day, and are often brought into other countries as great curiosities. Their manner of embalming was thus: they scooped out the brains with an iron scoop, out at the nostrils, and threw in medicaments to fill up the vacuum: they also took out the entrails, and, having filled the body with myrrh, cassia, and other spices, except frankincense, proper to dry up the humours, they pickled it in nitre, where it lay soaking for seventy days. The body was then wrapped up in bandages of fine linen and gums, to make it stick like glue, and so was delivered to the kindred of the deceased, entire in all its features, the very hairs of the eye-lids being preserved. They used to keep the bodies of their ancestors, thus embalmed, in little houses magnificently adorned, and took great pleasure in beholding them, alive as it were, without any change in their size, features, or complexion.

CREMATION is sometimes used for burning, particularly when applied to the ancient custom of burning the dead. This custom is well known to have prevailed among most eastern nations, and continued with their descendants after they had peopled the different parts of Europe.

Hence we find it prevailing in Greece, Italy, Gaul, Britain, Germany, Sweden, Norway, and Denmark, till Christianity abolished it.

Bleeding

Early editions often reflect an attitude of uncertainty. The editors seem to be simultaneously pressured by the legacy of the past and the intuition of a more scientific future. Under "Bleeding" the 4th edition (1801–1809) offers:

BLEEDING OF A CORPSE is a phenomenon said to have frequently happened in the bodies of persons murdered, which, on the touch, or even the approach, of the murderer, began to bleed at the nose, ears, and other parts; so as formerly to be admitted in England, and still allowed in some other parts, as a sort of detection of the criminal and proof of the fact. Numerous instances of these posthumous haemorrhagies are given by writers. But this kind of evidence ought to be of small weight.

Baldness

The current edition holds out no hope whatsoever; not a word of practical help. The 4th edition (1801–1809), under "Alopecia," is happily a bit more optimistic.

In cases where the baldness is total, a quantity of the finest burdock roots are to be bruised in a marble mortar, and then boiled in white wine until there remains only as much as will cover them. This liquor, carefully strained off, is said to cure baldness, by washing the head every night with some of it warm. A ley made by boiling ashes of vine branches in common water is also recommended with this intention. A fresh cut onion, rubbed on the part until it be red and itch, is likewise said to cure baldness.

A multitude of such remedies are everywhere to be found in the works of Valescus de Taranta, Rondeletius, Hollerius, Trincavellius, Celsus, Senertay, and other practical physicians.

Gout

The 11th edition (1910–1911), by reason of its eminent contributors, has remained legendary. One of its most famous pieces is unsigned. It deals with the unlikely subject of gout, a classically aristocratic disease. It treats the subject with a vividness that seems quaint to us today. Gout, as the brief article in Britannica's *current edition reminds us, is one of the oldest diseases in medical literature, which may in part account for the enthusiasm with which "Ignotus" ("Anonymous") handles the subject. His or her account retains some practical value inasmuch as the recommended curative agent, colchicum, is still widely used. From it is derived the modern substance colchicine.*

GOUT, the name rather vaguely given, in medicine, to a constitutional disorder which manifests itself by inflammation of the joints, with sometimes deposition of urates of soda, and also by morbid changes in various important organs. The term gout, which was first used about the end of the 13th century, is derived through the Fr. *goutte* from the Lat. *gutta,* a drop, in allusion to the old pathological doctrine of the dropping of a morbid material from the blood within the joints. The disease was known and described by the ancient Greek physicians under various terms, which, however, appear to have been applied by them alike to rheumatism and gout. The general term *arthritis* (ἄρθρου, a joint) was employed when many joints were the seat of inflammation; while in those instances where the disease was limited to one part the terms used bore reference to such locality; hence *podagra* (ποδάγρα, from πούς, the foot, and ἄγρα, a seizure), *chiragra* (χειρ, the hand), *gonagra* (γονυ, the knee), etc.

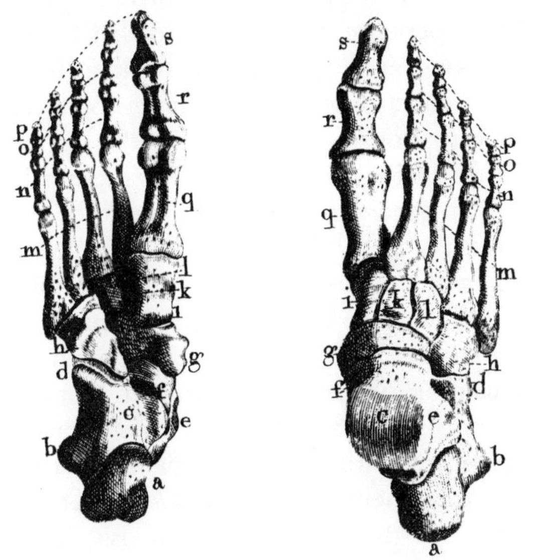

Hippocrates in his *Aphorisms* speaks of gout as occurring most commonly in spring and autumn, and mentions the fact that women are less liable to it than men. He also gives directions as to treatment. Celsus gives a similar account of the disease. Galen regarded gout as an unnatural accumulation of humours in a part, and the chalk-stones as the concretions of these, and he attributed the disease to overindulgence and luxury. Gout is alluded to in the works of Ovid and Pliny, and Seneca, in his 95th epistle, mentions the prevalence of gout among the Roman ladies of his day as one of the results of their high living and debauchery. Lucian, in his *Tragopodagra,* gives an amusing account of the remedies employed for the cure of gout.

In all times this disease has engaged a large share of the attention of physicians, from its wide prevalence and from the amount of suffering which it entails. Sydenham, the famous English physician of the 17th century, wrote an important treatise on the subject, and his description of the gouty paroxysm, all the more vivid from his having himself been afflicted with the disease for thirty-four years, is still quoted by writers as the most graphic and exhaustive account of the symptomatology of gout. Subsequently Cullen, recognizing gout as capable of manifesting itself in various ways, divided the disease into *regular gout,* which affects the joints only, and *irregular gout,* where the gouty disposition exhibits itself in other forms; and the latter variety he subdivided into *atonic gout,* where the most prominent symptoms are throughout referable to the stomach and alimentary canal; *retrocedent gout,* where the inflammatory attack suddenly disappears from an affected joint and serious disturbance takes place in some internal organ, generally the stomach or heart; and *misplaced gout,* where from the first the disease does not appear externally, but reveals itself by an inflammatory attack of some internal part. Dr Garrod, one of the most eminent authorities on gout, adopted a division somewhat similar to, though simpler than that of Cullen, namely, *regular gout,* which affects the joints alone, and is either acute or chronic, and *irregular gout,* affecting non-articular tissues, or disturbing the functions of various organs.

It is often stated that the attack of gout comes on without any previous warning; but, while this is true in many instances, the reverse is probably as frequently the case, and the premonitory symptoms, especially in those who have previously suffered from the disease, may be sufficiently precise to indicate the impending seizure. Among the more common of these may be mentioned marked disorders of the digestive organs, with a feeble and capricious appetite, flatulence and pain after eating, and uneasiness in the right side in the region of the liver. A remarkable tendency to gnashing of the teeth is sometimes observed. This symptom was first noticed by Dr Graves, who connected it with irritation in the urinary organs, which also is present as one of the premonitory indications of the gouty attack. Various forms of nervous disturbance also present themselves in the form of general discomfort, extreme irritability of temper, and various perverted sensations, such as that of numbness and coldness in the limbs. These symptoms may persist for many days and then undergo amelioration immediately before the impending paroxysm. On the night of the attack the patient retires to rest apparently well, but about two or three o'clock in the morning awakes with a painful feeling in the foot, most commonly in the ball of the great toe, but it may be in the instep or heel, or in the thumb. With the pain there often occurs a distinct shivering followed by feverishness. The pain soon becomes of the most agonizing character: in the words of Sydenham, "now it is a violent stretching and tearing of the ligaments, now it is a gnawing pain, and now a pressure and tightening; so exquisite and lively meanwhile is the part affected that it cannot bear the weight of the bedclothes, nor the jar of a person walking in the room."

When the affected part is examined it is found to be swollen and of a deep red hue. The superjacent skin is tense and glistening, and the surrounding veins are more or less distended. After a few hours there is a remission of the pain, slight perspiration takes place, and the patient may fall asleep. The pain may continue moderate during the day but returns as night advances, and the patient goes through a similar experience of suffering to that of the previous night, followed with a like abatement towards morning. These nocturnal exacerbations occur with greater or less severity during the continuance of the attack, which generally lasts for a week or ten days. As the symptoms decline the swelling and tenderness of the affected joint abate, but the skin over it pits on pressure for a time, and with this there is often associated slight desquamation of the cuticle. During the attacks there is much constitutional disturbance. The patient is restless and extremely irritable, and suffers from cramp in the limbs and from dyspepsia, thirst and constipation. The urine is scanty and high-coloured, with a copious deposit, consisting chiefly of urates. During the continuance of the symptoms the inflammation may leave the one foot and affect the other, or both may suffer at the same time. After the attack is over the patient feels quite well and fancies himself better than he had been for a long time before; hence the once popular notion that a fit of the gout was capable of removing all other ailments. Any such idea, however, is sadly belied in the experience of most sufferers from this disease. It is rare that the first is the only attack of gout, and another is apt to occur within a year, although by care and treatment it may be warded off. The disease, however, undoubtedly tends to take a firmer hold on the constitution and to return. In the earlier recurrences the same joints as were formerly the seat of the gouty inflammation suffer again, but in course of time others become implicated, until in advanced cases scarcely any articulation escapes, and the disease thus becomes chronic. It is to be noticed that when gout assumes this form the frequently recurring attacks are usually attended with less pain than the earlier ones, but their disastrous effects are evidenced alike by the disturbance of various important organs, especially the stomach, liver, kidneys and heart, and by the remarkable changes which take place in the joints from the formation of the so-called chalk-stones or tophi. These deposits, which are highly characteristic of gout, appear at first to take place in the form of a semifluid material, consisting for the most part of urate of soda, which gradually becomes more dense, and ultimately quite hard. When any quantity of this is deposited in the structures of a joint the effect is to produce stiffening, and, as deposits appear to take place to a greater or less amount in connexion with every attack, permanent thickening and deformity of the parts is apt to be the consequence. The extent of this depends, of course, on the amount of the deposits, which, however, would seem to be in no necessary relation to the severity of the attack, being in some cases even of chronic gout so slight as to be barely appreciable externally, but on the other hand occasionally causing great enlargement of the joints, and fixing them in a flexed or extended position which renders them entirely useless. Dr Garrod describes the appearance of a hand in an extreme case of this kind, and likens its shape to a bundle of French carrots with their heads forward, the nails corresponding to the stalks. Any of the joints may be thus affected, but most commonly those of the hands and feet. The deposits take place in other structures besides those of joints, such as along the course of tendons, underneath the skin and periosteum, in the sclerotic coat of the eye, and especially on the cartilages of the external ear. When largely deposited in joints an abscess sometimes forms, the skin gives way, and the concretion is exposed. Sir Thomas Watson quotes a case of this kind where the patient when playing at cards was accustomed to chalk the score of the game upon the table with his gouty knuckles.

The recognition of what is termed irregular gout is less easy than that form above described, where the disease gives abundant external evidence of its presence; but that other parts than joints suffer from gouty attacks is beyond question. The diagnosis may often be made in cases where in an attack of ordinary gout the disease suddenly leaves the affected joints and some new series of symptoms arises. It has been often observed when cold has been applied to an inflamed joint that the pain and inflammation in the part ceased, but that some sudden and alarming seizure referable to the stomach, brain, heart or lungs supervened. Such attacks, which correspond to what is termed by Cullen retrocedent gout, often terminate favourably, more especially if the disease again returns to the joints. Further, the gouty nature of some long-continued internal or cutaneous disorder may be rendered apparent by its disappearance on the outbreak of the paroxysm in the joints. Gout, when of long standing, is often found associated with degenerative changes in the heart and large arteries, the liver, and especially the kidneys, which are apt to assume the contracted granular condition characteristic of one of the forms of Bright's disease. A variety of urinary calculus—the uric acid —formed by concretions of this substance in the kidneys is a not unfrequent occurrence in connexion with gout; hence the well-known association of this disease and gravel.

The pathology of gout is discussed in the article on METABOLIC DISEASES. Many points, however, still remain unexplained. As remarked by Trousseau, "the production in excess of uric acid and urates is a pathological phenomenon inherent like all others in the disease; and like all the others it is dominated by a specific cause, which we know only by its effects, and which we term the gouty diathesis." This subject of diathesis (habit, or organic predisposition of individuals), which is regarded as an essential element in the pathology of gout, naturally suggests the question as to whether, besides being inherited, such a peculiarity may also be acquired, and this leads to a consideration of the causes which are recognized as influential in favouring the occurrence of this disease.

It is beyond dispute that gout is in a marked degree hereditary, fully more than half the number of cases being, according to Sir C. Scudamore and Dr Garrod, of this character. But it is no less certain that there are habits and modes of life the observance of which may induce the disease even where no hereditary tendencies can be traced, and the avoidance of which may, on the other hand, go far towards weakening or neutralizing the influence of inherited liability. Gout is said to affect the sedentary more readily than the active. If, however, inadequate exercise be combined with a luxurious manner of living, with habitual over-indulgence in animal food and rich dishes, and especially in alcoholic beverages, then undoubtedly the chief factors in the production of the disease are present.

Much has been written upon the relative influence of various forms of alcoholic drinks in promoting the development of gout. It is generally stated that fermented are more injurious than distilled liquors, and that, in particular, the stronger wines, such as port, sherry and madeira, are much more potent in their gout-producing action than the lighter class of wines, such as hock, moselle, etc., while malt liquors are fully as hurtful as strong wines. It seems quite as probable, however, that over-indulgence in any form of alcohol, when associated with the other conditions already adverted to, will have very much the same effect in developing gout. The comparative absence of gout in countries where spirituous liquors are chiefly used, such as Scotland, is cited as showing their relatively slight effect in encouraging that disease; but it is to be noticed that in such countries there is on the whole a less marked tendency to excess in the other pleasures of the table, which in no degree less than alcohol are chargeable with inducing the gouty habit. Gout is not a common disease among the poor and labouring classes, and when it does occur may often be connected even in them with errors in living. It is not very rare to meet gout in butlers, coachmen, etc., who are apt to live luxuriously while leading comparatively easy lives.

Gout, it must ever be borne in mind, may also affect persons who observe the strictest temperance in living, and whose only excesses are in the direction of over-work, either physical or intellectual. Many of the great names in history in all times have had their existence embittered by this malady, and have died from its effects. The influence of hereditary tendency may often be traced in such instances, and is doubtless called into activity by the depressing consequences of over-work. It may, notwithstanding, be affirmed as generally true that those who lead regular lives, and are moderate in the use of animal food and alcoholic drinks, or still better abstain from the latter altogether, are less likely to be the victims of gout even where an undoubted inherited tendency exists.

Gout is more common in mature age than in the earlier years of life, the greatest number of cases in one decennial period being between the ages of thirty and forty, next between twenty and thirty, and thirdly between forty and fifty. It may occasionally affect very young persons; such cases are generally regarded as hereditary, but, so far as diet is concerned, it has to be remembered that their home life has probably been a predisposing cause. After middle life gout rarely appears for the first time. Women are much less the subjects of gout than men, apparently from their less exposure to the influences (excepting, of course, that of heredity) which tend to develop the disease, and doubtless also from the differing circumstances of their physical constitution. It most frequently appears in females after the cessation of the menses. Persons exposed to the influence of lead poisoning, such as plumbers, painters, etc., are apt to suffer from gout; and it would seem that impregnation of the system with this metal markedly interferes with the uric acid excreting function of the kidneys.

Attacks of gout are readily excited in those predisposed to the disease. Exposure to cold, disorders of digestion, fatigue, and irritation or injuries of particular joints will often precipitate the gouty paroxysm.

With respect to the treatment of gout the greatest variety of opinion has prevailed and practice been pursued, from the numerous quaint nostrums detailed by Lucian to the "expectant" or do-nothing system recommended by Sydenham. But gout, although, as has been shown, a malady of a most severe and intractable character, may nevertheless be successfully dealt with by appropriate medicinal and hygienic measures. The general plan of treatment can be here only briefly indicated. During the acute attack the affected part should be kept at perfect rest, and have applied to it warm opiate fomentations or poultices, or, what answers quite as well, be enveloped in cotton wool covered in with oil silk. The diet of the patient should be light, without animal food or stimulants. The administration of some simple laxative will be of service, as well as the free use of alkaline diuretics, such as the bicarbonate or acetate of potash. The medicinal agent most relied on for the relief of pain is colchicum, which manifestly exercises a powerful action on the disease. This drug (*Colchicum autumnale*), which is believed to correspond to the hermodactyl of the ancients, has proved of such efficacy in modifying the attacks that, as observed by Dr Garrod, "we may safely assert that colchicum possesses as specific a control over the gouty inflammation as cinchona barks or their alkaloids over intermittent fever." It is usually administered in the form of the wine in doses of 10 to 30 drops every four or six hours, or in pill as the acetous extract (gr. ½-gr. i.). The effect of colchicum in subduing the pain of gout is generally so prompt and marked that it is unnecessary to have recourse to opiates; but its action requires to be carefully watched by the physician from its well-known nauseating and depressing consequences, which, should they appear, render the suspension of the drug necessary. Otherwise the remedy may be continued in gradually diminishing doses for some days after the disappearance of the gouty inflammation. Should gout give evidence of its presence in an irregular form by attacking internal organs, besides the medicinal treatment above mentioned, the use of frictions and mustard applications to the joints is indicated with the view of exciting its appearance there. When gout has become chronic, colchicum, although of less service than in acute gout, is yet valuable, particularly when the inflammatory attacks recur. More benefit, however, appears to be derived from potassium iodide, guaiacum, the alkalis potash and lithia, and from the administration of aspirin and sodium salicylate. Salicylate of menthol is an effective local application, painted on and covered with a gutta-percha bandage. Lithia was strongly recommended by Dr Garrod from its solvent action upon the urates. It is usually administered in the form of the carbonate (gr. v., freely diluted).

The treatment and regimen to be employed in the intervals of the gouty attacks are of the highest importance. These bear reference for the most part to the habits and mode of life of the patient. Restriction must be laid upon the amount and quality of the food, and equally, or still more, upon the alcoholic stimulants. "The instances," says Sir Thomas Watson, "are not few of men of good sense, and masters of themselves, who, being warned by one visitation of the gout, have thenceforward resolutely abstained from rich living and from wine and strong drinks of all kinds, and who have been rewarded for their prudence and self-denial by complete immunity from any return of the disease, or upon whom, at any rate, its future assaults have been few and feeble." The same eminent authority adds: "I am sure it is worth any *young* man's while, who has had the gout, to become a teetotaller." By those more advanced in life who, from long continued habit, are unable entirely to relinquish the use of stimulants, the strictest possible temperance must be observed. Regular but moderate exercise in the form of walking or riding, in the case of those who lead sedentary lives, is of great advantage, and all over-work, either physical or mental, should be avoided. *Fatiguez la bête, et reposez la tête* is the maxim of an experienced French doctor (Dr Debout d'Estrées of Contrexéville). Unfortunately the complete carrying out of such directions, even by those who feel their importance, is too often rendered difficult or impossible by circumstances of occupation and otherwise, and at most only an approximation can be made. Certain mineral waters and baths (such as those of Vichy, Royat, Contrexéville, etc.) are of undoubted value in cases of gout and arthritis. The particular place must in each case be determined by the physician, and special caution must be observed in recommending this plan of treatment in persons whose gout is complicated by organic disease of any kind.

Bacteriology

By the early twentieth century, bacteriology was a well-established science, already having numerous subdivisions. Here is how the 11th edition (1910–1911) introduces the subject. (B.L.F.)

The minute organisms which are commonly called "bacteria" are also known popularly under other designations, *e.g.* "microbes," "micro-organisms," "microphytes," "bacilli," "micrococci." All these terms, including the usual one of bacteria, are unsatisfactory; for "bacterium," "bacillus" and "micrococcus" have narrow technical meanings, and the other terms are too vague to be scientific. The most satisfactory designation is that proposed by Nägeli in 1857, namely "schizomycetes," and it is by this term that they are usually known among botanists; the less exact term, however, is also used and is retained in this article since the science is commonly known as "bacteriology." The first part of this article deals with the general scientific aspects of the subject, while a second part is concerned with the medical aspects.

I. The Study of Bacteria

The general advances which have been made of late years in the study of bacteria are clearly brought to mind when we reflect that in the middle of the 19th century these organisms were only known to a few experts and in a few forms as curiosities of the microscope, chiefly interesting for their minuteness and motility. They were then known under the name of "animalculae," and were confounded with all kinds of other small organisms. At that time nothing was known of their life-history, and no one dreamed of their being of importance to man and other living beings, or of their capacity to produce the profound chemical changes with which we are now so familiar. At the present day, however, not only have hundreds of forms or species been described, but our knowledge of their biology has so extended that we have entire laboratories equipped for their study, and large libraries devoted solely to this subject. Furthermore, this branch of science has become so complex that the bacteriological departments of medicine, of agriculture, of sewage, etc., have become more or less separate studies.

Antiseptics

Writing on the very eve (1928) of his discovery of penicillin, Scottish bacteriologist and Nobelist Alexander Fleming, later Sir Alexander (1881–1955), laid out the problem his work would begin to solve.

Fleming's co-author was Walter Sydney Lazarus-Barlow, a member of the British Ministry of Health and medical editor for the 14th edition (1929), from which this extract on "Antiseptics" is taken. (B.L.F.)

During recent years the study of antiseptics has gone mainly along two lines—to produce more efficient antiseptics for use in the ordinary way by external application, and to elaborate chemical substances which can be injected into the circulation and destroy the infecting microbes. At the same time many studies have been made on the natural antiseptics by which the body rids itself of infection. . . .

Sterilization

While antiseptics have not been very successful in killing bacteria in infected tissues in the body, they are invaluable in sterilizing apparatus, instruments and infected matter of many kinds outside the body. An infected water supply can be efficiently and economically sterilized by the use of a small quantity of chlorine; the infective excreta from cases of typhoid fever and similar diseases can be rendered harmless by treating them with carbolic acid or other similar antiseptic; catgut for use in surgical operations can only be sterilized by the use of chemical antiseptics, and there are innumerable other ways in which these chemicals fulfil their function of destroying bacteria.

Melancholy and Madness

The early editions of Britannica *reflected an understanding of mental illness that was considerably more compassionate than that of society at large. To be sure, however, it was no more accurate than the state of knowledge at the time. This is from the 1st edition (1768–1771). (B.L.F.)*

Melancholy and madness may be very properly considered as diseases nearly allied; for we find they have both the same origin; that is, an excessive congestion of blood in the brain: they only differ in degree, and with regard to the time of invasion. Melancholy may be looked upon as the primary disease, of which madness is only the augmentation.

When persons begin to be melancholy, they are sad, dejected, and dull, without any apparent cause; they tremble for fear, are destitute of courage, subject to watching, and fond of solitude; they are fretful, fickle, captious, and inquisitive; sometimes niggardly to an excess, and sometimes foolishly profuse and prodigal. They are generally costive; and when they discharge their excrements, they are often dry, round, and covered with a black, bilious humour. Their urine is little, acrid, and bilious; they are troubled with flatulencies, putrid and fetid eructations. Sometimes they vomit an acrid humour with bile. Their countenances become pale and wan; they are lazy and weak, and yet devour their victuals with greediness.

Those who are actually mad, are in an excessive rage when provoked to anger. Some wander about; some make a hideous noise; others shun the sight of mankind; others, if permitted, would tear themselves to pieces. Some, in the highest degree of the disorder, see red images before their eyes, and fancy themselves struck with lightning. They are so salacious, that they have no sense of shame in their venereal attempts. When the disease declines, they become stupid, sedate, and mournful, and sensibly affected with their unhappy situation.

The antecedent signs are, a redness and suffusion of the eyes with blood; a tremulous and inconstant vibration of the eye lids; a change of disposition and behaviour; supercilious looks, a haughty carriage, dis-

PASSIONS. Plate CCCLXXIX

A. Bell Prin. Wal. Sculptor fecit.

dainful expressions, a grinding of the teeth, unaccountable malice to particular persons; also little sleep, a violent head-ach, quickness of hearing, a singing of the ears; to these may be added incredible strength, insensibility of cold, and, in women, an accumulation of blood in the breasts, in the increase of this disorder. . . .

Both these disorders suppose a weakness of the brain, which may proceed from violent disorders of the mind, especially long-continued grief, sadness, dread, uneasiness and terror; as also close study and intense application of mind, as well as long protracted lucubrations. It may also arise from violent love in either sex, especially if attended with despair; from profuse evacuations of the semen; from an hereditary disposition; from narcotic and stupefactic medicines; from previous diseases, especially acute fevers. Violent anger will change melancholy into madness; and excessive cold, especially of the lower parts, will force the blood to the lungs, heart, and brain; whence oppressive anxieties, sighs, and shortness of breathing, tremors and palpitations of the heart; thus vertigoes and a sensation of weight in the head, fierceness of the eyes, long watchings, various workings of the fancy intensely fixed upon a single object, are produced by these means. To these may be added a suppression of usual haemorrhages, and omitting customary bleeding: hence melancholy is a symptom very frequently attending hysteric and hypochondriac disorders. . . .

Diseases of the mind have something in them so different from other disorders, that they sometimes remit for a long time, but return at certain periods, especially about the solstices, the times at which they first appeared. It may likewise be observed, that the raving fits of mad people, which keep the lunar period, are generally accompanied with epileptic symptoms.

Lunatic

From the 3rd edition (1788–1797):

LUNATIC, a person affected with that species of madness termed *lunacy*. The word is indeed properly applied to one that hath lucid intervals; sometimes enjoying his senses, and sometimes not; and that frequently supposed to depend on the influence of the moon.

Lunatic, in Law

Under the general term of *non compos mentis* (which Sir Edward Coke says is the most legal name) are comprized not only lunatics, but persons under frenzies, or who lose their intellects by disease; those that *grow* deaf, dumb, and blind, not being *born* so; or such, in short, as are judged by the court of chancery incapable of conducting their own affairs. To these also, as well as idiots, the king is guardian, but to a very different purpose. For the law always imagines, that these accidental misfortunes may be removed; and therefore only constitutes the crown a trustee for the unfortunate persons, to protect their property, and to account to them for all profits received, if they recover, or after their decease to their representatives. And therefore it is declared by the statute 17 Edw. II. c. 10. that the king shall provide for the custody and sustentation of lunatics, and preserve their lands, and the profits of them, for their use when they come to their right mind; and the king shall take nothing to his own use: and if the parties die in such estate, the residue shall be distributed for their souls by the advice of the ordinary, and of course (by the subsequent amendments of the law of administrations) shall now go to their executors or administrators.

On the first attack of lunacy, or other occasional insanity, when there may be hopes of a speedy restitution of reason, it is usual to confine the unhappy objects in private custody under the direction of their nearest friends and relations; and the legislature, to prevent all abuses incident to such private custody, hath thought proper to interpose its authority, by 14. Geo. III. c. 49. for regulating private mad-houses. But when the disorder is grown permanent, and the circumstances of the party will bear such additional expence, it is thought proper to apply to the royal authority to warrant a lasting confinement.

The method of proving a person *non compos* is very similar to that of proving him an idiot.

Insanity

It's interesting to compare our knowledge of insanity and our treatment of the insane with conditions in the middle of the last century. David Skae (1814–1873), a brilliant specialist in the study and treatment of insanity, wrote the article "Mental Diseases" for the 8th edition (1852–1860). An extract follows.

TREATMENT OF INSANITY

Public asylums, indeed, existed in most of the metropolitan cities of Europe; but the insane were more generally, if at all troublesome, confined in jails, where they were chained in the lowest dungeons, or made the butts and menials of the most debased criminals. Even in the public asylums, many of which were endowed by the munificence of philanthropists, the inmates were generally confined in low and damp cellars, sometimes isolated in cages or chained to the floor or wall; if harmless, they were huddled together, without regard to their habits, in cells not fitted to contain one tithe of the number immured in them. The medical treatment consisted, perhaps, in an annual bleeding and a few emetics; while the lash was systematically used, justified, and even recommended, as it had been by such authorities as the celebrated William Cullen. These unhappy victims of disease were exhibited to the public like wild beasts, and their passions irritated to gratify a morbid and vulgar curiosity. They were often killed by the ignorance and brutality of their keepers, sometimes during rough methods of forcing meat into them, sometimes by barbarous and violent beating. . . .

In concluding this brief historical retrospect, we cannot refrain from expressing our surprise that the study of mental diseases has been deemed of so little interest or importance hitherto, as to form no part of the curriculum of medical education in this country. Although the large metropolitan asylums afford ample means of illustrating courses of instruction in psychological medicine, the study of the subject has never been required by our licensing medical or surgical boards or universities. Lectures on mental diseases, both systematic and practical, have indeed been delivered in many of the continental medical schools; and of late years, in some of the large asylums of London and in that of Edinburgh, clinical lectures have been given; but attendance upon such courses of instruction is voluntary, with the exceptional case of candidates for appointments in the East India Company's service, who have been required during the last four years to attend an asylum for the insane for three months. This neglect seems altogether unaccountable, when we reflect upon the many collateral sciences students of medicine are compelled to master, of comparatively little value to them in actual practice, and the many diseases, accidents, and operations, toxicological and analytical investigations, they are carefully and minutely schooled in, which it may never fall to their lot, in a long life, to see or practise; while insanity, which affects 1 in every 400 or 500 of the population, and which, in some of its states or forms, they can hardly pass a week in medical practice without being consulted about,—often in circumstances requiring great judgment and skill,—is made no part of their medical education at all.

Wolf Children

Occasionally a new theory or a new explanation was injected into an existing article by an enthusiastic editor or publisher. In the case that follows, the intriguing item, debunking a hoary tradition, was supplied by anthropologist Margaret Mead (1901–1978). It was shoehorned into the article "Child Psychology" in the 14th edition, which was in print from 1929 through 1973. Professor Mead's sidebar feature was inserted into the 1968 printing and remained in the set through 1973. (B.L.F.)

Occasional reports from various parts of the world and over many years have described children said to have been reared by wolves or other animals. In outline these reports resemble accounts in earlier centuries of individuals found wandering naked and speechless in European forests. The Bear Boys of Lithuania (1657), Wild Peter (1724), the girl of Châlons-sur-Marne (1731), the Wild Boy of Aveyron (1798), and others excited extraordinary interest, particularly among early students of man. Observed, examined by the limited techniques of the period, and painstakingly described, they became widely known, and the details of their behaviour, more animal-like than human, led Linnaeus to classify them as a separate species, *Homo ferus,* feral man. In the 20th century reports came from India about feral children who had been stolen and reared by wolves. Modern anthropologists and psychologists no longer doubted that these wolf children belonged to our species, *Homo sapiens,* but they hoped that their history would shed light on the question of the relative importance of nature and nurture in individual human development. In the 1920s, two "wild" girls were found in Midnapur, India. One died soon afterward, but the other, known as Kamala, was reared by the Rev. J. A. Singh, whose careful notes on the process were published with an exhaustive analysis by Robert M. Zingg. Though she, too, died when she was about 18 years old, the record of her life was sufficiently persuasive to capture the interest of Arnold Gesell, who accepted the claim that the children actually had been reared by wolves and, interpreting Kamala's strange behaviour as the result of her wolf rearing, thought that her human traits had survived even though her maturation was slowed down.

Later research has effectively cleared up the question of whether human children have been reared by wolves or bears and has shown how these individuals came into being and how the stories about them originated.

It was known for a long time that children wandered away or were purposely abandoned at the edge of the forest. Their destruction could readily be explained as theft by a wolf, a belief strengthened by the occasional child found in a wild, desperate state. In 1943, David Mandelbaum outlined this explanation of the wolf mythology of India: the so-called wolf children were children who had been abandoned and later were found by other people. But it remained for a detailed, on-the-spot investigation by sociologist William Ogburn to verify this theory when, in 1958, looking into the case of a child allegedly found in a wolf den, he demonstrated that, actually, no one had witnessed the find. Each had heard the story from someone else. Independent evidence by the child analyst Bruno Bettelheim showed that the behaviour of emotionally damaged, autistic children—children so damaged that they fail to relate to other people and do not talk—matches the described behaviour of the wolf children. This provided a rationale for their strange behaviour. All these data, taken together with our growing knowledge about the species-characteristic behaviour of animals, finally dispels the old myth.

Wolf children are to be understood as children who were abandoned and who survived for weeks or months before they were found, just in time. The literature on the successive finds of these wild children remains a fascinating chapter in man's attempt to understand what part of human behaviour is innate.

Fig.: 5.
WOLF.

CHAPTER TWO

How We Behave

Woman

The 1st edition (1768–1771) was succinct:

WOMAN, the female of man. *See* HOMO.

It did touch on women's rights in the long article "Law" but hardly at all elsewhere, including under such titles as "Wife," "Widow," and "Marriage." Gradually, however, through the last quarter of the eighteenth century and all of the nineteenth, those rights expanded at a fairly steady pace. By the 9th edition (1875–1889) a voluminous article appeared under the heading "Women, Law relating to." It reviewed the history and gathering momentum of women's rights in England and discussed specific categories, including political rights, family rights, legal procedures, and criminal law. (B.L.F.)

That article began thus:

The law as it relates to women has been gradual in its operation, but its tendency has been almost uniformly in one direction. Disabilities of women, married or unmarried, have been one after another removed, until at the present day, in most civilized countries, the legal position of women differs little from that of men as far as regards private rights. Politically and professionally the sexes are still not upon an equality, but even in this aspect women have considerably greater rights than they once possessed, and the old theory of their intellectual and moral inferiority is virtually exploded. Those who defend their exclusion must now do so on other grounds.

It is worth noting that, in 1869, seven years before the first part of the 9th edition was distributed, John Stuart Mill had published his epochal The Subjection of Women.

In addition to multifarious other references to the subject, the current 15th edition of Britannica *devotes fourteen columns to an exhaustive discussion titled "Sex Differentiation: Women."*

Women in the 10th Edition

The 10th edition (1902–1903) was a ten-volume supplement to the thirty-five volumes of the famous 9th, and its editor was a brilliant and fiery young Englishman named Hugh Chisholm, who was an ardent supporter of women's rights. He saw to publication in the 10th of an article of more than 9,000 words titled "Women," which reviewed the profound changes under way in the society between 1871, when the 9th was begun, and 1902, when the 10th was issued. (B.L.F.)

Remarkable changes affected the lives and work of women in the second half of the 19th century. The industrial, religious, educational, and philanthropic work of women increased out of all proportion compared with what was done before that period, and it is desirable not only to know what has been accomplished, but to have also some knowledge of the agencies that have been instrumental in carrying it out. There is no complete history of the movement, though there is ample fragmentary information on certain subjects. The larger objects of women's work have occupied the attention of the public, while many of the equally useful but smaller objects attained are unknown.

Before the accession of Queen Victoria there was no systematic education for English women, but as the first half of the 19th century drew to a close, broader views began to be held on the subject, while the humanitarian movement, as well as the rapidly-increasing number of women, helped to put their education on a sounder basis. It became more thorough; its methods were better calculated to stimulate intellectual power; and the conviction that it was neither good, nor politic, for women to remain intellectually in their former state of ignorance, was gradually accepted by every one. The movement owed much to Frederick Denison Maurice. He was its pioneer; and Queen's College, which he founded, was the first to give a wider scope to the training of its scholars. Out of its teaching, and that of its professors (including Charles Kingsley), grew nearly all the educational advantages which women enjoy to-day; and to the women who were trained at Queen's College we owe some of the best teaching in England. Bedford College, Cheltenham College, the North London Collegiate School for Girls, the Girls' Public Day School Company's schools, are some of those which sprang into life in different parts of England, and were filled, as rapidly as they were opened, by the girls of the middle and professional classes. From their teaching came the final stage which gave women the same academic advantages as men. Somerville College and Lady Margaret Hall at Oxford, Girton and Newnham Colleges at Cambridge, Westfield College in London, St Hilda's College, St Hugh's Hall, Holloway College, Owens College, the Manchester and Birmingham and Victoria Universities, and other colleges for women in all parts of the United Kingdom, are some of the later but equally successful results of the movement. The necessity for testing the quality of the education of women, however, soon began to be felt. The University of Cambridge was the first to institute a special examination for women over eighteen, and its example was followed by Oxford; but while London, Dublin, Victoria, Edinburgh, Glasgow, and St Andrews Universities now grant degrees, Oxford and Cambridge do not.

❧ ❧ ❧

Women in the 11th Edition

By the time Hugh Chisholm was named to edit the great 11th edition (1910–1911), ownership of the Britannica *had passed from Edinburgh to London to the United States, and one of his first steps was to spend a year traveling around America to see the country at first hand, before returning to London to put together the new edition with the help of an American editor. Up to this time, female contributors had been noted for their rarity; for the 11th edition, Chisholm engaged thirty-four.*

Perhaps half a century ahead of his time among encyclopedists, Chisholm felt by this time that the Britannica *should drop its article "Women" because, as he put it, "they are so much an integral part of the human race that it is unnecessary to write of them as though they are race apart." However, he was persuaded by associates to continue the topic in the 11th and commissioned a new article of some 11,000 words. It began on a more indignant note than its precursors. (B.L.F.)*

The very word "woman" (O. Eng. *wifmann*), etymologically meaning a wife (or the wife division of the human race, the female of the species *Homo*), sums up a long history of dependence and subordination, from which the women of to-day have only gradually emancipated themselves in such parts of the world as come under "Western civilization." Though married life and its duties necessarily form a predominant element in the woman's sphere, they are not necessarily the whole of it; and the "woman's movement" is essentially a struggle for the recognition of equality of opportunity with men, and for equal rights irrespective of sex, even if special relations and conditions are willingly incurred under the form of partnership involved in marriage. The difficulties of obtaining this recognition are obviously duc to historical causes combined with the habits and customs which history has produced.

The dependent position of women in early law is proved by the evidence of most ancient systems which have in whole or in part descended to us. In the Mosaic law divorce was a privilege of the husband only, the vow of a woman might be disallowed by her father or husband, and daughters could inherit only in the absence of sons, and then they must marry in their tribe. The guilt or innocence of a wife accused of adultery might be tried by the ordeal of the bitter water. Besides these instances, which illustrate the subordination of women, there was much legislation dealing with, *inter alia,* offences against chastity, and marriage of a man with a captive heathen woman or with a purchased slave. So far from second marriages being restrained, as they were by Christian legislation, it was the duty of a childless widow to marry her deceased husband's brother. In India subjection was a cardinal principle. "Day and night must women be held by their protectors in a state of dependence," says Manu. The rule of inheritance was agnatic, that is, descent traced through males to the exclusion of females. The gradual growth of *stridhana,* or property of a woman given by the husband before or after marriage, or by the wife's family, may have led to the suttee, for both the family of the widow and the Brahmans had an interest in getting the life estate of a woman out of the way. Women in Hindu law had only limited rights of inheritance, and were disqualified as witnesses.

Home and Family Life

The foundation of the eighteenth-century home and family was, of course,

MARRIAGE, a contract both civil and religious, between a man and a woman, by which they engage to live together in mutual love and friendship, for the ends of procreation, etc. [1st edition, 1768–1771]

Monogamy in that era carried its original connotation from the Greek, i.e.,

the state or condition of those who have been only once married, and are restrained to a single wife. [1st edition]

The bias here is not necessarily intentionally masculine; owing to the high incidence of death in childbirth, few women survived their husbands. In any case, a monogamist did not remarry upon the death of his or her spouse.

Polygamy meant then what it does in our time:

a plurality of wives or husbands, in the possession of one man or woman, at the same time. [1st edition]

A stringent taboo set apart incest in all societies. (B.L.F.)

INCEST, the crime of venereal commerce between persons who are related in a degree wherein marriage is prohibited by the law of the country. [1st edition]

❧ ❧ ❧

Children

In earlier times Britannica*'s presumably highly cultivated readers seem to have relished information that nowadays we might list under pop culture. The article "Children" (3rd edition, 1788–1797) leads off* à la *Ripley. Its discussion of another aspect of the subject may elicit raised eyebrows from some of today's parents.*

CHILDREN, the plural of Child.

Mr Derham computes, that marriages, one with another, produce four children not only in England but in other parts also. . . .

In the genealogical history of Tuscany, wrote by Gamarini, mention is made of a nobleman of Sienna, named Pichi, who of three wives had 150 *children;* and that, being sent ambassador to the pope and the emperor, he had 48 of his sons in his retinue. . . .

Children are, in law, a man's issue begotten on his wife. As to *illegitimate children,* see BASTARD.

For the legal duties of parents to their children, see the articles PARENT and BASTARD.

As to the duties of children to their parents, they arise from a principle of natural justice and retribution. For those who gave us existence, we naturally owe subjection and obedience during our minority, and honour and reverence ever after; they who protected the weakness of our infancy, are entitled to our protection in the infirmity of their age; they who by sustenance and education have enabled their offspring to prosper, ought, in return, to be supported by that offspring, in case they stand in need of assistance. Upon this principle proceed all the duties of children to their parents, which are enjoined by positive laws.

Bastards

The 3rd edition (1788–1797) instructs us about one result of a careless liaison. (B.L.F.)

BASTARDY is a defect of birth objected to one born out of wedlock. Eustathius will have bastards among the Greeks to have been in equal favour with legitimate children, as low as the Trojan war; but the course of antiquity seems against him. Potter and others show, that there never was a time when bastardy was not in disgrace.

In the time of William the Conqueror, however, bastardy seems not to have implied any reproach, if we may judge from the circumstance of that monarch himself not scrupling to assume the appellation of bastard. His epistle to Alan count of Bretagne begins, *Ego Willielmus cognomento bastardus.*

Bastardy, in relation to its trial in law, is distinguished into general and special. *General* bastardy is a certificate from the bishop of the diocese, to the king's justices, after inquiry made, whether the party is a bastard or not, upon some question of inheritance. Bastardy *special* is a suit commenced in the king's courts against a person that calls another bastard.

Arms of BASTARDY should be crossed with a bar, fillet, or traverse, from the left to the right. They were not formerly allowed to carry the arms of their father, and therefore they invented arms for themselves; and this is still done by the natural sons of a king.

Right of BASTARDY, *Droit de batardise,* in the French laws, is a right, in virtue whereof the effects of bastards dying intestate devolve to the king or the lord.

Exposing of Children

The eighteenth century viewed with horror a fate that befell many children of an earlier millennium. From the 3rd edition (1788–1797): (B.L.F.)

EXPOSING OF CHILDREN, a barbarous custom practised by most of the ancients excepting the Thebans. . . .

When a child was born, it was laid on the ground; and if the father designed to educate his child, he immediately took it up; but if he forbore to do this, the child was carried away and exposed. The Lacedemonians indeed had a different custom: for with them all new-born children were brought before certain triers, who were some of the gravest men in their own tribe, by whom the infants were carefully viewed; and if they were found lusty and well-favoured, they gave orders for their education, and allotted a certain proportion of land for their maintenance; but if weakly or deformed, they ordered them to be cast into a deep cavern in the earth, near the mountain Taygetus, as thinking it neither for the good of the children themselves nor for the public interest, that defective children should be brought up. Many persons exposed their children only because they were not in a condition to educate them, having no intention that they should perish. It was the unhappy fate of daughters especially to be thus treated, as requiring more charges to educate and settle them in the world than sons.

The parents frequently tied jewels and rings to the children they exposed, or any other thing whereby they might afterwards discover them, if Providence took care for their safety. Another design in adorning these infants was either to encourage such as found them to nourish and educate them, if alive; or to give them human burial if dead. The places where it was usual to expose children were such as people frequented most. This was done in order that they might be found, and taken up by compassionate persons who were in circumstances to be at the expence of their education. With this intention the Egyptians and Romans chose the banks of rivers, and the Greeks the highway.

Love

The emotion of love is of general interest. Yet if you look the word up in the current 15th edition, you will find only four rather rarefied entries. They deal with love as viewed in Christian ethics and as treated in the philosophies of Augustine, Empedocles, and Plato. For the editors of the 3rd edition (1788–1797), however, love was a legitimate encyclopedic subject, worth five pages of grave discussion, often moralistic, and including a notable description of the tender emotion as seen from the medical viewpoint.

Read at a remove of two centuries, the essay is a striking admixture of common sense, nonsense, wisdom, arrogance, and insular ignorance. In the context of its own time it represented, and disseminated, enlightenment and understanding. (B.L.F.)

Animal desire is the actual energy of the sensual appetite: and that it is an essential part of the complex affection, which is properly called *love,* is apparent from this consideration, that though a man may have sentiments of esteem and benevolence towards women who are both old and ugly, he never supposes himself to be in love of any woman, to whom he feels not the sensual appetite to have a stronger tendency than to other individuals of her sex. On the other hand, that animal desire *alone* cannot be called the affection of love is evident; because he who gratifies such a desire without esteeming its object, and wishing to communicate at the same time that he receives enjoyment, loves not the woman, but himself. Mere animal desire has nothing in view but the species and the sex of its object. . . .

From the whole of this investigation, we think it appears, that the affection between the sexes which deserves the name of *love,* is inseparably connected with virtue and delicacy; that a man of loose morals cannot be a faithful or a generous lover: that in the breast of him who has ranged from woman to woman for the mere gratification of his sensual appetite, desire must have effaced all esteem for the female character; and that, therefore, the maxim too generally received, "that a reformed rake makes the best husband," has very seldom a *chance* to be true. . . .

Love, in Medicine

The symptoms produced by this passion as a disease, according to medical writers, are as follow: The eye-lids often twinkle; the eyes are hollow, and yet appear as if full with pleasure: the pulse is not peculiar to the passion, but the same with that which attends solicitude and care. When the object of this affection is thought of, particularly if the idea is sudden, the spirits are confused, the pulse changes, and its force and time are very variable: in some instances, the person is sad and watchful; in others, the person, not being conscious of his state, pines away, is slothful, and regardless of food; though the wiser, when they find themselves in love, seek pleasant company and active entertainments. As the force of love prevails, sighs grow deeper; a tremor affects the heart and pulse; the countenance is alternately pale and red; the voice is suppressed in the senses; the eyes grow dim; cold sweats break out; sleep absents itself, at least until the morning; the secretions become disturbed; and a loss of appetite, a hectic fever, melancholy, or perhaps madness, if not death, constitutes the sad catastrophe.

The 4th edition (1801–1809) makes more of a point of the differences between the sexes.

LOVE

Every one is conscious of a pleasing emotion when contemplating beauty either in man or woman; and when that pleasure is combined with the gratification of the sensual appetite, it is obvious that the sum of enjoyment must be greatly increased. The perception of beauty, therefore, necessarily directs the energy of the sensual appetite to a particular object; but still this combination is a mere selfish feeling, which regards its object only as the best of many similar instruments of pleasure. Before it can deserve the name of love, it must be combined with esteem, which is never bestowed but upon moral character and internal worth; for let a woman be ever so beautiful, and of course ever so desirable as an instrument of sensual gratification, if she be not possessed of the virtues and dispositions which are peculiar to her sex, she will inspire no man with a generous affection. With regard to the outlines, indeed, whether of internal disposition or of external form, men and women are the same; but nature, intending them for mates, has given them dispositions which, though concordant, are however different, so as to produce together delicious harmony. The man, more robust, is fitted for severe labour, and for field exercise; the woman, more delicate, is fitted for sedentary occupations, and particularly for nursing children. The man, bold and vigorous, is qualified for being a protector; the woman, delicate, and timid, requires protection. Hence it is that a man never admires a woman for possessing bodily strength or personal courage; and women always despise men who are totally destitute of these qualities. The man, as a protector, is directed by nature to govern; the woman, conscious of inferiority, is disposed to obey. Their intellectual powers correspond to the destination of nature. Men have penetration and solid judgment to fit them for governing, women have sufficient understanding to make a decent figure under a good government; a greater portion would excite dangerous rivalship between the sexes, which nature has avoided by giving them different talents. Women have more imagination and sensibility than men, which make all their enjoyments more exquisite; at the same time that they are better qualified to communicate enjoyment. Add another capital difference of disposition: The gentle and insinuating manners of the female sex tend to soften the roughness of the other sex; and wherever women are indulged with any freedom, they polish sooner than men.

These are not the only particulars that distinguish the sexes. With respect to the ultimate end of love, it is the privilege of the male, as superior and protector, to make a choice; the female preferred has no privilege but barely to consent or to refuse. Whether this distinction be the immediate result of the originally different dispositions of the sexes, or only the effect of associations inevitably formed, may be questioned; but among all nations it is the practice for men to court, and for women to be courted; and were the most beautiful woman on earth to invert this practice, she would forfeit the esteem, however by her external grace she might excite the desire, of the man whom she addressed. The great moral virtues which may be comprehended under the general term integrity are all absolutely necessary to make either men or women estimable; but to procure esteem to the female character, the modesty peculiar to their sex is a very essential circumstance. Nature hath provided them with it as a defence against the artful solicitations of the other sex before marriage, and also as a support of conjugal fidelity.

Sex

The 1st edition (1768–1771) came up with a cautious definition:

SEX, something in the body which distinguishes male from female.

Alternatives to Standard Monogamy

Here is the 1st edition (1768–1771) on what we usually call whorehouses:

STEWS were . . . places anciently permitted in England to women of professed incontinency, for the proffer of their bodies to all comers. These were under particular rules and laws of discipline, appointed by the lord of the manor.

The same edition on a more sociable alternative:

SERAGLIO, a Persian word, which signifies the palace of a prince or lord; in which sense the houses of the ambassadors of England, France, etc., are, at Constantinople, called their seraglios. But the term seraglio is used by way of eminence, for the palace of the grand seignor at Constantinople, where he keeps his court, in which his concubines are lodged, and where the youth are trained up for the principal posts of the empire. It is in form of a triangle, about two miles round, at the end of the promontory Chrysopolis, now called the Seraglio-point: the buildings extend to the top of the hill, and from thence there are gardens that reach to the sea. The outward appearance is not very beautiful, the architecture being irregular, consisting of separate edifices, in the manner of pavilions and domes. The old seraglio is the palace where the grand seignor's old mistresses are kept.

The ladies of the haram, which is the part allotted to the women, is a collection of young beautiful girls, who, on their admission, are committed to the charge of some old lady, and taught musick, dancing, and other accomplishments. These frequently play and dance before the grand seignor, while others entertain him with their conversation. Besides these ladies, there are a great many black eunuchs, and female slaves, in the seraglio, whose business it is to guard and wait upon them.

And on

BUGGERY is defined by Sir Edward Coke to be a carnal copulation against nature, either by the confusion of species, that is to say, a man or woman with a brute beast; or sexes, as a man with a man, or man unnaturally with a woman. It is said this sin against God and nature was first brought into England by the Lombards; and anciently, according to some writers, it was punishable with burning; but others say, with burying alive. It is, by statute, felony without benefit of clergy, and is always excepted out of a general pardon.

Bachelor

The 3rd edition (1788–1797) seems to suggest that bachelorhood was accorded a dour glance.

BACHELOR, or Batchelor, a common term for a man not married, or who is yet in a state of celibacy.—The Roman censors frequently imposed fines on old bachelors. . . . In England, there was a tax on bachelors, after 25 years of age, 12l. 10s. for a duke, a common person 1s. by 7 Will. III. 1695. In Britain, at present, they are taxed by an extra-duty on their servants. Every man of the age of 21 years and upwards, never having been married, who shall keep one male servant or more, shall pay 1l. 5s. for each above or in addition to the ordinary duties leviable for servants. Every man of the age of 21 years and upwards, never having been married, keeping one female servant, shall pay 2s. 6d. in addition to the former 2s. 6d.; 5s. in addition for each, if he has two female servants; and 10s. in addition for each for three or more female servants.

Satyriasis and Nymphomania

The 3rd edition (1788–1797) faced this pair of aberrations with the realism and practicality proper to its time. Particularly helpful in the case of nymphomania is the clear statement that matrimony is preferable to barley water.

SATYRIASIS

Satyriasis is a violent desire of venery in men, even so that reason is depraved by it. The pulse is quick, and the breathing short; the patient is sleepless, thirsty, and loathes his food; the urine is evacuated with difficulty, and a fever soon comes on. These symptoms, however, are probably not so much the consequence of satyriasis, as merely concomitant effects resulting from the same cause. And indeed this affection is most frequently the concomitant of a certain modification of insanity. The nature and cause of this affection are in most instances very little ascertained; but as far as we are acquainted with the treatment, it agrees very much with the affection next to be mentioned, which, of the two, is the most common occurrence.

NYMPHOMANIA

Furor Uterinus

The *furor uterinus* is in most instances either a species of madness or an high degree of hysterics. Its immediate cause is a preternatural irritability of the uterus and pudenda of women (to whom the disorder is proper), or an unusual acrimony of the fluids in these parts.—Its presence is known by the wanton behaviour of the patient: she speaks and acts with unrestrained obscenity; and as the disorder increases, she scolds, cries, and laughs, by turns. While reason is retained, she is silent, and seems melancholy, but her eyes discover an unusual wantonness. The symptoms are better and worse untill the greatest degree of the disorder approaches, and then by every word and action her condition is too manifest.—In the beginning a cure may be hoped for; but if it continue, it degenerates into a mania—In order to the cure, blood-letting is commonly had recourse to in proportion to the patient's strength. Camphor in doses of 15 or 20 grains, with nitre, and small doses of the tincture of opium, should be repeated at proper intervals. Some venture to give cerusa acetata in doses from three to five grains. Besides bleeding, cooling purges should also be repeated in proportion to the violence of symptoms, etc. What is useful in maniacal and hypochondriac disorders, is also useful here, regard being had to sanguine or phlegmatic habits, etc. When the delirium is at the height, give opiates to compose; and use the same method as in a phrenitis or a mania. Injections of barley-water, with a small quantity of hemlock-juice, according to Riverius, may be frequently thrown up into the uterus: this is called *specific;* but matrimony, if possible, should be preferred. For although this cannot be represented as a cure for the disease when in an advanced state, yet there is reason to believe that it has not unfrequently prevented it where it would otherwise have taken place.

Aphrodisiac

In the 11th edition (1910–1911) this article occupied a half page and, an editors' favorite, remained in the Britannica *for more than a generation. It was augmented by half in the 14th edition (1929), from which the following extract has been taken, and its basic facts still appear, in abbreviated form, in the 15th. (B.L.F.)*

APHRODISIAC, any of various forms of stimulation used chiefly to arouse sexual excitement. Aphrodisiacs may be classified in two principal groups: (1) psychophysiological (visual, tactile, olfactory, aural); and (2) internal (foods, alcoholic drinks, drugs, love potions, medical preparations).

By far the more important is the second group, as the preparation of erotic dishes has played a tremendous role in the sexual history of man. In spite of their vast popularity, almost no scientific studies have been written about them; most writings on the subject are little more than unscientific compilations of traditional material. . . .

With the exception of alcoholic drinks and certain narcotics such as marijuana, which may lead to sexual excitation through depression of inhibitory centres, modern medical science recognizes a very limited number of aphrodisiacs. These are, principally, cantharides and yohimbine. Yohimbine is a crystalline alkaloid substance derived from the bark of the yohimbé tree (*Corynanthe yohimbe*) found in central Africa, where it has been used for centuries by Africans to increase sexual powers. Although it has been promoted as an aphrodisiac, most investigators feel that any clinical change in sexual powers after its use is probably due to suggestion, since stimulatory effects are elicited only with toxic doses.

Maiden

The early editors were fascinated with cruel and unusual punishments, which they recounted in often graphic detail. This is from the 1st edition (1768–1771). (B.L.F.)

MAIDEN, an instrument used in Scotland for beheading criminals.

This is a broad piece of iron, about a foot square, very sharp on the lower part, and loaded above with a very heavy weight of lead. At the time of execution it is pulled up to the top of a narrow wooden frame, about ten feet high, and as broad as the engine, with mouldings on each side for the maiden to slide in. A convenience is made about four feet from the ground, for the prisoner to lay his neck; and there is a kind of bar so fastened as to keep him from stirring. The prisoner being thus secured, and the sign given, the maiden is let loose, which in a moment separates his head from his body.

❧ ❧ ❧

Maiden à la Française

The maiden's French equivalent offered not only an opportunity to describe a bloody punishment but another occasion for desecrating the morality of the despised French. From the Supplement to the 3rd edition (1801): (B.L.F.)

GUILLOTINE, a new term introduced into the languages of Europe by the mournful effects of fanaticism in the holy cause of liberty. Our readers are not ignorant that this is the name given by the National Assembly of France to the engine of decapitation, which those usurpers of the legislative authority decreed to be the sole punishment of those condemned to death for their crimes. . . .

Dr Guillotin, physician at Lyons, and member of the self-named National Assembly of France, thought himself honoured by the decree which associated his name with this instrument of popular vengeance. It was indeed proposed by him as an instrument of mercy, in a studied harangue, filled with that sentimental slang of philanthropy, which costs so little, promises so much, and has now corrupted all the languages of Europe. His invention is indeed one of the most expressive specimens of Gallic philanthropy, whose tender mercies are cruel; and was accordingly received with loud applauses, both from the house and from the galleries. . . .

We acknowledge, that in as far as this instrument lessens the duration of the horrid conflict with the king of terrors, and probably diminishes the corporeal sufferance, it may be called merciful (alas! the day!); but we question much, whether the dreadful agitation of soul is not rather increased by the long train of preparatory operations. The hands of the convict are tied behind his back: he is then stretched along on his face on a strong plank, and his precise position adjusted to the instrument. When fastened to the plank, it is pushed forward into its place under the fatal edge, his neck adjusted to the block, and a basket placed just before his eyes (for the face of Louis XVI. was not covered) to receive his head. This must employ a good deal of time, and every moment is terrible.

The construction has received many alterations and refinements; and has at last been made so compendious and portable, as to become part of the travelling equipage of a commissioner from the National Assembly, sent on a provincial or special visitation. Thus did the sovereign people become terrible in majesty.

Ducking

In describing ducking as a punishment, the 1st edition (1768–1771) had not yet taken note of the colonial American use of the ducking stool. (B.L.F.)

DUCKING, plunging in water, a diversion anciently practiced among the Goths, by way of exercise; but among the Celtae, Franks, and ancient Germans, it was a sort of punishment for persons of scandalous lives.

They were shut up, naked to the shift, in an iron cage, fastened to the yard of a shaloop, and ducked several times.

Ducking at the main-yard, among seamen, is a way of punishing offenders on board a ship; and is performed by binding the malefactor, by a rope, to the end of the yard, from whence he is violently let down into the sea, once, twice, or three times, according to his offence: and if the offence be very great, he is drawn underneath the keel of the ship, which they call keel-hauling.

Keel-hauling

With this item from the 2nd edition (1778–1783) we conclude our brief glance at our forebears' obsession with corporal punishment.

KEEL-HAULING, a punishment inflicted for various offences in the Dutch navy. It is performed by plunging the delinquent repeatedly under the ship's bottom on one side, and hoisting him up on the other, after having passed under the keel. The blocks, or pullies, by which he is suspended, are fastened to the opposite extremities of the main-yard, and a weight of lead or iron is hung upon his legs, to sink him to a competent depth. By this apparatus he is drawn close up to the yard-arm, and thence let fall suddenly into the sea, where, passing under the ship's bottom, he is hoisted up on the opposite side of the vessel. As this extraordinary sentence is executed with a serenity of temper peculiar to the Dutch, the culprit is allowed sufficient intervals to recover the sense of pain, of which indeed he is frequently deprived during the operation. In truth, a temporary insensibility to his sufferings ought by no means to be construed into a disrespect of his judges, when we consider that this punishment is supposed to have peculiar propriety in the depth of winter, whilst the flakes of ice are floating on the stream; and that it is continued till the culprit is almost suffocated for want of air, benumbed with the cold of the water, or stunned with the blows his head receives by striking the ship's bottom.

Cheering

The making of love, which creates, and the making of war, which destroys, are perhaps the two most consequential forms of human behavior, if we exclude eating. But Britannica, *yesterday and today, has also devoted much attention to our conduct in less fateful areas. The famous 11th edition (1910–1911), for example, has a rousing article on college yells.*

CHEERING, the uttering or making of sounds encouraging, stimulating or exciting to action, indicating approval or acclaiming or welcoming persons, announcements of events and the like. . . .

Rhythmical cheering has been developed to its greatest extent in America in the college yells, which may be regarded as a development of the primitive war-cry; this custom has no real analogue at English schools and universities, but the New Zealand football team in 1907 familiarized English crowds at their matches with a similar sort of war-cry adopted from the Maoris. In American schools and colleges there is usually one cheer for the institution as a whole and others for the different classes. The oldest and simplest are those of the New England colleges. The original yells of Harvard and Yale are identical in form, being composed of *rah* (abbreviation of *hurrah*) nine times repeated, shouted in unison with the name of the university at the end. The Yale cheer is given faster than that of Harvard. Many institutions have several different yells, a favourite variation being the name of the college shouted nine times in a slow and prolonged manner. The best known of these variants is the Yale cheer, partly taken from the *Frogs* of Aristophanes, which runs thus:

"Brekekekéx, ko-áx, ko-áx,
Brekekekéx, ko-áx, ko-áx,
O-óp, O-óp, parabaloū,
Yale, Yale, Yale,
Rah, rah, rah, rah, rah, rah, rah, rah, rah,
Yale! Yale! Yale!"

The regular cheer of Princeton is:

"H'ray, h'ray, h'ray, tiger,
Siss, boom, ah; Princeton!"

This is expanded into the "triple cheer":

"H'ray, h'ray, h'ray,
Tiger, tiger, tiger,
Siss, siss, siss,
Boom, boom, boom,
Ah, ah, ah,
Princetón, Princetón, Princetón!"

The "railroad cheer" is like the foregoing, but begun very slowly and broadly, and gradually accelerated to the end, which is enunciated as fast as possible. Many cheers are formed like that of Toronto University:

"Varsitý, varsitý,
V-a-r-s-í-t-y (spelled)
VARSITY (spelled *staccato*)
Vár-sí-tý,
Rah, rah, rah!"

Another variety of yell is illustrated by that of the School of Practical Science of Toronto University:

"Who are we? Can't you guess?
We are from the S. P. S.!"

The cheer of the United States Naval Academy is an imitation of a nautical syren. The Amherst cheer is:

"Amherst! Amherst! Amherst! Rah! Rah!
Amherst! Rah! Rah!
Rah! Rah! Rah! Rah! Rah! Rah! Amherst!"

Besides the cheers of individual institutions there are some common to all, generally used to compliment some successful athlete or popular professor. One of the oldest examples of these personal cheers is:

"Who was George Washington?
First in war,
First in peace,
First in the heárts of his countrymén,"

followed by a stamping on the floor in the same rhythm.

College yells are used particularly at athletic contests. In any large college there are several leaders, chosen by the students, who stand in front and call for the different songs and cheers, directing with their arms in the fashion of an orchestral conductor. This cheering and singing form one of the distinctive features of inter-collegiate and scholastic athletic contests in America.

Photography

George Eastman (1854–1932), who introduced the Eastman Kodak camera and thus effectively created the immensely popular hobby of amateur photography, wrote the article "Photography" for the 13th edition (a supplement to the 11th and 12th editions, 1926). It begins thus: (B.L.F.)

In this article photography is treated under four different heads. The first is introductory and general covering, among other topics, amateur, professional and aerial photography, radiography and amateur cinematography. The second deals with photographic manufacture; the third, with colour photography; and the fourth is an account of the general principles of photography in the light of recent knowledge.

I. Introductory and General

Photography is now applied to very many fields. It is employed in astronomy—in which photographic has almost superseded visual observation—microscopy, spectroscopy and many other fields of science, for a discussion of which reference must be made to the corresponding articles.

Amateur Photography. The use of photography for making personal records has extended very greatly since portable cameras and sensitive materials were introduced, and the tendency is continually towards a simplification of the work to be done by the user and a diminution in the amount of expert knowledge required to get good results. This has resulted in the establishment of commercial firms to develop and print photographs made by the amateur, so that the great majority of photographs are now taken by those whose knowledge of the subject is limited to that necessary for making the exposures. The cameras used are chiefly of the folding type using a cartridge of film and often of very small size.

The film can be loaded into the camera without the use of a dark room and removed after exposure for development. After an exposure has been made, an inscription may be written with a stylus on the red paper protecting the *autographic* film. The pressure of the stylus removes the dark-coloured wax from the "carbon" paper. An opening in the back of the camera where the writing is done is then exposed to light, which penetrates the translucent red paper and prints the inscription on the film. For development, the films are hung by clips in deep tanks and are then printed by artificial light upon gaslight or developing-out papers which are made in different degrees of contrast to suit the negatives obtained. As a general rule the photographic dealers will deliver prints from an exposed roll of film within two days. Enlargements are made upon bromide paper, frequently by means of enlarging cameras in which the focus is automatically maintained correct while the scale of magnification is varied. In addition to roll films, films in packs are largely used, each separate unit having a tab of paper attached to it by which it can be withdrawn after exposure. A small number of cameras still use plates or flat cut out films in suitable holders.

Almost all the cameras used in amateur photography are designed primarily for use in the hand and are only occasionally used upon tripods. In addition to the small portable cameras, many amateur photographers use reflex cameras and folding cameras fitted with focal plane shutters. A number of makers have introduced lenses working at very large apertures f/2 and f/2.5 and special cameras fitted with these lenses have been used for photography in ordinary rooms and under poor light conditions. Such equipment is very valuable under extreme conditions, but has the limitation that large aperture lenses have little depth of focus and consequently must be focused very exactly if good results are to be obtained.

The Olympics

In 1924 Harold Maurice Abrahams became an Olympic gold medalist, winning the 100-meter dash. He went on to become a broadcaster, a journalist, chairman of the British Amateur Athletic Association, and the author of The Olympic Games, 1896–1952. *He was one of the two heroic characters portrayed in the successful movie* Chariots of Fire. *Mr. Abrahams died in 1978.*

The current Britannica *article on "Olympic Games" is basically his work. Here are a few excerpts from it.*

Just how far back in history organized athletic contests were first held remains a matter of doubt, but it is reasonably certain that they occurred in Greece, at least, some 3,500 years ago.

However ancient in origin, by the end of the 6th century BC at least four of the Greek sporting festivals, sometimes known as classical games, had achieved major importance. They were the Olympic Games, held at Olympia; the Pythian Games at Delphi; the Nemean Games at Nemea; and the Isthmian Games at Corinth. Later, similar festivals were held in nearly 150 cities as far afield as Rome, Naples, Odessus, Antioch, and Alexandria.

The Olympic Games in particular were to become famous throughout the Greek world. There are records of the champions at Olympia from 776 BC to AD 217. The Games, held every four years, were abolished in AD 393 by the Roman emperor Theodosius I, probably because of their pagan associations. For the first 100 or 200 years, Olympic champions came from a dozen or more Greek cities, the majority from Sparta and Athens, but in the next three centuries, athletes were drawn from 100 cities in the Greek empire. And in the final 100 years or so before the games were discontinued, champions came from as far from Olympus as Antioch, Alexandria, and Sidon.

In 1887 the 24-year-old Baron Pierre de Coubertin conceived the idea of reviving the Olympic Games and spent seven years preparing public opinion in France, England, and the United States to support his plan. At an international congress in 1894, his plan was accepted and the International Olympic Committee was founded. The first modern Olympic Games were held in Athens in April 1896, with 13 nations sending nearly 300 representatives to take part in 42 events and 10 different sports. The revival of the Olympic Games led to the formation of many international bodies controlling their own amateur sports and to the creation of National Olympic Committees in countries throughout the world. . . . Boxing was introduced in 688 BC, and in 680 a chariot race. In 648 the pancratium (Greek *pankration*), a kind of all-strength, or no-holds-barred, wrestling, was included. Kicking and hitting were allowed; only biting and gouging (thrusting a finger or thumb into an opponent's eye) were forbidden. . . .

Sources generally agree that women were not allowed as competitors or, except for the priestess of Demeter, as spectators. In most events, the athletes participated in the nude. . . .

The Opening Ceremony

The form of the opening ceremony is laid down by the IOC in great detail, from the moment when the chief of state of the host country is received by the president of the IOC and the organizing committee at the entrance to the stadium, to the end of the proceedings when the last team files out. The rules provide that participants are not permitted to carry cameras into the arena, but this provision is always ignored.

When the head of state has reached his place in the tribune, he is greeted with the national anthem of his country, and the parade of competitors begins. The Greek team is always the first to enter the stadium, and, except for the host team, which is always last, the other nations follow in alphabetical order as determined by the language of the organizing country. Each contingent, dressed in its official uniform, is preceded by a shield with the name of its country, while an athlete carries its national flag. At the 1980 games, some of the countries protesting the Soviet Union's involvement in Afghanistan carried the Olympic flag in place of their national flag. The competitors march around the stadium and then form up in the centre of the ground facing the tribune.

The president of the organizing committee then delivers a brief speech of welcome, followed by another brief speech from the president of the IOC, who asks the chief of state to proclaim the Games open.

A fanfare of trumpets is sounded as the Olympic flag is slowly raised; pigeons are released, symbolically to fly to the countries of the world with the news that the Games are open.

The Olympic flame is then carried into the stadium by the last of the runners who have brought it from Olympia, Greece. The runner circles the track, mounts the steps, and lights the Olympic fire that burns night and day during the Games. In 1968 a woman carried the flame into the stadium, and in 1976 the flame was borne jointly by a male and a female athlete. In 1984, at the Games in Los Angeles, a female runner brought the flame into the stadium but passed it to a male, who ran up the steps to light the Olympic fire.

A Certain Game among the Scots

Although the early Britannica *editors often devoted fulsome attention to matters Scottish, the game of golf was not mentioned in the first two editions. It made a quaint, modest first appearance in the 3rd edition (1788–1797). (B.L.F.)*

The current Britannica, *in addition to a column in the* Micropaedia, *devotes to golf a considerable part of the major* Macropaedia *article on "Major Team and Individual Sports"—a clear indication of its startling expansion. The editors of the 3rd edition would be pleased if they knew that the current article was the work of Francis Moran, who, as a golf writer for* The Scotsman, *Edinburgh, was presumably himself a Scot. Here is the 3rd edition:*

GOLF, the name of a certain game among the Scots, and said to be peculiar to their country.—Among them it has been very ancient; for there are statutes prohibiting it as early as the year 1457, lest it should interfere with the sport of archery. It is commonly played on rugged broken ground, covered with short grass, in the neighbourhood of the seashore. A field of this sort is in Scotland called *links*. The game is generally played in parties of one or two on each side. Each party has an exceeding hard ball, somewhat larger than a hen's egg. This they strike with a slender and elastic club, of about four feet long, crooked in the head, and having lead run into it, to make it heavy. The ball being struck with this club, will fly to the distance of 200 yards, and the game is gained by the party who puts his ball into the hole with the fewest strokes. But the game does not depend solely upon the striking of the longest ball, but also upon measuring the strength of the stroke, and applying it in such direction as to lay the ball in smooth ground, whence it may be easily moved at the next stroke. To encourage this amusement, the city of Edinburgh, A.D. 1744, gave to the company of golfers a silver club, to be played for annually by the company, the victor to append a gold or silver piece to the prize. It has been played for every year since, except the years 1746, 1747. For their better accommodation, 22 members of the company subscribed L. 30 each in the year 1768, for building a house, where their meetings might be held. The spot chosen for this purpose was the southwest corner of Leith Links, where an area was taken in leu from the magistrates of Edinburgh, and a commodious house and tavern built upon it.

❧ ❧ ❧

A Saturnalian Amusement

Charles Apperley (1777–1843), using the pseudonym "Nimrod," was once a famous writer on the chase and other field sports. He appears in the 7th edition (1830–1842) as a defender of a diversion favored by many of his readers. The current Britannica*'s five columns on "Hunting" manage to take no position, either for or against.*

On Hunting

Nature has prepared many advantages and pleasures for the use of mankind, and given them the taste to enjoy them, and the sagacity to improve them; but of all the out-of-door amusements that have occupied the modern world, at least the male part of it, nothing has better stood the test of time than the noble diversion of hunting.

"Of all our fond diversions,
 A hunter's is the best:
In spite of wars and petty jars,
 That sport has stood the test."

And why has it stood the test? Not merely because the passion for the chase is interwoven closely with our nature; not because it originated in necessity, therefore originated in nature; but because it has been encouraged and approved of by the very best authorities, and practised by the greatest men. It cannot now, then, be supposed to dread criticism, or require support; neither can any solid objections be raised against a reasonable enjoyment of the sports of the field in general, provided what ought to be the pleasing relaxation of a man's leisure hours be not converted into the whole business of his life. But hunting, above all others, is a taste characteristically manly and appropriate to the gentlemen of Great Britain; and it has likewise another advantage over all other sports of the field, which adds much to its value in this land of liberty, and especially in the present age: it is a kind of Saturnalian amusement, in which the privileges of rank and fortune are laid aside, the best man in the chase being he who rides the best horse, and is best skilled in the use he should make of his superiority.

The Compleat Angler

The current Britannica *offers four and a third solid, informative columns on this sport. In the 7th edition (1830–1842) the writer preferred to choose as his vehicle what we would call the familiar essay and seems to be less interested in instructing than in charming us.*

ANGLING, or the art of fishing with rod and line, includes those branches of the piscatorial trade which are usually followed, not so much for profit, as for pleasant recreation. That the practice of "casting angles into the brook" had its origin in necessity, the mother of so many inventions, can hardly be doubted; but it is equally clear that the refined skill exhibited in this pursuit at the present day has been derived from leisure and the love of sport, aided by the more delicate gear which modern ingenuity has invented for the deception of the finny race.

The comparative merits of angling, and of the kindred occupations of the fowler and the huntsman, are not likely to be determined by any portraiture which a lover of these exciting amusements might draw of their various excellencies, but must depend on the tone and temper of mind possessed by different persons, and their greater or less accordance with individual tastes. This much, however, may be safely stated as a general and admitted truth, that the value of a pursuit increases in proportion as it becomes attainable by the mass of our fellow-creatures; and as angling is a much cheaper and more convenient pleasure than either hunting or shooting, it may, in so far as regards those advantages, claim a decided preference. Be it remembered that Dr Johnson's description of a rod with a fly at one end and a fool at the other is not admitted among the memorabilia of old Izaak Walton. . . .

As expert angling never was and never will be successfully taught by rule, but is almost entirely the result of assiduous and long-continued practice, we purpose being very brief in our disquisition on the subject. We shall commence by stating our belief that fly-fishing, by far the most elegant and interesting branch of the art, ought not to be regarded exclusively as an art of imitation. It no doubt depends on deception, which usually proceeds on the principle of one thing being successfully substituted in the likeness of another; but Bacon's distinctive definitions of simulation and dissimulation place the subject in a truer light. As simulation consists in the adoption or affectation of what is not, while dissimulation consists in the careful concealment of what really is—the one being a positive, the other rather a negative act—so the great object of the fly-fisher is to dissimulate in such a manner as to prevent his expected prey from detecting the artificial nature of his lure, without troubling himself by a vain effort to simulate or assume, with his fly, the appearance of any individual or specific form of insect life. There is, in truth, little or no connection between the art of angling and the science of entomology; and therefore the success of the angler, in by far the greater proportion of cases, does not depend on the resemblance which subsists between his artificial fly and the natural insect. This statement is no doubt greatly at variance, as well with the principles as the practice of all who have deemed fishing worthy of consideration, from the days of Isaiah and Theocritus, to those of Carrol and Bainbridge. But we are not the less decidedly of opinion, that in nine instances out of ten a fish seizes upon an artificial fly as upon an insect or moving creature *sui generis,* and not on account of its exact and successful resemblance to any accustomed and familiar object.

Football

Walter Camp (1859–1925) virtually invented American football, splitting it off from British rugby by such changes as devising the position and signal-calling role of quarterback, cutting team size to eleven from fifteen, and replacing the somewhat more boisterous free-for-all of the scrum with the scrimmage. Camp, a Yale graduate and briefly a medical student there, was Yale's first football head coach, and for many years he and one associate alone selected All-American college players. He brought his unique authority to the Britannica*'s description of the game in the 10th edition (1902–1903). By the time of the 11th edition (1910–1911), little remained to be added but the forward pass. (B.L.F.)*

Of course, the game has changed a great deal

since Camp's day. The current Britannica *devotes nine pages to the subject, taking due account of those factors that have made it part of both show business and big business.*

An extract from Camp's article follows, dealing only with the game as played in our country.

Football in America has had a peculiar history, and one showing the great tenacity of life possessed by this sport. At first such football as was played consisted merely in kicking the ball, and the play was without system. In the years 1871–72 certain rules were formulated, but they did not correspond to those in any other country, and were not on the whole satisfactory. Some of the colleges (to which the sport, until recently, was largely confined) formed an association, and adopted these rules. In 1875 Harvard and Yale met under rules taken partly from the Rugby Union and partly from the American game. These proved unsatisfactory, and the next year Harvard and Yale adopted the Rugby Union rules in their entirety. This was the foundation of the present American game. The players found that the Rugby Union rules, while much more satisfactory than anything that had been used, depended in a great measure upon traditional understanding and interpretations. American players were unwilling to be guided by anything except written regulations, and hence it was necessary to add to and explain the rules. Annual conventions were therefore held, and the rules were amplified and from time to time altered. Other colleges joined the Association, and the game became well established in the college world. The roughness and brutality displayed in playing were strongly commented upon in the newspapers, and at that time it was difficult to say whether the game would survive or not; but in another ten years it had made great progress, and then again it became the object of further newspaper assaults, and the Harvard team, through the action of the University authorities, was withdrawn from participation. This withdrawal lasted, however, for only a year. From that time the game has been characterized by lessening tendencies to roughness, by increasing skill, and by greater satisfaction to players and spectators. For some time past it has been, perhaps, the most popular sport in the college calendar, and has drawn crowds of from 35,000 to 40,000 people at the principal games. The Association disbanded some years ago, but a Rules Committee, invited by the University Athletic Club of New York, has made the necessary changes in the rules from time to time, and these have been accepted by the country at large. In the West associations have been formed, and still exist; but the game in the East is played principally under separate agreements between the contesting universities, all playing, however, under one code of rules.

The rules provide for a field 330 feet long by 160 feet wide, upon which teams composed of eleven men each contend for a period of two thirty-five minute halves, the total score at the end of the second half determining the victor. The scoring is by goals, touch-downs, and safety touch-downs. A goal is scored when the ball is kicked through the upright goal-posts and above the cross-bar connecting the posts at a distance of 10 feet above the ground; a touch-down when the ball is carried and touched to the ground behind the goal line;

a safety touch-down when the opponent is forced to carry the ball across his own goal line. The points and their values are: Goal from touch-down, 6 points; goal from field-kick, 5 points; touch-down from which no goal is kicked, 5 points; safety by opponents, 2 points. Any player when on-side can run with the ball, and his opponent may tackle him; if stopped, he must put the ball down, and a line-up or scrimmage is then formed. The ball may also be advanced by kicking. Infringement of the rules constitutes a foul, and various penalties are imposed.

Upon the above simple framework there has been built a most intricate system of play. The principle of the game is absolutely clear to the spectator, and therein lies its especial charm. There stands out boldly one cardinal object, namely, to advance the ball towards the opponent's goal. When this advance is attempted by means of kicking, the ball is usually sent as far as possible down into the opponent's territory, two or three men of the kicking side following it, and, in case it is muffed, endeavouring to secure it, or, if it be caught, to prevent the catcher from carrying it back on a run or returning the kick. The kicking game is most employed when the wind favours. It is also used to relieve the running game. A rule of the sport makes it obligatory upon the side which has failed to advance the ball five yards in three running attempts to surrender it. Hence it is usually to the advantage of the side in possession of the ball, when they have failed in two running attempts, and it looks unlikely that they would succeed in a third, to kick the ball as far as possible into the opponent's territory rather than to surrender it within a yard or so of its immediate position. The running game is more involved than the kicking game, it being the object of the captain to use all possible means to assault the opponents at points of weakness, to enable his runner to encircle the ends of the opponent's line, or to pierce that line at points where the attack can gather the most force, and the defence exhibits the least resistance. Certain signals are used which, presumably unknown to the opponents, indicate to the assaulting side just what the method of assault is to be, and thus enable the men to concentrate suddenly at the one point. This concentration is not finally brought about until after the ball has been put in play, so that the opponents have little chance to anticipate it.

The ball is handled with great accuracy, one man being selected to place the ball on the ground in a scrimmage and to snap it back with his hand to another player who delivers it, usually by a hand-pass or a short throw, to such individual as has been selected for the particular play. No man can pass the ball towards his opponent's goal, and any man is off-side and out of the play if he gets between the ball and his opponent's goal. He cannot then touch the ball until it touches an opponent, or until the man of his own side who has kicked it runs up ahead of him.

In order to measure properly the distance gained or lost the field is marked with white lines every five yards.

The officials consist of an umpire, whose principal duty it is to decide regarding fouls; a referee, who decides questions relating to the progress of the ball and the play; timekeepers and linesmen, who keep the time of the play and mark the exact progress of the ball for the benefit of the referee. The American game is far more involved and intricate than the Rugby, but offers correspondingly greater field for skilful play. Amateur athletic clubs have taken up the sport, and it is now the principal fall game throughout the United States.

Tennis

One of the world's foremost women's tennis champions, Helen Wills, was commissioned to describe U. S. lawn tennis for the 14th edition (1929). Helen Newington Wills Moody Roark (1905–), known briefly as "Little Miss Poker Face," won eight times at Wimbledon and took four French singles titles. For eight years (1927–1933 and 1935) she dominated female tennis competition. (B.L.F.)

Just when lawn tennis was introduced into the United States, and by whom, is a matter of conjecture. It is said that Miss Outerbridge spent the winter in Bermuda in 1874, and found the game being played there by British officers attached to the regiments stationed in Bermuda. She obtained from the regimental supply, some racquets and a net, which she brought back with her in the spring of that year. There was some difficulty in getting the outfit through the custom house, as no one knew what it was, or at what rate to assess duty on it. Miss Outerbridge obtained permission from her brother, who was a director of the Staten island cricket and baseball club, to mark off a court, and to set up her net in a corner of the grounds.

Shortly afterwards, James Dwight obtained a set from England. Dwight always claimed that the first court in the United States was laid out along one side of the Longwood cricket club's grounds. Others claimed the distinction for Nahant, near Boston. . . .

What the Davis Cup has done for men's tennis, the Wightman Cup has done for women's tennis. It was presented by Mrs. George W. Wightman for competition between women players of England and America, and was played for first at Forest Hills in 1923. The matches, which are annual, are played alternately at Wimbledon and at Forest Hills. In each series of matches, there are five singles and two doubles. The cup, which is a perpetual trophy, was won by the United States in 1923, 1926, 1927 and by England in 1924, 1925 and 1928.

CHAPTER THREE

Living Things

Botany

Beginning with the 1st edition (1768–1771) it was the editors' plan to treat large subjects comprehensively in full-scale treatises. This goal was realized in many subjects, among them botany. Succeeding editions extended the policy to more and more topics, meanwhile updating and occasionally reorganizing earlier treatises to accommodate new knowledge on subjects. This is the way the article "Botany" began in the 3rd edition (1788–1797). (B.L.F.)

In the utmost extent of the word, [Botany] signifies a knowledge of plants, and of the uses to which they may be applied, either in medicine, chemistry, or in the different arts. But as the medical virtues of plants fall properly under the province of the physician, their chemical properties belong to the chemist, etc.; hence the science of botany is commonly restricted to a bare knowledge of the different plants themselves, and of the distinguishing marks whereby each individual species may be known from each other. . . .

The utility of botanical classifications may be further illustrated from the following considerations.

1. With regard to *Food*. Many animals are endowed with an instinctive faculty of distinguishing with certainty whether the food presented to them be salutary or noxious. Mankind have no such instinct. They must have recourse to experience and observation. But they are not sufficient to guide us in every case. The traveller is often allured by the agreeableness of smell and taste to eat poisonous fruits. Neither will a general caution, not to eat any thing but what we know from experience to be salutary, answer in every emergency. A ship's company, in want of provisions, may be thrown upon an uninhabited coast or a desert island. Totally ignorant of the nature of the plants they meet with, diseases, or scarcity of animals, may make it absolutely necessary to use vegetable food. The consequence is dreadful: they must first eat before any certain conclusion can be formed. This is not the description of danger arising from an imaginary situation. Before the vegetables that grow in America, the East and West Indies, etc.

Fig. 3. Acanthus

became familiar to our sailors, many lives were lost by trials of this kind: neither has all the information received from experience been sufficient to prevent individual from still falling a prey to ignorance or rashness.—If the whole science of botany were as complete as some of its branches, very little skill in it would be sufficient to guard us infallibly from committing such fatal mistakes. There are certain orders and classes which are called *natural,* because every genus and species comprehended under them are not only distinguished by the same characteristic marks, but likewise possess the same qualities, though not in an equal degree. For example: Show a botanist the flower of a plant whose calyx is a double-valved glume, with three stamina, two pistils, and one naked seed; he can pronounce with absolute certainty, that the plant from which the flower was taken, bears seeds of a farinaceous quality, and that they may be safely used as food. In like manner, show him a flower with 12 or more stamina all inserted into the internal side of the calyx, tho' it belonged to

Fig. 1.
ALOE floribus sessilibus bilabiatis
or PEARL ALOE

Plate II.

Fig. 1. ACHILLEA NOBILIS or
purple Tansy leav'd Yarrow
Fig. 2.
ACONITUM PYRENAICUM
or
Yellow Pyrenean Aconite
A. Bell Sculp.t

a plant growing in Japan, he can pronounce without hesitation, that the fruit of it may be eat with safety. On the other hand, show him a plant whose flower has five stamina, one pistil, one petal, or flower-leaf, and whose fruit is of the berry kind, he will tell you to abstain from it, because it is poisonous. Facts of this kind render botany not only a respectable, but a most interesting, science.

2. With respect to *Medicine,* the same thing holds good. It is found by experience, that plants which are distinguished by the same characters in the flower and fruit have the same qualities, though not always in an equal degree as to strength or weakness; so that, upon inspection of the flower and fruit, a botanist can determine *à priori* the effects that will result when taken into the stomach.

Tobacco

All Earth's creatures, botanical or otherwise, are surprising, including ourselves.

Among the most surprising of human activities is smoking. Britannica*'s 1st edition (1768–1771) had some strong opinions about the use of tobacco. Here is an extract from the article "Nicotiana."*

Tobacco is either taken by way of snuff, as a sternutatory; or as a masticatory, by chewing it in the mouth; or by smoking it in a pipe. It is sometimes also taken in little longish pellets put up the nose, where it is found to produce very good effects, to attract a deal of water or pituita, unload the head, resolve catarrhs, and make a free respiration; for the subtile parts of the tobacco in inspiration, are carried into the trachea and lungs, where they loosen the peccant humours adhering thereto, and promote expectoration. Some have left this tobacco in their noses all night; but this is found to occasion vomiting the next morning. Another thing charged on this way of application, is, that it weakens the sight. When taken in great quantities in the way of snuff, it is found to prejudice the smelling, greatly diminishes the appetite, and in time gives rise to a phthisis. That taken in the way of smoke, dries and damages the brain. Borrhi, in a letter to Bartholine, mentions a person who through excess of smoking had dried his brain to that degree, that after his death there was nothing found in his skull but a little black lump, consisting of mere membranes.

Some people use the infusion of tobacco as an emetic; but it is a very dangerous and unjustifiable practice, and often produces violent vomiting, sickness, and stupidity.

Bates and Fuller give some receipts, in which tobacco is an ingredient, with mighty encomiums in asthmatic cases. A strong decoction of tobacco, with proper carminatives and cathartics, given clysterwise, sometimes proves of good effect in what is usually called the stone-cholic, and also in the iliac passion. A drop or two of the chymical oil of tobacco, being put on the tongue of a cat, produces violent convulsions, and death itself in the space of a minute; yet the same oil used in lint, and applied to the teeth, has been of service in the tooth-ach: though it must be to those that have been used to the taking of tobacco; otherwise, great sickness, retchings, vomitings, etc., happen; and even in no case is the internal use of it warranted by ordinary practice.

By the time of the 4th edition (1801–1809), the encyclopedic view seems to have changed a bit.

NICOTIANA, tobacco, a genus of plants belonging to the pentandria class, and in the natural method ranking under the 28th order, *Luridae.* See BOTANY *Index.*—There are seven species, of which the most remarkable is the *tabacum,* or common tobacco plant. This was first discovered in America by the Spaniards about the year 1560, and by them imported into Europe. It had been used by the inhabitants of America long before; and was called by those of the islands *yoli,* and *paetun* by the inhabitants of the continent. It was sent into Spain from Tabaco, a province of Yucatan, where it was first discovered, and from whence it takes its common name. Sir Walter Raleigh is generally said to have been the first that introduced it into England about the year 1585, and who taught his countrymen how to smoke it. . . .

The most common uses of this plant, are either as a sternutatory when taken by way of snuff, as a masticatory by chewing it in the mouth, or as effluvia by smoking it; and when taken in moderation, it is not an unhealthful amusement. Before pipes were invented, it was usually smoked in segars, and they are still in use among some of the southern nations.

If you look up the discussion of smoking in the current 15th edition, you will find that virtually the entire article deals with "health issues" and "controls."

❧ ❧ ❧

Semen

Biological usage has altered since the 2nd edition (1778–1783), when the major article on this topic dealt with plants. In the same edition, a much smaller article, "Semen Masculinum," gets only second billing. (B.L.F.)

SEMEN, in botany, the seed; the essence of the fruit of every vegetable; defined by Linnaeus to be a deciduous part of the plant, containing the rudiments of a new vegetable, and fertilized by the aspersion or sprinkling of the male-dust. The parts of a seed, properly so called, enumerated by Linnaeus, are as follows: 1. CORCULUM, the *punctum vitae,* or essence of the seed. 2. COTYLEDONES, the lobes. 3. HILUM, a mark or scar in the seed. 4. ARILLUS, Lin. the proper covering: *calyptra* of Tournefort. 5. CORONULA, PAPPUS, the crown of the seed. 6. ALA, the wing of the seed.

Besides the seed properly so called, two other terms are referred by Linnaeus to the general article of SEMEN, viz. 7. NUX, a nut, or seed covered with a hard bony skin. 8. PROPAGO, the seed of the mosses.

With respect to number, plants are either furnished with one seed, as sea-pink and bistort; two, as wood-roof and the umbelliferous plants; three, as spurge; four, as the lip-flowers of Tournefort and rough-leaved plants of Ray; or many, as ranunculus, anemone, and poppy.

The form of seeds is likewise extremely various, being either large or small, round, oval, heart-shaped, kidney-shaped, angular, prickly, rough, hairy, wrinkled, sleek, or shining, black, white, or brown. Most seeds have only one cell, or internal cavity; those of lesser burdock, valerian, lamb's

Plate IV.

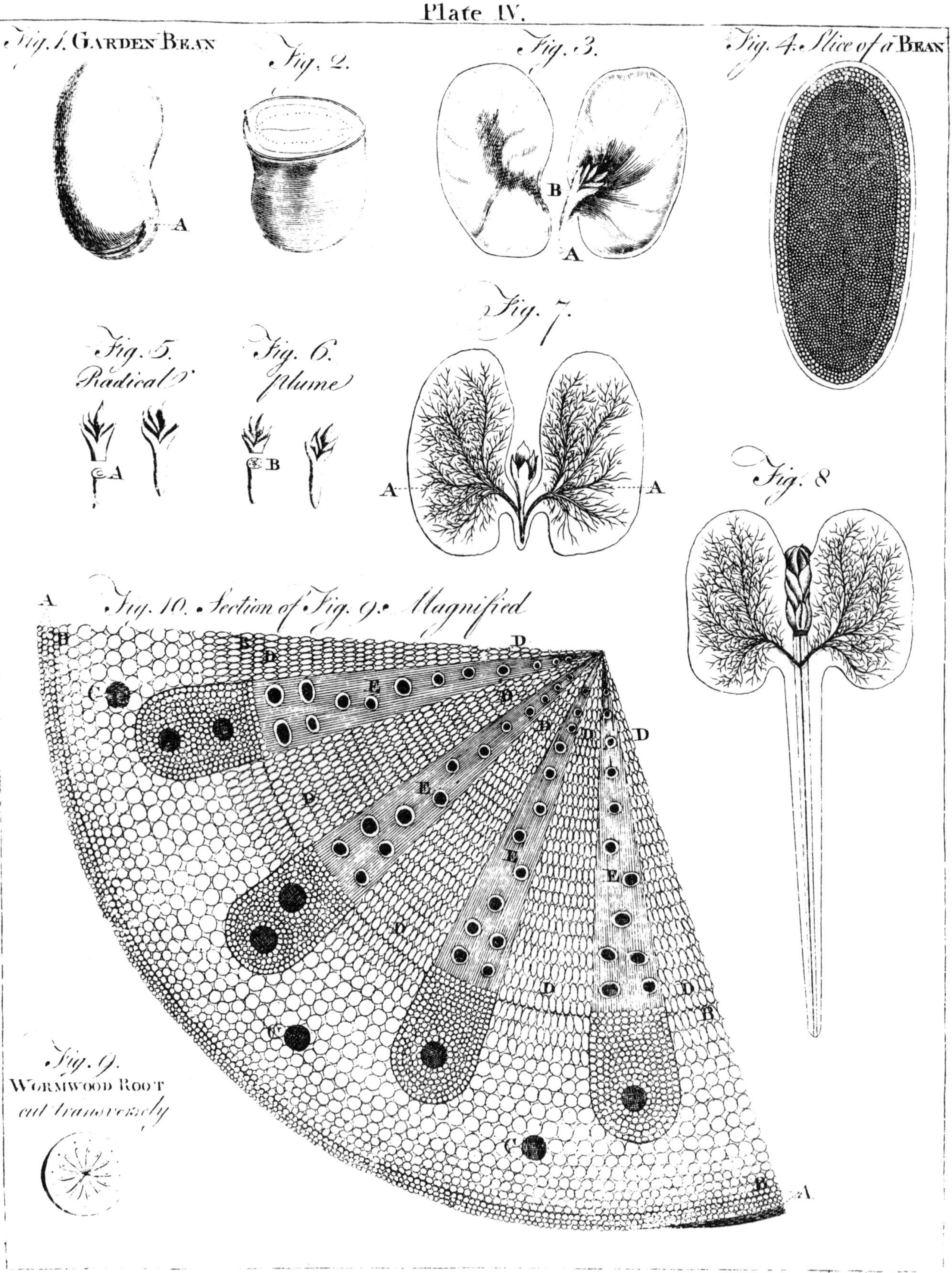
Fig. 1. Garden Bean
A
Fig. 2.
Fig. 3.
B
A
Fig. 4. Slice of a Bean
Fig. 5. Radicale
A
Fig. 6. plume
B
Fig. 7
A
A
Fig. 8
Fig. 10. Section of Fig. 9. Magnified
A
B
B
D
D
C
E
E
D
D
D
D
E
D
E
E
D
D
B
C
C
B
A
Fig. 9.
Wormwood Root
cut transversely

lettuce, cornelian cherry, and sebesten, have two.

With respect to substance, seeds are either soft, membranaceous, or of a hard bony substance; as in gromwell, tamarind, and all the nuciferous plants.

In point of magnitude, seeds are either very large, as in cocoa-nut; or very small, as in campanula, *ammannia,* rampions, and throat-wort.

With respect to situation, they are either dispersed promiscuously through the pulp, (*femina nidulantia*), as in water-lily; affixed to a suture or joining of the valves of the seed-vessel, as in the cross-shaped and pea-bloom flowers; or placed upon a *placenta,* or receptacle within the seed-vessel, as in tobacco, and thorn-apple.

Seeds are said to be naked (*femina nuda*) which are not contained in a cover, or vessel: such are those of the lip and compound flowers, the umbelliferous and rough-leaved plants; covered seeds (*femina tecta*) are contained in some vessel, whether of the capsule, pod, berry, apple, or cherry kind.

A simple seed is such as bears neither crown, wing, nor downy *pappus;* the varieties in seeds, arising from these circumstances, are particularly enumerated under their respective heads.

SEMEN *Masculinum,* in the animal oeconomy, is a white, liquid matter or humour, the thickest of any in the body, separated from the blood in the testicles, and reserved in proper vessels, to be the means of generation. By chemical analysis it is found to consist almost entirely of oil and volatile salts blended together by the mediation of a little phlegm.

Potato

The Britannica *was a source of practical as well as scholarly knowledge. For agriculturists, as a case in point, useful tips abounded. This extract is from the 3rd edition (1788–1797).*

. . . Potatoes, it is generally thought, came originally from North America, where they were not reckoned good for food. They were first (we are told) introduced into Ireland in the year 1565, and from thence into England by a vessel wrecked on the western coast, called *North Meols,* in Lancashire, a place and soil even now famous for producing this vegetable in great perfection. It was 40 years after their introduction, however, before they were much cultivated about London; and then they were considered as rarities, without any conception of the utility that might arise from bringing them into common use. At this time they were distinguished from the Spanish by the name of *Virginia potatoes,* or *battatas,* which is the Indian name of the Spanish sort. At a meeting of the Royal Society, March 18th, 1662–3, a letter was read from Mr Buckland, a Somerset gentleman, recommending the planting of potatoes in all parts of the kingdom to prevent famine. This was referred to a committee; and, in consequence of their report, Mr Buckland had the thanks of the society. . . .

The utility of potatoes to the common people is well known, and this utility has brought them into general use, and has extended them over every part of this kingdom. To promote this utility, and to make their cultivation more easy, a variety of experiments and inquiries have been made. Some of these we shall now lay before our readers, without repeating, however, what has been said on the same subject in the article AGRICULTURE. By many people the Irish purple potato is thought to be the sweetest and best; and of these the bright and middle-sized are directed to be set whole, in February, March, and April, in a fine deep tilth, in any soil. During the frost, the first setting should be covered with litter or fern. They should be set six inches deep, and a yard distant from each other every way, in a kind of hillocks like a molecast; and they must be moulded every month or fortnight, as high as possible. By July or August, under each hillock there will be nearly a bushel of potatoes. The white kidney potato runs all into stringy roots in loose ground, while the pink-coloured will do extremely well in the way we have now directed, and the smallest of them, though often given to hogs, unless they be otherwise improper or unhealthy, will be very good feed. The following experiments concerning the culture of potatoes are related in the Georgical Essays. . . .

"My gardener cut a large potato into nine pieces, which he planted with dung, in a drill, in the garden. By earthing up and laying the shoots, he produced 575 (A) sizeable potatoes, which weighed eight stone eight pound. Another of my servants produced, in the field, seven stone of good potatoes from the same number of sets. Though this experiment cannot always be executed in its full force in an extensive scale, it ought, notwithstanding, to be imitated as nearly as circumstances will allow. It shows, in the most distinguishing manner, the use of clean and careful husbandry."

❧ ❧ ❧

The Sleep of Plants

Daniel Ellis, Esq., was a respected botanist of Edinburgh and a fellow of the Royal Society. In his article "Vegetable Physiology," in the Supplement to the 4th, 5th, and 6th editions (1815–1824), he took note, rather cautiously, of an early nineteenth-century notion that plants, like animals, needed sleep. (B.L.F.)

Some writers, deeming plants to possess voluntary power, have from thence inferred that they require sleep. We have no proof, however, that they possess any such power; nor that, in the exercise of their ordinary functions, they experience that fatigue and exhaustion which renders sleep necessary to their restoration. All the spontaneous movements of vegetables previously described, seem to arise from the operation of physical agents, conjoined with those inherent properties which belong to them as living beings. These agents act variously on different plants; and hence some close their leaves and flowers from the abstraction of heat or moisture, and others from the exclusion of light; and this at various periods of the day, as well as through the night. Other plants exhibit spontaneous movements only in the flower, and at the season of fecundation, when suitable conditions of the atmosphere prevail: and though, in some instances, these motions continue for a time after the conditions required for their display may have been withdrawn, yet we must ascribe such motions rather to habit than to any thing that partakes of the nature of volition.

The diminution or suspension of action that occurs, through the night, to plants that inhabit temperate climes, cannot be received as a proof of sleep, induced by exhaustion of the vegetative powers; for even in such climes, vegetation, in favourable seasons, proceeds often by night as well as by day. In climates still more favourable, the same plants which produce fruits only once a-year with us, yield two or more crops; and in Norway and Lapland, where the sun, at certain periods, continues almost constantly above the horizon, the whole period between seed-time and harvest sometimes occupies only about fifty days. In such cases, little or no suspension of the vegetative functions can have taken place; nor have we the smallest reason to believe that the continued exercise of them is followed by fatigue or exhaustion sufficient to require sleep. What, therefore, has commonly been denominated the "sleep of plants," we can regard only as a diminution or suspension of the vegetative functions, arising from the abstraction, more or less complete, of those external agents, whose presence is essential to their full operation and display.

Sleepers

Sometimes terminology was quaint by our standards, though perfectly logical. From the 1st edition (1768–1771): (B.L.F.)

SLEEPERS, in natural history, a name given to those animals which sleep all winter; such as bears, marmots, dormice, bats, hedge-hogs, swallows, etc. These do not feed in winter, have no sensible evacuations, breathe little or none at all, and most of the viscera cease from their functions. Some of these creatures seem to be dead, and others return to a state like that of the foetus before birth: in this state they continue, till by length of time maturating the process, or by new heat the fluids are attenuated, and the functions begin where they left off.

Lacerta

Don't look up "Lacerta" today: Lizards are saurians, crocodiles are crocodilia; both, with snakes (and dinosaurs) are reptilia. For the 1st edition (1768–1771), however . . . (B.L.F.)

LACERTA, the lizard, in zoology, a genus of amphibious animals belonging to the order of reptilia, the characters of which are these: The body is naked, with four feet, and a tail. There are 49 species, *viz.*

1. The crocodylus, or crocodile, has a compressed jagged tail, five toes on the fore-feet, and four on the hind-feet. This is the largest animal of the lizard kind. One that was dissected at Siam, an account of which was sent to the Royal Academy at Paris, was

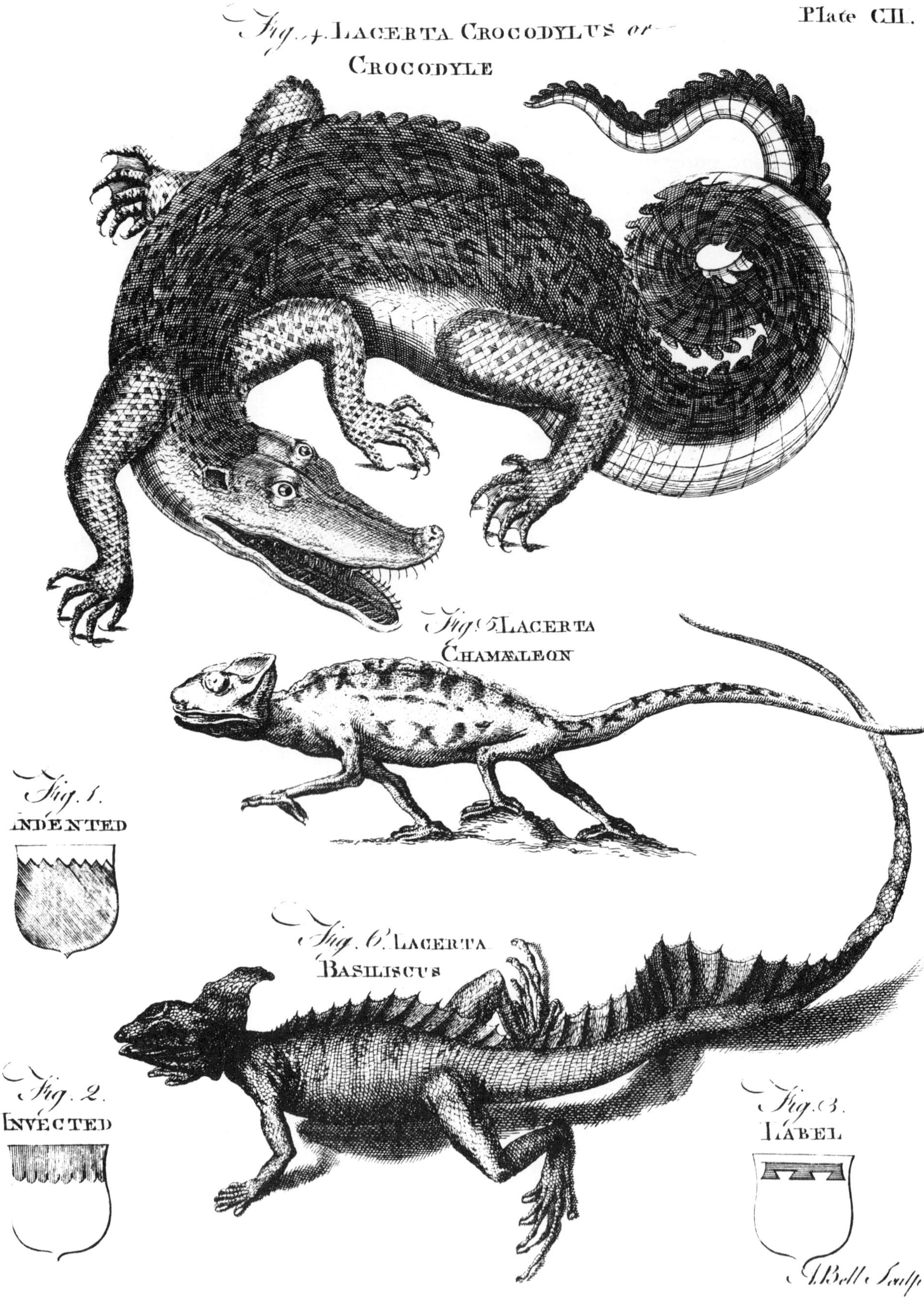
Plate CII.
Fig. 4. LACERTA CROCODYLUS or CROCODYLE
Fig. 5. LACERTA CHAMÆLEON
Fig. 1. INDENTED
Fig. 6. LACERTA BASILISCUS
Fig. 2. INVECTED
Fig. 3. LABEL
A. Bell Sculp.

eighteen feet and a half long, of which the tail was no less than five feet and a half, and the head and neck above two and a half. He was four feet and nine inches in circumference where thickest.

Herring

"Dead as a herring" was an eighteenth-century Britishism approximating the Americanism "dead as a mackerel." From the 1st edition (1768–1771) modern readers may, at last, find out why these fish have been so distinguished for their mortality. (B.L.F.)

CLUPEA, or herring, in ichthyology, a genus belonging to the order of abdominales. The upper jaw is furnished with a serrated mystache; the branchioflege membrane has eight rays; a scaly serrated line runs along the belly from the head to the tail; and the belly-fins have frequently nine rays. There are 11 species, *viz.*

1. The harengus, or common herring, has no spots, and the under jaw is longer than the upper one. A herring dies immediately after it is taken out of the water, whence the proverb arises, *As dead as a herring*. The flesh is every where in great esteem, being fat, soft, and delicate, especially if it is drest as soon as caught; for then it is incomparably better than on the next day.

Eels in Vinegar

In old encyclopedias, things are not always what they might seem at first glance to modern eyes; so "Eels in Vinegar," which appeared in the 2nd edition (1778–1783), was not a recipe—though the edition did contain some recipes. The invention and ever-widening use of the microscope brought with it discoveries that required newly invented words. The 1st edition (1768–1771) had defined one of these:

ANIMALCULE, an animal so minute in its size as not to be the immediate object of our senses. See MICROSCOPE.

Some of these minute creatures were named for what, in microcosm, they resembled in the "real world," i.e., *eels. We know these microscopic "eels" as nematodes. (B.L.F.)*

EEL-FISHING. See BOBBING and SNIGGLING.

The silver-eel may be catched with several sorts of baits, as powdered-beef, garden-worms, minnows, hens-guts, fish-garbage, etc. The most proper time for taking them is in the night, fastening your line to the bank-sides, with your laying-hook in the water: or a line may be thrown with good store of hooks, baited and plumbed, with a float to discover where the line lies, that they may be taken up in the morning.

MICROSCOPIC EELS *in sour Paste.* See ANIMALCULE

EELS IN VINEGAR are similar to those in sour paste. The taste of vinegar was formerly thought to be occasioned by the biting of these little animals, but that opinion has been long ago exploded. Mentzelius says, he has observed the actual transformation of these little creatures into flies: but as this hath never been observed by any other person, nor is there an instance of such a transformation in any other animalcule, it seems probable that Mentzelius hath been mistaken in his observations.

Fig. 41.

Fig. 42.

Fig. 43.

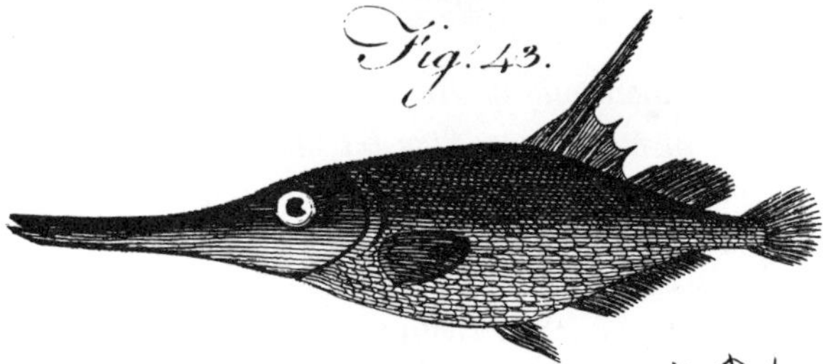

Fig. 44.

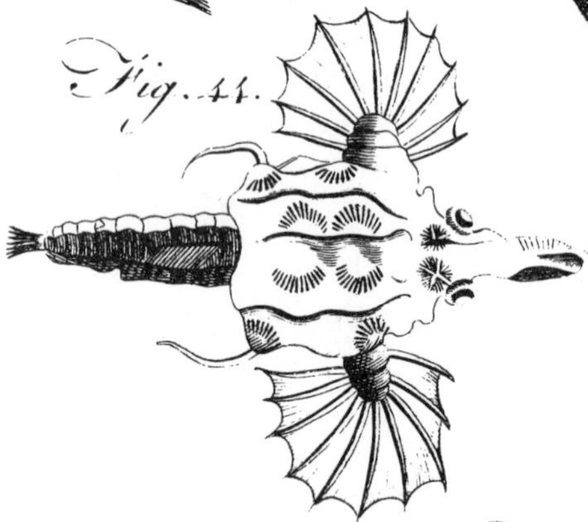

Fig. 45.

Fig. 46.

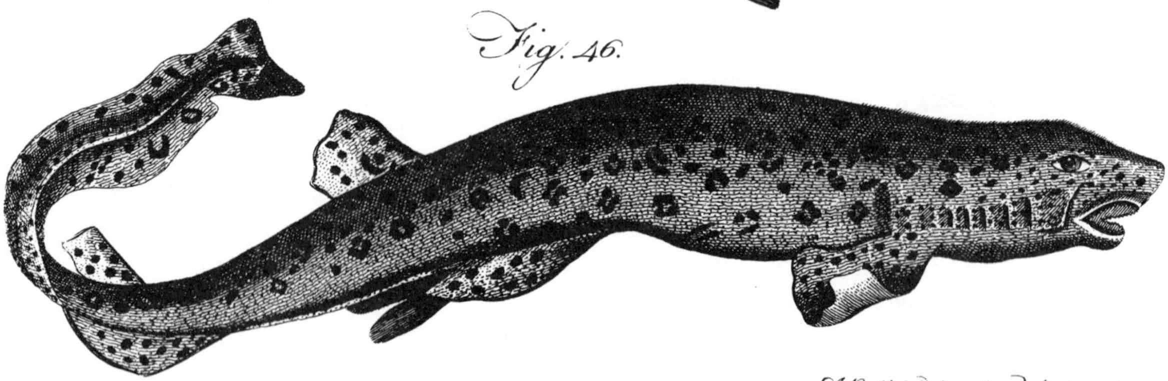

A. Bell Prin. Wal. Sculptor fecit.

Serpents

The 2nd edition (1778–1783) discussed animals in a manner that, however unscientific, may seem to modern readers to have succeeded in bringing out their characters. Here, for instance, is an extract from the article "Serpent," dealing with that creature's dietary habits.

A single meal, with many of the snake kind, seems to be the adventure of a season; it is an occurrence, of which they have been for weeks, nay sometimes for months, in patient expectation. When they have seized their prey, their industry for several weeks is entirely discontinued; the fortunate capture of an hour often satisfies them for the remaining period of their annual activity. As their blood is colder than that of most other terrestrial animals, and as it circulates but slowly through their bodies, so their powers of digestion are but feeble. Their prey continues, for a long time, partly in the stomach, partly in the gullet, and is often seen in part hanging out of the mouth. In this manner it digests by degrees; and in proportion as the part below is dissolved, the part above is taken in. It is not therefore till this tedious operation is entirely performed, that the serpent renews its appetite and its activity. But should any accident prevent it from issuing once more from its cell, it still can continue to bear famine, for weeks, months, nay for years together. Vipers are often kept in boxes for six or eight months, without any food whatever; and there are little serpents sometimes sent over to Europe from Grand Cairo, that live for several years in glasses, and never eat at all, nor even stain the glass with their excrements.

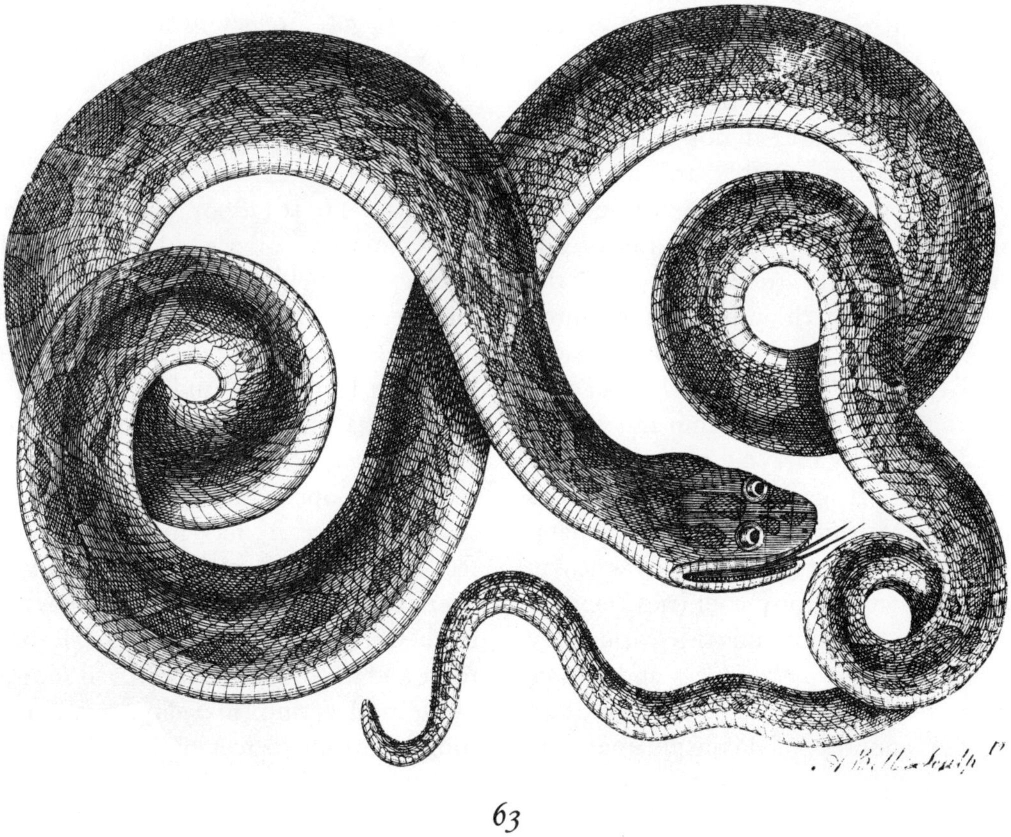

Frogs

Encyclopedias today, in their scientific articles, eschew the anecdote, and with good reason. But perhaps something is lost. If you refer to "Amphibians" in the Macropaedia *of the current edition, you will find a full but sternly sober treatment of frogs. If in its time you had consulted* Britannica's *2nd edition (1778–1783), you would have found a surprising article running to more than three pages. But you would have had to know that rana = frog. Here is an extract from it. (A "waite," by the way, was a term for a public or street musician.)*

RANA, the frog, in zoology, a genus belonging to the order of amphibia reptilia. The body is naked, furnished with four feet, and without any tail. There are 17 species. . . .

As frogs adhere closely to the backs of their own species, so we know they will do the same by fish. Walton mentions a strange story of their destroying pike; but that they will injure, if not entirely kill carp, is a fact indisputable, from the following relation. A very few years ago, on fishing a pond belonging to Mr Pit, of Encomb, Dorsetshire, great numbers of the carp were found each with a frog mounted on it, the hind legs clinging to the back, and the fore legs fixed in the corner of each eye of the fish, which were thin and greatly wasted, seized by carrying so disagreeable a load. These frogs Mr Pennant supposes to have been males disappointed of a mate.

The croaking of frogs is well known; and from that in fenny countries they are distinguished by ludicrous titles: thus they are styled *Dutch nightingales,* and *Boston waites. . . .*

In the country of Pennsylvania, and some other parts of North America, there is a very large species of frogs called the *bull-frog.* These make a monstrous roaring noise like a bull, only somewhat more hoarse. Their size is superior to that of any other of the genus, and they can spring forward three yards at a leap. By this means they will equal in speed a very good horse in its swiftest course. Their places of abode are ponds, or bogs with stagnant water; but they never frequent streams. When many of them are together, they make such a horrid noise, that two people cannot understand each other's speech.

Giants

Pioneer editors were more credulous than they are today, a circumstance that often produced interesting results. This sample, from the entry titled "Giant," comes from the 2nd edition (1778–1783).

REMAINS OF GIANTS

January 11, 1613, some masons digging near the ruins of a castle in Dauphiné, France, in a field which (by tradition) had long been called *the giant's field,* at the depth of 18 feet discovered a brick-tomb 30 feet long, 12 feet wide, and 8 feet high; on which was a grey stone, with the words *Theutobochus Rex* cut thereon. When the tomb was opened, they found a human skeleton entire, 25 feet and a half long, 10 feet wide across the shoulders, and five feet deep from the breast-bone to the back. His teeth were about the size each of an ox's foot, and his shin bone measured four feet. —Near Mazarino, in Sicily, in 1516, was found a giant 30 feet high; his head was

arms nor legs, and the head of that animal hath not the least resemblance to that of a man. If it be true, therefore, that a great number of the gigantic bones which we have mentioned have been seen by anatomists, and by them have been reputed real human bones, the existence of giants is proved.

the size of an hog-head, and each of his teeth weighed five ounces. Near Palermo, in the valley of Mazara, in Sicily, a skeleton of a giant 30 feet long was found, in the year 1548; and another of 33 feet high, in 1550; and many curious persons have preserved several of these gigantic bones.

The Athenians found near their city two famous skeletons, one of 34 and the other of 36 feet high.

At Totu, in Bohemia, in 758, was found a skeleton, the head of which could scarce be encompassed by the arms of two men together, and whose legs, which they still keep in the castle of that city, were 26 feet long. The skull of the giant found in Macedonia, September 1691, held 210 pounds of corn.

The celebrated Sir Hans Sloane, who treated this matter very learnedly, does not doubt these facts; but thinks the bones were those of elephants, whales, or other enormous animals.

Elephants' bones may be shown for those of giants; but they can never impose on connoisseurs. Whales, which, by their immense bulk, are more proper to be substituted for the largest giants, have neither

"Bedbuggs"

Today's Britannica *will tell you what bugs are—but not how to get rid of them. In olden days, scholars had a less theoretical bent. The very first edition suggested in a short article that the best remedy was cleanliness. The 3rd edition (1788–1797) knew precisely what should be done.*

BUG, or bugg, in zoology, the English name of a species of cimex.

Cheap, easy, and clean mixture for effectually destroying Buggs. Take of the highest rectified spirit of wine, (*viz.* lamp-spirits) that will burn all away dry, and leave not the least moisture behind it, half a pint; new distilled oil, or spirit, of turpentine, half a pint: mix them together; and break into it, in small bits, half an ounce of camphire, which will dissolve it in a few minutes; shake them well together; and with a piece of sponge, or a brush dipt in some of it, wet very well the bed or furniture wherein those vermin harbour and breed, and it will infallibly kill and destroy both them and their nits, although they swarm ever so much. But then the bed and furniture must be well and thoroughly wet with it (the dust upon them being first brushed and shook off), by which means it will neither soil, stain, nor in the least hurt, the finest silk or damask bed that is. The quantity here ordered of this mixture (that costs but about a shilling) will rid any one bed whatever, tho' it swarms with buggs.

Moles

The current Britannica *will tell you as much about moles as anyone would wish to know. But as we have seen in the case of the bedbug, it won't tell you how to root them out. The editors of the 3rd edition (1788–1797) very much concerned themselves with the problems of daily life, as the reader will see in*

MOLE, in zoology. See Talpa.
Moles in the fields may be destroyed by taking a head or two of garlic, onion, or leek, and putting it into their holes; on which they will run out as if frighted, and you may kill them with a spear or dog. Or pounded hellebore, white or black, with wheat-flour, the white of an egg, milk, and sweet-wine, or metheglin, may be made into a paste, and pellets as big as a small nut may be put into their holes: the moles will eat this with pleasure, and will be killed by it. In places where you would not dig nor break much, the fuming their holes with brimstone, garlic, or other unsavoury things, drives them away; and if you put a dead mole into a common haunt, it will make them absolutely forsake it.

Greyhound

Hundreds of what seem to us quaint entries throw clear light on the minds and daily interests of the Englishman (and, perhaps, the Englishwoman) of two centuries ago. Here, for example, from the 3rd edition (1788–1797), is "Greyhound," or "Gre-hound." (Note that you are referred not to "Dog" but to "Canis.")

GRE-HOUND See Canis. — Among a litter of gre-hound puppies, the best are always those which are lightest. These will make the nimblest dogs as they grow up. The gre-hound is best for open countries where there is little covert. In these places there will sometimes be a course after a hare of two or three miles or more, and both the dogs and the game in sight all the while. It is generally supposed that the gre-hound bitch will beat the dog in running; but this seems to be an error; for the dog is both longer made, and considerably stronger, than the bitch of the same kind. In the breeding these dogs the bitch is principally to be regarded; for it is found by experience, that the best dog and a bad bitch will not get so good puppies as an indifferent dog with a good bitch. The dog and bitch should be as nearly as may be of the same age; and for the breeding of fine and perfect dogs, they should not be more than four years old. An old bitch may be used with a young dog, but the puppies of a young bitch and an old dog will never be good for any thing.

The general food for a gre-hound ought to be chippings or raspings of bread, with soft bones and gristles; and those chippings ought always to be soaked in beef or mutton broth.

The proper exercise for a gre-hound is coursing him three times a-week, and rewarding him with blood; which will animate him in the highest degree, and encourage him to prosecute his game. But the hare also should ever have fair play.

She should have the law, as it is called; that is, have leave to run about twelve score yards before the dog is slipped at her, that he may have some difficulty in the course, and not pick up the game too easily. If he kills the hare, he must never be suffered to tear her; but she must be taken from him, his mouth cleaned of the wool, and the liver and lights given him by way of encouragement. Then he is to be led home, and his feet washed with butter and beer, and about an hour after he is to be fed.

When the dog is to be taken out to course, he should have nothing in the morning but a toast and butter, and then he is to be kennelled till taken out to the field. The kennelling these dogs is of great use, always giving them spirit and nimbleness when they are let loose: and the best way of managing a fine gre-hound is, never to let him stir out of the kennel, except at the times of feeding, walking, or coursing.

Unicorns and Other Mammalia

The opening paragraphs of "Mammalia" (4th edition, 1801–1809) give us an idea of how imperfect the state of knowledge was at the time. The last sentence is a startler. For an interesting summary of our present-day information about the unicorn, the reader is referred to Volume 12 of the 15th edition under "Unicorn."

The first class of the animal kingdom in the system of Linnaeus, containing those animals which have *breasts* or *paps,* (*mamme*) at which they suckle their young. In this class are included, not only what are called the *viviparous quadrupeds,* but the Bat tribe, and several marine animals, as Seals and Whales. In the present article, we are to give an account of all but the whales, or Cetacea, which have been already fully treated of under the article CETOLOGY.

INTRODUCTION

The relations that subsist between man and many of the animals arranged in this class, either from their utility as domestic servants, or from the warfare that they carry on against him, his property or his dependants, render the study of this part of natural history peculiarly important; while the extraordinary actions and faculties of some of these animals must make the history of them highly interesting to every one who examines nature with a curious or discerning eye.

Quadrupeds have, accordingly, engaged the particular attention of naturalists in every country and in every age, and as our acquaintance with them is less difficult than with most other classes of animated nature, it is not surprising that their form, habits, and manners are most familiar to us. Still, indeed, much remains in doubt respecting some of the foreign and rarer quadrupeds, and of some we know little more than the name. Even with regard to those which have been longest known and described, as the *lion,* the *elephant,* the *porcupine,* etc., the observations of modern naturalists and travellers have corrected several erroneous notions that had been generally received as certain. Long as this part of natural history has occupied the attention of mankind, there yet probably remain many gleanings to repay the industry of future inquirers. It is probable that the unexplored regions of Africa, America, and New Holland, may contain many quadrupeds either entirely unknown to us at present, or known only by the fossil remains that have been discovered in the bowels of the earth. There can, we think, be little doubt that the unicorn exists in Africa not far north of the Cape of Good Hope, and perhaps, at some distant period it may be as well known as the elephant or the hippopotamus is at present.

The Feathered Race

What started out in the 1st edition (1768–1771) as a rather spare taxonomic element of the article "Natural History," augmented by a few short articles on some particular birds, grew edition by edition into the 4th's (1801–1809) comprehensive treatise of more than a hundred pages under the title "Ornithology." (B.L.F.)

The term *Ornithology* is derived from the Greek ορνις, a bird, and ζολος, discourse, and denotes that part of Zoology which treats of birds.

Birds are two-footed animals, covered with feathers, and furnished with wings. Like quadrupeds and the cetaceous tribe, they have warm blood, a heart with two ventricles and two auricles, and lungs for the purpose of respiration; but they are distinguished from both by their feet, feathers, wings, and horny bill, as well as by the circumstance of their females being oviparous.

The elegant and beautiful colouring of many of the feathered race, the graceful ease of their flight, their various music, their tender solicitude for their offspring, their engaging instincts, their susceptibility of domestication, and their subservience to the sustenance of man, have, in all ages, contributed to interest the latter in the study of their history.

Of the naturalists, however, whose writings have descended to us from antiquity, Aristotle and Pliny are the only two who appear to have entered into any details on a subject so inviting and important.

Brute

To get a quick sense of the mental world of scholars of two centuries ago, one may compare the titles of their encyclopedia articles with ours. We would never think of including an article labeled "Brute," but they did. Here, in part, is how the 4th edition (1801–1809) handled the topic.

BRUTE, a general name for all animals except mankind.

Among brutes, the monkey kind bear the nearest resemblance to man, both in the external shape and internal structure, but more in the former than in the latter. In the monkey kind, the highest and the nearest approach to the likeness of man is the ouran outang, or *Homo Sylvestris.* — The structure and economy of brutes make the objects of what is called *Comparative Anatomy.*

16
4
2
4
1
1
5
3
3
6
32
33
18
3
17
8
10
10
7
8
15
11
9
12
13
14
19
20
31
21
22
23
29
25
27
24
25
28
30

Fig. 1.

FALCO LEUCOCEPHALUS
or
WHITE HEADED EAGLE

Fig. 2.

FALCO FURCATUS
or
SWALLOW TAILD HAWK

Fig. 3.

FALCO COLUMBARIUS
or
PIGEON HAWK

A. Bell Sculp.t

ORNITHOLOGY. Picæ. Plate CCCXCV.

A. Bell Prin. Wal. Sculptor fecit.

Philosophers have been much puzzled about the essential characteristics of brutes, by which they may be distinguished from man. Some define a brute to be an *animal not risible,* or *a living creature incapable of laughter;* others call them *mute animals.* The peripatetics allowed them a sensitive power, but denied them a rational one. The Platonists allowed them reason and understanding, though in a degree less pure and refined than that of men. Lactantius allows every thing to brutes which men have, except a sense of religion; and even this has been ascribed to them by some sceptics. Descartes maintained, that brutes are mere inanimate machines, absolutely destitute not only of reason but of all thought and perception, and that all their actions are only consequences of the exquisite mechanism of their bodies. . . .

The opinion of Descartes was probably invented, or at least adopted by him, to defeat two great objections: one against the immortality of the souls of brutes, if they were allowed to have any; the other against the goodness of God, in suffering creatures who had never sinned to be subjected to so many miseries.

Longevity

Under the rubric "Life-Span," the current Britannica *discusses this topic at length, sticking to the facts. The 3rd edition (1788–1797) was not handicapped by the problem of documentation. Here is*

LONGEVITY, WITH SOME OUTSTANDING EXAMPLES

From the different longevities of men in the beginning of the world, after the flood,

Names of the Persons	*Ages*	*Places of Abode*	*Living or Dead*
Thomas Parr	152	Shropshire	Died November 14. 1635 Phil. Trans. No. 44.
Henry Jenkins	169	Yorkshire	Died December 8. 1670 Phil. Trans. No. 221.
Robert Montgomery	126	Ditto	Died in —— 1670
James Sands	140	Staffordshire	} Do Fuller's Worthies p. 47
His Wife	120	Ditto	
Countess of Desmond	140	Ireland	Raleigh's Hist. p. 166
Ecleston	143	Ditto	Died —— 1691.
J. Sagar	112	Lancashire	——— 1668.
— Laurence	140	Scotland	Living —
Simon Sack	141	Trionia	Died May 30. 1764
Col. Thomas Winslow	146	Ireland	— Aug. 26, 1766
Francis Consist	150	Yorkshire	— Jan. — 1768
Christ. J. Drakenberg	146	Norway	— June 24. 1660.
Margaret Forster	136	Cumberland	} Both living 1771.
— her daughter	104	Ditto.	
Francis Bons	121	France	Died Feb. 6. 1769
John Brookey	134	Devonshire	Living —— 1777

Names of the Persons	*Ages*	*Places of Abode*	*Living or Dead*
James Bowels	152	Killingworth	Died Aug. 15. 1656
John Tice	125	Worcestershire	— March, 1774
John Mount	136	Scotland	— Feb. 27, 1776
A. Goldsmith	140	France	— June — 1776
Mary Yates	128	Shropshire	— — — 1776
John Bales	126	Northampton	— April 5, 1766
William Ellis	130	Liverpool	— Aug. 16, 1780
Louisa Truxo, a Negress	175	Tucomea, S. America	Living Oct. 5. 1780
Margaret Patten	138	Lockneugh near Paisley	Lynche's Guide to Health
Janet Taylor	108	Fintray, Scotland	Died Oct. 10, 1780
Richard Lloyd	133	Montgomery	Lynche's Guide to Health
Susannah Hilliar	100	Piddington, Northampsh.	Died Feb. 19. 1781
Ann Cockbolt	105	Stoke-Bruerne, *Ib.*	— April 5. 1775
James Hayley	112	Middlewich, Cheshire	— March 17. 1781

William Walker aged 112, not mentioned above, who was a soldier at the battle of Edge-hill

and in these ages, Mr. Derham draws an argument for the interposition of a divine Providence.

Immediately after the creation, when the world was to be peopled by one man and one woman, the ordinary age was 900 and upwards. —Immediately after the flood, when there were three persons to stock the world, their age was cut shorter, and none of those patriarchs but Shem arrived at 500. In the second century we find none that reached 240: in the third, none but Terah that came to 200 years; the world, at least a part of it, by that time being so well peopled, that they had built cities, and were cantoned out into distant nations. — By degrees, as the number of people increased, their *longevity* dwindled, till it came down at length to 70 or 80 years: and there it stood and has continued to stand ever since the time of Moses. —This is found a good medium, and by means hereof the world is neither overstocked, nor kept too thin; but life and death keep a pretty equal pace.

Revivification

All modern encyclopedias, influenced by the triumph of the scientific method, pride themselves on their adherence to the provable truth. In earlier days, encyclopedists seem to have been less inflexible. Here, for example, is an extract from a brief article headed "Revivification." It is from the Supplement to the 3rd edition (1801).

REVIVIFICATION, in physiology, the recalling to life of animals apparently dead. There are many kinds of insects which may be revivified, after all the powers of animation have been suspended for a considerable time. Common flies, small beetles, spiders, moths, bugs, etc., after being drowned in spirit of wine, and continuing apparently dead for more than a quarter of an hour, have been restored to life merely by being thrown among wood-ashes slightly warm.

While Dr Franklin resided in France, he

received from America a quantity of Madeira wine which had been bottled in Virginia. In some of the bottles he found a few dead flies, which he exposed to the warm sun, it being then the month of July; and in less than three hours these apparently dead animals recovered life which had been so long suspended. At first they appeared as if convulsed; they then raised themselves on their legs, washed their eyes with their fore feet, dressed their wings with those behind, and began in a little time to fly about.

But the most extraordinary instance of revivification that we ever heard of, is the following: In the warmer parts of France there is an insect very destructive to rye, which seems to begin its operations at the root of the plant, and gradually to proceed upwards to the ear. If the plant be completely dried while the insect is in the root or stem, the animal is irrecoverably killed; but after it has reached the grain, the case is very different. There have been instances, which are noticed in the Academy of Sciences, of these insects being brought to life in a quarter of an hour, by a little warm water, after the grains, in which they were lodged, had been kept dry for 30 years.

What is the metaphysician to think of these phaenomena, or what conclusion is he to draw from them with respect to the mind or sentient principle? If he be a sober man, he will draw no conclusion; and for this very good reason, that of the sentient principle of insects, and indeed of every animal but man, he knows nothing.

CHAPTER FOUR

The Physical World

The scientific revolution was set in motion by the sixteenth-century work of Copernicus and that of his successors Tycho Brahe, Kepler, and Galileo, which extended well into the seventeenth. Newton, in the late seventeenth and early eighteenth centuries, provided a mathematical and theoretical explanation for their discoveries. Then began what we may call the classical age of science. The word "science" at that time meant knowledge; what we call science was understood as the natural philosophy.

The natural philosophy was the province of all educated men, and the intellectuals of Europe were beginning to consolidate the exhilarating and unsettling revolution that had been upending European knowledge for a generation. It was a time when the educated and curious were conducting their own experiments in the natural philosophy, so as to understand the astonishing inventions and discoveries of the new pioneers, whose exploits they followed assiduously through personal correspondence, in such journals as the Philosophical Transactions *of the Royal Society, and in books.*

This era of widespread intellectual ferment lasted for a century, a time never really paralleled before or since. In the middle of it, 1768, the series of pamphlets that would constitute the first Encyclopaedia Britannica *began to appear. (B.L.F.)*

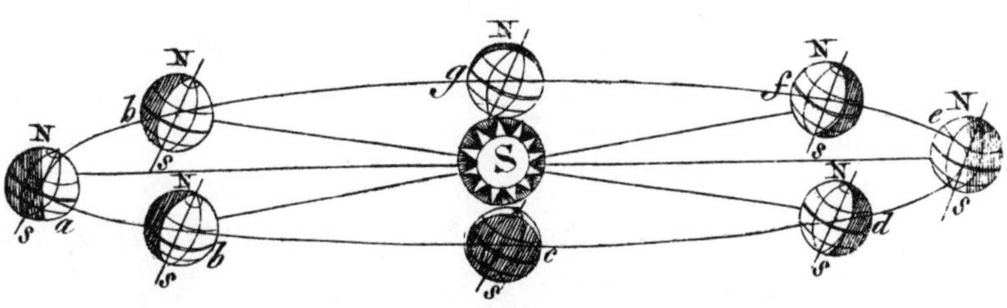

The Cosmos

We can get some idea of what the cosmos looked like in the late eighteenth century by reading Chapter I of the lengthy article on "Astronomy" in the 1st edition (1768–1771).

ASTRONOMY is the science which treats of the nature and properties of the heavenly bodies.

Chap. I. Of Astronomy in general

By astronomy we discover that the earth is at so great a distance from the sun, that if seen from thence it would appear no bigger than a point, although its circumference is known to be 25,020 miles. Yet that distance is so small, compared with the earth's distance from the fixed stars, that if the orbit in which the earth moves round the sun were solid, and seen from the nearest star, it would likewise appear no bigger than a point, although it is at least 162 millions of miles in diameter. For the earth, in going round the sun, is 162 millions of miles nearer to some of the stars at one time of the year than at another; and yet their apparent magnitudes, situations, and distances from one another still remain the same; and a telescope which magnifies above 200 times does not sensibly magnify them; which proves them to be at least 400 thousands times farther from us than we are from the sun.

It is not to be imagined that all the stars are placed in one concave surface, so as to be equally distant from us; but that they are scattered at immense distances from one another through unlimited space. So that there may be as great a distance between any two neighbouring stars, as between our sun and those which are nearest to him. Therefore an observer, who is nearest any fixed star, will look upon it alone as a real sun; and consider the rest as so many shining points, placed at equal distances from him in the firmament.

By the help of telescopes we discover thousands of stars which are invisible to the naked eye; and the better our glasses are, still the more become visible; so that no limits can be set either to their number or their distances.

The sun appears very bright and large in comparison of the fixed stars, because we keep constantly near the sun, in comparison of our immense distance from the stars. For a spectator, placed as near to any star as we are to the sun, would see that star a body as large and bright as the sun appears to us: and a spectator, as far distant from the sun as we are from the stars, would see the sun as small as we see a star, divested of all its circumvolving planets; and would reckon it one of the stars in numbring them.

The stars, being at such immense distances from the sun, cannot possibly receive from him so strong a light as they seem to have; nor any brightness sufficient to make them visible to us. For the sun's rays must be so scattered and dissipated before they reach such remote objects, that they can never be transmitted back to our eyes, so as to render these objects visible by reflexion. The stars therefore shine with their own native and unborrowed lustre, as the sun does; and since each particular star, as well as the sun, is confined to a particular portion of space, it is plain that the stars are of the same nature with the sun.

Plate XLVII.

Fig. 1.

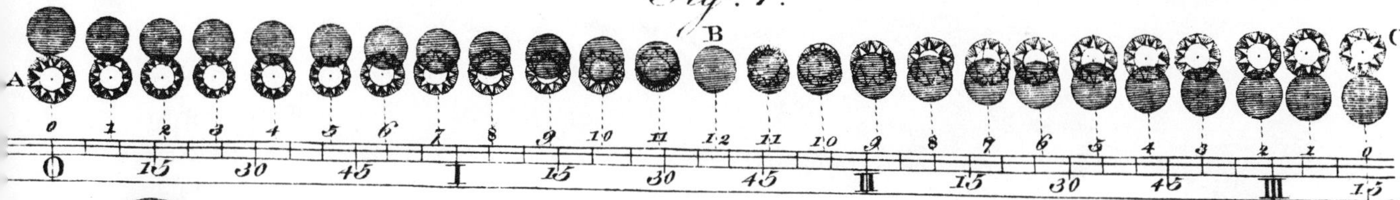

Fig. 2.

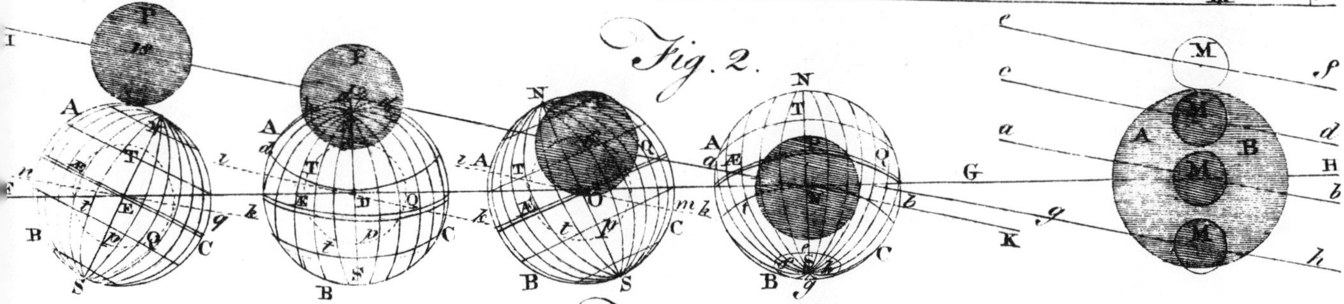

Fig 3

FERGUSONS ORRERY

A. Bell Sculp.

Plate XLII

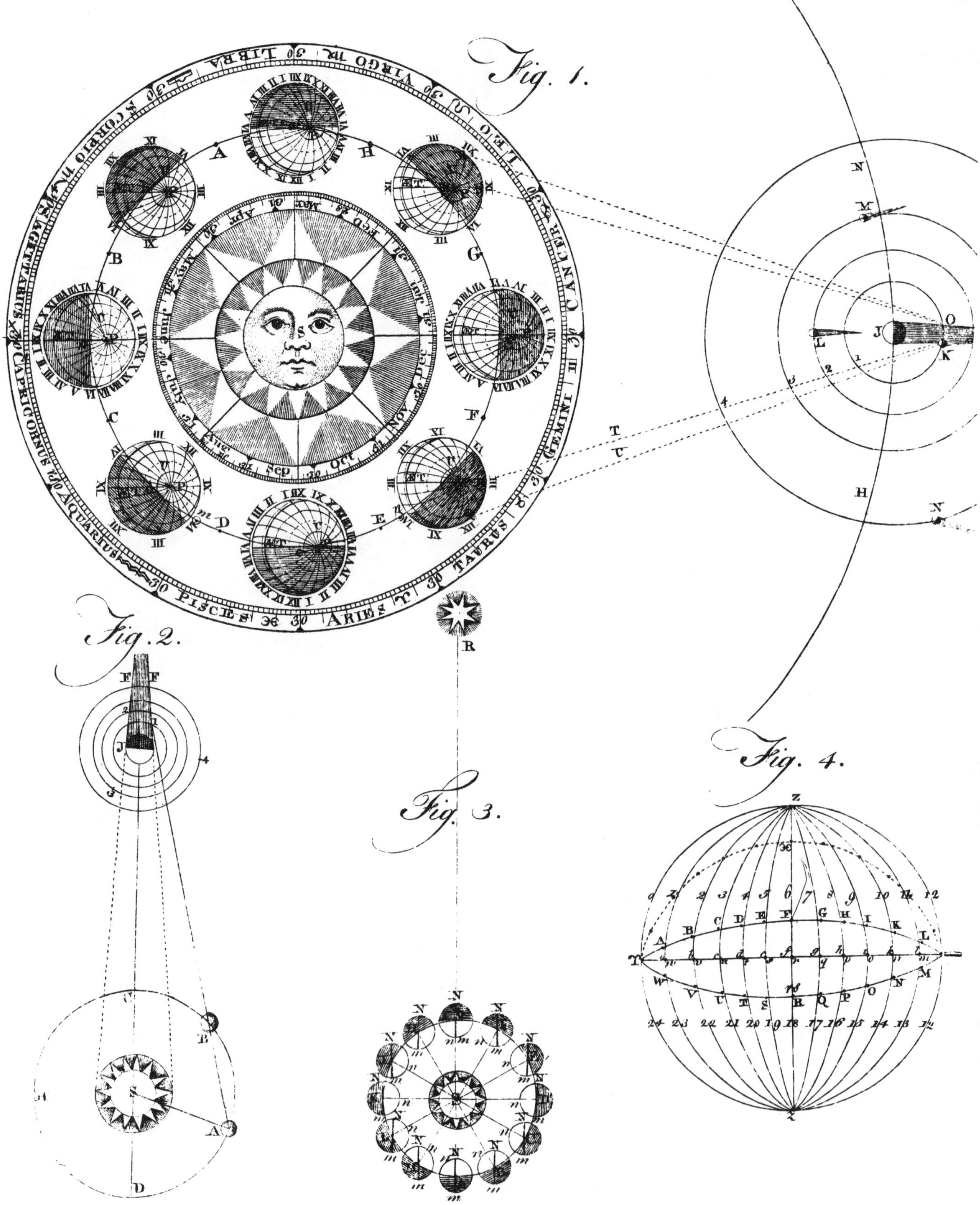

Fig. 1.
LIBRA
VIRGO
LEO
CANCER
GEMINI
TAURUS
ARIES
PISCES
AQUARIUS
CAPRICORNUS
SAGITTARIUS
SCORPIO
Fig. 2.
Fig. 3.
Fig. 4.

Plate. XLVI.

Fig. 1.

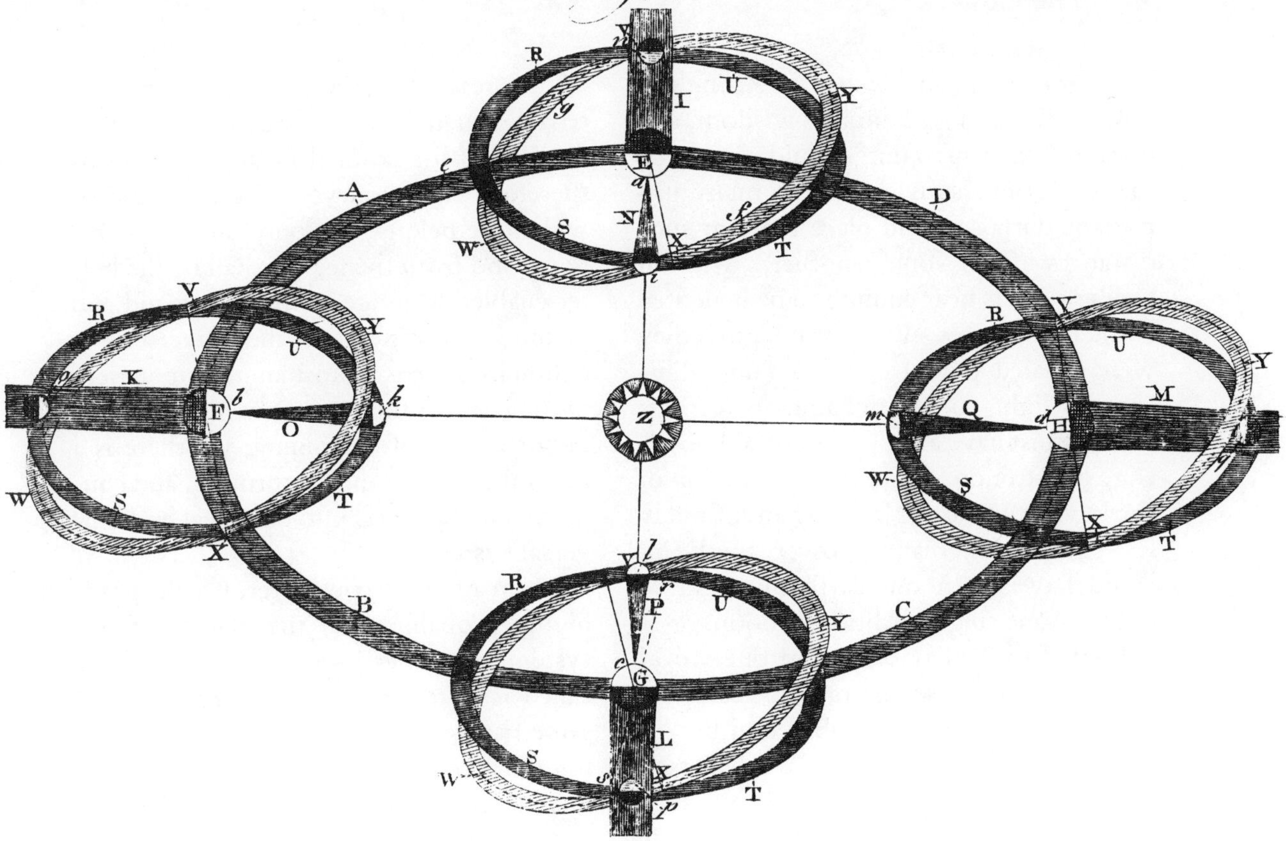

Fig. 2.

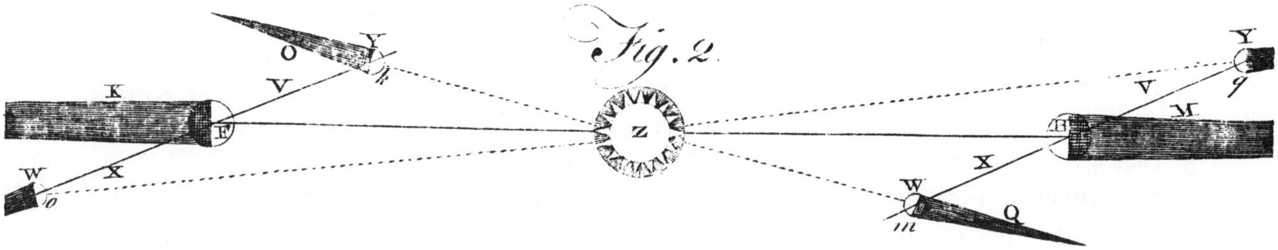

Fig. 3.

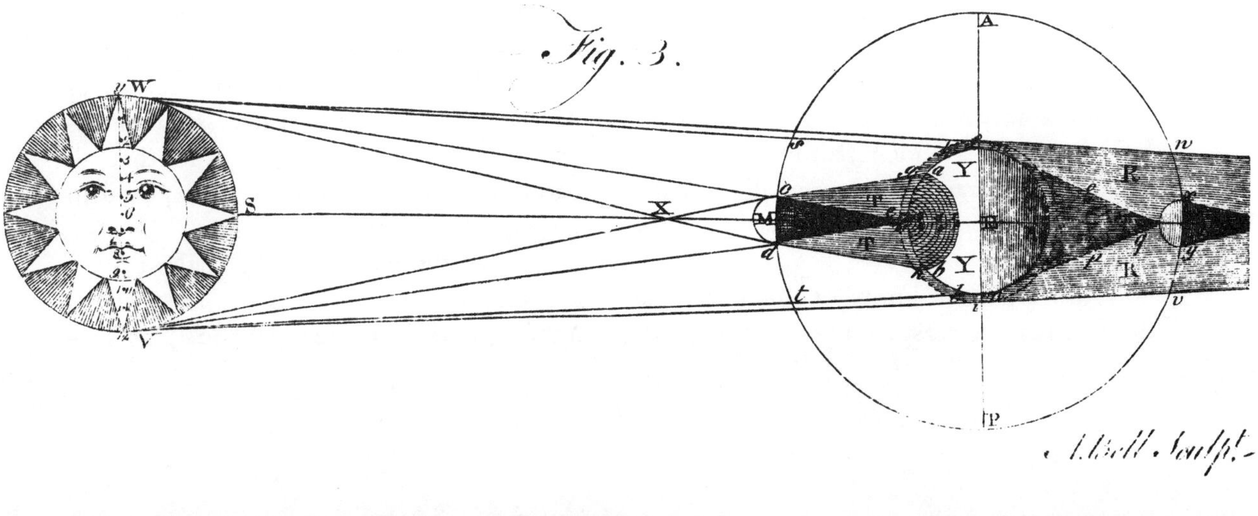

A. Bell Sculpt.

It is noways probable that the Almighty, who always acts with infinite wisdom, and does nothing in vain, should create so many glorious suns, fit for so many important purposes, and place them at such distances from one another, without proper objects near enough to be benefited by their influences. Whoever imagines they were created only to give a faint glimmering light to the inhabitants of this globe, must have a very superficial knowledge of astronomy, and a mean opinion of the Divine Wisdom; since, by an infinitely less exertion of creating power, the Deity could have given our earth much more light by one single additional moon.

Instead then of one sun and one world only in the universe, astronomy discovers to us such an inconceivable number of suns, systems, and worlds, dispersed through boundless space, that if our sun, with all the planets, moons, and comets belonging to it, were annihilated, they would be no more missed, by an eye that could take in the whole creation, than a grain of sand from the sea-shore: The space they possess being comparatively so small, that it would scarce be a sensible blank in the universe, although Saturn, the outermost of our planets, revolves about the sun in an orbit of 4884 millions of miles in circumference, and some of our comets make excursions upwards of ten thousand millions of miles beyond Saturn's orbit; and yet, at that amazing distance, they are incomparably nearer to the sun than to any of the stars; as is evident from their keeping clear of the attractive power of all the stars, and returning periodically by virtue of the sun's attraction.

From what we know of our own system, it may be reasonably concluded, that all the rest are with equal wisdom contrived, situated, and provided with accommodations for rational inhabitants. Let us therefore take a survey of the system to which we belong; the only one accessible to us; and from thence we shall be the better enabled to judge of the nature and end of the other systems of the universe. For although there is almost an infinite variety in the parts of the creation which we have opportunities of examining; yet there is a general analogy running through, and connecting all the parts into one great and universal system.

To an attentive considerer, it will appear highly probable, that the planets of our system, together with their attendants called *satellites* or *moons,* are much of the same nature with our earth, and destined for the like purposes. For they are solid opaque globes, capable of supporting animals and vegetable. Some of them are larger, some less, and some much about the size of our earth. They all circulate round the sun, as the earth does, in a shorter or longer time, according to their respective distances from him; and have, where it would not be inconvenient, regular returns of summer and winter, spring and autumn. They have warmer and colder climates, as the various productions of our earth require: And, in such as afford a possibility of discovering it, we observe a regular motion round their axes like that of our earth, causing an alternate return of day and night; which is necessary for labour, rest, and vegetation, and that all parts of their surfaces may be exposed to the rays of the sun.

Such of the planets as are farthest from the sun, and therefore enjoy least of his light, have that deficiency made up by several moons, which constantly accompany and revolve about them, as our moon revolves about the earth. The remotest planet has, over and above, a broad ring encompassing it; which like a lucid zone in the heavens reflects the sun's light very copiously on that planet; so that if the remoter planets have the sun's light fainter by day than we, they have an addition made to it morning and evening by one or more of their moons, and a greater quantity of light in the night-time.

On the surface of the moon, because it is nearer us than any other of the celestial bodies are, we discover a nearer resemblance of our earth. For, by the assistance of telescopes we observe the moon to be full of high mountains, large valleys, and deep cavities. These similarities leave us no room to doubt, but that all the planets and moons in the system are designed as commodious habitations for creatures endued with capacities of knowing and adoring their beneficent Creator.

Since the fixed stars are prodigious spheres of fire like our sun, and at inconceivable distances from one another as well as from us, it is reasonable to conclude they are made for the same purposes that the sun is; each to bestow light, heat, and vegetation, on a certain number of inhabited planets, kept by gravitation within the sphere of its activity.

This Terraqueous Globe

Earth scientists today know that our planet is some 4,600,000,000 years old. At the time of the 1st edition (1768–1771) their predecessors believed it was about 4,000 years old. The process of bridging that not inconsequential gap is revealed edition by edition in the Britannica.

The article "Earth" in the 1st edition supplied only a definition and a cross-reference to astronomy and geography. In its larger bulk (ten volumes vs. three) the 2nd edition (1778–1783) devoted fifteen pages to the article "Earth," summarizing ancient and modern theories of the planet's origin. Here is the introduction. (B.L.F.)

EARTH, in astronomy and geography, one of the primary planets; being this terraqueous globe which we inhabit.

The cosmogony, or knowledge of the original formation of the earth, the materials of which it was composed, and by what means they were disposed in the order in which we see them at present, is a subject which, though perhaps above the reach of human sagacity, has exercised the wit of philosophers in all ages. To recount the opinions of all the eminent philosophers of antiquity upon this subject would be very tedious: it may therefore suffice to observe, that, ever since the subject began to be canvassed, the opinions of those who have treated it may be divided into two classes. 1. Those who believed the earth, and whole visible system of nature, to be the Deity himself, or connected with him in the same manner that a human body is with its soul. 2. Those who believed the materials of it to have been eternal, but distinct from the Deity, and put into the present order by some power either inherent in themselves, or belonging to the Deity. Of the first opinion were Xenophanes, the founder of the *eleatic* sect, Strato of Lampsacus, the Peripatetics, etc. . . . They who held this opinion may again be divided into two classes: first, those who endeavoured to account for the gen-

Plate LXXXVII

Armillary **Sphere**

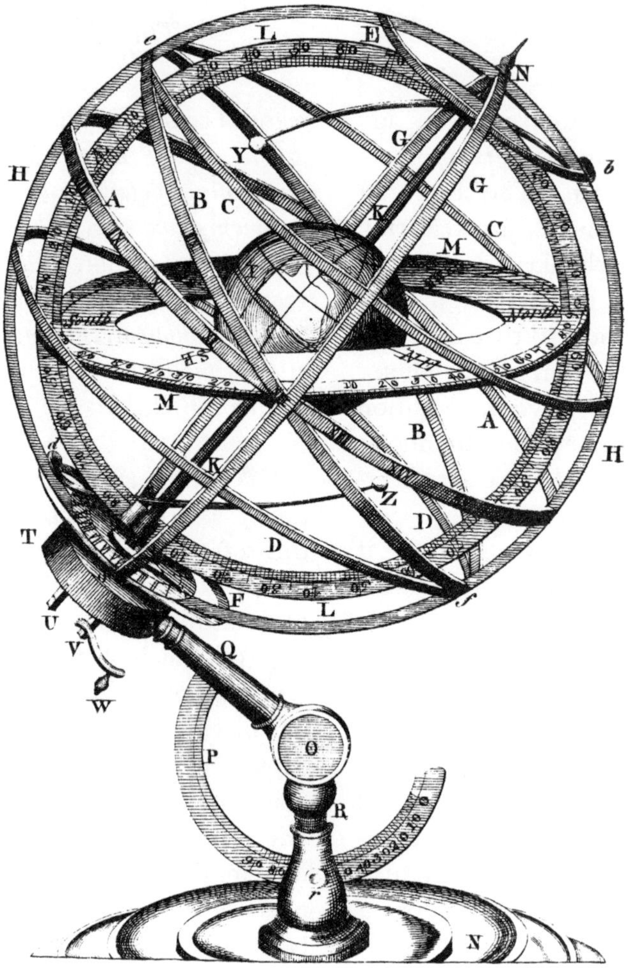

World

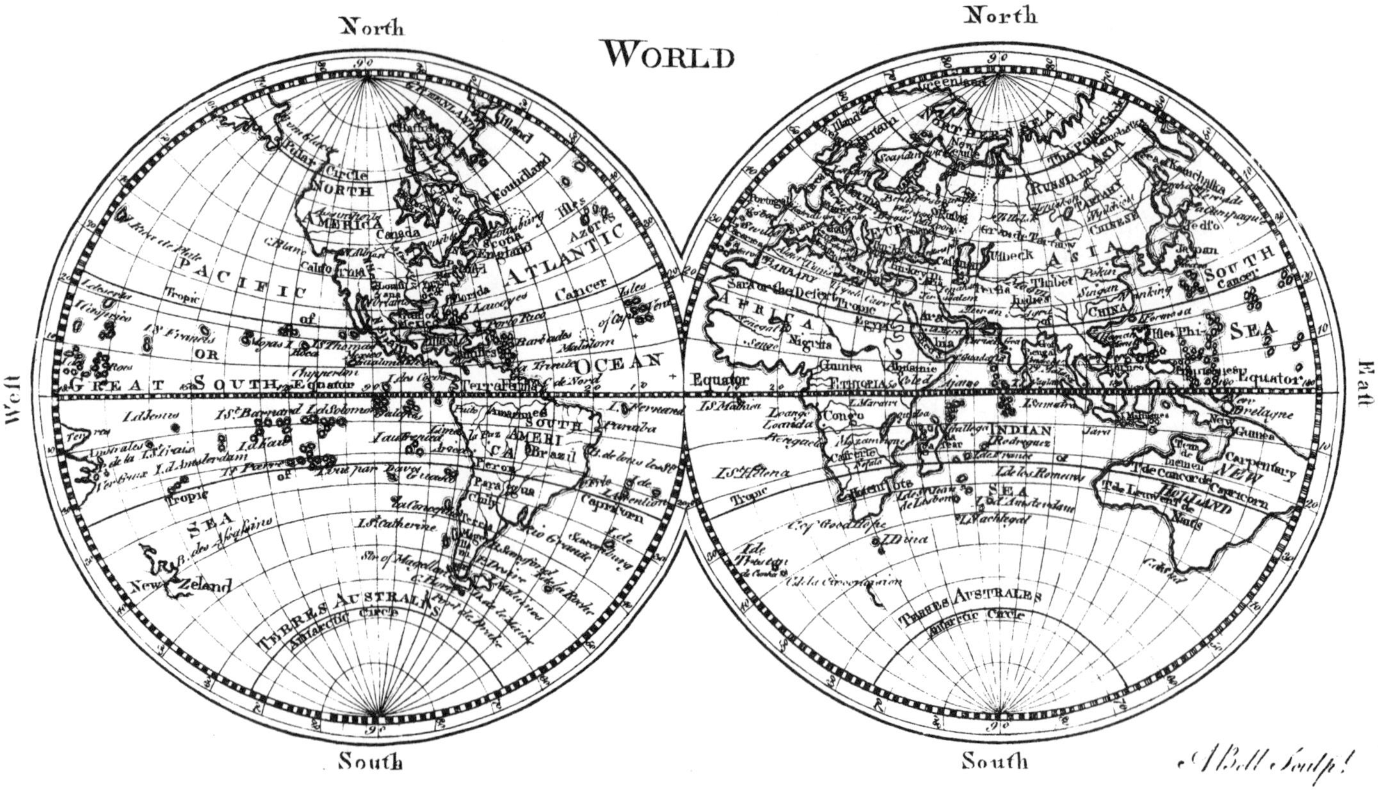

A. Bell Sculp.

eration of the world, or its reduction into the present form, by principles merely mechanical, without having recourse to any assistance from divine power; and secondly, those who introduced an intelligent mind as the author and disposer of all things. To the first of these classes belonged the cosmogony of the Babylonians, Phoenicians, and Egyptians; the particulars of which are too absurd to deserve notice.

Earthquakes

Human knowledge about that cataclysmic force, the earthquake, progressed slowly. The 1st edition (1768–1771) gave it a single sentence: "Earthquake, in natural history, a violent agitation or trembling of some considerable part of the earth generally attended with a terrible noise like thunder, and sometimes with an eruption of fire, water, wind, etc." The 2nd (1778–1783) had fourteen pages, mostly anecdote, with conjecture about the theories of the day, some of which implicated electricity.

Two centuries later, in the current 15th edition, the American geophysicist and seismologist Charles F. Richter (1900–1985), who in 1935 devised the logarithmic scale by which the severity of earthquake shocks is universally measured, set forth lucid answers to the age-old questions. (B.L.F.)

CAUSES OF EARTHQUAKES

Natural Causes: Rock Fracture and Volcanism

Earthquakes can originate in various ways, but one principal cause is responsible for all large earthquakes and for a majority of small ones. This is the fracturing of rocks in the outer part of the Earth as a result of the gradual accumulation of strain during geological processes. Sudden fracture occurs when strain exceeds the strength of the rocks; generally, rupture follows established lines and surfaces of weakness, which are active geologic faults. Fracture usually begins at depths of 17 to 34 kilometres (11 to 21 miles) or much more; but in large earthquakes, it often extends to the surface, and relative displacements of the two sides are observed along the line or zone of intersection between the fault and the surface. This fault displacement may be vertical, horizontal, or both.

The ultimate cause of distortion and faulting is the same as that responsible for the warping and breaking of the crust of the Earth during geological time, thereby producing mountain ranges and ocean basins. An earlier generation of workers confidently attributed all this to the wrinkling of the surface of a cooling and shrinking Earth. That idea gradually became untenable and has been replaced by variations of a hypothesis that the flow of heat within the Earth causes transfer of material by convection, and that these slow but inexorable motions provide the driving forces for geologic changes. The latest and most fruitful development, called plate tectonics, has revived the temporarily neglected idea of continental drift and combined it with the notions of sea-floor spreading and transform (offset) faulting, phenomena that are substantiated by the paleomagnetic history of oceanic rocks. . . .

The most important of the minor causes of earthquakes is volcanism. Earthquakes are caused not merely by explosions and other eruptive processes, but also by gradual displacements of subterranean volcanic material, or magma.

Emeralds

In the early days Britannica *articles on geological subjects ranged from giving practical advice to debunking the downright fanciful. (B.L.F.)*

"Emeralds" is from the 1st edition (1768–1771). The instructions for counterfeiting emeralds may contain a faint reflection of the persistence of alchemical practices.

EMERALD, in natural history, a genus of precious stones, of a green colour, and next in hardness to the ruby.

Our jewelers distinguish emeralds into two kinds, the oriental and occidental: the emeralds of the East-Indies are evidently finer than those of any other part of the world; but our jewellers, seldom meeting with these, call the American emeralds the oriental, and usually sell crystal accidentally tinged with green, under the name of the occidental emerald. . . .

To Counterfeit Emeralds

Take of natural crystal, four ounces; of red-lead, four ounces; verdegrease, forty-eight grains; crocus martis, prepared with vinegar, eight grains; let the whole be finely pulverized and sifted; put this into a crucible, leaving one inch empty: lute it well, and put it into a potter's furnace, and let it stand there as long as they do their pots. When cold, break the crucible, and you will find a matter of a fine emerald colour, which, after it is cut and set in gold, will surpass in beauty an oriental emerald.

❧ ❧ ❧

"Stones Are Stones"

These extracts come from the 3rd edition (1788–1797).

STONES, in natural history, bodies which are insipid, not ductile, nor inflammable, nor soluble in water. But as this is the definition given of earths by chemists and naturalists, we must refer the reader to the articles EARTH, and MINERALOGY, for a view of the classification of stones. Here we will only make a few observations concerning their natural history.

As philosophers have perplexed themselves much about the origin and formation of the earth (a subject certainly far beyond the ken of the human intellect, at least if we believe that it was made by the Almighty power of God), so they have also proposed theories to explain the origin of stones. When philosophers limit their inquiries within the boundaries of science, where they are led by the sober and safe conduct of observation and experiment, their conclusions may be solid and may be useful; but when, throwing experiment and observation aside, they rear a theory upon an airy nothing, or upon a single detached fact, their theories will vanish before the touch of true philosophy as a romantic palace before the rod of the enchanter. . . . We content ourselves with the old opinion, that the soul is a spiritual substance; that plants are plants, and that stones are stones.

We have been led into these remarks by finding that some philosophers say that stones are vegetables; that they grow and increase in size like a plant. This theory, we believe, was first offered to the world by M. Tournefort, in the year 1702, after returning from his travels in the east.[1]

"Snow, a Well-Known Meteor"

Meteorology had become an established science by the early nineteenth century, and was extensively treated in the Britannica. *In our own time, we may lose sight of the origins of its name. In the eighteenth century, any unfamiliar object in the sky was a meteor, from the Greek* meteoron, *"a phenomenon in the air." For instance, from the 2nd edition (1778–1783): (B.L.F.)*

SNOW, a well-known meteor, formed by the freezing of the vapours in the atmosphere. It differs from hail and hoar-frost in being as it were crystallized, which they are not. This appears on examination of a flake of snow by a magnifying glass; when the whole of it will appear to be composed of fine shining spicula diverging like rays from a centre. As the flakes fall down through the atmosphere, they are continually joined by more of these radiated spicula, and thus increase in bulk like the drops of rain or hailstones. Dr Grew, in a discourse of the nature of snow, observes, that many parts thereof are of a regular figure, for the most part so many little rowels or stars of six points, and are as perfect and transparent ice as any we see on a pond, etc.

1. To give a more distinct notion of Tournefort's theory, we shall subjoin his conclusions: From these observations (he says) it follows, that there are stones which grow in the quarries, and of consequence that are fed; that the same juice which nourishes them serves to rejoin their parts when broken; just as in the bones of animals, and the branches of trees, when kept up by bandages; and, in a word, that they vegetate. There is, then (he says), no room to doubt but that they are organized; or that they draw their nutritious juice from the earth.

River

To appreciate the changes that have taken place in Britannica*'s handling of scientific subjects over the last two centuries we might consider the treatment of "River" in the 3rd edition (1788–1797). It was so admired that much of the article was retained unchanged over some six decades. Today we would deny it the title of scientific prose. It seems to us a leisurely essay designed for leisurely gentlemen, and that is indeed the case. The entire article is replete with references to Lucretius, the Old Testament, Virgil, and other classical* loci, *with more than one casual Latin quotation. In those happy days C. P. Snow's notorious distinction between the two cultures did not exist. The sciences had not yet been divorced from the humanities. For all the following extract's floridity it does tell us something about rivers that is absent from today's sober and objective treatment.*

RIVER is a current of fresh water, flowing in a bed or channel from its source to the sea.

The term is appropriated to a *considerable* collection of waters, formed by the conflux of two or more BROOKS, which deliver into its channel the united streams of several rivulets, which have collected the supplies of many rills trickling down from numberless springs, and the torrents which carry off from the sloping grounds the surplus of every shower.

Rivers form one of the chief features of the surface of this globe, serving as voiders of all that is immediately redundant in our rains and springs, and also as boundaries and barriers, and even as highways, and in many countries as plentiful storehouses. They also fertilise our soil by laying upon our warm fields the richest mould, brought from the high mountains, where it would have remained useless for want of genial heat.

Being such interesting objects of attention, every branch acquires a proper name, and the whole acquires a sort of personal identity, of which it is frequently difficult to find the principle; for the name of the great body of waters which discharges itself into the sea is traced backwards to one of the sources, while all the contributing streams are lost, although their waters form the chief part of the collection.

But in general their origin and progress, and even the features of their character, bear some resemblance (as has been prettily observed by Pliny) to the life of man. The river springs from the earth; but its origin is in heaven. Its beginnings are insignificant, and its infancy is frivolous; it plays among the flowers of a meadow; it waters a garden, or turns a little mill. Gathering strength in its youth, it becomes wild and impetuous. Impatient of the restraints which it still meets with in the hollows among the mountains, it is restless and fretful; quick in its turnings, and unsteady in its course. Now it is a roaring cataract, tearing up and overturning whatever opposes its progress, and it shoots headlong down from a rock; then it becomes a sullen and gloomy pool, buried in the bottom of a glin. Recovering breath by repose, it again dashes along, till tired of the uproar and mischief, it quits all that it has swept along, and leaves the opening of the valley strewed with the rejected waste. Now, quitting its retirement, it comes abroad into the world, journeying with more prudence and discretion through cultivated fields, yielding to circumstances, and winding round what would trouble it to overwhelm or remove. It passes through the populous cities and all the busy haunts of man, tendering its services on every side, and becomes the support and ornament of the country. Now increased by numerous alliances, and advanced in its course of existence, it becomes grave and stately in its motions, loves peace and quiet; and in majestic silence rolls on its mighty waters, till it is laid to rest in the vast abyss.

Glacier

As in the rest of the Earth sciences, the Britannica*'s treatment of hydrology owed much to the journals of travelers who were meticulous observers. However well or badly their scientific conclusions meet the test of time, their reports often hold up beautifully as travel writing. (B.L.F.)*

From the 3rd edition (1788–1797):

Mr Coxe, who visited the glacier des Bois, informs us, that the appearance of it at a distance was so tremendous, that it seemed impracticable to cross it. Numerous and broad chasms intersected it in every direction; but entering upon it, the company found that courage and activity were only required to accomplish the task. They had large nails in their shoes and spiked sticks; which on this occasion were found to be particularly serviceable. . . . As our traveller proceeded on his journey, he was surprised by the noise of a large fragment of rock which had detached itself from one of the highest needles, and bounded from one precipice to another with great rapidity; but before it reached the plain, it was almost reduced to dust. "Having proceeded about an hour (says he) we were astonished with a view more magnificent than imagination can conceive: hitherto the glaciers had scarcely answered my expectations, but now they far surpassed them. Nature had clad herself in all her terrors. Before us was a valley of ice 20 miles in extent, bounded by a circular glacier of pure unbroken snow, named Takul, which leads directly to the foot of Mount Blanc, and is surrounded by large conical rocks, terminating in sharp points like the towers of an ancient fortification; to the right rose a range of magnificent peaks, their intervals filled with glaciers; and far above the rest, the magnificent summit of Mount Blanc, his highest point obscured with clouds. He appeared of such immense magnitude, that, at his presence, the circumjacent mountains, however gigantic, seemed to shrink before him, and *hide their diminished heads. . . .*"

They continued to ascend the valley of ice, the scene constantly increasing in magnificence and horror; and having walked about five miles on the ice, they arrived at last at the foot of the eminence named *Couvercle,* where they were obliged to quit the ice. The doing this was extremely dangerous, and at one place very tremendous. It was a bulging smooth rock, with a precipice of considerable depth terminated by a vast crevice in the ice, which seemed to stop all further progress: a small hollow in the middle, however, afforded room for one foot; and having fixed this, they sprung over to the other side, being helped and directed by the guides who went over first. Having gained the top of the Couvercle, they had a view of three of the glaciers, viz. that of *Talefre* to the left, *l'Echant* in front, and *Takul* on the right; all uniting that great one called the *Glacier ae Bois*. The Couvercle itself is a most extraordinary rock, having the appearance of a large irregular building with many sides; the substance of which is granite. Having reached the top, they were surprised with a thunder-storm, from whence they took shelter under an impending rock. The view was exceedingly magnificent; the glaciers appearing like a rugged expanse of frozen sea bounded by gigantic rocks, and terminated by Mount Blanc. A single rock appeared of a triangular figure covered with Alpine plants; and which by reason of its contrast with the rugged and snowy mountains in the neighbourhood, has obtained the name of the *Garden.*—During this, as well as other excursions among the Alps, Mr Coxe had occasion to observe that the colour of the sky was of a much deeper blue than in the lower regions.

Ice

In the 4th edition (1801–1809), a long article about the principal component of glaciers noted the need for ice as a refrigerant and reviewed experimental efforts to create it artificially.

The ether experiments recounted in the article led within a half century to successful commercial refrigeration. Unfortunately, the article began on a false note: a completely mistaken view of why ice floats. (B.L.F.)

ICE, in Physiology, a solid, transparent, and brittle body, formed of some fluid, particularly water, by means of cold. . . .

Gallileo was the first that observed ice to be lighter than the water which composed it: and hence it happens, that ice floats upon water, its specific gravity being to that of water as eight to nine. This rarefaction of ice seems to be owing to the air-bubbles produced in water by freezing; and which, being considerably large in proportion to the water frozen, render the body so much specifically lighter: these air-bubbles, during their production, acquire a great expansive power, so as to burst the containing vessels, though ever so strong.

The Birth of Physics

At the end of the eighteenth century, many separate elements of the natural philosophy—mechanics, electricity, magnetism, and optics—were coalescing into what we now call physics. Here is the introduction to "Physics" from the 3rd edition (1788–1797). (B.L.F.)

Taken in its most enlarged sense, [physics] comprehends the whole study of nature; and Natural Philosophy is a term of the same extent: but ordinary language, and especially in this country, employs both of these terms in a much narrower sense, which it is proper in this place to determine with some precision.

Under the article PHILOSOPHY, we gave a particular account of that view of nature in which the objects of our attention are considered as connected by causation; and we were at some pains to point out the manner in which this study may be successfully cultivated. By a judicious employment of the means pointed out in that article, we discover that the objects of our contemplation compose an Universe, which consists, not of a number of independent existences solitary and detached from each other, but of a number of substances connected by a variety of relations and dependencies, so as to form a whole which may with great propriety be called the System of Nature.

This assembling of the individual objects which compose the universe into one system is by no means the work of a hasty and warm fancy, but is the result of sober contemplation. The natural historian attempts in vain to describe objects, by only informing us of their shape, colour, and other sensible qualities. He finds himself obliged, in describing a piece of marble, for instance, to tell us that it takes a fine polish; that it strikes fire with steel; that it burns to quicklime; that it dissolves in aquafortis, and is precipitated by alkalis; that with vitriolic acid it makes gypsum, etc., etc., etc., and thus it appears that even the *description* of any thing, with the view of ascertaining its specific nature, and with the sole purpose of discrimination, cannot be accomplished without taking notice of its various relations to other things. But what do we mean by the *nature* of any thing? We are ignorant of its essence, or what makes it that thing and no other thing. We must content ourselves with the discovery of its *qualities* or *properties;* and it is the assemblage of these which we call its *nature*. But this is very inaccurate. These do not constitute its essence, but are the consequences of it. Yet this is all we shall ever know of its nature. Now the term *property* is nothing but a name expressing some relation which the substance under consideration has to other things. This is true of all such terms. Gravity, elasticity, sensibility, gratitude, and the like, express nothing but certain *matters of fact,* which may be observed respecting the object of our contemplation in different circumstances of situation with regard to other things. Our distinct notions of individuals, therefore, imply their relations to other things.

Electricity

This extract, from the 1st edition (1768–1771), is interesting on two counts: the conception of electricity as a fluid and the close-to-the-event description of Benjamin Franklin's pivotal experiment. "Virtue," of course, means "power" in this case.

Magnets have been observed to lose their virtue, or to have their poles reversed, by lightning. Dr Franklin did the same by electricity. By electricity he frequently gave polarity to needles, and reversed them at pleasure. A shock from four large jars, sent through a fine sewing needle, gave it polarity, so that it would traverse when laid on water. What is most remarkable in these electrical experiments upon magnets is, that if the needle, when it was struck, lay east and west, the end which was entered by the electric blast pointed north; but that if it lay north and south, the end which lay towards the north would continue to point north, whether the fire entered at that end or the contrary. He also observed, that the polarity was strongest when the needle was struck lying north and south, and weakest when it lay east and west. He takes notice, that, in these experiments, the needle, in some cases, would be finely blued, like the spring of a watch, by the electric flame; in which case the colour given by a flash from two jars only might be wiped off, but that a flash from four jars fixed it, and frequently melted the needles. The jars which the doctor used held seven or eight gallons, and were coated and lined with tinfoil.

To demonstrate, in the completest manner possible, the sameness of the electric

fluid with the matter of lightning, Dr Franklin contrived to bring lightning from the heavens, by means of an electrical kite, which he raised when a storm of thunder was perceived to be coming on. This kite had a pointed wire fixed upon it, by which it drew the lightning from the clouds. This lightning descended by the hempen string, and was received by a key tied to the extremity of it; that part of the string which was held in the hand being of silk, that the electric virtue might stop when it came to the key. He found that the string would conduct electricity even when nearly dry, but that when it was wet it would conduct it quite freely; so that it would stream out plentifully from the key at the approach of a person's finger.

At this key he charged phials, and from electric fire thus obtained he kindled spirits, and performed all other electrical experiments which are usually exhibited by an excited globe or tube.

Phlogiston

Surely no scientific development of the waning eighteenth century was more dramatic than the dawning comprehension of the process of combustion. Almost in a stroke, the alchemists' notion of the elements of air, earth, fire, and water fell away, and the idea of the invisible fluid phlogiston as the "principle of inflammability" went up in its own smoke. This mystical theory was finally exploded by Lavoisier (1743–1794). The 2nd edition (1778–1783) does its rather uncertain best to explain the moribund notion.

PHLOGISTON, a term used by chemists to express that invisible and very much unknown substance, which, in conjunction with heat or elementary fire, produces the phenomena of flame or ignition, and gives to metals their splendor; which, in other circumstances, contaminates the white colour of some earths and metallic calces, with black, brown, or other shades; and which in some cases renders the air noxious, and incapable of sustaining the life of animals, or supporting flame, etc., etc.

To give a definition of this *principle of inflammability,* as the phlogiston is frequently called, has hitherto been found impossible; because, it is so far from being the subject of investigation by itself, that no person has yet been able to procure it by itself; neither is it possible to expel it from any one body, without suffering it, in the very same moment, to combine with another. In the act of burning, for instance, phlogiston is discharged very copiously by any inflammable body; but some part, and that a very considerable one, goes to the composition of the flame. Part of the remainder is carried off by the air, and goes to the formation of soot; another part contaminates the air, and either converts part of the atmospherical air into what is called *fixable air,* or, according to others, *phlogisticates* it, while the fixable air is separated from the atmosphere itself, of which it is originally a component part: but in all this process, no part of the phlogiston is to be discovered by itself. In like manner, when iron is dissolved in the vitriolic acid, a great quantity of phlogiston is discharged: but in this case also it is altogether invisible, and incapable of being subjected to examination; the only result of this process being a kind of aërial vapour, by Dr Priestley and others called *inflammable air:*

and so, in all other phlogistic processes, though we are assured that the principle is discharged in great quantity, yet it constantly eludes our most diligent search.

From this invisibility of the phlogiston, it has been concluded, either that phlogiston is the matter of fire, heat, and light, or that these elements contain it in great quantity. The arguments for this opinion seem reducible to the following. 1. Phlogiston is in some cases capable of penetrating the substance of the closest bodies, in such a manner as to be capable of reducing calcined metals to their proper state. 2. The light of the sun appears to contain phlogiston; as it will turn the calx of silver black when exposed to it, even tho' the calx is included within a glass vessel stopped in the most careful manner. In like manner, the green colour which the leaves of plants acquire from the solar light is thought to be owing to a communication of phlogiston from it. 3. Dr Priestley has determined, that the electric fluid either is the phlogiston itself, or contains it; because an electric shock will either reduce metals to a calx, or restore them from a calcined to a metallic state.

By the time the pamphlets that constituted the 3rd edition (1788–1797) reached the letter P, *phlogiston was no more. These two brief extracts let us listen in on its last gasp and see how an encyclopedia buries a theory.*

PHLOGISTON, a term used by chemists to express a principle which was supposed to enter the composition of various bodies.

Since the existence of phlogiston, as a chemical principle in the composition of certain bodies, is now fully proved to be false, we shall not trouble our readers with any farther observations on it, except adding, that although the chemists were satisfied with the proofs they gave of its reality, they were never able to exhibit it in a separate state, or show it in a pure form, unmixed with other matter.

Burning

The reader will, quite naturally, find in the current Britannica *no entry for "Burning." Earlier editors handled the subject in a manner that today would hardly be called encyclopedic, though it has its charms. This excerpt is from the article on "Burning" that appeared in the 3rd edition (1788–1797). The addendum on "Brenning" is satisfactorily admonitory.*

(Stews, by the way, are what we now call whorehouses).

We have instances of persons burnt by fire kindled within their own bodies. A woman at Paris, who used to drink brandy to excess, was one night reduced to ashes by a fire from within, all but her head and the ends of her fingers. Signora Corn. Zangari, or, as others call her, *Corn. Bandi,* an aged lady, of an unblemished life, near Celena in Romagna, underwent the same fate in March 1731. She had retired in the evening into her chamber somewhat indisposed; and in the morning was found in the middle of the room reduced to ashes, all except her face, legs, skull, and three fingers. The stockings and shoes she had on were not burnt in the least. The ashes were light; and, on pressing between the fingers, vanished, leaving behind a gross stinking moisture with which the floor was smeared; the walls and furniture of the room being covered with a moist cineritious soot, which had not only stained the linen in the chests, but had penetrated into the closet, as well as into the room overhead, the walls of which were moistened with the same viscous humour. —We have various other relations of persons burnt to death in this unaccountable manner.

Sig. Mondini, Bianchini, and Maffei, have written treatises express to account for the cause of so extraordinary an event: common fire it could not be, since this would likewise have burnt the bed and the room; besides that it would have required many hours, and a vast quantity of fuel, to reduce a human body to ashes; and, after all, a considerable part of the bones would have remained entire, as they were anciently found after the fiercest funeral fires. Some attribute the effect to a mine of sulphur under the house; others, to a miracle; while others suspect that art or villany had a hand in it. A philosopher of Verona maintains, that such a conflagration might have arisen from the inflammable matters wherewith the human body naturally abounds. Sig. Bianchini accounts for the conflagration of the lady above-mentioned, from her using a bath or lotion of camphorated spirit of wine when she found herself out of order. Maffei supposes it owing to lightning, but to lightning generated in her own body, agreeable to his doctrine, which is, That lightning does not proceed from the clouds, but is always produced in the place where it is seen and its effects perceived. We have had a late attempt to establish the opinion, that these destroying internal fires are caused in the entrails of the body by inflamed effluvia of the blood; by juices and fermentation in the stomach; by the many combustible matters which abound in living bodies for the purposes of life; and, finally, by the fiery evaporations which exhale from the settlings of spirit of wine, brandies, and other hot liquors, in the tunica villosa of the stomach and other adipose or fat membranes; within which those spirits engender a kind of camphor, which in the night-time, in sleep, by a full respiration, are put in a stronger motion, and are more apt to be set on fire. Others ascribe the cause of such persons being set on fire to lightning; and their burning so entirely, to the greater quantity of phosphorus and other combustible matter they contained. —For our own part, we can by no means pretend to explain the cause of such a phenomenon: but for the interests of humanity we wish it could be derived from something external to the human body; for if, to the calamities of human life already known, we superadd a suspicion that we may unexpectedly, and without the least warning, be consumed by an *internal* fire, the thought is too dreadful to be borne.

Burning, or *Brenning,* in our old customs, denotes an infectious disease, got in the stews by conversing with lewd women, and supposed to be the same with what we now call the *venereal disease.*

In a manuscript of the vocation of John Bale to the bishopric of Osiory, written by himself, he speaks of Dr Hugh Weston, who was dean of Windsor in 1556, but deprived by cardinal Pole for adultery, thus: "At this day is leacherous Weston, who is more practised in the arts of breech-burning, than all the whores of the stews. He not long ago brent a beggar of St Botolph's parish."

Heat

The age-old puzzle of heat was eventually solved by Sir William Thomson, later Baron Kelvin (1824–1907), the Scottish engineer, mathematician, and physicist who devised the dynamical theory of heat, along with many other substantial scientific discoveries and formulations of the Victorian era. In the 9th edition (1875–1889) Kelvin handily dispatched the two previously held theories of heat. One was the "subtle elastic fluid" notion, the other that it was an "intestine" or internal commotion in matter. (B.L.F.)

Preliminary Regarding the Nature of Heat. —Dynamical Calorimetry

From the dawn of science till the close of last century two rival hypotheses had been entertained regarding the nature of heat, each with more or less of plausibility, but neither on any sure experimental basis:—one that heat consisted of a subtle elastic fluid permeating through the pores or interstices among the particles of matter, like water in a sponge; the other that it was an intestine commotion among the particles or molecules of matter. In the year 1799 Davy, in his first published work entitled *An Essay on Heat, Light, and Combinations of Light,* conclusively overthrew the former of these hypotheses, and gave good reason for accepting as true the latter, by his celebrated experiment of converting ice into water by rubbing two pieces of ice together, without communicating any heat from surrounding matter. A few years earlier Rumford had been led to the same conclusion, and had given very convincing evidence of it in his observation of the great amount of heat produced in the process of boring cannon in the military arsenal at Munich, and the experimental investigation on the excitation of heat by friction with which he followed up that observation. He had not, however, given a perfect logical demonstration of his conclusion, nor even quite a complete experimental basis on which it could be established with absolute certainty. According to the materialistic doctrine it would have been held that the heat excited by the friction was not *generated,* but was *produced,* squeezed out, or let flow out like honey from a broken honeycomb, from those parts of the solid which were cut or broken into small fragments, or rubbed to powder in the frictional process. If this were true, the very small fragments or powder would contain much less heat in them than an equal mass of continuous solid of the same substance as theirs. But unhappily the caloristic doctrine, besides its fundamental hypothesis, which we now know to be wrong, had given an absurd and illogical test for quantity of heat in a body, of which a not altogether innocuous influence still survives in our modern name "specific heat"; and Rumford actually, in trying to disprove the materialistic doctrine, was baffled by this sophism. That is to say, he measured the specific heat or "capacity for heat" of the powder, and he found that the powder took as much heat to warm it to a certain degree as did an equal mass of the continuous solid, and from this he concluded that the powder did not contain less heat than the continuous solid at the same temperature. This conclusion is so obviously unwarranted by the premises that it is difficult to imagine how Rumford could have for a moment put forward the "capacity for heat" experiment as proving it, or could have rested in the conclusion without a real proof, or at least the suggestion of a real proof. All that Rumford's *argument* proved was that the fundamental hypothesis of the "calorists" and their other altogether gratuitous doctrine of equality of "specific heat" as a test for equality of whole quantities of heat in matter could not be both true; and any one not inclined to give up the materialistic hypothesis might have cheerfully abandoned the minor doctrine, and remained unmoved by Rumford's argument. If Rumford had but melted a quantity of the powder (or dissolved it in an acid), and compared the heat which it took with that taken by an equal weight of the continuous solid, he would have had no difficulty in proving that the enormous quantity of heat which he had found to be excited by the friction had not been squeezed, or rubbed, or pounded, out of the solid matter, but was really brought into existence, and therefore could not be a material substance. He might even, without experiment, have pointed out that, if the materialistic doctrine were true, it would follow that sufficiently long-continued pounding of any solid substance by pestle and mortar, whether by hand or by aid of machinery, would convert it into a marvellous powder possessing one or other of two properties about equally marvellous. Either the smallest quantity of it thrown into an acid would constitute a freezing mixture of unlimited intensity,—the longer it had been pounded, the more intense would be its frigorific effect on being dissolved,—or the powder would be incapable of being warmed by friction, because it had already parted with all the heat which friction could rub out of it. The real effect of Rumford's argument seems to have been to salve the intellectual consciences of those who were not inclined to give up the materialistic doctrine, and to save them from the trouble of reading through Rumford's paper and thinking for themselves, by which they would have seen that his philosophy was better than his logic, and would inevitably have been forced to agree with him in his conclusion. It is remarkable that Davy's logic, too, was at fault, and on just the same point as Rumford's, but with even more transparently logical fallaciousness, because his argument is put in a more definitely logical form.

Ether Through the Ages

A dramatic example of the way in which Britannica *reflects the growth of scientific knowledge is provided by the three treatments of "Ether" printed below. Ether, in physics, was believed in the nineteenth century to be the infinitely elastic, massless medium through which electromagnetic waves were transmitted.*

The first entry, taken from the 3rd edition (1788–1797), seems to us as quaint as that same edition's solemn consideration of phlogiston. By the time of the 9th edition (1875–1889), the concept had come under strong attack. The new skeptical attitude is expressed by James Clerk Maxwell (1831–1879), from whose then-authoritative article we extract a few pithy paragraphs. Maxwell, author of the theory of electromagnetic radiation, is one of the greatest names in the history of the physical sciences, ranking with Newton and Einstein. At the age of fourteen he had already published his first scientific paper, On the Description of Oval Curves, *and many of us still remember from our high school physics Maxwell's fascinating Demon.*

The chain of evidence attesting to the existence of ether was soon to be conclusively broken. Our third extract, from the current 15th edition, performs the requisite post-Einsteinian obsequies.

AETHER is usually understood of a thin, subtile matter, or medium, much finer and rarer than air; which commencing from the limits of our atmosphere, possesses the whole heavenly space. —The word is Greek, αιθηρ, supposed to be formed from the verb αδθηρ, "to burn, to flame;" some of the ancients, particularly Anaxagoras, supposing it of the nature of fire.

The philosophers cannot conceive that the largest part of the creation should be perfectly void; and therefore they fill it with a species of matter under the denomination of *aether.* But they vary extremely as to the nature and character of this aether. Some conceive it as a body *sui generis,* appointed only to fill up the vacuities between the heavenly bodies; and therefore confined to the regions above our atmosphere. Others suppose it of so subtile and penetrating a nature, as to pervade the air and other bodies, and possess the pores and intervals thereof. Others deny the existence of any such specific matter; and think the air itself, by that immense tenuity and expansion it is found capable of, may diffuse itself through the interstellar spaces, and be the only matter found therein.

ETHER, or AEther (αἰθήρ, probably from αἴθω, I burn, though Plato in his *Cratylus* (410, b) derives the name from its perpetual motion—ὅτι ἀεὶ θεῖ περὶ τὸν ἀέρα ῥέων, ἀειθεὴρ δικαίωζ ἂν καλοῖτο), a material substance of a more subtle kind than visible bodies, supposed to exist in those parts of space which are apparently empty.

The hypothesis of an aether has been maintained by different speculators for very different reasons. To those who maintained the existence of a plenum as a philosophical principle, nature's abhorrence of a vacuum was a sufficient reason for imagining an all-surrounding aether, even though every other argument should be against it. To Descartes, who made extension the sole essential property of matter, and matter a necessary condition of extension, the bare existence of bodies apparently at a distance was a proof of the existence of a continuous medium between them.

But besides these high metaphysical necessities for a medium, there were more mundane uses to be fulfilled by aethers. AEthers were invented for the planets to swim in, to constitute electric atmospheres and magnetic effluvia, to convey sensations from one part of our bodies to another, and so on, till all space had been filled three or four times over with aethers. It is only when we remember the extensive and mischievous influence on science which hypotheses about aethers used formerly to exercise, that we can appreciate the horror of aethers which sober-minded men had during the 18th century, and which, probably as a sort of hereditary prejudice, descended even to the late Mr John Stuart Mill.

The disciples of Newton maintained that in the fact of the mutual gravitation of the heavenly bodies, according to Newton's law, they had a complete quantitative account of their motions; and they endeavoured to follow out the path which Newton had opened up by investigating and measuring the attractions and repulsions of electrified and magnetic bodies, and the cohesive forces in the interior of bodies, without attempting to account for these forces.

Newton himself, however, endeavoured to account for gravitation by differences of pressure in an aether; but he did not publish his theory, "because he was not able from experiment and observation to give a satisfactory account of this medium, and the manner of its operation in producing the chief phenomena of nature."

On the other hand, those who imagined aethers in order to explain phenomena could not specify the nature of the motion of these media, and could not prove that the media, as imagined by them, would produce the effects they were meant to explain. The only aether which has survived is that which was invented by Huygens to explain the propagation of light. The evidence for the existence of the luminiferous aether has accumulated as additional phenomena of light and other radiations have been discovered; and the properties of this medium, as deduced from the phenomena of light, have been found to be precisely those required to explain electromagnetic phenomena. . . .

Whatever difficulties we may have in forming a consistent idea of the constitution of the aether, there can be no doubt that the interplanetary and interstellar spaces are not empty, but are occupied by a material substance or body, which is certainly the largest, and probably the most uniform body of which we have any knowledge.

Whether this vast homogeneous expanse of isotropic matter is fitted not only to be a medium of physical interaction between distant bodies, and to fulfil other physical functions of which, perhaps, we have as yet no conception, but also, as the authors of the *Unseen Universe* seem to suggest, to constitute the material organism of beings exercising functions of life and mind as high or higher than ours are at present, is a question far transcending the limits of physical speculation.

ETHER, also spelled AEther, also called Luminiferous Ether, in physics, a theoretical, universal substance believed during the 19th century to act as the medium for transmission of electromagnetic waves (*e.g.*, light and X rays) much as sound waves are transmitted by elastic media such as air. The ether was assumed to be weightless, transparent, frictionless, undetectable chemically or physically, and literally permeating all matter and space. The theory met with increasing difficulties as the nature of light and the structure of matter became better understood; it was seriously weakened (1881) by the Michelson-Morley experiment, which was designed specifically to detect the motion of the Earth through the ether and which showed that there was no such effect.

With the formulation of the special theory of relativity by Einstein in 1905 and its acceptance by scientists generally, the ether hypothesis was abandoned as being unnecessary in terms of Einstein's assumption that the speed of light, or any electromagnetic wave, is a universal constant.

Atomic Energy

Francis William Aston (1877–1945) was an English chemist and physicist who developed the mass spectrograph to measure (with unprecedented accuracy) the mass of atoms and other fragments of molecules. For this accomplishment he won the Nobel Prize in 1922. Writing in 1924–1925, he saw with absolute clarity the future—ambiguities and all—of atomic energy. This extract is from the 13th edition (a supplement to the 11th and 12th editions, 1926). (B.L.F.)

Since Aston's time, of course, the subject of nuclear energy has taken on overwhelming importance. The index of Britannica*'s current edition lists almost four columns of references beginning with the word "nuclear." Oddly enough (after the first two major entries), the opening reference is "disasters," the closing one "nuclear winter." Something of Cassandra lived within F. W. Aston.*

With the coming of Relativity and the discovery of Isotopes the matter took a new aspect. The whole number rule removed the last obstacle in the way of the electrical theory of matter, that all atoms are composed of protons and electrons, the atoms of positive and negative electricity. According to Rutherford's nucleus atom theory, in the atom of a normal element all the protons and about half the electrons are packed together to form a central positively charged nucleus, which is surrounded by the remaining electrons. It can be shown that if we bring two charges of opposite sign as close together as they are in the nucleus, their fields will affect each other in such a way that the mass of the system will be reduced. This reduction is called the packing effect. In the atom of hydrogen with a nucleus of a single proton there can be no packing effect, so that it will be abnormally heavy. Measurements by means of the mass-spectrograph demonstrate conclusively that the mass of a hydrogen atom, consisting of one proton and one electron, is that accepted by chemists, namely 1.0077, whereas that of the helium atom, consisting of a nucleus of four protons and two electrons and two exterior electrons, is 4.00. Hence, whatever the explanation, it is certain that if it were possible to transmute hydrogen into helium, mass would be lost, and therefore, by the theory of relativity, energy liberated. On the latter theory, mass and energy are interchangeable, and the energy associated with a mass m is mc^2 where c is the velocity of light. For quantities of matter in ordinary experience this quantity of energy is prodigious. Take the case of one gramme atom of hydrogen, that is to say, the quantity of hydrogen in 9 cu.-cm. of water. If this is entirely transformed into helium the energy liberated will be

$$.0077 \times 9 \times 10^{20} = 6.93 \times 10^{18} \text{ ergs.}$$

Expressed in terms of heat this is 1.66×10^{11} calories or in terms of work 200,000 kilowatt hours. Within a tumbler of water lies sufficient energy to propel the "Mauretania" across the Atlantic and back at full speed. Here we have a supply equal even to the demands of astronomers. Eddington remarks that if only ten per cent of the hydrogen in the sun were transformed into helium, enough energy would be liberated to maintain its present radiation for a thousand million years. There can be little doubt that the vast energy of the stars is kept up by the loss of an insignificant fraction of their mass. Whether this process is a degradation of hydrogen, or simple annihilation of matter by the coalescence of protons and electrons, is unknown. How long it will be before man can release and control this energy, and to what uses he will put such vast potentialities, are subjects for the philosopher. The first step has already been taken, for Sir Ernest Rutherford has succeeded in causing transmutation in several elements, only, of course, in inconceivably small quantities, by bombardment with swift alpha rays. If scientific knowledge maintains its present rate of progress, the balance of probability is in favour of ultimate success, but this appears so far off that almost any speculation is permissible. It may be that the operation, once started, is uncontrollable and that the new stars which flare out from time to time are but the notification of successful large-scale experiments on far distant worlds. It may be that the highest form of life on our planet will one day discover supreme material power, or cataclysmic annihilation, in the same ocean wherein, we are told, its lowest forms originally evolved.

Embryonic Chemistry

When alchemical suppositions were finally discredited by advances in physics—chief among them the new understanding of combustion we witnessed in the previous pages—modern chemistry was free to emerge from the "calx" or ashes of the old. The 1st edition (1768–1771) presented the old order as it stood, while acknowledging that there were areas in which the received wisdom was not completely satisfactory. Here is the opening of the article "Chemistry." (B.L.F.)

The object and chief end of chemistry is to separate the different substances that enter into the composition of bodies; to examine each of them apart; to discover their properties and relations; to decompose those very substances, if possible; to compare them together, and combine them with others; to reunite them again into one body, so as to reproduce the original compound with all its properties; or even to produce new compounds that never existed among the works of nature, from mixtures of other matters differently combined.

But this analysis, or decomposition, of bodies is finite; for we are unable to carry it beyond a certain limit. In whatever way we attempt to go further, we are always stopped by substances in which we can produce no change, and which are incapable of being resolved into others.

To these substances we may give the title of *principles* or *elements.* Of this kind the principal are earth, water, air, and fire.

8

Fig. 1.

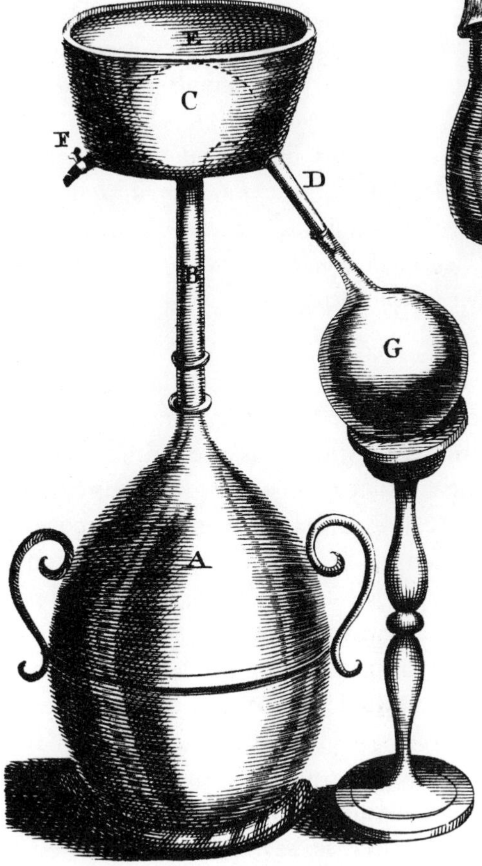

2

3

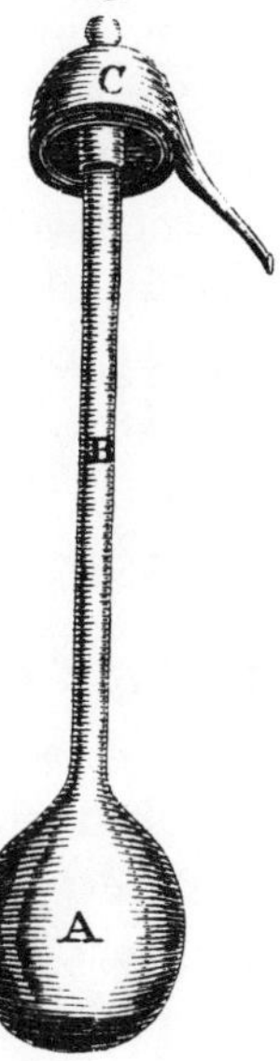

4

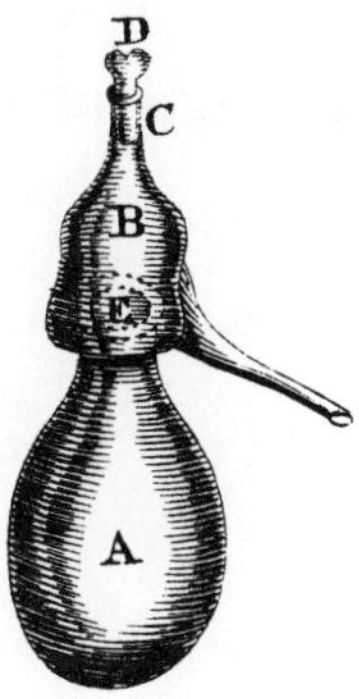

6

7

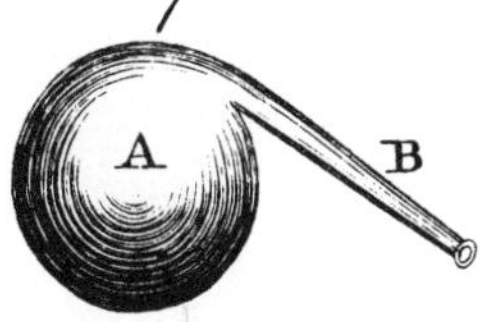

9

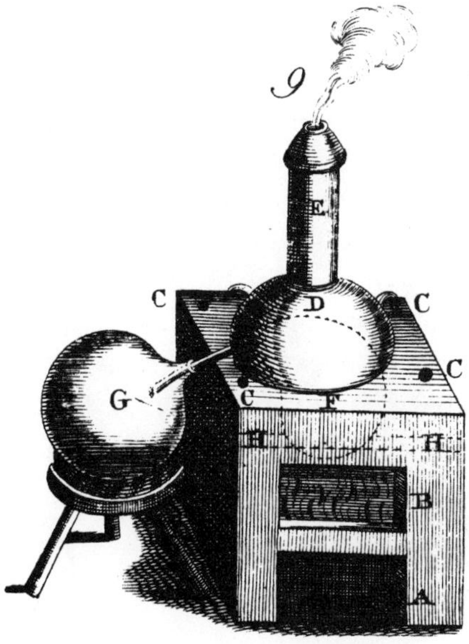

10

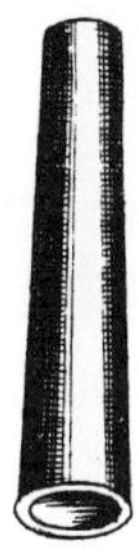

11

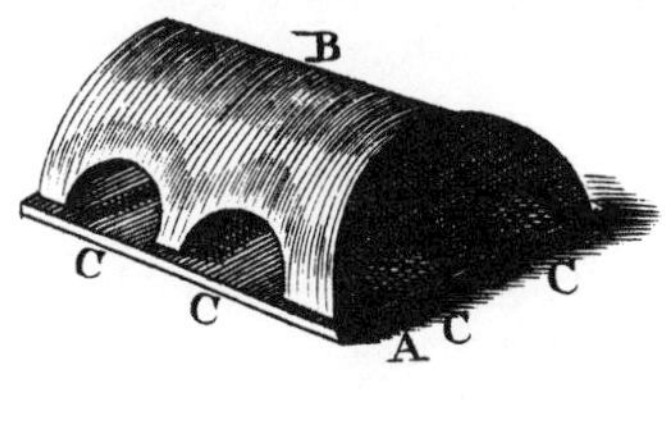

12

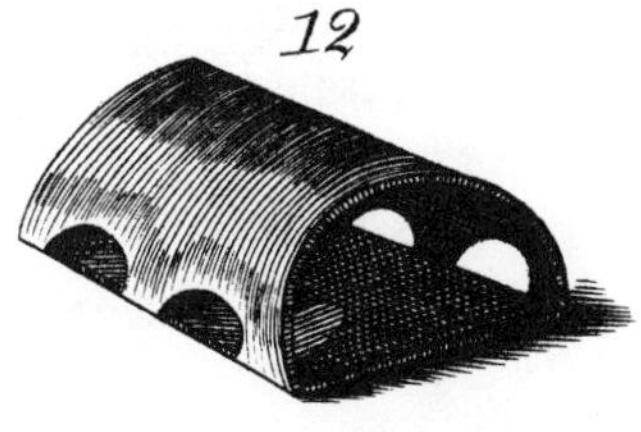

Detergent Dew

The editor of the Supplement to the 4th, 5th, and 6th editions (1815–1824) felt "Dew" to be a proper encyclopedic entry. Stress is laid on the utilitarian aspects of the subject, but the sly touch in the last sentence redresses the balance.

ALLEGED VIRTUES OF DEW

The dew of heaven has always been regarded as a fluid of the purest and most translucid nature. Hence it was celebrated for that abstergent property which, according to the vulgar persuasion, enables it to remove all spots and stains, and to impart to the skin the bloom and freshness of virgin beauty. Like the elixir of later times, it was conceived to possess the power of extending the duration of human life; and Ammianus Marcellinus ascribes the longevity and robust health of mountaineers, in comparison with the inhabitants of the plains, chiefly to the frequent aspersion of dew on their gelid bodies. Dew was also employed as a most powerful agent, in all their operations, by the alchemists; some of whom pretended that it possessed such a subtle and penetrating efficacy, as to be capable of dissolving gold itself. Following out the same idea, the people of remote antiquity fancied that the external application of dew had some virtue in correcting any disposition to corpulence. The ladies of those days, anxious to preserve their fine forms, procured this celestial wash, by exposing clothes or fleeces of wool to the humifaction of the night. It was likewise imagined, that grasshoppers feed wholly on dew, and owe their lean features perhaps to such spare diet.

Manure

In the physical world, manure remains of perennial interest. The Supplement to the 3rd edition (1801) devoted twelve columns to it, calling continually upon the authority of a certain Mr. Middleton, who seems to have been the last word on the subject. His views, crystallized in the final sentence of these extracts, might be considered anthropocentric.

MANURE is so essential to agriculture, that the want of it, or an improper manner of using it, is the principal cause of the sterility of a country. We have therefore treated of manures and their action at some length in the article AGRICULTURE in the *Encyclopaedia;* but as the theoretical part of that disquisition rests in a great measure on the doctrine of phlogiston, which is now exploded, it may not be improper to resume the subject here. . . .

What is a vegetable, considered chemically, according to the present state of our knowledge? It is, say the chemists, a compound of hydrogen, oxygen, and carbon, the proportions of which vary according to the agents which have concurred to its developement, and according to the matrix which received and assimilated them, in order to create those combinations which are varied to infinity, by their forms and properties, and known by the generic terms of salt, oil, and mucilage. . . .

Perhaps it would not be proper to dismiss this subject without noticing Mr Middleton's observations on various kinds of manure, which were published in the Transactions of the Society of Arts for the year 1799. This gentleman agrees with Mr Parmentier in recommending the *excrementitious matter of privies* as the most powerful of all manures on some kinds of soil; but he differs from him, and we believe from most writers on agriculture, when he affirms, that *wood ashes,* when spread on the grass in February or March, are of very little service, and that the ashes of *coal* and even of *peat* are of none upon any kind of land. He likewise affirms *soot* to be of very little value as a manure, *soapmakers waste* to be of none, or rather to be hurtful; and he seems to consider *malt-dust,* including the dust from the malt kilns, to be, after the soil of privies, one of the most powerful manures. He affirms, from his own experience, that, with respect to fertilising power, the soil of privies, compared with farm-yard dung, is in the proportion of five to one.

CHAPTER FIVE

Times and Places

Early Views

William Smellie, the editor of the Britannica's *1st edition (1768–1771), dismissed history and geography themselves rather brusquely. Here is the complete article on*

HISTORY, a description or recital of things as they are, or have been, in a continued orderly narration of the principal facts and circumstances thereof.

History, with regard to its subject, is divided into the history of Nature and the history of Actions. The history of Actions is a continued relation of a series of memorable events.

And here is

GEOGRAPHY, the doctrine or knowledge of the terrestrial globe; or the science that teaches and explains the properties of the earth, and the parts thereof which depend on quantity.

This definition was followed by nearly ten full pages of instructions and exercises under the heading "The Description and Use of the Globes and Armillary Sphere." (B.L.F.)

History

No subsequent Britannica *editor was as concise as Smellie, despite the unceasing demand for space, of which there was never enough. In fact, every editor for the next century allotted an increasing number of columns to these topics as topics. By the 3rd edition (1788–1797) the "History" article alone occupied sixty-one pages. Some extracts appear below. (B.L.F.)*

We encounter no mealy-mouthing in the 3rd edition. The historian is under an "absolute necessity" of accepting the Mosaic account as truth. It is amusing to note that the writer's categorical statements jog along serenely with his firm conviction that the historian must be "void of all passion or bias."

To comprehend the change in perspective that has occurred since 1788–1797, the reader may want to consult Jacques Barzun's "The Point and Pleasure of Reading History" in Part II of this volume.

HISTORY, in general, signifies an account of some remarkable facts which have happened in the world, arranged in the true order in which they actually took place, together with the causes to which they were owing, and the different effects they have produced as far as can be discovered. . . .

Sometimes, however, the word *history* is used to signify a description of things, as well as an account of facts. Thus Theophrastus calls his work in which he has treated of the nature and properties of plants, an *history of plants;* and we have a treatise of Aristotle, intitled an *history of animals;* and to this day the description of plants, animals, and minerals, are called by the general name of *natural history*.

But what chiefly merits the name of history, and what is here considered as such, is an account of the principal transactions of mankind since the beginning of the world; and which naturally divides itself into two parts, namely, *civil* and *ecclesiastical*. The first contains the history of mankind in their various relations to one another, and their behaviour, for their own emolument, or that of others, in common life; the second considers them as acting, or pretending to act, in obedience to what they believe to be the will of the Supreme Being. —Civil history, therefore, includes an account of all the different states that have existed in the world, and likewise of those men who in different ages of the world have most eminently distinguished themselves either for their good or evil actions. This last part of civil history is usually termed BIOGRAPHY.

History is now considered as a very considerable branch of polite literature: few accomplishments are more valued than an accurate knowledge of the histories of different nations; and scarce any literary production is more regarded than a well-written history of any nation. . . .

Concerning the number of years which have elapsed since the creation of the world, there have been many disputes. The compilers of the Universal History determine it to have taken place in the year 4305 B.C. so that, according to them, the world is now in the 6096th year of its age. Others think it was created only 4000 years B.C. so that it hath not yet attained its 6000th year. Be this as it will, however, the whole account of the creation rests on the truth of the Mosaic history; and which we must of necessity accept, because we can find no other which does not either abound with the grossest absurdities, or lead us into absolute darkness. The Chinese and Egyptian pretensions to antiquity are so absurd and ridiculous, that the bare reading must be a sufficient confutation of them to every reasonable person. . . . Some historians and philosophers are inclined to discredit the Mosaic accounts, from the appearances of volcanoes, and other natural phenomena: but their objections are by no means sufficient to invalidate the authority of the sacred writings; not to mention that every one of their own systems is liable to insuperable objections. . . . It is therefore reasonable for every person to accept of the Mosaic account of the creation as truth: but an historian is under an absolute necessity of doing it, because, without it, he is quite destitute of any standard or scale by which he might reduce the chronology of different nations to any agreement; and, in short, without receiving this account as true, it would be in a manner impossible at this day to write a general history of the world. . . .

TRUTH is, as it were, the very life and soul of history, by which it is distinguished from fable or romance. An historian therefore ought not only to be a man of probity, but void of all passion or bias. He must have the steadiness of a philosopher, joined with the vivacity of a poet or orator.

"Callifornia"

Here is the article "Callifornia" in its entirety, from the 1st edition (1768–1771).

CALLIFORNIA, a large country of the West Indies, lying between 116° and 138° W. long. and between 23° and 46° N. lat. It is uncertain whether it be a peninsula or an island.

The New World

British interest in the American colonies was high from the earliest times, and it remained high during the whole course of the American experiment. The encyclopedia related the good and the bad: the excesses of colonial days were recorded unblinkingly. Excerpts follow from the article "New England" in the 2nd edition (1778–1783). (B.L.F.)

The inhabitants of New England lived peaceably for a long time, without any regular form of policy. Their charter had indeed authorized them to establish any mode of government they might choose; but these enthusiasts were not agreed among themselves upon the plan of their republic, and government did not pay sufficient attention to them to urge them to secure their own tranquillity. At length they grew sensible of the necessity of a regular legislation; and this great work, which virtue and genius united have never attempted but with diffidence, was boldly undertaken by blind fanaticism. It bore the stamp of the rude prejudices on which it had been formed. There was in this new code a singular mixture of good and evil, of wisdom and folly. No man was allowed to have a share in the government except he were a member of the established church. Witchcraft, perjury, blasphemy, and adultery, were made capital offences; and children were also punished with death, either for cursing or striking their parents. Marriages, however, were to be solemnized by the magistrate. The price of corn was fixed at 2s. 11½ d. per bushel. The savages who neglected to cultivate their lands were to be deprived of them; and Europeans were forbidden under a heavy penalty to sell them any strong liquors or warlike stores. All those who were detected either in lying, drunkenness, or dancing, were ordered to be publicly whipped. But at the same time that amusements were forbidden equally with vices and crimes, one might be allowed to swear by paying a penalty of 11¾ d. and to break the sabbath for 2 l. 19 s. 9¾ d. Another indulgence allowed was, to atone, by a fine, for a neglect of prayer, or for uttering a rash oath. But it is still more extraordinary, that the worship of images was forbidden to the Puritans on pain of death; which was also inflicted on Roman Catholic priests, who should return to the colony after they had been banished; and on Quakers who should appear again after having been whipped, branded, and expelled. Such was the abhorrence for these sectaries, who had themselves an aversion for every kind of cruelty, that whoever either brought one of them into the country, or harboured him but for one hour, was liable to pay a considerable fine.

Those unfortunate members of the colony, who, less violent than their brethren, ventured to deny the coercive power of the magistrate in matters of religion, were persecuted with still greater rigour. This was considered as blasphemy by those very divines who had rather chosen to quit their country than to show any deference to Episcopal authority. This system was supported by the severities of the law, which attempted to put a stop to every difference in opinion, by inflicting capital punishment on all who dissented. Those who were either convicted, or even suspected, of entertaining sentiments of toleration, were exposed to such cruel oppressions, that they were forced to fly from their first asylum, and seek refuge in another. They found one on the same continent; and as New England had been first founded by persecution, its limits were extended by it.

This intemperate religious zeal extended itself to matters in themselves of the greatest indifference. A proof of this is found in the following public declaration, transcribed from the registers of the colony.

> It is a circumstance universally acknowledged, that the custom of wearing long hair, after the manner of immoral persons and of the savage Indians, can have been introduced into England only in sacrilegious contempt of the express command of God, who declares that it is a shameful practice for any man who has the least care for his soul to wear long hair. As this abomination excites the indignation of all pious persons; we, the magistrates, in our zeal for the purity of the faith, do expressly and authentically declare, that we condemn the impious custom of letting the hair grow; a custom which we look upon to be very indecent and dishonest, which horribly disguises men, and is offensive to modest and sober persons, in as much as it corrupts good manners. We therefore, being justly incensed against this scandalous custom, do desire, advise, and earnestly request all the elders of our continent, zealously to show their aversion for this odious practice, to exert all their power to put a stop to it, and especially to take care that the members of their churches be not infected with it; in order that those persons who, notwithstanding these rigorous prohibitions, and the means of correction that shall be used on this account, shall still persist in this custom, shall have both God and man at the same time against them.

This severity soon exerted itself against the Quakers. They were whipped, banished, and imprisoned. The behaviour of these new enthusiasts, who in the midst of tortures and ignominy praised God, and called for blessings upon men, inspired a reverence for their persons and opinions, and gained them a number of proselytes. This circumstance exasperated their persecutors, and hurried them on to the most atrocious acts of violence; and they caused five of them, who had returned clandestinely from banishment, to be hanged. This spirit of persecution was, however, at last suppressed by the interposition of the mother-country, from whence it had been brought. Charles II. moved with the sufferings of the Quakers, put a stop to them by a proclamation in 1661; but he was never able totally to extinguish the spirit of persecution that prevailed in America. . . .

There lived in a town of New England, called *Salem,* two young women who were subject to convulsions, accompanied with extraordinary symptoms. Their father, minister of the church, thought that they were bewitched; and having in consequence cast his suspicions upon an Indian girl who lived in his house, he compelled her by harsh treatment to confess that she was a witch. Other women, upon hearing this, immediately believed, that the convulsions, which proceeded only from the nature of their sex, were owing to the same cause. Three citizens, casually named, were immediately thrown into prison, accused of witchcraft, hanged, and their bodies left exposed to wild beasts and birds of prey. A few days after, 16 other persons, together with a counsellor, who, because he refused to plead against them, was supposed to share in their guilt, suffered in the same manner. From this instant, the imagination of the multitude was inflamed with these horrid and gloomy scenes. Children of ten years of age were put to death, young girls were stripped naked, and the marks of witchcraft searched for upon their bodies with the most indecent curiosity; and those spots of the scurvy which age impresses upon the bodies of old men were taken for evident signs of the infernal power. In default of these, torments were employed to extort confessions dictated by the executioners themselves. If the magistrates, tired out with executions, refused to punish, they were themselves accused of the crimes they tolerated; the very ministers of religion raised false witnesses against them, who made them forfeit with their lives the tardy remorse excited in them by humanity. Dreams, apparitions, terror, and consternation of every kind, increased these prodigies of folly and horror. The prisons were filled, the gibbets left standing, and all the citizens involved in gloomy apprehensions. The most prudent quitted the country stained with the blood of its inhabitants; and nothing less than the total and immediate subversion of the colony was expected, when, on a sudden, all eyes were opened at once, and the excess of the evil awakened the minds which it had first stupified. Bitter and painful remorse was the immediate consequence; the mercy of God was implored by a general fast, and public prayers were offered up to ask forgiveness for the presumption of having supposed that Heaven could have been pleased with sacrifices with which it could only have been offended.

Posterity will probably never know exactly what was the cause or remedy of this dreadful disorder. It had, perhaps, its first origin in the melancholy which those persecuted enthusiasts had brought with them from their own country, which had increased with the scurvy they had contracted at sea, and had gathered fresh strength from the inconveniences and hardships inseparable from a change of climate and manner of living. The contagion, however, ceased like all other epidemical distempers, exhausted by its very communication. A perfect calm succeeded this agitation; and the Puritans of New England have never since been seized with so gloomy a fit of enthusiasm.

But though the colony has renounced the persecuting spirit which hath stained all religious sects with blood, it has preserved some remains, if not of intoleration, at least of severity, which remind us of those melancholy days in which it took its rise. Some of its laws are still too severe.

The End of the Contest

The 4th edition (1801–1809) in its article "America" included a long and explicit history of the American Revolution, whose flavor may be tasted in the following excerpts. The 134-page article addressed both geography and political history, including the development and the text of the U.S. Constitution. It concluded with a map and an index four pages in length. The final paragraph displays an exquisite combination of amiability and patronage. (B.L.F.)

Notwithstanding the signal advantages that Lord Cornwallis had obtained over the Americans, his situation in Virginia began by degrees to be very critical; and the rather because he did not receive those reinforcements and supplies from Sir Henry Clinton, of which he had formed expectations, and which he conceived to be necessary to the success of his operations. Indeed, the commander in chief was prevented from sending those reinforcements to Lord Cornwallis which he otherwise might have done, by his fears respecting New York, against which he entertained great apprehensions that General Washington intended to make a very formidable attack. In fact, that able American general appears to have taken much pains, and to have employed great finesse, in order to lead Sir Henry Clinton to entertain this imagination. Letters, expressive of this intention, fell into the hands of Sir Henry, which were manifestly written with a design that they should be intercepted, and only with a view to amuse and deceive the British general. The project was successful; and by a variety of judicious military manoeuvres, in which he completely out-generalled the British commander, he increased his apprehensions about New York, and prevented him from sending proper assistance to Lord Cornwallis. . . .

In the mean time, the most effectual measures were adopted by General Washington for surrounding the British army under Lord Cornwallis. A large body of French troops, under the command of Lieutenant-general the count de Rochambeau, with a very considerable train of artillery, assisted in the enterprise. The Americans amounted to near 8000 continentals and 5000 militia. General Washington was invested with the authority of commander in chief of these combined forces of America and France. On the 29th of September, the investment of York Town was complete, and the British army quite blocked up. The day following, Sir Henry Clinton wrote a letter to Lord Cornwallis, containing assurances that he would do every thing in his power to relieve him, and some information concerning the steps that would be taken for that purpose. A duplicate of this letter was sent to his lordship by Major Cochran on the 3rd of October. That gentleman, who was a very gallant officer, went in a vessel to the capes, and made his way to Lord Cornwallis, through the whole French fleet, in an open boat. He got to York Town on the 10th of the month; and soon after his arrival had his head carried off by a cannon ball. . . .

It was on the 19th of October that Lord Cornwallis surrendered himself and his whole army, by capitulation, prisoners to the combined armies of America and France, under the command of General Washington. He made a defence suitable to the character he had before acquired for courage and military skill; but was compelled to submit to untoward circumstances and superior numbers. It was agreed by the articles of capitulation, that the British troops were to be prisoners to the United States of America, and the seamen to the French king, to whose officers also the British vessels found at York Town and Gloucester were to be delivered up. The British prisoners amounted to more than 6000; but many of them, at the time of surrender, were incapable of duty. A considerable number of cannon, and a large quantity of military stores, fell into the hands of the Americans on this occasion.

As no rational expectation now remained of a subjugation of the colonies, the military operations that succeeded in America were of little consequence. . . .

Such was the end of the contest between Great Britain and America: A contest in which the latter attained to an independant rank among the nations, that may be productive of more important consequences that can yet be foreseen; and in which the former, happily for herself, was forced to relinquish a sovereignty that served only to repress her own internal industry, and retard her prosperity. She has, in the event, only suffered a diminution of unwieldy empire, which has been more than compensated by an increase of population, commerce, revenues, and wealth. . . .

The convulsions of nations and the calamities and the crimes of mankind, always form the most interesting subject of history; and happy is that people concerning whom the historian finds little to relate. From the period of the acceptance of their constitution, the American states have, in a great degree, enjoyed that fortunate situation. On the 13th of September 1788, the old congress having received the ratification of the constitution from eleven states, declared it to be in force, and appointed the first Wednesday of the following January for choosing the electors, who were to assemble on the first Wednesday in February following, to elect the president and vice-president. The new congress was also appointed to meet on the first Wednesday of March following at New York. Accordingly on the first Wednesday of February 1789, George Washington, who had been the commander in chief of the armies of the United States, and president of the convention of Philadelphia that framed the constitution, was elected president, and John Adams, who had seconded Mr Jefferson in proposing the original declaration of American independence, was at the same time elected vice-president. The popularity of the president was deservedly very great; and, as all parties concurred in supporting the new constitution, much unanimity prevailed in the public councils.

American Education Two Centuries Ago

The 4th edition (1801–1809) summed it up thus:

The education of youth in America is conducted as in Scotland, with a view rather to introduce young persons quickly into life, than to render them men of profound learning. A young man in America hardly arrives at the age of 16 years before his parents are desirous of planting him in the counting-house of a merchant, or in the office of a lawyer: Hence he is never likely to resign himself to the sciences and to letters. He soon loses all other ideas than those which can hurry him on to the acquisition of a fortune. . . .

Hence it will not appear surprising, that there should be few learned men in the United States. Indeed, the number of learned, ingenious, and well-informed individuals, which is very considerable, that have appeared there, must be ascribed rather to their own native energy of character than to their education, or the state of society in which they were placed.

In the American schools, the instruction in Latin is seldom extended farther than the first classic authors, including Cornelius Nepos, Ovid, and some orations of Cicero. A little of Virgil and Horace are read in the colleges. The New Testament in Greek, and a little of Homer in some colleges, is the limit of classical instruction in that language. Mathematical instruction is usually confined to the Elements of Euclid, and the first principles of conic sections. Practical geometry, however, for the purposes of land-surveying and navigation, is much valued, on account of its connexion with those branches of business which lead to riches. Mechanics, hydrostatics, and hydraulics, are taught after the works of Nicolson, Ferguson, or Enfield. Medicine, however, and the branches of science connected with it, are said to be well taught in some American universities; and that profession has produced many respectable and well-informed men. Still it is probable, that however enlightened the Americans may account themselves, the nature of their pursuits is such, that a considerable time will elapse before they can exhibit any great number of men of profound and extensive learning. Such accomplishments, however, as their situation requires they possess in much perfection.

United States

In some respects, the most interesting bit of retrieval in this book is the opening section of a lengthy article by Charles Maclaren in the Supplement to the 4th, 5th, and 6th editions (1815–1824). Maclaren was a noted figure in Edinburgh's literary world, a staunch Whig, and the founder of The Scotsman, *the first independent liberal newspaper in Scotland. (He edited the 6th edition of the* Britannica, *(1820–1823), which was published simultaneously with the last volumes of the Supplement.)*

*Written perhaps 175 years ago, this statement about our country cannot help but induce meditation in today's reader. Particularly interesting is the last sentence of the introductory remarks here quoted. Its cautious prediction regarding Russia was made some years before Tocqueville (*Democracy in America, *1835–1840) issued a similar, more categorical prophecy.*

No single event in modern history has been of so much importance to mankind as the discovery of America. That great continent, which had been hid from the eyes of civilized nations for so many ages, comprises nearly one-third of the habitable globe. In soil and climate, it rivals the best parts of the old continent. It is not, like Asia and Africa, infested by the larger and more dangerous species of wild animals, nor deformed by vast deserts, which present insuperable obstacles to civilization. But its great and peculiar advantage lies in the unrivalled magnitude and number of its navigable rivers, which enable its most remote inland parts to hold commercial intercourse with each other, and with foreign states, with unparalleled ease and rapidity. The position of these great rivers, whose estuaries all open to the east, points out the western side of the old continent as the region with which it is destined by nature to be most closely connected. Two great classes of colonists, widely dissimilar in character and circumstances, came from Europe to occupy this new world. The Spaniards, who were first in order of time, took possession of the most populous and fertile regions; but their natural advantages were rendered abortive by political and moral evils,—a rapacious spirit, a corrupt religion, and a vicious system of government. The English, the other great class of colonists, owed their better fortunes in some measure to their apparent disadvantages. Having neither gold mines to work, nor wealthy Indians to rob, they cultivated with greater diligence the natural riches of the soil, and laid the foundation of future prosperity in habits of order and industry. Neglected by the government as a band of destitute refugees, they enjoyed what was then an unusual degree of civil and religious liberty. Their industry flourished, because it was unfettered and unburdened. They were well governed, because they were left to govern themselves. And if they wanted the aid of the mother country when that aid might sometimes have been useful, they were, on the other hand, exempted from those incessant exactions and vexations to which the Spanish colonists were exposed, from the ignorant, meddling, grasping, bigoted spirit of their European rulers. The troubles they experienced from the hostility of the Indians diminished as their own numbers increased, and, except at first, were never extremely detrimental. Their common dangers served in some measure as a bond of union among themselves, and perhaps favoured their social improvement, by acting as a slightly compressing force to prevent the indefinite diffusion of the population over a large surface. To their free spirit, virtuous habits, intelligence, and industry, the English colonists certainly owed much of their early success; but we must not forget that a series of fortunate changes, not directly the consequence of their own exertions, have greatly contributed to place them in the enviable situation they now occupy. Had the Dutch, French, Danish, and Swedish colonies planted in North America spread as fast and as far as those of England, and continued separate and independent, we should have seen, in the space between the Mississippi and the Atlantic, the same medley of nations and languages, with the same diversity of manners, religion, institutions, and clashing interests, which foster everlasting feuds and jealousies in Europe, engender desolating wars, load the people with oppressive taxes and military tyrannies, and present a formidable barrier to the circulation of knowledge and the progress of society. The conquests of England, which blended all these colonies into one nation, have secured to the United States an exemption from half the evils which afflict civil society in Europe, and prepared for them a career of peaceful grandeur and growing prosperity, which divided Europe cannot hope to enjoy, and which has had no parallel in the history of mankind. The people of the United States find themselves in a condition to devote their whole energies to the cultivation of their vast natural resources, undistracted by wars, unburdened by oppressive taxes, unfettered by old prejudices and corruptions. Enjoying the united advantages of an infant and a mature society, they are able to apply the highly refined science and art of Europe to the improvement of the virgin soil and unoccupied natural riches of America. They start unincumbered by a thousand evils, political and moral, which weigh down the energies of the old world. The volume of our history lies before them: they may adopt our improvements, avoid our errors, take warning from our sufferings, and with the combined lights of our experience and their own, build up a more perfect form of society. Even already, they have given some momentous and some salutary truths to the world. It is their rapid growth which has first developed the astonishing results of the productive powers of population. We can now calculate with considerable certainty, that America, which yet presents to the eye, generally, the aspect of an untrodden forest, will, in the short space of one century, surpass Europe in the number of its inhabitants. We even hazard little in predicting, that, before the tide of civilization has rolled back to its original seats, Assyria, Persia, and Palestine, an intelligent population of two or three hundred millions will have overspread the new world, and extended the empire of knowledge and the arts from Cape Horn to Alayska. Among this vast mass of civilized men, there will be but two languages spoken. The effect of this single circumstance in accelerating the progress of society can scarcely be calculated. What a field will then be opened to the man of science, the artist, the popular writer, who addresses a hundred millions of educated persons?—what a stimulus given to mental energy and social improvement, when every new idea, and every useful discovery, will be communicated instantaneously to so great a mass of intelligent beings, by the electric agency of the post and the press? With the united intellect and resources of a society framed on such a gigantic scale, what mighty designs will then be practicable? Imagination is lost in attempting to estimate the effects of such accumulated means and powers. One result, however, may be anticipated. America must then become the centre of knowledge, civilization, and power; and the present leading states of Europe (Russia perhaps excepted), placed on the arena amidst such colossal associates as the American Republics, will sink to a subordinate rank, and cease to exert any greater influence on the fate of the world than the Swiss Cantons do at the present day.

How to Treat Slaves

During the Britannica*'s early years, slavery, though outlawed in Britain and France, prevailed in America and the West Indies. Editorial distaste for the practice became increasingly apparent, but long before the general rise of abolitionist sentiment, the encyclopedia, in the article "Plantership" (2nd edition, 1778–1783), counseled humane treatment of slaves—for practical reasons. (B.L.F.)*

PLANTERSHIP, in the West Indies, denotes the management of a sugar plantation, including not only the cultivation of the cane, but the various processes for the extraction of the sugar, together with the making of sugar-spirits. See RUM, SACCHARUM, and SUGAR.

To effect a design so comprehensive, it is necessary for a planter to understand every branch of the art precisely, and to use the utmost attention and caution both in the laying down and executing of his plans. It is therefore the duty of a good planter to inspect every part of his plantation with his own eyes; to place his provisions, stores, and utensils, in regular order, and in safe repositories; that by preserving them in perfection, all kinds of waste may be prevented.

But as negroes, cattle, mules, and horses, are, as it were, the nerves of a sugar-plantation, it is expedient to treat that subject with some accuracy.

Of Negroes, Cattle, etc.

In the first place, then, as it is the interest of every planter to preserve his negroes in health and strength; so every act of cruelty is not less repugnant to the master's real profit, than it is contrary to the laws of humanity: and if a manager considers his own ease, and his employer's interest, he will treat all negroes under his care with due benevolence; for good discipline is by no means inconsistent with humanity: on the contrary, it is evident from experience, that he who feeds his negroes well, proportions their labour to their age, sex, and strength, and treats them with kindness and good-nature, will reap a much larger product, and with infinitely more ease and self-satisfaction, than the most cruel task-master, who starves his negroes, or chastises them with undue severity. Every planter then who wishes to grow rich with ease, must be a good oeconomist; must feed his negroes with the most wholesome food, sufficient to preserve them in health and vigour. Common experience points out the methods by which a planter may preserve his people in health and strength. Some of his most fruitful land should be allotted to each negro in proportion to his family, and a sufficient portion of time allowed for the cultivation of it; but because such allotment cannot in long droughts produce enough for his comfortable support, it is the incumbent duty of a good planter to have always his stores well filled with Guinea corn, yams, or eddoes, besides potatoes growing in regular succession; for plenty begets cheerfulness of heart, as well as strength of body; by which more work is effected in a day by the same hands, than in a week when enervated by want and severity. Scanty meals may sustain life; but it is evident, that more is requisite to enable a negro, or any other person, to go through the necessary labours. He therefore who will reap plentifully, must plant great abundance of provisions as well as sugar-canes: and it is nature's oeconomy so to fructify the soil by the growth of yams, plantains, and potatoes, as to yield better harvests of sugar, by that very means, than can be produced by many other arts of cultivation. . . .

However plenty of wholesome food may be conducive to health, there are also other means, equally necessary to strength and the longevity of negroes, well worth the planter's attention: and those are, to choose airy dry situations for their houses; and to observe frequently that they be kept clean, in good repair, and perfectly water-tight; for nastiness, and the inclemencies of weather, generate the most malignant diseases. If these houses are situated also in regular order, and at due distances, the spaces may at once prevent general devastations by fire, and furnish plenty of fruits and pot-herbs, to please an unvitiated palate, and to purify the blood. Thus then ought every planter to treat his negroes with tenderness and generosity, that they may be induced to love and obey him out of mere gratitude, and become real good beings by the imitation of his behaviour; and therefore a good planter, for his own ease and happiness, will be careful of setting a good example.

How the Scots Got Their Name

Whether from modesty or forgetfulness, the 1st edition (1768–1771) had little to say about Scotland: only a scant paragraph. The 2nd edition (1778–1783) made up for lost time and space, devoting some one hundred and eighty pages to the country—more than 1 percent of the entire encyclopedia. The great bulk of this was given to the colorful and frequently bloody history of Scotland, told in a lusty and often vigorously partisan fashion that makes much later historiography in and out of encyclopedias seem pale and bloodless by comparison. (B.L.F.)

SCOTLAND, the country of the Scots, or that part of Great Britain lying to the north of the Tweed; is situated between the 54th and 59th degrees of north latitude, and extends in length about 278 miles, and in some places near 180 in breadth; containing an area of 27,794 miles. On the south it is bounded by England; on the north, east, and west, by the Deucaledonian, German, and Irish seas.

It is extremely difficult to give any satisfactory account of the origin of the appellation of *Scots,* from which the country has derived its name. It has puzzled the most eminent antiquaries, whose conjectures serve rather to perplex than to clear up the difficulty. Nor is this to be wondered at, when Varro and Dionysius could not agree about the etymon of *Italia,* nor Plutarch and Solinus about that of *Rome.* All that we know with any degree of certainty, concerning the appellation of *Scot,* amounts to this—That it was at first a term of reproach, and consequently framed by enemies, rather than assumed by the nation distinguished by that name. The Highlanders, who were the genuine descendants of the ancient Scots, are absolutely strangers to the name, and have been so from the beginning of time. All those who speak the Gaelic language call themselves *Albanich* or *Gael,* and their country *Alba* or *Gaeldochd.*

The Picts, who possessed originally the northern and eastern, and in a latter period also the more southern, division of North Britain, were at first more powerful than the Caledonians of the west. It is therefore probable, that the Picts, from a principle of malevolence and pride, were ready to traduce and ridicule their weaker neighbours of Argyle. These two nations spoke the same language, the Gaelic. In that language *Scot,* or *Scode,* signifies a corner or small division of a country. Accordingly, a corner of north Britain is the very name which Giraldus Cambrensis gives the little kingdom of Argyle, which the six sons of Muredus king of Ulster were said, according to his information, to have erected in Scotland. *Scot* in Gaelic is much the same with *little* or *contemptible* in English; and *Scotlan,* literally speaking, signifies a *small flock;* metaphorically, it stands for a small body of men. (*Dr Macpherson's Dissert.*)

Others observe, that in the same language the word *Scuit* signifies a *wanderer,* and suppose that this may have been the origin of the name of *Scot;* a conjecture which they think is countenanced by a passage in Ammianus Marcellinus (l. xxvii.), who characterizes the men by the epithet of *roaming;* "per diversa vagantes." (*Mr Macpherson, and Mr Whitaker*).

All that we can say is, that for some one of the reasons couched under the above disparaging epithets, their malicious or sneering neighbours, the Picts or the Britons, may have given the appellation of *Scots* to the ancestors of the Scottish nation.

Pride and Prejudice

Here and there in the famous Supplement to the 4th, 5th, and 6th editions (1815–1824) could be seen two quite different elements that in their modern guises are familiar enough to late-twentieth-century readers: a pride bordering on zealotry for one's own culture and a complementary disdain for others. The article "Europe" was written by Charles Maclaren. His introduction, printed below, opened on a note that managed to be at once graceful and boosterish. Maclaren then immediately proceeded to denigrate the peoples of the entire rest of the world—except for European transplants. For the unwashed he saw no prospect of advancement save conquest by Europeans. (B.L.F.)

EUROPE

One of the great divisions of the globe. On a first view, Europe appears to be less favoured by nature than the other quarters of the globe over which it has obtained so great an ascendancy. It is much smaller in extent; its rocky and mountainous surface does not admit of those noble rivers, like inland seas, which lay open the remotest regions of Asia and America to the commerce of the world. Its vegetable productions are neither so various nor so exuberant; and it is poorly supplied with the precious metals, and with many of those commodities on which mankind set the greatest value. On the other hand, the climate of Europe, if it nourishes a less luxuriant vegetation, is of an equal and temperate kind, well adapted to preserve the human frame in that state of health and vigour which fits it for labour, and promotes the developement of the intellectual and moral powers. The mountains that intersect its surface were barriers which enabled infant communities to protect themselves from violence, and to lay the foundation of arts, knowledge, and civilization. If it has few large navigable rivers, its inland seas and bays are the finest in the world, and were the means of creating and nourishing that commercial spirit which has been one great source of its improvement. Though comparatively deficient in gold and silver, it is abundantly supplied with those useful metals and minerals which minister still more essentially to the wants of civilized life. Its apparent defects have become the source of real benefits, and the foundation of its grandeur. The disadvantages of its soil and climate have excited the industry of its inhabitants, given them clearer ideas of property, kindled a resolute spirit to defend their rights, and called into existence that skill and enterprise, and those innumerable arts and inventions, which have enabled the inhabitants of this apparently barren and rocky promontory to command the riches and luxuries of all the most favoured regions of the globe. . . . It is only in Europe that knowledge and the arts seem to be indigenous. Though they have appeared at times among some of the nations of Asia, they have either stopt short after advancing a few steps, or they have speedily retrograded and perished, like something foreign to the genius of the people. In Europe, on the contrary, they have sprung up at distant periods, and in a variety of situations; they have risen spontaneously and rapidly, and declined slowly; and when they disappeared, it was evident, they were but crushed for the time by external violence, to rise again when the pressure had subsided. It is only in Europe, and among colonies of Europeans, that the powers of the human mind, breaking through the slavish attachment to ancient usages and institutions, have developed that principle of progressive improvement of which it is impossible to calculate the final results. The rudest tribe in Europe, in which this principle has taken root, has a certain source of superiority over the most improved nations of Asia and Africa, where society remains perfectly stationary. If these nations are ever destined to advance in civilization, they must borrow from Europe those arts which she has invented, and which belong to civilized life in every climate. But the tenacious adherence of rude nations to the customs and superstitions of their ancestors will not allow us to hope that the benefits of civilization will be rapidly diffused in this way. It is more probable, that colonies from the older states of Europe will multiply, as the population becomes more and more redundant; and that these colonies will carry the arts and knowledge, the language and manners of Europe with them, to the other quarters of the world. From prejudices on both sides, it is found that two races in very different stages of civilization do not readily amalgamate; and it is therefore probable, that the feebler inhabitants of these countries, like the American Indians, will be gradually displaced by the continued encroachments of the more energetic race of Europe. Such a change, however, must take place slowly, and there is nothing in it to alarm humanity. The vast number of tribes that people Asia and Africa seem born only to be the victims of savage superstition and ferocious tyranny. No treatment they are likely to experience from European colonies can render their condition worse; and were the whole swarm of these nations to die out in the course of nature without being renewed, no great deduction would be made from the sum of human enjoyment. Should the state of things we have been contemplating, and which seems to arise naturally out of the circumstances of Europe, and the other quarters of the globe, be realized, it will be curious to reflect on the circle of changes which will then be completed. The ancient inhabitants of Europe, as well as the modern, were originally colonies sent off from the surplus population of Asia. Here they have thrown off their barbarism, invented and improved arts and sciences, and carried their social institutions to a high degree of perfection; and now, in the maturity of their strength, they are throwing back their surplus numbers upon Asia, to conquer and supplant the remains of those tribes from whom they originally sprung.

Canada as It Was

Of course Encyclopædia Britannica *maintained a high degree of interest in what remained of British North America after the U.S. Dec-*

laration of Independence. David Buchanan, a journalist and editor of the Edinburgh Courant, *lyrically recalled his observations of the extremes of climate in that vast country. The excerpt is from the article "Canada" in the Supplement to the 4th, 5th, and 6th editions (1815–1824). (B.L.F.)*

In Canada, the opposite extremes of heat and cold are felt in all their excess. The greatest heat experienced during the summer is from 96 to 102 degrees of Fahrenheit in the shade; but the usual summer heat varies from 75 to 80. In the winter, the mercury sometimes sinks to 31°, and it has even been known to fall so low as 36° below 0. It never continues, however, above one or two days at these extremes, and it is not above once or twice in a season that this excessive cold is felt. The medium temperature of winter may be estimated, in general, to be from 20 degrees above to 25 degrees below 0. The pure air and cloudless sky, which always accompany this intense frost, make it both pleasant and healthy, and render its effects on the human body much less severe than when the atmosphere is loaded with vapours. In the vicinity of the sea, towards the eastern coast of Lower Canada, fogs are frequently brought from the gulf of Lawrence, by the easterly wind. But to the westward they seldom prevail, and even at Quebec they are almost unknown. In Canada, the spring, summer, and autumn are comprehended in five months, from May to September. The rest of the year may be said to consist wholly of winter. The summer commences in May, and ends with September. In October, frost begins to be felt, although during the day, the rays of the sun still keep the weather tolerably warm. In the succeeding month of November, the frost increases in rigour, and one snow storm succeeds another, until the whole face of the country is covered, and the eye looks in vain for one solitary spot of verdure whereon to rest. These storms are generally accompanied by a violent tempest of wind, which, driving along the snow with immense velocity, renders them tenfold more gloomy and terrific. The most severe snow storms occur in November. They generally come from the north-east, from the frozen regions of Hudson's Bay and Labrador. This gloomy and disagreeable weather frequently continues to the middle or latter end of December, when the atmosphere clears; an intense frost succeeds—the sky becomes serene, pure, and frosty, and of a bright azure hue, and this cold and clear weather generally lasts till the month of May. The snow covers the ground to the depth of several feet, so that wheel-carriages can no longer be used. Their place is supplied by *carioles,* a sort of sledges, which, being placed on iron-runners, resembling in their form the irons of a pair of skaits, pass over the hardened snow without sinking deep. Those carriages are generally light open vehicles, drawn by one horse, to which the snow, after it is trodden for some time, and hardened by the frost, offers very little resistance. In these vehicles, the Canadians travel in the most agreeable manner, and with inconceivable rapidity. So light is the draught, that the same horse will go in one day 80, and sometimes 90 miles, and the inhabitants of this cold climate always take advantage of the winter season, when they can travel so easily and expeditiously, to visit their friends who live at a distance. Covered *carioles* are sometimes used to protect the travellers from the weather. But, in general, open carriages are preferred.

About the beginning of December, all the small rivers are completely frozen over and covered with snow. Even the great river St Lawrence is arrested in its course, and from the beginning of December till the middle of April, the navigable communication is interrupted by the frost. During this period, the river from Quebec to Kingston, and between the great lakes, except the Niagara and the rapids, is wholly frozen over. The great lakes are never entirely covered with ice; but it usually shuts up all the bays and inlets, and extends many miles towards the centre of those inland seas. In Lake Superior, which is furthest to the north, the ice extends 70 miles from the shore. It is seldom that the river is frozen over below Quebec. But the force of the tides is continually detaching the ice from its shores, and those immense masses are kept in such constant agitation that navigation is rendered quite impracticable. In some seasons, though rarely, the river is frozen completely over below Quebec; and this happens when large masses of ice come in contact, and fill the whole space between one side of the river and the other, in consequence of which the whole becomes stationary. If this takes place at neap tides, and in calm weather, the intense frost gives it solidity before it can be deranged by the rising tides; and when it has stood some days, it remains firm and immoveable, till it is dissolved and broken up by the warmth of the April sun. When the river is frozen over, it is of great advantage, both to the inhabitants of Quebec, and to those of the adjacent country, as it affords an easy mode of transporting into the town all sorts of bulky commodities, such as fire-wood, and other produce. It thus reduces the price of those necessary articles in Quebec, while by diminishing the price of carriage, it opens to the produce of the most distant parts of the country, a quick and easy access to all the most eligible markets.

The snow begins to melt in April, and the thaw is so rapid that it is generally gone by the second or third week. Vegetation then resumes its suspended powers; the fields are clothed with verdure, and spring can scarcely be said to exist before summer is at hand. In Upper Canada, the winters are much shorter than in Lower Canada, nor is the cold so intense. The spring opens, and the labours of the farmer commence six weeks or two months earlier than in the neighbourhood of Quebec. The climate is not liable to the same extremes either of heat or cold, and the weather in autumn is usually favourable for securing all the late crops.

Australia

Not for twenty-five years after the first settlement at Port Jackson did a British explorer penetrate farther than thirty leagues (ninety miles) into the interior of Australia. Sir John Barrow (1764–1848), the explorer and geographer, relates that first inland exploration. The excerpts are from his "Australasia" in the Supplement to the 4th, 5th, and 6th editions (1815–1824). (B.L.F.)

Of these journeys we are enabled to give a brief abstract. On the 19th November 1813, Mr Evans left Emu Island in the Nepean, and returned on the 8th January 1814, having performed a journey of 154 miles nearly west. At the end of 48 miles, he had cleared the ranges of mountains, which he says are granite, with loose flints and quartz pebbles strewed on the surface; and here, for the first time, he fell in with a small stream running to the westward. The farther he advanced the more beautiful the country became; both hill and dale were clothed with fine grass, the whole appearing at a little distance as if laid out into fields divided by hedge-rows; through every valley meandered trickling streams of fine water, all falling down towards the *Fish River,* so called by him from the vast abundance of fine fish resembling trout, which his party caught with ease whenever they had occasion for them. Many of the hills were capped with forest trees, chiefly of the Eucalyptus, and clumps of these mixed with Mimosas and the Casuarina, were interspersed along the feet of the hills and in the valleys, so as to wear the appearance of a succession of gentlemen's parks. The river, which at first consisted of a chain of pools, connected by small streamlets, had assumed in the neighbourhood of *Macquarrie's Plains,* the character of a considerable stream, and had become unfordable, which made it necessary to construct a bridge of large trees to transport the people, the horses, and baggage. Evans says, the country was now more beautiful than he had ever seen. A fine river, running in a deep channel over a gravelly bottom, and its banks skirted with trees, excepting at the sloping points of hills round which it winded, and which were covered with a fine green sod down to the margin, intermixed with the white daisy;—all this, added to the temperate climate, put him in mind of England. Farther on, and before they reached *Bathurst's Plains,* the river was increased considerably in size by the junction of another stream, which he called *Campbell's River;* and to the united streams, he gave the name of *Macquarrie's River,* the general direction of which appeared to be to the northward of west. Fish continued to abound of the same kind as those first caught, but of a size from 11 to 15 pounds each. Governor Macquarrie says, these fish resemble perch, are not unlike that usually called rock-cod, and have been caught from 17 to 25 pounds weight each. Large herds of emus were seen crossing the plains, and kangaroos in great abundance; but not a native human being appeared until on his return, when, near *Bathurst's Plains,* two women and four children were come upon by surprise, and were so terrified, that they fell down with fright. It was observed, that both the women had lost the right eye. Evans makes Bathurst's Plains near 150 miles from Emu Island; but Governor Macquarrie, who subsequently visited this place, states the measured distance from Sydney town to be only 140 miles. It is represented as an eligible situation for establishing a settlement, as the land is excellent; plenty of stone and timber for building, but no limestone; abundance of water, though the river, at the time of the Governor's visit, just at the close of an unusually dry season, was reduced to a chain of pools, the intermediate channels being dried up.

From hence Mr Evans was a second time dispatched, in May 1815, to follow the course of Macquarrie's River. He proceeded about 115 miles, from whence he could see across an extensive plain, 40 or 50 miles, at the extremity of which was a range of blue mountains, separated by an opening in the north-west, through which, he had no doubt, the river flowed; and he appears to have as little doubt, that it crosses the continent, and falls into the sea, somewhere in De Witt's Land, probably through Dampier's Opening, behind Rosemary Island. . . .

The country beyond *Bathurst* was even superior to that first explored. The vast herds of emus and kangaroos were truly astonishing. These animals, and the fish of the river, appeared to be the principal articles of subsistence for the natives. In one large plain, covered with kangaroos and emus, Evans discovered an immense quantity of a white substance, resembling comfits or sugar-plums, which he took to be manna, but which appears to be a pure saccharine substance,—an exudation probably from some particular plant. He passed whole mountains of fine blue limestone, and picked up topazes, crystals, and other pebbles, such as are met with on the coast of Bass's Strait. He also mentions forests of pines, the trees 40 feet high without a branch. Governor Macquarrie, however, observed, that as the soil and grass-lands improved, the timber trees decreased in size. (See the different works of *Dalrymple, Burney, Cook, D'Entrecasteaux,* and *Flinders.*)

If, however, but little is yet known of the interior of New Holland, and the detail of the western coast still requires to be filled up, the grand outline of this large Island, or, more properly, Continent, has been completed, and its limits correctly ascertained. It extends in latitude from Cape York in 10° 45′ south to Wilson's promontory in 39° 9′ south, and in longitude from Dirk Hartog's Island in Shark's Bay in 113° east, to point Look-out in Glasshouse Bay in 153° 35′ east; the mean breadth, from north to south, being about 1200, and length, from east to west, 2100 geographical miles, making an area equal to about three-fourths of the Continent of Europe. A remarkable sameness in all the productions of the three kingdoms of nature prevails in every part of its extensive coasts, and as remarkable a difference in two of them (the animal and vegetable) from those of the rest of the world.

The natives, wherever they have been met with, are of the very lowest description of human beings. In the journal of the Duyfhen, the north coast is described as thinly "inhabited by wild, cruel, black savages, by whom some of the crew were murdered;" and the ship Vianen, touching on the western coast about 21° south, observed "a foul and barren shore, green fields, and very wild, black, barbarous inhabitants." In 24° south, Polsert, who commanded the Batavia, saw four natives, whom he describes as "wild, black, and altogether naked, not covering even those parts which almost all savages conceal."

China 'Crost the Bay

Early editors mined their geography articles from the accounts of adventurers and travelers. The Supplement to the 4th, 5th, and 6th editions (1815–1824) was the first to assign most articles to outside authorities and the first to identify contributors. Since that day, it is the travelers themselves who have recounted their own observations. At first these experts were given carte blanche. *Many British travelers to the Far East saw its exotic cultures through a strange mix of xenophobia and absolute cultural and moral superiority. One of these was a famous geographer and travel writer of the early eighteenth century, Sir John Barrow (1764–1848), later a baronet, and the man for whom Point Barrow, Alaska (among others), was named. He was Second Secretary of the Admiralty, a founder of the Royal Geographic Society, and had been secretary to the British ambassador to China. Out of that background came his article "China," from the aforementioned Supplement. He was impressed by a relative freedom of the press; he patronized Confucius and Mencius ("Cong-foo-tse" and "Men-tse"); he cast a baleful eye on most of the arts; but he recognized that in dexterity and imitation, the Chinese excelled. (B.L.F.)*

In the current edition the two major articles on "China" and on "Chinese Literature" alone run to 205 double-column pages, in effect a fairly large book.

One of the most remarkable features of Chinese policy, is the encouragement given to the cultivation of letters, which are professedly the sole channel of introduction to political advancement in the state, and to the acquirement of office, rank, and honours of almost every description. The pursuits of literature throw open the highest offices in the state to the lowest of the people; and, with a few exceptions of particular favourites, or of Tartars connected by blood with the imperial family, it would appear that honours and offices are generally bestowed according to merit. With the prospect of such rewards, the number of competitors is very great, and a taste for letters is almost universally diffused among all ranks and denominations. Schools abound in every town and village, and the best education that China affords is to be had on the most moderate terms. In every part of the empire, certain magistrates are appointed by the government to call before them all candidates for employment, to direct them in their studies, and twice a year to hold public examinations, when small presents are distributed to the most deserving. As a farther encouragement to literature, the press is left free to all, and any one may print what he pleases, taking his chance for the consequences. That this unrestrained liberty of the press should exist in one of the most arbitrary governments that is known, is a remarkable phenomenon in the history of nations. . . .

We can form no estimate of the state of literature in China, from the paraphrastic translations of ill-chosen books, and the commentaries on them, made by the Jesuits and other Catholic missionaries; the trite morality of Cong-foo-tse and Mentse; the wise sayings of this emperor, and the wicked doings of that, which are contained in the *Ou-king* and the *Se-Choo,* their ancient canonical books, convey no better idea of the state of China or of its literature, than the Domesday Book does of that of England. . . .

Dr Burney has well observed, that, the more barbarous the age and the music, the more powerful its effects;

"For still the less they understand
The more they admire the slight of hand."

In China the music is still barbarous enough, whatever the people may be who can admire it. It has neither science nor system; but, from a strange confused account given by Pere Amiot, of the generation and true dimensions of the tones (not one word of which, as he afterwards acknowledges, he could understand), the Abbé Roussier concludes, that, like the music of the Greeks, it appears to be the remaining fragments of a complete system, belonging to a people more ancient than either of them. . . .

As a favourable specimen of Chinese music, the following national song of *Moo-lee-wha* is here inserted:

This air was played by Lord Amherst's band, and delighted the Chinese more than any other. . . .

In a country where every kind of luxury is discouraged, and some of them constitute a crime; where property is so precarious as rarely to descend to three generations; and where the useful only is affected to be considered as valuable, no great progress can be looked for in the fine arts. For the same reason that their poetry is deficient in invention, imagination, and dignity of sentiment, and their music of harmony, the sister art of painting is wanting in all the requisites that are considered to be necessary to form a good picture. Indeed, it could not well be otherwise; as, independent of their contracted ideas, they offend against every principle of perspective which, with the effects produced by a proper disposition of light and shade, they affect to consider unnatural. That it is not from want of talent that their drawings and paintings are so extravagantly outré, is sufficiently proved by the facility and accuracy with which the painters of Canton copy any picture put into their hands, whether on paper, glass, or canvas; and, so far from the Abbé Grozier's Parisian idea being true, that their best works are executed in Pekin, the very reverse is the case: all the arts, manufactures, even down to common printing, being worse executed in the capital than in any other city of the empire; and the reason is obvious enough; for the moment that a man acquires a superior reputation, he is summoned to the palacc, where, within its spacious precincts, his talents must be exercised for the emperor alone. Here their arts and manufactures remain stationary, while the artists of Canton, being in the habit of copying from better models, are superior to any that the imperial palace can boast. . . .

Superior as the temples and palaces of the Hindus and Mahometans in India and Persia, and indeed throughout Asia, are to those of the Chinese, the dwellings of the latter are infinitely more comfortable in every respect than those of the former. Their stoves for warming the apartments and for cooking, their beds and furniture, bespeak a degree of refinement and comfort unknown to other oriental nations; but the great characteristic difference is, that the Chinese sit on chairs, eat off tables, burn wax candles, and cover the whole body with clothing.

Their naval architecture wears the stamp of great antiquity, and is exceedingly grotesque. They have, in fact, made little progress in maritime navigation, from the inveterate dislike of the government to all foreign intercourse, and to all innovation. . . .

Whatever depends on mere imitation and manual dexterity, can be executed as well, and as neatly, by a Chinese, as by the most skilful artists of the western world; and some of them in a style of very superior excellence. No people, for example, have carried the art of dyeing, or of extracting dyeing materials from so great a variety of animal, mineral, and vegetable substances, as the Chinese have done; and this merely from a practical knowledge of chemical affinities, without troubling themselves with theories derived from scientific principles. In like manner, practice has taught them how to detect the exact proportion of alloy that may be mixed with gold and silver, and how to separate it. We import from China their native cinnabar, but our vermillion, extracted from it, is not to be compared with theirs for brilliancy and deepness of colour, which is supposed to be given to it by long and patient trituration under water. Again, their beautiful blues on their porcelain are more transparent, deep, and vivid, than the same blues applied to our pottery ware; yet we supply the Chinese with the same cobalt frits from which our own colours are extracted. It has been supposed, that the greater or less brilliancy of the colours used for painting porcelain, depends more on the nature of the glaze on which they are laid, than on their own intrinsic merits. Here, then, we have something still to learn from the Chinese. The biscuit of their porcelain, too, is much superior in whiteness, hardness, and transparency to any which has been made in Europe. The Swansea porcelain comes the nearest to it in these respects, supposed to be owing, in some degree, to a proportion of magnesian earth being mixed with the aluminous and silicious ingredients. In form and decoration, which depend on a taste and feeling which the Chinese are strangers to, we far surpass them.

In the cutting of ivory into fans, baskets, pagodas, nests of nine or more hollow moveable balls, one within the other, beautifully carved, the artists of Europe cannot pretend to vie with the Chinese; yet it does not appear that they practise any other means than that of working in water with small saws. As little can Europeans pretend to rival their large horn lanterns, of several feet in diameter, perfectly transparent in every part, without a flaw or opaque spot, and without a seam; yet a small portable stove or furnace,—an iron boiler, and a pair of common pincers, are all the tools that are required for the manufacture of those extraordinary machines. In silver fillagree they are, at least, equal to the Hindoos, and their lacquered cabinets, and other articles, are excelled only in Japan.

Barbary

Egypt and the Barbary States lying west of it were where the Near East merged into Africa proper. It was a land of enchantment, unknown perils, and mystery. The Britannica *described its people. The excerpts are from the article "Barbary States" in the Supplement to the 4th, 5th, and 6th editions (1815–1824). (B.L.F.)*

The population of the Barbary States is made up of a number of distinct races. A particular survey of each will therefore be necessary, in order to afford any complete view of the subject.

The first and most numerous class are the Moors. This is an European term, derived from the ancient *Mauri,* of whom probably no traces are now to be found. It is applied to the inhabitants of the cities of Barbary, and the country in their immediate vicinity. Their manners and habits of life have been described in considerable detail in the body of the work, under the head of MOROCCO. Generally speaking, a Mahometan city presents an uniform aspect. Everywhere the same silence and seclusion, the same absence of all gaiety, bustle, and animation; narrow and dirty streets, bordered on each side by lines of dead wall,—each individual burying himself in the interior of his family, and shrouding his existence, as it were, from every other eye; while the female sex, who, in Europe, form the ornament of society, are immured in the apartments of the haram, bought and sold almost as slaves. With all this is combined an outward deportment of great gravity, solemnity, and decorum, with which neither the sentiments nor actions are found to correspond. All this is more particularly true of the cities of Morocco; for in Algiers and Tunis, an unsettled government, and the habits of a seafaring life, have produced, especially in the lower orders, a greater appearance of activity and turbulence, though without any departure from the general tenor of oriental habits.

The *Letters* lately published, written by a female relation of Mr Tully, formerly consul at Tripoli, give a very lively picture of the manners of a Barbary court, and particularly of female society. This she had very peculiar access to observe, through the intimate footing on which she lived with the ladies of the palace. The wives of the bashaw, and the other grandees, are generally Georgian or Circassian captives, who are purchased at Constantinople at an early age, and trained in all those accomplishments which fit them for the harams of the great. By the Mahometan law, each individual may have four wives, and an equal number of concubines; but there is one principal wife, who alone shares the sovereign power. She has usually the same origin with the others, and enters the haram as a slave, but succeeds, by address and superior powers of captivation, in raising herself to this envied dignity. It is unlawful for the daughters of the sovereign to marry a subject; and as they do not usually form alliances with foreign states, they have no resource but to marry Turks and renegadoes, the refuse of the society. They thus often choose as companions for life, persons unworthy even to appear in their company. Accordingly, the husband is ruled with the most absolute sway, and treated usually worse than their slaves; to all which he quietly submits, in consideration of the lucrative offices to which this connection secures his advancement.

The toilet of a Moorish lady is said to be formed entirely after the ancient model. No dressing-table is used; but a number of slaves attend, to each of whom a different office is assigned. One plaits and perfumes the hair, another arranges the eyebrows, a third paints them, and so on. A profusion of the richest Arabian perfumes and scented waters is used, and powdered cloves, in vast quantity, are stuffed into the hair. The eyelashes are, by a very tedious process, painted black, and, by pulling out a number of the hairs, are formed into a particular shape. This operation, though attended with very acute pain, is cheerfully submitted to. In short, a Moorish lady cannot be fully dressed under several hours; and her appearance is then so completely altered, that her nearest relations could scarcely be able to recognise her.

These ladies are represented, in the letters alluded to, as by no means spending their time, as usually supposed, in listless indolence. It is their task to overlook the numerous slaves who grind, spin, and perform all the necessary domestic offices. They are particularly expected to superintend the culinary operations, in order to guard against poison, the administering of which at meals is not unusual in these countries. These cares, with those of their family, fill up the time of the more amiable and domestic members of the haram; while those of a lighter turn find full occupation in the difficult and dangerous intrigues to which their disposition prompts them. With a few exceptions, however, they seem tolerably cheerful; and the view which these letters give of their character is, on the whole, favourable.

Plus Ça Change

In the 8th edition (1852–1860) there appeared an article by a distinguished expert on libraries, Edward Edwards, which comprehensively and intelligently reviewed newspaper history around the world. Here is a remarkable excerpt.

Thirty years later, the American revolution rekindled the local bigotry of faction, beneath the mask of patriotism, with even more than its former fierceness. At this period the *Manchester Mercury* published special supplements from time to time, as intelligence came from the seat of war; and whenever the news was unfavourable to the Americans, prefixed headings to the supplements, which served the double purpose of exulting in their defeat and exciting popular hatred against such of the townsmen as were known, or supposed, to regard the colonists in the light of an injured people. Thus, on the 7th January 1777, an extra sheet was published, entitled "No. 1312. —*A New Year's Gift for all true lovers of their King and Country, and a Receipt in full to the most wicked, daring, and unnatural Rebellion that ever disgraced the Annals of History, fomented and abetted by a Junto of Republicans on this side the Atlantic.* Joseph Harrop, printer of the *Manchester Mercury,* with unspeakable pleasure again presents his friends, gratis, with the following *London Gazette Extraordinary,*" etc. In the next paper this paragraph was inserted:—

> We are assured by a gentleman just arrived from America, that when Washington found himself reduced to the necessity of quitting his strong entrenchments near King's Bridge, he declared that all was over with the colonies, and dropped some intimation of not wishing to survive the misfortunes of the day . . . Mr Washington, notwithstanding his amour with Mrs Gibbons, is, we hear, married to a very amiable lady; but it is said that Mrs Washington, being a warm loyalist, has been separated from the General since the commencement of the present troubles, and lives very much respected in the city of New York.

The next supplement begins thus:—"Ye republican fomenters and abettors of rebellion, blush and tremble at your deeds." And another:—"The hour is now approaching when all those vile republican miscreants, as well on this as on the other side the Atlantic (who have fomented . . . a most wicked and horrid rebellion against the best of kings and the best of ministers), must answer for all their mal-practices," etc. . . .

The printing-office of the *Manchester Herald,* which had been started on the 31st March 1792, as the advocate of moderate reform, was partially destroyed by a mob in the month of December following; the local authorities of the town standing by and applauding the act; and the paper itself ceased to appear in March 1793.

Czechoslovakia

After the 1820s, the editors' choice for any contributor was a (or the) preeminent authority on the subject at hand. Sometimes they were academics, sometimes practitioners.

The article "Czechoslovakia" in the 13th edition (1926) was written by Czechoslovakia's first president, Tomás G. Masaryk (1850–1937).

Masaryk served from 1918 to 1935. Reading his words today, written in the third person and devoid of any self-serving note, we at once think of Vaclav Havel, a Czech philosopher-statesman cast precisely in the mold of his great predecessor.

Prof. Masaryk and the Western Powers

The necessity for systematic action abroad, and mainly in Western Europe, was soon realised by Prof. Masaryk, the leader of the small Realist party, who, as a member of Parliament and of the Austro-Hungarian delegations, had for many years past—especially during the Bosnian annexationist crisis—been an opponent of reactionary Austria and especially of its provocative and dishonourable foreign policy. As early as the autumn of 1914 it was clear to him that the War would not be decided on the Russian front, but in the West, and that it would last longer than was imagined by those who, guided by Slavonic sympathies, relied mainly on the strength of Russia. Apart from friendly relations with France, and relations and sympathies with Russia which had developed before the War as a result of the political, economic, but mainly cultural co-operation with the Slavonic nations expressed in the neo-Slavism of Dr. Kramár, Czech political leaders had no concrete arrangements with foreign countries for the eventuality of war. Prof. Masaryk could therefore only make use of the modest bonds of sympathy and friendship with the countries in Western Europe.

Accordingly in 1914 he got into touch with his French and English friends in the course of two journeys to Holland, of which he availed himself for supplying the earliest information to official, especially British, circles. His journey to Italy in Dec. 1914 was also intended to be of an informative character. Being warned on returning by way of Switzerland, where he continued to study the situation, that the Austrian police had orders to arrest him on his return, Masaryk decided to remain abroad and to organise the Czech campaign against Austria-Hungary, keeping, as far as possible, in continual touch with the underground activities at home concentrated in the "Maffia," a secret society which originated from the clandestine meetings of Czech politicians and their friends. The aim of his action was to make known to public opinion and political and official circles in the Entente countries the claims of the Czechoslovak nation, and to make the Czechoslovak question a subject of diplomatic negotiations on the part of the competent official circles of the Entente, which would effect its solution on international lines.

Organisation Outside Austria-Hungary

For this purpose Masaryk proceeded to organise Czechoslovak settlers or residents abroad in order to make use of their resources and their influence in favour of his programme, and particularly to obtain a financial basis for his action and for direct armed intervention against Austria in the ranks of the Entente. When the Czechoslovaks abroad were joined by a large number of Czechoslovak soldiers who crossed over to the Allied side, it was possible to consider the formation of special military units and a separate Czechoslovak army within the framework of the Allied armies.

In all the Entente states there were spontaneous organisations of Czechs and Slovaks for the purpose of actively supporting the Allies in the struggle against the Central Powers. In Russia, at the very beginning of the War, there came into existence what was known as the Czech brigade, a body, however, which was more propagandist than military in character. In France large numbers of Czechs joined the Foreign Legion and many Czechs entered the army in England and Canada. In the latter country they consisted largely of volunteers from among the Czechoslovak settlers in the United States, which were then still neutral. But the Czechs and Slovaks of America soon had an opportunity of doing important work, particularly in taking upon themselves the major part of the financial burden of the campaign. This had great moral significance, because it made the Czechoslovak movement independent of financial help from the Allies. Matters were made easier by the circumstance that Russia and France very soon adopted a relatively favourable attitude to the Czechoslovaks, who nominally were subjects of an enemy State, and by this concession they gained freedom of movement and organisation.

The Formation of Foreign Committees

The year 1915 resulted in a mobilisation of resources and the distribution of work for the Czechoslovak movement abroad, rather than in any positive successes. Masaryk inaugurated an open struggle against Austria-Hungary in the spirit of humanitarian and democratic ideals on the occasion of the Hus celebrations in Switzerland, and he prepared for further activities in the Press and by lectures. Up to the arrival of Dr. Beneš in the autumn of 1915 the headquarters of this work were in Switzerland, but after the arrival of Dr. Beneš and of the agrarian deputy Josef Durich who left Bohemia with the knowledge and support of Czech political circles there, Masaryk chose London as his seat of action, while Beneš as secretary of the central foreign committee proceeded to Paris with Štefánik, the Slovak scientist, who served as an aviator in the French army. Durich was entrusted with the task of concentrating the work that had hitherto been accomplished in Russia by means of a unified Czech committee.

Steps were very soon taken to form a Czechoslovak foreign committee for the purpose of carrying on a united struggle against Austria. This idea was indicated by Masaryk in a circular addressed in March 1915 to a number of persons in the Czechoslovak settlements abroad and on Nov. 14 1915 the committee issued a manifesto, signed by Masaryk and Durich, by the leaders of the Czech colonies in the Entente states and notably also by the Czechs and Slovaks in America. This was the first official pronouncement by the Czechs abroad against Austria-Hungary, in favour of the Entente, and of the independence of the Czechoslovak state. This manifesto, which had also the approval of the Czechs in Austria-Hungary, was issued at a moment when not only was the result of the War not decided but the situation for the Allied states was not altogether favourable. At the beginning of Jan. 1916 the foreign committee was transformed into a National Czech Council, the president of which was Masaryk, the vice-president Josef Durich, and the general secretary was Dr. Beneš. The Slovaks were represented on agreement, to grant the military and material assistance asked for by Masaryk. The military help promised by the Entente was not forthcoming, with the exception of a small Japanese contingent, but abundant quantities of supplies and equipment were given. The victory of the Czechoslovak troops on the Volga and in Siberia caused a sensation in the Allied states, so that the Czech success had a considerable moral significance and denoted the strengthening of the Czech cause. What made the Czech achievement particularly valuable was that it had prevented the Soviet Govt., and thus also Germany, from obtaining the keenly desired contact with the Siberian supplies of raw materials and foodstuffs, and also that the vast numbers of German prisoners of war in the Siberian camps could not be used for strengthening the German army. As an example of the appreciation which the work of the Czechoslovak legions met with among the Allies, reference may be made to a telegram of Lloyd George on Sept. 11 1918, in which he thanked the National Council for the inestimable services rendered by the legions to the Allies.

Recognition by the Powers

Great Britain had previously, in a pronouncement of Lord Robert Cecil on May 22 1918, officially recognised the right of the Czechoslovak nation to complete independence. When on May 29 1918 the Govt. of the United States approved the anti-Austrian resolution passed by the Congress of Oppressed Nations in Rome, which had been organised in April of that year by Dr. Beneš on the initiative of Prof. Denis, the War Council at Versailles associated itself with this American proclamation, while the Prime Ministers of France, England and Italy, and indeed of all the Allied nations, declared their sympathies with the Czechoslovak and Yugoslav aims for liberation. At the same time the British Govt. announced its willingness to recognise the National Council as the leading body of the Czechoslovak movement and also of the army that was fighting on the side of the Entente. The first country to grant actual recognition in this sense was France (June 29 1918), the Government of which recognised the right of the Czechoslovak nation to independence, and the National Council as the supreme body controlling general interests and as the first basis of the future government. On June 30 President Poincaré with the representatives of the French Cabinet handed over the colours to the 21st Czechoslovak regiment at Darney, and on the following day the British Govt. expressed its agreement with the speech made by President Poincaré on this occasion. . . .

Finally, on Oct. 14 Dr. Beneš notified the Entente States of the establishment of an interim Czechoslovak Govt. in Paris in accordance with the decision of the President of the National Council on Sept. 26, and Dr. Beneš as Minister for Foreign Affairs was appointed the first Czechoslovak Minister to the Entente States. This interim Czechoslovak Govt. was recognised by the French Govt. on Oct. 15, and by the Italian Govt. on Oct. 24, while on Oct. 18 1918 the interim Govt. itself proclaimed the independence of the Czechoslovak nation by a declaration dated at Washington.

Cities

Blake Ehrlich was a freelance journalist and author of Paris on the Seine, London on the Thames, *and other books. He died in 1974 and, like hundreds of other good journalists of his period, is forgotten. For* Britannica*'s 15th edition he did a number of "city pieces." Normally such articles, purely factual, hope merely to be useful to both the student and the tourist. But Ehrlich took a colorless genre and, by giving it a touch all his own, managed to transform it into something far livelier. Here is his introduction to "Lisbon," followed by a few representative paragraphs on Athens, Edinburgh, Dublin, Florence, and Rome.*

LISBON

The capital, chief port, and largest city of Portugal, Lisbon (Portuguese Lisboa) stands on the westernmost point of land of the European continent, where the Tagus River flows into the Atlantic Ocean. In the eight miles (13 kilometres) from the sea upstream to the city, the river is almost straight and about two miles wide. Just beyond the soaring gateway to Lisbon, the 25th of April Bridge (formerly called the Salazar Bridge), which is the longest suspension bridge in western Europe, the waters suddenly broaden into a bay seven miles wide called the Mar de Palha (Straw Sea)—named for the sheen of its water, not its pollution. It is one of the continent's most beautiful harbours.

Scenically spectacular though it may be, the hill-cradled basin of burnished water also serves as a modern port. Amid the freighters, warships, liners, and ferryboats, a persistently picturesque note is struck by the *fragatas* with their Phoenician silhouettes, black hulls, and sepia sails; they perform most of the harbour's lighterage. The port maintains an intimacy with its city that was common in the days before steam. Vessels tie up at quays open to the everyday life of the town, where the clang of the trolley cars blends with the sound of ships' bells. At dawn, fishing smacks deposit their catch at the town's front doorstep for noisy auction to Lisbon dealers, while the fishwives wait to fill the baskets they will peddle through the streets.

Later the fish market gives way to the equally colourful and clamorous fruit and vegetable market.

The People

For centuries the citizens have been discussing the symptoms of an affliction they say is endemic in their strip of the Iberian Peninsula: *saudade,* very approximately translated as "melancholy," a variety of a state of anxiety tempered by fatalism. *Saudade* is said to be reflected in the music called *fado,* which is sung in its original form only in Lisbon, and in Lisbon only in two hillside plebeian precincts, Alfama and Bairro Alto. The word *fado* means "fate," usually an unkind fate described in the songs that are throbbingly sung to a penetrating but melodic music.

One aspect of the Lisbonese character readily noticeable on the streets is self-respect, a nonaggressive esteem for human dignity. It can be seen in the waiter's pride in his deftness and in the cleanliness of the white shirt worn by the beggar gently soliciting alms among the café tables. (Lisbon, judged by net median family income, is the capital of western Europe's poorest people.) The pride is visible in the bearing and enthusiasm of the newspaper vendor, though he may be among the 40 percent illiterate in the Portuguese population.

Among the more affluent citizenry there are some indications that *saudade* may have soured into a sense approaching inferiority, and that the pride behind the facade of courtesy prickles with a dueller's sensitivity. Their baleful stares at tourists can be a reminder that much of Lisbon's history is a list of wars, uprisings, and assassinations.

A cross section of the population is visible during the late afternoon thronging of men in the Chiado neighbourhood, on the heights, and on the Rossio (city square), just below. Originally, the strolling began around three o'clock as a sort of peripatetic club for the professional men who could take time off to visit the intellectual coffeehouses. Today the coffeehouses have almost all gone, and the listless crowd scenes begin after office hours with a less distinguished cast.

On the character of the city of Athens Ehrlich writes:

ATHENS

Athens, when approached from the Middle East, is the first European city, with tall buildings, newspaper kiosks, modern shops, and modishly dressed citizens. Approached from Europe, it seems, if not exactly the first Oriental city, at any rate not quite European, in its ill-fitting, locally tailored modernity. The European notes a medley of characterless concrete and out-of-style dress, with the smell of spitted meat and spices in narrow, unpaved streets as clamorous as bazaars and a few streets away from the centre.

Nevertheless, it is wrong to say that Athens is a mixture of East and West: it is Greek and, more particularly, Athenian. The Athenians, after all, nurtured Western civilization. Yet, some three centuries after the death of Pericles (429 BC), they entered upon a period of bondage that lasted almost 2,000 years. Athens was freed in 1833, and in the following 135 years it was the scene of 14 revolutions, another brutal foreign occupation, and a civil war of especial savagery. This long history of passion and suffering has had considerable effect on the Athenian character. The core of that character is an implacable will to survive, buttressed by a profound sense of loyalty (especially to the family) and patriotism. The Greek Orthodox Church, which is directed by a synod sitting in Athens, was a main force in keeping alive the Greek language, tradition, and literature when such things were forbidden, and most people still support it.

The millennia of oppression, instead of driving the Athenians into obtuse moroseness, have honed their wit and rendered them tough but supple, while centuries of privation have only preserved their warmth and generosity. The long oral tradition, alive even under the invader, has reflected and stimulated a taste for rich talk. Of course, the poetic impulse to make a good story better leads to considerable exaggeration in daily conversation, suiting a vanity that goes with a sharp-edged sense of personal and family honour and the spoiling of children. The ancient heroes, too, were vain about both themselves and honour, boasting as much about outwitting the enemy as about outfighting him. Cunning, as in the *Odyssey,* is still a virtue there.

The first paragraph on Edinburgh bears the mark of Ehrlich's style, though the whole article has been updated and vetted by Archie Rule Turnbull, the recognized authority on Edinburgh.

EDINBURGH

A city long renowned for a somewhat inflexible respectability—when West Princes Street Gardens were turned over to the general public in 1876, smoking was forbidden—Edinburgh concurrently maintained a fascinating netherworld of ribaldry and drunkenness. A poet or jurist of sufficient distinction might succeed in inhabiting both worlds. Such "Edinburgh characters" abounded during the flourishing neoclassical period of the 18th and 19th centuries known as the Augustan age, when the city's authors, critics, publishers, teachers, physicians, and scientists formed an intellectual elite of world influence. With the subsequent relapse of the city into a more provincial role, such noted eccentrics have become virtually extinct. . . .

Several decades earlier, in the 1720s, the town had reformed and developed its university on the faculty system (the medical faculty was instituted in 1726). This change made possible Edinburgh's contribution to that extraordinary intellectual and cultural flowering known as the Scottish Enlightenment. The Edinburgh Enlightenment itself was very much an Old Town affair. A characteristic of Old Town life was that each multistoried building housed a cross section of Edinburgh society: the very poor at street level or up in the attics; the wealthy on the main floor above street level; and others in between, according to a system whereby the lower the income the less desirable the floor occupied. All shared a common stair and ate and drank in common at the same taverns. Something of this commonness—plainness as well as coarseness—was apparent in Edinburgh's outbreak of intellectual inquiry: a strong, broad, confident ability to grasp the first principles of things and to explain them in the common language, preferably through conversation and debate. So

David Hume grasped that there were no uncaused events; Adam Smith recognized the implications of division of labour; Adam Ferguson the danger of "alienation" inherent in labour; William Robertson the degree to which environmental factors shaped economic history; Joseph Black the principle of latent heat; and James Hutton the enormous antiquity of the Earth. As well as these, Edinburgh was the university of the poet James Thomson; of James Boswell, the biographer of Dr. Johnson; the novelist and poet Oliver Goldsmith; the jurist and writer Lord Kames; the French novelist Benjamin Constant; and Benjamin Rush, an American signatory of the Declaration of Independence.

Toward the end of the 18th century those able to afford the price of a house in the New Town deserted the Old Town. For the first time in five centuries Edinburgh became socially segregated and, in the political climate of the French Revolution, the city's intellectual elite became authoritarian and antiradical. For 30 years into the 19th century Edinburgh continued to dominate the literary world in Britain, with Sir Walter Scott as its greatest figure, but by the beginning of Queen Victoria's reign, Edinburgh's intellectual fervour had subsided. The pace of social segregation slowed as well in 1833, when the Town Council, which had sponsored the building of the New Town, went bankrupt.

And here he is on Dublin:

DUBLIN

The preeminent city of the republic of Ireland, Dublin (Baile Átha Cliath) is the last capital of the Western world whose winter streets are still smudged with the smoke of home fires, redolent of burning peat. It is also the legendary capital of English conversation. How long such agreeable vestiges of the past will endure is problematical: Dublin, so long a relic of a fading colonialism, is moving toward its long-denied future. There have been other occasions when Dublin, roused by some freshening of economic or political winds, has hurried to catch up with the rest of the world. What effect the current surge of modernization will have upon the charm of Dublin depends in large measure on the quality of the urban civilization it is hurrying to embrace. . . .

The People

Of all the charms of Dublin, the most pervasive and durable is the citizenry itself, a people who are notoriously hospitable and generous. Their speech is often helplessly poetic. Their celebrated conversations frequently are about religion, which is still a force in Irish life, and often touch on that other Irish trinity of interests: horses, politics, and personalities. But the Dubliners' humour is built on a long heritage of sorrow. After a thousand years of strife and treachery, their wit conceals an ingrained wariness.

A new prosperity, free health care, social insurance, and modern housing have substantially improved the lot of Dublin's poor. An erroneous impression of continued widespread misery is nevertheless abetted by the dress of manual labourers, who habitually wear worn, soiled street garb on the job instead of special work clothes. The traditional harpers, or ballad singers, have moved off the streets of Dublin and into the singing pubs, but its beggars—usually native gypsies, who were once called tinkers but are now referred to as "itinerants"—are still abroad in the streets.

Much of the city's charm has also been the tempo of its life—urban, yet leisurely, with the numerous pubs and churches offering a ready excuse from more mundane pursuits. The beat of Dublin life, however, has been subtly accelerating, a change largely due to the growth of the city's businesses.

No one but Blake Ehrlich could have thought of ending his discussion of the economy of Florence thus:

FLORENCE

Artisans who fashion the gold, silver, jewelry, straw, intarsia (Florentine mosaic), leather goods, glass, pottery, and embroidery complain that they are being squeezed out of existence by the pressures of modern economic life. They can still be seen through the open doors of their workrooms engaged in the tasks and poised in the attitudes shown in the carvings on the 15th-century facade of the guildsmen's church, Or San Michele.

The passersby in these same narrow streets—they display the agility of fish in passing one another and the cars and delivery vans—have the strong-boned Tuscan faces of the Renaissance sculptures and paintings. Although the days of Florentine power long ago evaporated, the men of this city retain much of the swagger of swordsmen of the bygone age, and their dandyism psychically clothes them in hose and doublet. Their vanity, patently masculine, is made visible at the early evening hour, when they troop to the cafés while performing the rites of hair smoothing, lapel patting, and trouser adjusting.

Here's how he writes about the people of Rome. The last paragraph, ending the article, is characteristic.

ROME

The People

The knowledge that Rome is eternal, that nothing lasts but nothing changes, gives rise to the local watchword, *pazienza* ("patience"). In this overcrowded, understaffed city, *pazienza* is demonstrated everywhere, every day. Except for brief, lowering, summer-lightning flashes of an underlying volatility, the Roman is apt to be cheery and courteous, a little less operatic in his reactions than many other Italians.

In Rome, as in the rest of Italy, all children are godsends and are demonstrably, publicly loved, patted, petted, cuddled, and kissed. Unmonied families make sacrifices to provide the biggest possible dolls and the flashiest possible tricycles. This continues far into life, with the man playing the role of adored but respectful princeling to his queen mother and imperious but indulgent king to his wife and children. In society outside the family the important thing is *bella figura,* or keeping face. Thus the *dottore* (the only degree the university of Rome gives is the doctorate) salutes the street sweeper as *capo* ("chief"), a gesture of respect called for by the uniform.

For 1,000 years, to be a citizen of Rome was to hold the keys to the world, to live in safety, pride, and relative comfort. Today there is still considerable pride in being a *Romano di Roma,* a Roman Roman. Among such are the "black nobility," families with papal titles who form a society within high society, shunning publicity and not given to great intimacy with the "white nobility," whose titles were conferred by mere temporal rulers. . . .

The least-liked fountain figure in Rome, unpopular since it was installed in 1587, is on the triumphal arch fountain in the Piazza S. Bernardo, commissioned by Sixtus V. The figure is a pallid Moses, apparently in imitation of Michelangelo's, and its sculptor, Prospero Bresciano, is said to have been so hurt by the public's jeers that he died of a broken heart.

CHAPTER SIX

Some Ideas

Money Then

Prudent Scotsmen that they were, the early publishers and editors of Encyclopaedia Britannica *paid careful attention to ideas in the field of economics. The 1st edition (1768–1771) devoted seventeen pages to the topic "Money." The 2nd (1778–1783) increased the length by half, with most of the article addressing the theory of money, carefully integrating and elaborating on the elements of the earlier one. An extract follows. (B.L.F.)*

THEORY OF MONEY

I. Of Artificial or Material Money

I. As far back as our accounts of the transactions of mankind reach, we find they had adopted the precious metals, that is, silver and gold, as the common measure of value, and as the adequate equivalent for every thing alienable.

The metals are admirably adapted for this purpose: they are perfectly homogeneous: when pure, their masses, or bulks, are exactly in proportion to their weights: no physical difference can be found between two pounds of gold, or silver, let them be the production of the mines of Europe, Asia, Africa, or America: they are perfectly malleable, fusible, and suffer the most exact division which human art is capable to give them: they are capable of being mixed with one another, as well as with metals of a baser, that is, of a less homogeneous nature, such as copper: by this mixture they spread themselves uniformly through the whole mass of the composed lump, so that every atom of it becomes proportionally possessed of a share of this noble mixture; by which means the subdivision of the precious metals is rendered very extensive.

Their physical qualities are invariable: they lose nothing by keeping; they are solid and durable; and tho' their parts are separated by friction, like every other thing, yet still they are of the number of those which suffer least by it.

If money, therefore, can be made of any thing, that is, if the proportional value of things vendible can be measured by any thing material, it may be measured by the metals.

II. The two metals being pitched upon as the most proper substances for realising the ideal scale of money, those who undertake the operation of adjusting a standard, must constantly keep in their eye the nature and qualities of a scale, as well as the principles upon which it is formed.

The unit of the scale must constantly be the same, altho' realised in the metals, or the whole operation fails in the most essential part. This realising the unit is like adjusting a pair of compasses to a geometrical scale, where the smallest deviation from the exact opening once given must occasion an incorrect measure. The metals, therefore, are to money what a pair of compasses is to a geometrical scale.

This operation of adjusting the metals to the money of account implies an exact and determinate proportion of both metals to the money-unit, realised in all the species and denominations of coin, adjusted to that standard.

The smallest particle of either metal added to, or taken away from, any coins, which represent certain determinate parts of the scale, overturns the whole system of material money. And if, notwithstanding such variation, these coins continue to bear the same denominations as before, this will as effectually destroy their usefulness in measuring the value of things, as it would overturn the usefulness of a pair of compasses, to suffer the opening to vary, after it is adjusted to the scale representing feet, toises, miles, or leagues, by which the distances upon the plan are to be measured.

III. Debasing the standard is a good term; because it conveys a clear and distinct idea. It is diminishing the weight of the pure metal contained in that denomination by which a nation reckons, and which we have called the *money-unit.* Raising the standard requires no farther definition, being the direct contrary.

IV. Altering the standard (that is, raising or debasing the value of the money-unit)

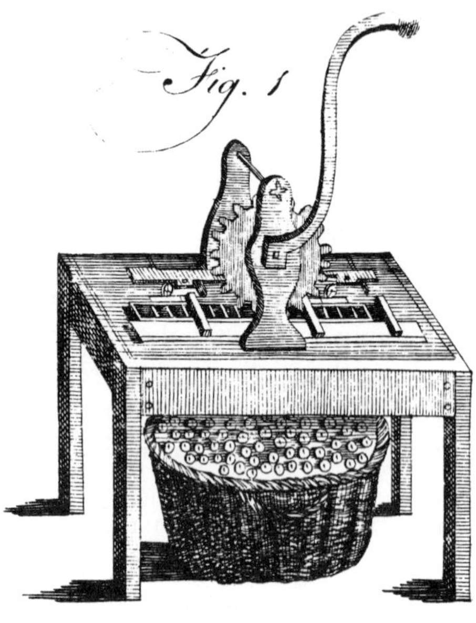

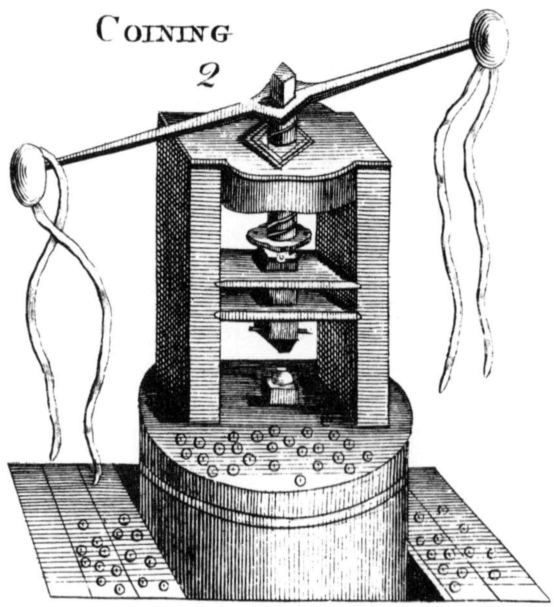

3

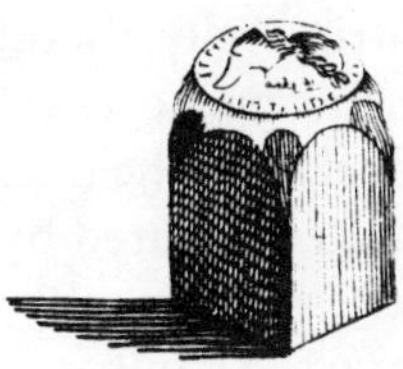

4

is like altering the national measures or weights. This is best discovered by comparing the thing altered with things of the same nature which have suffered no alteration. Thus if the foot of measure was altered at once over all England, by adding to it, or taking from it, any proportional part of its standard length, the alteration would be best discovered by comparing the new foot with that of Paris, or of any other country, which had suffered no alteration. Just so, if the pound Sterling, which is the English unit, shall be found any how changed, and if the variation it has met with be difficult to ascertain because of a complication of circumstances, the best way to discover it, will be to compare the former and the present value of it with the money of other nations which has suffered no variation. This the course of exchange will perform with the greatest exactness.

V. Artists pretend, that the precious metals, when absolutely pure from any mixture, are not of sufficient hardness to constitute a solid and lasting coin. They are found also in the mines mixed with other metals of a baser nature, and the bringing them to a state of perfect purity occasions an unnecessary expence. To avoid, therefore, the inconvenience of employing them in all their purity, people have adopted the expedient of mixing them with a determinate proportion of other metals, which hurts neither their fusibility, malleability, beauty, or lustre. This metal is called *alloy;* and, being considered only as a support to the principal metal, is accounted of no value in itself. So that eleven ounces of gold, when mixed with one ounce of silver, acquires, by that addition, no augmentation of value whatever.

This being the case, we shall, as much as possible, overlook the existence of alloy, in speaking of money, in order to render language less subject to ambiguity.

And Now

In the current edition of Britannica *the major article on "Money" runs to fourteen columns and is the work of* Nobelist Milton Friedman *(1912–). From it we extract the introductory paragraph and, for purposes of comparison to the 2nd edition (1778–1783), his treatment of metallic money.*

The subject of money has fascinated wise men from the time of Aristotle to the present day because it is so full of mystery and paradox. The piece of paper labelled one dollar or 100 francs or 10 kroner or 1,000 yen is little different, as paper, from a piece of the same size torn from a newspaper or magazine, yet it will enable its bearer to command some measure of food, drink, clothing, and the remaining goods of life while the other is fit only to light the fire. Whence the difference?

The easy answer, and the right one, is that people accept money as such because they know that others will. The pieces of paper are valuable because everyone thinks they are, and everyone thinks they are because in his experience they always have been. At bottom money is, then, a social convention, but a convention of uncommon strength that people will abide by even under extreme provocation. The strength of the convention is, of course, what enables governments to profit by inflating the currency. But it is not indestructible. When great variations occur in the quantity of these pieces of paper—as they have during and after wars—they may be seen to be, after all, no more than pieces of paper. People will then seek substitutes—like the cigarettes and cognac that for a time became the medium of exchange in Germany after World War II. As John Stuart Mill wrote:

> There cannot, in short, be intrinsically a more insignificant thing, in the economy of society, than money; except in the character of a contrivance for sparing time and labour. It is a machinery for doing quickly and commodiously, what would be done, though less quickly and commodiously, without it: and like many other kinds of machinery, it only exerts a distinct and independent influence of its own when it gets out of order. (*Principles of Political Economy*, W. J. Ashley [ed.], 1909, p. 488).

Mill was perfectly correct, although one must add that there is hardly a contrivance man possesses that can do more damage to a society when it goes wrong. . . .

Metallic Money

The use of metals as money has occurred throughout history. As Aristotle observed,

> The various necessities of life are not easily carried about, and hence men agreed to employ in their dealings with each other something which was intrinsically useful and easily applicable to the purposes of life, for example, iron, silver, and the like. Of this the value was at first measured by size and weight, but in process of time they put a stamp upon it, to save the trouble of weighing and to mark the value.

The use of metal for money can be traced back to more than 2,000 years before the birth of Christ. But standardization and certification in the form of coinage, as referred to by Aristotle, did not occur except perhaps in isolated instances until the beginning of the 7th century BC. Historians generally assign to Lydia, a Greek state in Asia Minor, priority in using coined money. The first coins were made of electrum, a natural mixture of gold and silver, and were crude, bean-shaped ingots bearing a primitive punchmark certifying to either weight or fineness or both.

The use of coins enabled payment to be by "tale," or count, rather than weight, greatly facilitating commerce. But this in turn encouraged clipping (shaving off tiny slivers from the sides or edges of coins) and sweating (shaking a bunch of coins together in a leather bag and collecting the dust that was thereby knocked off) in the hope of passing on the lighter coin at its face value. Gresham's law (that "bad money drives out good" when there is a fixed rate of exchange between them) came into operation, and heavy, good coins were held for their metallic value, while light coins were passed on. The coins became lighter and lighter, and prices higher and higher. Then payment by weight would be resumed for large transactions, and there would be pressure for recoinage. These particular defects were largely ended by the "milling" of coins (making serrations around the circumference of a coin), which began in the late 17th century.

A more serious matter was the attempt by the sovereign to benefit from the monopoly of coinage. In this respect, Greek and Roman experience offers an interesting contrast. Though Solon, on taking office in Athens in 594 BC, did institute a partial debasement of the currency, for the next four centuries, until the absorption of Greece into the Roman Empire, the Athenian *drachma* had an almost constant silver content (67 grains of fine silver until Alexander, 65 grains thereafter) and became the standard coin of trade in Greece and in much of Asia and Europe as well. Even after the Roman conquest, the *drachma* continued to be minted and widely used.

The Roman experience was very different. Not long after the silver *denarius,* patterned after the Greek *drachma,* was introduced in 269 BC, the prior copper coinage (*aes,* or *libra*) began to be debased until, by the time the empire began, its weight had been reduced from one pound to half an ounce. The silver *denarius* and the gold *aureus* (introduced about 87 BC) suffered only minor debasement until the time of Nero (AD 54), when almost continuous tampering with the coinage began. The metal content of the gold and silver coins was reduced, and the proportion of alloy was increased to three-fourths or more of its weight. Debasement in Rome (as ever since) was a reflection of the state's inability or unwillingness to finance its expenditures through explicit taxes. But the debasement in turn worsened Rome's economic situation and undoubtedly contributed to the collapse of the empire.

❧ ❧ ❧

Bulls and Bears

The article in the 1st edition (1768–1771) explaining stocks and their markets in Exchange Alley reveals the early origins of such familiar modern terms as "bull" and "bear." At the time of this writing, the idea of "bull" as a speculative buyer of a stock expected to increase in value, and "bear" as the reverse, was about fifty years old and the terms were growing in popular use. (B.L.F.)

STOCKS or Public Funds in England. As there are few subjects of conversation more general than the value of stocks, and hardly any thing so little understood, we shall here give account of them in as clear and concise a manner as possible; presenting our readers with the rationale of the stocks, and a short history of the several companies, describing the nature of their separate funds, the uses to which they are applied, and the various purposes they answer, both with respect to the government, the companies themselves, and the community in general. . . .

The method of depositing money in the bank, and exchanging it for notes (though they bear no interest) is attended with many conveniencies; as they are not only safer than money in the hands of the owner himself, but as the notes are more portable and capable of a much more easy conveyance, since a bank note for a very large sum may be sent by the post, and, to prevent the designs of robbers, may, without damage, be cut in two, and sent at two several times. Or bills, called bank post-bills, may be had by application at the bank, which are particularly calculated to prevent losses by robberies, they being made payable to the order of the person who takes them out at a certain number of days after sight; which gives an opportunity to stop bills at the bank if they should be lost, and prevents their being so easily negotiated by strangers as common bank notes are: and whoever considers the hazard, the expence and trouble there would be in sending large sums of gold and silver to and from distant places, must also consider this as a very singular advantage. Beside which, another benefit attends them; for if they are destroyed by time, or other accidents, the bank will, on oath being made of such accident, and security being given, pay the money to the person who was in possession of them. . . .

By the word *stock* was originally meant a particular sum of money contributed to the establishing a fund to enable a company to carry on a certain trade, by means of which the person became a partner in that trade, and received a share of the profit made thereby, in proportion to the money employed. . . .

But as every capital stock or fund of a company is raised for a particular purpose, and limited by parliament to a certain sum, it necessarily follows, that when that fund is compleated, no stock can be bought of the company; though shares already purchased may be transferred from one person to another. This being the case, there is frequently a great disproportion between the original value of the shares, and what is given for them when transferred: for if there are more buyers than sellers, a person who is indifferent about selling will not part with his share without a considerable profit to himself; and, on the contrary, if many are disposed to sell, and few inclined to buy, the value of such shares will naturally fall, in proportion to the impatience of those who want to turn their stock into specie.

These observations may serve to give our readers some idea of the nature of that unjustifiable and dishonest practice called *stock jobbing,* the mystery of which consists in nothing more than this: The persons concerned in that practice, who are denominated stock-jobbers, make contracts to buy or sell, at a certain distant time, a certain quantity of some particular stock, against which time they endeavour, according as their contract is, either to raise or lower such stock, by raising rumours and spreading fictitious stories in order to induce people either to sell out in a hurry, and consequently cheap, if they are to deliver stock, or to become unwilling to sell, and consequently to make it dearer, if they are to receive stock.

The persons who make these contracts are not in general possessed of any real stock; and when the time comes that they are to receive or deliver the quantity they have contracted for, they only pay such a sum of money as makes the difference between the price the stock was at when they made the contract, and the price it happens to be at when the contract is fulfilled; and it is no uncommon thing for persons not worth 100 l. to make contracts for the buying or selling 100,000 l. stock. In the language of Exchange Alley, the buyer in this case is called the Bull, and the seller the Bear.

Beside these, there are another set of men, who, though of a higher rank, may properly enough come under the same denomination. These are your great monied men, who are dealers in stock, and contracters with the government whenever any new money is to be borrowed. These indeed are not fictitious, but real buyers and sellers of stock; but by raising false hopes, or creating groundless fears, by pretending to buy or sell large quantities of stock on a sudden, by using the forementioned set of men as their instruments, and other like practices, are enabled to raise or lower the stocks one or two per cent, at pleasure.

Income Taxes

A critical issue of the early nineteenth century was the source of government revenues. John R. McCulloch (1789–1864), a native Scotsman who became the first professor of political economy at London University, was an influential analyst and observer of the economic landscape of the early and middle nineteenth century. In the 7th edition (1830–1842) he wrote this ringing denunciation of income tax, which he found preposterous. (B.L.F.)

The reader may perhaps be disposed to regard this section as superfluous. All incomes being derived from rent, profit, or wages, it may seem that the previous discussions have exhausted the subject; and that, in order to estimate the operation of the tax in any particular instance, we have merely to ascertain the source whence the income of the party is derived, and then to apply the principles already laid down. But this would be a most fallacious conclusion.

. . . Incomes arising from the rent of land and houses, mortgages, funded property, and such like sources, may be learned with tolerable precision; but it neither has been, and, we are bold to say, never will be, possible to determine the incomes of farmers, manufacturers, dealers of all sorts, and professional men, with any thing like even the rudest approximation to accuracy. It is in vain to attempt to overcome this insuperable difficulty by instituting an odious inquiry into the affairs of individuals. It is not, indeed, very likely that any people, not altogether enslaved, would tolerate, in ordinary circumstances, such inquisitorial proceedings; but whether they did or did not, the result would be the same. The investigations would be worthless; and the commissioners of an income-tax would in the end have nothing to trust to but the declarations of the parties. Hence it is that the tax would fall with its full weight upon men of integrity, while the *millionaire* of "easy virtue" would well nigh escape it altogther. It would, in fact, be a tax on honesty, and a bounty on perjury and fraud; and, if carried to any considerable height—to such a height as to render it a prominent source of income—it would undoubtedly generate the most barefaced prostitution of principle, and would do much to obliterate that nice sense of honour which is the only sure foundation of national probity and virtue.

Political Economy

Although Adam Smith (1723–1790) published his epochal Inquiry into the Nature and Causes of the Wealth of Nations *only the year before the 2nd edition (1778–1783) began to appear, the philosopher and his book were included in the preface acknowledging the "List of Authors" whose work the editor had mined so freely—as Smith himself had mined and for the first time systematized the work of other political economists. The theory and philosophy of this commanding intellectual presence of Glasgow and Edinburgh was reflected in every aspect of* Britannica*'s economic coverage throughout the nineteenth century.*

This excerpt is from the article "Political Economy," in the Supplement to the 4th, 5th, and 6th editions (1815–1824), by John R. McCulloch, author of the preceding article on income taxes. McCulloch's major writings included annotated editions of Smith's Wealth of Nations *and the works of David Ricardo. (B.L.F.)*

At length, in 1776, our illustrious countryman Adam Smith published the *Wealth of Nations*—a work which has done for Political Economy what the *Principia* of Newton did for Physics, and the *Esprit des Loix* of Montesquieu for Politics. In this work the science was, for the first time, treated in its fullest extent, and many of its fundamental principles placed beyond the reach of cavil and dispute. In opposition to the French economists, Dr Smith showed, that *labour* is the only source of wealth, and that the desire inherent in the breast of every individual to improve his fortune and rise in the world is the cause of its accumulation. He next traced the means by which the powers of labour may be rendered most effective, and showed that it is productive of wealth when employed in manufactures and commerce, as well as when employed in the cultivation of the land. Having established these principles, Dr Smith showed, in opposition to the commonly received opinions of the merchants, politicians, and statesmen of his time, that wealth did not consist in the abundance of gold and silver, but in the abundance of the various necessaries, conveniencies, and enjoyments of human life; he showed that individuals are always the best judges of what is for their own interest, and that, in prosecuting branches of industry advantageous to themselves, they necessarily prosecute such as are advantageous to the public. From thence Dr Smith drew his grand inference, that every regulation intended to force industry into particular channels, or to determine the species of commercial intercourse to be carried on between different parts of the same country, or between distant and independent countries, is impolitic and pernicious—injurious to the rights of individuals—and adverse to the progress of *real* opulence and lasting prosperity.

The fact that traces of most of these principles, and even that the distinct statement of many of those that are most important, may be found in the works of previous writers, does not in the least detract from the real merits of Dr Smith. In adopting the discoveries of others, he has made them his own; he has demonstrated the truth of principles on which his predecessors had, in most cases, stumbled by chance; has disentangled and separated them from the errors by which they were incumbered; has traced their remote consequences, and pointed out their limitations; has shown their practical importance and real value—their mutual dependence and relation; and has reduced them into a consistent, harmonious, and magnificent system. We do not mean to say that Dr Smith has produced a perfect work. Undoubtedly there are errors, and those, too, of no slight importance, in the *Wealth of Nations*. The principles to which we have just referred, and which form the basis of the work, are unimpeachable; but Dr Smith has not always reasoned correctly from them, and he has occasionally introduced others, which a more careful observation and analysis has shown to be ill-founded. But, after every allowance has been made for these defects, enough still remains to justify us in considering Dr Smith as the real founder of the science. If he has not left us a perfect work, he has, at all events, left us one which contains a greater mass of useful and universally interesting truths than has ever been given to the world by any other individual; and he has pointed out and smoothed the route, by following which, subsequent philosophers have been enabled to perfect much that he had left incomplete, to rectify the mistakes into which he had fallen, and to make many new and important discoveries. Whether, indeed, we refer to the soundness of its leading doctrines, to the liberality and universal applicability of its practical conclusions, or to the powerful and beneficial influence it has had on the progress and perfection of economical science, and still more on the policy and destiny of nations, Dr Smith's work must be placed in the foremost rank of those that have done most to liberalise, enlighten, and enrich mankind. . . .

It was long a prevalent opinion among moralists, that the labour bestowed on the production of luxuries, and consequently their consumption, was unproductive. But this opinion is now almost universally abandoned. Unless, indeed, all comforts and enjoyments are to be proscribed, it is impossible to say where necessaries end, and luxuries begin. But if we are to understand by necessaries such products only as are absolutely required for the support of human life, every thing but wild fruits, roots, and water, must be deemed superfluous; and in this view of the matter, the peasantry of Ireland, who live only on potatoes and butter-milk, must be considered as contributing much more to the national wealth than the peasantry of Britain! The mere statement of such a doctrine is sufficient for its refutation. Every thing that stimulates exertion is advantageous. The mere necessaries of life may be obtained with comparatively little labour; and those savage and uncivilized hordes, who have no desire to possess its comforts, are proverbially and notoriously indolent and dissipated. To make men industrious—to make them shake off that lethargy which is natural to them, they must be inspired with a taste for the luxuries and enjoyments of civilized life. When this is done, their artificial wants will become equally clamorous with those that are strictly necessary, and they will increase exactly as the means of gratifying them increase. Wherever a taste for comforts and conveniencies has been generally diffused, the wants and desires of man become altogether unlimited. The gratification of one leads directly to the formation of another. In highly civilized societies, new products and new modes of enjoyment are constantly presenting themselves as motives to exertion, and as means of rewarding it. Perseverance is, in consequence, given to all the operations of industry; and idleness, and its attendant train of evils, almost entirely disappear.

War

In today's Britannica *the brief biography of Sir Ian Hamilton begins: "British general, commander in chief of the Mediterranean Ex-*

peditionary Force in the unsuccessful campaign against Turkey in the Gallipoli Peninsula during World War I." It ends: "He was recalled on Oct. 16, 1915, and was given no further command. He wrote Gallipoli Diary, *2 vol. (1920)."*

He also wrote the article "War" for the 13th edition (1926), which was designed to supply perspective on World War I. His knowledge of the subject was matched by a commanding literary style and a sharp awareness of the follies of his superiors. The article also contains remarkable flashes of insight and prescience. (B.L.F.)

There is a human voice, incisive, even indignant, behind these sentences. The following brief extracts give us a clue as to how an intelligent man viewed the aftermath of World War I and the prospects for the future.

The years 1914–8 have dug so deep a trench across the history of civilisation that the epithet "pre-War" implies a remoteness not to be measured in time. Nothing has suffered more from this ageing process than military literature. . . .

Because good Europeans hate war in 1926 it does not follow that they hated war in 1914 or that they will hate it in 1964. . . .

Those who have seen with their own eyes and suffered in their own bodies know the ugly truths of war, but they cannot convey their knowledge to the young generation. The old lack imagination to tell; the young lack imagination to believe. Nothing will stop war save a Second Advent of Christ. The year 1926 finds war in the melting pot where it is much more likely to take on a new shape than to corporate. Great Britain and the United States should use this respite to overhaul their machinery. Let neither of those great, but strangely improvident, nations imagine that because they mean to do the right thing by humanity they will on that account escape the challenge of the sword. . . .

The doctrine of the "nation in arms" was first made completely possible by railways. Its idea is that the State has a lien on all men of military age; that the State should earmark those wanted for war, and that the rest should carry on "business as usual." But, since the World War, the brains of the suave Attilas who, in bowler hats and kid gloves, perambulate our modern cities, have hatched out a new thought. The "nation in arms" is to become the "nation at war." Next time the whole tribe are to go, literally, under fire. Next time all the life, all the machinery, fuel, food, wealth, transport of the State are to be drawn into the net and developed for purposes of destruction. This is the fixed goal of military intention, but it may be that the process will be reversed. Instead of the "nation in arms" being further expanded into the "nation at war," it may be that we shall have to revert to small, highly technicalised armies. For, in the view of the present writer, the combination of mobility, fire-power and protection against bullet and poison gas, which the internal combustion engine has given to aeroplanes, tanks and mechanical supply and transport units, will render our existing types of fleets and marching troops—horse, foot and artillery—as helpless as were the peasants of the Jacquerie when they encountered knights in impenetrable armour moving rapidly on horseback. . . .

Never, in the history of the art of war,

has the world been treated to so much war and so little art as in the conduct of the World War. One reason was the lack of artists. An artist with a pen uses as few words as possible, an artist with a pencil as few lines, an artist with a sword as few lives. But would even a Marlborough, who had so biting an experience of the infirmities of councils, have struggled against a French Plan XVII, a British Cabinet, and a British War Office from which the brain had been removed? . . .

An Intense Individualist

The British Govt., yielding to an impulse, mainly emotional, pulled Lord Kitchener off his ship to conduct the war. The appointment gave confidence to the whole Empire, as well as to Lord Kitchener's old comrades in arms who remembered his flashes of instinct, his stonewall fortitude, his driving power, his industry —all his many just claims to be a superman. But the nation and many soldiers did not realise how intensely individualistic Lord Kitchener had remained. His mind entirely rejected the sweeping changes which took place in the British War Office and command headquarters in 1904. . . .

Unfortunately post-War Govts. have given no indication of the drift of their policy except that they are "drifting" towards the obligations of Locarno. . . . Since the War there has been less cohesion and less enthusiasm, because men can never do their best when they feel instinctively that their chiefs do not know what they are driving at. The bulk of them are quite well enough educated to feel sure that the next European war will be decided in the clouds and yet they see their chiefs in the Navy and Army each struggling for the lion's share of the military budget. The phantom Super-Chief of the Imperial general staff in commission cannot judge between them, for he is a trinity holding, on that point, three diametrically opposed views. War may be a long way off but since this article began to be written it has drawn a little closer. Were it only for the sake of tactics there is crying need that the British get their military house in order, especially in its top storey. The rank and file and lower deck ratings are the most splendid stuff imaginable. The officers have war experience. The masses of trained fighters are still fit to take the field. But there is no head. Only the Prime Minister can be head in war, and he is not equipped for the task nor kept in practice during peace. He has neither a Defence Minister nor a living Super-Chief of the General Staff to take his ideas on policy and give him back a technical view of their bearings upon his defence force estimates. . . .

An army must be built up round something. The fabrics of Greek Art and Roman Law rose from the foundation of the heavily armed hoplite and the steel-clad legionary. In 378 A.D. heavy cavalry swept these pillars of society out of military significance until 1314 A.D. After that came the day of infantry again first in conjunction with archers, afterwards as fighters of dual functions, the bullet and the bayonet their weapons. These survivals of Blenheim, Waterloo and Mons were, at least until a few months ago, the supreme arbiters of war in the eyes of British military authority. But let the student look up, for Victory is winged. Sea and land forces have become the servants of the air force. The navy will be represented more and more by fleets of seaplane carriers. The functions of armies will be to push on as fast as petrol can drive their machines to seize advanced bases and depots, whence ever more extended air raids can be delivered. The atom round which the British defence forces must be grouped is no longer a human being—it is an internal combustion engine.

Government

Britannica's first edition (1768–1771) included some remarks on government that remain cogent today. They derive, as did in part our own early political thinking, from John Locke (1632–1704). The basic phrase "lives, liberties and properties" appears in the Fifth and Fourteenth Amendments to the Constitution, though the nouns are there changed to the singular.

In 1768 the writer opened his discussion with a bland definition of government. The current edition prefers to advance no definition. Readers will note that in the following excerpt only one gender is recognized.

GOVERNMENT, in general, is the polity of a state, or an orderly power constituted for the public good.

Civil government was instituted for the preservation and advancement of men's civil interests, and for the better security of their lives, liberties, and properties. The use and necessity of government is such, that there never was an age or country without some sort of civil authority: but as men are seldom unanimous in the means of attaining their ends, so their difference in opinion in relation to government, has produced a variety of forms of it. . . . They may, in general, be reduced to one of these heads: either the civil authority is delegated to one or more, or else it is still reserved to the whole body of the people; whence arises the known distinction of government into monarchy, aristocracy, and democracy. . . .

Governments are commonly divided into two classes, arbitrary and free governments; but there are many different sorts of each. Thus the governments of France and Spain are generally called arbitrary; though they differ as much from the governments of Turkey and other eastern empires, where absolute despoticism prevails, as they do from the government of England, and other European nations, where liberty is said to flourish in its fullest perfection.

Politics and Morality

That moral considerations were extremely important to seventeenth- and eighteenth-century Britons was evident in everything they said and wrote. This preoccupation is reflected in the founding documents of the United States, whose colonists were, after all, educated Britons. The language of the early editions of Encyclopædia Britannica, *such as the 4th edition (1801–1809), quoted here, often bears a striking resemblance to those documents. (B.L.F.)*

POLITY, or Policy, denotes the peculiar form and constitution of the government of any state or nation; or the laws, orders, and regulations, relating thereto—Polity differs only from politics, as the theory from the practice of any art.

Of the nature of our social duties, both private and political, we have already spoken at some length (*see* Moral Philoso-

PHY). . . . We shall only further remark in this place upon the necessity of always joining politics and morality together. This view of the subject is indeed antiquated and neglected; but the connection has always been externally respected, even by those who have separated them the most widely. Politics and morality, far from standing in opposition to each other, have the most intimate connection, and exhibit the relation which the *part* bears to the *whole;* that is to say, that politics are only a part or a branch of morality. No truth can be more evident than this; for as morality is the guide of human life, the principle of order, and the universal source of real improvement and genuine happiness to all mankind, every thing relative to the direction of individuals, or the government of nations, must be comprehended within its sphere, and must be subservient to its laws. All the schemes and projects of pretended political wisdom, that deviate from or violate the rules of this master-science, turn out in the issue often to the detriment of their contrivers, always to that of the nation; and it is a palpable and absurd error to think of advancing the happiness of one country at the expence of the general good of mankind. The experience of ages, and the history of the world, confirm these assertions; from which, and from daily observation, we obtain a convincing proof of the wisdom of the good old maxim, both in its application to individuals and to nations, that "honesty is the best policy."

❧ ❧ ❧

Slavery

In the early part of the nineteenth century one of America's greatest problems was earnestly, often violently, discussed in British intellectual circles. The subjoined excerpt from the Supplement to the Britannica*'s 4th, 5th, and 6th editions (1815–1824) was written by Charles Maclaren (1782–1866), first editor of* The Scotsman *and a fellow of the Royal Society of Edinburgh. Forming part of a large article, "United States," it reflects a controversial, even misguided, point of view.*

Humane Treatment of Negro Slaves in the U.S. Creates a Problem

It may be safely said, that the superior humanity of the Americans in the treatment of the blacks is the greatest obstacle to that abolition of slavery which they so ardently wish to accomplish, and that, were their slaves worked and fed like those in the West Indies, the race of blacks, instead of multiplying ten-fold in the course of one century, would be entirely extinguished. The existence of slavery is a bequest from Britain; it is not the crime of the Americans, but their misfortune. It is an evil which they deplore, and of which they would gladly rid themselves if they knew how. The difficulty is, how to dispose of the slaves, whom many would be willing to manumit. The plan of carrying them back to a colony on the African coast seems absolutely chimerical; and the strong distinction of colour, with the rooted prejudices of the whites, form an insuperable bar to such an amalgamation of the two races as took place when the serfs of Western Europe were incorporated with the freemen in the fifteenth and sixteenth centuries.

Language

The tone of any good modern encyclopedia is characterized by detachment from emotion, a hallmark of style that is associated with the triumph of the scientific method. Since we tend to take this approach for granted, it's interesting to look back on an entry such as "Language" from the Britannica*'s first edition (1768–1771). The eighteen-page article begins by discussing the subject philosophically enough but then surrenders to a kind of linguistic chauvinism that would appall any reputable scholar of today.*

. . . The English is perhaps possessed of a greater degree of excellence, blended with a greater number of defects, than any of the languages we have hitherto mentioned. As the people of Great Britain are a bold, daring, and impetuous race of men; subject to strong passions, and, from the absolute freedom and independence which reigns among all ranks of people throughout this happy isle, little solicitous about controlling these passions;—our language takes its strongest characteristical distinction from the genius of the people; and, being bold, daring, and abrupt, is admirably well adapted to express those great emotions which spring up in an intrepid mind at the prospect of interesting events. Peculiarly happy too in the full and open sound of the vowels, which forms the characteristic *tone* of the language, and in the strong use of the aspirate H in almost all those words which are used as exclamations, or marks of strong emotions upon interesting occasions, that particular class of words called *interjections* have, in our language, more of that fulness and unrestrained freedom of tones, in which their chief power consists, and are pushed forth from the inmost recesses of the soul in a more forcible and unrestrained manner, than any other language whatever. Hence it is more peculiarly adapted for the great and interesting scenes of the *drama* than any language that has yet appeared in the globe. Nor has any other nation ever arrived at that perfection which the English may justly claim in that respect; for however faulty our dramatic compositions may be in some of the critical niceties which relate to this art,—in nervous force of diction, and in the natural expression of those great emotions which constitute its soul and energy, we claim, without dispute, an unrivalled superiority.

Patience

In the Britannica*'s early years, what we would call moralism or even preaching fell under the heading of knowledge. Self-improvement and instruction were not separated. Here, for example, from the 3rd edition (1788–1797) is an extract from a homily on "Patience." (The current edition has two references to "Patience." One concerns a card game, the other a poem in Middle English.)*

PATIENCE, that calm and unruffled temper with which a good man bears the evils of life, from a conviction that they are at least permitted, if not sent, by the best of Beings, who makes all things work together for good to those who love and fear him.

The evils by which life is embittered

may be reduced to these four: 1. Natural evils, or those to which we are by nature subject as men, and as perishable animals. The greatest of these are, the death of those whom we love, and of ourselves. 2. Those from which we might be exempted by a virtuous and prudent conduct, but which are the inseparable consequences of imprudence or vice, which we shall call punishments; as infamy proceeding from fraud, poverty from prodigality, debility and disease from intemperance. 3. Those by which the fortitude of the good are exercised; such as the persecutions raised against them by the wicked. To these may be added, 4. The opposition against which we must perpetually struggle, arising from the diversity of sentiments, manners, and characters of the persons among whom we live.

Under all these evils patience is not only necessary but useful: it is necessary, because the laws of nature have made it a duty, and to murmur against natural events is to affront providence; it is useful, because it renders our sufferings lighter, shorter, and less dangerous.

Is your reputation sullied by invidious calumnies? rejoice that your character cannot suffer but by false imputations. You are arraigned in a court of judicature, and are unjustly condemned: passion has influenced both your prosecutor and your judge, and you cannot forbear repining that you suffer although innocent. But would it have been better that you should have suffered being guilty? Would the greatest misfortune that can befal a virtuous man be to you a consolation? The opulence of a villain, the elevated station to which he is raised, and the honours that are paid to him, excite your jealousy, and fill your bosom with repinings and regret. What! say you, are riches, dignity, and power, reserved for such wretches as this? Cease these groundless murmurs. If the possessions you regret were real benefits, they would be taken from the wicked and transferred to you.

Education

Although Britannica *has always been viewed by its editors as an instrument of education, the 1st edition accorded the term "Education" hardly a paragraph. By the time of the 3rd edition (1788–1797), however, it was felt to merit forty-two pages. It faithfully reflected "the best wisdom of the day about the ends of education and the means as well." Some of that "best wisdom" now seems to many of us grotesque. In this extract from the 3rd edition note the sunny assumption that "the boy" is a member of the class of gentlemen. The remainder of the excerpt, dealing with the education of women, is useful in allowing us to measure the progress we have made in two centuries. It is sure to raise the blood pressure of all feminists.*

But while caution is to be used in bestowing rewards and inflicting punishments, still rewards and punishments are indispensably necessary in the management of the child. Inspire your boy with a sense of shame, and with a generous thirst for praise. Caress and honour him when he does well; treat him with neglect when he acts amiss. This conduct will produce much better effects than if you were at one time to chide and beat him; at another, to reward him with a profusion of sweetmeats and playthings.

Think not that children are to be taught

propriety of conduct by loading their memory with rules, directing them how to act on every particular occasion. Burden them not with rules, but impress them with habits.

Be not desirous of forming them at too early an age, to all that politeness and propriety of manners which you wish to distinguish them when they become men. Let them be taught an easy, graceful carriage of body: but give yourself no concern, though they now and then blunder against the punctilios of good breeding; time will correct their aukwardness.

With regard to that important question, whether children ought to be sent to a public school, or are likely to be better trained up in a domestic education? so impossible is it for one master to extend his attention to a number of boys, and so likely is the contagion of vice to be caught among the crowd of a public school, that a private seems more favourable than a public education to virtue, and scarce less favourable to learning. . . .

Ladies have sometimes distinguished themselves as prodigies of learning. Many of the most eminent geniuses of the French nation have been of the female sex. Several of our countrywomen have also made a respectable figure in the republic of letters. Yet we cannot approve of giving girls a learned education. To acquire the accomplishments which are more proper for their sex, will afford sufficient employment for their earlier years. If they be instructed in the grammar of their mother-tongue, and taught to read and speak it with propriety; be taught to write a fair hand, and to perform with readiness the most useful operations of arithmetic: if they be instructed in the nature of the duties which they owe to God, to themselves, and to society; this will be almost all the literary instruction necessary for them. Yet we do not mean to forbid them an acquaintance with the literature of their country. The periodical writers, who have taught all the duties of morality, the decencies of life, and the principles of taste, in so elegant and pleasing a manner, may with great propriety be put into the hands of our female pupil. Neither will we deny her the historians, the most popular voyages and travels, and such of our British poets as may be put into her hands without corrupting her heart or inflaming her passions. But could our opinion or advice have so much influence, we would endeavour to persuade our countrymen and countrywomen to banish from among them the novelists, those panders of vice, with no less determined severity than that with which Plato excludes the poets from his republic, or that with which the converts to Christianity, mentioned in the Acts, condemned their magical volumes to the flames. Unhappily, novels and plays are almost the only species of reading in which the young people of the present age take delight; and nothing has contributed more effectually to bring on that dissoluteness of manners which prevails among all ranks.

But we will not discover so much austerity as to express a wish that the education of the female sex should be confined solely to such things as are plain and useful. We forbid not those accomplishments which are merely ornamental, and the design of which is to render them amiable in the eyes of the other sex. When we consider the duties for which they are destined by nature, we find that the art of pleasing constitutes no inconsiderable part of these;

and it would be wrong, therefore, to deny them those arts, the end of which is to enable them to please. Let them endeavour to acquire taste in dress: to dress in a neat graceful manner, to suit colours to her complexion, and the figure of her clothes to her shape, is no small accomplishment for a young woman. She who is rigged out by the taste and dexterity of her maid and her milliner, is nothing better than a doll sent abroad to public places as a sample of their handy-work. Dancing is a favourite exercise: nay, we might almost call it the favourite study of the fair sex. . . .

Music, also, is an art in which the youth of the female sex are pretty generally instructed; and if their voice and ear be such as to enable them to attain any excellence in vocal music, it may conduce greatly to increase their influence over our sex, and may afford a pleasing and elegant amusement to their leisure-hours. . . .

Drawing is another accomplishment which generally enters into the plan of female education.

Like Father, Like Son

James Mill (1773–1836), the historian and early Utilitarian philosopher, wrote more major articles for the celebrated Supplement to the 4th, 5th, and 6th editions of 1815–1824 than any other contributor. One of these articles, on government, became an influential book. He was already well known as an uncommonly lucid writer, and at the time that he wrote the article "Education" for the Supplement he was busily practicing what he preached, seeing to every detail of the education of his brilliant son, the preeminent Utilitarian philosopher (and early feminist) John Stuart Mill (1806–1872). That education was going forward at home, in the very room where the elder Mill was writing his Britannica *essays. The one on education began thus: (B.L.F.)*

The end of education is to render the individual, as much as possible, an instrument of happiness, first to himself, and next to other beings.

The properties, by which he is fitted to become an instrument to this end, are, partly, those of the body, and, partly, those of the mind.

Happiness depends upon the condition of the Body, either immediately, as where the bodily powers are exerted for the attainment of some good; or mediately, through the mind, as where the condition of the body affects the qualities of the mind.

Education, in the sense in which it is usually taken, and in which it shall here be used, denotes the means which may be employed to render the *mind,* as far as possible, an operative cause of happiness. The mode in which the *body* may be rendered the most fit for operating as an instrument of happiness is generally considered as a different species of inquiry, and is thought to belong to physicians and others, who study the means of perfecting the bodily powers.

Education, then, in the sense in which we are now receiving it, may be defined, the best employment of all the means which can be made use of, by man, for rendering the human mind to the greatest possible degree the cause of human happiness. Every thing, therefore, which operates, from the first germ of existence, to the final extinction of life, in such a manner as to affect those qualities of the mind on which happiness in any degree depends, comes within the scope of the present inquiry. The grand question of education embraces nothing less than this—namely, What can be done by the human powers, by aid of all the means which are at human disposal, to render the human mind the instrument of the greatest degree of happiness? It is evident, therefore, that nothing, of any kind, which operates at any period of life, however early, or however late, ought to be left out of the account. Happiness is too precious an effect, to let any cause of it, however small, run to waste and be lost. The means of human happiness are not so numerous that any of them can be spared. Not to turn every thing to account, is here, if any where, bad economy, in the most emphatical sense of the phrase.

The field, it will easily be seen, is exceedingly comprehensive. It is everywhere, among enlightened men, a subject of the deepest complaint, that the business of education is ill performed; and that, in this, which might have been supposed the most interesting of all human concerns, the practical proceedings remain far behind the actual state of the human mind. It may be remarked, that, notwithstanding all that has been written on the subject, even the *theory* of education has not kept pace with the progress of philosophy; and it is unhappily true, that the *practice* remains to a prodigious distance behind the theory. One reason why the theory, or the combination of ideas which the present state of knowledge might afford for improving the business of education, remains so imperfect, probably is, that the writers have taken but a partial view of the subject; in other words, the greater number have mistaken a part of it for the whole. And another reason of not less importance is, that they have generally contented themselves with vague ideas of the object or end to which education is only useful as means. One grand purpose of the present inquiry will be to obviate all these mistakes; and, if not to exhibit that comprehensive view, which we think is desirable, but to which our limits are wholly inadequate; at any rate, to conduct the reader into that train of thought which will lead him to observe for himself the ultimate boundaries of the field; and, conceiving more accurately the end, to form a better estimate of what is desirable as the means.

Arithmetic

Scientists everywhere, especially since Newton and Leibniz and the development of calculus, have recognized the centrality of mathematics to the advancement of the sciences. In the Supplement to the 4th, 5th, and 6th editions (1815–1824) John Leslie, one of Edinburgh's great physicists and mathematicians, put forward a new "philosophical exposition of the principles of numerical calculations." (B.L.F.)

The current Britannica *devotes almost nineteen columns to "Arithmetic." It is remarkably comprehensive, supremely orderly, and rewards anyone willing to do a little mental work. But the casual reader who would like, as it were, to be seduced into reading about the subject is not given great encouragement. Leslie, writing almost two centuries ago, had the gift of linking his formidable subject with our odd human nature.*

The reader is also directed to Whitehead's article on "Mathematics" to be found in Part II of this book.

PALPABLE ARITHMETIC

The idea of number, though not the most easily acquired, remounts to the earliest epochs of society, and must be nearly coëval with the formation of language. The very savage, who draws from the exercise of fishing or hunting a precarious support for himself and family, is eager, on his return home, to count over the produce of his toilsome exertions. But the leader of a troop is obliged to carry farther his skill in numeration. The systematic practice of war and murder has ever distinguished our species from other animals of prey. The chieftain who prepares to attack a rival tribe, marshals his followers; and, after the bloody conflict has terminated, he reckons up the slain, and marks his unhappy and devoted captives. If those numbers were small, they could easily be represented by very portable emblems, by round pebbles, by dwarf-shells, by fine nuts, by hard grains, by small beans, or by knots tied on a string. But to express the larger numbers, it became necessary, for the sake of distinctness, to place those little objects or counters in regular rows, which the eye could comprehend at a single glance; as, in the telling of money, it would soon have become customary to dispose the rude counters, in two, three, four, or more ranks, as circumstances might suggest. The attention would then be less distracted, resting chiefly on the number of marks presented by each separate row.

Language insensibly moulds itself to our wants. But it was impossible to furnish a name for each particular number: No invention could supply such a multitude of words as would be necessary, and no memory could ever retain them. The only practical mode of proceeding was to have recourse, as on other occasions, to the powers of classification. By conceiving the individuals of a mass to be distributed into successive ranks and divisions, a few component terms might be made sufficient to express the whole. We may discern around us traces, accordingly, of the progress of numeration, through all its gradations.

The earliest and simplest mode of reckoning was by *pairs,* arising naturally from the circumstance of both hands being employed for the sake of expedition. It is now familiar among sportsmen, who use the names of *brace* and *couple,* words that signify *pairing* or *yoking.*—To count by *threes* was another step, though not practised to the same extent. It has been preserved, however, by the same class of men, under the term *leash,* meaning the strings by which *three* dogs and no more can be held at once in the hand.—The numbering by *fours* has had a more extensive application: It was evidently suggested by the custom, in rapid tale, of taking a pair in each hand. Our fishermen, who generally reckon in this way, call every *double pair* of herrings, for instance, a *throw* or *cast;* and the term *warp,* which, from its German origin, has exactly the same import, is employed to denote *four,* in various articles of trade.

Those simple arrangements would, at their first application, carry the reckoning but a very little way. To express larger numbers, it was necessary to repeat the process of classification. The ordinary steps, by which language ascends from particular to general objects, might point out the right path. A collection of *individuals* forms a *species;* a cluster of *species* makes a *genus;* a bundle of *genera* composes an *order;* and a group of *orders* perhaps constitutes a *class*. Such is the method indispensably required in framing the successive arrangement of the almost unbounded subjects of Natural History. A similar mode is pursued in the subdivision and distribution of the members of a vast army.

In following out the classification of numbers, it seemed easy and natural, after the first step had been made, to repeat the same procedure. If a heap of pebbles were disposed in certain rows, it would evidently facilitate their enumeration, to break each of those rows into similar parcels, and thus carry forward the successive subdivision till it stopped. The heap, so analysed by a series of partition, might then be expressed with a very few low numbers easily formed, and capable of being distinctly retained. The particular system adopted, would soon become clothed with terms borrowed from the vernacular idiom. . . .

In the ruder periods of society, a gradation of counters, accommodated to such a process of numerical analysis, was supplied by pebbles, grains, or shells of different sizes. This series, however, is very limited, and would soon confine the range of decomposition. To reach a greater extent, it was necessary to proceed by a swifter analysis; to distribute the counters, for instance, successively into ten or twenty rows, and to make pebbles, shells, or other marks, having their size only doubled perhaps or tripled, to represent values increased ten or twenty fold. Beyond this stage in the progress of numeration, none of the various tribes dispersed over the vast American Continent seem ever to have passed. In the Old World, it is probable that a long pause of improvement had ensued among the nations which were advanced to the same point in the arts of life. But the necessity, in such arithmetical notation, of employing the natural objects to signify a great deal more than their relative size imports, would lead at last to a most important step in the ascent. Instead of distinguishing the different orders of counters by their *magnitude,* they might be made to derive an *artificial value* from their *rank* alone. It would be sufficient, for that purpose, to employ marks all of the same kind, but disposed on a graduating series of vertical bars or columns. The augmented value which these marks acquire in rising through the successive bars, would evidently be quite arbitrary, depending, in every case, on a key to be fixed by convention. This point in the chain of discovery was attained by the Greeks at a very early period, and communicated to the Romans, who continued, during their whole career of empire, to practise a sort of tangible arithmetic, which they transmitted to their successors in modern Europe. The Chinese also have, from the remotest antiquity, been accustomed to employ a similar mode of calculation, which they are said to manage with singular skill and address.

Who Owns an Idea?

The status of intellectual property, i.e., *useful inventions or original works of literature or music, was much debated in the British Isles, and it was given substantial attention by* Encyclopædia Britannica, *which itself was repeatedly "pirated" or issued in unauthorized and uncompensated editions. In the Supplement to the 4th, 5th, and 6th editions (1815–1824) the author of "Copyright" related a brief history of the controversy, and then adopted a dialogue format to probe more deeply. The writer of this article was Joseph Lowe, a barrister.*

By the time this article was written, the American Constitution had adopted the idea of copyright for a fixed term in Article I, Section 8 (Powers of Congress). (B.L.F.)

. . . To avoid perplexity, we shall endeavour to comprise the *pros* and *cons* in these various discussions, in a kind of regular succession, adopting the plan of appending a rejoinder to each argument, as the best method of doing justice to both sides.

Objection. Ideas cannot be the object of property; they are not visible, tangible, or corporeal. (Judge Yates.)

Answer. Whatever admits of exclusive enjoyment may be property. (Hargrave.)

O. Another person may arrive, by his own process of thought, at similar conclusions, would you deny to him what you granted to his predecessor?

A. There is very little apprehension of such a coincidence; the plans and the results of study admit of as infinite variety as the human countenance; the same views, or the same conclusions, will never come from two persons, or even from the same person at different times, in the same language. At all events, an arbitrator or a court of justice can be at no loss to decide, whether a second publication on the same subject comes within the description of plagiarism.

O. A literary composition is undoubtedly the property of the writer, so long as it remains in MS.; but by the act of publishing, he gives it to the world; he lets the bird fly; his property is gone. (Judge Yates.)

A. He gives the public the free use of the knowledge contained in his book; but this is a very different thing from the profit as publisher. The ten shillings paid for a volume entitles the reader to the use of its contents, but can certainly give him no claim to the hundred pounds which may be expected from a new edition. (Lord Mansfield, Judges Willes, Blackstone, and Aston.)

O. It is not clear that common law ever sanctioned the exclusive enjoyment of copyright; the only titles appear to have been the royal patent and the licence of the Stationers' Company. (Lord Camden.)

A. It seems to have been always taken for granted by Chancery and other courts, that an exclusive right existed. There was a confirmatory example in the highest quarter; the King is perpetual proprietor of the right of publishing acts of Parliament and all public documents. (Lord Mansfield, Judges Willes, Blackstone, and Aston.)

O. The patentees of mechanical inventions possess but a limited term; none of them ever advanced a claim to perpetuity. (Judge Yates.)

A. Such patentees are much sooner reimbursed than authors; the fruit of their invention is of a more direct practical application. Besides, the stranger who makes a duplicate of a machine, incurs a much greater relative expence than the stranger who reprints an edition of a book,—in the one the materials form the chief part of the cost; in the other, they are comparatively insignificant, and copies may be multiplied by the thousand.

O. The statute of the 8th of Queen Anne, expressly limits the duration of copyright; it enacts that the protecting penalties shall be in force during fourteen years, and no longer. (Judge Yates.)

A. This is, no doubt, the apparent meaning of the statute, but the preamble of the act declares, that it is passed for the protection of literature; to make the act an instrument for curtailing a literary privilege would certainly be at variance with its general language. (Lord Mansfield.)

O. If such property be admitted for a time, is not the term of fourteen years sufficient? What good could the public expect from the writings of men so selfish as to call for a perpetual monopoly?

A. Monopoly is not the proper word; the object may be attained, as will be shown presently, under modifications which insure to the public a complete supply of books at reasonable prices.

O. "Glory," said Lord Camden, "is the reward of science, and those who deserve it scorn all meaner views."

A. Reputation is, and always will be, the grand stimulus to literary exertion, but it requires long-continued exertion; and if we do not enable a writer to live by his works, we confine the possibility of acquiring reputation to a very small class—to the rich, or to those who derive an income from other means. Such, in fact, has hitherto been the case; standard works have been attempted only by men who, like Gibbon, possessed patrimony, or who, like Robertson and Hume, arrived at the possession of income from other sources. No one imagines that our military or naval officers follow their profession for the sake of pay; yet no one would propose to abridge it on the ground of reputation being their primary object.

O. "It was not for gain," said Lord Camden, "that Bacon, Newton, Milton, and Locke, instructed the world."

A. Each of these distinguished men were obliged to trespass on the time devoted to literature, and to seek an income from public employments. How much better would it have been could they have given an undivided and uninterrupted attention to their favourite pursuits?

In comparing these various arguments, the balance is evidently on the side of the advocates of exclusive right in every point except one—the interpretation of the statute of Queen Anne. There the words, "fourteen years and no longer," are too pointed to admit of the construction put on them by Lord Mansfield. In the beginning of 1774, when the question came before the House of Lords, the judges attended and delivered their opinions at length, Lord Mansfield advocating the cause of permanency, while Judge Yates, now supported by his brethren, Baron Eyre and Baron Perrot, asserted once more the necessity of limitation. . . . The House, however, appear to have been alarmed at the idea of perpetuity, and finally decided, that the exclusive right should last only "fourteen years, with a contingent fourteen, if the author happened to be alive at the end of the first period."

Civilization

J. H. Robinson (1863–1936), son of a bank president, became one of the intellectual pillars which support our present broadly based con-

ception of history. In a series of influential books (see his pioneering The New History, *1912) and a lifetime of teaching he extended our perspectives so that we no longer think of history as largely diplomatic, dynastic, and military.* Britannica *assigned him to write on "Civilization," a daunting task. Some of his theses, rooted in the James-Dewey pragmatism of his period, remain controversial. As a whole, however, his article was not only trail-breaking but retains its relevance. In certain respects it ranks as the most important one in the 1929 printing of the 14th edition. It is very long, but we venture to reproduce it in its entirety.*

This Encyclopaedia is in itself a description of civilization, for it contains the story of human achievement in all its bewildering developments. It shows what men during hundreds of thousands of years have been learning about themselves, their world and the creatures which share it with them. They have reached out into remote space and studied nebulae whose light reaches them after a million years; they have, on the other hand, dissected atoms and manipulated electrons as they might handle pebbles. In the present magnificent series of volumes man's inventions are reviewed from the rudest chipped flint to the most delicately adjusted microscope; his creation of multiform beauties of design, colour and word, his ways of dealing with his fellows, his co-operations and dissensions; his ideals and lofty aspirations, his inevitable blunders and disappointments; in short, all his gropings, disheartening failures and unbelievable triumphs are recalled.

Several thousand contributors have been brought together to do each his special part in writing some thirty-five million words on what mankind has hitherto done and said. It might therefore seem at first sight superfluous, and indeed impossible, to treat civilization itself as a separate topic in a few pages. But there is danger that owing to the overwhelming mass of information given in these volumes certain important underlying considerations may be lost sight of. There are highly significant questions concerning the nature and course of human development, the obstacles which have lain in the way of advance; the sources of success and frustration, which could hardly be brought together in dealing with any of the special aspects of human culture. Accordingly an attempt will be made under this caption to scan civilization as a single, unique and astonishing achievement of the human species.

To begin with, it is a startling fact that civilization, which sets off man in so astounding a manner from all other animals, should only lately have begun to be understood. We are immersed in it from infancy; we take it for granted, and are too near it to see it, except in this detail and that. Even to-day, with all our recently acquired knowledge, those who strive most valiantly in imagination to get outside civilization so that they may look upon it dispassionately and appraise it as a whole, are bewildered by its mysteries. As for the great mass of intelligent people, they still harbour many ancient illusions and misapprehensions from which they can only be weaned with great reluctance.

The object of the present article is to describe the newer ways of viewing civilization, its general nature, origin, progress, transmission and chief developments, in the light of information which has been accumulating during the past fifty or sixty years. The study of man himself has been revealing quite as many revolutionary facts and hypotheses during the past half century as the scientific investigation of the world in which he lives. The history of human achievement has been traced back, at least in vague outline, hundreds of thousands of years; man's original uncivilized nature and equipment have been studied and compared with the behaviour of his nearer relatives; new conjectures have emerged in regard to the functioning of speech and the nature and origin of human reasoning; careful investigations of primitive civilizations have cast great light on more complicated ones; the tremendous importance of childhood and its various implications in the development of civilization have been elaborated.

These and many other discoveries conspire to recast our conception of civilization, its past progress and its future possibilities.

It is instructive to note that the word civilization is by no means an old one. Boswell reports that he urged Dr. Johnson to insert the term in his dictionary in 1772, but Johnson refused. He preferred the older word "civility." This, like "urbanity," reflects the contempt of the townsman for the rustic or barbarian; it is an invidious term, although in a way justified by the fact that only where cities have grown up have men developed intricate civilizations. The arduous and dispersed tasks of the hunter, shepherd and peasant folk do not afford the leisure, or at least the varied human contacts, essential to the generation of new ideas and discoveries. But modern anthropologists have pointed out that peoples without cities, such as the tribes of Polynesia and the North American Indians, are really highly "civilized," in the sense that upon sympathetic examination, they are found to have subtle languages, ingenious arts, admirably suited to their conditions, developed institutions, social and political; religious practices and confident myths, no better and no worse substantiated than many that prevail today among the nations of Europe. All these betoken and presuppose a vastly long development. Among English speaking people the first to point this out clearly was E. B. Tylor, who published his famous *Primitive Society,* in 1871, the same year in which Darwin's *Descent of Man* appeared. These two books would alone have served, by different approaches, to give the word civilization a far more profound meaning than it had ever had before.

New Conception of Civilization

There could be no real understanding of the fundamental characteristics of civilization until the fact was well established and digested that could we trace back man's lineage far enough we should find it merging into that of wild animals, without artificial shelters, clothes or speech; dependent for sustenance on the precarious daily search for food. It requires a considerable effort of the imagination to picture the human race without these seeming necessities of even primitive civilization. Without fire and tools men must have existed as did a wild girl discovered near Châlons, France, in 1731. She possessed a monkey-like agility which enabled her to catch birds and rabbits; these she skinned with her nails and gobbled raw, as would a dog. She delighted to suck the blood from living pigeons, and had no speech except hideous screams and howls.

This conception of man's former animal existence is gradually supplanting the older one, based upon ancient Hebrew tradition, that the first man and first woman were special creations with fully developed minds, speech and reason, which enabled them forthwith to dress the garden in which they found themselves, to name its animal denizens, and to talk with one another, and with God himself in the cool of the evening. This view is still passively accepted by an overwhelming majority of Americans and Europeans and is at present hotly defended by a powerful group in the United States.

The former assumption was that man was *by nature* endowed with a *mind* and with *reason*. These distinguished him sharply from the animals, which did wondrous things it is true, but not as a result of reason. Their behaviour was guided, it was argued, by instinct. Darwin says that "the very essence of an instinct is that it is followed independently of reason." But if we agree, as manifold evidence seems to force us to do, that long, long ago men behaved and lived like wild animals, are we not forced to ask if they did not live wholly according to what Darwin calls "instincts"? And if once upon a time our ancestors lived solely by their animal equipment, did they as yet have a mind and reason? May not the human mind be something that has very gradually developed as a result of man's peculiar animal make-up and capacities? May not his reason be but another name for his slowly accumulated knowledge and beliefs and his ways of dealing with them and building upon them? In any case the discovery that our ancestors once lived like wild animals raises entirely new and difficult questions as to the nature, origin and interpretation of those powers of his known as mind and reason, which have enabled him to seek out those inventions and come upon beliefs and practices which have produced in the aggregate civilization.

In short, it seems to be more and more apparent that mind and reason were not part of man's original equipment, as are his arms and legs, his brain and tongue, but have been slowly acquired and painfully built up. They are themselves *inventions*—things he has come upon. Like other inventions *they are part and parcel of civilization*—not innate in man but dependent for their perpetuation on education in the widest sense of that term. This is so novel an idea that many readers may find it difficult to grasp, but when grasped it alters one's whole estimate of human progress. We ordinarily think of civilization as made up of mechanical devices, books and pictures, enlightened religious ideas, handsome buildings, polite conduct, scientific and philosophical knowledge, social and political institutions, ingenious methods of transportation and the rest. We think that all these things are due to man's possession of a mind, which no animal has, and as a result of the exercise of reason. In a way this is true enough, only we must reconceive mind and reason and regard them just as truly a part of the gradual elaboration of civilization as a House of Commons or a motor car, and quite as subject to improvement. At the risk of making a seemingly irrelevant philosophical digression, which is really most essential to a modern understanding of civilization, something may be said of the newer conception of mind and its variant, reason.

The word mind was originally a verb, not a noun; it meant action, not a thing or agent. It was remembering and purposing, and taking note of—as for instance "I minded"—that is, remembered, or paid attention to, or was concerned by. But as time went on philosophers made a noun of the good old verb. It was conceived as that incorporeal substance which was the seat of a person's consciousness, thoughts, feelings, and especially of his reasoning. The body was set over against the mind whose orders it was supposed to execute. The Scottish philosopher of common sense, Reid, says explicitly that "we do not give the name of mind to thought, reason or desire; but to that power which both perceives and wills." Even John Stuart Mill says in his *Logic* that "mind is the mysterious something which feels and thinks."

Recently there has been a tendency to reduce the noun mind once more to a series of verbs—desiring, remembering, feeling, thinking, distinguishing, inferring, planning—and to regard the assumption of "a mysterious something" as unfounded, unnecessary and a serious embarrassment. Relieved of this embarrassment it is possible to begin to bridge the gulf between the original behaviour of the human race and that of mankind to-day. Descartes and all the older philosophers believed that man had always had a mind as good as theirs. They sought to tell him how to employ it in the pursuit of truth. Mind was to them a sort of divine instrument, conferred solely upon man, that could be sharpened and efficiently used by following the laws of logic; but they could not think of it as something accumulated, so to speak, through the many thousands of years since man made his first contributions to the upbuilding of civilization.

The way is now cleared for a new view of civilization which would not have been possible 50 or 60 years ago. Civilization is no longer contrasted with "rusticity," "barbarity" or "savagery," but with man's purely animal heritage. Modern men are still animals, they have to eat and sleep, protect themselves from the inclemencies of the weather, and defend themselves from attacks of their fellow creatures and other animals, and to rear a new generation, if the species is to be perpetuated. They closely resemble kindred animals in much of their physical structure, in their important organs, breathing, digestion and the circulation of their blood. All these peculiarities are hereditarily transmitted no matter how much or how little men may be civilized. On the other hand, civilization—language, religion, beliefs, morals, arts and manifestations of the human mind and reason—none of these can be shown to be handed down as biological traits. They can only be transmitted to a new generation by imitation or instruction.

All mankind to-day has a double heritage. The one comes to us without any effort on our part, as do the spider's peculiar characteristics or those of birds, or of any of our fellow mammals, come to them. It is secure and tends to remain the same for thousands of years. Civilization, on the other hand, is precarious; it must be assimilated anew by each one of us for himself in such a degree as circumstances permit. It can increase indefinitely but it may also fall off tremendously, as the history of man amply testifies. It is a legacy that can be lost as well as kept and increased.

To illustrate: it may be that before human beings had acquired any of this loseable thing, civilization, they would pick up a stick to strike an assailant or hurl a stone at him. They might have found themselves riding astride floating tree trunks to cross a stream. Certain persons would occur, let us say, in each generation who would do all these things without ever having seen them done. These acts would be classed in man's animal heritage. But should we find traces of men who chipped a flint nodule into a hatchet head, and hollowed out their log with such a hatchet, or with fire, we should have to class these acts among the arts of civilization since they presuppose so much accumulated experience and ingenuity that they could not be inborn. The art of making a rude boat might consequently be wholly lost, as surely many inventions must have lapsed, if a single generation passed without constructing one.

It seems now an imperative fact that all civilization—the total social and traditional heritage, would fall away immediately and completely should a thoroughgoing forgetfulness, an overwhelming amnesia and profound oblivion overtake humanity. Only their natural equipment would be left. As Graham Wallas suggests, those least civilized would have a possible chance of surviving. It is only uncivilized man that might go on indefinitely. We are all by nature wild animals *plus;* and our taming weakens us for the ancient struggle in the forest, naked and bare-handed.

❧ ❧ ❧

Peculiar Items of Man's Bodily Form

At this juncture the question arises, what was there peculiar in man's physical make-up that enabled him to initiate civilization and build up a mind which he could use to increase his resources so far beyond that of any other animal? Before proceeding we should recollect that the ways of all living creatures are manifold and astonishing. Even a single-celled organism can marvellously adjust itself to altered conditions. It seems to learn by experience, it appears to have a sort of memory, it is modified by happenings which interrupt its comfortable routine. It is ingenious in defending itself, in seeking food and reproducing. It is, in short, purposive in its conduct. The tiger and the frog are able to adjust themselves to very different modes of life, and so are the orioles and cacti. Before man began to accumulate civilization we are forced to assume that he too made terms with the daily need of adjustment which faced him, otherwise we should not be here to write the tale. These are the salient essentials of *Life,* and man is a part of what Julian Huxley calls "the stream of life." All these possibilities lay behind the development of man's intelligence. They are the hinterland from which civilization emerged and to which it ever tends to retreat.

In order to begin and carry on the accumulation of civilization, man had of necessity to be so constructed physically that he could *perceive* more clearly than his predecessors, make more accurate distinctions and so remember and imagine better; for all these are essential to talking and thinking. The awareness of animals is of a low, vague type, and so must pristine man's have been. The one-celled animals behave in a purposive way, but they have no eyes or ears or noses. They must live in silence and darkness like a human blind, deaf mute. They will nevertheless take in certain food and reject other things. They perceive and act without, so far as we can see, being conscious of their actions. They make the necessary decisions without deciding in a human sense. They have no nervous system, but, as has lately been discovered, the promise of one. The creatures most like ourselves have eyes, ears and noses, and evidently see, hear and smell; and they have an elaborate nervous system. Of these resources they make constant use. But compared with man they are ill-qualified to make careful distinctions and discriminations and remember clearly. They take note of far fewer factors in their situation. They must act somewhat as our digestive system does. It is a sort of animal within us which performs wondrous feats when given food. It works purposively, as does our heart and blood circulation. We can become *conscious* of these unconscious achievements when we choke, because the switch is not thrown promptly enough to prevent a morsel from going down our windpipe instead of taking the route to the stomach. Palpitation of the heart is a conscious suggestion of the faithful pump, which rarely reminds us of its constant attention to business. Let it neglect two or three beats and we are dead.

The essentials of man's physical equipment for initiating and piling up civilization have been dwelt upon by many writers. He has sensitive hands, and (after he got securely on his hind legs) he could use them far more freely than if he had to employ them as auxiliary feet. His thumb can be readily placed against any one of his fingers. There is no such expert feeler and handler as he to be found among his kindred. He could learn much of shape and form, of softness and hardness, of weight, texture, heat and cold, toughness, rigidity and flexibility, which could be but vaguely sensed with hoof or paw. Had he had ears that he could turn about like a jack-rabbit, and a prehensile tail, he might have been able to learn faster. And all these things were the beginning of knowledge. He could not only strike but hurl. His eyes were so placed that he was always looking through a stereoscope, so to speak, and seeing things in the round. His vocal organs promised a great range of delicate discrimination in the sounds he made. Then he was a helpless dependent for many years on his elders so that their acquired ways could become his.

Lastly there is man's brain with its complex cerebral cortex and its association paths, which develop astonishingly as a child grows up. The cortex is the prime correlator of impressions, and is modified through individual experience in a higher degree than any other part of the nervous system. Its functioning is still very mysterious, but no one doubts its essential rôle in the process of human learning and the increase of intelligence. Its operations are not, however, autonomous but closely associated with the experiences of the whole human organism and dependent on those singular capacities of mankind already mentioned.

So it becomes apparent that after hundreds of millions of years during which nature's experiments have been going on in physical structure and function, which have enabled creatures of the most diverse types to meet the absolute requisites of life—growing up and reproducing their species—a kind of animal finally appeared on the earth so constructed that he could become civilized. Man's biological make-up represents a unique combination of physical characteristics. Most of these, as we have seen, occur in other mammals. Even those which seem peculiar to him would not serve, however, as a foundation for the development of civilization except in a highly complex union. Cows might have a human cerebral cortex, foxes apposable thumbs, birds stereoscopic eyes, dogs vocal organs similar to ours, and yet civilization would be far beyond their reach. Man can teach all of them tricks. They themselves can learn something as their life goes on. Chimpanzees may under favourable circumstances, as Köhler has shown, make very simple, human-like inferences; but none of them could initiate and perpetuate the arts and sciences as a heritage of their species.

Progress and Conservatism

Such then was man's original equipment for getting civilized. He had, obviously, no means of foreseeing the enterprise in which he was engaged. His evolution as a civilized being was no more premeditated than his rise from earlier simian ancestors. There seems to be sufficient evidence that for hundreds of thousands of years changes in his mode of life were so gradual and rare as to pass unperceived. Each generation accepted the conditions in which it was reared without thought of betterment. Our modern hope of "progress"—an indefinite increase of human knowledge and its application to the improvement of man's estate—was practically unknown even to the Greeks and Romans. From the 13th century onward a few writers dwelt upon the promise of the future, but they were outclamoured by those convinced that human woes were attributable to a departure from ancient standards. The Humanists strove to re-establish the wisdom of the classical writers, and the Protestants sought to revive the beliefs and practices of the early Christians. Only three centuries ago did Bacon unroll a programme of aggressive search for the hitherto unknown, which had any very wide influence. In the 18th century the conception of reform and progress found illustrious spokesmen, and their anticipations of coming changes in the economy of human life were destined, as it proved, to be far outrun by the events of the 19th and early 20th centuries.

We can, however, still note on all hands illustrations of man's confidence in routine sanctified by ancient authorities; his suspicion of innovation in wide realms of belief and practice. This dogged obstinacy in clinging to his habits, and his general suspicion of the unfamiliar, are exactly what might have been anticipated when we consider his animal origin. This trait has served to slow down the process of change, but at the same time has greatly increased the security and permanence of each achievement. Here we find a possible explanation of the great rôle that the veil of sacredness has played in man's development. He has cast it over beliefs and practices and so hid them from pert scrutiny and criticism. The number of those who can tolerate somewhat critical thinking here and there, has, nevertheless, greatly increased of late, but they are still few indeed. What we call to-day a conservative or reactionary mood must have been characteristic of mankind from the beginning. It corresponds to animal inclinations.

Among animal proclivities there is, however, from the one-celled organisms upward, a life-saving tendency to make random movements, extensions and contractions, to hasten hither and thither, in the pursuit of food and mates. This restlessness and groping are among man's legacies also. They offset his routine and static habits, and lie behind and back of the inventions and discoveries he has made. There is, too, especially obvious among the higher animals, something auguring what in man becomes curiosity. The danger of attack made preliminary scouting a valuable asset in survival. So men were by nature wont to pry and try and fumble, long before they scientifically analysed and experimented.

There can be no doubt that hundreds of thousands of years were required for man to reach even the lowest degree of culture to be found among the simplest tribes today. The discovery of fossil skulls, teeth and bones at different geological levels shows that more or less ape-like men have been on earth for from half a million to a million years. Several species, such as the Java man, the Heidelberg man and the much later Neanderthal race are now extinct. The only vestiges of their handiwork consist in chipped flint tools, becoming better made and more varied as time went on. There is no way of telling what other arts, beliefs and practices were associated with a particular assortment of flint utensils. Sollas, in his *Ancient Hunters,* has sought to draw ingenious analogies between these prehistoric weapons and the civilizations of the Tasmanians, Australians, Eskimos, etc.

The so-called Cro-Magnon race had finely developed skulls quite as good as those of to-day. To them are ascribed the remarkable paintings and drawings found in caves of southern France and northern Spain. They are believed to be from 25 to 30 thousand years old. Halving this period we come upon traces of ground and polished stone tools, coincident with the relinquishment of hunting as man's exclusive pursuit and a settling down to sow and reap, spin and weave. Halving it again, we get news of the use of copper, the precursor of the metals on which our civilization largely rests. This can but be a rough chronology subject to much revision as time goes on and the earth is more thoroughly searched for evidences of man's past.

To get the matter clearly before one, let us imagine, as the writer has suggested elsewhere, that 500,000 years of developing culture were compressed into 50 years. On this scale mankind would have required 49 years to learn enough to desert here and there his inveterate hunting habits and settle down in villages. Half through the fiftieth year writing was discovered and practised within a very limited area, thus supplying one of the chief means for perpetuating and spreading culture. The achievements of the Greeks would be but three months back, the prevailing of Christianity, two; the printing press would be a fortnight old and man would have been using steam for hardly a week. The peculiar conditions under which we live did not come about until Dec. 31 of the fiftieth year.

There is a school of anthropologists, the

diffusionists, who would derive all the higher types of civilization—writing, metallurgy, the construction of imposing stone buildings—from a single region, Egypt. They have collected much evidence to show that through the commerce of the Phoenicians, Egyptian inventions spread eastward into India, China and Japan, then across the Pacific to form the basis of Maya culture in Central America. The merits of the "diffusionist" arguments cannot be considered here. G. Elliot Smith, one of the best known advocates of this theory, dwells on the common lack of inventiveness and the reluctance of mankind to adopt new ideas, his tenacious hold on old ones and "his thick armour of obstinacy." "To obtain recognition of even the most trivial of innovations it is the common experience of almost every pioneer in art, science or invention to have to fight against a solid wall of cultivated prejudice and inherent stupidity."

All anthropologists are well aware of this hostility to change, which we may regard, as shown above, as a natural trait of mankind. They also admit the wide dissemination of inventions through commerce and conquest. Nevertheless many maintain that the same or similar discovery has been made independently in different parts of the earth, as the result of similar needs and conditions. When we have examined the exigencies of successful inventions in the following section we shall see that however commonplace they are now, with the accumulation of the past to build upon and modern facilities to work with, they were beyond measure difficult at the start when mankind still led the life of an animal. When once made and adopted by some tribe it is far easier to think of them as being introduced to other peoples than to assume that their presence represents an independent discovery.

Civilization depends upon the discoveries and inventions man has been able to make, together with the incalculable effects these have had upon his daily conduct, thoughts and feelings. As knowledge and ingenuity increased he departed further and further from his original wild animal life. The manner in which he began to learn is a matter of conjecture, since the manufacture of tools and weapons, the invention of language and artificial ways of producing fire, far antedate any written accounts of advances in man's education. The same may be said of the much more recent spinning, weaving and farming. As we have seen, it required hundreds of thousands of years to reach the degree of civilization represented by these achievements. Their importance, however, cannot be overestimated, since they formed the absolutely essential basis of all later developments. We may feel a certain pride in contemporary inventions, but let us remember that we owe to savage hunters and illiterate neolithic farmers the accumulation of knowledge and skill without which none of our modern experimentation would be possible. Where would we be without fire, speech, clothes and bread!

Since invention, discovery and the increase of knowledge are the stuff of which civilization is made, it is pertinent to our theme to consider how they occur. There is plenty of evidence available in the reports which discoverers now make of the manner in which they reach their conclusions. There is also evidence of how their results are received and acted upon by others. All explorers must be exceptionally curious and at the same time patient gropers. The curiosity observable in most children tends to die away, but survives in one form or another in rare instances through life. These exceptional persons possess a drive alien to their fellows. They may be the handyman of a village or a member of a highly endowed research staff. They avail themselves of what has already been found out; the village mechanical genius does not have to invent a monkey-wrench or bit of insulating tape, nor does the biologist need to know much about the optical principles of his lenses, much less invent or manufacture them. The geologist before he makes any discoveries is familiar with hundreds of treatises on his subject. It would be generally conceded by investigators that their discoveries are seemingly accidental. They do not know what they are going to find, and quite commonly find what they were not looking for, even as Saul, chasing lost asses, came upon a kingdom. All this applies to every kind of increase of knowledge, whether it have to do with the operations of so-called Nature or with novel suggestions in the realms of philosophy or art. All are the result of curiosity, patient examination and thought. At best they are no more than foot-notes and glosses added to existing human knowledge. This is now so varied and voluminous that no single person can compass it except in this detail and that. Should he attempt to do so, all chance of adding to it would be excluded.

But an invention or discovery or the rectification of an ancient error, does not become a part of civilization until it has been accepted by the tribe and been added to its habits of action and thought. Plenty of shocking tales could be recalled of professional and popular opposition to innovations on grounds which now seem grotesque. We owe discoveries to individual men and women, but new information and skill can only be propagated and disseminated in a favourable culture medium. Many instances could be cited of promising knowledge which has so far failed to get a footing in civilization.

The influence of particular discoveries and mechanical devices is by no means confined to their more immediate and obvious applications. It is impossible to foresee what wide-ranging effects they may ultimately exert on human life. Fire will cook a meal, harden an earthen bowl, keep a group of naked savages warm, frighten off prowling animals, soften or melt metals; it may also consume sacrifices to the gods, or form the central interest of a stately temple and be replenished by an order of vestal virgins. It may play its part in the symbolism of the theologian and the poet. The Indians of the North American plains were deeply affected by the introduction of the horse, and African tribes by fire-arms and whisky. The motor car and telephone altered social relations. The perfecting of the steam engine revolutionized the transport of men and their wares; it promoted city life; further, it caused Marx to write a big book which became the gospel of a momentous social upheaval, which threatened the peace of mind of all nations.

The invention of clothes—quite material things, whether of linen, wool, silk or cotton—not only created great industries but enabled men by changing their hide artificially to establish social distinctions akin to biological genera and species. Through clothes entered in prudery and the pious horror of bare bodies which has wrought consternation and disaster among the dark-skinned folk. After the World War women's skirts were gradually shortened. The warmth of houses and vehicles permitted this. One of the conventional distinctions between girls and women was thus obliterated. The unveiling of women's faces in Mohammedan countries, the breaking down of *purdah* in India—all these material changes imply modifications of woman's life and of the attitude of the sexes to one another. They forecast further important changes in traditional civilization.

In view of these facts, and indefinitely more that each one can easily add for himself, it would seem that what are esteemed the "nobler" aspirations and creations of mankind, whether in art and literature or the pursuit of truth, are all not only dependent upon "material" inventions but so strangely interwoven with them and their effects that it is no easy thing to separate the higher and the lower, except in imagination. What is sometimes called "the higher life of man" arises from his more humble and practical knowledge and skill; accordingly the old distinction between the material and spiritual seems to be greatly attenuated as they are both seen to merge into the newer conception of civilization as a whole. This will become even more apparent when we come to deal with words.

Rôle of Childhood

One of the essential conditions for the perpetuation of civilization is the long period of dependence through which the human child must pass before it gains sufficient bodily strength and intelligence to achieve merely animal self-sufficiency and make its own way. Without the constant and prolonged succour of adults it would speedily perish. This means that the extended period of helpless susceptibility to his surroundings makes it possible vastly to modify a child's original disposition. A mouse is sexually mature in six weeks and fully grown in three months. Calves and colts walk about shortly after birth. The gorilla, on the other hand, has a prolonged childhood, requires ten or twelve years before it is able to breed, and goes on growing, like man, for a few years after. He lacks, however, in spite of his prolonged childhood, the other essential traits which have enabled mankind to initiate, increase and transmit civilization.

We are all born uncivilized and would remain so through life were we not immersed in civilization. There is a long time in which we may, according to the place where we are born, be moulded into a well authenticated Papuan, Chinaman, or Parisian. We cannot choose whether we shall find ourselves talking like a Hottentot, a Russian or a German. And we learn to do in all things as those do among whom we are brought up. We cannot but accept their respective customs, scruples, and ideas, for all these are imposed upon us before we have any choice or discretion. We must perforce follow the ways of our elders, who themselves were once children and gained their civilization before any discrimination or comparison with other than the prevailing habits was possible. This is the inexorable rule, and it accounts for many of the striking characteristics of civilization.

If the assimilation of culture is closely associated with the dependence and adaptability of childhood there need be no great surprise that accumulating evidence seems to indicate that when bodily maturity is once reached, the increase of knowledge and intelligence slackens or even almost ceases in many cases. By 13 or 14 the child has acquired an overwhelming part of the knowledge, impressions, cautions and general estimates of his fellow creatures and the world in which he lives, which he continues to harbour with slight modifications during his lifetime. When as a result of the participation of the United States in the World War it became necessary to test the competence of a great number of young men an unforeseen contribution was made to our insight into civilization. Of the 1,700,000 examined, 45% did not show themselves (to quote an eminent authority, Dr. Henry H. Goddard) "much above the 12-year-old limit." Those tested, it must be remembered, did not include idiots or "morons," but the average run of youths accepted by their fellows as normal. While tests may be as yet inadequate they but confirm the observable fact that the inculcation of culture is associated with bodily growth and especially with the strange changes in the cells of the forebrain and their intercommunications. These developments are tremendous from infancy to maturity in so-called normal cases.

Only in exceptional instances does mind-building continue steadily after childhood and adolescence. We have had time before 13 to take over the standardized sentiments of our elders, to learn all that they know, to accept their views of religion, politics, manners, general proprieties and respectabilities. The common run of mankind can, however, be taught tricks as time goes on and acquire special expertness. But a great part of our childish conceptions retain a permanent hold on us. There is usually little encouragement to alter them. We leave most of them unrevised, though we have to make adjustments as the years elapse. Human beings seem on the whole easily subdued to routine and the routine is established, as it would seem, by the time we are grown up. That the *ability* to learn, however, falls off very slowly after adulthood has been recently shown by E. L. Thorndike.

The experts in advertising, the publishers of "tabloid" newspapers and the contrivers of moving picture films seem to conform to the supposition that what appeals to a 12- or 13-year-old child is admirably adapted to the intelligence and tastes of the multitude. This means that the overwhelming majority of men and women assimilate in childhood the common and familiar forms of civilization or culture in the midst of which they find themselves, but hardly outrun them as life goes on. Perhaps one in a hundred may allow his opinions to be altered by assiduous reading, or take pains to cultivate his insight into art and literature and scientific discoveries. But all these and other contributions to one's personal civilization are outside the range of the human animal in general. Indeed the mere upkeep of our present complicated culture must depend upon a very trifling percentage of the population. Were a few thousand carefully selected infants in the various progressive countries of the world to be strangled at birth not only would advances in industry, arts and letters cease but a decline would set in owing to the lack of those to make the essential readjustments in our industries and their financing; to keep up laboratories and books at their present standards. Accordingly the great majority of human beings can barely maintain at best the civilization in which they were reared. Even the innovators considered above, are unable to escape from the toils in which they were so easily enmeshed and which they regard not as entanglements and restraints but as comforts and assurances. It would be faithless and disloyal to regard them otherwise. Only peculiar temperaments under highly favourable conditions question what they have been taught. They can do this only on a most modest scale as a result of continued curiosity and study. A physicist may reach a new theory of the constitution of atoms and yet cling stolidly to the notions of religion he had acquired at ten years of age; he may even engage in subtle philosophical speculation and remain a hot defender of the *mores* of the most commonplace persons 50 years ago.

If these points be well taken the whole contrast between Society and the individual which has been played up in various rather futile ways takes on a new aspect. From the standpoint of civilization each individual owes his entire equipment as a civilized being to others. Biologically even, he is vastly modified by his domestication, in habits, impulses and moods. The so-called "instinct of the herd," which Trotter has made famous, tends to become an unnecessary hypothesis. For every child is made by others in their own image. How gregarious mankind was before the onset of civilization it is impossible to say; but the prolonged infantile weakness implied multiform dependence upon others. Of course there is really no such thing as Society in the sense of some powerful and precious personality for whose welfare the so-called individual is invited to make appropriate sacrifices of personal preferences. What we have to do is to make terms with the notions of "the good" and "the bad" which those profess with whom we are thrown. These rules of conduct and sentiment constitute Society. They have their heavy sanctions if violated or impeached—disgrace, persecution, imprisonment and even death. The methods of eluding Society constitute a highly interesting chapter in the history of civilization. It is not difficult for the shrewd, and seems greatly to enrich life for certain temperaments, whether one be a burglar, a storyteller, or a philosopher. Wholesale deceit has established the reputation and fame of many a hero from Jacob and Ulysses to those in high places to-day. Boldness of thought is less likely as yet to arouse primitive enthusiasm.

Words Viewed as Deeds

One of the most stupendous elements in civilization has hitherto been only casually mentioned—words. Without language civilization could hardly even have begun and certainly could never have attained its higher forms. Speech underlies thinking and conscious planning and research. It does more. It creates a world of ideas which interpenetrates and seems to transcend that of the facts of human experience. What pass for facts are indeed so moulded by our notions of them that recent philosophers are less and less confident in their efforts to separate the functioning of ideas from that of facts. Much has been discovered of late which serves to revolutionize the older theories of language and thinking, and to eliminate some of the age-long quandaries in which philosophers have found themselves involved. These new views can be only briefly suggested here.

The Fourth Gospel opens, "In the beginning was the Word; . . . All things were made by it; . . . In it was life; and the life was the light of men." Goethe declared that in the beginning was the deed. The most recent writers who deal with speech would seek to shed new light on civilization by recognizing that words have always been deeds. They have always been regarded as wonder-working acts; they create things which without them could never exist; they are the chief light of man—and his darkness as well.

Making noises is a conspicuous animal trait. Katydids, frogs, whippoorwills, dogs, and many other creatures exhibit a tireless patience in this matter. Man, too, is a great chatterer. His fellow men may be bored by his talk, but they are likely to be scared by his silence. It is portentous and bodes no good. To keep still is an unfriendly act. So, as Malinowski has pointed out, one of the many functions of utterances has been reassurance and the expression of companionability. The cries of animals as related to their needs and behaviour are only just beginning to be carefully studied. Whitman and Craig have discovered a marvellous correlation between the ejaculations of pigeons and their ways of life. Köhler, Yerkes and others are attending to our nearer relatives. But all that needs be noted here is that human language must have emerged from the spontaneous sounds made by pre-man.

Only when men began to make pictures of events and gestures, and painfully developed writing from the pictures, have we the least actual evidence of language. The Egyptian inscriptions illustrate picture writing and its later and most ingenious metamorphosis into sound symbols—an alphabet. This happened five or six thousand years ago. But it is clear from the Egyptian language that its surprising complexity and sophistication imply an antecedent development of incalculable length, to judge from the slowness of man's material inventions.

While the beginnings of language are hidden from us by the lapse of hundreds of thousands of unrecorded years, there are several new ways of coming to a far better understanding of them than hitherto. There are historical and contemporaneous sources of information which have been exploited of late and serve to revolutionize the older views. For example, the so-called primitive languages (until recently, never reduced to writing), afford a sufficient proof that words are fundamentally acts, closely related to man's other conduct. Then, watching the way that babies—the Latins aptly called them *infantes,* or speechless creatures—learn to talk, greatly reenforces and corroborates the evidence derived from the study of "illiterate" tribes. Lastly, anyone who has learned the trick, can substantiate the same thing if he tests the babble always going on around him.

We have already noted one way in which speech is a mode of action, a friendly gesture, not an expression of thought or conveyance of ideas as philosophers have taught us. "How do you do?" is not a question to be answered under usual circumstances. One concurs in the obvious statement, which conveys no fresh information, "Fine day, sir." These are just tailwaggings, like taking off one's hat, bowing, smiling and hand-shaking. We can, however, do far more with language; we at times can strike with a word more safely and more effectively than with our fist; by words we can cower, and dodge, and elude danger. Those in highest standing in all communities make a living by words, unwritten and written. Whole professions confine their activities to words,—clergymen, teachers (of the older type), lawyers, politicians; brokers deal in alternately saying "buy" or "sell." Doubtless other things lie behind this trafficking, but words are effective acts, or so intimately intertwined with them, that it is impossible to say where one sets in and the other ends. Pure talk and written words seem often to do the business without the intervention of so-called things. The magic operations and achievements of words can be observed everywhere and in all ages. Jacob and Esau struggled bitterly to win a blessing from their blind old father. His words were momentous. They might cause unborn generations to bow down before his son's offspring or doom him and his children to perpetual slavery.

As a clergyman of the 18th century remarked, "Words have a certain bewitchery or fascination which makes them operate with a force beyond what we can naturally give account of." Joy and infinite woe follow in their train; from which our wordless ancestors must have been spared. The main emotional structure of civilization—so poignant and so unique an element in human life—is largely reared on words. They serve to establish new orders of sensitiveness and excitability. Words increase the clarity of our memory to a tremendous degree and at the same time they vivify imagination, which could exist on no considerable scale without them. With these word-created adjuncts we can elaborate our hopes, fears, scruples, self-congratulations, jealousies, remorses and aspirations far beyond anything that seems justified to the onlooker; we can project them backward into the past and forward into the future. Words can rear more glorious palaces and dig deeper, darker dungeons than any made with hands.

Talking and Thinking

What has so far been said of the recent views of language helps to explain the newer interpretation of the old terms mind and reason. These seem to be processes, as we have seen, rather than agents. They are ways of doing things rather than things themselves. John Dewey calls his admirable little book on mind, *How We Think*. When older philosophers began to think about thinking, and how by thinking we reached truth, they commonly found themselves writing very long books, very hard to read; and they called their great theme epistemology or the theory of cognition. The effective thinking which has built up civilization has not, however, relied upon their treatises; nor has it been influenced by them. Two or three considerations only can be touched upon here which impress recent students in investigating thinking.

Thinking and words go together. For thinking, to be clear, has to rely upon names and their various associations with one another. For instance, grocer's bill, cheque-book, fountain-pen, envelope, stamp, letter-box are names put together in a particular sequence. Of late there has been a good deal of discussion as to whether thinking was not always talking quite noiselessly to ourselves. A child will first utter sounds at random, then begin to find that the sounds he makes bring things; then he gets to naming with vast enthusiasm; then he prattles too freely and inopportunely to please his elders; then he may merely move his lips—as many childish people continue to do—and finally hold his tongue. It can be shown, however, by appropriate tests that this suppressed talking is accompanied by muscular adjustments of the vocal organs which indicate a silent execution of the words and sentences. We can say openly "That's too bad," or mutter it, or adjust our organs so as to say it if we wished. This suppressed talking seems to be thinking. That all thinking is merely talking to ourselves many will doubt or deny. While some minor reservations are justifiable there is an overwhelming mass of evidence, derived for instance from the study of deaf mutes, that fortifies the contention stated above—no words, no thinking.

But thinking can easily be seen to be of several varieties. There is the meandering succession of recollections, vague apprehensions, hopes, preferences, disappointments and animosities which has come to be called *reverie*. It underlies other and more exacting forms of thinking. It is found on inspection to consist of recollections, anticipations, excuses for past or contemplated conduct, reflections on the unfairness of our fellow creatures and of the world in general; or assurances that all is well and must in the nature of things remain so. Ordinary daily planning is an essential form of thought—making homely decisions and adjustments. Underneath, we can perceive the reverie flowing as a sort of undercurrent—for thinking is very complicated.

We occasionally turn our thinking to trying to find out something that we do not yet know. This may be the result of mere personal suspicions and vulgar curiosity, or of an honest desire to improve a defective social situation, or learn more of light waves, Chinese paintings, psychoneuroses or investments. In dealing with the workings of the physical universe a special kind of thinking, the mathematical, has produced results that tend to safeguard the investigator from the usual prejudices which beset us in all thinking. It is a peculiar, highly refined language, or way of talking about things, by employing the vocabulary of sines and cosines, logarithms, constants, variables, roots, powers, etc. It has proved to be a wonderfully fruitful way of talking about light, for instance, and the nature of "matter" and "force" and in dealing with engineering problems. Few are addicted to this type or any other variety of scientific thinking. Most practical inventions seem to proceed from our power to experiment by thinking; to fumble and stumble mentally, and sometimes succeed. This mental trying-out is a kind of trial and error. It cannot proceed long without various external acts to check up the guesses and inferences produced by meditation.

One of the most novel and promising methods of learning more about all kinds of thinking is abnormal psychology. Illusional and obsessive thinking which fill the mad-houses appear to be only the exaggerations of the thinking of those at large. The psychiatrists hold out hopes of discovering through their special knowledge, and a study of infants and children, ways of eliminating or reducing some of the vices of civilization as it has hitherto developed. To them civilization is in many of its manifestations a species of mild madness; these can only be eliminated by a great change in the way children are brought up, so as to obviate the maladjustments and distress incident to a rapidly altering cultural environment.

Men and women think not only when they are awake but when they are asleep. Their sleeping thoughts and visions and experiences we have learned to set off sharply—far too sharply as it would appear—from waking thought. Primitive man did not do this. He did not deem his dreams mere illusions, comical or distressing, to be banished when he opened his eyes. They were not negligible to him but quite as real and instructive for conduct as what he saw in the day-time. Indeed they had a weight and authority superior to the pronouncements of daily experience; and they served vastly to widen it. What civilization would have been without the manifold influences of dreams it is quite impossible to guess. Had man been dreamless would he have had his religions, his symbolism and his allegories, his poetry and much of his art? This much at least is assured that the beliefs and practices of primitive peoples are in many cases directly attributable to their dreams. Later beliefs and practices of more elaborately civilized peoples can usually be traced back to primitive ideas, which seem to be the soil from which they sprang. So we have to conclude that dreams are one of the most remarkable factors that have entered into the fabrication of civilization as we know it to-day.

When asleep we find ourselves visiting distant places; for instance when walking the streets of Paris we suddenly wake in New York. How could early men escape the conviction that they had a second self which could wander forth from the body, leaving it behind in the hut, while the "spirit" led for a time an emancipated and adventurous existence freed from the slow and lumpish flesh? Then in dreams the dead appear to us in full life and activity. They may admonish or fortify us; rebuke our departure from the old ways, or fill us with assurance of success. The North American Indians shared the confidence of the ancient Hebrews and Romans in dreams. In India and China the veneration of ancestors forms a highly practical obstacle to the introduction of Western institutions. So have we here, without the possibility of much question as to the main issues, a fair explanation of the original belief in the spirit or soul and its survival of death. We have much more. We have the dawn of the gods and the demi-gods, and the whole foundation of beliefs about supernatural beings and their converse with men; their anger and the possibility of their propitiation by sacrifice.

Looking Forward

In the preceding sections of this article certain important considerations are enumerated which escaped until recently the attention of students of mankind. They are clear enough when once pointed out. But it has always been a tragic trait of civilization that the obvious has been difficult to perceive, for it is too familiar to catch our attention. It requires a peculiar penetration to discover what in all discussions we are unconsciously taking for granted. And what we are most prone to take for granted are unrevised childish impressions.

There is much complaint of the childishness of mankind, which has become more conspicuous with the democratic assumption that everyone should have his say. Langdon-Davies' *New Age of Faith,* and E. C. Ayres' *Science the False Messiah,* to cite two examples, dwell with some petulance and bitterness on the easy gullibility and obstinate ignorance of humanity. They assume standards of intelligence which obviously do not prevail, as one reads popular newspapers, sermons and political speeches. They are disappointed, but have no reason to be surprised. Why should an ex-animal not have made grotesque mistakes as he floundered about with words and besetting mysteries and hardened orthodoxies? Then, as we have seen, civilization is mainly acquired in childhood and perforce ever haunted with infantile longings and misapprehensions. When there is an issue between his dreams and visions and his waking experiences why should man not prefer the former? As a matter of fact those reputed as great and deep thinkers have dealt mainly, until very recently, with imaginary beings, with events that never happened; with empty concepts, allegories and symbols and false analogies. John Dewey has in his *Reconstruction in Philosophy* deduced philosophy and ethics from savage antecedents and shown how these have interpenetrated later speculations. The hardly to be overcome prejudice which attributes to mind and body separate existence and regards them of diverse substance is the easily explained and inevitable mistake of a savage. The will, the unconscious, the moral sense, regarded as agents, belong to the category of primitive animistic conceptions. Even causation as it used to be conceived is but an expression of the naïve urge to blame or praise some particular person or thing for this or that event. We are now learning to think in terms of situations. For example when Edward Carpenter wrote many years ago on *Civilization, its Cause and Cure,* he yielded to a venerable usage. It has become apparent enough that civilization has had no one cause but is the result of a situation of cosmic complexity. There can be no one cure for its recognized defects. A recent Italian writer, Pareto, has filled two large volumes with instances of the misapprehensions upon which current sociological treatises are based.

As humanity, or at least their leaders, become more fully aware of the nature and origin of civilization and the manner in which it has hitherto developed they will discover firmer foundations on which to build, more efficient ways of eradicating the inevitable and congenial errors of the race, and of stimulating patient and fruitful reconstruction and reform. So far mankind has stumbled along, enslaved by its past rather than liberated by it for further advances. The reasons for this are beginning to become more apparent than ever before and might as time goes on be made the basis of a type of education, especially in man's early years, which would greatly forward and direct the progress of civilization rather than retard its development.

CHAPTER SEVEN

Technology

The Machine

The emergence of modern technology can be seen as both cause and effect of the Industrial Revolution. The abundance of coal as fuel, the harnessing of steam, the arrival of a new iron age—or more correctly an age of iron and steel—the wave of invention that created new machines and unending improvements on them, and the organization of a system of factories made possible a newly efficient use of labor. This phenomenal restructuring of business, industry, the economy, and society itself coincided with the appearance of the 1st through the 7th editions of Encyclopædia Britannica. *(B.L.F.)*

At the center of the Industrial Revolution stands the machine. The subjoined excerpt from the Supplement to the 3rd edition (1801) helps us understand how people viewed machines in earlier days.

The denomination Machine is now vulgarly given to a great variety of subjects . . . but in the language of modern Europe, it seems restricted either to such tools or instruments as are employed for executing some philosophical purpose, or of which the construction employs the simple mechanical powers in a conspicuous manner, in which their operation and energy engage the attention. An electrical machine, a centrifugal machine, are of the first class; a threshing machine, a fire machine, are of the other class. It is nearly synonymous, in our language, with engine; a term altogether modern, and in some measure honourable, being bestowed only, or chiefly, on contrivances for executing work in which ingenuity and mechanical skill are manifest. . . .

By far the greatest number of our most serviceable engines consist chiefly of parts which have a motion of rotation round fixed axes, and derive all their energy from levers virtually contained in them. And these acting parts are also material, requiring force to move them, over and above what is necessary for producing the acting force at the working part of the machine. The modifications which this circumstance frequently makes of the whole motions of the machine, are indicated in the article ROTATION in an elementary way; and the propositions there investigated will be found almost continually involved in the complete theory of the operation of a machine. Lastly, it will be proper to consider attentively the propositions contained in the article STRENGTH OF MATERIALS, that we may combine them with those which relate wholly to the working of the machine; because it is from this combination only that we discover the strains which are excited at the various points of support, and of communication, and in every member of the machine. We suppose all these things already understood.

The Steam Engine

Among the pleasures to be derived from venturing through the early editions of the Britannica *is the one we think of as "being present at the creation."*

Steam engines had been around as novelties for centuries, but the first practical ones were invented by the Englishmen Thomas Savery in 1698 and Thomas Newcomen about 1712. About the time the proprietors of the first Britannica *were looking for an editor, James Watt (1736–1819) was beginning a succession of improvements that brought new and real efficiency to the steam engine, making it the power plant of the Industrial Revolution.*

Watt agreed to revise the Britannica*'s 3rd edition (1788–1797) article on steam power but died before finishing the job. His preparatory notes, relating his successful experiments, were nevertheless included in the later updating done for the 7th edition (1830–1842). These notes are presented "as is" in the first person. Here are some excerpts. (B.L.F.)*

In the winter of 1764–5, I made experiments at Glasgow on the subject, in the course of my endeavours to improve the steam-engine, and as I did not then think of any *simple* method of trying the elasticities of steam at temperatures less than that of boiling water, and had at hand a digester by which the elasticities at greater heats could be tried, I considered that, by establishing the ratios in which they proceeded, the elasticities at lower heats might be found nearly enough for my purpose. I therefore fitted a thermometer to the digester, with its bulb in the inside, placed a small cistern with mercury also within the digester, fixed a small barometer tube with its end in the mercury, and left the upper end open. I then made the digester boil for some time, the steam issuing at the safety-valve, until the air contained in the digester was supposed to be expelled. The safety-valve being shut, the steam acted upon the surface of the mercury in the cistern, and made it rise in the tube. When it reached to 15 inches above the surface of the mercury in the cistern, the heat was 236°; and at 30 inches above that surface, the heat was 252°. Here I was obliged to stop, as I had no tube longer than 34 inches, and there was no white glass made nearer than Newcastle-upon-Tyne. I therefore sealed the upper end of the tube hermetically, whilst it was empty, and when it was cool immersed the lower end in the mercury, which now could only rise in the tube by compressing the air it contained. The tube was somewhat conical; but, by ascertaining how much it was so, and making allowances accordingly, the following points were found, which, though not exact, were tolerably near for an *aperçu*. At 29½ inches (with the sealed tube) the heat

Hornblower's
STEAM ENGINE.

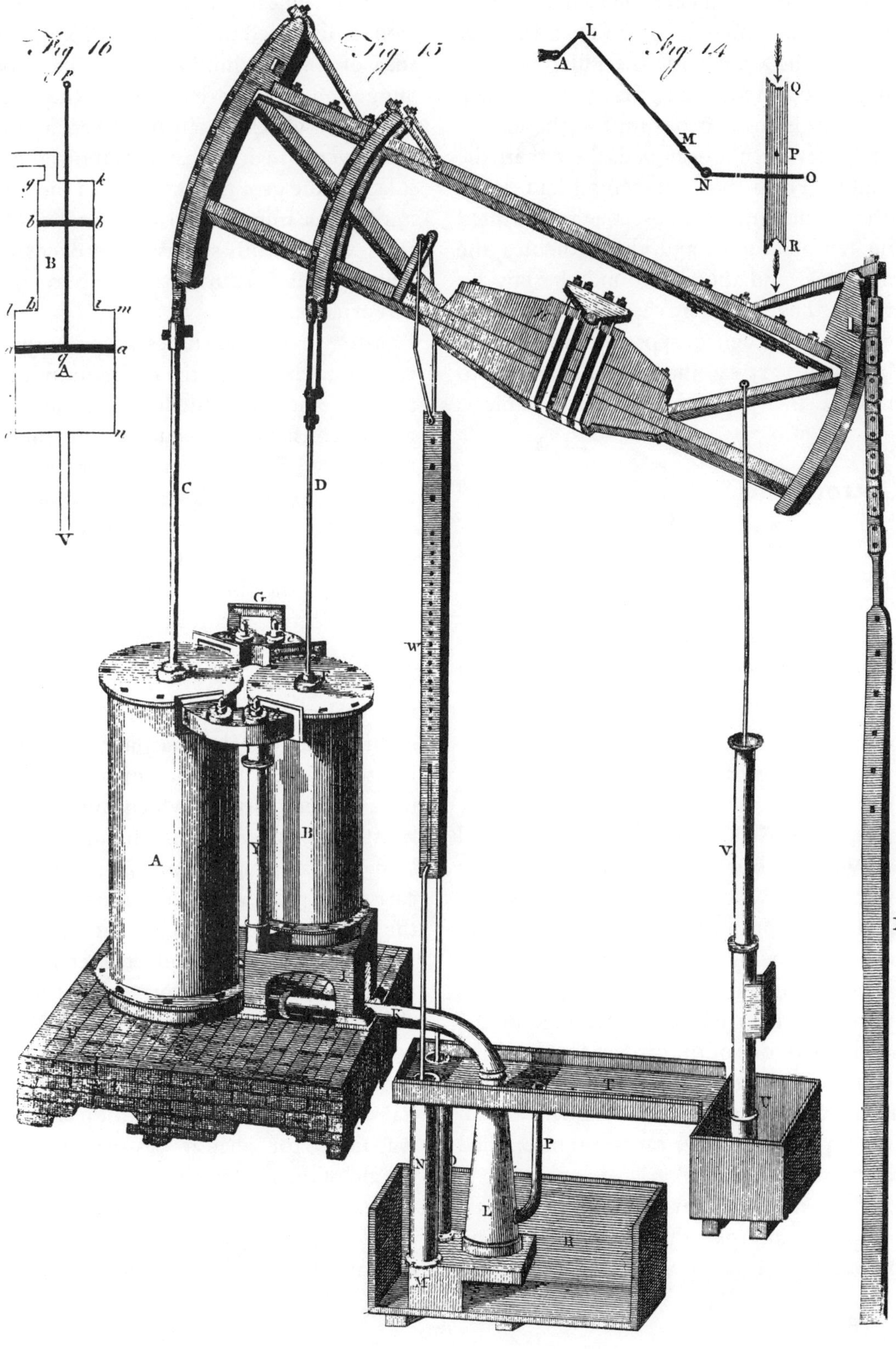

was 252°, at 75½ inches the heat was 264°, and at 110½ inches 292°. (That is, after making allowances for the pillar of mercury supported, and the pillar which would be necessary to compress the air into the space which it occupied, these were the results.) From these elements I laid down a curve, in which the abscissae represented the temperatures, and the ordinates the pressures, and thereby found the law by which they were governed, sufficiently near for my then purpose. It was not till the years 1773–4, that I found leisure to make further experiments on this subject.

Cotton Jenny

Prolific inventors contrived one improvement after another. It's interesting to note how the 7th edition (1830–1842) viewed the two great names associated with improvements in "Cotton Manufacture," the title of the article from which these excerpts are taken. (B.L.F.)

James Hargreaves, a weaver at Stanhill, near Church, in Lancashire, an illiterate man, possessed of no great mechanical knowledge, had adapted the stock cards used in the woollen manufacture, to the carding of cotton, and had besides greatly improved them. By his invention a person was able to do double the work, and with more ease than by hands carding. In the stock cards, one of the cards is fixed, whilst the other, being suspended by a cord over a pulley, is worked by the carder; and in this way two or three cards can be applied to the same stock. . . .

There had been several unsuccessful attempts to improve the mode of spinning before the year 1767, when James Hargreaves, whom we have already mentioned, invented the "*Spinning Jenny*." The idea of this machine is said to have been suggested to him by seeing a common spinning wheel which had been accidentally overturned, continue its motion while it lay on the ground. If such was the cause, it marks a mind of no common description, which from so casual an occurrence could elicit an invention of so much importance.

After several unsuccessful attempts to carry into execution the conception he had formed, he succeeded in producing a rudely constructed *jenny* of eight spindles, turned by bands from a horizontal wheel. In it the eight rovings were passed between two pieces of wood laid horizontally the breadth of the machine; and these being grasped in the spinner's hand, and drawn out by him, formed the rovings into threads. The structure of this "jenny" was soon afterwards greatly improved, and it was at last brought to work as many as eighty spindles. This machine, although of limited powers when compared with the beautiful inventions which succeeded it, must be considered as the first and leading step in that progress of discovery which carried improvement into every branch of the manufacture—which, as it proceeded, changed the nature and character of the means of production, by substituting mechanical operations for human labour—which caused the manufactured article to become more and more a product of capital. The progress of invention after this was rapid; for when it was seen that, with the aid of the few mechanical combinations we have mentioned, the spinner had been enabled to increase his power of production nearly eighty fold, the attention of those engaged in other branches of manufacture was awakened to the possibility of introducing changes equally beneficial into their peculiar employments.

Hargreaves' invention occasioned great alarm among those who earned their subsistence by the old mode of spinning, and even produced popular commotion. A mob broke into his house and destroyed his machine; and some time after, when a better knowledge of the advantage of his invention had begun to bring his "spinning jenny" into general use, the people rose a second time, and scouring the country, broke to pieces every carding and spinning machine they could find. Hargreaves himself had by this time removed to Nottingham, where he was engaged in erecting a small spinning work, about the same period that Mr Arkwright came to settle there, being also driven from Lancashire by the fear of similar violence.

The "jenny" in a short time put an end to the spinning of cotton by the common wheel, and the whole wefts used in the manufacture continued to be spun upon that machine, until the invention of the "mule jenny," by which it was in its turn superseded. Hargreaves died in great poverty a few years after his removal to Nottingham.

While Hargreaves was producing the common jenny, Mr Arkwright (afterwards Sir Richard Arkwright) was employed in contriving that wonderful piece of mechanism, the spinning frame, which, when put in motion, performs of itself the whole process of spinning, leaving to the workman only the office of supplying the material, and of joining or piecing the thread when it happens to break.

The extraordinary person to whom we owe this invention was born in the year 1732, at Preston, in Lancashire, of parents in poor circumstances, and was the youngest of thirteen children. He was brought up to the humble occupation of a barber, and up to the time when he made his discovery he continued to derive his subsistence from the exercise of this employment. Living in a manufacturing district, it is probable that his attention was drawn to the mechanical contrivances around him; and that hearing from every one complaints of the deficient supply of cotton yarn, he was stimulated to contrive a plan for increasing the production, by changing the mode of spinning. . . .

The originality of Mr Arkwright's mind, as well as the merit of his invention of the spinning frame, appear most striking when we consider the little resemblance between this machine and the common spinning wheel. His discovery did not consist in improving an instrument which already existed, but in the invention of an entirely new means for performing the same process in a better manner. When this is kept in view, it seems extraordinary that such a contrivance should have been the production of a person in his circumstances. His after inventions for preparing the cotton, which are sometimes spoken of as the most wonderful parts of the process of cotton spinning, do not appear to us so striking as this first effort of his genius.

The Invention of Gunpowder

John Macculloch, M.D., F.R.S., "late Chemist to the Board of Ordnance," brought authoritative knowledge to a treatise on "Gunpowder" which, after setting forth the history

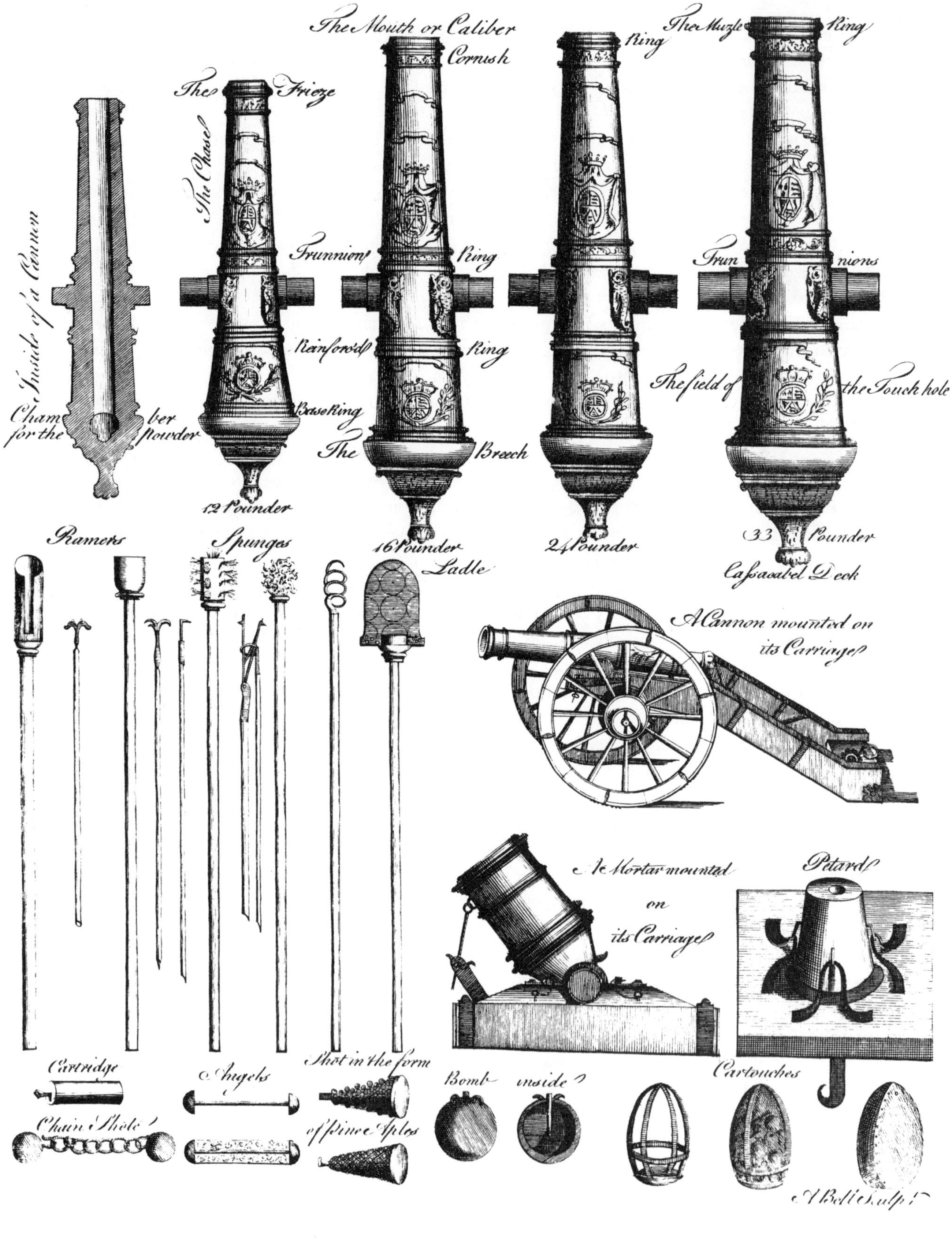
The Mouth or Caliber
Cornish
The Muzle
Ring
Ring
The Frieze
The Chase
Inside of a Cannon
Trunnions
Ring
Trun nions
Reinforc'd
Ring
The field of the Touch hole
Cham ber for the powder
Base Ring
The Breech
12 Pounder
16 Pounder
24 Pounder
33 Pounder
Ramers
Spunges
Ladle
Cascabel Deck
A Cannon mounted on its Carriage
A Mortar mounted on its Carriage
Petard
Cartridge
Angels
Shot in the form of Pine Aples
Bomb
inside
Cartouches
Chain Shot
A Bell Sculp.

of the stuff as was then known, supplied the formulas in current use by various nations. This excerpt is from the Supplement to the 4th, 5th, and 6th editions (1815–1824). (B.L.F.)

The invention of gunpowder is popularly ascribed to Barthold Schwartz, a German monk and alchemist, and the date of the discovery is further supposed to have been in 1320. The prior claims of our countryman, Roger Bacon, such as they are, are however unquestionable; as this substance is described in his writings about the year 1270; or eighty years before the time of the supposed discovery of Schwartz. But even Bacon has as little title to this invention as his supposed rival; nor, indeed, when we examine his own description of this then wonderful compound, do we perceive that he makes any claim to have been the discoverer. On the contrary, he quotes it as a well known substance, in common use all over the world for making squibs to amuse children. So pertinacious are vulgar errors. . . .

The earliest date to which we can refer the knowledge of gunpowder, in defect of a sufficiently remote acquaintance with Oriental History, is 355 A.C.; although, from the very nature of this evidence, it follows that it was then not only known to the eastern nations, but that it must have long been so; since, even at that early period, it was applied to warlike purposes. In the code of Hindoo laws, indeed, where it is mentioned, it is referred to a period which Oriental antiquaries have considered as coincident with the time of Moses.

❧ ❧ ❧

Lamps for Lighting Streets

We often complain that crime might be alleviated if our streets were better lit. It's interesting, in our technologically advanced age, to get a glimpse of how city streets were actually lighted almost two centuries ago. The subjoined excerpts are from the article "Lamps" in the Supplement to the 4th, 5th, and 6th editions (1815–1824).

Till within the last six years, the street lamps, used in London and in other parts of Britain, consisted almost uniformly of a deep inverted bell-shaped glass lantern blown of one piece, and suspended by the edge in an iron ring; with a tin conical cover perforated to give issue to the smoke, and within the lantern, a flat oil vessel with two or more wick holders or beaks, projecting from its circumference. Many districts of London are lighted with lamps of this form; other districts employ several kinds of street lamps of a different form. The first of these new kinds were made under the direction of Lord Cochrane, and employed to light the streets in the parish of Saint Anne, Soho, London.

The lanterns which serve to protect the light from wind and weather in the new lamps in one district of London, are composed of four lateral panes and a bottom of glass, joined together by sheet iron, so that the lantern is in form of a truncated pyramid, inverted like the lanterns of the street lamps in Paris. In lanterns of this form some light is intercepted, and a shadow is thrown on the street by the metal that unites the panes. This defect does not occur in the lanterns of street lamps most commonly used in England, and made of one piece of glass blown into the form of a spheroid. The spheroidal lanterns deflect the light more, because they are more unequal in thickness, but this is a smaller inconvenience: the lanterns blown of one piece of glass are more easily cleaned. Many of the lanterns for gas lights are also made of panes in the above mentioned form; some are cylindroids blown of one piece with a hole in the bottom to admit air. In some of the new lamps, in London, which have lanterns of one piece of glass, the form of the lantern is nearly cylindrical; in others, the lantern is not so deep as the lanterns of the old form. The new lamps have reflectors placed above the light, for the purpose of reflecting the light downwards on the foot pavement. These reflectors are of various forms, in some of the lamps, the four plane surfaces of the inside of the pyramidal cover of the lantern are made bright, and serve to reflect the light downwards. In other lamps the ceiling of the lantern is a reflector in form, having a small portion of a large curved surface with a chimney in the middle to give issue to the smoke. Others have two, and sometimes three, concave conoidal reflectors, whose vertices meet over the light, the axes of two of the reflectors being parallel to the direction of the street: at the point where the reflectors meet there is a chimney through which the smoke ascends. The reflectors require to be frequently wiped in order to keep them bright. . . .

In England whale oil is used as the combustible material in the streetlamps; of late naptha, obtained from the distillation of pit coal, has been used in a district of London which is lighted with Major Cochrane's lamps. This naptha is a clear and colourless liquid, and is found to give a good light; it requires to be prepared with particular attention; that made at the gas light work is said to be too easily inflammable. In Paris rape seed oil, and poppy seed oil, are used: these expressed oils are made in the north-eastern part of France and in Flanders. In the south of Europe olive oil of inferior quality and walnut oil are used. Street lamps lighted with the gas distilled from pit coal are now (1821) employed in the principal streets of London, Edinburgh, Glasgow, Liverpool, Manchester, Birmingham, Sheffield, and other cities in Britain. The use of coal gas for giving light had made very little progress in France in 1818, being scarcely employed even in Paris, and we believe not at all at Lyons, although pit coal is abundant and commonly used as fuel there.

The Art and Science of Measurement

Along with a host of technological contrivances to do things better, faster, easier, and less expensively, one of the most important products of the Scientific Revolution was the invention and improvement of devices to measure accurately. These advances, which amounted to a technological revolution, in turn helped amplify and extend the Scientific Revolution itself, and made possible the Industrial Revolution.

A number of the basic measuring instruments are addressed here.

In the first edition (1768–1771) precision was, to a considerable extent, more literary than physical. As for uniformity . . . (B.L.F.)

ACRE, a measure of land used in several provinces of France, particularly in

Plate CIV.

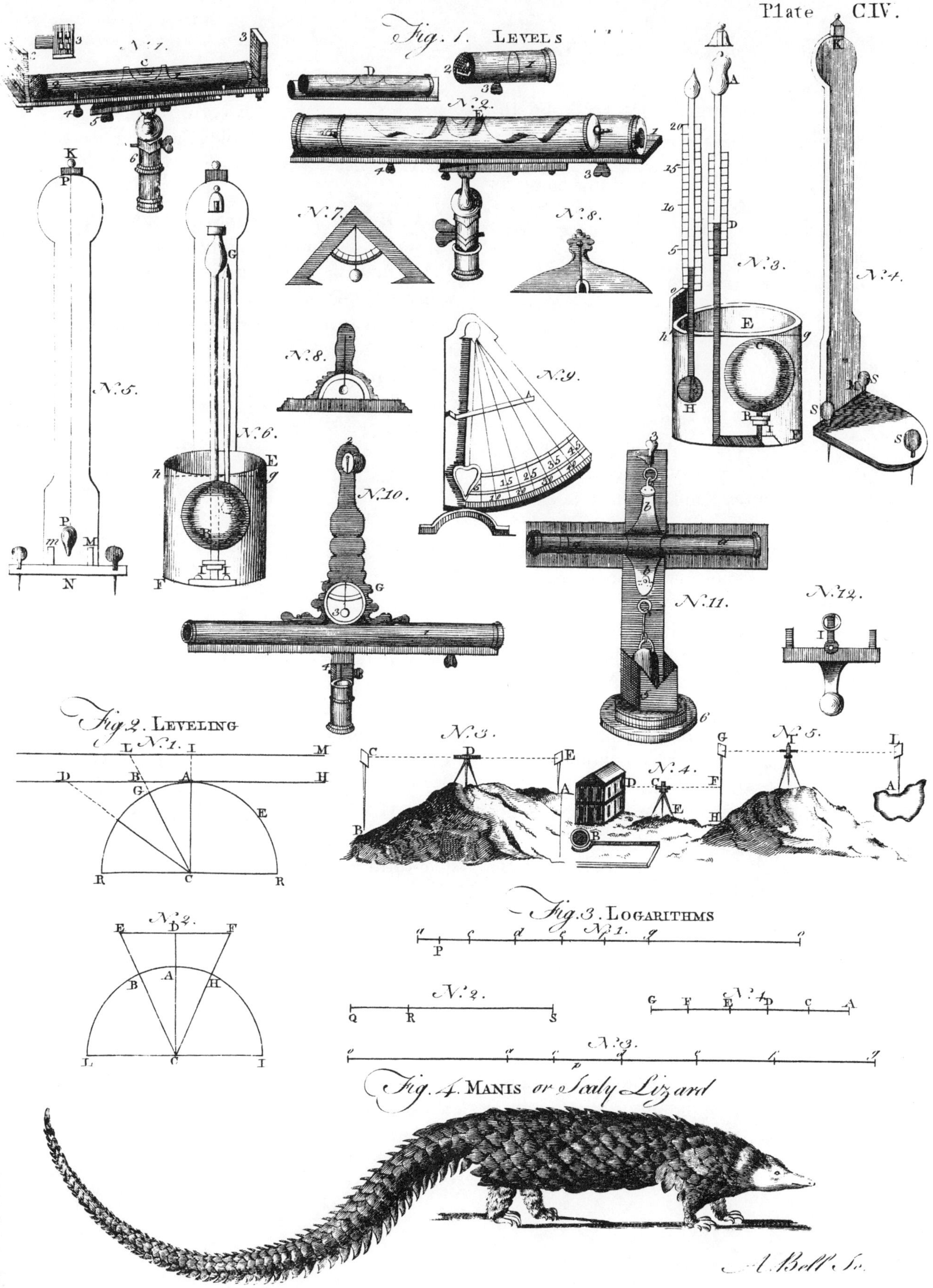
Fig. 1. Levels
N.º 1.
N.º 2.
N.º 3.
N.º 4.
N.º 5.
N.º 6.
N.º 7.
N.º 8.
N.º 8.
N.º 9.
N.º 10.
N.º 11.
N.º 12.
Fig. 2. Leveling
N.º 1.
N.º 2.
N.º 3.
N.º 4.
N.º 5.
Fig. 3. Logarithms
N.º 1.
N.º 2.
N.º 3.
N.º 4.
Fig. 4. Manis or Scaly Lizard
A. Bell Sc.

Normandy. It is larger or less according to the different places; but commonly contains 160 perches.

THE ACRE OF WOODS IN FRANCE, consists of four roods, called *vergies;* the rood is 40 perches, the perch 24 feet, the foot 12 inches, the inch 12 lines.

ACRE, the universal measure of land in Britain. An acre in England contains 4 square roods, a rood 40 perches or poles of 16½ feet each by statute. Yet this measure does not prevail in all parts of England, as the length of the pole varies in different counties, and is called *customary measure,* the difference running from the 16½ feet to 28. The acre is also divided into 10 square chains, of 22 yards each, that is 4840 square yards. An acre in Scotland contains 4 square roods; 1 square rood is 40 square falls; 1 square fall, 36 square ells; 1 square ell, 9 square feet, and 73 square inches; 1 square foot, 144 square inches. The Scots acre is also divided into 10 square chains; the measuring chain should be 24 ells in length, divided into 100 links, each link 8 inches; and so 1 square chain will contain 10,000 square links.

The English statute acre is about 3 roods and 6 falls standard measure of Scotland.

GALLON, a measure of capacity both for dry and liquid things, containing four quarts; but these quarts, and consequently the gallon itself, are different, according to the quality of the thing measured: for instance, the wine gallon contains 231 cubic inches, and holds eight pounds averdupois, of pure water: the beer and ale gallon contains 282 solid inches, and holds ten pounds three ounces and a quarter averdupois, of water: and the gallon for corn, meal, etc. 272¼ cubic inches, and holds nine pounds thirteen ounces of pure water.

MILE, *mille passus,* a measure of length or distance, containing eight furlongs, etc.

The English statute-mile is fourscore chains, or 1760 yards; that is, 5280 feet.

We shall here give a table of the miles in use among the principal nations of Europe, in geometrical paces, 60,000 of which make a degree of the equator.

	Geometrical paces.
Mile of Russia	750
of Italy	1000
of England	1250
of Scotland and Ireland	1500
Old league of France	1500
The small league, *ibid.*	2000
The mean league, *ibid.*	2500
The great league of France	3000
Mile of Poland	3000
of Spain	3248
of Germany	4000
of Denmark	5000
of Hungary	6000

INCH, a well known measure of length; being the twelfth part of a foot, and equal to three barley-corns in length.

Two centuries (and more) supplied not only better perspective but explicit accuracy. Here's how the current 15th edition handles "Inch."

INCH, unit of British Imperial and U.S. Customary measure equal to 1/36 of a yard. The unit derives from the old English *unce,* or *ynche,* which came from the Latin *uncia,* meaning "one-twelfth." (The same Latin word was the source of another English unit name, the ounce.) The old En-

RAMSDENS Machine *for dividing Mathimatical Instruments*

Plate CCLV

Fig. 1.

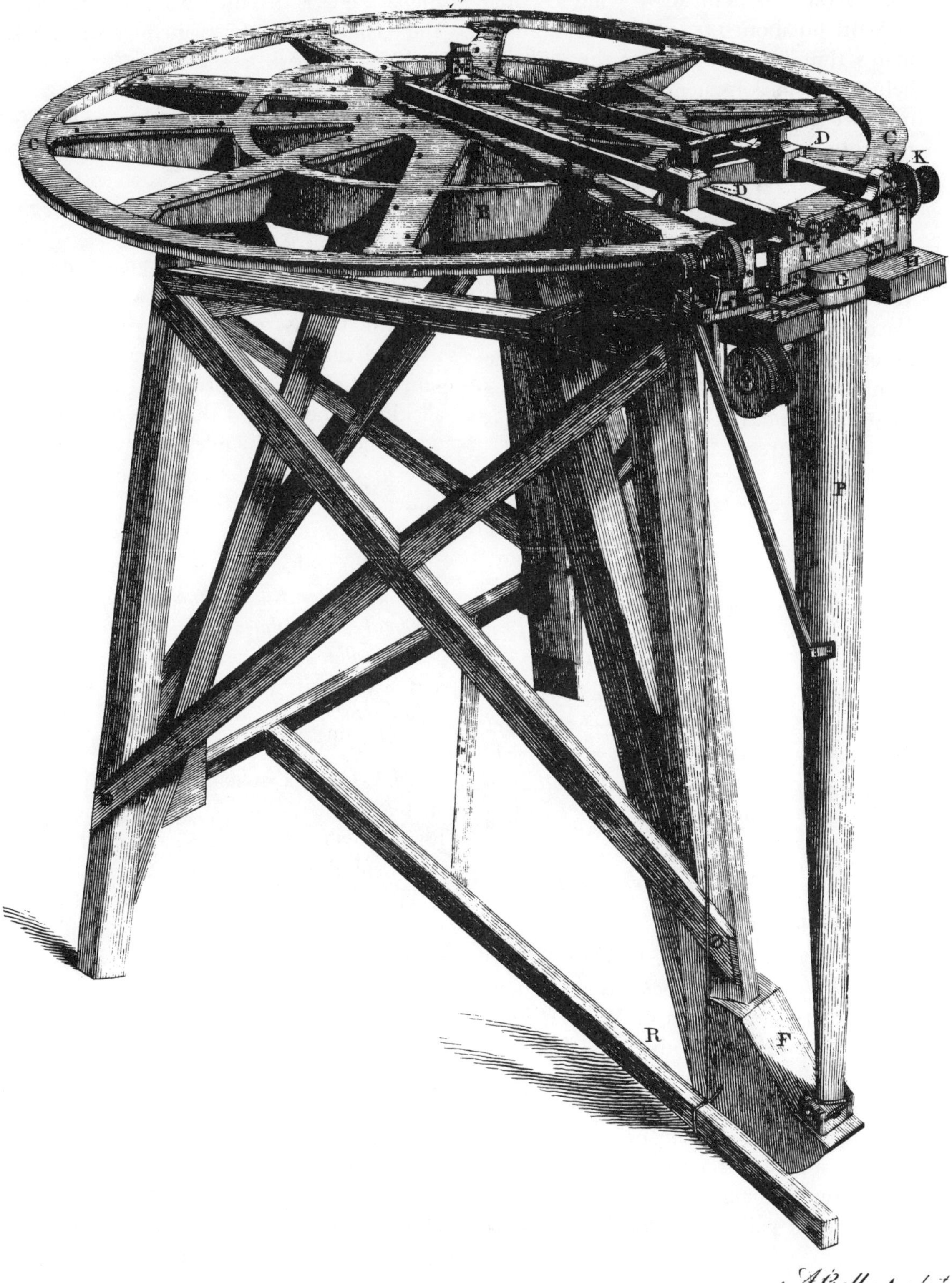

A Bell Sculp^t.

glish *ynche* was defined by King David I of Scotland about 1150 as the breadth of a man's thumb at the base of the nail. To help maintain consistency of the unit, the measure was usually achieved by adding the thumb breadth of three men—one small, one medium, and one large—and then dividing the figure by three. During the reign of King Edward II, in the early 14th century, the inch was defined as "three grains of barley, dry and round, placed end to end lengthwise." At various times the inch has also been defined as the combined lengths of 12 poppyseeds. Since 1959 the inch has been defined officially as 2.54 centimetres.

Time

The accurate measurement of time was also of critical importance to the advancement of science, and the editor of the 1st edition (1768–1771) was at some pains to explain how clocks worked. But the necessary article—or perhaps the engravings to illustrate it—was not ready when the alphabetical sequence of publication arrived at the Cs in middle or late 1769. As a result, we have:

CLOCK, a kind of movement, or machine, serving to measure time.

The invention of clocks is attributed to Pacificus, archdeacon of Verona, who lived in the time of Lotharius: others ascribe it to Boethius, about the year 510: be that as it will, it is certain, that the art of making clocks, such as are now in use, was either first invented, or at least retrieved in Germany, about 230 years ago; and the invention of pendulum clocks, so late as the last age, is disputed between Huygens and Galileo. For the principles of Clock and Watch Work, see WATCH.

By the end of 1771 the research and artwork were complete.

CLOCKWORK

A clock is a machine constructed in such a manner, and regulated by such uniform movements, as to measure time and all its subdivisions with great exactness. The same definition comprehends watches of all kinds; and indeed they are both made upon the same principles. We shall therefore give a view of both these machines under this article.

The article then went on for two full pages detailing the construction of a clock operated by a weight and regulated by a pendulum.

The editor of the 2nd edition (1778–1783) was more precise and provided more historical information.

CLOCK, a machine constructed in such a manner, and regulated by such uniform movements, as to measure time, and all its subdivisions, with great exactness.

The invention of clocks with wheels is referred to Pacificus, archdeacon of Verona, who lived in the time of Lotharius son of Louis the Debonnair, on the credit of an epitaph quoted by Ughelli, and borrowed by him from Panvinius. They were at first called nocturnal dials, to distinguish them from sun-dials, which shewed the hour by the sun's shadow. Others ascribe the invention to Boethius, about the year 510.

. . . It is certain that the art of making

CLOCK and WATCH-WORK.

Plate LXXX.

Fig. 1.

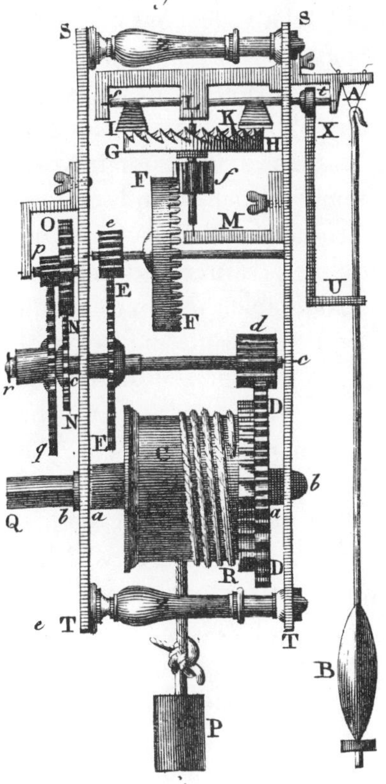

Fig. 2.

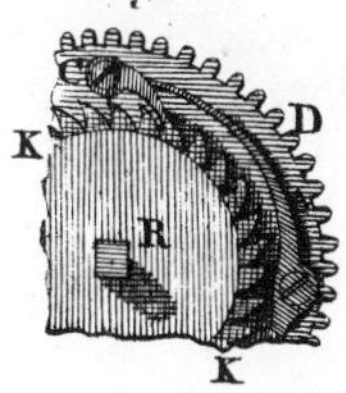

Fig. 3.

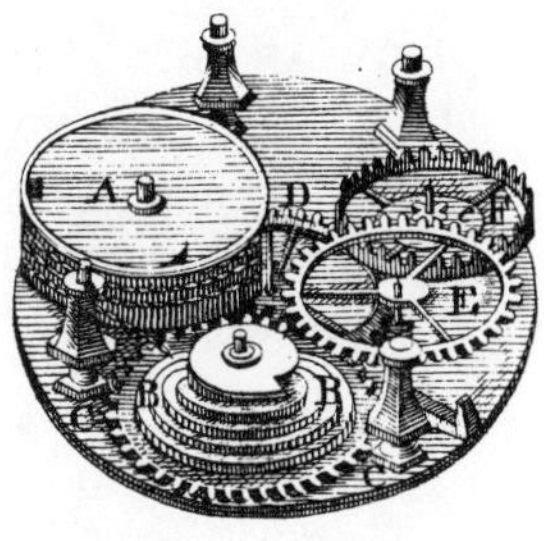

Fig. 4.

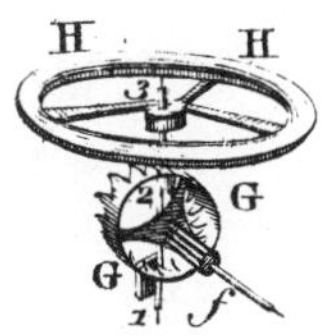

Fig. 5.

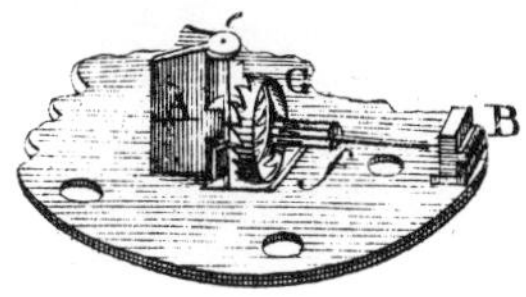

Fig. 6.

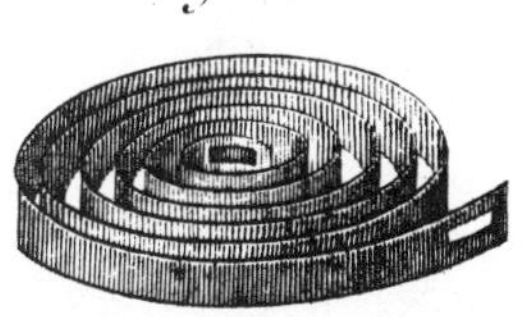

Fig. 7.

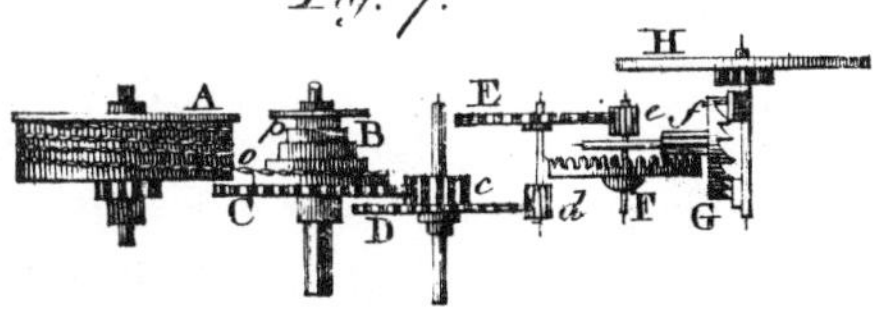

Fig. 8.

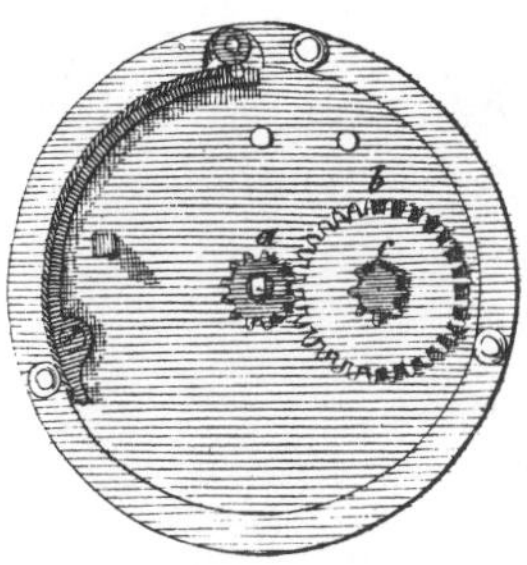

Fig. 9.

Fig. 10.

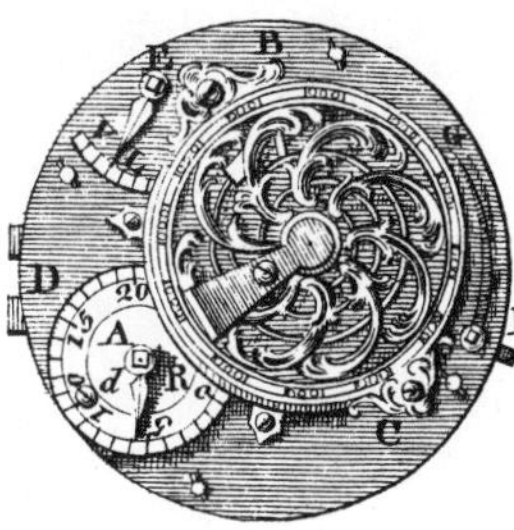

Fig. 11.

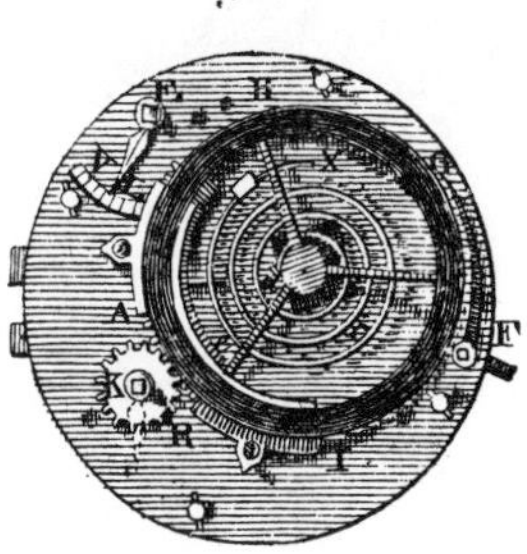

Fig. 12.

Fig. 13.

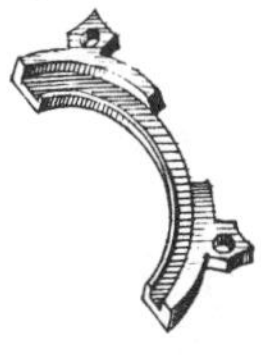

Fig. 14.

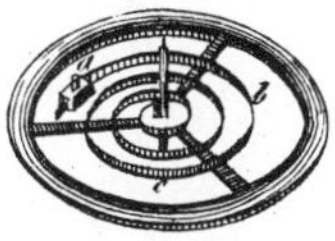

Fig. 15.

Fig. 16.

A. Bell Sc.

clocks, such as are now in use, was either first invented, or at least retrieved, in Germany about 200 years ago. The water-clocks, or clepsydrae, and sun-dials, have both a much better claim to antiquity. . . .

The invention of pendulum-clocks is owing to the happy industry of the last age: the honour of it is disputed by Huygens and Galileo. The former, who has written a volume on the subject, declares it was first put in practice in the year 1657, and the description thereof printed in 1658. . . .

But his additional research also turned up lore and descriptions he could not resist sharing. (B.L.F.)

The first pendulum-clock made in England, was in the year 1622, by Mr Fromantil a Dutchman.

Amongst the modern clocks, those of Strasburg and Lyons are very eminent for the richness of their furniture, and the variety of their motions and figures. In the first, a cock claps his wings, and proclaims the hour; the angel opens a door, and salutes the virgin; and the holy Spirit descends on her, etc. In the second, two horsemen encounter, and beat the hour on each other: a door opens, and there appears on the theatre the virgin, with Jesus Christ in her arms; the magi, with their retinue, marching in order, and presenting their gifts; two trumpeters sounding all the while to proclaim the procession. These, however, are excelled by two lately made by English artists, and intended as a present from the East India company to the emperor of China. The clocks we speak of are in the form of chariots, in which are placed, in a fine attitude, a lady, leaning her right hand upon a part of the chariot, under which is a clock of curious workmanship, little larger than a shilling, that strikes and repeats, and goes eight days. Upon her finger sits a bird finely modelled, and set with diamonds and rubies, with its wings expanded in a flying posture, and actually flutters for a considerable time on touching a diamond button below it; the body of the bird (which contains part of the wheels that in a manner give life to it) is not the bigness of the 16th part of an inch. The lady holds in her left hand a gold tube not much thicker than a large pin, on the top of which is a small round box, to which a circular ornament set with diamonds not larger than a sixpence is fixed, which goes round near three hours in a constant regular motion. Over the lady's head, supported by a small fluted pillar no bigger than a quill, is a double umbrella, under the largest of which a bell is fixed at a considerable distance from the clock, and seems to have no connection with it; but from which a communication is secretly conveyed to a hammer, that regularly strikes the hour, and repeats the same at pleasure, by touching a diamond button fixed to the clock below. At the feet of the lady is a gold dog; before which from the point of the chariot are two birds fixed on spiral springs; the wings and feathers of which are set with stones of various colours, and appear as if flying away with the chariot, which, from another secret motion, is contrived to run in a straight, circular, or any other direction; a boy that lays hold of the chariot behind, seems also to push it forward. Above the umbrella are flowers, and ornaments of pearls, rubies, and other precious stones; and it terminates with a flying dragon set in the same manner. The whole is of gold, most curiously executed, and embellished with gold, rubies, and pearls.

The Barometer

Measurement of atmospheric pressure was so essential to physical experimentation that Evangelista Torricelli's invention of the barometer in the early seventeenth century was one of the most important opening wedges of the Scientific Revolution. Every edition of the Britannica *had an article on the subject, and hosts of other articles treating physics dealt in passing with barometric measurements. In a long disquisition in the Supplement to the 4th, 5th, and 6th editions (1815–1824), the great physicist John Leslie reviewed the literature on this important subject; in his opening paragraph he rather grandly disparaged the earlier efforts. (B.L.F.)*

The *Encyclopaedia* contains such an account of the discovery and construction of this most valuable instrument, as could be drawn from the popular treatises of natural philosophy in the English language. But, unfortunately, our compilers of elementary works have seldom taken the trouble to remount to the original sources of information, and have frequently, by substituting their own fancies, or servilely copying the mistakes of others, contrived to disfigure egregiously the relation of facts, and the history of the progress of invention. We now purpose, therefore, as far as our limits will admit, to remodel the article; and, passing rather slightly over the description of the different kinds of barometers, and other practical details already given, to dwell more especially on the successive steps which led to the fine discovery of atmospheric pressure, and its application to physical science. . . .

In the course of his article Leslie described Blaise Pascal's various influential experiments with Torricelli's barometer, and then went on, in fine Protestant dudgeon against the Church of Rome, to recount some of young Pascal's resulting tribulations with the Jesuits. (B.L.F.)

Pascal, then only twenty-four years of age, proposed to write a treatise on the subject of those inquiries; but thought proper, in the meantime, to publish a short abstract of it, which appeared in 1647, and involved him in a wretched controversy. Father Nöel, rector of the Jesuits' College at Paris, keenly attacked it, armed with all the miserable sophisms of the schools, and the absurd dogmas of the Romish church. He contended, that the space above the mercurial column was corporeal, because it was visible and admitted light; that a void being a mere non-entity, cannot have different degrees of magnitude; that the separation produced in the experiments was violent and unnatural; and he presupposed that the atmosphere, like blood, containing a mixture of the several elements, the fire and the finer part of the air were detached from it, and violently forced through the pores of the glass, to occupy the deserted space. To enforce these puerile arguments, the reverend Jesuit did not scruple to employ the poisoned weapon which his order has often wielded with deadly effect,—the hinting an oblique charge of heresy. This rude attack only roused Pascal, and disposed him boldly to throw off the fetters of inveterate opinion. . . .

But Pascal did not rest satisfied with mere reasoning, however strictly conducted; and he soon devised an experiment which should palpably mark, under different circumstances, the varying effects of atmospheric pressure. It occurred to him, that, if the mercury in the Torricellian tube were really supported by the counterpoising weight of the atmosphere, it would be affected by the mass of superincumbent fluid, and must therefore partially subside in the higher elevations. He was impatient to have his conjecture tried in a favourable situation, and, in November 1647, he wrote a letter communicating those views to his brother-in-law, Perier, who filled an office of considerable trust in the province, and commonly resided at Clermont in Auvergne, in the immediate vicinity of the Puy de Dôme, a lofty conical mountain, which rose, according to estimation, above the altitude of 500 toises. Various avocations, however, prevented that intelligent person from complying with his instructions, till the following year. Early in the morning of the 19th of September 1648, a few curious friends joined him in the garden of a monastery, situate near the lowest part of the city of Clermont, where he had brought a quantity of mercury, and two glass tubes hermetically sealed at the top. These he filled and inverted, as usual, and found the mercury to stand in both at the same height, namely, 26 inches and 3¾ lines, or 28 English inches. Leaving one of the tubes behind, in the custody of the subprior, he proceeded with the other to the summit of the mountain, and repeated the experiment, when his party were surprised and delighted to see the mercury sink more than three inches under the former mark, and remain suspended at the height of 23 inches and 2 lines, or 24.7 English inches. In his descent from the mountain, he observed, at two several stations, that the mercury successively rose; and, on his return to the monastery, he found it stood exactly at the same point as at first. Encouraged by the success of this memorable experiment, Perier repeated it on the highest tower of Clermont, and noted a difference of two lines at an elevation of 20 toises. Pascal, on his part, as soon as the intelligence reached him at Paris, where he then chanced to be, made similar observations on the top of a high house, and in the belfry of the church of St Jacques des Boucheries, near the border of the Seine; and so much was he satisfied with the results, that he proposed already the application of the barometer for measuring the relative height of distant places on the surface of the globe.

The investigation of the existence and effects of atmospheric pressure was now completed, and it threw a sudden blaze over the whole contexture of physical science.

Make Your Own Telescope

Continuing progress in astronomy relied heavily on advances in the development of telescopes, and in the early nineteenth century such activity was widespread. At this time the Britannica *was an important medium for disseminating knowledge of new improvements not only to laymen and amateurs but also to astronomers themselves. The great English astronomer Sir John F. W. Herschel (1792–1871), in his article "Telescope" for the 8th edition (1852–1860), shared useful information on fabricating the speculum or mirror for a reflecting telescope—spiced with a tart critical comment on the work of one of his colleagues. (B.L.F.)*

. . . The raw material of metallic specula at present in use is an alloy of pure copper with pure tin. . . . In making the mixture it is indispensable to cast the metal first into ingots, and then to remelt it (which requires a much lower heat than that required for the first melting, which must be that of melting copper), adding a small quantity of tin to replace that destroyed by oxidation, and stirring the melted metal before pouring with a wooden pole (as in the "poleing" of copper castings).

The destruction of the more brittle metal, by cracking in a close mould, is owing to the violent tension induced in the internal portions of the mass by the simultaneous fixation of the *whole external crust,* while the interior remains fluid, and which cannot then contract in dimension without solution of continuity. Mr Potter (Brewster's *Jour.,* N.S. iv. 18, 1831), by casting the metal into a mould, the lower surface of which consisted of a thick mass of steel, succeeded in determining the rapid fixation of the lower surface, and the subsequent abstraction of the heat by conduction through it in the same direction, and thus solidifying the mass in successive strata from below upwards, allowing each new stratum to accommodate itself in some degree to the already contracted state of the previous one. Dr Macculloch (*Journ. of Science,* June 1828) had previously recommended quick cooling to the fixing point, not to obviate fracture, but to prevent crystallization, but without a word as to the mode of accomplishing it.[1]

1. In all other respects his paper is a wonderful example of what a multitude of words can do towards obliterating meaning.

The Continuing Revolution in Communication

It is not hard to argue that the communication revolution began with Gutenberg, but that until the age of unceasing technological change was ushered in by the Scientific and Industrial Revolutions, substantive improvements in printing, such as cutting type from metal instead of wood, were relatively modest. Basic printing methods were described in the following extract from the 2nd edition (1778–1783), which was followed by a history of the art, taking note of Far Eastern developments not known with certainty in the West. (B.L.F.)

To all those who have ever worked on Encyclopædia Britannica, *as has the General Editor of this book, the second subjoined paragraph will be felt as a statement moving in its aptness and concision.*

PRINTING, the art of taking impressions from characters or figures, moveable and immoveable, on paper, linen, silk, etc. There are three kinds of printing: the one from moveable letters, for books; another from copper-plates, for pictures; and the last from blocks, in which the representation of birds, flowers, etc. are cut, for printing calicoes, linen, etc. The first is called *common* or *letter-press* printing; the second, *rolling-press* printing; and the last, *calico,* etc. printing. The principal difference between the three consists in this, that the first is cast in relievo, in distinct pieces; the second engraven in creux; and the third cut in relievo, and generally stamped, by placing the block upon the materials to be printed, and striking upon the back of it.

LETTER-PRESS PRINTING

Of the above branches, this is the most curious, and deserves the most particular notice; for to it are owing chiefly our deliverance from ignorance and error, the progress of learning, the revival of the sciences, and numberless improvements in arts, which, without this noble invention, would have been either lost to mankind, or confined to the knowledge of a few.

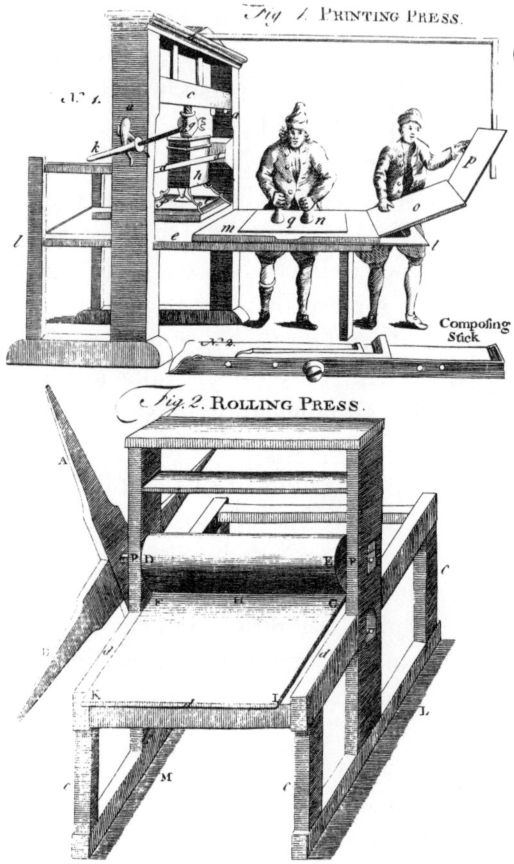

Magazines in the Eighteenth Century

A major beneficiary of the advances in printing was the periodical press. The state of that institution in eighteenth-century Britain was assessed by the pious editor and future bishop George Gleig. He wrote this critique about 1799. The Reign of Terror and the de-Christianization (however brief) of France were in the immediate past, and Napoleon was about to seize power. This explains his stern word for France. Note the rectitudinous dismissal of the Monthly Magazine. *Excerpts are from the Supplement to the 3rd edition (1801). (B.L.F.)*

JOURNALS, the title of periodical publications. *See* ENCYCLOPEDIA. The principal British Journals are: *The History of the Works of the Learned,* begun at London in 1699. *Censura Temporum,* in 1708. About the same time there appeared two new ones; the one under the title of *Memoirs of Literature,* containing little more than an English translation of some articles in the foreign Journals, by M. de la Roche; the other, a collection of loose tracts, intitled, *Bibliotheca Curiosa,* or a Miscellany. These, however, with some others, are now no more, but are succeeded by the *Annual Register,* which began in 1758; the *New Annual Register,* begun in 1780; the *Monthly Review,* which began in the year 1749, and gives a character of all English literary publications, with the most considerable of the foreign ones: the *Critical Review,* which began in 1756, and is nearly on the same plan: as also the *London Review,* by Dr Kenrick, from 1775 to 1780; *Maty's Review,* from Feb. 1782 to Aug. 1786; the *English Review,* begun in Jan. 1783; and the *Analytical Review,* begun in May 1788, dropt in 1798, and revived in 1799, under the title of the *New Analytical Review;* but again dropt after two or three months trial: the *British Critic,* begun in 1792, and still carried on with much spirit and ability; the *Anti-Jacobin Review and Magazine,* commenced in 1798, for the meritorious purpose of counteracting the pernicious tendency of French principles in politics and religion: the *New London Review,* January 1799; *A Journal of Natural Philosophy, Chemistry, and the Arts,* which was begun in 1797 by Mr Nicholson, and has been conducted in such a manner, that it is one of the most valuable works of the kind to be found in any language; the *Philosophical Magazine,* begun in 1798 by Mr Tilloch, and carried on upon much the same plan, and with much the same spirit, as Nicholson's Journal.

Besides these, we have several monthly pamphlets, called *Magazines,* which, together with a chronological series of occurrences, contain letters from correspondents, communicating extraordinary discoveries in nature and art, with controversial pieces on all subjects. Of these, the principal are those called the *Gentleman's Magazine,* which began with the year 1731; the *London Magazine,* which began a few months after, and has lately been discontinued; the *Universal Magazine,* which is nearly of as old a date; the *Scotch Magazine,* which began in 1739, and is still continued; the *European Magazine;* and the *Monthly Magazine,* a miscellany of much information, but not of good principles.

"A Disgrace to the Country"

A distinguished journalist, James Browne (1793–1841), editor of the Scots Magazine *and later of the* Caledonian Mercury, *had a kind word for both magazines and newspapers. However, he took a very harsh view of the press in America. The reader may wish to compare it with the judgments expressed in the current edition, where newspapers are considered under the more general rubric "Publishing." The following excerpts are from the 7th edition (1830–1842) under "Newspapers."*

One of the most remarkable characteristics of modern, as compared with ancient times, is the periodical press, an engine affecting society in all its relations, and forming one of the most important safeguards of public liberty. Under this head are usually included reviews, magazines, and other publications of a similar kind, as well as newspapers. But although, upon certain grave and important questions, the former sort of periodicals may contribute more to enlighten the public mind, and to guide public opinion into safe and proper channels; yet the wide diffusion of newspapers, their rapid communication of intelligence on subjects of immediate interest, their hasty and rough but often vigorous comments on the leading events of the day, and the means which they thus afford of acting immediately and constantly upon the public mind, in all its varied states, render them much more powerful as instruments of political influence, and thus secure to them a prominence to which, intrinsically, they are by no means entitled. They circulate every kind of information with equal celerity and regularity; they bring to every man's home and fireside intelligence of all that is passing in the great world, whether at home or abroad, in war, in politics, in government, in commerce, and in the common affairs of life; they are registers of extraordinary events, as well as of ordinary occurrences, of discoveries and inventions, as well as accidents, offences, calamities, or crimes;

they often diversify their contents with scientific and literary notices; and from the variety of facts and information which they contain, they are indispensable to many classes of society, and more or less agreeable or instructive to all. . . .

The increase of newspapers in the United States has been much more rapid than in England. The total number of newspapers annually issued in the Union has been estimated at from 55,000,000 to 60,000,000, whereas the total number issued in Great Britain and Ireland during the year 1833 was only 34,515,221. It follows that, making allowance for the difference of population, every individual in America has, at an average, more than twice the supply of newspapers enjoyed by each person in England. From the low price of the American, as compared with the English and even the French newspapers, they are liberally patronised by all classes, and are to be seen in almost every dwelling and counting-house, and in all hotels, taverns, and shops. But we must not estimate the value nor the influence of newspapers by their quantity alone. Regard must likewise be had to its quality, which indeed is the principal consideration to be attended to. But in whatever degree the American may exceed the English or French journals in number, they sink immeasurably below them in point of quality. In the United States the state of the newspaper press is such that it can scarcely descend lower; indeed it may be considered as a disgrace to the country. These journals, with but few exceptions, indulge in the most offensive, and often brutal personalities. Instead of examining the principles of measures, they assail the character and misrepresent the motives of those by whom they are introduced; and, in fact, it would be difficult to name an individual of any distinction who has not been libelled and calumniated by a large portion of the press, to a degree which can scarcely be imagined. The magnitude of the evil, however, will in all probability lead to its cure. It can scarcely be supposed that an intelligent and well-instructed people will long continue to patronise a press which traffics in misrepresentation, scurrility, and exaggeration, and which, besides the outrages it commits against individuals, opposes a serious obstacle to wise government and well-considered improvement.

The Typewriter

At a time when the typewriter is being supplanted by the word-processor and the personal computer, it's salutary to reflect that the typewriter was once a revolutionary invention. Early Britannicas *followed its development with professional interest. This extract is from "Writing Machines," 9th edition (1875–1889).*

The principal substitute for the pen, however, is the machine now generally known as the type-writer, which in its present form dates only from 1873, but it has within that time come into extensive use, especially in America, the country of its origin. Numerous attempts to produce type-writing machines had been previously made both in England and America. So long ago as 1714 one Henry Mill took out a patent for a machine which he described as "an artificial machine or method for the impressing or transcribing of letters, singly or progressively, one after another as in writing, whereby all writings whatsoever may be engrossed in paper or parchment so neat and exact as not to be distinguished from print"; but his instrument is said to have been clumsy and useless, and led to no practical result. In 1867 the idea was taken up by Messrs C. Latham Sholes and Samuel W. Soulé, printers in Milwaukee, and Mr Carlos Glidden, and, after many experiments and failures, a practical working machine was elaborated in 1873, which, being originally made by Messrs E. Remington and Sons, of Ilion, N.Y., is known as the Remington standard type-writer. The success of this machine has induced many inventors to enter the field, and now three principal classes of type-writers are more or less in use. These are (1) type-bar machines, (2) cylinder machines, and (3) wheel machines. The Remington is the type and original of all type-bar machines, which are so called because the steel types are fixed at the extremity of a bar or rod of iron. These bars are in the Remington arranged in a circle around a common centre, and by striking the key of any particular letter, a lever is moved which raises the type-bar, and causes the type at its point to strike on an inked ribbon, and impresses the letter on the paper, which lies against an india-rubber roller. The type-bars are so hinged that all the types as they are struck hit precisely the same spot, so that were the paper to remain stationary the impressions of all the types struck would be superimposed on each other; but, by an automatic mechanism, the cylinder with the paper moves a space to the left after the impression of each type, and the depression of a wooden bar similarly moves the cylinder a space after each word without impressing any sign. In the recent forms of the Remington machine, each type bar carries two types, capital and lower case, or other duplicate signs, the one a little behind the other, and when a capital letter is to be printed the depression of a key shifts the position of the cylinder so as to bring the second type in contact with the ink ribbon. In this way from one set of keys two sets of type can be with facility acted upon. With practice, an average writing speed of forty words per minute can easily be attained on the Remington type-writer, and very expert writers have been able to keep up a speed of from sixty to seventy words for a short time. It is safe to say that type-writing can be ordinarily done at about three times the speed of ordinary handwriting.

The Telegraph

Since the most ancient times, the keenest interest has attended efforts to speed communication across long distances. Hence the telegraph. These extracts are from the article "Telegraph," 3rd edition (1788–1797). (B.L.F.)

TELEGRAPH (derived from πηλε and γραφω), is the name very properly given to an instrument, by means of which information may be almost instantaneously conveyed to a considerable distance.

The telegraph, though it has been generally known and used by the moderns only for a few years, is by no means a modern invention. There is reason to believe that amongst the Greeks there was some sort of telegraph in use. The burning of Troy was certainly known in Greece very soon after it happened, and before any person had returned from thence. . . .

About 40 years afterwards M. Amontons proposed a new telegraph. His method was this: Let there be people placed in several stations, at such a distance from one another, that by the help of a telescope a man in one station may see a signal made in the next before him; he must immediately make the same signal, that it may be seen by persons in the station next after him, who are to communicate it to those in the following station, and so on. These signals may be as letters of the alphabet, or as a cipher, understood only by the two persons who are in the distant places, and not by those who make the signals. . . .

It was not, however, till the French revolution that the telegraph was applied to useful purposes. Whether M. Chappe, who is said to have invented the telegraph first used by the French about the end of 1793, knew any thing of Amontons's invention or not, it is impossible to say; but his telegraph was constructed on principles nearly similar. The manner of using this telegraph was as follows: At the first station, which was on the roof of the palace of the Louvre at Paris, M. Chappe, the inventor, received in writing, from the committee of public welfare, the words to be sent to Lisle, near which the French army at that time was. An upright post was erected on the Louvre, at the top of which were two transverse arms, moveable in all directions by a single piece of mechanism, and with inconceivable rapidity. He invented a number of positions for these arms, which stood as signs for the letters of the alphabet; and these, for the greater celerity and simplicity, he reduced in number as much as possible. The grammarian will easily conceive that sixteen signs may amply supply all the letters of the alphabet, since some letters may be omitted not only without detriment but with advantage. These signs, as they were arbitrary, could be changed every week; so that the sign of B for one day might be the sign of M the next; and it was only necessary that the persons at the extremities should know the key. . . .

Were telegraphs brought to so great a degree of perfection, that they could convey information speedily and distinctly; were they so much simplified, that they could be constructed and maintained at little expence—the advantages which would result from their use are almost inconceivable.

A Galvanic Telegraph

The subjoined paragraph was inserted into the article "Telegraph" at the last moment before the article was set in type. The Wheatstone experiment it described was performed in 1837, and its actual, and successful, application to railroad signalling was only being completed as the final volume (XXI) of the 7th edition (1830–1842) went to press. (B.L.F.)

It has been supposed that electricity might be the means of conveying intelligence, by passing given numbers of sparks through an insulated wire in given spaces of time. A gentleman of the name of Ronalds has written a small treatise on the subject; and several persons on the Continent and in England have made experiments on Galvanic or Voltaic telegraphs, by passing the stream through wires in metal pipes to the two extremities or stations, into phials of water; but there is reason to think that, ingenious as the experiments are, they are not likely ever to become practically useful. Since this was written, Professor Wheatstone has succeeded in contriving a Galvanic telegraph that works admirably, and will no doubt be applied to all the great lines of rail-road in the kingdom. It is simple in its construction, not liable to error, very portable, and carries round the margin of a circle the letters of the whole alphabet in rapid succession, so that each word is speedily conveyed to any distance.

Wireless Telephony

By the time of the 11th edition, Guglielmo Marconi (1874–1937) had astonished the world by sending a wireless telegraph signal across the Atlantic. For the 13th edition he himself, by then a Nobel laureate in physics (1909), explained not only wireless telegraphy but also the newer and more remarkable phenomenon of wireless telephony. The article concludes with an exciting and, to us, amusing look at the near future. The excerpts are from the article "Wireless Telegraphy and Telephony," by Guglielmo Marconi and Henry M. Dowsett, in the 13th edition (1926). (B.L.F.)

The employment of the Poulson arc generator from 1906 onwards gave an impetus to the development of wireless telephony, and an appreciable advance was made by the invention by Majorana in 1908 of a heavy current liquid microphone which enabled speech to be transmitted from Rome to Sicily, a distance of 300 miles. In 1909 the Colin-Jeance arc apparatus was in use from Toulon to a French cruiser 100 m. away; in 1910 successful tests were carried out in the United States over a distance of 490 m., and in 1912 the Vanni liquid microphone used with an arc transmitter enabled speech to be carried on from Rome to Tripoli—600 miles.

Development along new and more practical lines followed the invention by Meissner in 1913 of the valve oscillator and its use as a carrier wave generator for communicating between Berlin and Nauen, and the necessity for a heavy current microphone also disappeared with the arrival of the valve amplifier. In 1914 Marconi carried out a number of tests with valve transmitters and receivers on Italian war vessels up to a range of 45 miles.

The outbreak of war brought European long range telephone tests to a temporary standstill, but the American tests were continued, and in Oct. 1915, by employing 300 valves in the oscillator and modulator circuits, speech communication was effected when transmission conditions were favourable from Arlington to Eiffel Tower, Paris, a distance by great circle of 3,080 m.; also during the same series of tests long distance telephony from New York to Arlington by land line and Arlington to Hawaii by wireless was achieved, the total distance being over 5,000 miles. . . .

Future Progress

An enormous field of development lies ahead. Navigation by sea and air will be aided by the installation of rotating wireless beams which signal a different code for each point of the compass; by special beacon stations automatically transmitting known code signals on reserved wavelengths for direction-finding purposes; and by the use on board ship of automatic call devices for S.O.S. signals.

Point to point wireless telegraph communications for economic and interference reasons are likely to be established to a rapidly increasing extent by short wave beams, transmission on alternative wavelengths being provided if propagation absorption conditions make this necessary.

Automatic operating speeds up to 2,000 words per min. if called for can be achieved, and if traffic becomes heavy enough multiplex transmission by applying different modulating frequencies to the same carrier wave may be employed.

It is expected that the British Post Office trans-Atlantic wireless telephone service will be operating commercially within a year or so.

Transmission of line drawings and photographs and whole pages of messages by wireless is already an accomplished fact, and is being adapted for commercial use to trans-Atlantic circuits by the Radio Corporation of America working in conjunction with the Marconi Company.

The invaluable aid that a popular broadcast service, comprising distributed transmitting stations under a centralised control, can render a Government at a time of national emergency, was effectively demonstrated in Great Britain during the General Strike of 1926, and the experience then gained is likely to influence future broadcast regulations.

Finally reference may be made to wireless television, which is still (in 1926) in the laboratory stage, and must take several years to develop; but when mature will prove to be a very useful and popular extension of the art of broadcasting and radio transmission in general.

❧ ❧ ❧

The Early Days of Television

The experiments with wireless television to which Marconi alluded in the 13th edition (1926) had made enough progress just a few years later to justify a substantial article under the title "Television" in the 14th edition (1929). That article reported on the ongoing experiments and the obstacles to truly effective systems of transmission and reception of images.

A few years later, the decision was adopted to reprint the Britannica *annually, opening the way to annual revisions. "Television" was updated a few times, and in the 1948 printing of the 14th edition an entirely new article appeared, written by the man who invented both the transmission tube (iconoscope) and the television receiver (kinescope) that enabled television to work entirely by electronics. That was Vladimir Zworykin (1889–1982), director of research at the Radio Corporation of America. These extracts are from the 1948 article "Television," co-authored by Zworykin and G. A. Morton. (B.L.F.)*

Essentially three steps are involved in television, namely: (1) the analysis of the light image into electrical signals; (2) the transmission of the electrical signals to the points of reception; and (3) the synthesis of a visible reproduction of the original image from the electrical signals. . . .

As early as 1905 Boris Rosing proposed the use of a Braun cathode-ray tube as a means of reconstructing television images, and demonstrated by experiment that this was feasible. In 1911 Campbell-Swinton suggested a special cathode-ray tube which would function as an image pick-up device. The proposed tube was of theoretical interest only and was never reduced to practice. It was not until the early 1920s that electronic pick-up tubes were actually shown to be operative. The first electronic device of this type was the iconoscope, invented by V. K. Zworykin in 1923. This was followed in 1928 by a totally different form of pick-up tube, termed a dissector tube, invented by P. T. Farnsworth.

Television developed rapidly under the impetus given it by the new electronic pick-up and viewing devices. By the latter part of the 1930s, just before World War II, regular programs were being broadcast, under commercial licence, from New York City and Schenectady, N.Y., Philadelphia, Pa., Chicago, Ill., and San Francisco, Calif., in the United States; in England by the BBC from London, and also from a number of points in continental Europe. In the United States and England many thousand home receivers were in private hands and were in regular use receiving these programs. Program material included: sporting events, such as the outdoor pick-up of football, baseball and tennis, and indoor pick-up of boxing, wrestling and hockey, news events, studio production of plays, dance recitals, musical shows and general entertainment features as well as moving-picture film programs.

During the war years, 1940–45, commercial television activities were drastically curtailed. However, research in the field of television continued because of its potential military value. As a result of this work, television emerged from World War II with many important improvements which have been applied to television broadcasting to make possible a greater range of subject material, and better reproduced images. . . .

The problem of analyzing a picture into information suitable for electrical transmission and later resynthesis does not have a unique solution. However, the process known as scanning is the only one which by 1946 had proved to be satisfactory, and is the only one that will be discussed in this article.

The process of scanning is that of exploring the image area by means of a sensitive analyzing element which moves in a continuous or discontinuous line covering the entire surface of the picture. In general the size of the sensitive exploring element is equal to or smaller than a picture element. The analyzing element generates either directly or indirectly an electrical signal which corresponds to the brightness of the area of the image at which it is located. As the analyzing element traces out the scanning pattern over the surface of the picture the electrical signal varies, forming a characteristic complex wave known as the video signal.

At the picture reproducer or receiver the reproducing element moves over the viewing area in a scanning pattern which is geometrically similar to that at the transmitter. The brightness or its equivalent (i.e., optical transmission, reflectivity, etc.) of the reproducing element is a monotonic function of the instantaneous amplitude of the video signal. The motion of this element is so synchronized with that of the exploring element that when instantaneous amplitude of the video signal associated with a particular point in the picture being transmitted reaches it, the reproducing element is at the corresponding point of the viewing area. Therefore a reproduction of the picture being transmitted is formed on the viewing area of the receiver.

❧ ❧ ❧

Transportation: Opening the Air Age

Although modest mechanical improvements in the means of highway travel were made throughout Encyclopaedia Britannica*'s first century, the revolution set off by the internal combustion engine did not occur until after the time of the 9th edition of 1875–1889. Curiously enough, however, the invention of the railway and the revolutions in sea and air travel began virtually with the* Britannica*'s 1st edition of 1768–1771. The pages of every edition are filled with reports of the newest developments in these modes of transportation.*

While it was occurring to Andrew Bell to publish an encyclopedia in Edinburgh, Henry Cavendish was determining that hydrogen was lighter than air, a discovery that led Joseph Black and others to conclude that a lightweight sac of hydrogen ought to float in air. James Tytler, an Edinburgh chemist and contemporary of these men, was editor of the Britannica*'s 2nd edition and a portion of the 3rd. He was interested in the possibility of flight, and wrote the article "Flying" in the 3rd, describing the flight of birds, then recounting various speculations on human flight, including those of Britain's famous scientific pioneer, Roger Bacon.*

What did Tytler mean by his interjection of "Fa" after Friar Bacon's famous and fanciful claim that man had already succeeded in flying? It hardly seems a credulous endorsement, an attitude sometimes attributed to Tytler.

This excerpt is from the 2nd edition (1778–1783). If Tytler, a trained scientist, was no naif, he nonetheless grew wholly absorbed with the possibilities of human flight and when the 2nd edition was complete he became a passionate experimenter with balloons. He may even have been the first Briton to ascend in one—briefly and almost disastrously. As a consequence he came to be called "Balloon Tytler." (B.L.F.)

As for Tytler's "Fa": Could it have been an earlier version of our "Faugh!"? In any case we suddenly hear an unashamed human voice.

Friar Bacon, who lived near 500 years ago, not only affirms the art of flying possible, but assures us, that he himself knew how to make an engine wherein a man sitting might be able to convey himself through the air like a bird; and further adds, that there was then one who had tried it with success. The secret consisted in a couple of large thin hollow copper-globes exhausted of air; which being much lighter than air, would sustain a chair, whereon a person might sit. Fa. Francisco Lana, in his *Prodromo,* proposes the same thing, as his own thought. He computes, that a round vessel of plate-brass, 14 foot in diameter, weighing three ounces the square foot, will only weigh 1848 ounces; whereas a quantity of air of the same bulk, will weigh 2155⅔ ounces; so that the globe will not only be sustained in the air, but will carry with it a weight of 373⅔ ounces; and by increasing the bulk of the globe, without increasing the thickness of the metal, he adds, a vessel might be made to carry a much greater weight.—But the fallacy is obvious: a globe of the dimensions he describes, Dr Hook shews, would not sustain the pressure of the air, but be crushed inwards. Beside, in whatever ratio the bulk of the globe were increased, in the same must the thickness of the metal, and consequently the weight, be increased: so that there would be no advantage in such augmentation.

The same author describes an engine for

flying, invented by the Sieur Besnier, a smith of Sable, in the county of Maine.

The philosophers of king Charles the second's reign were mightily busied about this art. The famous bishop Wilkins was so confident of success in it, that he says, he does not question but, in future ages, it will be as usual to hear a man call for his wings, when he is going a journey, as it is now to call for his boots.

A Balloon Ascent

Here is more from Tytler's "Aerostation" article (3rd edition, 1788–1797), recreating for us the sensation of ballooning in 1785.

Mr Baldwin's Ascent from Chester

On the 8th of September 1785, at forty minutes past one P.M. Mr Baldwin ascended from Chester in Mr Lunardi's balloon. After traversing in a variety of different directions, he first alighted, at 28 minutes after three, about twelve miles from Chester, in the neighbourhood of Frodsham; then reascending and pursuing his excursion, he finally landed at Rixton-moss, five miles N.N.E. of Warrington, and 25 miles from Chester. Our limits will not admit of relating many of his observations; but the few following are some of the most important and curious. The sensation of ascending is compared to that of a strong pressure from the bottom of the car upwards against the soles of his feet. At the distance of what appeared to him seven miles from the earth, though by the barometer scarcely a mile and a half, he had a grand and most enchanting view of the city of Chester and its adjacent places below. The river Dee appeared of a red colour; the city very diminutive; and the town entirely blue. The whole appeared a perfect plain, the highest building having no apparent height, but reduced all to the same level, and the whole terrestrial prospect appeared like a coloured map. Just after his first ascent, being in a well-watered and maritime part of the country, he observed a remarkable and regular tendency of the balloon towards the sea; but shortly after rising into another current of air, he escaped the danger: this upper current, he says, was visible to him at the time of his ascent, by a lofty sound stratum of clouds flying in a safe direction. The perspective appearance of things to him was very remarkable. The lowest bed of vapour that first appeared as cloud was pure white, in detached fleeces, increasing as they rose: they presently coalesced, and formed, as he expresses it, a sea of cotton, tufting here and there by the action of the air in the undisturbed part of the clouds. The whole became an extended white floor of cloud, the upper surface being smooth and even. Above this white floor he observed, at great and unequal distances, a vast assemblage of thunder-clouds, each parcel consisting of whole acres in the densest form: he compares their form and appearance to the smoke of pieces of ordnance, which had consolidated as it were into masses of snow, and penetrated through the upper surface or white floor of common clouds, there remaining visible and at rest. Some clouds had motions in slow and various directions, forming an appearance truly stupendous and majestic. Mr Baldwin also gives a curious description of his tracing the shadow of the bal-

MOSTGOLFIER'S BALLOON.

BLANCHARD'S BALLOON.

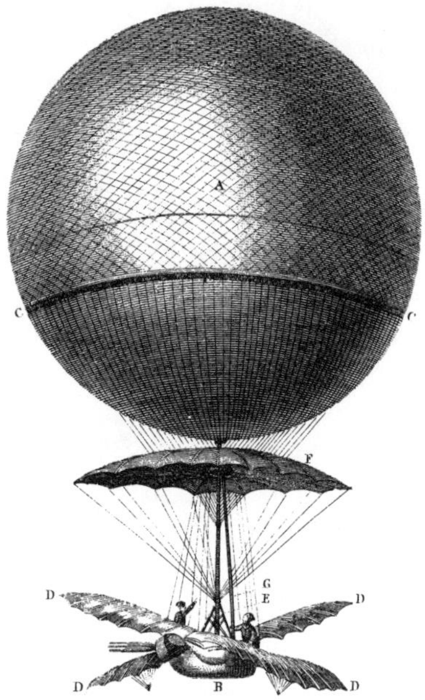

References to Blanchards Balloon

A *The Balloon made of Taffeta 26 Feet in diameter covered with a Net*

B *The Car suspended by longitudinal Cords from the Hoop C.*

D.D.D.D. *The Wings moved by Rack-work E.*

F *A Parachute or Umbrella to break the force of descent if the Balloon should burst*

G *A Tube communicating with the inside of the Balloon*

GARNERIN'S PARACHUTE
in ascending

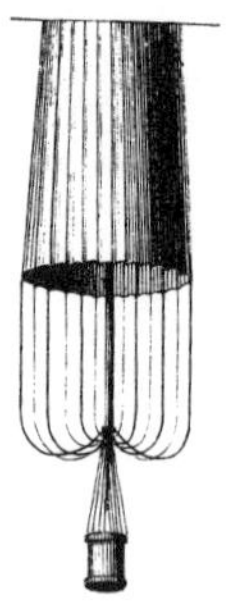

GARNERIN'S PARACHUTE
in descending

LUNARDI'S BALLOON.

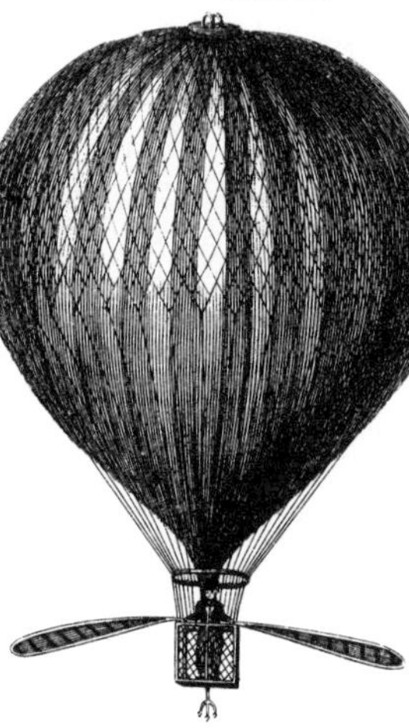

CHARLES' & ROBERT'S BALLOON.

loon over tops of volumes of clouds. At first it was small, in size and shape like an egg; but soon increased to the magnitude of the sun's disc, still growing larger, and attended with a most captivating appearance of an iris encircling the whole shadow at some distance round it, the colours of which were remarkably brilliant. The regions did not feel colder, but rather warmer, than below. The sun was hottest to him when the balloon was stationary. The discharge of a cannon when the balloon was at considerable height, was distinctly heard by the aeronaut; and a discharge from the same piece, when at the height of 30 yards, so disturbed him as to oblige him for safety to lay hold firmly of the cords of the balloon. At a considerable height he poured down a pint-bottle full of water; and as the air did not oppose a resistance sufficient to break the steam into small drops, it mostly fell down in large drops. In the course of the balloon's tract it was found much affected by the water (a circumstance observed in former aerial voyages). At one time the direction of the balloon kept continually over the water, going directly towards the sea, so much as to endanger the aeronaut; the mouth of the balloon was opened and he in two minutes descended into an under current blowing from the sea: he kept descending, and landed at Bellair farm in Rinsley, 12 miles from Chester. Here he lightened his car by 31 pounds, and instantly reascending, was carried into the interior part of the country, performing a number of different manoeuvres. At his greatest altitude he found his respiration free and easy. Several bladders which he had along with him crackled and expanded very considerably. Clouds and land, as before, appeared on the same level. By way of experiment, he tried the upper valve two or three times, the neck of the balloon being close; and remarked, that the escape of the gas was attended with a growling noise like millstones, but not near so loud. Again, round the shadow of the balloon, on the clouds he observed the iris. A variety of other circumstances and appearances he met with, is fancifully described; and at 53 minutes past three he finally landed.

Flying

When the great 9th edition (1875–1889) began to appear, its first volume featured a new "Aeronautics" article by one of the most distinguished balloon pilots of the day, James Glaisher, a fellow of the Royal Society, first president of the Royal Meteorological Society, and a founder of the Aeronautical Society of Great Britain. Glaisher, who had himself ascended in a balloon to the remarkable altitude of 37,000 feet in 1862, touched on the development and use of the parachute. Early experiments with flight were fraught with danger, as will be seen below. (B.L.F.)

Jordaki Kuparento, a Polish aeronaut, is the only person who ever made any real use of a parachute. He ascended from Warsaw on July 24, 1808, in a fire-balloon, which, at a considerable elevation, took fire; but being provided with a parachute, he was enabled to effect his descent in safety.

The next experiment made with a parachute was that which resulted in the unfortunate death of Mr Robert Cocking. . . . The great defect of Garnerin's umbrella-shaped parachute was its violent oscillation during descent, and Mr Cocking considered that if the parachute were made of a conical form (vertex downwards), the whole of this oscillation would be avoided; and if it were made of sufficient size, there would be resistance enough to check too rapid a descent. He therefore constructed a parachute on this principle, the radius of which at its widest part was about 17 feet. It was stated in the public announcements previous to the experiment that the whole weighed 223 lb; but from the evidence at the inquest it appeared that the weight must have been over 400 lb. Mr Cocking's weight was 177 lb, which was so much additional. On July 24, 1837, the trial took place; and the Nassau balloon, with Mr Green and Mr Spencer, a solicitor, in the car, and having suspended below it the parachute, in the car of which was Mr Cocking, rose from the ground at twenty-five minutes to eight in the evening. A good deal of difficulty was experienced in rising to a suitable height, partly in consequence of the resistance to the air offered by the expanded parachute, and partly owing to its weight. Mr Cocking wished the height to be 8000 feet; but when the balloon reached the height of 5000 feet, it being then nearly over Greenwich, Mr Green called out to Mr Cocking that he should be unable to ascend to the requisite height if the parachute was to descend in daylight. Mr Cocking accordingly let slip the catch which was to liberate him from the balloon. The parachute for a few seconds descended very rapidly but still evenly, until suddenly the upper rim seemed to give way, and the whole apparatus collapsed (taking a form resembling an umbrella turned inside out, and nearly closed), and the machine descended with great rapidity, oscillating very much. When about two or three hundred feet from the ground, the basket became disengaged from the remnant of the parachute, and Mr Cocking was found in a field at Lee, literally dashed to pieces. . . .

We may remark that a descending balloon half-full of gas either does rise, or can with a little management be made to rise, to the top of the netting and take the form of a parachute, thus materially lessening the rapidity of descent. Mr Wise, in fact, having noticed this, once purposely exploded his balloon when at a considerable altitude, and the resistance offered to the air by the envelope of the balloon was sufficient to enable him to reach the ground without injury. And a similar thing took place in one of Mr Glaisher's high scientific ascents (April 18, 1863), when, at a height of about 2 miles, the sea appeared directly underneath; the gas was let out of the balloon as quickly as possible, and the velocity of descent was so great, that the 2 miles of vertical height were passed through in four minutes. On the balloon reaching the ground at Newhaven, close to the shore, it was found to be nearly empty. The balloon had, in fact, for the last mile or more, merely acted as a parachute; the shock was a severe one, and all the instruments were broken, but nothing serious resulted to the occupants of the car.

Numerous attempts have been made both to direct balloons and contrive independent flying machines. After the invention of the balloon by the brothers Montgolfier, it was at once thought that no very great difficulty would be found in devising a suitable steering apparatus; in fact, it was supposed that to rise into the air and remain there was the chief difficulty, and that, this being accomplished, the power of directing the aerostat would be a secondary achievement that must follow before long. Accordingly, in most of the early balloons the voyagers took up oars, sails, or paddles, which they diligently worked while in the air; sometimes they thought an effect was produced, and sometimes not. If we consider the number of different currents in the atmosphere, it is no wonder that some should have announced with confidence that their course was changed from that of the wind by means of the sails or oars that they used; in fact, it is not very often that the whole atmosphere up to a considerable height is moving *en masse* in the same direction, so that generally the course taken by the balloon, as determined merely by joining the places of ascent and descent, is not identical with the direction of the wind, even when it is the same at both places. Although there is no reason why balloons should not be so guided by means of mechanical appliances attached to them as to move in a direction making a small angle with that of the wind, still it must have been evident to any one who has observed a balloon during inflation on a windy day, that any motion in which it would be exposed to the action of a strong current of air must result in its destruction. It has therefore gradually become recognised that the balloon is scarcely a step at all towards a system of aerial navigation; and many have thought that the principles involved in the construction of a flying machine must be very different from the simple statical equilibrium that subsists when a balloon is floating in the air. "To navigate the air the machine must be heavier than the air," has frequently been regarded as an axiom; and there can be no doubt that an apparatus constructed of such light material as is necessary for a balloon must either be destroyed or become ungovernable in a high wind. Recently, however, M. Dupuy de Lôme, an eminent French engineer, has constructed and made experiments with a balloon which he considers satisfies some of the conditions. The balloon is spindle-shaped, the longer axis being horizontal, and it contains about 120,000 cubic feet. The car is suspended below the middle of the balloon, and there are provided a rudder and a screw. The rudder consists of a triangular sail placed beneath the balloon and near the rear, and is kept in position by a horizontal yard, about 20 feet long, turning round a pivot in its forward extremity; the height of the sail is 16 feet, and its surface 160 square feet. Two ropes for working the rudder extend forward to the seat of the steerer, who has before him a compass fixed to the car, the central part of which will contain fourteen men. The screw is carried by the car, and is driven by four or eight men working at a capstan. A trial was made with the machine on February 2, 1872, on a windy day, and M. de Lôme considered that he had been enabled by his screw and rudder to alter his course about 12°. (See *Report of the Aeronautical Society, 1872).*

Whatever difficulties may present themselves in regulating the horizontal movement of the balloon, there can be no doubt that the vertical motion could be obtained by means of a screw or other mechanical means; and the power of being able to ascend or descend without loss of ballast would be a considerable gain. In the opinion of many, however, the balloon is not worth improvement; and as ballooning is now generally practised merely as a spectacle by which the aeronaut or showman gains his living, it is not likely that any advancement will be made.

Of flying machines, in which both bouyancy and motion were proposed to be obtained by purely mechanical means, the number has been very great. Most of the projects have been chimerical, and were due to persons possessed of an insufficient knowledge of the principles of natural philosophy, both theoretically and practically. They serve, however, to show how great a number of individuals must have paid attention to the matter, and even at the present time several patents are taken out annually on the subject.

Success at Last

Finally, the classic 11th edition (1910–1911) could report success with the flying machine in its article "Flight and Flying." (B.L.F.)

To Lilienthal in Germany belongs the double credit of demonstrating the superiority of arched over flat surfaces, and of reducing gliding flight to regular practice. He made over 2000 glides safely, using gravity as his motive power, with concave, batlike wings, in some cases with superposed surfaces. . . .

It was with a machine of the latter type that he was upset by a sudden gust of wind and killed in 1896. . . .

Similar experiments were meanwhile conducted by Wilbur and Orville Wright of Dayton, Ohio, in whose hands the glider developed into a successful flying machine. These investigators began their work in 1900, and at an early stage introduced two characteristic features—a horizontal rudder in front for steering in the vertical plane, and the flexing or bending of the ends of the main supporting aeroplanes as a means of maintaining the structure in proper balance. Their machines to begin with were merely gliders, the operator lying upon them in a horizontal position, but in 1903 a petrol motor was added, and a flight lasting 59 seconds was performed. In 1905 they made forty-five flights, in the longest of which they remained in the air for half an hour and covered a distance of 24½ m. The utmost secrecy, however, was maintained concerning their experiments, and in consequence their achievements were regarded at the time with doubt and suspicion, and it was hardly realized that their success would reach the point later achieved. . . .

But the best results were obtained by the Wright brothers—Orville Wright in America and Wilbur Wright in France. On the 9th of September 1908 the former, at Fort Myer, Virginia, made three notable flights; in the first he remained in the air 57½ minutes and in the second 1 hour 3 minutes, while in the third he took with him a passenger and covered nearly 4 m. in 6 minutes. Three days later he made a flight of 45 m. in 1 hour 14⅓ minutes, but on the 17th he had an accident, explained as being due to one of his propellers coming into contact with a stay, by which his machine was wrecked, he himself seriously injured, and Lieutenant Selfridge, who was with him, killed. Four days afterwards Wilbur Wright at Le Mans in France beat all previous records with a flight lasting 1 hour 31 minutes 25⅘ seconds, in which he covered about 56 m.; and subsequently, on the 11th of October, he made a flight of

Multiple-wing Gliding Machine.

Chanute's Gliding Machine.

Langley's Aërodrome.

1 hour 9 minutes accompanied by a passenger. On the 31st of December he succeeded in remaining in the air for 2 hours 20 minutes 23 seconds.

Wilbur Wright's machine, that used by his brother being essentially the same, consisted of two slightly arched supporting surfaces, each 12½ metres long, arranged parallel one above the other at a distance of 1⅘ metres apart. As they were each about 2 metres wide their total area was about 50 sq. metres. About 3 metres in front of them was arranged a pair of smaller horizontal aeroplanes, shaped like a long narrow ellipse, which formed the rudder that effected changes of elevation, the driver being able by means of a lever to incline them up or down according as he desired to ascend or descend. The rudder for lateral steering was placed about 2½ metres behind the main surfaces and was formed of two vertical pivoted aeroplanes. The lever by which they were turned was connected with the device by which the ends of the main aeroplanes could be flexed simultaneously though in opposite directions; *i.e.* if the ends of the aeroplanes on one side were bent downwards, those on the other were bent upwards. By the aid of this arrangement the natural cant of the machine when making a turn could be checked, if it became excessive. The four-cylinder petrol engine was placed on the lower aeroplane a little to the right of the central line, being counterbalanced by the driver (and passenger if one was carried), who sat a little to the left of the same line. Making about 1200 revolutions a minute, it developed about 24 horse-power, and was connected by chain gearing to two wooden propellers, 2½ metres in diameter and 3½ metres apart; the speed of which was about 450 revolutions a minute. The whole machine, with aeronaut, weighed about 1100 lb, the weight of the motor being reputed to be 200 lb.

A feature of the year 1909 was the success obtained with monoplanes having only a single supporting surface, and it was on a machine of this type that the Frenchman Blériot on July 25th flew across the English Channel from Calais to Dover in 31 minutes. Hubert Latham all but performed the same feat on an Antoinette monoplane. The year saw considerable increases in the periods for which aviators were able to remain in the air; and Roger Sommer's flight of nearly 2½ hours on August 7th was surpassed by Henry Farman on November 3rd, when he covered a distance estimated at 137¼ m. in 4 hr. 17 min. 53 sec. In both these cases biplanes were employed. Successful aviation meetings were held, among other places, at Reims, Juvisy, Doncaster and Blackpool; and at Blackpool a daring flight was made in a wind of 40 m. an hour by Latham. This aviator also proved the possibility of flying at considerable altitudes by attaining on December 1st a height of over 1500 ft. but this record was far surpassed in the following January by L. Paulhan, who on a biplane rose to a height of 1383 yds. at Los Angeles. In the course of the year three aviators were killed—Defèvbre and Ferber in September and Fernandez in December; and four men perished in September by the destruction of the French airship "République," the gas-bag of which was ripped open by a broken propeller. In January 1910 Delagrange was killed by the fracture of one of the wings of a monoplane on which he was flying. On April 27th–28th,

1910, Paulhan successfully flew from London to Manchester, with only one stop, within 24 hours, for the *Daily Mail*'s £10,000 prize.

A Species of Road

George Buchanan (1790–1852), distinguished civil engineer and fellow of the Royal Society of Edinburgh, writing on "Railway" for the Supplement to the 4th, 5th, and 6th editions (1815–1824), gives us a sense of the pristine.

EARLY RAILWAYS

A railway is a species of road or carriage-way, in which the track of the carriage-wheels being laid with bars, or rails, of wood, stone, or metal, the carriage is more easily drawn along this smooth surface than over an ordinary road. . . .

The railways in Britain are so numerous, that it would exceed our limits to specify the particular lines. In the Newcastle coal district, on the river Wear, in the coal and mining districts of Yorkshire and Lancashire, as well as of Derbyshire and Staffordshire, there are numerous railways branching off from the navigable rivers and canals to the different mines. . . .

On some of the railways near Newcastle, the waggons are drawn by means of a steam-engine working in a waggon by itself, the wheels of which are driven by the engine, and acting on a rack laid along the railway, impel forward both the engine and the attached waggons: in some cases the wheels of the waggon operate without rail work, by the mere friction between them and the railway. The steam-engines employed for this purpose are of the high pressure kind; these requiring no condensing apparatus. But this application of steam has not yet arrived at such perfection as to have brought it into general use.

The Confused Start of Steam Navigation

We Americans at once think of Robert Fulton, but the story is a bit more complicated, especially when written by a Brit.

The Supplement to the 4th, 5th, and 6th editions (1815–1824) carries an unsigned article, "Steam-Navigation," which explicates its tangled subject. Fulton does appear on the scene.

From a manuscript *Memorial on Steam-Navigation,* drawn up by Mr Symington, with the perusal of which we have been favoured, we make the following extract:

"Mr Miller being then very much engaged improving his newly purchased estate in Dumfries-shire, and I also employed to construct large machinery for the use of the lead-mines at Wanlockhead, the idea of carrying the experiments, at that time, any farther, was entirely given up, till meeting with the late Thomas Lord Dundas of Kerse, who wished that I would construct a steam-boat for dragging vessels on the Forth and Clyde Canal, in place of horses. Agreeably to his Lordship's request, a series of experiments, which cost nearly L. 3000, were set on foot in the year 1801, and ending in 1802, upon a larger scale, and more improved plan, having a steam cylinder 22 inches diameter, and four feet stroke; a complete model of which, with a set of ice-breakers attached, may be seen (if not in Lord Dundas's house, Arlington

Street) in the Royal Institution, London, which proved itself very much adapted for the intended purposes, as will appear from the following simple yet authentic narrative. Having previously made various experiments, in March 1802, at Lock No. 20, Lord Dundas, the great patron and steam-boat promoter, along with Archibald Speirs, Esq. of Elderslee, and several gentlemen of their acquaintance being on board, the steam-boat took in drag two loaded vessels, *Active* and *Euphemia* of Grangemouth, Gow and Espline masters, each upwards of 70 tons burthen, and with great ease carried them through the long reach of the Forth and Clyde Canal, to Port-Dundas, a distance of 19½ miles, in six hours, although the whole time it blew a very strong breeze right a-head of us; so much so, that no other vessels could move to windward, in the canal, that day, but those we had in tow; which put beyond the possibility of doubt the utility of the scheme in canals or rivers, and ultimately on open seas. . . ."

It is indisputable, therefore, that Mr Symington was the first person who had the merit of successfully applying the power of the steam-engine to the propulsion of vessels. The boat which he constructed was, like that proposed by Hulls, really a *Tug*. It is much to be regretted, that there existed not enterprise enough at that time in Scotland to encourage the ingenious artizan to repeat his experiments on the Clyde. All the subsequent improvements, however, in steam-navigation may be fairly traced to Mr Symington's attempt, and we cannot help thinking that he has a strong claim on the national gratitude. He is still alive, and we fear not in the most flourishing circumstances. Should the state decline rewarding such meritorious services, the opulent proprietors of steam-boats might well evince their liberality and discernment, by bestowing on him some recompence.

Considering the importance to America of navigating her mighty rivers, it is not surprising that the application of the power of steam to the propulsion of boats should, by persevering efforts, have been first carried into successful practice in that continent. This was achieved by the activity and zeal of Mr Fulton, who appears evidently, however, to have derived all his primary knowledge of the subject from Scotland.

Mr Symington's *Memorial,* above referred to, gives the following remarkable statement:

"When engaged in these last experiments in 1802, I was called upon by Mr Fulton, who very politely made himself known, and candidly told me that he was lately from North America, and intended to return thither in a few months, but having heard of our steam-boat operations, could not think of leaving this country without first waiting upon me in expectation of seeing the boat, and procuring such information regarding it as I might be pleased to communicate; he at same time mentioned, however advantageous such invention might be to Great Britain, it would certainly become more so in North America, on account of the many extensive navigable rivers in that country; and as timber of the first quality, both for building the vessels, and also for fuel to the engine, could be purchased there for a small expence, he was decidedly of opinion it could hardly fail, in a few years, to become very beneficial to trade in that part of the world; and that his carrying the plan to North America could not turn out otherwise than to my advantage; as, if I inclined it, both the making and superintendence of such vessels would naturally fall upon me, provided my engagements with steam-boats at home did not occupy so much of my time as to prevent me from paying any attention to those which might afterwards be constructed abroad.

"Mr Fulton having thus spoken, in compliance with his most earnest request, I caused the engine fire to be lighted up, and in a short time thereafter, put the steam-boat in motion, and carried him from Lock No. 16, where the boat then lay, four miles west the canal, and returned to the place of starting, in one hour and twenty minutes, to the great astonishment of Mr Fulton, and several gentlemen, who, at our outset, chanced to come on board.

"During the above trip, Mr Fulton asked if I had any objections to his taking notes respecting the steam-boat, to which question I said, none; as I considered the more publicity that was given to any discovery intended for general good, so much the better; and having the privilege secured by letters-patent, I was not afraid of his making any encroachment upon my right in the British dominions; though in the United States, I was well aware, I had no power of control. In consequence, he pulled out a memorandum-book, and, after putting several pointed questions respecting the general construction and effect of the machine, which I answered in a most explicit manner, he jotted down particularly every thing then described, with his own remarks upon the boat, while moving with him on board, along the canal; but he seems to have been altogether forgetful of this, as, notwithstanding his fair promises, I never heard any thing more of him, till reading in a newspaper an account of his death.

"From the above incontrovertible facts, which can be corroborated by a number of people of respectability living at this day, it is very evident that commerce is not indebted to North America for the invention of steam-packets, it being hereby established beyond the possibility of doubt, to be truly British, both in idea and practice, and that Mr Fulton's steam-vessel did not make its first appearance in the Hudson River earlier than 1806 or 1807, four years at least posterior to his having been on board the Charlotte Dundas steam-boat, and minutely examined it, when at work upon the Forth and Clyde Canal, and 18 years later than the date of the first experiments made by me upon steam-boats, on the lake at Dalswinton, Dumfries-shire, in Great Britain. . . ."

The Motor Car

Various experiments with steam carriages were carried out in the prosperous scientific climate of the seventeenth and eighteenth centuries, and in the nineteenth century even more prototypes were built. But the motor vehicle that became the mainstay of modern land transport had to await the development of the internal (as opposed to external) combustion engine. The Britannica*'s first article on motor vehicles appeared in the 10th edition (1902–1903), but nowhere is the early history presented more gracefully and concisely than in the article "Motor Car" in the 14th edition (1929). It was written by Charles F. Kettering (1876–1958),* *the auto pioneer and inventor and legendary head of research for the General Motors Corporation.*

Following this excerpt, Kettering went on to describe in considerable detail the engine and other main components of the vehicle, as well as various production considerations. Another article in the 14th was "Mass Production," ghost-written for the signature of Henry Ford and printed later in this book. (B.L.F.)

Reflecting the modern world's passionate, ongoing love affair with the automobile, *Britannica*'s current edition devotes almost twenty-seven columns to the subject, treating it under the more general title of "Transportation." We think of it as peculiar to our time, but the idea of a self-powered vehicle is part of our mythic tradition. It is first recorded in the *Iliad*. In a single day, Homer informs us, Vulcan made one hundred and twenty tricycles which

> Wondrous to tell instinct with spirit rolled
> From place to place, around the blest abodes,
> Self-moved, obedient to the beck of gods.

It is difficult to assign definite dates for events in the progress of the automobile. Many men were working on the same problems in different places. This brief outline can point out only the trends and major developments. The self-propelled vehicle dates back to the middle of the 18th century. Credit for the first "road wagon" propelled by its own engine, is generally given to Nicholas Cugnot, a Frenchman, who about 1770 built a three-wheeled carriage, with a cumbersome steam power plant operating on the single front wheel. It is claimed that this steam carriage could run at the rate of 2½ m. per hour, but it had to stop every hundred feet or so to make steam. Cugnot's second vehicle, produced in 1771, is still preserved in the Conservatoire des Arts et Métiers, Paris. (Some histories of the automobile state that his first car is still preserved and not his second car.) During the latter half of the 18th century a few other attempts were made to build steam carriages, many of which were not capable of operating under their own power. The next century, however, saw a number of steam vehicles put to practical use in transporting passengers. Among these early experimenters were: Oliver Evans in America, making a car in 1787; Trevithick, England (1801); Gordon, England (1824); James, England (1824); Gurney, England (1828); James, America (1829); Summers and Ogle, England (1831); Hancock, England (1824–36); Church, England (1832); Maceroni and Squires, England (1834); Dudgeon, America (1857); and Butler, England (1883). Gurney put three steam coaches into operation on a route near London covering about 3,644 miles. Around the same time Walter Hancock built the first of nine steam carriages that were to operate on a route regularly.

Starting about 1831, the English parliament enacted laws which practically eliminated the steam coaches from the roads. Among these might be mentioned the Red Flag Law, which required that a man precede the horseless carriage, carrying a red flag by day and a red lantern by night. In addition, the toll roads and bridges raised the charges for the steam carriages until they could no longer operate at a profit. As a result, there was little development of the horseless carriages in England until after 1896, then the restrictive law was repealed. In Germany and France interest

turned toward the internal combustion engine to replace the cumbersome power plant of these early steam vehicles. In 1885–86 Gottlieb Daimler (Germany), patented his high speed internal combustion engine, which is generally credited with revolutionizing automotive transportation. Nevertheless, there is some disagreement among historians on this point. Some state that in 1875 Siegfried Narkus (Austria) built a four-wheeled vehicle powered by an internal combustion engine. Benz (Germany), in 1885, produced a tricycle with an internal combustion engine. Credit is commonly given to Krebs for the first petrol or gasoline automobile incorporating many of the essential features of the modern car. In 1894 he designed the Panhard car with a vertical engine under a bonnet or hood, at the front, and a modern type chassis. The car also had the common type of sliding gear transmission operated by the right hand, clutch and brake pedals, and a foot accelerator.

About 1896 or 1897 considerable work was carried on in Germany, France, England and the United States on the development of vehicles driven by internal combustion engines. These cars varied greatly in detailed design; some had the same general arrangement as the Panhard, while others were patterned on the familiar horse-drawn carriages which they were expected to supplant. The motor car is not the product of a single inventor nor even of men within a single century. Among the European pioneers there were: Daimler, Benz, Maybach, Krebs, Panhard, Levassor, Royce, Serpollet, De Dion, Bouton, Gibbon and Roots; and among the American pioneers were Duryea, Olds, Haynes, Winton, Ford, King, Maxwell, Apperson, Riker, Clarke, Stanley, White and Franklin. These automobiles were produced, of course, in very small numbers because of the limited manufacturing facilities and of the small consumer demand.

In 1903 the Association of Licensed Automobile Manufacturers was formed in America to grant licences to manufacture motor cars under the Selden patent (U.S. patent No. 549,160, Nov. 5, 1895), and for eight years was a powerful force in the development of the new industry. By limiting licences to concerns which were held to be "good and reliable," the association doubtless protected both the automobile industry and its customers from unscrupulous exploitation, and stabilized somewhat the general conditions of production and market competition. The National Automobile Chamber of Commerce was organized in 1913 to succeed the association (strictly speaking, the National Automobile Chamber of Commerce succeeded the Automobile Board of Trade, which succeeded the Association of Licensed Automobile Manufacturers). Among its activities was the "cross-licence" agreement whereby any member might use the patents held by any other member, without paying a royalty. While never adhered to quite universally, this agreement still (1928) holds for patents issued previous to 1925. At that time the life of the agreement ran out; and it was not renewed mostly on account of the commercial aspect of large private developments.

Until 1909–12 the automotive industry was, in general, chiefly concerned with developing a product that at least would operate. Some cars, of course, were marketed in this period; these in essential details were nearly as satisfactory as cars designed in recent years. During the experimental period, cars of every description were produced with alternatively chain, bevel gear or friction drive: bar, tiller or wheel steering; planetary or sliding gear transmissions; and with the number of cylinders ranging from one to eight, with a few twelves and sixteens. The prejudice against a new and radical invention, poor road conditions, the comparatively high original cost, the cost of maintenance and the general unreliability of the cars, all tended to retard rapid introduction of motor vehicles. The sporting phase of the automobile was recognized long before it was commonly appreciated that the automobile provides a thoroughly reliable, economical, comfortable and rapid means of individual transportation.

After 1909–12 the production of sufficient cars for a growing demand and marketing and distributing facilities became of great importance. Problems of time payments and the extensive purchasing of cars on an instalment payment basis, trade in used cars, dealer organization and advertising have been demanding the attention of manufacturers, in addition to problems of quantity production and engineering. During this period also the internal combustion engine has almost entirely superseded both steam and electric motors for propelling automobiles. The electric vehicle is confined, for the most part, to use for short distances, over improved roads. The expansion and growth of the motor car has, in a large measure, proceeded abreast with the building of good roads, development of alloy steels and improvement of rubber. The need for rapid and reliable individual, or private, transport has existed for a long time; and when the automobile was recognized as fulfilling that need, its adoption was rapid not only in Europe and America, but in late years, all over the world.

CHAPTER EIGHT

The Arts

Art

Especially to those whose interests lie outside what we now call the arts, the modern meaning of the term "art" is extremely narrow. "Art" means painting and "artists" are painters. To the editor of the first Encyclopædia Britannica *(1768–1771), the term was catholic:*

ART, a system of rules serving to facilitate the performance of certain actions.

Thus in the late eighteenth century a human activity of enormous affective power was defined in twelve rather abstract, quiet words. Note the period's stress on "rules" and systems. In the current edition one of the Propaedia's ten parts of the circle of learning is devoted to art. If collected, the articles on the subject throughout the set would comprise a large volume. To sense how our attitude to art differs from that of the English neoclassical era try Mark Van Doren's "The World of Art" in the Propaedia. (B.L.F.)

❧ ❧ ❧

The Literary Arts

Literature was not a title in the 1st edition (1768–1771), although its several elements were treated, e.g.:

NOVEL, in matters of literature, a fictitious history of a series of entertaining events in common life, wherein the rules of probability are or ought to be strictly preserved.

ROMANCE, in matters of literature, a fabulous relation of certain adventures designed for the entertainment and instruction of the readers. . . .

With succeeding editions, and somewhat more space as the editions grew slowly in size, more attention was paid to the field. At first, preeminent authorities were identified and quoted, often extensively, sometimes without soliciting permission. (B.L.F.)

This was the case with the article "Romance" in the 4th edition (1801–1809). The author, Isaac D'Israeli (1766–1848), was the father of Benjamin. The editor, after a florid compliment to D'Israeli's delightful Curiosities of Literature, *then proceeded to quote from it at length, presumably without either permission or pay. Two brief extracts:*

ROMANCE has been elegantly defined the offspring of fiction and love. Men of learning have amused themselves with tracing the epocha of romances. In this research they have displayed more ingenuity than judgement; and some have fancied that it may have existed as far back as the time of Aristotle; Dearchus, one of his disciples, having written several works of this amusing species. . . .

From romances, which had now exhausted the patience of the public, sprung novels. They attempted to allure attention by this inviting title, and reducing their works from ten to two volumes. The name of romance disgusted; and they substituted those of histories, lives, memoirs, and adventures. In these works they quitted the unnatural incidents, the heroic projects, the complicated and endless intrigues, and the exertion of noble passions; heroes were not now taken from the throne, they were sought for even amongst the lowest ranks of the people. On this subject, I shall just observe, that a novel is a very dangerous poison in the hand of a libertine; it may be a salutary medicine in that of a virtuous writer.

Bard-Bashing

From the start, the Britannica *treated specific aspects of literature. Often these usually compact entries were unstinting in their criticism even of the greatest literary names. In the article "Comparison" in the 1st edition (1768–1771), the editor, William Smellie, devoted many pages to taking Shakespeare to task for his sins. (B.L.F.)*

Intellectuals in the eighteenth century, still greatly influenced by the medieval conception of the liberal arts, paid more attention to rhetoric than we do. They also felt uneasy when poets digressed from the path of "good sense." Mr. Smellie has little confidence in Shakespeare's command over simile and metaphor. His lengthy discussion, of which only the beginning is given here, is studded with such phrases as "this comparison has scarce any force . . . this error . . . an useless image. . . ."

COMPARISON, in a general sense, the consideration of the relation between two persons or things, when opposed and set against each other, by which we judge of their agreement or difference.

Instruction is the principal, but not the only end of comparison. It may be employed with success in putting a subject in a strong point of view. A lively idea is formed of a man's courage by likening it to that of a lion; and eloquence is exalted in our imagination by comparing it to a river overflowing its bank, and involving all in its impetuous course. The same effect is produced by contrast: A man in prosperity becomes more sensible of his happiness, by comparing his condition with that of a person in want of bread. Thus comparison is subservient to poetry as well as to philosophy. . . .

But it will be a better illustration of the present head, to give examples where comparisons are improperly introduced. Similes are not the language of a man in his ordinary state of mind, dispatching his daily and usual work: for that reason, the following speech of a gardener to his servant, is extremely improper:

> Go bind thou up yon dangling apricocks,
> Which, like unruly children, make their sire
> Stoop with oppression of their prodigal weight:
> Give some supportance to the bending twigs.
> Go thou, and, like an executioner,
> Cut off the heads of too-fast-growing sprays,
> That look too lofty in our commonwealth:
> All must be even in our government.
>
> *Richard II, act 3. sc. 7.*

The fertility of Shakespear's vein betrays him frequently into this error.

Shakespeare draws similar fire from James Tytler, editor of the 2nd edition (1778–1783). There the subject is narration. (B.L.F.)

NARRATION, in oratory, poetry, and history, a recital or rehearsal of a fact as it happened, or when it is supposed to have happened.

Concerning Narration and Description, we have the following rules and observations in the Elements of Criticism.

1. The first rule is, That in history the reflections ought to be chaste and solid; for while the mind is intent upon truth, it is little disposed to the operations of the imagination. Strada's Belgic history is full of poetical images, which, being discordant with the subject, are unpleasant; and they have a still worse effect, by giving an air of fiction to a genuine history. Such flowers ought to be scattered with a sparing hand, even in epic poetry; and at no rate are they proper, till the reader be warmed, and by an enlivened imagination be prepared to relish them: in that state of mind, they are agreeable; but while we are sedate and attentive to an historical chain of facts, we reject with disdain every fiction.

2. Vida, following Horace, recommends a modest commencement of an epic poem: giving for a reason, That the writer ought to husband his fire. Besides, bold thoughts and figures are never relished till the mind be heated and thoroughly engaged, which is not the reader's case at the commencement. Homer introduces not a single simile in the first book of the Iliad, nor in the first book of the Odyssey. On the other hand, Shakespeare begins one of his plays with a sentiment too bold for the most heated imagination:

> *Bedford.* Hung be the heav'ns with black, yield day to night!
> Comets, importing change of times and states,
> Brandish your crystal tresses in the sky,
> And with them scourge the bad revolting stars,
> That have consented unto Henry's death!
> Henry the Fifth, too famous to live long!
> England ne'er lost a king of so much worth.
>
> *First part Henry VI.*

The passage with which Strada begins his history, is too poetical for a subject of that kind; and at any rate too high for the beginning of a grave performance.

❧ ❧ ❧

The Dictionary

Besides editing the 1st edition (1768–1771), William Smellie wrote many of the unsigned articles, and his strong biases suffuse many others. He was quite equal to the task of patronizing Samuel Johnson. Here is the opening section of "Dictionary." (The reader is spared the five pages of examples that follow his introductory remarks).

DICTIONARY, in its original acceptation, is the arranging all the words of a language according to the order of the alphabet, and annexing a definition or explanation to each word. When arts and sciences began to be improved and extended, the multiplicity of technical terms rendered it necessary to compile dictionaries either of science in general, or of particular sciences, according to the views of the compiler. For further particulars concerning dictionaries of this kind, see the *Preface.*

Dictionary of the English Language

The only attempt which has hitherto been made towards forming a regular dictionary of the English language, is that of the learned Dr Samuel Johnson. But although it is executed in a masterly manner, yet as it cannot be expected that an undertaking of this nature could be brought to perfection by one man, we shall venture to suggest a few circumstances which, if duely attended to, may perhaps be of some utility.

The design of every dictionary of language, is to explain in the most accurate manner, the meaning of every word, and to show the various ways in which it can be combined with others, in as far as this tends to alter its meaning. The dictionary which does this in the most accurate manner, is the most complete. Therefore the principal study of a lexicographer ought to be, to discover a method which will be best adapted for that purpose. Dr Johnson, with great labour, has collected the various meanings of every word, and quoted the authorities: But, would it not have been an improvement if he had given an accurate definition of the precise meaning of every word; pointed out the way in which it ought to be employed with the greatest propriety; shewed the various deviations from that original meaning, which custom had so far established as to render allowable; and fixed the precise limits beyond which it could not be employed without becoming a vicious expression? With this view, it would have been necessary to exhibit the nice distinctions that take place between words which are nearly synonymous. Without this, many words can only be defined in such a manner, as that they must be considered as exactly synonymous. We omit giving any quotations from Johnson to point out these defects; but shall content ourselves with giving a few examples, to shew how, according to our idea, a dictionary of the English language ought to be compiled.

Grammar: An Art and a Science

Grammar has not only been a central element of a sound education but also a subject in which most of the Britannica*'s editors have particularly excelled. Smellie was one of those, and it is probable that he wrote all of the article "Grammar" himself—eighteen pages plus a foldout table amounting to nearly six more pages. (He does not list a grammar among the*

150-odd books his foreword acknowledges as sources.)

Here is the preface to Smellie's article, untouched between the 1st (1768–1771) and 9th (1875–1889) editions. (B.L.F.)

GRAMMAR is the art of speaking or writing any language with correctness and propriety; and the purpose of language is to communicate our thoughts.

Grammar, considered as an art, necessarily supposes the previous existence of language; and as its design is to teach any language to those who are ignorant of it, it must be adapted to the genius of that particular language of which it treats. A just method of grammar, therefore, without attempting any alterations in a language already introduced, furnishes certain observations called rules, to which the methods of speaking used in that language may be reduced; and this collection of rules is called the *grammar* of that particular language. For the greater distinctness with regard to these rules, grammarians have usually divided this subject into four distinct heads: *Orthography,* or the art of combining letters into syllables, and syllables into words; *Etymology,* or the art of deducing one word from another, and the various modifications by which the sense of any one word can be diversified consistently with its original meaning or its relation to the theme whence it is derived; *Syntax,* or what relates to the construction or due disposition of the words of a language into sentences or phrases; and *Prosody,* or that which treats of the quantities and accents of syllables, and the art of making verses.

But grammar, considered as a science, views language only as significant of thought. Neglecting particular and arbitrary modifications introduced for the sake of beauty or elegance, it examines the analogy and relation between words and ideas; distinguishes between those particulars which are essential to language and those which are only accidental; and thus furnishes a certain standard, by which different languages may be compared, and their several excellencies or defects pointed out. This is what is called Philosophical or Universal Grammar.

Painting

Benjamin Robert Haydon (1786–1846) was an English painter of historical scenes—and of modest ability—who was an outstanding writer of the broadest acquaintance with the whole British art world of the early nineteenth century. In the 7th edition (1830–1842) he surveyed the history of painting in a brilliant thirty-eight-page treatise, "Painting," that was studded with cameolike portraits of the great painters of the ages.

The article was carried intact into the 8th edition (1852–1860), which began to appear six years after the unfortunate man, a repeated visitor to debtors' prisons and never able to manage his financial affairs, took his life. A short addendum by a lesser critic countered some of Haydon's views with more modern theoretical positions. (B.L.F.)

It is interesting to compare Haydon's style and judgments with those of William Hazlitt, his illustrious near-contemporary, whose article on the fine arts appears in Part II. Many critics feel that Haydon comes off very well indeed. Painters generally write poorly but Haydon was an exception; he was more skillful with a pen than a brush, as his remarkable Autobiography *suggests. His brief biography in* Britannica*'s current edition stresses the fact that he wrote the article from which the following extracts are drawn.*

PAINTING is the art of conveying thought by the imitation of things through the medium of form and colour, light and shadow. Colour, and light and shadow, can by themselves do little more than excite sensations of harmony and sentiment, independently of action, passion, or story; but if founded upon form, thoughts become clear, expressions of passion intelligible, and actions, gestures, and motions of the human frame defined and decided. *Form* therefore is the basis of painting, sculpture, architecture, and design of every description. . . .

In what country Painting first originated, is nearly as difficult to discover, as it is to find a country where it never existed at all. . . .

The Egyptians appear to have done every thing with reference to form. Their painting was at best but coloured sculpture. They seem to have been aware of the mortality of colours, and to have said, "As colours must go, let us cut out the designs in stone, so that at least form may remain in our granite sculpture, and defy every thing but the convulsion of the earth." First the designer drew the outline in red, then the master artist corrected it, then the sculptor cut it, then the painter coloured it, gods blue, goddesses yellow, men red, and draperies green and black; and such is the extreme dryness of the climate, that a traveller says, he saw in Nubia, a bas-relief half cut, with the red outline left for the rest, and that he wetted his finger and put it up, and immediately obliterated a part of the red chalk.

The Egyptians would seem to have been a severe people, as hard as their own granite. They had an awful feeling of respect for the wisdom of their ancestors; they hated reform; no physician dared to prescribe a new medicine, and no painter dared to invent a new thought. Plato says, that the pictures of his day in Egypt were just the same as from ages immemorial; and, according to Winkelman, another cause of their inferiority in painting, was the little estimation in which painters were held, and their extreme ignorance. Not a single painter of eminence has reached us, and but one sculptor, viz. Memnon, author of three statues at the entrance of the great temple at Thebes. In the knowledge of the figure it is impossible they could be great; for there is proof that they dared not touch the dead body for dissection, and even the embalmers risked their lives from the hatred of the populace. . . .

The superiority of the Greeks in art is always attributed to the secondary causes of climate and government, forgetting the one important requisite, without which the influence of the most genial climate, or the patronage of the most perfect government could avail little; we mean natural and inherent genius. If the Athenians, the Rhodians, the Corinthians, and the Sicyonians owed their excellence in art to the climate, why did not the same climate produce equal perfection in the Spartans and Arcadians? If climate be the secret, why are not all people under the same latitude equally gifted and equally refined? Climate may be more or less favourable to intellectual development, but is never the cause of its existence. Government may elicit genius by fostering and reward, but can never create it. All the lamentation about the climate of England, Scotland, or Flanders, did not prevent Hogarth's appearance in the first, Wilkie's in the second, or Rubens' in the last of these countries; nor could all the beauty of climate in Greece or Italy, ever have made Mengs a Raffaelle, or David the Titian of modern times. . . .

The Greeks were idolaters, and their love of beauty was a principle of their religion. The more beautiful a face or form could be rendered in painting or sculpture, the better chance had the artist of the blessing of the gods here, and their immortal rewards hereafter. As beauty was so much prized by this highly-endowed people, those who were gifted with it became ambitious of making it known to great artists, and by them to the world. Artists fixed the fame of beauty in man or woman, and even children who gave promise of being beautiful were allowed to contest for a prize, and the child who won it had a statue erected to him. Many people were complimented by being named from the beauty of any particular part, and Winkelman quotes an instance, where one was called Χαριτοβλεφαρος that is, "having eyelids where the graces sat." . . .

The whole history of ancient art shews the estimation in which the unsophisticated judgment of the public was held. Aristotle says, "The multitude is the surest judge of the productions of art;" "If you do not get the applause of the public," says some one else, "what celebrity can you attain?" and Cicero makes the public the supreme judge. . . .

After so many vicissitudes of fortune, painting now began to shew symptoms of revival. Frescos had been executed in Rome in 498, and in 795; and there was a head of Christ painted in St. John Lateran, and still to be there seen, which gave evidence of great feeling. But the grand impulse was given in the year 1066, when St. Didier sent for Greek artists to adorn Monte Casino at Subiaco. The example was followed. Pisa, Venice, Amalfi, Genoa, and Milan, all municipal corporations rivalled each other; and when Pisa sent to Greece to collect as many splendid remains of art as could be obtained to adorn the dome of the city, Buschetto, a celebrated Greek architect, was engaged to superintend their embarcation, to accompany them during the voyage, and to land them safely for the purchasers. Buschetto was received with so much enthusiasm, that he founded a school of sculpture, which existed for two hundred years; and ultimately out of this very Greek school, came the great artist Nicolo Pisano, the head of the Italico-Pisan school. From this moment art, after having sunk to the lowest barbarism, went on improving till the taking of Constantinople by Mahommed II., an event which scattered the Greeks collected at that court all over Europe. Hundreds went to Italy as painters, sculptors, chasers, and mosaic painters; and by their struggles for existence, inoculated Italian artists with some remnant of their taste for beauty, decayed as it was. Cimabue was their pupil, and Giotto was his. The Catholic church wanted artists, and genius again began to shew itself. One man of genius appeared after another, till Michel Angelo, Leonardo, Raffaelle, Titian, and Corregio, were the glorious results. And though it cannot be denied that the high aspirations of Christianity, by placing every thing human on its proper level on earth, in comparison with eternal happiness, had justly prostrated the splendid beauty of Pagan art, by exposing its idolatrous tendencies; though the sufferings, and the agonies of its founder and its martyrs had revived its pathos with higher objects than mere beauty of form or face, and saved painting and sculpture from extinction; yet it must be acknowledged, that the beauty of Christian art has never rivalled the indisputable perfection of the Pagans. To their enthusiastic overestimate of the religious value of physical, as emblematic of moral beauty, is their perfection attributable; but if it can only be revived by some similar delusion, the result will in our opinion more than atone for any thing that seems doubtful or questionable in the principle. . . .

Pisa now began to decline, and the Florentines took possession of that city in 1406. Hated and detested by their conquerors, the spirit of the citizens sunk into the greatest depression; the artists left the city, and the school entirely decayed. The Florentines now rose in the ascendant. The Medici began to appear. Cosimo, the father of his country and the protector of genius, gave fresh energy to art, science, and public affairs. Lorenzo followed, and their house became the refuge and resort of all who were celebrated in painting, poetry, sculpture, architecture, and philosophy. Masaccio, the two Piselli, the two Lippi, Binozzo, Sandro, and Ghirlandaio, received from the Medici protection and employment. The pictures of the time have perpetual portraits of the Medici. The citizens became animated with the same spirit; frescoes covered the churches, and smaller works filled the houses. Up sprung, too, that host of painters, marble-cutters, bronze-casters, and chasers, by which the principles of design passed from Pisa to Florence; and out blazed before the world Donatello, Brunelleschi, Ghiberti. The most exquisite productions of sculpture, marble, and bronze followed. . . .

Leonardo was born in 1452. He was a natural son, and had all the eccentricity, sloth and fire, weakness and energy, idleness and diligence of that class. A poet, a musician, a mathematician, an hydraulist, a mechanic, a modeller, and a painter; he excelled in all. Keen, eager, minute, searching and indefatigable, handsome in face, beautiful in person, tall in figure, athletic and skilled in manly exercises, a graceful dancer, a splendid horseman, and an harmonious singer; he equally delighted the people, infatuated the women, and bewitched the sovereign. And yet with all this vast power, the gift of his Creator, he was so deficient in concentration of mind, that he seemed to have no power of collecting its rays sufficiently long to make discoveries in any thing. He was the scholar of Verocchio, by whom he was infected with a lazy love of design in preference to the vigorous energy of using the brush. He passionately loved geometry, horses, and soldiers; and in his horses he never left nature like Raffaelle, Julio Romano, or Michel Angelo, but gave them their natural characteristics of fleshy nostrils and projecting eyes. . . .

The fact is, that such men as Leonardo are great geniuses, but not the greatest. The evidence of superior genius is the power of intellectual concentration. Such powers had Newton, Milton, Bacou, Locke, Watt, Michel Angelo, Napoleon,

Raffaelle, Titian, Rubens, Vandyke, and our own Reynolds. Such men only are examples, and not beacons; such men only are blessings to their species. . . .

Michel Angelo, after his day's study in the gardens which Lorenzo had opened for the youth of Florence, retired to the coins, cameos, and fragments of the palace. With his acuteness, energy, and perception, it is not wonderful that he soon perceived the inferiority of the forms of his master, in comparison with the full beauty of the form, the result of perfect construction in the antique. He corrected with his boyish hand the narrow meagreness of Ghirlandio; and announced, thus early, that self-will and vigorous decision, which enabled him subsequently to accomplish whatever he undertook. Here was the germ of that mighty power which placed the Pantheon in the air, as he predicted and realized in the dome of St. Peter's. Here was the embryo fearlessness, that brought him through the vast ceiling of the Sistine Chapel in fresco, though when he began it, he had never painted in fresco before. Michel Angelo was one of those rare beings who are wanted when they come, and have opportunities put in their way adequate to develope the powers with which they are gifted. Julius II. was as wonderful a man as Michel Angelo; and they mutually inspired each other. What Julius willed, Michel Angelo was as ready to perform; and what the inspirations of Michel Angelo's genius suggested, the vigorous pope, whose fine old venerable head a helmet would have suited better than a tiara, had comprehension to value. They were both fierce, both self-willed, both proud and haughty, both independent and ungovernable. If Julius wished what Michel Angelo was in no humour to do, he would not do it; and if Michel Angelo wanted to execute, on sound principles of art, what the aged pontiff did not comprehend, he would do it, in spite of denunciations of banishment, or threats of displeasure. They were made for each other, they understood each other, and they were attached to each other; they quarrelled, became friends, and quarrelled again. "When will the ceiling be finished?" said Julius, as he trod on the scaffolding with a stamp that made the boards tremble, after climbing to the top, where the great artist lay on his back on a mattress, hard at work, painting with vigour. "When I can," said Michel Angelo, irritated at the interruption. "When thou canst," thundered out the pope; "Art thou minded to be hanged?"

This was the man for Michel Angelo. Conscious of his age, conscious that death followed him wherever he went, he began, proceeded with, and finished all he undertook, as if he had not an hour to live. By his perpetual watching, he hurried Michel Angelo through the ceiling of the chapel in twenty months, a time by no means equal to that which ought to have been devoted to it. The hurry is visible in the fierce, rapid execution; and that which was entirely owing to the impetuosity of his old patron, has been attributed as a merit and a principle to the great painter. Such is the infatuation of praise when a man is really great. Of this astonishing work, it seems that enough can never be said; though language has been exhausted to do it justice. Fuseli was the first who cleared up the mystery of the composition, in a style that places the commentator on a level with the inventor. "It exhibits," he says, "the origin, the progress, and the final dispensation of theocracy." But Fuseli's character of Michel Angelo is overdone. It is an effort to express the deepest feelings in the strongest language; and in all such efforts the language invariably becomes inflated and turgid. . . .

We now come to the Venetian, a great school of colour, light and shadow, impasto, and execution, completing the imitation of reality; and in summing up the character of Italian and Greek art, we shall see that these components of imitation, each of which characterised an Italian school, were combined in all schools, as a necessary requisite in the perfection of Grecian imitation.

The most ancient work of Venetian art known, is in Verona, in the cellar of a monastery, (Santi Nazario a Celso). It is inaccessible to the public, but can be seen in the woodcuts of Dionisi. In the part which formed the oratorio of the faithful, has been painted the mystery of redemption; it is a work of 1070, when the Doge Silvo invited Grecian mosaic painters to adorn St. Mark; men who though rude in art, could nevertheless paint. Thus commenced the art in Venice, whither, after Constantinople was taken by the Venetians in 1204, Greek painters and sculptors, as well as orefici, flocked in crowds.

In the thirteenth century, painters had increased so much, that a company was formed, like the English constituent body to which Hogarth belonged, and laws and constitutions were made. Things were proceeding in this train when Giotto, returning from Avignon, painted at Verona and Padua. Nothing of his, however, is left in Verona; but at Padua the remains of his works are still quite fresh in fresco, and full of grace and vigour. Such was the early beginning of this great school, in which it will be seen that Greeks, as usual, had the first hand. Various names sprung up in this period, but the Bellinis are the most important. . . .

Titian began in the style of his master Bellini, with the most minute finish; a capital basis for future practice, if a man have comprehension to know when to leave it, as Titian did. To shew the young artist that it is never too late to improve, let him compare the Bacchus and Ariadne in our National Gallery, when he could not draw finely, with the Pietro Martyre when he could. In modern art, he was the only painter who hit the characteristic of flesh. Every great painter's flesh is paint; Titian's had real circulation of blood under the skin. On comparing the Ganymede, in our National Gallery, fine as it came from Titian's pencil, with the Theodosius by Vandyke, which is close to it, as fine a specimen of Vandyke's fire of brush as can be seen, the heavy leathern look of Vandyke's colour excited astonishment. In the flesh of Ganymede, colour, oil, brush, and canvass, were all entirely forgotten; it quivered, it moved with the action of the limbs. In Vandyke, the materials of art are uppermost; you think of them, you wonder at the touch, you forget the subject, the expressions as it were scenting of the painter's room and the easel. And so you do with all the Flemings, but never with Titian. Though we have fine Titians in England, the Diana being at Lord Egerton's, and a head at the Duke of Sutherland's; yet it must be confessed, that the Louvre possesses Titians more perfect, especially the entombing of Christ. In Josephine's collection at Malmaison, there were a Venus and Cupid, as perfect as our Ganymede, and not injured by *restoring,* the fatal propensity of the French. In Titian whenever you see the blues sober and in harmony, the picture is uninjured; whenever you see them harsh and too brilliant, they have been rubbed, and the last tone has been taken off. . . .

The giant of Titian's school was Tintoretto, who gave such early indications of self-will and genius, that Titian, mean and jealous, turned him out of the house. Raffaelle would not have done this; he did not turn out Julio Romano. But Tintoretto was not to be crushed by the bad passions of his envious master; and took it very properly as an evidence of his talent. And what did Titian get by his paltry meanness? Nothing but pity. Tintoretto, young as he was, immediately formed a plan of his own, for combining the drawing of Michel Angelo with the colour of Titian. He devoted the day to the one, and many parts of many nights, and often whole ones, to the other. In a few years, the result was the Miracle of the Slave and the Crucifixion. Although the execution of Tintoretto looked daring and impudent by the side of the modest, senatorial dignity of Titian, yet there was a grand, defined dash about it. . . . His pictures seem to be a mass of fore-shortenings, affected twistings, dashing darks, and splashing lights, with a hundred horse power of execution; bearded heads, Venetian armour, silks, satins, angels, horses, architecture, dogs, water, and brawny-armed and butcher-legged gondoliers, without pathos, passion, or refinement. He used to put little models in boxes, and light them in different holes, for effect. Like all Italians, he was accustomed to model and hang up his models by threads for fore-shortening. His style of form was a mixture of the pulpiness of the Venetian, and the long, anotomical, bony look of the Florentine school. He cannot be depended upon for correctness of proportions, but he was a grand and daring genius; and his conduct, when oppressed by Titian, should ever be held up as an example for the aspiring youth, when trodden upon by his elders. . . .

Rembrandt van Rhyn, was next to Rubens, in point of art, and more than equal to him in originality. Whether in portrait, landscape, or historical pictures large and small, he was like nobody; as wonderful as any, and sometimes superior to all. His bistre-drawings are exquisite, his etchings unrivalled; his colour, light and shadow, and surface, solemn, deep, and without example; but in the naked form, male or female, he was an Esquimaux. His notions of the delicate form of women, would have frightened an Arctic bear. Let the reader fancy a Billingsgate fish-woman, descending to a bath at a moment's notice, with hideous feet, large knees and bony legs, a black eye, and a dirty night-cap—and he will have a perfect idea of Rembrandt's conception of female beauty. . . .

We come now to the British School, which, though the last founded in Europe, is inferior to none in variety of power.

There is no doubt that the art would have advanced in Britain side by side with the continental nations, if we had continued Catholics; in fact, we were doing so, when Wickliffe's opposition to the Catholic priests roused up the people to hate and detest every thing connected with their system. Painting of course came under this furious denunciation, and through successive ages went on till the period of the Reformation. . . .

As an inventor, Hogarth is by far the greatest of the British school; although in aim and object, colour, surface, and all the requisites of a great painter, infinitely below Reynolds. It would be useless to detail the perfections of a man so admired all over the earth, and who will only cease to be a delight with its existence. It is astonishing how hereditary is the hatred of academies. The painters in revenge for Hogarth's opposition, swore that he was no painter, and swear so to this hour. The absurdity of this criticism can be proved by the Marriage à la Mode, whilst the picture of the husband and wife after a rout, is as beautifully touched as any in that class of art can be. He has not the clearness of Teniers, nor the sharpness of Wilkie; his touch is blunt, and his colour deficient in richness; but you feel not the want whilst looking at him; and although his expression is often caricature, yet in the above picture it is perfection. Hogarth unfortunately believed himself infallible; but his wretched beauty of Drury Lane for Pharaoh's daughter at the Foundling, his miserable Sigismunda, and his Paul before Felix, we hope convinced him of his forte. If he was *serious* in these pictures, which we very much doubt, he deserved a strait waistcoat and a low diet as the only treatment for his hallucination.

Water-Color Painting

When it comes to the nuts and bolts of the visual arts it's always useful to listen to a leading practitioner. Britannica *frequently provides this opportunity. In the 1957 printing of the 14th edition (1929), as part of a longer article on water-color painting, Adolf Dehn (1895–1968) discussed technique. We subjoin its opening paragraphs.*

Transparent water colour allows for a freshness and luminosity in its washes and for a deft calligraphic brushwork which makes it a most alluring medium. Too often artists, dazzled by the ease of attaining atmospheric effects, degenerated into creating slight and pretty transcriptions of nature. Consequently water colour was condescendingly thought of as the anemic and gaudy little sister of oil painting.

During the 20th century, especially after 1940, a revitalization in water-colour painting came about. The painters liberated themselves of tight purists' notions and started adding ink, pencil, pastel, crayon and opaque white to gain new effects. The biggest change came in the general use of gouache and casein colours. As a result the average water-colour exhibition probably contained more opaque than transparent water colours and acquired the same serious respect which oil painting had always had.

There is one basic difference between transparent water colour and all other heavy painting mediums—its transparency. The oil painter can paint one opaque colour over another until he has achieved his desired result. The whites are created with opaque white.

The water-colourists' approach is the opposite. Instead of building up he leaves out. The white paper creates the whites. The darkest accents may be placed on the paper with the pigment as it comes out of the tube or with very little water mixed with it. Otherwise the colours are diluted with water. The more water in the wash, the more the paper affects the colour; for example, vermilion, a warm red will gradually turn into a cool pink as it is thinned with more water.

The knowledge which comes through much experience, of how all colours change through dilution and the awareness that the wet wash is fresher and brighter than the dried-in wash, is necessary to successful painting. Timing—knowing when to place a wash of one colour next to a wash of another colour or over it—requires experience. If the original wash is very wet a complete merging of the two will occur; if it is still damp the edges will become fuzzy; if it is dry the newly laid wash or line will be sharp and clear.

Laying an even wash over a large area, as in a sky, should be done rapidly with a big flat brush so that one stroke is placed against the preceding one before it will have dried into the paper. If the whole area is dampened with water beforehand it can be covered with greater ease. If a graduated wash from light to dark is desired, the wash can be spread upward by starting with the lighter colour and gradually intensifying it to the darkest tone. Then by tilting the drawing board at a 45° angle, an even merging of colour will occur.

Although the most unique and beautiful attribute of water colour is the luminosity of the washes and the skilful calligraphy of the brush strokes, some painters deliberately glaze over certain colour areas with thin washes, thereby destroying some of the luminosity of such areas. The resulting heavier and more mat surface, *e.g.*, in the ground area of a landscape, sets off the luminosity of the sky.

Scrubbing out colours partially or completely with a dampened sponge creates fuzzy atmospheric effects which may be desirable. The hard surface of the paper is lost, however, and transparency is lessened.

The dry brush technique—the use of the brush containing pigment but little water, dragged over the rough surface of the paper—creates various granular effects similar to a crayon drawing. Whole compositions can be made in this way. This technique also may be used over dull washes to enliven them.

A razor blade is a valuable tool. The blade dug into a wet wash will create different textures as in foliage. Absorbent tissues can be used effectively to create shapes, as in clouds, by pressing the tissue onto the wet wash and lifting the colour.

It is often said that transparent watercolour painting is the most difficult medium of painting. Great knowledge and experience plus a nimbleness of hand and brain are required for success. The watercolourist may start with a well-conceived plan of action but should always be ready to shift his approach if, and most probably when, the washes run away from him. He must then be able to use the new possibilities which the unforeseen makes possible, thus remaining master of a situation which might otherwise cause failure.

The 2nd Edition on Music

The 1st edition (1768–1771) featured an article on "Musick" of more than thirty-five pages, augmented by seventeen plates illustrating notes, keys, "cliffs" (clefs), chords, melodies, and rhythms. This was enormously expanded in the 2nd edition (1778–1783), which presented a long and separate history of "Music," as it was now spelled, along with a lengthy and entirely new section on musical theory.

James Tytler, the editor of the 2nd edition and the author of this article, clearly wrote from a sound musical knowledge of his own, and quoted from various learned contemporaries including Benjamin Franklin. (B.L.F.)

We subjoin his introductory remarks. They turn out to be largely an admonitory lecture on that bugaboo of all eighteenth-century Britons, the unfortunate Jean-Jacques Rousseau.

MUSIC

The art of combining sounds in a manner agreeable to the ear. This combination may be either simultaneous or successive: in the first case, it constitutes harmony; in the last, melody. But though the same sounds, or intervals of sound, which give pleasure when heard in succession, will not always produce the same effect in harmony; yet the principles which constitute the simpler and more perfect kinds of harmony, are almost, if not entirely, the same with those of melody. By *perfect harmony*, we do not here mean that plenitude, those complex modifications of harmonic sound which are admired in practice; but that harmony which is called *perfect* by theoricians and artists; that harmony which results from the coalescence of simultaneous sounds produced by vibrations in the proportions of thirds, fifths, and octaves, or their duplicates.

The principles upon which these various combinations of sound are founded, and by which they are regulated, constitute a science, which is not only extensive but profound, when we would investigate the principles from whence these happy modifications of sound result, and by which they are determined; or when we would explore the sensations, whether mental, or corporeal, with which they affect us. The ancient definitions of music are not proportioned in their extent to our present ideas of that art; but M. Rousseau betrays a temerity highly inconsistent with the philosophical character, when from thence he infers, that their ideas were vague and undetermined. Every soul susceptible of refinement and delicacy in taste or sentiment, must be conscious that there is a music in action as well as in sound; and that the ideas of beauty and decorum, of harmony and symmetry, are, if we may use the expression, equally constituent of visible as of audible music. These illustrious minds, whose comprehensive prospects in every science where taste and propriety prevail took in nature at a single glance would behold with contempt and ridicule those narrow and microscopic views of which alone their successors in philosophy have discovered themselves capacious. With these definitions, however, we are less concerned, as they bear no proportion to the ideas which are now entertained of music. Nor can we follow M. Rousseau, from whatever venerable sources his authority may be derived, in adopting his Egyptian etymology for the word *music*. The established derivation from *Musa* could only be questioned by a paradoxical genius. Is the fact sufficiently authenticated, that music had been practised in Egypt before it was known in Greece? And though it were true, would it follow from thence, that the Greeks had borrowed the name as well as the art from Egypt? If the art of music be so natural to man that vocal melody is practised wherever articulate sounds are used, there can be little reason for deducing the idea of music from the whistling of winds through the reeds that grew on the river Nile. And indeed, when we reflect with how easy a transition we may pass from the accents of speaking to diatonic sounds, when we observe how early children adapt the language of their amusements to measure and melody however rude, when we consider how early and universally these practices take place, there is no avoiding the conclusion, that the idea of music is connatural to man, and implied in the original principles of his constitution. We have already said, that the principles on which it is founded, and the rules by which it is conducted, constitute a science. The same maxims when applied to practice form an art.

Adagio

In the 1st edition (1768–1771) the term "adagio" is thus defined:

. . . in music, an Italian adverb, signifying *softly, leisurely;* and is used to denote the slowest of all times, except the grave.

From the final three words alone we can beautifully conceive the temper of the Scottish editors.

The Musical Glasses

Benjamin Franklin (1706–1790) never wrote directly for the Britannica *(like Samuel Johnson, he would have been a great editor) but he is so generously quoted in the article "Harmonica" (3rd edition, 1788–1797) that we may call him an honorary contributor. The editor tells us that "in a letter to Father Beccaria" Franklin gives "a minute and elegant account of the Harmonica" (a contemporary invention) and then goes on to describe a "new instrument," quite different, of course, from our modern mouth harmonica. These extracts leap the centuries to give us the flavor of one aspect of the versatile doctor.*

. . . You have doubtless heard the sweet tone that is drawn from a drinking-glass, by pressing a wet finger round its brim. One Mr Puckeridge, a gentleman from Ireland, was the first who thought of playing tunes formed of these tones. . . .

Mr E. Delaval, a most ingenious member of our Royal Society, made one in imitation of it with a better choice and form of glasses, which was the first I saw or heard. Being charmed with the sweetness of its tones, and the music he produced from it, I wished to see the glasses disposed in a more convenient form, and brought together in a narrower compass, so as to admit of a greater number of tones, and all within reach of hand to a person sitting before the instrument; which I accomplished, after various intermediate trials, and less commodious forms, both of glasses and construction, in the following manner.

The glasses are blown as near as possible in the form of hemispheres, having each an open neck or socket in the middle. The thickness of the glass near the brim is about the tenth of an inch, or hardly quite so much, but thicker as it comes nearer the neck; which in the largest glasses is about an inch deep, and an inch and a half wide within. . . . The largest glass is nine inches diameter, and the smallest three inches. Between these there are 23 different sizes, differing from each other a quarter of an inch in diameter. To make a single instrument there should be at least six glasses blown of each size; and out of this number one may probably pick 37 glasses (which are sufficient for three octaves with all the semitones) that will be each either the note one wants, or a little sharper than that note, and all fitting so well into each other as to taper pretty regularly from the largest to the smallest. . . .

The glasses being chosen, and every one marked with a diamond the note you intend it for, they are to be tuned by diminishing the thickness of those that are too sharp. This is done by grinding them round from the neck towards the brim, the breadth of one or two inches as may be required; often trying the glass by a well tuned harpsichord, comparing the note drawn from the glass by your finger with the note you want, as founded by that string of the harpsichord. . . .

Harmonica.

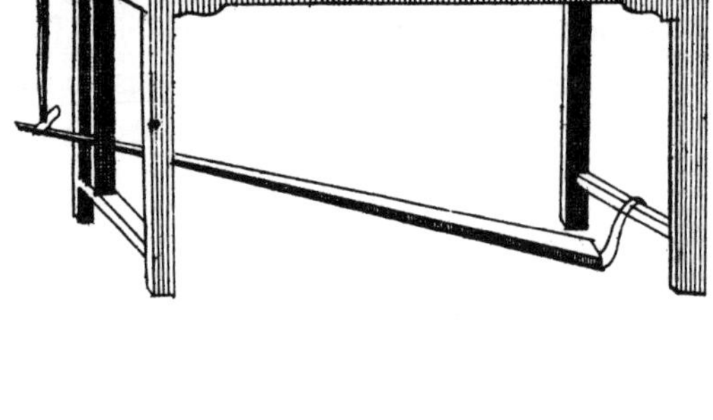

The glasses being thus tuned, you are to be provided with a case for them, and a spindle on which they are to be fixed. My case is about three feet long, eleven inches every way wide within at the biggest end, and five inches at the smallest end; for it tapers all the way, to adapt it better to the conical figure of the set of glasses. This case opens in the middle of its height, and the upper part turns up by hinges fixed behind. The spindle is of hard iron, lies horizontally from end to end of the box within, exactly in the middle, and is made to turn on brass gudgeons at each end. It is round, an inch diameter at the thickest end, and tapering to a quarter of an inch at the smallest.—A square shank comes from its thickest end through the box, on which shank a wheel is fixed by a screw. This wheel serves as a fly to make the motion equable, when the spindle, with the glasses, is turned by the foot like a spinning wheel. My wheel is of mahogany, 18 inches diameter, and pretty thick, so as to conceal near its circumference about 25 lb. of lead.—An ivory pin is fixed in the face of this wheel, about four inches from the axis. Over the neck of this pin is put the loop of the string that comes up from the moveable step to give it motion. The case stands on a neat frame with four legs.

To fix the glasses on the spindle, a cork is first to be fitted in each neck pretty tight, and projecting a little without the neck, that the neck of one may not touch the inside of another when put together, for that would make a jarring. These corks are to be perforated with holes of different diameters, so as to suit that part of the spindle on which they are to be fixed. When a glass is put on, by holding it stiffly between both hands, while another turns the spindle, it may be gradually brought to its place. . . . The glasses thus are placed one in another; the largest on the biggest end of the spindle, which is to the left hand: the neck of this glass is towards the wheel; and the next goes into it in the same position, only about an inch of its brim appearing beyond the brim of the first; thus proceeding, every glass when fixed shows about an inch of its brim (or three quarters of an inch, or half an inch, as they grow smaller) beyond the brim of the glass that contains it; and it is from these exposed parts of each glass that the tone is drawn, by laying a finger on one of them as the spindle and glasses turn round.

My largest glass is G a little below the reach of a common voice, and my highest G, including three complete octaves. . . .

This instrument is played upon by sitting before the middle of the set of glasses, as before the keys of a harpsichord, turning them with the foot, and wetting them now and then with a spunge and clean water. The fingers should be first a little soaked in water, and quite free from all greasiness; a little fine chalk upon them is sometimes useful, to make them catch the glass and bring out the tone more readily. Both hands are used, by which means different parts are played together. Observe, that the tones are best drawn out when the glasses turn *from* the ends of the fingers, not when they turn *to* them.

The advantages of this instrument are, that its tones are incomparably sweet beyond those of any other; that they may be swelled and softened at pleasure by stronger or weaker pressures of the finger, and continued to any length; and that the instrument, being once well tuned, never again wants tuning.

Opera

Sir Donald Francis Tovey (1875–1940) was by all accounts the most knowledgeable and penetrating writer on music in his day, and perhaps in any day. Somewhat to his chagrin, his criticism and program notes were so highly regarded as to overshadow his equally remarkable abilities as pianist, conductor, and composer. Since such diverse talents are rarely combined in a single individual, however, it was inevitable that the lucidity and wit of his literary style—itself a rarity in the realm of criticism—should win the wider audience. The invitation to contribute a number of articles on musical topics to the 11th edition (1910–1911) may well have been the original stimulus for his turning to the pen. The articles were collected in volume form in 1944, and they constitute, together with the six volumes of his Essays in Musical Analysis, *an invaluable, if lamentably small, body of work. The major part of his article on "Opera" follows. (R. McH.)*

OPERA (Italian for "work"), a drama set to music, as distinguished from plays in which music is merely incidental. Music has been a resource of the drama from the earliest times, and doubtless the results of researches in the early history of this connexion have been made very interesting, but they are hardly relevant to a history of opera as an art-form. If language has meaning, an art-form can hardly be said to exist under conditions where the only real connexions between its alleged origin and its modern maturity are such universal means of expression as can equally well connect it with almost everything else. We will therefore pass over the orthodox history of opera as traceable from the music of Greek tragedy to that of miracle-plays, and will begin with its real beginning, the first dramas that were set to music in order to be produced as musical works of art, at the beginning of the 17th century.

There seems no reason to doubt the story, given by Doni, of the meetings held by a group of amateurs at the house of the Bardi in Florence in the last years of the 16th century, with the object of trying experiments in emotional musical expression by the use of instruments and solo voices. Before this time there was no real opportunity for music-drama. The only high musical art of the 16th century was unaccompanied choral music: its expression was perfect within its limits, and its limits so absolutely excluded all but what may be called static or contemplative emotion that "dramatic music" was as inconceivable as "dramatic architecture." But the literary and musical *dilettanti* who met at the house of the Bardi were not mature musical artists; they therefore had no scruples, and their imaginations were fired by the dream of restoring the glories of Greek tragedy, especially on the side of its musical declamation. The first pioneer in the new "monodic" movement seems to have been Vincenzo Galilei, the father of Galileo. This enthusiastic amateur warbled the story of Ugolino to the accompaniment of the lute, much to the amusement of expert musicians; but he gained the respect and sympathy of those whose culture was literary rather than musical. His efforts must have been not unlike a wild caricature of Mr. W. B. Yeats's method of reciting poetry to the psaltery. The first public production in the new style was Jacopo Peri's *Euridice* (1600), which was followed by a less successful effort of Caccini's on the same subject. To us it is astonishing that an art so great as the polyphony of the 16th century could ever have become forgotten in a new venture so feeble in its first steps. Sir Hubert Parry has happily characterized the general effect of the new movement on contemporary imagination as something like that of laying a foundation-stone—the suggestion of a vista of possibilities so inspiriting as to exclude all sense of the triviality of the present achievement. Meanwhile those composers who retained the mastery of polyphonic music tried to find a purely vocal and polyphonic solution of the problem of music-drama; and the *Amfiparnasso* of Orazio Vecchi (written in 1594, the year of Palestrina's death, and produced three years later) is not alone, though it is by far the most remarkable, among attempts to make a music-drama out of a series of madrigals. From the woodcuts which adorn the first edition of the *Amfiparnasso* it has been conjectured that the actors sang one voice each, while the rest of the harmony was supplied by singers behind the stage; and this may have been the case with other works of this kind. But the words of Vecchi's introductory chorus contradict this idea, for they tell the audience that "the theatre of this drama is the world" and that the spectators must "hear instead of seeing."

With the decadence of the madrigal, Monteverde brought a real musical power to bear on the new style. His results are now intelligible only to historians, and they seem to us artistically nugatory; but in their day they were so impressive as to render the further continuance of 16th-century choral art impossible. At the beginning of the 17th century no young musician of lively artistic receptivity could fail to be profoundly stirred by Monteverde's *Orfeo* (1602), *Arianna* (1608) and *Il Combattimento di Tancredi e Clorinda* (1624), works in which the resources of instruments were developed with the same archaic boldness, the same grasp of immediate emotional effect and the same lack of artistic organization as the harmonic resources. The spark of Monteverde's genius produced in musical history a result more like an explosion than an enlightenment; and the emotional rhetoric of his art was so uncontrollable, and at the same time so much more impressive in suggestion than in realization, that we cannot be surprised that the next definite step in the history of opera took the direction of mere musical form, and was not only undramatic but anti-dramatic.

The system of free musical declamation known as *recitative* is said to have been used by Emilio del Cavalieri as early as 1588, and it was in the nature of things almost the only means of vocal expression conceivable by the pioneers of opera. Formal melody, such as that of popular songs, was as much beneath their dignity as it had been beneath that of the high art from which they revolted; but, in the absence of any harmonic system but that of the church modes, which was manifestly incapable of assimilating the new "unprepared discords," and in the utter chaos of early experiments in instrumentation, formal melody proved a godsend as the novelty of recitative faded. Tunes were soon legalized at moments of dramatic repose when it was possible for the actors to indulge in either a dance or a display of vocalization; it was in the tunes that the strong harmonic system of modern tonality took shape; and by the early days of Alessandro Scarlatti, before the end of the 17th century, the art of tune-making had perennially blossomed into the musically safe and effective form of the *aria*. From this time until the death of Handel the history of opera is simply the history of the aria; except in so far as in France, under Lully, it is also the history of ballet-music, the other main theatrical occasion for the art of tune-making. With opera before Gluck there is little interest in tracing schools and developments, for the musical art had as mechanical a connexion with drama as it had with the art of scene-painting, and neither it nor the drama which was attached to it showed any real development at all, though the librettist Metastasio presented as imposing a figure in 18th-century Italian literature as Handel presented in Italian opera. Before this period of stagnation we find an almost solitary and provincial outburst of life in the wonderful patchwork of Purcell's art (1658–1695). Whether he is producing genuine opera (as in the unique case of *Dido and Aeneas*) or merely incidental music to plays (as in the so-called opera *King Arthur*), his deeply inspired essays in dramatic music are no less interesting in their historic isolation from everything except the influence of Lully than they are admirable as evidences of a genius which, with the opportunities of 50 years later or 150 years earlier, might assuredly have proved one of the greatest in all music. Another sign of life has been appreciated by recent research in the interesting farcical operas (mostly Neapolitan) of certain early 18th-century Italian composers, which have some bearing on the antecedents of Mozart.

The real reason for the stagnation of high opera before Gluck is that the forms of music known before 1750 could not express dramatic change without losing artistic organization. The "spirit of the age" can have had little to do with the difficulty, or why should Shakespeare not have had a contemporary operatic brother-artist during the "Golden Age" of music? The opportunity for reform came with the rise of the sonata style. It was fortunate for Gluck that the music of his time was too vigorously organized to be upset by new discoveries. Gluck was a much greater artist than Monteverde, but he too was not overloaded with academic mastery; indeed, though historians have denied it, Monteverde was by far the better contrapuntist and seems rather to have renounced his musical powers than to have struggled for need of them. But instead of memories of a Golden Age, Gluck had behind him 150 years of harmonic and orchestral knowledge of good and evil. He also had almost as clear a sense of symphonic form as could find scope in opera at all; and his melodic power was generally of the highest order. It is often said that his work was too far in advance of his time to establish his intended reform; and, if this means that undramatic Italian operas continued to outnumber those dramatic masterpieces which no smaller man could achieve, the statement is as true as it is of every great artist. If, however, it is taken to mean that because Mozart's triumphs do not lie in serious opera he owes nothing to Gluck, then the statement is misleading. The influence of Gluck on Mozart was profound, not only where it is relevant to the particular type of libretto, as in *Idomeneo,* but also on the broad dramatic basis which includes Greek tragedy and the 18th-century comedy of manners. Mozart, whose first impulse was always to make his music coherent in itself, for some time continued to cultivate side by side with his growing polyphony and freedom of movement certain Italian formalities which, though musically effective and flattering to singers, were dramatically vicious. But these features, though they spoil *Idomeneo,* correspond to much that in Gluck's operas shows mere helplessness; and in comic opera they may even become dramatically appropriate. Thus in *Cosi fan tutte* the florid arias in which the two heroines protest their fidelity are the arias of ladies who do protest too much; and in *Die Zauberflöte* the extravagant vocal fireworks of the Queen of Night are the displays of one who, in the words of the high priest Sarastro, "hopes to cajole the people with illusions and superstition." In the article MOZART we have discussed other evidences of his stagecraft and insight into character, talents for which his comic subjects gave him far more scope than those of classical tragedy had given to Gluck. Mozart always extracts the utmost musical effect from every situation in his absurd and often tiresome libretti (especially in vocal *ensemble*), while his musical effects are always such as give dramatic life to what in other hands are conventional musical forms. These merits would never have been gainsaid but for the violence of Wagner's earlier partisans in their revolt from the uncritical classicism of his denser and noisier opponents. Wagner himself stands as far aloof from Wagnerian Philistinism as from uncritical classicism. He was a fierce critic of social conditions and by no means incapable of hasty iconoclastic judgments; but he would have treated with scant respect the criticism that censures

Mozart for superficiality in rejecting the radically unmusical element of mordant social satire which distinguishes the *Figaro* of Beaumarchais from the most perfect opera in all classical music.

It cannot be said that in any high artistic sense Italian comic opera has developed continuously since Mozart. The vocal athleticism of singers; the acceptance and great development by Mozart of what we may call symphonic (as distinguished from Handelian) forms of aria and *ensemble;* and the enlargement of the orchestra; these processes gave the Italian composers of Mozart's and later times prosaically golden opportunities for lifting spectators and singers to the seventh heaven of flattered vanity, while the music, in itself no less than in its relation to the drama, was steadily degraded. The decline begins with Mozart's contemporary and survivor, D. Cimarosa, whose ideas are genuine and, in the main, refined, but who lacks power and resource. His style was by no means debased, but it was just so slight that contemporaries found it fairly easy. His most famous work, *Il Matrimonio Segreto,* is an *opera buffa* which is still occasionally revived, and it is very like the sort of thing that people who despise Mozart imagine *Figaro* to be. Unless it is approached with sympathy, its effect after *Figaro* is hardly more exhilarating than that of the once pilloried spurious "Second Part" to the *Pickwick Papers*. But this is harsh judgment; for it proves to be a good semi-classic as soon as we take it on its own merits. It is far more musical, if less vivacious, than Rossini's *Barbiere;* and the decline of Italian opera is more significantly foreshadowed in Cimarosa's other *chef-d'oeuvre,* the remarkable *opera seria, Gli Orazzi ed i Curiazzi.* Here the arias and *ensembles* are serious art, showing a pale reflection of Mozart, and not wholly without Mozart's spirit; the choruses, notably the first of all, have fine moments; and the treatment of conflicting emotions at one crisis, where military music is heard behind the scenes, is masterly. Lastly, the abrupt conclusion at the moment of the catastrophe is good and was novel at the time, though it foreshadows that sacrifice of true dramatic and musical breadth to the desire for an "effective curtain," and that mortal fear of anti-climax which in classical French opera rendered a great musical finale almost impossible. But the interesting and dramatic features in *Gli Orazzi* are unfortunately less significant historically than the vulgarity of its overture, and the impossibility, after the beautiful opening chorus, of tracing any unmistakably tragic style in the whole work except by the negative sign of dullness.

Before Cimarosa's overwhelming successor Rossini had retired from his indolent career, these tendencies had already reduced both composers and spectators to a supreme indifference to the mood of the libretto, an indifference far more fatal than mere inattention to the plot. Nobody cares to follow the plot of Mozart's *Figaro;* but then no spectator of Beaumarchais's *Mariage de Figaro* is prevented by the intricacy of its plot from enjoying it as a play. In both cases we are interested in the character-drawing and in each situation as it arises; and we do no justice to Mozart's music when we forget this interest, even in cases where the libretto has none of the literary merit that survives in the transformation of Beaumarchais's comedy into an Italian libretto. But with the Rossinian decline all charitable scruples of criticism are misplaced, for Italian opera once more became as purely a pantomimic concert as in the Handelian period; and we must not ignore the difference that it was now a concert of very vulgar music, the vileness of which was only aggravated by the growing range and interest of dramatic subjects. The best that can be said in defence of it was that the vulgarity was not pretentious and unhealthy, like Meyerbeer's; indeed, if the famous "Mad Scene" in Donizetti's *Lucia di Lammermoor* had only been meant to be funny it would not have been vulgar at all. Occasionally the drama pierced through the empty breeziness of the music; and so the spirit of Shakespeare, even when smothered in an Italian libretto unsuccessfully set to music by Rossini, proved so powerful that one spectator of Rossini's *Otello* is recorded to have started out of his seat at the catastrophe, exclaiming "Good Heavens! the tenor is murdering the soprano!" And in times of political unrest more than one opera became as dangerous as an over-censored theatre could make it. An historical case in point is brilliantly described in George Meredith's *Vittoria.* But what has this to do with the progress of music? The history of Italian opera from after its culmination in Mozart to its subsidence on the big drum and cymbals of the Rossinians is the history of a protected industry. Verdi's art, both in its burly youth and in its shrewd old age, is far more the crown of his native genius than of his native traditions; and, though opinions differ as to the spontaneity and depth of the change, the paradox is true that the Wagnerization of Verdi was the musical emancipation of Italy.

After Mozart the next step in the development of true operatic art was neither Italian nor German, but French. The French sense of dramatic fitness had a wonderfully stimulating effect upon every foreign composer who came to France. Rossini himself, in *Guillaume Tell,* was electrified into a dramatic and orchestral life of an incomparably higher order than the rollicking rattle of serious and comic Italian opera in its decline. He was in the prime of life when he wrote it, but it exhausted him and was practically his last important work, though he lived to a cheerful old age. The defects of its libretto were grave, but he made unprecedented efforts to remedy them, and finally succeeded, at the cost of an entire act. The experience was very significant; for, from the time of Gluck onwards, while it cannot be denied that native and naturalized French operatic art has suffered from many forms of musical and dramatic debasement, we may safely say that no opera has met with success in France that is without theatrical merit. And the French contribution to musical history between Gluck and Rossini is of great nobility. If Cherubini and Méhul had had Gluck's melodic power, the classics of French opera would have been the greatest achievements in semi-tragic music-drama before Wagner. As it is, their austerity is not that of the highest classics. It is negative, and tends to exclude outward attractiveness rather because it cannot achieve it than because it contains all things in due proportion. Be this as it may, Cherubini had a real influence on Beethoven; not to mention that the libretti of *Fidelio* and *Les Deux journées* were originally by the same author, though *Fidelio* underwent great changes in translation and revision. It is impossible to say what French opera might have done for music through Beethoven if *Fidelio* had not remained his solitary (because very nearly unsuccessful) operatic monument; but there is no doubt as to its effect on Weber, whose two greatest works, *Der Freischütz* and *Euryanthe,* are two giant strides from Cherubini to Wagner. *Euryanthe* is in respect of *Leit-motif* almost more Wagnerian than *Lohengrin,* Wagner's fourth published opera. It failed to make an epoch in history because of its dreary libretto, to which, however, the highly dramatic libretto of *Lohengrin* owes a surprising number of points.

The libretti of classical opera set too low a literary standard to induce critics to give sufficient attention to their aesthetic bearings; and perhaps the great scholar Otto Jahn is the only writer who has applied a first-rate literary analysis to the subject (see his *Life of Mozart*); a subject which, though of great importance to music, has, like the music itself, been generally thrust into the background by the countless externals that give theatrical works and institutions a national or political importance independent of artistic merit and historical development. Much that finds prominent place in the orthodox history of opera is really outside the scope of musical and dramatic discussion; and it may therefore be safely left to be discovered under non-musical headings elsewhere in this Encyclopaedia. Even when what passes for operatic history has a more real connexion with the art than the history of locomotion has with physical science, the importance of the connexion is often overrated. For example, much has been said as to the progress in German opera from the choice of remote subjects like Mozart's *Die Entführung aus dem Serail* to the choice of a subject so thoroughly German as *Der Freischütz:* but this is only part of the general progress made, chiefly in France, towards the choice of romantic instead of classical subjects. Whatever the intrinsic interest of musical ethnology, and whatever light it may throw upon the reasons why an art will develop and decline sooner in one country than in another, racial character will not suffice to produce an art for which no technique as yet exists. Nor will it suffice in any country to check the development or destroy the value of an art of which the principles were developed elsewhere. No music of Mozart's time could have handled Weber's romantic subjects, and all the Teutonism in history could not have prevented Mozart from adopting and developing those Italian methods that gave him scope. Again, in the time of Lully, who was the contemporary of Molière, the French genius of stagecraft was devoted to reducing opera to an effective series of ballets; yet so little did this hamper composers of real dramatic power that Quinault's libretto to Lully's very successful *Armide* served Gluck unaltered for one of his greatest works 90 years later. If Lully owes so little to Cambert as to be rightly entitled the founder of French opera, if Gluck is a greater reformer than his predecessor Rameau, if Cherubini is a more powerful artist than Méhul, and if, lastly, Meyerbeer developed the vices of the French histrionic machinery with a plausibility which has never been surpassed, then we must reconcile our racial theories with the historic process by which the French *Grand Opéra,* one of the most pronounced national types in all music, was founded by an Italian Jew, reformed by an Austrian, classicized by another Italian, and debased by a German Jew. This only enhances the significance of that French dramatic sense which stimulated foreign composers and widened their choice of subjects, as it also preserved all except the Italian forms of opera from falling into that elsewhere prevalent early 19th-century operatic style in which there was no means of guessing by the music whether any situation was tragic or comic. From the time of Meyerbeer onwards, trivial and vulgar opera has been as common in France as elsewhere; but there is a world of difference between, for example, a garish tune naïvely intended for a funeral march, and a similar tune used in a serious situation with a dramatic sense of its association with other incidents in the opera, and of its contrast with the sympathies of spectators and actors. The first case is as typical of 19th-century musical Italy as the second case is of musical France and all that has come under French influence.

As Wagner slowly and painfully attained his maturity he learned to abhor the influence of Meyerbeer, and indeed it accounts for much of the inequality of his earlier work. But it can hardly have failed to stimulate his sense of effect; and without the help of Meyerbeer's outwardly successful novelties it is doubtful whether even Wagner's determination could have faced the task of his early work, a task so negative and destructive in its first stages. We have elsewhere described how if music of any kind, instrumental or dramatic, was to advance beyond the range of the classical symphony, there was need to devise a kind of musical motion and proportion as different from that of the sonata or symphony as the sonata style is different from that of the suite. All the vexed questions of the function of vocal ensemble, of the structure of the libretto, and of instrumentation, are but aspects and results of this change in what is as much a primary category of music as extension is a primary category of matter. Wagnerian opera, a generation after Wagner's death, was still an unique phenomenon, the rational influence of which was not yet sifted from the concomitant confusions of thought prevalent among many composers of symphony, oratorio, and other forms of which Wagner's principles can be relevant only with incalculable modifications. With Wagner the history of classical opera ends and a new history begins, for in Wagner's hands opera first became a single art-form, a true and indivisible music-drama, instead of a kind of dramatic casket for a collection of *objets d'art* more or less aptly arranged in theatrical tableaux. . . .

With Wagnerian polyphony and continuity music became capable of treating words as they occur in ordinary speech, and repetitions have accordingly become out of place except where they would be natural without music. But it is not here that the real gain in freedom of movement lies. That gain has been won, not by Wagner's negative reforms alone, but by his combination of negative reform with new depths of musical thought; and modern opera is not more exempt than classical opera from the dangers of artistic methods that have become facile and secure. If the libretto has the right dramatic movement, the modern composer need have no care beyond what is wanted to avoid interference with that movement. So long as the music arouses no obviously incompatible emotion and has no breach of continuity, it may find perfect safety in being meaningless. The necessary stagecraft is indeed not common, but neither is it musical. Critics and public will cheerfully agree in ascribing to the composer all the qualities of the dramatist; and three allusions in the music of one scene to that of another will suffice to pass for a marvellous development of Wagnerian *Leit-motif.*

Modern opera of genuine artistic significance ranges from the light song-play type admirably represented by Bizet's *Carmen* to the exclusively "atmospheric" impressionism of Debussy's *Pélleas et Mélisande.* Both these extremes are equally natural in effect, though diametrically opposite in method: for both types eliminate everything that would be inadmissible in ordinary drama. If we examine the libretto of *Carmen* as an ordinary play we shall find it to consist mainly of actual songs and dances, so that more than half of the music would be necessary even if it were not an opera at all. Debussy's opera differs from Maeterlinck's play only in a few omissions such as would probably be made in ordinary non-musical performances. His musical method combines perfect Wagnerian continuity with so entire an absence of *Leit-motif* that there are hardly three musical phrases in the whole opera that could be recognized if they recurred in fresh contexts. The highest conceivable development of Wagnerian continuity has been attained by Strauss in *Salome* and *Elektra;* these operas being actually more perfect in dramatic movement than the original plays of Wilde and Hofmannsthal. But their use of *Leit-motif,* though obvious and impressive, is far less developed than in Wagner; and the polyphony, as distinguished from the brilliant instrumental technique, is, like that technique, devoted mainly to realistic and physically exciting effects that crown the impression in much the same way as skilful lighting of the stage. Certainly Strauss does not in his whole time-limit of an hour and three-quarters use as many definite themes (even in the shortest of figures) as Wagner uses in ten minutes.

It remains to be seen whether a further development of Wagnerian opera, in the sense of addition to Wagner's resources in musical architecture, is possible. The uncompromising realism of Strauss does not at first sight seem encouraging in this direction; yet his treatment of Elektra's first invocation of Agamemnon produces a powerful effect of musical form, dimly perceived, but on a larger scale than even the huge sequences of Wagner. In any case, the best thing that can happen in a period of musical transition is that the leading revolutionaries should make a mark in opera. Musical revolutions are too easy to mean much by themselves; there is no purely musical means of testing the sanity of the revolutionaries or of the critics. But the stage, while boundlessly tolerant of bad music, will stand no nonsense in dramatic movement. (The case of Handelian opera is no exception, for in it the stage was a mere topographical term.) In every period of musical fermentation the art of opera has instantly sifted the men of real ideas from the aesthetes and doctrinaires; Monteverde from the prince of Venosa, Gluck from Gossec, and Wagner from Liszt. As the ferment subsides, opera tends to a complacent decadence; but it will always revive to put to the first and most crucial test every revolutionary principle that enters into music to destroy and expand.

❧ ❧ ❧

The Theatre

The theatre was given only a few lines in the 1st edition (1768–1771), but by the 3rd (1788–1797) it was treated at considerable length. Under that title appeared an excellent review of theatrical history, surely written by the editor, George Gleig. (B.L.F./Ed.)

THEATRE, a place in which shows or dramatic representations are exhibited.

For the origin of the dramatic art we always turn our eyes to Greece, the nursery of the arts and sciences. It may indeed have been known among more ancient nations, but no records remain sufficient to support this opinion. The different states of Greece asserted their claim to the honour of having given it birth, but the account of the Athenians is most generally received. It derived its origin from the hymns which were sung in the festivals of Bacchus in honour of that deity. While these resounded in the ears of the multitude, choruses of Bacchants and Fauns, ranged round certain obscene images which they carried in triumphal procession, chanted lascivious songs, and sometimes sacrificed individuals to public ridicule.

This was the practice in the cities; but a still greater licentiousness reigned in the worship paid to the same divinity by the inhabitants of the country, and especially at the season when they gathered the fruits of his beneficence. Vintagers, besmeared with wine-lees, and intoxicated with joy and the juice of the grape, rode forth in their carts, and attacked each other on the road with gross sarcasms, revenging themselves on their neighbours with ridicule, and on the rich by publishing their injustice. . . .

The origin of the English stage is hid in obscurity. It was not, however, copied from the Grecian or Roman; for it was evidently different in form as well as in matter, and may with more propriety be deduced from a Gothic original. It appears that there were theatrical entertainments in England almost as early as the conquest; for we are told by William Stephanides or Fitz-Stephen, a monk, who in the reign of Henry II. wrote his *Descriptio Nobilissima Civitatis Londonie,* that "London, instead of the common interludes of the theatre, had plays of a more holy kind; representations of the miracles of confessors, and the sufferings of martyrs. At this time there were also certain sets of idle people, who travelled the countries and were called *Mummers,* a kind of vagrant comedians, whose excellence consisted altogether in mimickry and humour.

It is probable that, soon after this time, the dramatic representations called *Mysteries* were exhibited: These mysteries were taken from scripture-history: some represented the creation of the world, with the fall of Adam and Eve; some the story of Joseph; and others even the incarnation and sufferings of the Son of God. These pieces were exhibited in a manner so ridiculous as to favour libertinism and infidelity, as appears by a petition of the chaunters of St Paul's cathedral to Richard II. in 1378 praying, that "some unexpert people might be prohibited from representing the history of the Old Testament to the prejudice of the said clergy, who had been at great expence to represent it publicly at Christmas." . . .

For the state of the theatre during the time of Shakespeare, see PLAYHOUSE; where a full account of it is given from the late valuable edition of our illustrious poet's works by Mr Malone. During the whole reign of James I. the theatre was in great prosperity and reputation: dramatic authors abounded, and every year produced a number of new plays; it became a fashion for the nobility to celebrate their weddings, birth-days, and other occasions of rejoicing, with masques and interludes, which were exhibited with surprising expence; our great architect, Inigo Jones, being frequently employed to furnish decorations, with all the luxuriance of his invention and magnificence of his art. The king and his lords, and the queen and her ladies, frequently performed in these masques at court, and the nobility at their private houses; nor was any public entertainment thought complete without them. This taste for theatrical entertainments continued during great part of the reign of king Charles the first; but, in the year 1633, it began to be opposed by the Puritans from the press; and the troubles that soon after followed entirely suspended them till the restoration of king Charles the second in 1660.

The king, at his restoration, granted two patents, one to Henry Killigrew, Esq; and the other to Sir William Davenant, and their heirs and assigns, for forming two distinct companies of comedians. Killigrew's were called the *King's Servants,* and Davenant's the *Duke's Company*. About ten of the company called the *King's Servants* were on the royal household establishment, having each ten yards of scarlet cloth, with a proper quantity of lace allowed them for liveries; and in their warrants from the lord chamberlain they were styled *gentlemen of the great chamber*.

Till this time no woman had been seen upon the English stage, the characters of women having always been performed by boys, or young men of an effeminate aspect, which probably induced Shakespeare to make so few of his plays depend upon female characters, as they must have been performed to great disadvantage. The principal characters of his women are innocence and simplicity, such are Desdemona and Ophelia; and his specimen of fondness and virtue in Portia is very short. But the power of real and beautiful women was now added to the stage; and all the capital plays of Shakespeare, Fletcher, and Ben Jonson, were divided between the two companies, by their own alternate choice, and the approbation of the court. . . .

It has been frequently a subject of debate, whether the stage be favourable to morals. We do not mean to enter into the controversy; but we shall make an observation or two. It will be allowed by all, that the intention of the players in acting, is to procure money; and the intention of the audience in attending the theatre, is to seek amusement. The players then will only act such plays as they believe will answer their intention. And what sort of plays are these? They are such as correspond with the opinion, manners, and taste, of the audience. If the taste of the audience be gross, therefore the plays will be gross; if delicate and refined, they will be the same. And if we go back to the time of Shakespeare, we shall find that this has been uniformly the case. The conclusion, then, which we draw, is this, if the taste of the audience be pure, free from licentiousness, the plays will be the same, and the stage will be favourable to virtue.

Actresses

What interests us in the subjoined article is not only that the editor felt it to be a legitimate entry but also that its main function was to afford an opportunity for moralizing. Obviously today's actresses occupy a social position quite other than that here indicated—indeed, two of them became First Ladies of the United States—but that is not a theme a modern editor would deem worthy of encyclopedic treatment. Indeed, the current Britannica *does not even have a reference to Actress. In its comprehensive article "Theatrical Production" it discusses "The Performer" and recognizes no difference between the genders.*

This excerpt is taken from the 4th edition (1801–1809).

ACTRESS, in a general sense, a female who acts or performs something.

ACTRESS, in the Drama, a female performer. Women actors were unknown to the ancients, among whom men always performed the female character; and hence one reason for the use of masks among them.

Actresses are said not to have been introduced on the English stage till after the restoration of King Charles II. who has been charged with contributing to the corrupting of our manners by importing this usage from abroad. But this can be but partly true: the queen of James I. acted a part in a pastoral; and Prynn, in his Histriomastix, speaks of women actors in his time as prostitutes; which was one occasion of the severe prosecution brought against him for that book.

There are some very agreeable and beautiful talents, of which the possession commands a certain sort of admiration; but of which the exercise for the sake of gain is considered, whether from reason or prejudice, as a sort of public prostitution. The pecuniary recompense, therefore, of those who exercise them in this manner, must be sufficient, not only to pay for the time, labour, and expence of acquiring the talents, but for the discredit which attends the employment of them as the means of subsistence. The exorbitant rewards of players, opera-singers, opera-dancers, etc., are founded upon these two principles; the rarity and beauty of the talents, and the discredit of employing them in this manner. It seems absurd at first sight, that we should despise their persons, and yet reward their talents with the most profuse liberality. While we do the one, however, we must of necessity do the other. Should the public opinion or prejudice ever alter with regard to such occupations, their pecuniary recompense would quickly diminish. More people would apply to them, and the competition would quickly reduce the price of their labour. Such talents, though far from being common, are by no means so rare as is imagined. Many people possess them in great perfection, who disdain to make this use of them; and many more are capable of acquiring them, if any thing could be made honourably by them.

Dance

The world of Terpsichore has been treated with increasing sophistication in succeeding editions. The level of sophistication was not high in the early days.

An obviously and perhaps wistfully second-hand account of dancing girls followed the twelve-page article on dance itself appearing in the 3rd edition through the 6th. Both extracts given here are from the 4th edition (1801–1809). (B.L.F.)

The current edition devotes twelve pages to "Dance, the Art of," and another thirteen to "Dance, the History of Western." These pages (and, in fact, the entire set) bear witness to the benefits bestowed on encyclopedias by the development of photography, both black and white and color. However, there's not much about dancing girls.

DANCE, or Dancing, as at present practised, may be defined "an agreeable motion of the body, adjusted by art to the measures or tone of instruments, or of the voice."—But, according to what some reckon more agreeable to the true genius of the art, dancing is "the art of expressing the sentiments of the mind, or the passions, by measured steps or bounds that are made in cadence, by regulated motions of the body, and by graceful gestures; all performed to the sound of musical instruments or of the voice."

There is no account of the origin of the practice of dancing among mankind. It is found to exist among all nations whatever, even the most rude and barbarous; and, indeed, however much the assistance of art may be necessary to make any one perfect in the practice, the foundation must certainly lie in the mechanism of the human body itself.

The connexion that there is between certain sounds and those motions of the human body called *dancing,* hath seldom or never been inquired into by philosophers, though it is certainly a very curious speculation. The power of certain sounds not only over the human species, but even over the inanimate creation, is indeed very surprising. It is well known, that the most solid walls, nay the ground itself, will be found to shake at some particular notes in music. This strongly indicates the presence of some universally diffused and exceedingly elastic fluid, which is thrown into vibrations by the concussions of the atmosphere upon it, produced by the motion of the sounding body.—If these concussions are so strong as to make the large quantity of elastic fluid vibrate that is dispersed through a stone wall or a considerable portion of earth, it is no wonder they should have the same effect upon that invisible and exceedingly subtle matter that pervades and seems to reside in our nerves.

Some there are that have their nerves constructed in such a manner, that they cannot be affected by the sounds which affect others, and some scarce with any; while others have such an irritability of the nerves in this case, that they cannot, without the greatest difficulty, sit or stand still when they hear a favourite piece of music played. . . .

As to performers and their personal qualifications: The first point to which it is directed to pay attention when one takes up the profession of a dancer (at least so soon as he becomes capable of reflection), is his bodily formation: If one is conscious of any natural defect which seems irremediable by art, it will be best immediately to renounce every idea that may have been formed of the advantage arising from popular approbation. But where personal defects can be reformed by application, study, or the advice and assistance of judicious masters, then it becomes an essential concern quickly to exert every effort, before the parts to be corrected have acquired strength and consistence, before nature has unalterably taken her bent, and the error becomes too habitual and inveterate.

Among other personal defects, there are two which deserve particular notice: The first is that of being *jarreté,* "knock-knee'd"; the other of being *arqué,* or "bow-legged." . . .

Dancing Girls of Egypt

Dancing-girls are employed all over the east, as affording great diversion at all public entertainments. They are all prostitutes; and by the laws of their society, are bound to refuse no one for their price, which is rated according to their beauty and other accomplishments. There are even particular sets of them appropriated to the service of the Gentoo temples, and the use of the Bramin priests who attend them. These poor creatures say that they were first debauched by their *god,* and afterwards by him consigned over to the use of the priests who belong to his temples.

These dancing-girls, whether in a settled or unsettled condition, live in a band or community under the direction of some superannuated female of the same profession, under whom they receive a regular education, and are trained up in all the arts of love and pleasing, like scholars in an academy. Thus they acquire the art of captivating the affections of the other sex to such a degree, that nothing is more common than for one of the princes or chief people of the country to take a liking to one of these girls, and waste immense sums on her, though at the same time their own haram is stocked with beauties far superior, and who are besides possessed of the natural modesty of the sex, to which the others have not the smallest pretensions. Thus some of these girls acquire immense wealth. In the neighbourhood of Goa, for instance, on a part of the continent bordering on the district of that island, the dancing-girls founded a village, after being driven from Goa by the zeal of the archbishop. Here they reside in a body corporate, and attend the parties of pleasure of the noblemen and principal inhabitants, for it is not every one's purse that can afford them. Here many of them acquire considerable fortunes by this scandalous traffic, and throw it into a common stock for the sake of carrying on merchandise; being concerned in shipping and the most profitable voyages, for which they have regular factors and brokers.

The dress of these women varies according to the country they live in; but in all it is the most gorgeous imaginable. They are loaded with jewels, literally from top to toe, since even on their toes they wear rings. Their necks are adorned with carcanets, their arms with bracelets, and their ancles with chains of gold and silver, often enriched with precious stones. They also wear nose-jewels, which at first have an odd appearance, but to which the eye is soon reconciled. In Indostan, these dancing-girls, as well as the other women of the country, have a peculiar method of preserving and managing their breasts, which at the same time makes no inconsiderable part of their finery. They inclose them in a pair of hollow cases, exactly fitted to them; made of very light wood, linked together and buckled at the back. These at once confine their breasts so that they cannot grow to any disgustfully exuberant size; though, from their smoothness and pliancy, they play so freely with every motion of the body, that they do not crush the tender texture of the flesh in that part, like the stiff whalebone stays in use among the Europeans. The outside of them is spread over with a thin plate of gold or silver, or set with gems, if they can afford it. Another occasional ornament the dancing-girls put on, particularly when they resort to their gallants, viz. a necklace of many loose turns, composed of flowers strung together, which they call *mogrees,* somewhat resembling Spanish double jessamy, but of a much stronger and more agreeable fragrant odour, and far preferable to any perfumes. "They have nothing," says Mr Grose, "of that nauseous boldness which characterizes the European prostitutes, their style of seduction being all softness and gentleness."

Ballroom Dancing

The famous ballroom dancer Irene Castle (1893–1969) contributed the section headed "Modern Dancing" to the article "Dance" in the 14th edition (1929). (B.L.F.)

She and her husband Vernon (1887–1918) originated the one-step, the castlewalk, and the turkey trot, and popularized the maxixe and the tango. Reading the article today may make some of us feel that ballroom dancing has fallen on less illustrious days. It is worth noting that Irene's original last name was Foote and Vernon's, Blythe. Her article, titled "Modern Dancing," is reproduced in full except for the instructions.

The first three decades of the 20th century have been remarkable in the development of ballroom dancing, as well as the ballet and other forms of stage dancing. This may be attributed to a number of things, but more especially to a certain freedom in "steps" and a greater variety of dance music.

The Steps

Ballroom dancing has, for the most part, become less complicated and more dignified. The best dancers are those who apparently dance with no effort. Dance floors are more crowded, and to-day there is no room for the grotesque antics displayed by the Grizzly Bear, Bunny Hug and Texas Tommy, popular in the first decade of the 20th century. The exaggerated swaying of shoulders, the complicated steps, the violent exercise and noticeable efforts put forth in dancing, all are out of place today. The feet are kept close to the floor, the shoulders maintain their natural position, the extended arm is not pushed forward and back, or "pump-handled" up and down, and, with a graceful ease of manner, very few "steps" are necessary. With a group of couples on the ballroom floor, there is no longer that unison of action, that necessity of conforming with the other dancers in a particular "step" that is determined by the music. There may be just as many variations in these few simple steps as there are couples dancing, but rhythm is maintained throughout. For example, present-day orchestras seldom play the waltz, because it is poorly supported, but when it is played, many of the dancers fox-trot.

The One-step and the Fox-trot are the most popular dances, the latter being used far in excess of any other dance, but a remarkably wide variation is practised in these simple steps. Such a tendency toward less athletic steps has meant a greater attraction for the ballroom and consequently a steady growth of interest in modern dancing. The second decade of the 20th century saw a more complicated programme, such as the Hesitation Waltz, the Maxixe (which never should have been done except as an exhibition dance) and the Tango. The latter seemed ideally suited to the ballroom, but never gained a firm footing in America. Originating in Argentina, it seems dependent upon the Latin temperament for success. Dancers in the United States were intrigued by it and tried in every way to master it, but somehow never caught the rhythm and proper swing.

The Charleston created more of a furore than any dance brought out in recent years, but again did not prove suitable to the ballroom floor and consequently died out almost as suddenly as it appeared. The dance was not new, having been performed among the negroes of the Southern States for years, and being brought to the front by an enthusiast who saw in it great possibilities as a stage attraction. It was never graceful, and decidedly too energetic to be included in modern ballroom dances. The same may be said of the Black Bottom. Even as an attraction suited only for the stage, it created considerable adverse criticism because of its suggestive qualities when executed according to the original dance. Both these dances were really more talked about than danced, but for a short while they gained world-wide fame. Like most fads, they were more harmful than constructive, and have little to do with the history of the dance.

The Fox-trot, an outgrowth of negro music, and earlier connected with such names as Ragtime, Blues and Jazz, has been danced since about 1913 and is firmly established in the programme of modern dances. It is typically American in rhythm, is danced in 4/4 time and played in two distinct tempos—slow fox-trot, perhaps the more popular, and fast fox-trot. The predominance of this as a modern ballroom dance calls for a simple description of how it is performed. . . .

The Castle Walk is sometimes danced to a one-step. It is to the one-step what the Boston is to a fox-trot, depending on the change of weight or the accent of the beat. From 1913 to 1915 it was the most popular form of the one-step. It looked ridiculous at first, but was such fun to do that it spread like magic throughout the dancing world. Walking was its main feature, but one walked on one's toes, lifting up (as if starting to skip) instead of coming down on the beat, giving a childish, carefree swing that was irresistible. The lady partner went backwards most of the time, and the square step was not needed, dancers rounding the corners like an aeroplane banking a turn. It required considerable room, but was of such a joyous motion that it produced no end of merriment. It was originated by Vernon and Irene Castle.

In 1928 many of the old dances were revived in London, and during the course of an evening such old-timers as the *Polka,* the *Galop* and various forms of the barn-dance were performed. The revival met with considerable enthusiasm in London, the ensemble dance producing an act that was both novel and amusing.

The Music

The traditional dance band of strings and piano has been supplanted by the "jazz" band to a great extent, especially in the United States. This consists of various combinations, the most common of which is piano, violin, saxophone, banjo and trap drum. The drummer uses a side-drum, a bass drum and cymbals played with the feet and various other instruments on which he beats a tattoo with his drumsticks in alternation with the side-drum, adding considerably to the rhythm of the ensemble. The radio has created added impetus in dance orchestras, resulting in unusual cleverness on the part of the different players in extemporizing variations on the tune. Broadcasting stations assign certain hours for dance music and the radio orchestra is especially effective in furnishing a great variety of music for dancing in the home.

The Aesthetic Basis of Photographic Art

Perhaps no one has written more authoritatively on photography's aesthetic foundation than Edward Weston (1886–1958). His article on "Photographic Art," written for the 14th edition (1929), first appeared in the 1940 printing. Extracts from it follow.

The notion, advanced long ago, that the camera would kill painting, has proved false. From Weston's discussion—he was influenced by Charles Sheeler and other modernists of his time—it becomes clear that great photography, rather than being inimical to painting, is nourished by, and nourishes, it.

Anyone who has mastered a few simple instructions can make printable negatives with a pocket kodak. Because it is impossible for the untrained beginner to achieve such acceptable results in any other medium, photography has sometimes been called "the easy art." But to bridge the gulf between the taking of such casual snapshots and the production of photographs that can be classed as art is certainly no easy task. To the mastering of his tools and the perfecting of his technique, the photographer must devote just as much time and effort as does the musician or the painter. Since the nature of the photographic process determines the artist's approach, we must have some knowledge of the inherent characteristics of the medium in order to understand what constitutes the aesthetic basis of photographic art.

Photography must always deal with things—it cannot record abstract ideas—but far from being restricted to copying nature, as many suppose, the photographer has ample facilities for presenting his subject in any manner he chooses.

First, an infinite number of compositions can be achieved with a single stationary subject by varying the position of the camera, the camera angle, or the focal length of the lens. Second, any or all values can be altered by change of light on the subject, or the use of a colour filter. Third, the registering of relative values in the negative can be controlled by length of exposure, kind of emulsion used, and method of developing. And finally, the relative values in the negative can be further modified by allowing more or less light to affect certain parts of the image in printing. The photographer is restricted to representing objects of the real world, but in the manner of portraying those objects he has vast discretionary powers; he can depart from literal recording to whatever extent he chooses without resorting to any method of control that is not of a photographic (*i.e.,* optical or chemical) nature.

But the artist's use of these controlling powers must be conditioned by two factors: (1) the nature of his recording process, and (2) the nature of his image. There is a frequent cause of mistaken understanding in the belief that the camera's image reproduces nature as the human eye sees it. On the contrary, its ability to record things as the unaided human eye can never see them is one of the most important attributes of photography. The human eye can focus on but one small area at a time; consequently we observe an object or a scene only by letting our eyes rove over it in a series of short jumps. The assortment of images thus recorded are flashed to the brain which sorts and edits them, automatically discarding some as of no importance and emphasizing others, according to its individual conditioning. The impersonal camera-eye makes no such distinctions; every detail within its field of vision can be recorded instantly and with great clarity. In the time the eye takes to report an impression of houses and a street the camera can record them completely, from their structure, spacing, and relative sizes, to the grain of the wood, the mortar between the bricks, the dents in the pavement. The image that is thus registered has certain characteristics that at once distinguish it from the products of all other graphic processes. In its ability to register fine detail and in its ability to render an unbroken sequence of infinitely subtle gradations, the photograph cannot be equalled by any work of the human hand. For this reason any manual interference with the image at once destroys those very qualities that give the true photograph value as an art form.

From these two facts we may draw an obvious deduction: if the recording process is instantaneous and the nature of the image such that it cannot survive corrective handwork, then it is clear that the artist must be able to visualize his final result in advance. His finished print must be created in full *before* he makes his exposure, and the controlling powers enumerated above must be used, not as correctives, but as predetermined means of carrying out that original visualization. As in the mastery of any other graphic form, years of experience are necessary in photography before technical considerations can be made entirely subordinate to pictorial aims. The ability to previsión the finished print is the photographer's most important qualification and in order to attain it he must concentrate on learning to *see* in terms of his tools and processes. . . .

Exposure records the photographer's seeing; developing and printing execute it; so no matter how fine the original vision, if it has not been faithfully carried out in subsequent procedures the resulting print will suffer. The clarity of image and delicacy of gradation that characterize a fine photograph demand a special kind of surface for their best presentation. A rough surface destroys the integrity of the image; a smooth surface retains it. A shiny or reflecting surface enhances the beauty of image quality, while a dull or absorbing surface tends to obscure it.

For beautiful image quality, the best of the old daguerreotypes have never been equalled. The positives were made directly on the metal base and the small pictures were esteemed for their exquisite rendering of fine detail. The photo-painters, who did away with all things characteristically photographic, often used papers of independently beautiful surface texture for their prints. The result of such a combination is that the paper competes with the image instead of becoming a part of it. . . .

Conception and execution so nearly coincide in this direct medium that an artist with unlimited vision can produce a tremendous volume of work without sacrifice of quality. But the camera demands for its successful use a trained eye, a sure, disciplined technique, keen perception, and swift creative judgement. The artist who would use his photographic powers to the full must have all these, plus the first requisite for the artist in any medium—something to say.

The Motion Picture as Art

One of the demands met by the 13th edition (1926) was treating the new technology and art form of motion pictures. The noted critic Gilbert Seldes (1893–1970) discussed the latter aspect in "The Motion Picture as Art," part of the longer article "Motion Pictures." He was pessimistic about the artistic future of the medium, early voicing views that critics would continue to express in the ensuing years. (B.L.F.)

Gilbert Seldes discussed the motion picture in his trail-blazing The Seven Lively Arts, *published in 1924. Since his time, of course, cinema has been greatly affected by internationalization and the triumphant advent of color and sound, both foreseen by Seldes. As evidence of film's importance to our lives, the current* Britannica *devotes sixty-seven pages, a small volume, to the subject. While that article is magnificently comprehensive, the work of authoritative academics, it lacks the Seldesian brio. The reader may also want to refer to Lillian Gish's more lyrical treatment, printed in Part II of this volume. Extracts from Seldes follow.*

From a toy, the motion picture developed into an industry in accordance with two major principles: the scientific, leading to perfection of the instrument; and the commercial, tending to the maximum of financial return in the shortest possible time. There was little energy to spare for the consideration of the third, the aesthetic, principle. . . .

Natural Potentiality. A logical critic, observing the machinery in complete ignorance of its history, would say that the name itself, especially in the common form of "moving pictures," told nearly the whole story; a camera taking pictures and a projector giving to those pictures the sense of action—movement governed by light. Assuming that the result was to be an art, this critic would hold essential the independence of the motion picture; just as music cannot always be "incidental music" or painting only illustration, the motion picture would have to develop a separate existence, drawing inspiration, perhaps, from the other arts, but fundamentally independent. It would share with painting its communication through the eye; with sculpture its power to create forms; with the dance the interest of movement. These three relations, it is understood, derive from the nature of the instrument rather than from any use to which the instrument may be put; they do not imply that the motion picture must be sculptural, pictorial or choreographic; only that it may be all of these without violence to its inner nature. They do imply as the essence of the picture that it must be all visual: the use of light and movement in the creation of visual images is the essence of the motion picture as an art form.

The Value of the "Absolute" Film. Thirty years after the birth of the motion picture this essence is the goal of a few experimenters, chiefly in France and Germany. Theorists and experts are trying to create the absolute film, as far removed from the commercial film as a fugue of Bach is from "Il Trovatore" or a cubist painting from "The Doctor." . . . The machinery of the motion picture was quite properly accepted as a supremely credible record of the actual; scenes, events, phenomena, were made visible and the screen became an aid to education, an invaluable record of history, and even an instrument of discovery in the natural sciences. It was put into the service of phenomenal truth, and functioned perfectly.

It was only when this service, in all its perfection, was employed in place of the imagination, in the domain of art, that it became a disservice. The motion picture always transposes its material, either mechanically, as a phonograph does, or imaginatively, as an artist does. The impressive fact that the camera could reproduce the actual, led to its use, almost from the start, as an instrument of photographic realism, against creativeness. This was natural in a civilisation devoted largely to mechanical progress and in a country negligent of the imaginative arts; but it neglected a prime value in the instrument itself, to wit, its capacity to transpose, to distort, to displace the object upon which its eye was trained. The motion picture was, in its very beginnings, used by magicians as a new trick, a new way to create "illusion." Almost at once, however, this use was abandoned; the real magic of the picture was suggested—and forgotten. . . .

Importance of Movement. The melodrama and the thriller were important because, whatever their story, they expressed it all in movement, rather than in gesture, facial expression or subtitles. The scenarios were such as needed movement, utilising the screen's capacity to present simultaneous parallel activities, bringing them together in climax. The formula was lacking in adaptability, the material was intellectually contemptible; but the expression was completely kinematographic, not literary, not theatrical. This was true also in the spectacle films. The difference between the poetic beauties of "Cabiria" (on a scenario by Gabriele d'Annunzio) and the non-literary, kinematographic excellence of "The Birth of a Nation" (which was adapted with exceptional propriety from a bad novel) is marked. In the latter (1915) D. W. Griffith exploited the characteristic quality of the American spectacle film; its use of the melodramatic element of suspense in direct connection with the spectacle itself. The "last minute rescue" has always been well managed by American directors, generally by subdividing it into parts—the victims, the attacker, the rescuers—and alternating these in scenes of accelerating rhythm. This is "good movie" and distinguishes the American spectacle from the German, which often handles masses better, creates the sense of multitudes or expanse with none of the gross lavishness of second-rate American directors, but lacks excitement proportionate to its duration and scope. . . .

Economy and Effect. It was in the thriller and the melodrama that the American moving picture learned also to unroll its plot succinctly. Padding is common enough; but no one comparing the average American and the average European film can fail to note that, when they want to, American directors are able to present their effects with superior conciseness and economy. There is also, in American films, an appreciable working up to climax and, their chief virtue, a neatness of execution, in which phrase may be included a multitude of technical devices, cleverness in general methods, discovery of settings which lend themselves to dramatic action, expertness in camera work, absolute clarity of the projected film, ingenuity, inventiveness. Even in their sum these qualities fall short of the meanest artistic stature; they are good qualities none the less. They were, or most of them, inherent in the silly Westerns and serials of the picture's earliest day.

The Right Road. It is the writer's belief that the first halting steps of the motion picture were along the proper, the kinematographic, road from which it has since been diverted, to which it must return, enriched by experience, if it is to have a future. Another early type fortifies this belief: the slapstick. It is no accident that the one figure in the pictures to which some degree of immortality is universally accorded should have come from slapstick: Charlie Chaplin. These comedies, especially in their beginnings, were close to the type of the *commedia dell'arte;* they were almost all improvised before the camera. In them developed a type of playing which was purely kinematographic, and could be related to the stage only by way of American burlesque. Slapstick was remarkable also because it instantly saw the motion picture as a medium for fantasy, grotesque no doubt, but in essence fantastic. The properties of the physical world, all reality, were annihilated by the tricks of the camera for specific comic effect; retarded and accelerated motion, the repertory of the stopped camera, all suspended the mind of the spectator, as a pun might or a paradox, between the intellectual certainty that a thing is impossible and the visual certainty—it is here that the credibility of the camera becomes significant—that it has just happened. The thriller employed what was hazardous or difficult; slapstick brought to the film the impossible and the unreal. Fantasy appeared elsewhere as dream and as fairy-tale, with no impropriety but, except in rare instances (Crainquebille among them), without imagination. In slapstick, fantasy was built out of the elements of common life and flourished with extraordinary imaginative vigour. Whether the material was worthy of this treatment has been debated; to some observers slapstick shows an honest vulgarity far more endearing than the pretentiousness, the intellectual fatuity, the errors of taste, the bad manners of its more serious counterparts in the films.

Dangers of Realism. The use of indifferent materials in the usual American feature film was made doubly dangerous by the pedestrian realism of the direction. The motion picture seemed in 1920 to be destined forever to photography, to lack all bearing on created art. (It is worth noting that except for scientific purposes the motion picture cannot be exact; absolute fidelity in photographing "He walked six miles before breakfast" would result in unbearable tedium.) Fore-shortening, indirect suggestion, the creation of images capable of evoking the desired emotion—all the processes of the arts must find their counterparts in the films and will be governed, after the ruling direction of the mechanism, by the physiology of the eye, and by the psychology of attention; that is, if the picture is an art in the old sense. There are critics, wholly favourable to the motion picture, who consider that its real future is in developing outside of the sphere of the fine arts and in conscious hostility to their precepts. The break in 1920 came with the exportation of a German film, the famous "Cabinet of Doctor Caligari."

Without immediate effect on public or producers, this film is memorable because of its effect on the critics; it may be said that "Caligari" created motion-picture criticism in England and America. French critics hold it in low esteem because of its elaborate scenario; yet even they allow its chief virtues: that it worked chiefly through the camera (although the subtitles in the American presentation were lengthy and frequent) and broke entirely with realism on the screen. The change was marked by the use of cubist and expressionist settings in place of actual built or discovered "locations." The settings were psychologically correct for the story; the picture was perfect in the moments when its chief players, Conrad Veidt and Werner Kraus, so played before the distorted backgrounds as to give the whole picture a logical, complete, acceptable rhythm of its own, a life of its own, recognisable not as reality, but as a possible reality, an escape from or transposition of reality. "Caligari" was notable because it was artistically right in showing that the picture was most effective when it was not photographic; it was psychologically right because it brought the imagination of the spectator into play. It has been shown in Europe for six years (and finally made into play); it is in no sense a failure. That it failed in America may be ascribed, by critics hostile to the naturalistic film, to the stultification of popular taste in the preceding 10 years of the film's wanderings on the wrong road. "Caligari" means that the motion picture must be created, not photographed; painted backgrounds are incidental.

Five years later another German film, superficially less striking, claimed universal attention: "The Last Laugh" ("The Last Man" is another name for it). Films without subtitles had appeared before; the distinction of this one was that everything the picture had to say, and it said some subtle things, was said by means of the camera. What is more, the correlation of scenes was perfect, the separate sequences held together, and needed no connection or explanation. The American director, aware of American distaste for long series of pictures without subtitles, is prone to let his story hang loosely, trusting to its titles to draw it together. The slower-moving Scandinavian and German films are closely knitted in the sequences of the picture and can give psychological explanations which the faster American films skip or explain in words.

Importance of Imagination. The artistic film will be characterised by imagination and will express itself visually, *i.e.,* through the camera. Ingenuity has already used the camera, notably in the excellent trick films presented for the trick alone; the news pictures have also learned kinematographic methods well. Creation has lagged behind, partly because there have been so many temporarily acceptable substitutes. The imaginative communication of emotions in "The Last Laugh" may prove a failure; but a few thousand dollars invested in a railway wreck is likely to make a picture a success. The director, at present the most interesting figure in the motion picture, has always known this. The future of the picture depends upon his capacity to free himself from tricks, from detailed scenarios, bad acting, "screen personalities" and other misfortunes. More, it depends upon his intelligence to see that the completed film must be a unit, not a series of separate scenes which a scenario-writer has invented and an editor-cutter will piece together for a title-writer to render reasonable as a plot. The motion picture conceived as a unit will have internal growth, development, rhythm; the relation between its parts and between the durations of its parts will have purpose; the bearing of the parts on the whole will be effective; the picture will have both style and form. At present few directors have manners so definite that their work can be identified without recourse to their tricks. Actual style, a personal way of expressing something experienced or observed, is almost entirely lacking, and that a picture as a whole should have form is a heresy still unheard in Hollywood.

Style and Form. The future of the picture as an art depends, nevertheless, on the growth of elements of style and form, such as, with natural differences, distinguish the other arts: economy of means, sobriety, seriousness of purpose—all the other tests for an artistic creation are certain to vary with the individual artist, but the moving picture will not begin to be an art until it is conceived as the communication of a precise emotion or experience (communication by a group of artists or by a director through a group of interpreters of his vision). The expression of such a personal vision in a highly personal style distinguishes Chaplin as actor; a bluntness of perception, an imperfect sense of form, make him less than supreme as a director. But one looks vainly elsewhere for more than the beginnings of his qualities. Perhaps a half-dozen directors in America, twice as many in all Europe, seem at moments to approach the question of the motion picture as an art, but none offers a solution to it.

Except for striving for the film which shall have the illusion of depth, science seems satisfied with the motion picture. (The twin mistakes—the film synchronised with a talking-machine and the colour-film—may be perfected; but as each relieves the director of an obligation, instead of compelling him to fulfil one, they are not necessary developments of the film as art.) At the same time, the film as commerce may become stabilised; the pioneer days when companies were hastily organised to make the most of a nine days' wonder are over. With these two effective agencies reduced to secondary places, the moving picture as an art may flourish. So long as it remains a popular art, it will require novelty. Its greatest novelty, at the moment, must be an artistic one.

CHAPTER NINE

Articles of Faith

The View from Edinburgh

From its inception the Britannica *has treated religion fully, carefully, and seriously. But its modern tradition of objectivity took much more than a century to evolve. Today's editors aim to present every responsible view of subjects about which there are more views than one. And they hope to do so without obviously endorsing one over another.*

In the early days a strenuous effort was made to present at least a synopsis of what was known about every topic, no matter how arcane, and to describe exotic beliefs that were important enough to merit attention. But the Britannica *itself represented a single point of view. It was that shared by the elite of eighteenth-century Scotsmen: a pious, Protestant Christianity.*

Thus when the Britannica talked of the Romish Church or, worse, of pagan religions, the practices and beliefs of these exotic groups were seen and explained as though they were in a museum of curiosities or the half-fanciful tales of some intrepid traveler.

The editors maintained a sort of incredulous distance from such subjects as the Popish persuasion or the Mussulman or the Hindoo, but there was no malice in it. The Britannica *was simply reporting what could be known of the facts to the true believers in Edinburgh, Glasgow, and outlying Scotland, and to other God-fearing Britons.*

The Roman Catholics were not really equated with the heathens of the East for, after all, Rome had been the source of reformed Christianity. Treatment of Judaism was somewhat different, also, inasmuch as it was the very foundation of Christianity. Nonetheless, when the early Britannica *came to religious subjects, the view from Edinburgh was explicitly Christian and explicitly Protestant.*

Heaven was a special case because the word had a secular as well as a sacred meaning.

The extracts on heaven and hell are from the 1st edition (1768–1771). (B.L.F.)

HEAVEN literally signifies the expanse of the firmament, surrounding our earth, and extended every way to an immense distance.

The Hebrews acknowledged three heavens: the first, the aerial heaven, in which the birds fly, the winds blow, and the showers are formed; the second, the firmament in which the stars are placed; the third, the heaven of heavens, the residence of the Almighty, and the abode of saints and angels.

Heaven is considered by Christian divines and philosophers, as a place in some remote part of infinite space, in which the omnipresent Deity is said to afford a nearer and more immediate view of himself, and a more sensible manifestation of his glory, than in the other parts of the universe. This is often called the empyrean, from that splendor with which it is supposed to be invested; and of this place the inspired writers give us the most noble and magnificent descriptions.

The pagans considered heaven as the residence only of the celestial gods, into which no mortals were admitted after death, unless they were deified. As for the souls of good men, they were consigned to the elysian fields.

HELL, the place of divine punishment after death. . . .

The Jews placed hell in the centre of the earth, and believed it to be situated under waters and mountains. . . . They likewise acknowledged seven degrees of pain in hell, because they find this place called by seven different names in scripture. Though they believed that infidels, and persons eminently wicked, will continue for ever in hell; yet they maintained, that every Jew who is not infected with some heresy, and has not acted contrary to the points mentioned by the rabbins, will not be punished therein for any other crimes above a year at most.

The Mahometans believe the eternity of rewards and punishments in another life. In the Koran it is said, that hell has seven gates, the first for the Mussulmans, the second for the Christians, the third for the Jews, the fourth for the Sabians, the fifth for the Magians, the sixth for the pagans, and the seventh for the hypocrites of all religions.

Among Christians, there are two controverted questions in regard to hell; the one concerns locality, the other the duration of its torments. The locality of hell, and the reality of its fire, began first to be controverted by Origen. That father, interpreting the scripture account metaphorically, makes hell to consist not in external punishments, but in a consciousness or sense of guilt, and a remembrance of past pleasures. Among the moderns, Mr Whiston advanced a new hypothesis. According to him, the comets are so many hells appointed in their orbits alternately to carry the damned into the confines of the sun, there to be scorched by its violent heat, and then to return with them beyond the orb of Saturn, there to starve them in these cold and dismal regions. Another modern author, not satisfied with any hypothesis hitherto advanced, assigns the sun to be the local hell. As to the second question, *viz.* the duration of hell-torments, we have Origen again at the head of those who deny that they are eternal; it being that father's opinion, that not only men, but devils, after a due course of punishment suitable to their respective crimes, shall be pardoned and restored to heaven. The chief principle upon which Origen built his opinion, was the nature of punishment, which he took to be emendatory, applied only as physic for the recovery of the patient's health. The chief objection to the eternity of hell torments among modern writers, is the disproportion between temporary crimes and eternal punishments. Those who maintain the affirmative, ground their opinions on scripture accounts, which represent the pains of hell under the figure of a worm which never dies, and a fire which is not quenched; as also upon the words, "These shall go away into everlasting punishment, but the righteous into life eternal."

Christianity

The 1st edition (1768–1771) devoted a large share of its three fat volumes to religious topics. Indeed some fourteen pages were allotted to the article "Theology."

After a brief introduction, it described the minimum attainments needed by a theologian. In doing so it helped answer a question students of the early Britannicas *often raise: Why did clergymen, very many of them theologians, bulk so large in the roster of early contributors to the encyclopedia?*

The answer is that they were educated far beyond the nonclerical professions. Physicians and surgeons needed no graduate education; scientists needed no Ph.D. as a passport to the laboratory; but the theologian in 1770 needed an education at least equal to the highest standards of the late twentieth century. (B.L.F.)

Here follows, from the 1st edition, the intimidating opening section of "Theology; or, The Study of Religion":

To ascend by a chain of reasoning from things visible to things invisible, from palpable to impalpable, from terrestrial to celestial, from the creature even up to the Creator, is the business of theology: it is not surprising, therefore, that the union of many doctrines is necessary completely to form such a science. To understand, and properly to interpret, the scriptures or revelation, demands not less sagacity than assiduity. The gift of persuasion is also essential to the ministers of the gospel. And lastly, the civil government has committed to their care certain functions of society, which relate, or seem to relate, either to the doctrines or morality of the gospel. They assemble, for example, in bodies to form consistories; they judge in matrimonial cases; they carry consolation and hope to the souls of the sick; they prepare for death those criminals which justice sacrifices to public safety; they take upon themselves the charge of Ephori, with the inspection of some pious foundations: they distribute alms; they administer the sacraments, etc.

To discharge fully so many duties, the theologian has need, 1. Of several preparatory studies; 2. Of some theoretic sciences; and, 3. Of many doctrines which have for their object his ministerial office. The first are,

1. The languages; and among these,
   - (a) His native language, in which he is to preach and exercise his ministry, and with which he ought to be perfectly acquainted.
   - (b) The Latin language, which is the language of the learned world in general.
   - (c) The Greek language, in order to understand the new Testament.
   - (d) The Hebrew language, of which the Talmudian and Rabbinical idioms are a part.
   - (e) The Arabic language.
   - (f) The Syriac language.
   - (g) The French language. And,

(h) The English language. The two latter of which now appear necessary to every man of letters, and particularly to a theologian, on account of the excellent works which are wrote in those languages.

2. The principal parts of philosophy; as,
   (a) Logic.
   (b) Metaphysics.
   (c) Moral philosophy.
3. Rhetoric and eloquence, or the art of speaking correctly, of writing with elegance, and of persuasion.

To which may be added,

4. The elements of chronology, and universal history.
5. The study of the Jewish antiquities.

He who would devote himself to the important employment of a theologian, and has the noble ambition to excel in it, should early impress on his mind these truths: that the years which are passed at an university are few; that they run rapidly away; that they are entirely engrossed by the theoretic sciences; and that he who does not carry with him to the university a fund of knowledge in the preparatory parts of learning, commonly brings very little away, when his age or his parents oblige him to quit it.

The theoretic sciences of a theologian are,

1. The dogmatic, or the theory of theology; which some Latin authors name also *thetica,* or *systematica.*
2. The exegesis, or the science of attaining the true sense of the holy scriptures.
3. The hermeneutic, or the art of interpreting and explaining the scriptures to others. This differs in general but little from the exegesis, and in some respects is quite the same.
4. Polemic theology, or controversy.
5. Natural theology.
6. Moral theology.
7. The history of the church under the Old and New Testaments.

The practical sciences are,

1. Homiletic theology.
2. Cathechetic theology.
3. Casuistic theology.

We do not here particularly name the *patristic theology, (theologia patrum feu patristica*), because all Christian communions are not agreed in their opinions concerning the degree of authenticity and infallibility that is to be attributed to these ancient fathers of the church. The Protestants believe, that these primitive theologians were liable to error in their sentiments as well as those of our days; and, in all probability, that they were less skilful, less learned, less clear, and less accustomed to close reasoning, than the latter, as philosophy was then more imperfect. But as we find in the writings of these fathers, many elucidations of the doctrine of the primitive apostles, and many irrefragable testimonies of the authenticity of divers remarkable events, which serve to establish the truth of Christianity; and as we there see, moreover, the origin of errors, of arbitrary ceremonies, and of many doctrines that have been introduced into the Christian church; the reading and the study of these fathers cannot but be of great utility to the theologian. To a virtuous citizen, who unites such various sciences, and employs them in pointing out to his fellow citizens the path that leads to temporal and eternal felicity; in a word, to a wise theologian, what veneration is not due?

First of the Human Race

Most late eighteenth-century scholars accepted the King James Version of the Bible as literal truth. Certainly the Britannica *and virtually all of its subscribers did so. (B.L.F.)*

The article "Adam" in the 2nd edition (1778–1783) begins thus:

ADAM, the first of the human race, was formed by the Almighty on the sixth day of the creation. His body was made of the dust of the earth; after which, God animated or gave it life, and Adam then became a rational creature.—His heavenly Parent did not leave his offspring in a destitute state to shift for himself; but planted a garden, in which he caused to grow not only every tree that was proper for producing food, but likewise such as were agreeable to the eye, or merely ornamental. In this garden were assembled all the brute creation; and, by their Maker, caused to pass before Adam, who gave all of them names, which were judged proper by the Deity himself.—In this review, Adam found none for a companion to himself. This solitary state was seen by the Deity to be attended with some degree of unhappiness; and therefore he threw Adam into a deep sleep, in which state he took a rib from his side, and healing up the wound, formed a woman of the rib he had taken out. On Adam's awaking, the woman was brought to him; and he immediately knew her to be one of his own species, called her his bone and his flesh, giving her the name of *woman* because she was taken out of man.

The first pair being thus created, God gave them authority over the inferior creation, commanding them to subdue the earth, also to increase and multiply, and fill it. They were informed of the proper food for the beasts and for them; the grass, or green herbs, being appointed for beasts; and fruits, or seeds, for man. Their proper employment also was assigned them; namely, *to dress the garden, and to keep it.*

Pan

In accord with their own classical education, early editors accorded careful treatment to mythological figures, properly identifying them as pagan, and not failing to relate their amorous and other adventures. The article on Pan in the 2nd edition (1778–1783) begins:

PAN, in Pagan worship, the son of Mercury and Penelope (the wife of Ulysses), who was ravished by that god in the form of a white goat, while she was keeping her father's flocks. He was educated on Mount Menelaus, in Arcadia, by Sinoe, and the other nymphs, whom he attracted by his music. He afterwards distinguished himself in the war with the giants, when he entangled Typhon in his nets. He attended Bacchus in his Indian expedition; and when the Gauls were about to pillage the temple of Delphos, he struck them with such a sudden consternation by night, that they fled, though none pursued them. He had a contest with Cupid; but was conquered by the little god, who punished him, by inspiring him with a passion for the nymph Syrinx, who treated him with disdain: but he closely pursuing her, overtook her by the river Ladon, when, invoking the Naiads, she was changed into a tuft of reeds, which the disappointed lover grasped in his arms; but observing, that as they trembled with the wind, they formed a murmuring sound, he made of them the pipe for which he became so famous. He charmed Luna in the shape of a beautiful ram, and had several other amours.

Pan is represented with a smiling ruddy face, a thick beard, with the horns, legs, feet, and tail of a goat; holding a shepherd's crook in one hand, and his pipe of unequal reeds in the other.

Apollo

Here are extracts from the article "Apollo" in the 3rd edition (1788–1797).

APOLLO, in mythology, a Pagan deity worshipped by the Greeks and Romans. Cicero mentions four of his name: the most ancient of whom was the son of Vulcan; the second a son of Corybas, and born in Crete; the third an Arcadian, called *Nomian,* from his being a great legislator; and the last, to whom the greatest honour is ascribed, the son of Jupiter and Latona. . . . As Apollo is almost always confounded by the Greeks with the sun, it is no wonder that he should be dignified with so many attributes. It was natural for the most glorious object in nature, whose influence is felt by all creation, and seen by every animated part of it, to be adorned as the fountain of light, heat, and life. The power of healing diseases being chiefly given by the ancients to medicinal plants and vegetable productions, it was natural to exalt into a divinity the visible cause of their growth. Hence he was also styled the *God of Physic;* and that external heat which cheers and invigorates all nature, being transferred from the human body to the mind, gave rise to the idea of all mental effervescence coming from this god; hence, likewise, poets, prophets, and musicians, are said to be *Numine afflati,* inspired by Apollo.

Whether Apollo was ever a real personage, or only the great luminary, many have doubted. Indeed, Vossius has taken great pains to prove this god to be only a metaphorical being, and that there never was any other Apollo than the sun. . . .

To the other perfections of this divinity the poets have added beauty, grace, and the art of captivating the ear and the heart, no less by the sweetness of his eloquence, than by the melodious sounds of his lyre. However, with all these accomplishments, he had not the talent of captivating the fair, with whose charms he was enamoured. But the amours and other adventures related of this god during his residence on earth, are too numerous, and too well known, to be inserted here.

Islam

The newest of the great world religions, Islam, was first treated in the Britannica's *1st edition (1768–1771) under the eighteenth-century English transliteration of the Arabic name of its scriptures, Alcoran (al Qur'an, or the Koran). The 2nd edition (1778–1783) had nine pages on the faith, which set out by listing its cardinal elements. (B.L.F.)*

MAHOMETANISM, or MAHOMETISM, the system of religion broached by Mahomet, and still adhered to by his followers. See MAHOMET, and ALCORAN.

Mahometanism is professed by the

Turks, Persians, and several nations among the Africans, and many among the East-Indians.

The Mahometans divide their religion into two general parts, faith and practice: of which the first is divided into six distinct branches; Belief in God, in his angels, in his scriptures, in his prophets, in the resurrection and final judgment, and in God's absolute decrees. The points relating to practice are, Prayer, with washings, &c. alms, fasting, pilgrimage to Mecca, and circumcision.

I. Of the Mahometan *Faith*. 1. That both Mahomet and those among his followers who are reckoned orthodox, had and continue to have just and true notions of God and his attributes, appears so plain from the Koran itself, and all the Mahometan divines, that it would be loss of time to refute those who suppose the God of Mahomet to be different from the true God, and only a fictitious deity or idol of his own creation.

2. The existence of angels, and their purity, are absolutely required to be believed in the Koran; and he is reckoned an infidel who denies there are such beings, or hates any of them, or asserts any distinction of sexes among them. They believe them to have pure and subtile bodies, created of fire; that they neither eat nor drink, nor propagate their species; that they have various forms and offices, some adoring God in different postures, others singing praises to him, or interceding for mankind. They hold, that some of them are employed in writing down the actions of men; others in carrying the throne of God, and other services.

The four angels, whom they look on as more eminently in God's favour, and often mention on account of the offices assigned them, are, Gabriel, to whom they give several titles, particularly those of the *holy spirit,* and the *angel of revelations,* supposing him to be honoured by God with a greater confidence than any other, and to be employed in writing down the divine decrees; Michael, the friend and protector of the Jews; Azrael, the *angel of death,* who separates men's souls from their bodies; and Irasil, whose office it will be to sound the trumpet at the resurrection. The Mahometans also believe, that two guardian angels attend on every man, to observe and write down his actions, being changed every day, and therefore called *al Moakkibat,* or "the angels who continually succeed one another."

The devil, whom Mahomet names *Eblis,* from his *despair,* was once one of those angels who are nearest to God's presence, called *Azazil;* and fell, according to the doctrine of the Koran, for refusing to pay homage to Adam at the command of God.

Besides angels and devils, the Mahometans are taught by the Koran to believe an intermediate order of creatures, which they call *jin* or *genii,* created also of fire, but of a grosser fabric than angels, since they eat and drink, and propagate their species, and are subject to death. Some of these are supposed to be good, and others bad, and capable of future salvation or damnation, as men are; whence Mahomet pretended to be sent for the conversion of genii as well as men.

Hinduism

The civilized inhabitants of Edinburgh relied on their more venturesome compatriots, and on writers of antiquity, for their knowledge of the exotic peoples and practices of the far corners of the world. Given the vagaries of memory (and translation), it is hardly surprising that the early encyclopedists of Edinburgh treated Hinduism, one of the world's oldest religions, haltingly and imperfectly. The term did not appear in the 1st edition (1768–1771), but the religion did, as we see by the following excerpts.

BRAMINS, the name of the priests among the idolatrous Indians; the successors of the ancient brachmans. See Brachmans.

BRACHMANS, a sect of Indian philosophers known to the ancient Greeks by the name of Gymnosophists. . . . The modern brachmans make up one of the casts or tribes of the banians. . . .

BANIANS, a religious sect in the empire of the Mogul, who believe in metempsychosis; and will therefore eat no living creature, nor kill even noxious animals; but endeavour to release them, when in the hands of others.

The 3rd edition (1788–1797) devoted a dozen pages to the subject, contributing more information somewhat more accurately. Some excerpts follow. (B.L.F.)

HINDOOS, or Gentoos, the inhabitants of that part of India known by the name of *Hindostan* or the *Mogul's empire,* who profess the religion of the Bramins, supposed to be the same with that of the ancient Gymnosophists of Ethiopia.

From the earliest period of history these people seem to have maintained the same religion, laws, and customs, which they do at this day: and indeed they and the Chinese are examples of perseverance in these respects altogether unknown in the western world. In the time of Diodorus Siculus they are said to have been divided into seven casts or tribes; but the inter-

course betwixt Europe and India was in his time so small, that we may well suppose the historian to have been mistaken, and that the same tenacity for which they are so remarkable in other respects has manifested itself also in this. At present they are divided only into four tribes; 1. The Bramin; 2. The Khatry; 3. The Bhyse; and, 4. The Soodera. All these have distinct and separate offices, and cannot, according to their laws, intermingle with each other; but for certain offences they are subject to the loss of their cast, which is reckoned the highest punishment they can suffer; and hence is formed a kind of fifth cast named *Pariars* on the coast of Coromandel, but in the Shanscrit or sacred language *Chandalas*. These are esteemed the dregs of the people, and are never employed but in the meanest offices. There is besides a general division which pervades the four casts indiscriminately; and which is taken from the worship of their gods *Vishnou* and *Sheevah;* the worshippers of the former being named *Vishnou-bukht;* of the latter *Sheevah-bukht.*

Of these four casts the bramins are accounted the foremost in every respect; and all the laws have such an evident partiality towards them, as cannot but induce us to suppose that they have had the principal hand in framing them. . . .

No Hindoo is allowed to quit the cast in which he was born upon any account. All of them are very scrupulous with regard to their diet; but the bramins much more so than any of the rest. They eat no flesh, nor shed blood; which we are informed by Porphyry and Clemens Alexandrinus was the case in their time. Their ordinary food is rice and other vegetables, dressed with *ghee* (a kind of butter melted and refined so as to be capable of being kept for a long time), and seasoned with ginger and other spices. The food which they most esteem, however, is milk as coming from the cow; an animal for which they have the most extravagant veneration, insomuch that it is enacted in the code of Gentoo laws, that any one who exacts labour from a bullock that is hungry or thirsty, or that shall oblige him to labour when fatigued or out of season, is liable to be fined by the magistrates.

Other Worlds

The occult was regarded with a kind of horrid fascination by Britannica *editors from the beginning—deprecated usually, but always covered, as in this extract from the 1st edition: (B.L.F).*

MAGIC, originally signified only the knowledge of the more sublime parts of philosophy; but as the magi likewise professed astrology, divination and sorcery, the term magi became odious, being used to signify an unlawful diabolical kind of science, acquired by the assistance of the devil and departed souls.

The excerpts that follow are from the 3rd edition (1788–1797). This edition was so prescient that it even included a comment on a presidential couple of our own time: "This art, which owed its origin to the practices of knavery on credulity, is now universally exploded by the intelligent part of mankind."

ASTROLOGY, a conjectural science, which teaches to judge of the effects and influences of the stars, and to foretel future events by the situation and different aspects of the heavenly bodies.

This science has been divided into two branches, *natural* and *judiciary*. To the former belongs the predicting of natural effects; as, the changes of weather, winds, storms, hurricanes, thunder, floods, earthquakes, etc. This art properly belongs to natural philosophy; and is only to be deduced *à posteriori,* from phenomena and observations. Judiciary or judicial astrology, is that which pretends to foretel moral events; i. e. such as have a dependence on the free will and agency of man; as if they were directed by the stars. This art, which owed its origin to the practices of knavery on credulity, is now universally exploded by the intelligent part of mankind. . . .

Second Sight, in Erse called *Taisch,* is a mode of seeing superadded to that which nature generally bestows. This gift or faculty, which is neither voluntary nor constant, is in general rather troublesome than agreeable to the possessors of it, who are chiefly found among the inhabitants of the Highlands of Scotland, those of the Western Isles, of the Isle of Man, and of Ireland. It is an impression made either by the mind upon the eye, or by the eye upon the mind, by which things distant or future are perceived, and seen as if they were present. A man on a journey far from home falls from his horse; another, who is perhaps at work about the house, sees him bleeding on the ground, commonly with a landscape of the place where the accident befals him. Another seer, driving home his cattle, or wandering in idleness, or musing in the sunshine, is suddenly surprised by the appearance of a bridal ceremony, or funeral procession, and counts the mourners or attendants, of whom, if he knows them, he relates the names; if he knows them not, he can describe the dresses. Things distant are seen at the instant when they happen. . . .

SPECTRE, an apparition, something made preternaturally visible to human sight, whether the ghosts of dead men or beings superior to man.

A belief that supernatural beings sometimes make themselves visible, and that the dead sometimes revisit the living, has prevailed among most nations, especially in the rudest stages of society. It was common among the Jews, among the Greeks, and among the Romans, as we find from the Scriptures, and from the poems of Homer and Virgil. Celestial appearances were indeed so often exhibited to the Jews, that the origin of their belief is not difficult to be explained. . . .

It appears from the writings of modern travellers who have visited rude and savage nations, that the belief of spectres is no less common among them. Mr Bruce tells us, that the priest of the Nile affirmed, that he had more than once seen the spirit of the river in the form of an old man with a white beard. Among the Mahometans the doctrine of spectres seems to be reduced to a regular system, by the accounts which they give of genii. Whoever has read the Arabian Nights Entertainments must have furnished his memory with a thousand instances of this kind. Their opinions concerning genii seem to be a corrupted mixture of the doctrines of the Jews and ancient Persians. In Christian countries, too, not withstanding the additional light which their religion has spread, and the great improvement in the sciences to which it has been subservient, the belief of ghosts and apparitions is very general, especially among the lower ranks. They believe that evil spirits sometimes make their appearance in order to terrify wicked men, especially those who have committed murder.—They suppose that the spirits of dead men assume a corporeal appearance, hover about church yards and the houses of the deceased, or haunt the places where murders have been committed. (See GHOST.) In some places it is believed that beings have been seen bearing a perfect resemblance to men alive. In the Highlands of Scotland, what is called the second sight is still believed by many (see SECOND SIGHT); viz. that future events are foretold by certain individuals by means of spectral representation.

When Did We Fall?

The 4th edition (1801–1809), considering this question under "Antediluvians," was not entirely sure but argues the point with notable cogency.

How long our first parents retained their innocence, we are nowhere told. Many assert that they fell on the very first day of their creation. But Moses mentions so many transactions on that day, as must have engrossed the whole of their attention, and prevented them from falling into such temptations as arise from indolence and want of reflection. Besides, if, in such circumstances as they were placed, they could not refrain from an open violation of the Divine law for the space of one day, it would bespeak a deceitfulness of heart in them greater than in most of their posterity.

Life in the Ark

It is salutary to be reminded that at one time what we now call fundamentalist Christianity was accepted as a given by the intelligent, well-educated social and professional class that produced and bought the Britannica. *The current edition, under "Ararat, Mount," is quietly cautious about the story of the Flood. It allows that "Ararat has been scaled by several explorers, some of whom claim to have sighted the remains of the Ark." The 4th edition (1801–1809) was more confident.*

The dimensions of the ark, as given by Moses, are 300 cubits in length, 50 in breadth, and 30 in height; which some have thought too scanty, considering the number of things it was to contain; and hence an argument has been drawn against the authority of the relation. To solve this difficulty, many of the ancient fathers and the modern critics have been put to very miserable shifts: But Buteo and Kircher have proved geometrically, that taking the common cubit of a foot and a half, the ark was abundantly sufficient for all the animals supposed to be lodged in it. Snellius computes the ark to have been above half an acre in area. Father Lamy shows, that it was 110 feet longer than the church of St Mary at Paris, and 64 feet narrower: and if so, it must have been longer than St Paul's church in London, from west to east, and broader than that church is high in the inside, and 54 feet of our measure in height; and Dr Arbuthnot computes it to have been 81062 tons. . . .

By the description Moses gives of the ark, it appears to have been divided into three stories, each ten cubits or 15 feet high; and it is agreed on, as most probable, that

Fig. 1. Noah's Ark floating on the waters of the Deluge   Plate XXXVIII.

the lowest story was for the beasts, the middle for the food, and the upper for the birds, with Noah and his family; each story being subdivided into different apartments, stalls, etc., though Josephus, Philo, and other commentators, add a kind of fourth story under all the rest; being, as it were, the hold of the vessel, to contain the ballast and receive the filth and faeces of so many animals: but F. Calmet thinks, that what is here reckoned a story, was no more than what is called the *keel* of ships, and served only for a conservatory of fresh water.

Prayer

Prayer was a solemn and universal duty, and after describing its proper elements, the Britannica *in its 4th edition (1801–1809) sternly addressed sophists who argued against its necessity. (B.L.F.)*

PRAYER, a solemn address to God, which, when it is of any considerable length, consists of *adoration, confession, supplication, intercession,* and *thanksgiving.* . . .

That prayer is a duty which all men ought to perform with humility and reverence, has been generally acknowledged as well by the untaught barbarian as by the enlightened Christian; and yet to this duty objections have been made by which the understanding has been bewildered in sophistry and affronted with jargon. "If God be independent, omnipotent, and possessed of every other perfection, what pleasure, it has been asked, can he take in our acknowledgment of these perfections? If he knows all things past, present, and future, where is the propriety of our confessing our sins unto him? If he is a benevolent and merciful Being, he will pardon our sins, and grant us what is needful for us without our supplications and intreaties; and if he be likewise possessed of infinite wisdom, it is certain that no importunities of ours will prevail upon him to grant us what is improper, or for our sakes to change the equal and steady laws by which the world is governed. . . ."

Such are the most plausible objections which are usually made to the practice of prayer; and though they have been set off with all the art of the metaphysical wrangler . . . they appear to us such gross sophisms as can operate only on a very unthinking head, or on a very corrupt heart. For if God certainly exists, and there is not a mathematical theorem capable of more rigid demonstration, it is obvious that no man can think of such a being without having his mind strongly impressed with the conviction of his own constant dependence upon him; nor can he "contemplate the heavens, the work of God's hands, the moon, and the stars which he has ordained," without forming the most sublime conceptions that he can of the Divine power, wisdom, and goodness, etc. . . .

Having evinced the duty of adoration, confession, supplication, and intercession, we need not surely waste our readers' time with a formal and laboured vindication of thanksgiving. Gratitude for benefits received is so universally acknowledged to be a virtue, and ingratitude is so detestable a vice, that no man who lays claim to a moral character will dare to affirm that we ought not to have a just sense of the goodness of God in preserving us from the numberless dangers to which we are exposed, and "in giving us rain from heaven, and fruitful seasons, filling our hearts with food and gladness."

Jesus

By the time of the 7th edition (1830–1842) the learned clergy were prepared to deal forthrightly with the occasional manifest inconsistency within the Christian tradition. But swallowing the outrageous conclusions of the worst of the secularists was still beyond the pale.

The following excerpts are from the article "Jesus" in the 7th edition. The author was the Rev. David Welsh, professor of ecclesiastical history at the University of Edinburgh. He was moderator of the General Assembly of the Church of Scotland, but he helped lead a secession from that body to found the Free Protesting Church of Scotland, and was its first moderator. (B.L.F.)

JESUS, the Divine Author of the Christian religion, was born at Bethlehem, a city of the tribe of Judah, about six miles south-east from Jerusalem. His mother was a Jewish virgin named Mary, the betrothed wife of Joseph, both in the humblest rank of life, though both of the royal race of David. The date of his birth is not mentioned in the sacred record; and there has been a difference of opinion among the learned who have engaged in the inquiry, respecting the precise period when it took place. It is now, however, generally agreed upon, that it must be fixed a few years earlier than is indicated by the epoch of our era, which, according to the common computation, corresponds with A. U. 754. We know that Jesus was born before the death of Herod the Great; and it appears from Josephus, that Herod died before the Jewish passover A. U. 750. From calculations founded on other parts of the gospel history, and particularly on a comparison between Luke, iii. 1 and 23, many have supposed that the nativity was in A. U. 747; and in this opinion some have been confirmed by the conjecture of Kepler, that the conjunction between Jupiter and Saturn, which took place in that year, was the star seen by the wise men; though it may be justly questioned how far the principles of scriptural interpretation admit of the supposition that the phenomenon referred to corresponds with the particulars mentioned by St Matthew. In regard to the day or month in which the Saviour was born, a subject to which the devotion of a large proportion of the Christian world has attached much importance, we have no means of accurate knowledge. The description given of shepherds watching their flocks by night, is inconsistent with the idea that it could have been in December or January, or during the heat of the summer months; as we know that in these periods the herds were no longer left in the fields. At other times of the year the flocks might be turned out to pasture day and night in the south of Palestine; but there is no circumstance referred to by any of the evangelists to determine whether it was in spring or in autumn that Jesus was born.

The chronological error in the vulgar era, and in the season for celebrating the festival of Christmas, does not in any way affect the truth of the gospel history; and cannot indeed appear strange, when it is considered that several centuries elapsed before the method of computing time by the birth of Christ was introduced, and that the festival of the nativity was not observed in the primitive church. . . .

The character of Christ, as exhibited in the Gospels, presents to us the only example, anywhere to be found, of the perfection of humanity; and the contemplation of it has ever been considered by his followers as one of the most edifying and delightful exercises of piety. A constant regard to the will of God, and a delight in doing it, form the distinguishing features of his character. With this was connected the absence of all sordid, or selfish, or ambitious aims, and an enlarged and enlightened philanthropy. There is perhaps nothing more remarkable in the life of Jesus than the apparently inconsistent qualities which are blended together in one harmonious whole. We see in him the most unbending constancy united with great tenderness of feeling—hatred of sin, and compassion for the offender—a heart superior to all the allurements of pleasure, with a condescending indulgence for the innocent relaxations of life—a mind of universal philanthropy, alive to all the domestic charities—views that extended to the whole human race, and a generous compliance with national and individual peculiarities. It is difficult to conceive that the portraiture presented to us in the sacred history can be contemplated without benefit; but the chief benefit will be lost if it is forgotten that he whose life was the model of every virtue laid down that life for the sins of the world.

Eden College

Richard Whately (1787–1863) was a logician, theological writer, and Archbishop of

Dublin. To the 8th edition (1852–1860) he contributed a lengthy "Dissertation; exhibiting a general view of the Rise, Progress, and Corruptions of Christianity." From it we excerpt an interesting view of the education of our first parents. The archbishop adds still another proof of the existence of God.

The Instruction of Our First Parents

The earliest history of mankind, by far, that we possess, is that contained in the Book of Genesis. It is extremely brief and scanty; especially the earliest portion of it. But it plainly represents the first of the human race, when in the Garden of Eden, as receiving direct communications from God. We have no detailed account, however, of the instruction they received; and even part of what the history does record is but obscurely intimated. For example, it is rather hinted than expressly stated, that the use of language was imparted to them by revelation. This, however, is generally understood to be the meaning of the passage (Gen. ii. 20), in which it is said that God brought unto Adam the beasts and birds, to see what he would call them, and that Adam gave them names.

But our first parents, or their children, must have received direct from God a great deal of instruction of which no particulars are related. For besides being taught something of religious and moral duty (Gen. ii. 16; iv. 7), it is evident that they must have learned something of the arts of life. The first generations of mankind were certainly not left at all in the condition of mere *savages,* subsisting on such wild fruits and animals as they might chance to meet with. We read concerning the first two sons of Adam, that the one was occupied in tilling the ground, and the other in keeping cattle.

And even independently of the Bible history, we might draw the same conclusion from what is matter of actual experience, and as it were before our eyes at this day. For it appears that mere savages, if left to themselves without any instruction, never did, and never can, civilise themselves. And, consequently, the *first* of the human race that did acquire any degree of civilisation, since they could not have had instruction from other *men,* must have had a superhuman instructor. But for such an instructor, all mankind would have been savages at this day. The mere fact that civilised men do exist, is enough to prove, even to a person who had never heard of the Bible, that, at some time or other, men must have been taught something by a superior Being: in other words, that there must have been a *revelation.*

The Bible

While the first eight editions of Encyclopædia Britannica *were being created, several bodies of criticism were growing that suggested the Holy Bible was not free of error after all. These criticisms were variously addressed by editors, such as George Gleig, and distinguished contributors like Archbishop Whately, and all concluded that the essential truth was that Moses did write the Pentateuch, or at least the four books after Genesis. This remained the firm conviction of most of the God-fearing people of the British Isles.*

Then, as the 9th edition (1875–1889) started to appear a volume at a time, the Britannica *delivered a bombshell into the ranks of the faithful. William Robertson Smith (1846–1894) was a brilliant young professor of Oriental languages and Old Testament exegesis at the Free Church College of Aberdeen. The editor of the 9th edition, the English scholar Thomas Spencer Baynes, had engaged Smith to write on a number of biblical topics. The centerpiece was to be the article "Bible," a review of the enormous strides made in biblical scholarship since the time of Archbishop Whately's dissertation twenty years earlier. Smith was a perfect choice, and the article was admired by both modernist and traditional scholars who reviewed it before publication.*

However, the article accepted the validity of the kind of textual biblical criticism that had been going on, especially in Germany, for years, and when it appeared in Volume III the fifteen-page article enraged some of the most conservative clergymen in Smith's own Free Church. A virtual heresy trial ensued and stormed on for several years. Finally, Smith vindicated himself before his peers, who nevertheless remained divided over the issue. The article was remarkable in its lucidity and remains remarkable for the degree to which it is still sound, even in the light of modern biblical criticism. This controversy of the 1880s still echoes today in the antagonism of champions of biblical infallibility toward scholarly criticism of the Bible. (B.L.F.)

In 1881 Smith, owing to Baynes's illness, was appointed joint editor of Britannica *and later remained as editor in chief until the completion of the 9th edition in 1889. Some crucial extracts from his historic article follow.*

The word Bible, which in English, as in Medieval Latin, is treated as a singular noun, is in its original Greek form a plural—τὰ βιβλία, *the (sacred) books,*—correctly expressing the fact that the sacred writings of Christendom are made up of a number of independent records, which set before us the gradual development of the religion of revelation. The origin of each of these records forms a distinct critical problem; and for the discussion of these questions of detail the reader is referred to the articles on separate Biblical books. The present article seeks to give a general account of the historical and literary conditions under which the unique literature of the Old and New Testaments sprang up, and of the way in which the Biblical books were brought together in a canonical collection and handed down from age to age. The Biblical development is divided into two great periods by the manifestation and historical work of Christ. In its pre-Christian stage the religion of revelation is represented as a *covenant* between the spiritual God and His chosen people the Hebrews. In accordance with this and in allusion to Jer. xxxi. 31, Jesus speaks of the new dispensation founded in His death as a new *covenant* (1 Cor. xi. 25). Hence, as early as the 2d century of our era the two great divisions of the Bible were known as the books of the Old and of the New Covenant respectively. Among Latin-speaking Christians the Greek word for covenant was often incorrectly rendered *testament,* and thus Western Christendom still uses the names of the Old and New Testaments. . . .

The expansion of the Talmudic twenty-four to the thirty-nine Old Testament books of the English version is effected by reckoning the minor prophets one by one, by separating Ezra from Nehemiah, and by subdividing the long books of Samuel, Kings, and Chronicles. . . . The Pentateuch and the so-called earlier prophets form together a single continuous narrative. It is plain, however, that the whole work is not the uniform production of one pen, but that in some way a variety of records of different ages and styles have been combined to form a single narrative. Accordingly, Jewish tradition bears that Moses wrote the Pentateuch, Joshua the book named after him, Samuel the book of Judges, and so forth. As all Hebrew history is anonymous,—a sure proof that people had not yet learned to lay weight on questions of authorship,—it is not probable that this tradition rests on any surer ground than conjecture; and, of course, a scribe who saw in the sacred books the whole outcome of Israel's history would naturally leap to the conclusion that the father of the Law was the author of the Pentateuch, and that the other leaders of Israel's history could not but be the writers of a great part of the Scriptures. A more careful view of the books themselves shows that the actual state of the case is not so simple. . . . In truth, an author who wrote after the occupation of Canaan could never have designed a history which should relate all God's promises to Israel and say nothing of their fulfilment. But in its present shape the Pentateuch is certainly subsequent to the occupation, for it uses geographical names which arose after that time (Hebron, Dan), refers to the conquest as already accomplished (Deut. ii. 12, *cf.* Num. xv. 32; Gen. xii. 6), and even presupposes the existence of a kingship in Israel (Gen. xxxvi. 31). And with this it agrees, that though there are marked differences of style and language within the book of Joshua, each style finds its counterpart in some section of the Pentateuch. In the subsequent books we find quite similar phenomena. The last chapters of Judges cannot be separated from the book of Samuel, and the earlier chapters of Kings are obviously one with the foregoing narrative; while all three books contain passages strikingly akin to parts of the Pentateuch and Joshua (*cf.*, for example, the book of Deuteronomy with Josh. xxiii., 1 Sam. xii., 1 Kings viii.) Such phenomena not only prove the futility of any attempt to base a theory of authorship on the present division into books, but suggest that the history as we have it is not one narrative carried on from age to age by successive additions, but a fusion of several narratives which partly covered the same ground and were combined into unity by an editor. This view is supported by the fact, that even as it now stands the history sometimes gives more than one account of the same event, and that the Pentateuch often gives several laws on the same subject. . . . Thus the legislation of Exod. xx.–xxiii. is partly repeated in ch. xxxiv., and on the passover and feast of unleavened bread we have at least six laws, which if not really discordant, are at least so divergent in form and conception that they cannot be all from the same pen. . . . Of historical duplicates the most celebrated are the twofold history of the creation and the flood, to which we must recur presently. . . .

And now a single word on the way in which these various elements, mirroring so many sides of the national life, and dating from so various ages, came to be fused into a single history, and yet retained so much of their own identity. The Semitic genius does not at all lie in the direction of organic structure. In architecture, in poetry, in history, the Hebrew adds part to part instead of developing a single notion. The temple was an aggregation of small cells, the longest Psalm is an acrostic, and so the longest Biblical history is a stratification and not an organism. This process was facilitated by the habit of anonymous writing, and the accompanying lack of all notion of anything like copyright. If a man copied a book it was his to add and modify as he pleased, and he was not in the least bound to distinguish the old from the new. If he had two books before him to which he attached equal worth, he took large extracts from both, and harmonized them by such additions or modifications as he felt to be necessary. But in default of a keen sense for organic unity very little harmony was sought in points of internal structure, though great skill was often shown, as in the book of Genesis, in throwing the whole material into a balanced scheme of external arrangement. On such principles minor narratives were fused together one after the other, and at length in exile a final redactor completed the great work, on the first part of which Ezra based his reformation, while the latter part was thrown into the second canon. The curious combination of the functions of copyist and author which is here presupposed did not wholly disappear till a pretty late date; and where, as in the books of Samuel, we have two recensions of the text, one in the Hebrew and one in the Septuagint translation, the discrepancies are of such a kind that criticism of the text and analysis of its sources are separated by a scarcely perceptible line. . . . On the other hand, a fresh and creative development, alike in point of form and of thought, is found in the book of Job, which, in grandly dramatic construction, and with wonderful discrimination of character in the several speakers, sums up the whole range of Hebrew speculation on the burning question of Old Testament religion, the relation of affliction to the justice and goodness of God and to the personal merit and demerit of the sufferer. Like the other noblest parts of the Old Testament, the book of Job has a comparatively early date. It was known to Jeremiah, and may be plausibly referred to the 7th century B.C.

In the book of Job we find poetical invention of incidents, attached for didactic purposes to a name apparently derived from old tradition. There is no valid *a priori* reason for denying that the Old Testament may contain other examples of the same art. The book of Jonah is generally viewed as a case in point. Esther, too, has been viewed as a fiction by many who are not over sceptical critics; but on this view a book which finds no recognition in the New Testament, and whose canonicity was long suspected by the Christian as well as by the Jewish Church, must sink to the rank of an apocryphal production. . . .

If we find, then, that after the prophecy of Zechariah i.–viii., which is complete in itself, there begins at ch. ix. a *new* oracle, quite distinct in subject and style, which speaks of an alliance between Judah and Israel as a thing subsisting in the prophet's own time, which knows no oppressor later than Assyria and Egypt, and rebukes forms of idolatry that do not appear after the Exile;—if, in short, the whole prophecy becomes luminous when it is placed a little after the time of Hosea, and remains absolutely dark if it is ascribed to Zechariah, we are surely entitled to let it speak for itself. When the principle is admitted other applications follow, mainly in the book of Isaiah, where the anonymous chapters, xl.–lxvi., cannot be understood in a natural and living way except by looking at them from the historical stand-point of the Exile. . . .

The Text of the Old Testament

Semitic alphabets have no full provision for distinguishing vowels, and the oldest writing, before orthography became fixed, was negligent in the use even of such vowel-letters as exist. For a long time, then, not only during the use of the old Phoenician character, but even after the more modern square or Babylonian letters were adopted, the written text of the Bible was *consonantal only,* leaving a certain scope for variety of pronunciation and sense. But even the consonantal text was not absolutely fixed. The loose state of the laws of spelling and the great similarity of several letters made errors of copying frequent. The text of Micah, for example, is often unintelligible, and many hopeless errors are older than the oldest versions. But up to the time of the Alexandrian version, MSS. were in circulation which differed not merely by greater or less accuracy of transcription, but by presenting such differences of recension as could not arise by accident. The Greek text of Jeremiah is vastly different from that of the Hebrew Bible, and it is not certain that the latter is always best. In the books of Samuel the Greek enables us to correct many blunders of the Hebrew text, but shows at the same time that copyists used great freedom with details of the text. For the Pentateuch we have, in the copies of the Samaritans, a third recension, often but not always closely allied to the Greek. The three recensions show important variations in the chronology of Genesis; and it is remarkable that the *Book of Jubilees*, a Jewish treatise, which cannot be much older than the Christian era, perhaps not much older than the destruction of the Jewish state, sometimes agrees with the Samaritan or with the Alexandrian recension. Up to this time, then, there was no absolutely received text. But soon after the Christian era all this was changed, and by a process which we cannot follow in detail, a single recension became supreme. . . .

Jewish Versions

Versions of the Old Testament became necessary partly because the Jews of the Western Dispersion adopted the Greek language, partly because even in Palestine the Old Hebrew was gradually supplanted by Aramaic. The chief seat of the Hellenistic Jews was in Egypt, and here arose the Alexandrian version, commonly known as the Septuagint or Version of the LXX, from a fable that it was composed, with miraculous circumstances, by seventy-two Palestinian scholars summoned to Egypt by Ptolemy Philadelphus. In reality there can be no doubt that the version was gradually completed by several authors and at different times. The whole is probably older than the middle of the 2d century B.C. . . .

Jewish disciples were accustomed to retain the oral teaching of their masters with extraordinary tenacity and verbal exactness of memory (Mishna, *Aboth,* iii. 8; *Edaioth,* i. 3), and so the words of Jesus might for some time be handed down by merely oral tradition. But did the gospel continue to be taught orally alone up to the time when the extant gospels were written? or must we assume the existence of earlier evangelical writings forming a link between oral tradition and the narratives we now possess? The earliest external evidence on this point is given in the prologue to Luke's gospel, which speaks of many previous essays towards a regularly digested evangelical history on the basis of the tradition (whether exclusively oral or partly written is not expressed) of eye-witnesses who had followed the whole course of Christ's ministry. It seems to be implied that if the eye-witnesses wrote at all, they, at least so far as was known to Luke, did not compose a regular narrative but simply threw together a mass of reminiscences. This understanding of the words of the evangelist agrees very well with the uniform tradition of the old church as to the second gospel, viz., that it was composed by Mark from material furnished by Peter. This tradition goes back to Papias of Hierapolis, about 150 A.D., but it is a fair question whether the second gospel as we have it is not an enlarged edition of Mark's original work. On the other hand ecclesiastical tradition recognizes the apostle Matthew as the author of the first gospel, but does so in a way that really bears out the statements of Luke. For the tradition that Matthew wrote the first gospel is always combined with the statement that he wrote in Hebrew (Aramaic). But from the time of Erasmus the best Greek scholars have been convinced that the gospel is not a translation. Either, then, the whole tradition of a directly apostolic Aramaic gospel is a mistake, caused by the existence among the Judaizing Christians in Palestine of an apocryphal "Gospel according to the Hebrews," which was by them ascribed to Matthew, but was, in fact, a corrupt edition of our Greek gospel; or, on the other hand, what Matthew really wrote in Aramaic was different from the book that now bears his name, and only formed an important part of the material from which it draws. The latter solution is naturally suggested by the oldest form of the tradition; for what Papias says of Matthew is that he wrote *τὰ λόγια, the oracles,*—an expression which, though much disputed, seems to be most fairly understood not of a complete gospel but of a collection of the words of Christ. And if so, all the earliest external evidence points to the conclusion that the synoptical gospels are non-apostolic digests of spoken and written apostolic tradition, and that the arrangement of the earlier material in orderly form took place only gradually and by many essays. With this the internal evidence agrees. The three first gospels are often in such remarkable accord even in minute and accidental points of expression, that it is certain either that they copied one another or that all have some sources in common. The first explanation is inadequate, both from the nature of the discrepancies that accompany the agreement of the three narratives, and from the impossibility of assigning absolute priority to any one gospel. For example, even if we suppose that the gospel of Mark was used by the other two authors, or conversely that Mark was made up mainly from Matthew and Luke, it is still necessary to postulate one or more earlier sources to explain residuary phenomena. And the longer the problem is studied the more general is the conviction of critics, that these sources cannot possibly have been merely oral.

It appears from what we have already seen, that a considerable portion of the

New Testament is made up of writings not directly apostolical, and a main problem of criticism is to determine the relation of these writings, especially of the gospels, to apostolic teaching and tradition. But behind all such questions as the relative priority of Matthew or of Mark, the weight to be assigned to the testimony of Papias, and so forth, lies a series of questions much more radical in character by which the whole theological world is at present agitated. Can we say of all the New Testament books that they are either directly apostolic, or at least stand in immediate dependence on genuine apostolic teaching which they honestly represent? or must we hold, with an influential school of modern critics, that a large proportion of the books are direct forgeries, written in the interest of theological tendencies, to which they sacrifice without hesitation the genuine history and teaching of Christ and his apostles? . . . But on the whole, what evidence does exist is of a kind to push back all the more important writings to an early date. The gospel of John, for example, is one of the books which negative critics are most determined in rejecting. Yet the fairest writers of the school (Hilgenfeld, Keim) admit that it was known to Justin Martyr in the middle of the 2d century, though they think that besides our four gospels he had a fifth of apocryphal character. But references of an earlier date can hardly be denied; and the gospel may be traced almost to the beginning of the century by the aid of fragments of the Gnostic Basilides and of the epistles of Ignatius. The Tübingen school, indeed, maintain that the fragments preserved by Hippolytus are not from Basilides, but from a later writer of his school, and utterly reject the Ignatian epistles. But it cannot be said that they have proved their case beyond dispute. They have at most shown that, if the gospel *must on other grounds* be taken as spurious, the external evidence may be pushed aside as not absolutely insuperable. On the other hand they try to bring positive proof that certain books were unknown in circles where, if genuine, they must have circulated. But such a negative is in its very nature difficult to prove. Probably the strongest argument of the kind is that brought to show that Papias did not know the gospel of John. But we know Papias only through Eusebius; and though the latter is careful to mention all references to disputed books, it does not appear that it was part of his design to cite testimony to a book so universally allowed as John's gospel. And Papias does give testimony to the first epistle of John, which is hardly separable from the gospel. On the whole, then, we repeat that, on the most cardinal points, the external evidence for the New Testament books is as strong as can fairly be looked for, though not, of course, strong enough to convince a man who is sure *a priori* that this or that book is unhistorical and must be of late date. . . .

Buddhism

Snippets from the life of Gautama Buddha and the great religion founded in his name appear here and there in the early Britannica *editions, but it is not until the great scholarly 9th (1875–1889) that the faith appears by name and receives a statement that is both lucid and grand in its reflection of that very old system of belief. The following excerpts are from the article "Buddhism," by T. W. Rhys Davids, professor of Pali and Buddhist literature at University College, London.*

BUDDHISM is the name of a religion which formerly prevailed through a large part of India, and is now professed by the inhabitants of Ceylon, Siam, and Burma (the southern Buddhists), and of Nepāl, Tibet, China, and Japan (the northern Buddhists). It arose out of the philosophical and ethical teachings of Siddhārtha Gautama, the eldest son of Suddhōdana, who was rāja in Kapilavastu and chief of the tribe of the Sākyas, an Aryan clan seated during the 5th century B.C. on the banks of the Kohain about 100 miles N. of the city of Benāres, and about 50 miles S. of the foot of the Himālaya Mountains.

We are accustomed to find the legendary and the miraculous gathering, like a halo, around the early history of religious leaders, until the sober truth runs the risk of being altogether neglected for the glittering and edifying falsehood. Buddha has not escaped the fate which has befallen the founders of other religions; and as late as the year 1854 the late Professor Wilson of Oxford read a paper before the Royal Asiatic Society of London in which he maintained that the supposed life of Buddha was a myth, and "Buddha himself merely an imaginary being." No one, however, would now support this view; and it is admitted that, under the mass of miraculous tales which have been handed down regarding him, there is a basis of truth already sufficiently clear to render possible an intelligible history, which will become clearer and clearer as older and better authorities are made accessible. . . .

The two ideas of the utter vanity of all earthly good and the inevitable law of rebirth, decay, and death will be seen to lead naturally to the belief in Nirvāna. If life be an evil, and death itself be no delivery from life, it is necessary to go further back to discover the very origin, the seed, so to speak, of existence; and by destroying that to put an end at last to the long train of misery in which we are compelled to go again and again through the same weary round of experiences, always ending in disappointment. This seed of existence Buddhism finds in "Karma," the sum of merit and demerit, which, as each one's demerit is the greater of the two, often comes practically to much the same thing as sin or error. It forms the second link in the Buddhist chain of causation, and arises itself from ignorance. Destroy that ignorance which brings with it such a progeny, cut the links of this chain of existence, root out karma with the mistaken cleaving to life, and there will be deliverance at last—deliverance from all sorrow and all trouble in the eternal rest of Nirvāna. Anything less than this would be a mockery of hope; for there is no life outside the domain of transmigration, and by the inevitable law of change that which causes existence of any kind would itself be the cause also of decay, and bring with it after a time the whole chain of evils from which the tired heart of man seeks relief.

To reach this end, to destroy karma, and thus to attain Nirvāna, there is only one way—the fourfold path already explained above, which is also summed up in the Buddhist books in the eight divisions, "right views, right thoughts, right speech, right actions, right living, right exertion, right recollection, and right meditation."

By these means ignorance will be overcome and karma destroyed, and after the organized being has been dissolved in death, there will be nothing left to bring about the production of another life. For it must be understood that while Buddhism occasionally yielded so far to popular phraseology as to make use of the word soul, it denies altogether that the word is anything more than a convenient expression, or that it has any counterpart in fact. Birth is not rebirth, but new birth; transmigration of soul becomes a transfer of karma; metempsychosis gives way to metamorphosis. As one generation dies and gives way to another—the heir of the consequences of all its vices and all its virtues, the exact result of pre-existing causes—so each individual in the long chain of life inherits all of good or evil that all its predecessors have done or been, and takes up the struggle towards enlightenment precisely there where they have left it. There is nothing eternal, but the law of cause and effect, and change; the kosmos itself is passing away; even karma can be destroyed; nothing is, everything becomes. And so with this organized life of ours, it contains within itself no eternal germ; it passes away like everything else, there only remains the accumulated result of all its actions. One lamp is lighted at another; the second flame differs from the first, to which it owes its existence. A seed grows into a tree and produces a seed from which arises another tree different from the first, though resulting from it. And so the true Buddhist saint does not mar the purity of his self-denial by lusting after a positive happiness which he himself is to enjoy hereafter. He himself will cease to be, but his virtue will live and work out its full effect in the decrease of the sum of the misery of sentient beings.

Judaism

The religion of the Jews was always treated under such titles as "Jews" or "Hebrews" or titles of particular topics. Not until the 13th edition (1926) did the title "Judaism" appear, and the accompanying article was the first on the subject written by a Jewish scholar instead of a Protestant Christian authority on the Old Testament. This contributor was chief rabbi of the United Hebrew Congregations of the British Empire, Joseph Herman Hertz. His article was written sparely and beautifully, and the echoes it stirs are the more haunting when it is read today, more than fifty years after the Holocaust of the Nazis. When Rabbi Hertz wrote, the Kristallnacht lay a scant dozen years in the future. (B.L.F.)

JUDAISM: 1910–1925—It is no exaggeration to say that the 15 years under review have been to Israel a period of woe and disaster, as well as of consolation and hope, such as no similar period since the Dispersion.

Russia

The darkest part of the picture is Russia, the fountain in modern times of the old Jewish life and, before the War, the home of one-half of the world's Jewish population. When the period opened, Mendel Beilis, and with him Judaism as a religion and the whole Jewish people, stood arraigned in the courts of the Tsar at Kieff to answer the hideous charge of ritual murder. In vain the friends of humanity in England, France and Germany protested that this accusation of religious cannibalism was an utterly baseless libel on Judaism, an insult to Western culture, and a dishonour to those who formulate it. The Russian bureaucracy recoiled from no means that would insure the conviction of Beilis, as it would have furnished a convenient apologia for pogroms, past and future. However, in Nov. 1913, an all-Russian jury acquitted Beilis.

One other instance to show the atmosphere in which Russian Judaism had to live during the last years of the Romanoffs. In the same year, at the International Congress for the Suppression of the White Slave Traffic held in London, Hertz called the attention of the world to the infamy of the Tsarist "yellow ticket," by which any Jewish woman, if she was willing to be registered as a prostitute, was permitted free and unrestricted residence throughout the Empire; whereas all other Jews and Jewesses were confined to the pale of Settlement, which was one of the fiercest battlegrounds of the World War.

The Jewish cities were taken and retaken by the rival armies, with attendant bombardments, burnings and pillagings. Added to these were the summary expulsions and calculated inhumanities which the Russian military authorities perpetrated against the Jewish population. As a result, scores of important communities were ruined, and their religious institutions, their rabbinical academies, together with every form of Jewish cultural activity, destroyed to their foundations. Of the surviving communities, hundreds were later annihilated during the massacres of the Jewish population in the Ukraine during the years 1919–21, massacres that for thoroughness and extent are surpassed by those in Armenia alone.

The Russian revolution completed this break-up of Russian Jewry and its religious life. At first constitutional, the revolution brought full religious emancipation to all, but in the unique persecution of all religion that began soon after the Bolshevists came into power, Judaism had to suffer most. Jewish communists have, from the first, taken a sinister delight in the proscription of all Jewish religious teaching—whether in the rabbinical colleges, in the elementary religious schools or even in homes. Synagogues were confiscated and converted into workmen's clubs (as late as Sept. 14 1925), and even into stables.

During 1925 the bitter fight against religion seemed to have relaxed somewhat, and Christian and Mahommedan bodies are now allowed to give religious instruction to small "groups" of their children after school hours. In the case of Jews, however, two children have been declared to constitute a school, and subject to the dire penalties for teaching religion or Bible to children at a school. Religious instruction is therefore given clandestinely, underground or in lofts and at midnight, as in the days of the Inquisition. In Dec. 1925 two teachers were sentenced at Kieff to six months imprisonment with hard labour for this offence; and 200 children were imprisoned at Podolia, for refusing to betray the name and whereabouts of their religious teachers. Zionists were pursued with a Tsar-like ferocity, hundreds of them having been banished to Siberia. The use of Hebrew as a bourgeois language is suppressed.

These persecutions called forth among the faithful remnant a new fervour and a deeper self-sacrifice for their faith; but Jewish institutional religion became paralysed in Soviet Russia, and the religious outlook for the growing generation is dark indeed. Before the War, the intense religious and intellectual life of Russian Jewry was duly reflected in the works of a whole galaxy of rabbinical, Hebrew and Yiddish writers. With the outbreak of hostilities all Hebrew and Yiddish publications of any kind were forbidden. After the revolution there was a brief literary revival, which was soon strangled by the Bolshevists.

Poland, Baltic and Balkan States

Jewish religious life has in the main resumed its pre-War aspect in Poland, the Baltic and the Balkan countries, despite the economic ruin of a large portion of the Jewries wrought by racial hatred and social unrest in those politically immature states. In Poland a widely ramified net of Hebrew-speaking schools, both elementary and secondary, has been founded by the *Tarbuth* organisation, and is recognised by the Government. In Greece, the only large, and autonomous Jewish community of Salonika is declining in consequence of the failure of the Greek Govt. to keep the solemn pledges it gave to respect the Jewish Sabbath. Its important rabbinate is unfilled. In Turkey, the status of all religions has undergone violent transformation under the secularising Kemalist *régime*. The activities of the Chief Rabbinate, which hitherto had practically the same powers as the Patriarchates of other denominations, were limited to ecclesiastical matters, and the congregations were organised on autonomous lines. The Chief Rabbi, Chacham Bashi Bijerano, introduced far-reaching reforms in the Jewish law of divorce. These have, however, not found recognition with the rabbinic authorities of other lands.

France and Central Europe

Judaism in France has been strengthened by the accession of the important religiously conservative congregations of Alsace-Lorraine; as well as by the Moroccan communities now under French control. In 1924, the Grand Rabbi of France, M. Israel Levi, appealed to the leaders of east European orthodoxy to consider the enactment, in accordance with rabbinic law, of modifications in certain aspects of the Jewish marriage and divorce law (Agunah). Italian Jewry found itself threatened by the new education law, with its compulsory Catholic instruction. . . .

The United States

The 3,600,000 Jews of America have now their own English version of the Bible, the result of many years' labour on the part of a group of scholars, among them Solomon Schechter and Joseph Jacobs. America has acquired great Jewish libraries, that of the New York Jewish Theological Seminary (including the Elkan Adler collection) being the largest in the world. The older rabbinical colleges are workshops of Jewish learning. To these have been added the Yitzchak Elchanan Yeshivah and the Jewish Institute of Religion, representing the two religious poles in American Judaism. . . .

The New Diaspora

Eastern European Jewish emigrants, fleeing from racial hatred and economic ruin, find the doors of the United States all but barred and bolted to them. In consequence, they are scattered and dispersed to distant lands where grave dangers await their Jewishness and Judaism. Outside the Argentine Republic, the fresh arrivals find in most Latin-American countries little organised Jewish life and, too often, total abandonment of Judaism on the part of the earlier settlers. The Jewish Colonisation Assn. of Paris appointed I. Raffalovich as Grand Rabbin of Brazil to lay the religious foundations of the new Jewish centres in the youngest diaspora. Mention must also be made of the praiseworthy efforts of Dr. J. Faitlovich to bring the forgotten Jewish tribes of Abyssinia—the Falashas—into touch with the general body and religious currents of European Jewry.

Palestine

The brightest spot on the Jewish horizon throughout this period is Palestine. The beginnings of the Jewish revival in the Holy Land date from long before the Balfour Declaration, when Eliezer ben Yehudah began his gigantic undertaking to make Hebrew the language of everyday speech, as well as of instruction in schools. One half of his monumental *Dictionary of the Hebrew Language, Ancient, Mediaeval and Modern,* was published in his life-time. Palestine became the home of Ahad Ha'am—the philosopher of Zionism—and of Ch. N. Bialik, the great neo-Hebrew poet. A Rabbinate for the whole of Palestine was called into existence, with A. I. Kook (Ashkenazi) and Jacob Meir (Sephardi) as joint Chief Rabbis. A Communities' Ordinance will, it is hoped, be promulgated, providing a democratic religious organisation for the Jewish population of the Holy Land.

The zenith of the spiritual revival was reached when the Hebrew University was opened by the Earl of Balfour on April 1 1925. It may be some time before the Jerusalem University fulfils the hope of being the sanctuary of the Jewish genius; but a land focuses a people and calls forth, as nothing else can, its spiritual potentialities. It is the ardent faith of the architects of the New Palestine that the resurrection of the Jewish people on its own soil will reopen its sacred fountains of creative energy. As of old, only a remnant will return to the land of their fathers. But it is the national rejuvenation of that remnant that may open a new chapter in the annals of the human spirit.

CHAPTER TEN

Some Lives

Biographies have been a focus of particular attention, and not infrequently of controversy, at various points in the history of Encyclopædia Britannica. *The editor of the 1st edition (1768–1771) omitted them as a matter of policy and refused to edit the 2nd when the publishers decided to include biographies. When biographies of persons still living were introduced in the 10th edition (a ten-volume supplement to the 9th, published in 1902–1903) some critics were outraged—but the new policy continued. The 11th edition of 1910–1911 was especially famous for its biographies.*

The biographies included here were chosen not as a cross-section of the whole range of subjects, but rather as a sampling of authors and a look at how the encyclopedists' biographic standards and treatments evolved over two centuries, and on occasion to present archaic language that is diverting to late-twentieth-century eyes and ears. (B.L.F.)

Pope Joan

From the 2nd edition (1778–1783), this account offers a fine example of two qualities absent (or almost so) from Britannica *today: bias and humor. For a thorough, straight-faced account of the facts go to Volume 6 of the 15th edition, but this makes better reading.*

JOAN (Pope), called by Platina *John VIII,* is said to have held the holy see between Leo IV. who died in 855, and Benedict III. who died in 858. Marianus Scotus says, she sat two years five months and four days. Numberless have been the controversies, fables, and conjectures, relating to this pope. It is said that a German girl, pretending to be a man, went to Athens, where she made great progress in the sciences; and afterward came to Rome in the same habit. As she had a quick genius, and spoke with a good grace in the public disputations and lectures, her great learning was admired, and every one loved her extremely; so that after the death of Leo, she was chosen pope, and performed all offices as such. Whilst she was in possession of this high dignity, she was got with child; and as she was going in a solemn procession to the Lateran church, she was delivered of that child, between the Coliseum and St Clement's church, in a most public street, before a crowd of people, and died on the spot, in 857. By way of embellishing this story, may be added the precaution reported to have been afterward taken to avoid such another accident. After the election of a pope, he was placed on a chair with an open seat, called the *groping chair,* when a deacon came most devoutly behind and satisfied himself of the pontiff's sex by feeling. This precaution, however, has been long deemed unnecessary, because the cardinals now always get bastards enough to establish their virility before they arrive at the pontificate.

Elizabeth I

An interesting contrast in styles is provided by the 2nd edition (1778–1783) account of the death of Queen Elizabeth I and that to be found in the current edition. Earlier writers were particularly good on deathbed scenes.

Elizabeth continued to reign with great glory till the year 1603; but all her greatness could not prevent her from being extremely miserable before her death. She had caused her greatest favourite, and probably her lover, the earl of Essex, to be executed. Though this execution could not be called unjust, the queen's affection (on being informed that he had at last thrown himself entirely on her clemency) returned to such a degree, that she thenceforth gave herself entirely over to despair. She refused food and sustenance; she continued silent and gloomy; sighs and groans were the only vent she gave to her despondence; and she lay for ten days and nights upon the carpet, leaning on cushions, which her maids brought her. Perhaps the faculties of her mind were impaired by long and violent exercise; perhaps she reflected with remorse on some past actions of her life, or perceived, but too strongly, the decays of nature, and the approach of her dissolution. She saw her courtiers remitting in their assiduity to her, in order to pay their court to James the apparent successor. Such a concurrence of causes was more than sufficient to destroy the remains of her constitution; and her end was now visibly seen to approach. Feeling a perpetual heat in her stomach, attended with an unquenchable thirst, she drank without ceasing, but refused the assistance of her physicians. Her distemper gaining ground, Cecil and the lord admiral desired to know her sentiments with regard to the succession. To this she replied, That as the crown of England had always been held by kings, it ought not to devolve upon any inferior character, but upon her immediate heir the king of Scotland. Being then advised by the archbishop of Canterbury to fix her thoughts upon God, she replied, that her thoughts did not in the least wander from him. Her voice soon after left her; she fell into a lethargic slumber, which continued some hours; and she expired gently without a groan, in the 70th year of her age, 45th of her reign.

Here in its entirety, from the 15th edition, is acknowledged authority Elizabeth Jenkins's description of Elizabeth I's final hours.

The last service she performed for her country was on her deathbed, at Richmond Palace in Surrey, on March 23, 1603. Almost speechless, she was asked to make a sign if she acknowledged [James VI of Scotland] as her successor. She made the gesture that lent her authority to a peaceful succession and died early the next morning.

Richard Savage

One of the most abused, and most abusive, men in the history of English letters was the subject of one of the first biographies to appear in the Britannica. *It reflects perfectly the biographical style of its period.*

Our extracts are from the 2nd edition (1778–1783). The editor here was heavily indebted to Dr. Johnson, whose work cited in the closing paragraph is still considered one of the finest short biographies in our language. (B.L.F.)

SAVAGE, RICHARD, one of the most remarkable characters that is to be met with perhaps in all the records of biography, was the son of Anne countess of Macclesfield, by the earl of Rivers, according to her own confession; and was born in 1698. This confession of adultery was made in order to procure a separation from her husband the earl of Macclesfield: yet, having obtained this desired end, no sooner was her spurious offspring brought into the world, than, without the dread of shame or poverty to excuse her, she discovered the resolution of disowning him; and, as long as he lived, treated him with the most unnatural cruelty. She delivered him over to a poor woman to educate as her own; and prevented the earl of Rivers from leaving him a legacy of L. 6000, by declaring him dead. She endeavoured to send him secretly to the plantations; but this plan being either laid aside or frustrated, she placed him apprentice with a shoemaker. In this situation, however, he did not long continue; for his nurse dying, he went to take care of the effects of his supposed mother; and found in her boxes some letters which discovered to young Savage of his birth, and the cause of its concealment.

From the moment of this discovery it was natural for him to become dissatisfied with his situation as a shoemaker. He now conceived that he had a right to share in the affluence of his real mother; and therefore he directly, and perhaps indiscreetly, applied to her, and made use of every art to awaken her tenderness and attract her regard. . . .

Mean time, while he was assiduously endeavouring to rouse the affections of a mother in whom all natural affection was extinct, he was destitute of the means of support, and reduced to the miseries of want. We are not told by what means he got rid of his obligation to the shoemaker, or whether he ever was actually bound to him; but we now find him very differently employed in order to procure a subsistence. In short, the youth had parts, and a strong inclination towards literary pursuits, especially poetry. He wrote a poem; and afterwards two plays, *Woman's a Riddle* and *Love in a Veil:* but the author was allowed no part of the profits from the first; and from the second he received no other advantage than the acquaintance of Sir Richard Steel and Mr Wilks, by whom he was pitied, caressed, and relieved. However, the kindness of his friends not affording him a constant supply, he wrote the tragedy of *Sir Thomas Overbury;* which not only procured him the esteem of many persons of wit, but brought him in 200 *l.* . . . But Savage was, like many other wits, a bad manager, and was ever in distress. As fast as his friends raised him out of one difficulty, he sunk into another; and, when he found himself greatly involved, he would ramble about like a vagabond, with scarce a shirt on his back. . . . The profits of his Tragedy and his Miscellanies together, had now, for a time, somewhat raised poor Savage both in circumstances and credit; so that the world just began to behold him with a more favourable eye than formerly, when both his fame and life were endangered by a most unhappy event. A drunken frolic in which he one night engaged, ended in a fray, and Savage unfortunately killed a man, for which he was condemned to be hanged; his friends earnestly solicited the mercy of the crown, while his mother as earnestly exerted herself to prevent his receiving it. The countess of Hertford at length laid his whole case before queen Caroline, and Savage obtained a pardon.

Savage had now lost that tenderness for his mother, which the whole series of her cruelty had not been able wholly to repress; and considering her as an implacable enemy, whom nothing but his blood could satisfy, threatened to harrass her with lampoons, and to publish a copious narrative of her conduct, unless she consented to allow him a pension. This expedient proved successful; and the lord Tyrconnel, upon his promise of laying aside his design of exposing his mother's cruelty, took him into his family, treated him as an equal, and engaged to allow him a pension of 200 *l.* a year. This was the golden part of Savage's life. He was courted by all who endeavoured to be thought men of genius, and caressed by all who valued themselves upon a refined taste. In this gay period of his life he published the *Temple of Health and Mirth*, on the recovery of lady Tyrconnel from a languishing illness; and *The Wanderer*, a moral poem, which he dedicated to lord Tyrconnel, in strains of the highest panegyric: but these praises he in a short time found himself inclined to retract, being discarded by the man on whom they were bestowed. . . . He, moreover, now thought himself at liberty to take revenge upon his mother.—Accordingly he wrote *The Bastard*, a poem, remarkable for the vivacity in the beginning, (where he finely enumerates the imaginary advantages of base birth), and for the pathetic conclusion, wherein he recounts the real calamities which he suffered by the crime of his parents.—The reader will not be displeased with a transcript of some of the lines in the opening of the poem, as a specimen of this writer's spirit and manner of versification.

Blest be the bastard's birth! thro'
    wond'rous ways,
He shines excentric like a comet's blaze.
No sickly fruit of faint compliance he;
He! stamp'd in nature's mint with ecstasy!
He lives to build, not boast a gen'rous race;
No tenth transmitter of a foolish face.

He, kindling from within, requires no
flame,
He glories in a bastard's glowing name.
—Nature's unbounded son, he stands
alone,
His heart unbias'd, and his mind his own.
—O mother! yet no mother!—'tis to you
My thanks for such distinguish'd claims
are due.

This poem had an extraordinary sale; and its appearance happening at the time when his mother was at Bath, many persons there took frequent opportunities of repeating passages from the Bastard in her hearing. This was perhaps the first time that ever she discovered a sense of shame, and on this occasion the power of wit was very conspicuous; the wretch who had, without scruple, proclaimed herself an adulteress, and who had first endeavoured to starve her son, then to transport him, and afterwards to hang him, was not able to bear the representation of her own conduct; but fled from reproach, though she felt no pain from guilt; and left Bath with the utmost haste, to shelter herself among the crowds of London.

Some time after this, Savage formed the resolution of applying to the queen; who having once given him life, he hoped she might farther extend her goodness to him by enabling him to support it.—With this view, he published a poem on her birthday, which he entitled *The Volunteer-Laureat;* for which she was pleased to send him 50 *l.* with an intimation that he might annually expect the same bounty. But this annual allowance was nothing to a man of his strange and singular extravagance. His usual custom was, as soon as he had received his pension, to disappear with it; and secrete himself from his most intimate friends, till every shilling of the 50 *l.* was spent; which done, he again appeared, pennyless as before. . . . His wit and parts, however, still raised him new friends, as fast as his misbehaviour lost him his old ones. Yet such was his conduct, that occasional relief only furnished the means of occasional excess; and he defeated all attempts made by his friends to fix him in a decent way. . . .

His distress now became so great, and so notorious, that a scheme was at length concerted for procuring him a permanent relief. It was proposed that he should retire into Wales, with an allowance of *50 l. per annum,* on which he was to live privately, in a cheap place, for ever quitting his town-haunts, and resigning all farther pretensions to fame. This offer he seemed gladly to accept; but his intentions were only to deceive his friends, by retiring for a while, to write another tragedy, and then to return with it to London in order to bring it upon the stage. . . . At length, with great reluctance, he proceeded to Swansey; where he lived about a year, very much dissatisfied with the diminution of his salary; for he had, in his letters, treated his contributors so insolently, that most of them withdrew their subscriptions. Here he finished his tragedy, and resolved to return with it to London: which was strenuously opposed by his great and constant friend Mr Pope; who proposed that Savage should put this play into the hands of Mr Thomson and Mr Mallet in order that they might fit it for the stage, that his friends should receive the profits it might bring in, and that the author should receive the produce by way of annuity. This kind and prudent scheme was rejected by Savage, with the utmost contempt.—He declared he would not submit his works to any one's correction; and that he would no longer be kept in leading-strings. . . . Necessity came upon him before he was aware; his money was spent, his cloaths were worn out, his appearance was shabby, and his presence was disgustful at every table. He now began to find every man from home, at whose house he called; and he found it difficult to obtain a dinner. . . . He remained for some time, at a great expence, in the house of the sheriff's officer, in hopes of procuring bail; which expence he was enabled to defray, by a present of five guineas from Mr Nash at Bath. No bail, however, was to be found; so that poor Savage was at last lodged in Newgate, a prison so named in Bristol. . . .

While he remained in this not intolerable prison, his ingratitude again broke out, in a bitter satire on the city of Bristol. . . . This satire he entitled *London and Bristol Compared;* and in it he abused the inhabitants of the latter, with such a spirit of resentment, that the reader would imagine he had never received any other than the most injurious treatment in that city.

When Savage had remained about six months in this hospitable prison, he received a letter from Mr Pope, (who still continued to allow him 20 *l.* a year) containing a charge of very atrocious ingratitude. What were the particulars of this charge, we are not informed; but, from the notorious character of the man, there is reason to fear that Savage was but too justly accused. He, however, solemnly protested his innocence, but he was very unusually affected on this occasion. In a few days after, he was seized with a disorder, which at first was not suspected to be dangerous: but growing daily more languid and dejected, at last a fever seized him; and he expired on the 1st of August 1743, in the 46th year of his age.

Thus lived, and thus died, Richard Savage, Esq; leaving behind him a character strangely chequered with vices and good qualities. Of the former we have seen a variety of instances in this abstract of his life; of the latter, his peculiar situation in the world gave him but few opportunities of making any considerable display. He was, however, undoubtedly a man of excellent parts, and had he received the full benefits of a liberal education, and had his natural talents been cultivated to the best advantage, he might have made a respectable figure in life. He was happy in an agreeable temper and a lively flow of wit, which made his company much coveted; nor was his judgment both of writings and of men, inferior to his wit: but he was too much a slave to his passions, and his passions were too easily excited. He was warm in his friendships, but implacable in his enmity; and his greatest fault, which is indeed the greatest of all faults, was ingratitude. He seemed to think everything due to his merit, and that he was little obliged to any one for those favours which he thought it their duty to confer on him: it is therefore the less to be wondered at, that he never rightly estimated the kindness of his many friends and benefactors, or preserved a grateful and due sense of their generosity towards him.

The works of this original writer, after having long lain dispersed in magasines and fugitive publications, have been lately collected and published in an elegant edition, in 2 vols; to which are prefixed, the admirable Memoirs of Savage, written by Dr Samuel Johnson.

Anne Boleyn

The queens who were variously wife, daughter, and grandniece to Henry VIII have inevitably received major attention from Britannica *editors since the 2nd edition (the first having, as noted, banned biographies* per se.*) These excerpts are from the 3rd edition (1788–1797).*

In treating Anne Boleyn the current Britannica *is, of course, devoid of the anti-Catholic bias so marked in earlier handlings. But it is more mealymouthed with respect to her moral character.*

BOLEYN, ANNE, queen of Henry VIII. of England; memorable in the English history, as the first cause of the reformation, as the mother of queen Elizabeth under whom it was completely established, and also on account of her own sufferings. She was the daughter of Sir Thomas Boleyn, and born in 1507. She was carried into France at seven years of age by Henry VIII's sister, who was wife of Louis XII. . . . The year of her return is not well known: some will have it to have been in 1527, others in 1525. This much is certain, that she was maid of honour to queen Catharine of Spain, Henry VIII's first wife; and that the king fell extremely in love with her. She behaved herself with so much art and address, that by refusing to satisfy his passion, she brought him to think of marrying her: and the king, deceived by her into a persuasion that he should never enjoy her unless he made her his wife, was induced to set on foot the affair of his divorce with Catharine, which at last was executed with great solemnity and form. A celebrated author observes, that "That which would have been very praise-worthy on another occasion, was Anne Boleyn's chief crime: since her refusing to comply with an amorous king, unless he would divorce his wife, was a much more enormous crime than to have been his concubine. A concubine (says he) would not have dethroned a queen, nor taken her crown or her husband from her; whereas the crafty Anne Boleyn, by pretending to be chaste and scrupulous, aimed only at the usurpation of the throne, and the exclusion of Catharine of Arragon and her daughters from all the honours due to them." In the mean time, Henry could not procure a divorce from the Pope; which, we know, made him resolve at length to disown his authority, and to fling off his yoke. Nevertheless he married Anne Boleyn privately upon the 14th of November 1532, without waiting any longer for a release from Rome; and as soon as he perceived that his new wife was with child he made his marriage public. He caused Anne Boleyn to be declared queen of England on Easter-eve 1533, and to be crowned the first of June following. She was brought to bed upon the 7th of September of a daughter, who was afterwards queen Elizabeth; and continued to be much beloved by the king, till the charms of Jane Seymour had fired that prince's heart in 1536. . . . When she was imprisoned, she is said to have acted very different parts; sometimes seeming devout and shedding abundance of tears, then all of a sudden breaking out into a loud laughter. A few hours before her death, she said, that the executioner was very handy: and besides, that she had a very small neck; at the same time feeling it with her hands, and laughing heartily. However, it is agreed that she died with great resolution; taking care to spread her gown about her feet, that she might fall with decency. . . . Roman Catholic writers have taken all occasions to rail at this unhappy woman, as well through vexation at the schism which she occasioned, as for the sake of defaming and dishonouring Queen Elizabeth by this means; and they have triumphed vehemently, that in the long reign of that queen, no endeavours were used to justify her mother. But either Queen Elizabeth or her ministers are greatly to be admired for prudence in this respect; since it is certain, that Anne Boleyn's justification could never have been carried on without discovering many things which must have been extremely prejudicial to the queen, and have weakened her right instead of establishing it. For though the representations of the Papists are in no wise to be regarded, yet many things might have been said to the disadvantage of her mother, without transgressing the laws of true history; as that she was a woman gay even to immodesty, indiscreet in the liberties she took, and of an irregular and licentious behaviour.

Alexander the Great

In earlier editions the assessment of great careers often boasted a forthright quality missing in our more judicious era. This is from the 4th edition (1801–1809).

To sum up the character of this prince, we cannot be of opinion, that his good qualities did in anywise compensate for his bad ones. Heroes make a noise; their actions glare, and strike the senses forcibly; while the infinite destruction and misery they occasion lie more in the shade, and out of sight. One good legislator is worth all the heroes that ever did or will exist.

Goethe Then and Now

The great essayist and critic Thomas De Quincey (1785–1859) was a voluminous contributor of literary biographies to the 7th and 8th editions. He was a copious writer, and his fame had already been secured by the original version of Confessions of an English Opium-Eater *in* London Magazine *in 1821. His criticism was informed, brilliant, and often so opinionated as to be almost idiosyncratic. (B.L.F.)*

These extracts from the 8th edition (1852–1860) instruct us in the mutability of judgment. We cannot predict what Britannica *will say a century from now, but at the moment it would seem clear that De Quincey was quite wrong in his verdict that "the reputation of Goethe must decline for the next generation or two, until it reaches its just level."*

It now remains to say a few words by way of summing up his pretensions as a man, and his intellectual power in the age to which he belonged. His rank and value as a moral being are so plain as to be legible to him who runs. Everybody must feel that his temperament and constitutional tendency was of that happy quality, the animal so nicely balanced with the intellectual, that with any ordinary measure of prosperity he could not be otherwise than a good man. . . . Yet at the same time we cannot disguise from ourselves that the moral temperament of Goethe was one which demanded prosperity: had he been called to face great afflictions, singular temptations, or a billowy and agitated course of life, our belief is that his nature would have been found unequal to the strife; he would have repeated the mixed and moody character of his father. Sunny prosperity was essential to his nature; his virtues were adapted to that condition. And happily that was his fate. He had no personal misfortunes; his path was joyous in this life; and even the reflex sorrow from the calamities of his friends did not press too heavily on his sympathies; none of these were in excess either as to degree or duration. . . .

Goethe, however, in a moral estimate, will be viewed pretty uniformly. But Goethe intellectually, Goethe as a power acting upon the age in which he lived, that is another question. Let us put a case; suppose that Goethe's death had occurred many years ago, say in the year 1785, what would have been the general impression? Would Europe have felt a shock? Would Europe have been sensible even of the event? Not at all: it would have been obscurely noticed in the newspapers of Germany, as the death of a novelist who had produced some effect about ten years before. In 1832, it was announced by the post-horns of all Europe as the death of him who had written the *Wilhelm Meister,* the *Iphigenie,* and the *Faust,* and who had been enthroned by some of his admirers on the same seat with Homer and Shakespeare, as composing what they termed the *trinity of men of genius.* And yet it is a fact, that, in the opinion of some amongst the acknowledged leaders of our own literature for the last twenty-five years, the *Werther* was superior to all which followed it, and for mere power was the paramount work of Goethe. For ourselves, we must acknowledge our assent upon the whole to this verdict; and at the same time we will avow our belief that the reputation of Goethe must decline for the next generation or two, until it reaches its just level.

In Goethe's case the problem of assessment or evaluation is complicated by the fact that there is too much to sum up; he lived so many lives. Elizabeth M. Wilkinson, co-author of Goethe: Poet and Thinker, *handled it thus (15th edition):*

A day will come, Carlyle predicted in a letter to Ralph Waldo Emerson, when "you will find that this sunny-looking courtly Goethe held veiled in him a Prophetic sorrow deep as Dante's." And since World War II there have been many attempts to replace the image of the serene optimist by that of the tortured skeptic. The one is as inadequate as the other—as inadequate as T.S. Eliot's conclusion that he was sage rather than poet—though this is perhaps inevitable when a writer is such a master of his own medium that even his prose proves resistant to translation. Even his Werther knew that the realities of existence are rarely to be grasped by Either-Or. And the reality of Goethe himself certainly eludes any such attempt. If he was a skeptic, and he often was, he was a hopeful skeptic. He looked deep into the abyss, but he deliberately emphasized life and light. He lived life to the full at every level, but never to the detriment of the civilized virtues. He remained closely in touch with the richness of his unconscious mind, but he shed on it the light of reflection without destroying the spontaneity of its processes. He was, as befits a son of the Enlightenment, wholly committed to the adventure of science; but he stood in awe and reverence before the mystery of the universe. Goethe nowhere formulated a system of thought. He was as impatient of the sterilities of logic chopping as of the inflations of metaphysics, though he acknowledged his indebtedness to many philosophers, including Kant. But here again he was not to be confined. Truth for him lay not in compromise but in the embracing of opposites. And this is expressed in the form of his *Maximen* ("maxims"), which, together with his *Gespräche* ("conversations"), contain the sum of his wisdom. As with proverbs, one can always find among them a twin that expresses the complementary opposite. And they have something of the banality of proverbs, too. But it is, as André Gide observed, "*une banalité supérieure.*" What makes it "superior" is that the thought has been felt and lived and that the formulation betrays this. And for all his specialized talents, there was a kind of "superior banality" about Goethe's life. If he himself felt it was "symbolic" and worth presenting as such in a series of autobiographical writings, it was not from arrogance but from a realization that he was an extraordinarily ordinary man in whom ordinary men might see themselves reflected. Not an ascetic, a mystic, a saint, or a recluse, not a Don Juan or a poet's poet but one who to the best of his ability had tried to achieve the highest form of *l'homme moyen sensuel*—which is perhaps what Napoleon sensed when after their meeting in Erfurt he uttered his famous "*Voilà un homme!*"

❧ ❧ ❧

Two Views of George Washington

The Washington biography in the 8th edition (1852–1860) was written by Edward Everett (1794–1865). He was one of the first American contributors to Encyclopædia Britannica. *He had been both a member of the U.S. House of Representatives and a Senator, a governor of Massachusetts, the U.S. minister to England, and president of Harvard University. He also was the most famous orator of his day. The oratorical style of his time was long, mellifluous, stem-winding, florid, and dramatic. Thus he wrote as well. His fulsome and ornate style can be seen from the final paragraphs of his twenty-six-page panegyric. (B.L.F.)*

. . . Without adopting Virgil's magnificent but scornful contrast between scientific and literary skill on the one hand and those masterful arts on the other, by which victories are gained and nations are governed, we must still admit that the chieftain who, in spite of obstacles the most formidable, and vicissitudes the most distressing, conducts great wars to successful issues;—that the statesman who harmonizes angry parties in peace; skillfully moderates the counsels of constituent assemblies, and without the resources of rhetoric, but by influence mightier than authority, secures the formation and organization of governments, and in their administration establishes the model of official conduct for all following time—is endowed with a divine principle of thought and action as distinct in its kind as that of Demosthenes or Milton. It is the genius of a consummate manhood. Analysis may describe its manifestations in either case, but cannot define the ulterior principle. It is a final element of character. We may speak of prudence, punctuality, and self-control, of bravery and disinterestedness, as we speak of an eye for colour and a perception of the graceful in the painter; a sensibility to the sublime, the pathetic, and the beautiful in discourse; but behind and above all these there must be a creative and animating principle at least as much in character as in intellect or art. The qualities which pertain to genius are not the whole of genius, in the one case any more than the other. The arteries, the lungs, and the nerves, are essential to life, but they are not life itself—that higher something which puts all the organic functions of the frame in motion. In the possession of that mysterious quality of character manifested in a long life of unambitious service, which, call it by whatever name, inspires the confidence, commands the respect, and wins the affection of contemporaries, and grows upon the admiration of successive generations, forming a standard to which the merit of other men is referred, and a living proof that pure patriotism is not a delusion, nor virtue an empty name, no one of the sons of men has equalled George Washington.

To sense at once the difference between generational styles the reader might consult the fifteen-column Washington biography in the current edition. It is by a truly responsible writer, Allan Nevins. Nevins (1890–1971) was perhaps the leading American historian of his generation, a two-time Pulitzer Prize winner (for historical biographies) and the author of a classic eight-volume history of the American Civil War. Here is an excerpt from his article's final paragraph.

. . . Retiring in March 1797 to Mount Vernon, he devoted himself for the last two and a half years of his life to his family, farm operations, and care of his slaves. In 1798 his seclusion was briefly interrupted when the prospect of war with France caused his appointment as commander in chief of the provisional army, and he was much worried by the political quarrels over high commissions; but the war cloud passed away. On December 12, 1799, he exposed himself on horseback for several hours to cold and snow and, returning home exhausted, was attacked late next day with quinsy or acute laryngitis. He was bled heavily four times and given gargles of "molasses, vinegar and butter," and a blister of cantharides (a preparation of dried beetles) was placed on his throat, his strength meanwhile rapidly sinking. He faced the end with characteristic serenity, saying, "I die hard, but I am not afraid to go," and later: "I feel myself going. I thank you for your attentions; but I pray you to take no more trouble about me. Let me go off quietly. I cannot last long." After giving instructions to his secretary, Tobias Lear, about his burial, he died at 10:00 PM on December 14.

Hypatia

The clergyman, novelist, and publicist Charles Kingsley (1819–1875) was a rather odd duck. We no longer read Hypatia *(1853), though his strange children's books* The Water-Babies *(1863) and* Westward Ho! *(1859) are still around. The 8th edition (1852–1860) was perfectly receptive to the eccentricity reflected in his account of Hypatia, the Neoplatonist phi-*

losopher who, the 15th edition tells us, "was the first notable woman in mathematics." Here is an excerpt from Kingsley.

HYPATIA is one of those whose names are glorified rather by wrongs than by merits; and had she not died, few would now know, and fewer care, whether she ever lived. [She was a teacher of Neoplatonic philosophy in Christian Alexandria and was cruelly murdered by a mob during a riot in A.D. 415.]

Her tragedy is well known by the account of Gibbon, drawn from *Socrates,* bk. vii., §15; and from Theodoret, who asserts Cyril's complicity. Theodoret knew Cyril [bishop of Alexandria] well enough to suspect him of anything; at least, to say of him, after his death, that "the only fear was that hell would find him too unpleasant a guest, and send him back to earth." And certainly all we know of him justifies the sneer; at least, it seems certain that Cyril protected her murderers.

Hypatia's death seems to have happened thus:—The minds of the Nitrian monks, and of the Alexandrian populace, had been inflamed by her intimacy with Orestes, the prefect, who was at open war with Cyril. Hating her both as what she was, the championess of an eclectic Polytheism; and as what she was not, a profligate woman, they laid wait for her at the door of that lecture-room in the Mouseion, where (to the envy of Cyril) her admirers' chariots and slaves were wont to wait. She was seized, stript naked, dragged into the Kaisareion (then a Christian church), and torn piece-meal, with fragments of shells and pottery. The flesh was scraped from the bones, and what remained burned in the Kinaron.

Thus ended, or seems to have ended, the last noble woman whom Greek paganism produced. But, indeed, Hypatia is at best but a myth and a shade; and two centuries more saw her transfigured into the famous Saint Catharine of Alexandria [an unproved theory]; the Christians whom she opposed into pagan philosophers confuted; Cyril into Maxentius the persecutor, the pot-sherds of the Kinaron into the toothed wheels miraculously broken by lightning from heaven; and Hypatia installed for a thousand years to come as one of the four virgin saints of Christendom. So does the whirligig of Time bring round its revenges; and every noble soul, even under a feigned name and circumstance, has its nobleness acknowledged, and does—not the work which it intended, but the work of which it was really capable.

Robert Burns

Robert Burns (1759–1796) was but a lad of nine when the first Britannica *began to appear in 1768, but he was a sometime drinking companion of James Tytler, editor of the 2nd edition (1778–1783), and by his death at a mere thirty-seven in 1796, he was already Scotland's incorrigible pride and poet. He was the subject of biographic sketches in subsequent editions of the* Encyclopædia, *starting with the Supplement to the 3rd edition (1801).*

These excerpts are from the article "Burns, Robert" by John Nichol (1833–1894), professor of English Language and Literature at the University of Glasgow, in the 9th edition (1875–1889). (B.L.F.)

The passages here given offer a fine example of the vein of criticism to be expected from a good academic who was also proud of being a Scottish patriot. It is suffused with Victorian emotion, a kind of warmth not always approved of by later editors of Britannica. *Still, the current edition carries an account by the acknowledged Burns expert David Daiches, which is no less moving than Professor Nichol's. Burns is well-named: No one has ever written coldly about him.*

Robert Burns was born on the 25th of January 1759, in a cottage about two miles from Ayr, the eldest son of a small farmer, William Burness, of Kincardineshire stock, who wrought hard, practised integrity, wished to bring up his children in the fear of God, but had to fight all his days against the winds and tides of adversity. . . .

From these hard tasks and his fiery temperament, craving in vain for sympathy in a frigid air grew the strong temptations on which Burns was largely wrecked,—the thirst for stimulants and the revolt against restraint which soon made headway and passed all bars. In the earlier portions of his career, a buoyant humour bore him up; and amid thick-coming shapes of ill he bated no jot of heart or hope. He was cheered by vague stirrings of ambition, which he pathetically compares to the "blind groping of Homer's Cyclops round the walls of his cave." Sent to school at Kirkoswald, he became, for his scant leisure, a great reader—eating at meal-times with a spoon in one hand and a book in the other,—and carrying a few small volumes in his pocket to study in spare moments in the fields. "The collection of songs," he tells us, "was my *vade mecum.* I pored over them driving my cart or walking to labour, song by song, verse by verse, carefully noting the true, tender, sublime, or fustian." He lingered over the ballads in his cold room by night; by day, whilst whistling at the plough, he invented new forms and was inspired by fresh ideas, "gathering round him the memories and the traditions of his country till they became a mantle and a crown." It was among the furrows of his father's fields that he was inspired with the perpetually quoted wish—

"That I for poor auld Scotland's sake
Some useful plan or book could make,
Or sing a sang at least." . . .

Sir Walter Scott bears a similar testimony to the dignified simplicity and almost exaggerated independence of the poet, during this *annus mirabilis* of his success. "As for Burns, *Virgilium vidi tantum,* I was a lad of fifteen when he came to Edinburgh, but had sense enough to be interested in his poetry, and would have given the world to know him. I saw him one day with several gentlemen of literary reputation, among whom I remember the celebrated Dugald Stewart. Of course we youngsters sat silent, looked, and listened. . . ."

. . . When, in 1787, the second edition of the *Poems* came out, the proceeds of their sale realized for the author £400. On the strength of this sum he gave himself two long rambles, full of poetic material—one through the border towns into England as far as Newcastle, returning by Dumfries to Mauchline, and another a grand tour through the East Highlands, as far as Inverness, returning by Edinburgh, and so home to Ayrshire.

In 1788 Burns took a new farm at Ellisland on the Nith, settled there, married, lost his little money, and wrote, among other pieces, "Auld Lang Syne" and "Tam O' Shanter." . . .

On the 4th of July he was seen to be dying. On the 12th he wrote to his cousin for the loan of £10 to save him from passing his last days in jail. On the 21st he was no more. On the 25th, when his last son came into the world, he was buried with local honours, the volunteers of the company to which he belonged firing three volleys over his grave. . . .

The poet passed away in darkness, but his name will never disappear from our literature. He stands before us as a feature of Nature; and the fact that he cannot be moved from the hearts of his countrymen, that they recognize and respect a man who has refused to mutilate human nature, and who at once celebrates and strives to harmonize its ethnical and Christian elements, marks a gulf still fixed between Scotland and the Spain with which Mr Buckle has associated it. "The generous verse of Burns," says Dr Craik, "springs out of the iron-bound Calvinism of the land like flowing water from Horeb's rock."

Mary Shelley

The following article from the 9th edition (1875–1889) is scanty on information about Mary Shelley's early life, but gives an interesting literary appreciation. (Note the accurate assessment of Frankenstein*). It is unsigned. (B.L.F.)*

SHELLEY, MARY WOLLSTONECRAFT (1797–1851), the second wife of the poet Shelley (*q.v.*), born in London, August 30, 1797, deserves some notice on her own account, as a writer of romance, chiefly imaginative. When she was in Switzerland with Shelley and Byron in 1816, a proposal was made that various members of the party should write a romance or tale dealing with the supernatural. The result of this project was that Mrs Shelley wrote *Frankenstein*, Byron the beginning of a narrative about a vampyre, and Dr Polidori, Byron's physician, a tale named *The Vampyre*, the authorship of which used frequently in past years to be attributed to Byron himself. *Frankenstein*, published in 1818, when Mrs Shelley was at the utmost twenty-one years old, is a very remarkable performance for so young and inexperienced a writer; its main idea is that of the formation and vitalization, by a deep student of the secrets of nature, of an adult man, who, entering the world thus under unnatural conditions, becomes the terror of his species, a half-involuntary criminal, and finally an outcast whose sole resource is self-immolation. This romance was followed by others: *Valperga, or the Life and Adventures of Castruccio, Prince of Lucca* (1823), an historical tale written with a good deal of spirit, and readable enough even now; *The Last Man* (1826), a fiction of the final agonies of human society owing to the universal spread of a pestilence,—this is written in a very stilted style, but bears some traces of the imagination which fashioned *Frankenstein; The Fortunes of Perkin Warbeck* (1830); *Lodore* (1835); and *Falkner* (1837). Besides these novels there was the *Journal of a Six Weeks' Tour,* which is published in conjunction with Shelley's prose-writings; also *Rambles in Germany and Italy* in 1840–42–43 (which shows an observant spirit, capable of making some true forecasts of the future), and various miscellaneous writings. After the death of Shelley, for whom she had a deep and even enthusiastic affection, marred at times by defects of temper, Mrs Shelley in the autumn of 1823 returned to London. At first the earnings of her pen were her only sustenance; but after a while Sir Timothy Shelley made her an allowance, which would have been withdrawn if she had persisted in a project of writing a full biography of her husband. She was a loving and careful mother, and shared the prosperous fortunes of her son, when, upon the death of Sir Timothy in 1844, he succeeded to the baronetcy. She died in February 1851.

George Eliot

The life of George Eliot was treated in the 11th edition (1910–1911) by "John Oliver Hobbes," the pen-name of P. M. T. Craigie (Pearl Mary Teresa Craigie, 1867–1906). She was an Anglo-American novelist and playwright who, like her subject, felt it advisable to use a male pseudonym. Her article is noteworthy on two counts. It strikes a quiet, nonaggressive, but firm feminist note, and it is one of the few Britannica *articles of its period by a woman. The current* Britannica *carries no reference to Craigie's work and career, which is a pity.*

Since the time when she wrote, however appreciatively, of George Eliot, the reputation of Eliot has risen strongly. Middlemarch *is now included in* Great Books of the Western World, *published by* Encyclopædia Britannica. *In* Britannica's *current edition the reader will find an excellent account of George Eliot, reflecting today's judgment, by Gordon Haight, author of the now-standard biography.*

ELIOT, GEORGE, the pen-name of the famous English writer, *née* Mary Ann (or Marian) Evans (1810–1880), afterwards Mrs J. W. Cross, born at Arbury Farm, in Warwickshire, on the 22nd of November 1819. . . . She received an ordinary education at respectable schools till the age of seventeen, when her mother's death, and the marriage of her elder sister, called her home in the character of housekeeper. This, though it must have sharpened her sense, already too acute, of responsibility, was an immense advantage to her mind, and, later, to her career, for, delivered from the tiresome routine of lessons and class-work, she was able to work without pedantic interruptions at German, Italian and music, and to follow her unusually good taste in reading. . . .

Marian Evans was subdued all through her youth by a severe religious training which, while it pinched her mind and crushed her spirit, attracted her idealism by the very hardness of its perfect counsels. It is not surprising to find, therefore, that when Mr Evans moved to Coventry in 1841, and so enlarged the circle of their acquaintance, she became much interested in some new friends, Mr and Mrs Charles Bray and Mr Charles Hennell. Mr Bray had literary taste and wrote works on the *Education of the Feelings,* the *Philosophy of Necessity,* and the like. Mr Hennell had published in 1838 *An Enquiry concerning the Origin of Christianity.* Miss Evans, then twenty-two, absorbed immediately these unexpected, and, at that time, daring habits of thought. So compelling was the atmosphere that it led to a complete change in her opinions. Kind in her affection, she was relentless in argument. She refused to go to church (for some time, at least), wrote painful letters to a former governess—the pious Miss Lewis—and barely avoided an irremediable quarrel with her father, a churchman of the old school. Here was rebellion indeed. But rebels come, for the most part, from the provinces where petty tyranny, exercised by small souls, show the scheme of the universe on the meanest possible scale. George Eliot was never orthodox again; she abandoned, with fierce determination, every creed, and although she passed, later, through various phases, she remained incessantly a rationalist in matters of faith and in all other matters. It is nevertheless true that she wrote admirably about religion and religious persons. She had learnt the evangelical point of view; she knew—none better—the strength of religious motives; vulgar doubts of this fact were as distasteful to her as they were to another eminent writer, to whom she refers in one of her letters (dated 1853) as "a Mr Huxley, who was the centre of interest" at some "agreeable evening." Her books abound in tributes to Christian virtue, and one of her own favourite characters was Dinah Morris in *Adam Bede*. . . .

Balzac created a whole world; George Eliot did not create, but her exposition of the upper and middle class minds of her day is a masterpiece of scientific psychology. . . . The death of Mr Lewes in 1878 was also the death-blow to her artistic vitality. She corrected the proofs of *Theophrastus Such* (a collection of essays), but she wrote no more. About two years later, however, she married Mr J. W. Cross, a gentleman whose friendship was especially congenial to a temperament so abnormally dependent on affectionate understanding as George Eliot's. But she never really recovered from her shock at the loss of George Lewes, and died at 4 Cheyne Walk, Chelsea, on the 22nd of December 1880.

No right estimate of her, whether as a woman, an artist or a philosopher, can be formed without a steady recollection of her infinite capacity for mental suffering, and her need of human support. The statement that there is no sex in genius, is on the face of it, absurd. George Sand, certainly the most independent and dazzling of all women authors, neither felt, nor wrote, nor thought as a man. Saint Teresa, another great writer on a totally different plane, was pre-eminently feminine in every word and idea. George Eliot, less reckless, less romantic than the Frenchwoman, less spiritual than the Spanish saint, was more masculine in style than either; but her outlook was not, for a moment, the man's outlook; her sincerity, with its odd reserves, was not quite the same as a man's sincerity, nor was her humour that genial, broad, unequivocal humour which is peculiarly virile. Hers approximated, curiously enough, to the satire of Jane Austen, both for its irony and its application to little everyday affairs. Men's humour, in its classic manifestations, is on the heroic rather than on the average scale: it is for the uncommon situations, not for the daily tea-table. . . . Jane Austen despised the greater number of her characters: George Eliot suffered with each of hers. Here, perhaps, we find the reason why she is accused of being inartistic. She could not be impersonal. . . .

Again, George Eliot was a little scornful to those of both sexes who had neither special missions nor the consciousness of this deprivation. Men are seldom in favour of missions in any field.

George Sand

Remarkable pieces by scholars now forgotten have studded Britannica'*s pages over more than two centuries. Here, for example, are excerpts from Francis Storr's biography of George Sand in the historic 11th edition (1910–1911). The author was a member of Trinity College, Cambridge, and editor of the* Journal of Education. *By the standards of the time his estimate of George Sand was sound and illuminating. In our country she is little read today, but Storr's account suggests to us what earlier generations prized in her ingenuous fiction.*

SAND, GEORGE (1804–1876), the pseudonym of Madame Amandine Lucile Aurore Dudevant, *née* Dupin, the most prolific authoress in the history of literature, and unapproached among the women novelists of France. Her life was as strange and adventurous as any of her novels, which are for the most part idealized versions of the multifarious incidents of her life. In her self-revelations she followed Rousseau, her first master in style, but while Rousseau in his *Confessions* darkened all the shadows, George Sand is the heroine of her story, often frail and faulty, but always a woman more sinned against than sinning. Thanks, however, to her voluminous correspondence that has recently been published and to family documents that her French biographers have unearthed, there are now full materials for tracing the history of her public and private career, and for forming a clear and unbiased estimate of her character and genius. . . .

Passing by her infantine recollections, which go back further than even those of Dickens, we find her at the age of three crossing the Pyrenees to join her father who was on Murat's staff, occupying with her parents a suite of rooms in the royal palace, adopted as the child of the regiment, nursed by rough old sergeants, and dressed in a complete suit of uniform to please the general.

For the next ten years she lived at Nohant, near La Châtre in Berri, the country house of her grandmother. Here her character was shaped; here she imbibed that passionate love of country scenes and country life which neither absence, politics nor dissipation could uproot; here she learnt to understand the ways and thoughts of the peasants, and laid up that rich store of scenes and characters which a marvellously retentive memory enabled her to draw upon at will. The progress of her mind during these early years well deserves to be recorded. Education, in the strict sense of the word, she had none. A few months after her return from Spain her father was killed by a fall from his horse. He was a man of remarkable literary gifts as well as a good soldier. "Character," says George Sand, "is in a great measure hereditary: if my readers wish to know me they must know my father." . . .

From the free out-door life at Nohant she passed at thirteen to the convent of the English Augustinians at Paris, where for the first two years she never went outside the walls. Nothing better shows the plasticity of her character than the ease with which she adapted herself to this sudden change. The volume which describes her conventual life is as graphic as Miss Brontë's *Villette,* but we can only dwell on one passage of it. Tired of mad pranks, in a fit of home-sickness, she found herself one evening in the convent chapel.

"I had forgotten all: I knew not what was

passing in me; with my soul rather than my senses, I breathed an air of ineffable sweetness. All at once a sudden shock passed through my whole being, my eyes swam, and I seemed wrapped in a dazzling white mist. I heard a voice murmur in my ear, '*Tolle, lege.*' I turned round, thinking that it was one of the sisters talking to me—I was alone. I indulged in no vain illusion; I believed in no miracle; I was quite sensible of the sort of hallucination into which I had fallen; I neither sought to intensify it nor to escape from it. Only I felt that faith was laying hold of me—by the heart, as I had wished it. I was so filled with gratitude and joy that the tears rolled down my cheeks. I felt as before that I loved God, that my mind embraced and accepted that ideal of justice, tenderness and holiness which I had never doubted, but with which I had never held direct communion, and now at last I felt that this communion was consummated, as though an invincible barrier had been broken down between the source of infinite light and the smouldering fire of my heart . . ."

Such is the story of her conversion as told by herself. It reads more like a chapter from the life of Ste Thérèse or Madame Guyon than of the author of *Lélia*. Yet no one can doubt the sincerity of her narrative, or even the permanence of her religious feelings under all her many phases of faith and aberrations of conduct. A recent critic has sought in religion the clue to her character and the mainspring of her genius. Only in her case religion must be taken in an even more restricted sense than Matthew Arnold's "morality touched by emotion." For her there was no categorical imperative, no moral code save to follow the promptings of her heart. "Tenderness" she had abundantly. . . .

Again in 1820 Aurore exchanged the restraint of a convent for freedom, being recalled to Nohant by Mme de Francueil, who had no intention of letting her granddaughter grow up a *dévote*. She rode across country with her brother, she went out shooting with Deschatres, she sat by the cottage doors on the long summer evenings and heard the flax-dressers tell their tales of witches and warlocks. . . .

Casimir Dudevant, whom she married on the 11th of December 1822, was the natural son of a Baron Dudevant. He had retired at an early age from the army and was living an idle life at home as a gentleman farmer. Her husband, though he afterwards deteriorated, seems at that time to have been neither better nor worse than the Berrichon squires around him, and the first years of her married life, during which her son Maurice and her daughter Solange were born, except for lovers' quarrels, were passed in peace and quietness, though signs were not wanting of the coming storm. . . . So long as the conventionalities were preserved she endured it, but when her husband took to drinking and made love to the maids under her very eyes she resolved to break a yoke that had grown intolerable. . . . She endeavoured unsuccessfully to eke out her irregularly paid allowance by those expedients to which reduced gentlewomen are driven—fancy-work and painting fans and snuff-boxes; she lived in a garret and was often unable to allow herself the luxury of a fire. It was only as a last resource that she tried literature. Her first apprenticeship was served under Delatouche, the editor of *Figaro*. He was a native of Berri, like herself, a stern but kindly taskmaster who treated her much as Dr Johnson treated Fanny Burney. . . . On the staff of *Figaro* was another compatriot with whom she was already intimate as a visitor at Nohant. Jules Sandeau was a clever and attractive young lawyer. Articles written in common soon led to a complete literary partnership, and 1831 there appeared in the *Revue de Paris* a joint novel entitled *Prima Donna* and signed Jules Sand. Shortly after this was published in book form with the same signature a second novel, *Rose et Blanche*. The sequel to this literary alliance is best recounted in George Sand's own words: "I resisted him for three months but then yielded; I lived in my own apartment in an unconventional style." Her first independent novel, *Indiana* (1832), was written at the instigation of Delatouche, and the world-famous pseudonym George (originally Georges) Sand was adopted as a compromise between herself and her partner. The "George" connoted a Berrichon as "David" does a Welshman. The one wished to throw *Indiana* into the common stock, the other refused to lend his name, or even part of his name, to a work in which he had had no share. The novel was received with instant acclamation, and Sainte-Beuve only confirmed the judgment of the public when he pronounced in the *Globe* that this new author (then to him unknown) had struck a new and original vein and was destined to go far. Delatouche was the first to throw himself at her feet and bid her forget all the hard things he had said of her. *Indiana* is a direct transcript of the author's personal experiences (the disagreeable husband is M. Dudevant to the life), and an exposition of her theory of sexual relations which is founded thereon. . . .

Her liaison with Jules Sandeau, which lasted more than a year, was abruptly terminated by the discovery in their apartment on an unexpected return from Nohant of *une blanchisseuse quelconque*. For a short while she was broken hearted:—"My heart is a cemetery!" she wrote to Sainte-Beuve. "A necropolis," was the comment of her discarded lover when years later the remark was repeated to him . . .

But a new chapter in her life was now to open. In her despair she turned for comfort and counsel to Sainte-Beuve, now constituted her regular father confessor. This ghostly Sir Pandarus recommended new friendships, but she was hard to please. Dumas was "trop commis-voyageur," Jouffroy too serenely virtuous and Musset "trop dandy." Mérimée was tried for a week, but the cool cynic and the perfervid apostle of women's rights proved mutually repulsive. Alfred de Musset was introduced, and the two natures leapt together as by elective affinity. The moral aspect has been given by Mr Swinburne in an epigram:—"Alfred was a terrible flirt and George did not behave as a perfect gentleman."

Towards the end of 1833 George Sand, after winning the reluctant consent of Musset's mother, set out in the poet's company for Italy, and in January 1834 the pair reached Venice, staying first at the Hôtel Danieli and then in lodgings. At first it was a veritable honeymoon; conversation never flagged and either found in the other his soul's complement. But there is a limit to love-making, and George Sand, always practical, set to work to provide the means of living. Musset, though he depended on her exertions, was first bored and then irritated at the sight of this *terrible rache à écrire,* whose pen was going for eight hours a day, and sought diversion in the cafés and other less reputable resorts of pleasure. The consequence was a nervous illness with some of the symptoms of delirium tremens, through which George Sand nursed him with tenderness and care. But with a strange want of delicacy, to use the mildest term, she made love at the same time to a young Venetian doctor whom she had called in, by name Pagello. The pair went off and found their way eventually to Paris, leaving Musset in Italy, deeply wounded in his affections, but, to do him justice, taking all the blame for the rupture on himself. George Sand soon tired of her new love, and even before she had given him his congé was dying to be on again with the old. She cut off her hair and sent it to Musset as a token of penitence, but Musset, though he still flirted with her, never quite forgave her infidelity and refused to admit her to his deathbed. . . .

Of George Sand's style a foreigner can be but an imperfect judge, but French critics, from Sainte-Beuve, Nisard and Caro down to Jules Lemaitre and Faguet, have agreed to praise her spontaneity, her correctness of diction, her easy opulence—the *lactea ubertas* that Quintilian attributes to Livy. The language of her country novels is the genuine *patois* of middle France rendered in a literary form. . . .

As a painter of nature she has much in common with Wordsworth. She keeps her eye on the object, but adds, like Wordsworth, the visionary gleam, and receives from nature but what she herself gives. Like Wordsworth she lays us on the lap of earth and sheds the freshness of the early world. She, too, had found love in huts where poor men dwell, and her miller, her bagpipers, her workers in mosaic are as faithful renderings in prose of peasant life and sentiment as Wordsworth's leech-gatherer and wagoners and gleaners are in verse. Her psychology is not subtle or profound, but her leading characters are clearly conceived and drawn in broad, bold outlines. No one has better understood or more skillfully portrayed the artistic temperament—the musician, the actor, the poet—and no French writer before her had so divined and laid bare the heart of a girl. . . .

George Sand died at Nohant on the 8th of June 1876. To a youth and womanhood of storm and stress had succeeded an old age of serene activity and then of calm decay. Her nights were spent in writing, which seemed in her case a relaxation from the real business of the day, playing with her grandchildren, gardening, conversing with her visitors—it might be Balzac or Dumas, or Octave Feuillet or Matthew Arnold—or writing long letters to Sainte-Beuve and Flaubert. "Calme, toujours plus de calme," was her last prayer, and her dying words, "Ne détruisez pas la verdure."

Arthur MacArthur

The following brief article about Arthur MacArthur appeared in the 14th edition (1929–1973, 1962 printing) written by the subject's son, General Douglas MacArthur (1880–1964). This is interesting enough. Just as interesting is its impeccably detached tone, so at variance with the general's usual Victorian style.

MacARTHUR, ARTHUR (1845–1912), U.S. army officer, was born at Chicopee Falls, Mass., June 2, 1845. He served throughout the American Civil War in the 24th Wisconsin volunteer infantry, being advanced through the ranks from lieutenant to colonel of the regiment when but 20 years of age. His regiment gained fame in Gen. Philip Sheridan's division of the Army of the Cumberland where he was affectionately known as the "Boy Colonel of the West." He was wounded three times, brevetted four times, and cited for "gallant and meritorious service" in the battles of Perryville, Stone River, Missionary Ridge, Resaca, Dalton, Jonesboro, Kenesaw Mountain, Atlanta and Franklin. He was awarded the Medal of Honor for seizing the colours of his regiment at a critical moment and planting them on the captured works on the crest of Missionary Ridge. At the close of the war he entered the regular army and from 1866 to 1886 participated in Indian campaigns in the southwest. At the outbreak of the Spanish-American War (1898) he was appointed a brigadier general and assigned to the Philippine command. His brigade captured the town of Malate and thus prepared the way for the taking of Manila. He was cited by Gen. Wesley Merritt for gallantry and conspicuous service and appointed a major general to command the 2nd division. When the insurrection under Gen. Emilio Aguinaldo broke out in February of 1899 he commanded the main column which defeated the insurgents. He succeeded Gen. E. S. Otis in command of the 8th corps, the army of the Philippines, and as the military governor. In the latter capacity (1900–01) he helped to lay the foundations for a free and independent Philippine republic, introducing the writ of habeas corpus, revising the Spanish law and establishing the free public school system and other democratic concepts. During the Russo-Japanese War he was detailed as a special observer with the Japanese army. In 1906 he was appointed a lieutenant general and became the senior ranking officer of the U.S. army. He retired from the army in 1909 and died Sept. 5, 1912, at Milwaukee, Wis.

Bismarck

For the article on Bismarck the current Britannica *sought out the distinguished British historian A. J. P. Taylor (1906–1990), author of* Bismarck. *Many of the set's biographies conclude with an "assessment," an "appraisal." That is the most problematic part of the assignment, for subjectivity inevitably enters. In their assessments writers generally try to steer a middle course between pat received opinion and a radically revisionist view of the subject. Here is how a first-rate biographer-historian solved the problem.*

Bismarck was a political genius of the highest rank, but he lacked one essential quality of the constructive statesman: he had no faith in the future. The revolutions of 1848 convinced him that the old order could not be preserved unchanged, and all his later policy was shaped by this conviction. He went with the modern forces of liberalism and democracy solely to draw their sting. Like Metternich he regarded them as evil; unlike Metternich he turned them to his own purposes. He is sometimes compared with the leaders of the English governing classes, who under Sir

Robert Peel also made a compromise with liberalism and democracy. But there was a basic difference. In England there was a genuine compromise, in Germany only a trick. The German people were defrauded, given a shadow instead of the substance.

Bismarck was at his greatest in foreign policy. There he understood, as no one else did, "the art of the possible." He never aspired to dominate Europe; he was content to balance between the great powers. Though he had no moral objection to war, he preferred to get his way by diplomacy and went to war only for limited aims when it was necessary to his policy. The system of alliances that he built up was designed to secure the peace of Europe, and he played the powers off against each other with matchless skill. In fact, though no believer in eternal peace, he was the principal architect of the halcyon age that gave Europe 26 years of peace after the Congress of Berlin.

In domestic affairs his record is less inspiring. He had a lust for power that grew on him with the years. He wanted Prussia to be supreme in Germany. He wanted the king to be supreme in Prussia; but most of all he wanted to be supreme over the king. His boasted loyalty to the crown vanished as soon as William II showed signs of independence, but he was equally ruthless, though more subtle, with William I. He spoke contemptuously of the old Emperor's intelligence and did not shrink from the most unscrupulous tricks in order to keep his hold. His suspicion of possible rivals was unbounded, and he persecuted them out of public life one after the other. In his latter years all his energies went into the search for the "German Gladstone cabinet," which he was convinced was being prepared against him, a search all the more degrading in that this cabinet was always a creation of his imagination. He battered down any politician who dared to cross him and refused to allow the Reichstag to pay a posthumous tribute to Eduard Lasker, a sincere National Liberal who had done much for the empire but had shown some independence. Yet Bismarck himself changed course whenever it suited him. He repudiated old friends and old policies without scruple and often showed the disloyalty that he denounced in others. He lived in the age of democracy and German power, and he devoted his life to making these two forces as harmless as possible. Despite his ringing, self-confident phrases, he was at heart a despairing conservative, caring only for the past, dreading the future, and trying to retard its arrival. Gladstone said of him, "He made Germany great and Germans small."

Samuel Pepys

When one thinks of Samuel Pepys, the name of Sir Arthur Bryant (1899–1985), author of a standard three-volume life of Pepys, at once comes to mind. Responsible for the Pepys article in the current Britannica, *he solves the problem of appraisal rather differently from Professor Taylor. He lets his subject do most of the talking.*

The diary by which Pepys is chiefly known was kept between his 27th and 36th years. Written in Thomas Shelton's system of shorthand, or tachygraphy, with the names in longhand, it extends to 1,250,000 words, filling six quarto volumes in the Pepys Library. It is far more than an ordinary record of its writer's thoughts and actions; it is a supreme work of art, revealing on every page the capacity for selecting the small, as well as the large, essential that conveys the sense of life; and it is probably, after the Bible and James Boswell's *Life of Samuel Johnson,* the best bedside book in the English language. One can open it on any page and lose oneself in the life of Charles II's London, and of this vigorous, curious, hardworking, pleasure-loving man. Pepys wanted to find out about everything because he found everything interesting. He never seemed to have a dull moment; he could not, indeed, understand dullness. One of the more comical entries in his diary refers to a country cousin, named Stankes, who came to stay with him in London. Pepys had been looking forward to showing him the sights of the town—

> But Lord! what a stir Stankes makes, with his being crowded in the streets, and wearied in walking in London, and would not be wooed by my wife and Ashwell to go to a play, nor to White Hall, or to see the lions, though he was carried in a coach. I never could have thought there had been upon earth a man so little curious in the world as he is.

Pepys possessed the journalist's gift of summing up a scene or person in a few brilliant, arresting words. He makes us see what he sees in a flash; his Aunt James, "a poor, religious, well-meaning, good soul, talking of nothing but God Almighty, and that with so much innocence that mightily pleased me"; and his sister Pall, "a pretty, good-bodied woman and not over thick, as I thought she would have been, but full of freckles and not handsome in the face." He could describe with wonderful vividness a great scene: as, for example, the day Gen. George Monck's soldiers unexpectedly marched into a sullen City and proclaimed there should be a free Parliament—"And Bow bells and all the bells in all the churches as we went home were a-ringing; it was past imagination, both the greatness and suddenness of it." He described, too, the Restoration and coronation; the horrors of the Plague; and the Fire of London, writing down his account—so strong was the artist in him—even as his home and its treasures were being threatened with destruction:

> We saw the fire as only one entire arch of fire from this to the other side of the bridge, and in a bow up the hill for an arch of above a mile long: it made me weep to see it. The churches, houses, and all on fire and flaming at once; and a horrid noise the flames made, and the cracking of houses at their ruine.

Above all, Pepys possessed the artist's gift of being able to select the vital moment. He makes his readers share the very life of his time: "I staid up till the bell-man came by with his bell just under my window as I was writing of this very line, and cried, 'Past one of the clock, and a cold, and frosty, windy morning.' " He tells of the guttering candle, "which makes me write thus slobberingly"; of his new watch—"But Lord! to see how much of my old folly and childishness hangs on me still that I cannot forebear carrying my watch in my hand in the coach all the afternoon and seeing what o'clock it is one hundred times"; of being awakened in the night—

> About 3 o'clock this morning I waked with the noise of the rain, having never in my life heard a more violent shower; and then the cat was locked in the chamber and kept a great mewing and leapt upon the bed, which made me I could not sleep a great while.

Pepys excluded nothing from his journal that seemed to him essential, however much it told against himself. He not only recorded his major infidelities and weaknesses; he put down all those little meannesses of thought and conduct of which all men are guilty but few admit, even to themselves. He is frank about his vanity—as, for example, in his account of the day he went to church for the first time in his new periwig: "I found that my coming in a perriwig did not prove so strange to the world as I was afeared it would, for I thought that all the church would presently have cast their eyes upon me, but I found no such thing"; about his meannesses over money, his jealousies, and his injustices—"Home and found all well, only myself somewhat vexed at my wife's neglect in leaving her scarfe, waistcoat and night dressings in the coach today; though I confess she did give them to me to look after." For he possessed in a unique degree the quality of complete honesty. He is both Everyman and the recording angel; his diary paints not only his own infirmities but the frailty of all mankind.

Albert Einstein

Peter Michelmore, among the most successful of Einstein's many biographers, faced with the daunting task of summarizing the life and work of Einstein, in the 15th edition, preferred to use his subject's own words—and to remarkable effect.

Compared with his renown of a generation earlier, Einstein was virtually neglected and said himself that he felt almost like a stranger in the world. His health deteriorated to the extent that he could no longer play the violin or sail his boat. Many years earlier, chronic abdominal pains had forced him to give up smoking his pipe and to watch his diet carefully.

On April 18, 1955, Einstein died in his sleep at Princeton Hospital. On his desk lay his last incomplete statement, written to honour Israeli Independence Day. It read in part: "What I seek to accomplish is simply to serve with my feeble capacity truth and justice at the risk of pleasing no one." His contribution to man's understanding of the universe was matchless, and he is established for all time as a giant of science. Broadly speaking, his crusades in human affairs seem to have had no lasting impact. Einstein perhaps anticipated such an assessment of his life when he said "Politics are for the moment. An equation is for eternity."

PART TWO

Best Foot Forward

JACQUES BARZUN
ON
History

Jacques Barzun (1907–   ), French-born educator, historian, translator, musicologist, and essayist, is presently University Professor Emeritus at Columbia University, capping a brilliant academic career which included his tenure at Columbia as Dean of Faculties and Provost (1958–1967). Among his many books some of the most notable are Teacher in America *(1945),* Berlioz and the Romantic Century *(2 vols., 1950, 1969), and* Simple and Direct *(1975), one of the few manuals in existence that really help us to think and therefore write better. Among American historians he is outstanding for the felicity and clarity of his style. This essay, titled "The Point and Pleasure of Reading History," is Barzun's introduction to Part Nine of the 15th edition of the* Britannica, *"The History of Mankind."*

Everything that we call the arts and the humanities comes out of some natural desire and acquires value by satisfying it. Painting and music and literature are important not because there are museums and concert halls and libraries to be kept supplied but because human beings want to draw and sing and tell stories as well as enjoy seeing others fulfill these native and universal impulses.

Among the humanities, history holds a special place in that its origin within each of us is not even dependent on impulse. A person may lack altogether the wish to sing or the knack of telling a story, but everybody without exception finds occasion to say: "I was there; I saw it; I remember it very well." In saying (or even thinking) these words, every man is a historian. History is inescapably a part of consciousness. The Greeks expressed this truth by describing Clio, the muse of history, as the daughter of memory.

Without going into the subtleties of how we are able to remember and what the contents of memory actually are, it is clear that as soon as we take thought about our experiences, whether the farthest back or the nearest and most immediate, we are dealing with what is past. The so-called present vanishes in the very act of reflecting upon it, and the future is all surmise and imagination. Hence the greater our interest in the facts and truths of human existence—our own existence included—the greater, necessarily, is our concern with the past. "To live in the past" ought not, therefore, to be the phrase of reproach that it commonly is. The larger part of the thoughtful life that one leads during the intervals of action cannot be anything but some form of living in the past. If this part of our lives is to be criticized, it should be in words different from the cliché. One should ask, *How* does he or she live in the past? *What past* does he or she recall, prefer, imagine?

It is at this point that history as the organized story of the whole human past comes in to contribute its pleasures and its illumination to the thoughtful life. A person who remembered only his own past would be pretty poor indeed—living on a starvation diet. Actually, it is a question whether such a life is not an impossible supposition. Everybody remembers pieces of other people's pasts; everybody, whether he means to or not, finds that he has learned about his country, his town, his street, his business office, or his factory many things that came to pass well before his time. To possess that information, if it is accurate, is in essence a knowledge of history. It differs in extent but not in kind from a knowledge of how Rome rose and fell. And this relation tells us what reading history affords in the first instance. Just as knowing about our neighbours' and friends' histories adds to our sense of reality, so does reading history: it gives us vicarious experience.

If we add to the habitual, unconscious intake of personal and local history the daily filling of the mind by news reports—which is contemporary history and which usually brings with it fragments of a remoter past—we begin to see that every man who lives in a modern, communicative society is forced to become in some sense a conscious historian. His interest begins with himself and his environment, but it is soon stretched out, haphazardly, into such domains of history as chance or special interests have developed. And special interests need not mean explicitly intellectual ones; baseball and chess, model trains and furniture, pottery and boat-building have their heroes and revolutions too, and whoever cares about these activities or artifacts for themselves inevitably becomes engrossed in their histories.

It is of course true that when we ordinarily speak of someone having an interest in history we mean the political, social, or cultural history of great civilizations; and for a long time history was arbitrarily taken to mean the sequence that leads from the ancient civilizations of the eastern Mediterranean to the modern ones of the West. It is a tremendous spectacle, even though concentrated on a relatively small territory. But now that certain dynamic elements of Western civilization have aroused the rest of the world to both imitation and resistance, it has become imperative to widen the panorama and see behind the vast and confused modern scene the several histories of the great Eastern civilizations as well as the traditions and vicissitudes of the African societies.

Two questions readily occur at the mere thought of so much to know. Can a reader who is not a professional historian find his way in this huge maze of names, dates, and facts? And if he can, why should he? The answer to the first question is the old reply of the mathematician to the nervous student: "What one fool can do, another can." A real compliment is concealed in this gruff retort, for what it implies is that given an interest, a motive, any man can inform himself about any part of world history through secondary accounts such as are digested in an encyclopaedia. There is no obligation to master every detail, to dispute or criticize sources—in a word, to ape the professional, who, for the best of reasons, limits himself to a small segment of the whole. A *reader* of history is one who follows with his mind the steps another took on his voyage of discovery; and this is easier in history than in mathematics, for history is told in plain words and deals with ordinary human relationships.

So the main difficulty lies in the second question: Why embark on the journey? The answers are numerous and varied, for temperaments differ, as do "special interests" in the sense referred to above. But there is one answer that covers the rest; it is the answer suggested by what was said earlier about every man's unconscious absorption of haphazard fragments of history. The best motive for reading history deliberately is curiosity about the portions missing from one's own picture of the past. Curiosity: How did things come to be as they are? How was it when they were different? Is it true that once upon a time men did thus and so? History deals with particulars, and most recorded particulars contain puzzles, contradictions, enormities, all of them spurs to curiosity: the Hudson River in the state of New York was named after the navigator often called Hendrik Hudson, who first sailed up the stream. But why Hendrik and not Henry? Well, Henry was his baptismal name; how did he acquire the other and why? The full answer leads really to a comprehensive view of exploration and colonization by the national states at the dawn of the modern age—the aims, drives, desires, errors, follies, cruelties, and incalculable consequences of a great movement that occupies two and a half centuries and that has continued in different forms down to the landings on the Moon.

The most striking feature of history is its fusion of purposeful direction and unexpected drift. For example, read about Plato, Aristotle, and the ancient mathematicians, and you will discover how their speculations and discoveries have been transformed and amplified into the methods and systems that we still work with. But you will also be told how at various times these same streams of thought or belief generated entirely new and remote, strange and absurd consequences. Again, ancient astrology led to the science of astronomy, and science (as we think) replaces superstition. Yet astrology fills columns in 20th-century newspapers and the minds of their millions of readers. What is the explanation? We lack the pythoness of Delphi, in whom Socrates believed or affected to believe, and we have no official college of augurs to scan the entrails of birds as a guide to future political action, but fortune-tellers are never out of business and we do have Gallup polls. Truly, the wonders of cultural history are infinite.

To conjure up these beliefs and institutions in this comparative fashion is not to equate them with one another or across the centuries; it is rather to stress the identity in diversity that is the principle of human affairs and that makes human history accessible to any willing reader. In different times and places, men are the same and also different. The differences are due to the varying emphases given by one people at one time to some element of life and feeling or to some form of its expression. This is most easily seen in the plastic arts. Think of the representations of the human body in Egypt, Greece, medieval Europe, the west coast of Africa, pre-Columbian America, and the art galleries of world capitals in the second half of the 20th century: is it the same human body or different? The question is really idle, for it is both and neither. In paint or marble there is strictly no human body, only a view of it, a feeling about it. Similarly, what we see in history is not so much Man distorted in one way or another as *men* who existed *only as we see them;* that is, in their society and culture, under their skies and gods, never staying put for more than a short time, never to be reduplicated elsewhere or at a later time, even when the effort to imitate is strong and shrewd—as in the Italian Renaissance, which tried to restore the ancient culture of Greece and Rome.

Despite this irreducible plasticity, diversity, and restlessness, we draw historical parallels, we make comparisons. That we can do so is what persuades us of the unity and continuity of history. When we find the Celtic druids and the Aztecs making human sacrifices to their gods we say we recognize a human tendency, though we profess to abhor it. Yet some future reader of history might be tempted to compare with those ancient peoples our contemporary revolutionists, who sacrifice 400,000 kulaks (or some other hapless group) for the good of the tribe and its eternal prosperity. But we also notice a strange difference: we know that fanatical faith presides over each type of human sacrifice, ancient and modern, but even as we condemn we think we understand the modern more readily: we know its background, have heard its advocates. It is one of the illuminations of history, not merely to know abstractly, but, by learning the local shape of things, to feel how the reality of each time and place differs; how the faiths diverge in contents and origins and thus in persuasiveness. We may now lump together the Celts and the Aztecs, but they were far apart in thought and character: in short, nothing is truly comparable; in history everything is *sui generis*.

The wise reader of history keeps his equilibrium between these two extremes of likeness and difference. He tries to see the unfamiliar in the familiar, and vice versa. He stands away from his own prejudices and satisfies his curiosity by trying to sympathize with what is farthest away or most alien. This is very hard to do when what is before us is a bloody sacrifice, a massacre, a piece of treachery or cynical greed that violates our sensibilities as well as our moral principles. But to sympathize is not to condone or approve, it is only to acknowledge in oneself the ever-present possibility of the same feeling or action. Certainly the enlightened 20th century has no warrant for looking down on times and places where treachery and massacre were commonplace. And it is a sobering observation to find in both past and present the evidence that inhumanities have been and are being committed by the brutish and civilized alike, the ignorant and the educated, the cynical and the devout, the selfish and the heroic.

A principal good derived from history is thus an increase in self-knowledge, through a fellow-feeling with men singly and in groups as history tells about them. That self-knowledge in turn makes the reader of history less ready to find "monsters of error" in his own time and place. Let it be said again, he need not condone or accept with indifference, but he is spared one of the very errors that perpetuates man's inhumanity to man—fanatical self-righteousness.

On the constructive side, what history tells is the long series of efforts to overcome the constraints of nature and the difficulties of living in society. Those efforts we call civilizations. They start small. In the West they first take the form of city-states. They clash, with one another or with the barbarians "outside." Trade and war, war and trade expand the scope of power, government, and law. Great men introduce broader conceptions of citizenship, morals, and religions. Others invent practical devices of administration, manufacture, and—again—war. Still others discover the workings of nature, create mathematics or art or systems of philosophy. A concentration of such activities over a given territory is what is meant by a high civilization—Egypt, Greece, the Hellenistic Age, Rome, the Saracens, the High Middle Ages, the Renaissance. And also China, Japan, the Khmers, India, the Mayas, the Incas, and so on.

Along this hazardous and always violent course, innumerable characters rise and play their parts. Their fates provide stories within the story. Visibly, biographies are the bricks of which history is made, for the story of mankind can only be the stories of men. But by a paradox of man's social existence, the life of communities is not a simple sum of individual lives. The reader of history must therefore imagine from the printed page characteristic acts, moods, errors, disasters, achievements that are nobody's doing and everybody's doing. This imagining is another important good bestowed by historical reading, for it dispels the illusion that H.G. Wells called the "governess view" of history: They (the bad people) are doing this terrible thing to Us (the good people). The fallacy in it is to suppose that any large group acts as with one mind, clear in purpose and aware of consequences. Such a projection of the single ego upon whole masses is a form of provincialism that is encountered in most political discussions and certainly in all social prejudices: "If the President would only act . . . if those people would only see reason. . . ." A reader of history is cured of this simple-mindedness by developing a new sense—the historical sense—of how mankind in the mass behaves, neither free nor fatally pushed, and in its clearest actions mysterious even to itself.

It is this peculiarity that, while marking the difference between history and biography (where acts can be deemed individual and responsible), has led many minds to postulate a meaning in history, a meaning discoverable but obscured by the multiplicity and confusion of facts. A famous passage in Cardinal Newman's *Apologia* records in admirable prose the feelings that lead to the elaboration of philosophies of history; for Newman it is of course the traditional Christian interpretation that unifies the multiplicity and resolves the confusion:

> To consider the world in its length and breadth, its various history, the many races of man, their starts, their fortunes, their mutual alienation, their conflicts; and then their ways, habits, governments, forms of wor-

> ship; their enterprises, their aimless courses, their random achievements and acquirements, the impotent conclusion of long-standing facts, the tokens so faint and broken, of a superintending design, the blind evolution of what turn out to be great powers or truths, the progress of things, as if from unreasoning elements, not towards final causes, the greatness and littleness of man, his far-reaching aims, his short duration, the curtain hung over his futurity, the disappointments of life, the defeat of good, the success of evil, physical pain, mental anguish, the prevalence and intensity of sin, the pervading idolatries, the corruptions, the dreary hopeless irreligion, that condition of the whole race, so fearfully yet exactly described in the Apostle's words, "having no hope and without God in the world,"—all this is a vision to dizzy and appal; and inflicts upon the mind the sense of a profound mystery, which is absolutely beyond human solution.

Other famous philosophies, from Vico's and Hegel's to Marx's and Spengler's, discover a direction in history, or a principle of action, and often a goal or terminus (as in Marx), after which history as we know it shall cease and a kind of second Eden be restored.

To the practical writer or reader of history these philosophies appeal mainly by their suggestiveness; they are valued for their scattered insights and analogies. As systems they negate the very spirit of history, which seeks the concrete and particular, the opposite of system and abstraction. True, there have been historians who took a middle course and attempted to find empirical regularities in history—again with occasionally suggestive results—but very soon their methods begin to do violence to the facts in order to group them and count them and treat them like identities in physical science. When the physical world itself has not yet been fully systematized, to assume or "find" a system in history without the means and the liberties that science uses is to think like neither a scientist nor a historian. It is in fact an attempt to remove the difficulty of history at the cost of destroying its unique merit and interest.

By the "liberties" that science takes is meant the experimenter's elimination of all but a very few components in a given trial, so as to ascertain precisely the nature and amount of a given effect. When this is done, the result is usually stated in causal terms—so much of this, under such and such conditions, will produce so much of that. Hardly anyone needs to be told that history defies a similar treatment. Its elements cannot be exactly measured, and although each historical situation presents to the discerning eye a variety of clear conditions or factors, the isolating of *a* cause for what happens is beyond reach.

That is but another way of saying that history is and must remain a story. And a story, if properly told, is a whole, to be understood as a whole—synthetically, not analytically. History in this regard resembles the arts. We say we "analyze" a work of art, but that is to speak metaphorically. We can enjoy and understand the products of art only as wholes. In history, the artful story is offered as a true story, and great pains are taken to see that it is true. But except in the broadest sense, the historical wholes are not given as such in the record; they are devised by the historian, to make the welter of facts intelligible and hence able to be remembered. Clio was not only the muse of history but also of eloquence, by which the Greeks meant good, intelligible prose, to be spoken before an audience unused to books. The same requirements still hold; written history must be readable with pleasure, or Clio is defeated.

But, it will be said, from many diverse writers will come divergent stories, rival interpretations. That is true, for only a divine mind could know "how it actually happened." But this limitation of history is also a merit, for it can thereby be written and read over and over again in as many versions as are plausible or accessible. There is and will be no final statement; the perspective forever changes, and with it the interest of history renews itself into infinity. As the philosopher William James once remarked, "What has been concluded that we should conclude about it?"

ANTHONY BURGESS
ON
The Novel

The current Britannica *is particularly fortunate in having writers who can effectively handle the major literary genres. (See later in this book Howard Nemerov's essay on poetry.) The novel, an interestingly chaotic form, offered a challenge well met by the English novelist, man of letters, linguist, Joycean, and musician Anthony Burgess (1917–). Burgess is a kind of English Norman Mailer, not afraid of exhibiting temperament and an often bizarre independence. His reputation was established with* A Clockwork Orange *(1962; filmed 1971). His lengthy article on the novel (15th edition), reprinted here in full, is a remarkable job of boxing the compass. No one could have done better in 8,000 words.*

The novel is a genre of fiction, and fiction may be defined as the art or craft of contriving, through the written word, representations of human life that instruct or divert or both. The various forms that fiction may take are best seen less as a number of separate categories than as a continuum or, more accurately, a cline, with some such brief form as the anecdote at one end of the scale and the longest conceivable novel at the other. When any piece of fiction is long enough to constitute a whole book, as opposed to a mere part of a book, then it may be said to have achieved novelhood. But this state admits of its own quantitative categories, so that a relatively brief novel may be termed a novella (or, if the insubstantiality of the content matches its brevity, a novelette), and a very long novel may overflow the banks of a single volume and become a *roman fleuve,* or river novel. Length is very much one of the dimensions of the genre.

The term novel is a truncation of the Italian word *novella* (from the plural of Latin *novellus,* a late variant of *novus,* meaning "new"), so that what is now, in most languages, a diminutive denotes historically the parent form. The *novella* was a kind of enlarged anecdote like those to be found in the 14th-century Italian classic Boccaccio's *Decameron,* each of which exemplifies the etymology well enough. The stories are little new things, novelties, freshly minted diversions, toys; they are not reworkings of known fables or myths, and they are lacking in weight and moral earnestness. It is to be noted that, despite the high example of novelists of the most profound seriousness, such as Tolstoy, Henry James, and Virginia Woolf, the term novel still, in some quarters, carries overtones of lightness and frivolity. And it is possible to descry a tendency to triviality in the form itself. The ode or symphony seems to possess an inner mechanism that protects it from aesthetic or moral corruption, but the novel can descend to shameful commercial depths of sentimentality or pornography. It is the purpose of this article to consider the novel not solely in terms of great art but also as an all-purpose medium catering for all the strata of literacy.

Such early ancient Roman fiction as Petronius' *Satyricon* of the 1st century AD and Lucius Apuleius' *Golden Ass* of the 2nd century contain many of the popular elements that distinguish the novel from its nobler born relative the epic poem. In the fictional works, the medium is prose, the events described are unheroic, the settings are streets and taverns, not battlefields and palaces. There is more low fornication than princely combat; the gods do not move the action; the dialogue is homely rather than aristocratic. It was, in fact, out of the need to find—in the period of Roman decline—a literary form that was anti-epic in both substance and language that the first prose fiction of Europe seems to have been conceived. The most memorable character in Petronius is a *nouveau riche* vulgarian; the hero of Lucius Apuleius is turned into a donkey; nothing less epic can well be imagined.

The medieval chivalric romance (from a popular Latin word, probably *Romanice,* meaning written in the vernacular, not in traditional Latin) restored a kind of epic view of man—though now as heroic Christian, not heroic pagan. At the same time, it bequeathed its name to the later genre of continental literature, the novel, which is known in French as *roman,* in Italian as *romanzo,* etc. (The English term romance, however, carries a pejorative connotation.) But that later genre achieved its first great flowering in Spain at the beginning of the 17th century in an antichivalric comic masterpiece—the *Don Quixote* of Cervantes, which, on a larger scale than the *Satyricon* or *The Golden Ass,* contains many of the elements that have been expected from prose fiction ever since. Novels have heroes, but not in any classical or medieval sense. As for the novelist, he must, in the words of the contemporary British-American W.H. Auden,

> Become the whole of boredom, subject to
> Vulgar complaints like love, among the Just
> Be just, among the Filthy filthy too,
> And in his own weak person, if he can,
> Must suffer dully all the wrongs of Man.

The novel attempts to assume those burdens of life that have no place in the epic poem and to see man as unheroic, unredeemed, imperfect, even absurd. This is why there is room among its practitioners for writers of hard-boiled detective thrillers such as the contemporary American Mickey Spillane or of sentimental melodramas such as the prolific 19th-century English novelist Mrs. Henry Wood, but not for one of the unremitting elevation of outlook of a John Milton.

Elements of the Novel

Plot. The novel is propelled through its hundred or thousand pages by a device known as the story or plot. This is frequently conceived by the novelist in very simple terms, a mere nucleus, a jotting on an old envelope: for example,

Charles Dickens' *Christmas Carol* (1843) might have been conceived as "a misanthrope is reformed through certain magical visitations on Christmas Eve"; or Jane Austen's *Pride and Prejudice* (1813) as "a young couple destined to be married have first to overcome the barriers of pride and prejudice"; or Fyodor Dostoyevsky's *Crime and Punishment* (1866) as "a young man commits a crime and is slowly pursued in the direction of his punishment." The detailed working out of the nuclear idea requires much ingenuity, since the plot of one novel is expected to be somewhat different from that of another, and there are very few basic human situations for the novelist to draw upon. The dramatist may take his plot ready-made from fiction or biography—a form of theft sanctioned by Shakespeare—but the novelist has to produce what look like novelties.

The example of Shakespeare is a reminder that the ability to create an interesting plot, or even any plot at all, is not a prerequisite of the imaginative writer's craft. At the lowest level of fiction, plot need be no more than a string of stock devices for arousing stock responses of concern and excitement in the reader. The reader's interest may be captured at the outset by the promise of conflicts or mysteries or frustrations that will eventually be resolved, and he will gladly—so strong is his desire to be moved or entertained—suspend criticism of even the most trite modes of resolution. In the least sophisticated fiction, the knots to be untied are stringently physical, and the denouement often comes in a sort of triumphant violence. Serious fiction prefers its plots to be based on psychological situations, and its climaxes come in new states of awareness—chiefly self-knowledge—on the parts of the major characters.

Melodramatic plots, plots dependent on coincidence or improbability, are sometimes found in even the most elevated fiction; E.M. Forster's *Howards End* (1910) is an example of a classic British novel with such a plot. But the novelist is always faced with the problem of whether it is more important to represent the formlessness of real life (in which there are no beginnings and no ends and very few simple motives for action) or to construct an artifact as well balanced and economical as a table or chair; since he is an artist, the claims of art, or artifice, frequently prevail. But there are ways of constructing novels in which plot may play a desultory part or no part at all. The traditional picaresque novel—a novel with a rogue as its central character—like Alain Lesage's *Gil Blas* (1715) or Henry Fielding's *Tom Jones* (1749), depends for movement on a succession of chance incidents. In the works of Virginia Woolf, the consciousness of the characters, bounded by some poetic or symbolic device, sometimes provides all the fictional material. Marcel Proust's great *roman fleuve, À la recherche du temps perdu* (1913–27; *Remembrance of Things Past*), has a metaphysical framework derived from the time theories of the philosopher Henri Bergson, and it moves toward a moment of truth that is intended to be literally a revelation of the nature of reality. Strictly, any scheme will do to hold a novel together—raw action, the hidden syllogism of the mystery story, prolonged solipsist contemplation—so long as the actualities or potentialities of human life are credibly expressed, with a consequent sense of illumination, or some lesser mode of artistic satisfaction, on the part of the reader.

Character. The inferior novelist tends to be preoccupied with plot; to the superior novelist the convolutions of the human personality, under the stress of artfully selected experience, are the chief fascination. Without character it was once accepted that there could be no fiction. In the period since World War II, the creators of what has come to be called the French *nouveau roman* (*i.e.*, new novel) have deliberately demoted the human element, claiming the right of objects and processes to the writer's and reader's prior attention. Thus, in books termed *chosiste* (literally "thing-ist"), they make the furniture of a room more important than its human incumbents. This may be seen as a transitory protest against the long predominance of character in the novel, but, even on the popular level, there have been indications that readers can be held by things as much as by characters. Henry James could be vague in *The Ambassadors* (1903) about the provenance of his chief character's wealth; if he wrote today he would have to give his readers a tour around the factory or estate. The popularity of much undistinguished but popular fiction has nothing to do with its wooden characters; it is machines, procedures, organizations that draw the reader. The success of Ian Fleming's British spy stories in the

1960s had much to do with their hero, James Bond's car, gun, and preferred way of mixing a martini.

But the true novelists remain creators of characters—prehuman, such as those in William Golding's *Inheritors* (1955); animal, as in Henry Williamson's *Tarka the Otter* (1927) or Jack London's *Call of the Wild* (1903); caricatures, as in much of Dickens; or complex and unpredictable entities, as in Tolstoy, Dostoyevsky, or Henry James. The reader may be prepared to tolerate the most wanton-seeming stylistic tricks and formal difficulties because of the intense interest of the central characters in novels as diverse as James Joyce's *Ulysses* (1922) and *Finnegans Wake* (1939) and Laurence Sterne's *Tristram Shandy* (1760–67).

It is the task of literary critics to create a value hierarchy of fictional character, placing the complexity of the Shakespearean view of man—as found in the novels of Tolstoy and Joseph Conrad—above creations that may be no more than simple personifications of some single characteristic, like some of those by Dickens. It frequently happens, however, that the common reader prefers surface simplicity—easily memorable cartoon figures like Dickens' never-despairing Mr. Micawber and devious Uriah Heep—to that wider view of personality, in which character seems to engulf the reader, subscribed to by the great novelists of France and Russia. The whole nature of human identity remains in doubt, and writers who voice that doubt—like the French exponents of the *nouveau roman* Alain Robbe-Grillet and Nathalie Sarraute, as well as many others—are in effect rejecting a purely romantic view of character. This view imposed the author's image of himself—the only human image he properly possessed—on the rest of the human world. For the unsophisticated reader of fiction, any created personage with a firm position in time-space and the most superficial parcel of behavioral (or even sartorial) attributes will be taken for a character. Though the critics may regard it as heretical, this tendency to accept a character is in conformity with the usages of real life. The average person has at least a suspicion of his own complexity and inconsistency of makeup, but he sees the rest of the world as composed of much simpler entities. The result is that novels whose characters are created out of the author's own introspection are frequently rejected as not "true to life." But both the higher and the lower orders of novel readers might agree in condemning a lack of memorability in the personages of a work of fiction, a failure on the part of the author to seem to add to the reader's stock of remembered friends and acquaintances. Characters that seem, on recollection, to have a life outside the bounds of the books that contain them are usually the ones that earn their creators the most regard. Depth of psychological penetration, the ability to make a character real as oneself, seems to be no primary criterion of fictional talent.

Scene, or setting. The makeup and behaviour of fictional characters depend on their environment quite as much as on the personal dynamic with which their author endows them: indeed, in Émile Zola, environment is of overriding importance, since he believed it determined character. The entire action of a novel is frequently determined by the locale in which it is set. Thus, Gustave Flaubert's *Madame Bovary* (1857) could hardly have been placed in Paris, because the tragic life and death of the heroine have a great deal to do with the circumscriptions of her provincial milieu. But it sometimes happens that the main locale of a novel assumes an importance in the reader's imagination comparable to that of the characters and yet somehow separable from them. Wessex is a giant brooding presence in Thomas Hardy's novels, whose human characters would probably not behave much differently if they were set in some other rural locality of England. The popularity of Sir Walter Scott's "Waverley" novels is due in part to their evocation of a romantic Scotland. Setting may be the prime consideration of some readers, who can be drawn to Conrad because he depicts life at sea or in the East Indies; they may be less interested in the complexity of human relationships that he presents.

The regional novel is a recognized species. The sequence of four novels that Hugh Walpole began with *Rogue Herries* (1930) was the result of his desire to do homage to the part of Cumberland, in England, where he had elected to live. The great Yoknapatawpha cycle of William Faulkner, a classic of 20th-century American literature set in an imaginary county in Mississippi, belongs to the category as much as the once-popular confections about Sussex that were written about the same time by the English novelist Sheila Kaye-Smith.

Many novelists, however, gain a creative impetus from avoiding the same setting in book after book and deliberately seeking new locales. The English novelist Graham Greene apparently needed to visit a fresh scene in order to write a fresh novel. His ability to encapsulate the essence of an exotic setting in a single book is exemplified in *The Heart of the Matter* (1948); his contemporary Evelyn Waugh stated that the West Africa of that book replaced the true remembered West Africa of his own experience. Such power is not uncommon: the Yorkshire moors have been romanticized because Emily Brontë wrote of them in *Wuthering Heights* (1847), and literary tourists have visited Stoke-on-Trent, in northern England, because it comprises the "Five Towns" of Arnold Bennett's novels of the early 20th century. Others go to the Monterey, California, of John Steinbeck's novels in the expectation of experiencing a *frisson* added to the locality by an act of creative imagination. James Joyce, who remained inexhaustibly stimulated by Dublin, has exalted that city in a manner that even the guidebooks recognize.

The setting of a novel is not always drawn from a real-life locale. The literary artist sometimes prides himself on his ability to create the totality of his fiction—the setting as well as the characters and their actions. In the Russian expatriate Vladimir Nabokov's *Ada* (1969) there is an entirely new space-time continuum, and the English scholar J.R.R. Tolkien in his *Lord of the Rings* (1954–55) created an "alternative world" that appeals greatly to many who are dissatisfied with the existing one. The world of interplanetary travel was imaginatively created long before the first moon landing. The properties of the future envisaged by H.G. Wells's novels or by Aldous Huxley in *Brave New World* (1932) are still recognized in an age that those authors did not live to see. The composition of place can be a magical fictional gift.

Whatever the locale of his work, every true novelist is concerned with making a credible environment for his characters, and this really means a close attention to sense data—the immediacies of food and drink and colour—far more than abstractions like "nature" and "city." The London of Charles Dickens is as much incarnated in the smell of wood in lawyers' chambers as in the skyline and vistas of streets.

Narrative method and point of view. Where there is a story, there is a storyteller. Traditionally, the narrator of the epic and mock-epic alike acted as an intermediary between the characters and the reader; the method of Fielding is not very different from the method of Homer. Sometimes the narrator boldly imposed his own attitudes; always he assumed an omniscience that tended to reduce the characters to puppets and the action to a predetermined course with an end implicit in the beginning. Many novelists have been unhappy about a narrative method that seems to limit the free will of the characters, and innovations in fictional technique have mostly sought the objectivity of the drama, in which the characters appear to work out their own destinies without prompting from the author.

The epistolary method, most notably used by Samuel Richardson in *Pamela* (1740) and by Jean-Jacques Rousseau in *La nouvelle Héloïse* (1761), has the advantage of allowing the characters to tell the story in their own words, but it is hard to resist the uneasy feeling that a kind of divine editor is sorting and ordering the letters into his own pattern. The device of making the narrator also a character in the story has the disadvantage of limiting the material available for the narration, since the narrator-character can know only those events in which he participates. There can, of course, be a number of secondary narratives enclosed in the main narrative, and this device—though it sometimes looks artificial—has been used triumphantly by Conrad and, on a lesser scale, by W. Somerset Maugham. A, the main narrator, tells what he knows directly of the story and introduces what B and C and D have told him about the parts that he does not know.

Seeking the most objective narrative method of all, Ford Madox Ford used, in *The Good Soldier* (1915), the device of the storyteller who does not understand the story he is telling. This is the technique of the "unreliable observer." The reader, understanding better than the narrator, has the illusion of receiving the story directly. Joyce, in both his major novels, uses different narrators for the various chapters. Most of them are unreliable, and some of them approach the impersonality of a sort of disembodied parody. In *Ulysses,* for example, an episode set in a maternity hospital is told through the medium of a parodic history of English prose style. But, more often than not, the sheer ingenuity of Joyce's techniques draws attention to the manipulator in the shadows. The reader is aware of the author's cleverness where he should be aware only of the characters and their actions. The author is least noticeable when he is employing the stream of consciousness device, by which the inchoate thoughts and feelings of a character are presented in interior monologue—apparently unedited and sometimes deliberately near-unintelligible. It is because this technique seems to draw fiction into the psychoanalyst's consulting room (presenting the raw material of either art or science, but certainly not art itself), however, that Joyce felt impelled to impose the shaping devices referred to above. Joyce, more than any novelist, sought total objectivity of narration technique but ended as the most subjective and idiosyncratic of stylists.

The problem of a satisfactory narrative point of view is, in fact, nearly insoluble. The careful exclusion of comment, the limitation of vocabulary to a sort of reader's lowest common denominator, the paring of style to the absolute minimum—these puritanical devices work well for an Ernest Hemingway (who, like Joyce, remains, nevertheless, a highly idiosyncratic stylist) but not for a novelist who believes that, like poetry, his art should be able to draw on the richness of word play, allusion, and symbol. For even the most experienced novelist, each new work represents a struggle with the unconquerable task of reconciling all-inclusion with self-exclusion. It is noteworthy that Cervantes, in *Don Quixote,* and Nabokov, in *Lolita* (1955), join hands across four centuries in finding most satisfactory the device of the fictitious editor who presents a manuscript story for which he disclaims responsibility. But this highly useful method presupposes in the true author a scholarly, or pedantic, faculty not usually associated with novelists.

Scope, or dimension. No novel can theoretically be too long, but if it is too short it ceases to be a novel. It may or may not be accidental that the novels most highly regarded by the world are of considerable length—Cervantes' *Don Quixote,* Dostoyevsky's *Brothers Karamazov,* Tolstoy's *War and Peace,* Dickens' *David Copperfield,* Proust's *À la recherche du temps perdu,* and so on. On the other hand, since World War II, brevity has been regarded as a virtue in works like the later novels of the Irish absurdist author Samuel Beckett and the *ficciones* of the Argentine Jorge Luis Borges, and it is only an aesthetic based on bulk that would diminish the achievement of Ronald Firbank's short novels of the post–World War I era or the Evelyn Waugh who wrote *The Loved One* (1948). It would seem that there are two ways of presenting human character—one, the brief way, through a significant episode in the life of a personage or group of personages; the other, which admits of limitless length, through the presentation of a large section of a life or lives, sometimes beginning with birth and ending in old age. The plays of Shakespeare show that a full delineation of character can be effected in a very brief compass, so that, for this aspect of the novel, length confers no special advantage. Length, however, is essential when the novelist attempts to present something bigger than character—when, in fact, he aims at the representation of a whole society or period of history.

No other cognate art form—neither the epic poem nor the drama nor the film—can match the resources of the novel when the artistic task is to bring to immediate, sensuous, passionate life the somewhat impersonal materials of the historian. *War and Peace* is the great triumphant example of the panoramic study of a whole society—that of early-19th-century Russia—which enlightens as the historian enlightens and yet also conveys directly the sensations and emotions of living through a period of cataclysmic change. In the 20th century, another Russian, Boris Pasternak, in his *Doctor Zhivago* (1957), expressed—though on a less than Tolstoyan scale—the personal immediacies of life during the Russian Revolution. Though of much less literary distinction than either of these two books, Margaret Mitchell's *Gone with the Wind* (1936) showed how the American Civil War could assume the distanced pathos, horror, and grandeur of any of the classic struggles of the Old World.

Needless to say, length and weighty subject matter are no guarantee in themselves of fictional greatness. Among American writers, for example, James Jones's celebration of the U.S. Army on the eve of World War II in *From Here to Eternity* (1951), though a very ambitious project, repels through indifferent writing and sentimental characterization; Norman Mailer's *Naked and the Dead* (1948), an equally ambitious military novel, succeeds much more because of a tautness, a concern with compression, and an astringent objectivity that Jones was unable to match. Frequently the size of a novel is too great for its subject matter—as with Marguerite Young's *Miss MacIntosh, My Darling* (1965), reputedly the longest single-volume novel of the 20th century, John Barth's *Giles Goatboy* (1966), and John Fowles's *Magus* (1965). Diffuseness is the great danger in the long novel, and diffuseness can mean slack writing, emotional self-indulgence, sentimentality.

Even the long picaresque novel—which, in the hands of a Fielding or his contemporary Tobias Smollett, can rarely be accused of sentimentality—easily betrays itself into such acts of self-indulgence as the multiplication of incident for its own sake, the coy digression, the easygoing jogtrot pace that subdues the sense of urgency that should lie in all fiction. If Tolstoy's *War and Peace* is a greater novel than Fielding's *Tom Jones* or Dickens' *David Copperfield,* it is not because its theme is nobler, or more pathetic, or more significant historically; it is because Tolstoy brings to his panoramic drama the compression and urgency usually regarded as the monopolies of briefer fiction.

Sometimes the scope of a fictional concept demands a technical approach analogous to that of the symphony in music—the creation of a work in separate books, like symphonic movements, each of which is intelligible alone but whose greater intelligibility depends on the theme and characters that unify them. The French author Romain Rolland's *Jean-Christophe* (1904–12) sequence is, very appropriately since the hero is a musical composer, a work in four movements. Among works of English literature, Lawrence Durrell's *Alexandria Quartet* (1957–60) insists in its very title that it is a tetralogy rather than a single large entity divided into four volumes; the concept is "relativist" and attempts to look at the same events and characters from four different viewpoints. Anthony Powell's *Dance to the Music of Time,* a multivolume series of novels that began in 1951 (collected 1962), may be seen as a study of a segment of British society in which the chronological approach is eschewed, and events are brought together in one volume or another because of a kind of parachronic homogeneity. C.P. Snow's *Strangers and Brothers,* a comparable series that began in 1940 and continued to appear throughout the '50s and into the '60s, shows how a fictional concept can be realized only in the act of writing, since the publication of the earlier volumes antedates the historical events portrayed in later ones. In other words, the author could not know what the subject matter of the sequence would be until he was in sight of its end. Behind all these works lies the giant example of Proust's *roman fleuve,* whose length and scope were properly coterminous with the author's own life and emergent understanding of its pattern.

Myth, symbolism, significance. The novelist's conscious day-to-day preoccupation is the setting down of incident, the delineation of personality, the regulation of exposition, climax, and denouement. The aesthetic value of his work is frequently determined by subliminal forces that seem to operate independently of the writer, investing the properties of the surface story with a deeper significance. A novel will then come close to myth, its characters turning into symbols of permanent human states or impulses, particular incarnations of general truths perhaps only realized for the first time in the act of reading. The ability to perform a quixotic act anteceded *Don Quixote,* just as *bovarysme* existed before Flaubert found a name for it.

But the desire to give a work of fiction a significance beyond that of the mere story is frequently conscious and deliberate, indeed sometimes the primary aim. When a novel—like Joyce's *Ulysses* or John Updike's *Centaur* (1963) or Anthony Burgess' *Vision of Battlements* (1965)—is based on an existing classical myth, there is an intention of either ennobling a lowly subject matter, satirizing a debased set of values by referring them to a heroic age, or merely providing a basic structure to hold down a complex and, as it were, centrifugal picture of real life. Of *Ulysses,* Joyce said that his Homeric parallel (which is worked out in great and subtle detail) was a bridge across which to march his 18 episodes; after the march the bridge could be "blown skyhigh." But there is no doubt that, through the classical parallel, the account of an ordinary summer day in Dublin is given a richness, irony, and universality unattainable by any other means.

The mythic or symbolic intention of a novel may manifest itself less in structure than in details which, though they appear naturalistic, are really something more. The shattering of the eponymous golden bowl in Henry

James's 1904 novel makes palpable, and hence truly symbolic, the collapse of a relationship. Even the choice of a character's name may be symbolic. Sammy Mountjoy, in William Golding's *Free Fall* (1959), has fallen from the grace of heaven, the mount of joy, by an act of volition that the title makes clear. The eponym of *Doctor Zhivago* is so called because his name, meaning "the living," carries powerful religious overtones. In the Russian version of the Gospel According to St. Luke, the angels ask the women who come to Christ's tomb: "Chto vy ischyote zhivago mezhdu myortvykh?"—"Why do you seek the living among the dead?" And his first name, Yuri, the Russian equivalent of George, has dragon-slaying connotations.

The symbol, the special significance at a subnarrative level, works best when it can fit without obtrusion into a context of naturalism. The optician's trade sign of a huge pair of spectacles in F. Scott Fitzgerald's *Great Gatsby* (1925) is acceptable as a piece of scenic detail, but an extra dimension is added to the tragedy of Gatsby, which is the tragedy of a whole epoch in American life, when it is taken also as a symbol of divine myopia. Similarly, a cinema poster in Malcolm Lowry's *Under the Volcano* (1947), advertising a horror film, can be read as naturalistic background, but it is evident that the author expects the illustrated fiend—a concert pianist whose grafted hands are those of a murderer—to be seen also as a symbol of Nazi infamy; the novel is set at the beginning of World War II, and the last desperate day of the hero, Geoffrey Firmin, stands also for the collapse of Western civilization.

There are symbolic novels whose infranarrative meaning cannot easily be stated, since it appears to subsist on an unconscious level. Herman Melville's *Moby Dick* (1851) is such a work, as is D.H. Lawrence's novella *St. Mawr* (1925), in which the significance of the horse is powerful and mysterious.

Uses of the Novel

As an expression of an interpretation of life. Novels are not expected to be didactic, like tracts or morality plays; nevertheless, in varying degrees of implicitness, even the "purest" works of fictional art convey a philosophy of life. The novels of Jane Austen, designed primarily as superior entertainment, imply a desirable ordered existence, in which the comfortable decorum of an English rural family is disturbed only by a not too serious shortage of money, by love affairs that go temporarily wrong, and by the intrusion of self-centred stupidity. The good, if unrewarded for their goodness, suffer from no permanent injustice. Life is seen, not only in Jane Austen's novels but in the whole current of bourgeois Anglo-American fiction, as fundamentally reasonable and decent. When wrong is committed, it is usually punished, thus fulfilling Miss Prism's summation in Oscar Wilde's play *The Importance of Being Earnest* (1895), to the effect that in a novel the good characters end up happily and the bad characters unhappily: "that is why it is called fiction".

That kind of fiction called realistic, which has its origins in 19th-century France, chose the other side of the coin, showing that there was no justice in life and that the evil and the stupid must prevail. In the novels of Thomas Hardy there is a pessimism that may be taken as a corrective of bourgeois Panglossianism—the philosophy that everything happens for the best, satirized in Voltaire's *Candide* (1759)—since the universe is presented as almost impossibly malevolent. This tradition is regarded as morbid, and it has been deliberately ignored by most popular novelists. The "Catholic" novelists such as François Mauriac in France, Graham Greene in England, and others—see life as mysterious, full of wrong and evil and injustice inexplicable by human canons but necessarily acceptable in terms of the plans of an inscrutable God. Between the period of realistic pessimism, which had much to do with the agnosticism and determinism of 19th-century science, and the introduction of theological evil into the novel, writers such as H.G. Wells attempted to create a fiction based on optimistic liberalism. As a reaction, there was the depiction of "natural man" in the novels of D.H. Lawrence and Ernest Hemingway.

For the most part, the view of life common to American and European fiction since World War II posits the existence of evil—whether theological or of that brand discovered by the French Existentialists, particularly Jean-Paul Sartre—and assumes that man is imperfect and life possibly absurd. The fiction of the Communist states is based on a very different assumption, one that seems naïve and old-fashioned in its collective optimism to readers in the disillusioned democracies. It is to be noted that in the Soviet Union aesthetic evaluation of fiction has been replaced by ideological judgment. The works of the popular British writer A.J. Cronin, since they seem to depict personal tragedy as an emanation of capitalistic infamy, are rated higher than those of Conrad, James, and their peers. The novel as an art form stands or falls by its capacity to express a view of life acceptable to the Soviet authorities.

As entertainment or escape. In a period that takes for granted that the written word should be "committed"—to the exposure of social wrong or the propagation of progressive ideologies—novelists who seek merely to take the reader out of his dull or oppressive daily life are not highly regarded, except by that reading public that has never expected a book to be anything more than a diversion. Nevertheless, the provision of laughter and dreams has been for many centuries a legitimate literary occupation. It can be condemned by serious devotees of literature only if it falsifies life through oversimplification and tends to corrupt its readers into belief that reality is as the author presents it. The novelettes once beloved of mill girls and domestic servants, in which the beggar maid was elevated to queendom by a king of high finance, were a mere narcotic, a sort of enervating opium of the oppressed; the encouragement of such subliterature might well be one of the devices of social oppression. Adventure stories and spy novels may have a healthy enough astringency, and the very preposterousness of some adventures can be a safeguard against any impressionable young reader's neglecting the claims of real life to dream of becoming a secret agent. The subject matter of some humorous novels—such as the effete British aristocracy created by P.G. Wodehouse, which is no longer in existence if it ever was—can never be identified with a real human society; the dream is accepted as a dream. The same may be said of Evelyn Waugh's early novels—such as *Decline and Fall* (1928) and *Vile Bodies* (1930)—but these are raised above mere entertainment by touching, almost incidentally, on real human issues (the relation of the innocent to a circumambient malevolence is a persistent theme in all Waugh's writing).

Any reader of fiction has a right to an occasional escape from the dullness or misery of his existence, but he has the critical duty of finding the best modes of escape—in the most efficiently engineered detective or adventure stories, in humor that is more than sentimental buffoonery, in dreams of love that are not mere pornography. The fiction of entertainment and escape frequently sets itself higher literary standards than novels with a profound social or philosophical purpose. Books like James Buchan's *Thirty-nine Steps* (1915), Graham Greene's *Travels with My Aunt* (1969), Dashiell Hammett's *Maltese Falcon* (1930), and Raymond Chandler's *Big Sleep* (1939) are distinguished pieces of writing that, while diverting and enthralling, keep a hold on the realities of human character. Ultimately, all good fiction is entertainment, and if it instructs or enlightens it does so best through enchanting the reader.

As propaganda. The desire to make the reader initiate certain acts—social, religious, or political—is the essence of all propaganda, and, though it does not always accord well with art, the propagandist purpose has often found its way into novels whose prime value is an aesthetic one. The *Nicholas Nickleby* (1839) of Charles Dickens attacked the abuses of schools to some purpose, as his *Oliver Twist* (1838) drew attention to the horrors of poorhouses and his *Bleak House* (1853) to the abuses of the law of chancery. The weakness of propaganda in fiction is that it loses its value when the wrongs it exposes are righted, so that the more successful a propagandist novel is, the briefer the life it can be expected to enjoy. The genius of Dickens lay in his ability to transcend merely topical issues through the vitality with which he presented them, so that his contemporary disclosures take on a timeless human validity—chiefly through the power of their drama, character, and rhetoric.

The purely propagandist novel—which Dickens was incapable of writing—quickly becomes dated. The "social" novels of H.G. Wells, which propounded a rational mode of life and even blueprinted utopias, were very quickly exploded by the conviction of man's irredeemable irrationality that World War I initiated and World War II corroborated, a conviction the author himself came to share toward the end of his life. But the early scientific romances of Wells remain vital and are seen to have been prophetic. Most of the fiction of the Soviet Union, which either glorifies the regime or refrains from criticizing it, is dull and unreal, and the same may be said of Communist fiction elsewhere.

Propaganda too frequently ignores man as a totality, concentrating on him aspectively—in terms of politics or sectarian religion. When a didactic attack on a system, as in Harriet Beecher Stowe's attack on slavery in the United States in *Uncle Tom's Cabin* (1852), seems to go beyond mere propaganda, it is because the writer makes the reader aware of wrongs and injustices that are woven into the permanent human fabric. The reader's response may be a modification of his own sensibility, not an immediate desire for action, and this is one of the legitimate effects of serious fiction. The propagandist Dickens calls for the immediate righting of wrongs, but the novelist Dickens says, mainly through implication, that all men—not just schoolmasters and state hirelings—should become more humane. If it is possible to speak of art as possessing a teaching purpose, this is perhaps its only lesson.

As reportage. The division in the novelist's mind is between his view of his art as a contrivance, like a Fabergé watch, and his view of it as a record of real life. The versatile English writer Daniel Defoe, on the evidence of such novels as his *Journal of the Plague Year* (1722), a re-creation of the London plague of 1665, believed that art or contrivance had the lesser claim and proceeded to present his account of events of which he had had no direct experience in the form of plain journalistic reportage. This book, like his *Robinson Crusoe* (1719) and *Moll Flanders* (1722), is more contrived and cunning than appears, and the hurried, unshaped narrative is the product of careful preparation and selective ordering. His example, which could have been a very fruitful one, was not much followed until the 20th century, when the events of the real world became more terrifying and marvellous than anything the novelist could invent, and seemed to ask for that full imaginative treatment that only the novelist's craft can give.

In contemporary American literature, John Hersey's *Hiroshima* (1946), though it recorded the actual results of the nuclear attack on the Japanese city in 1945, did so in terms of human immediacies, not scientific or demographic abstractions, and this approach is essentially novelistic. Truman Capote's *In Cold Blood* (1965) took the facts of a multiple murder in the Midwest of the United States and presented them with the force, reality, tone, and (occasionally) overintense writing that distinguish his genuine fiction. Norman Mailer, in *The Armies of the Night* (1968), recorded, in great personal detail but in a third-person narration, his part in a citizens' protest march on Washington, D.C. It would seem that Mailer's talent lies in his ability to merge the art of fiction and the craft of reportage, and his *Of a Fire on the Moon* (1970), which deals with the American lunar project, reads like an episode in an emergent *roman fleuve* of which Mailer is the central character in a story made up of true public events.

The presentation of factual material as art is the purpose of such thinly disguised biographies as Somerset Maugham's *Moon and Sixpence* (1919), undisguised biographies fleshed out with supposition and imagination like Helen Waddell's *Peter Abelard* (1933), and a great number of autobiographies served up—out of fear of libel or of dullness—as novels. Conversely, invented material may take on the lineaments of journalistic actuality through the employment of a Defoe technique of flat understatement. This is the way of such science fiction as Michael Crichton's *Andromeda Strain* (1969), which uses sketch maps, computer projections, and simulated typewritten reports.

As an agent of change in the language and thought of a culture. Novelists, being neither poets nor philosophers, rarely originate modes of thinking and expression. Poets such as Chaucer and Shakespeare have had much to do with the making of the English language, and Byron was responsible for the articulation of the new romantic sensibility in it in the early 19th century. Books like the Bible, Karl Marx's *Kapital,* and Adolf Hitler's *Mein Kampf* may underlie permanent or transient cultures, but it is hard to find, except in the early Romantic period, a novelist capable of arousing new attitudes to life (as opposed to aspects of the social order) and forging the vocabulary of such attitudes.

With the 18th-century precursors of Romanticism—notably Richardson, Sterne, and Rousseau—the notion of sentiment entered the European consciousness. Rousseau's *Nouvelle Héloïse* (1761) fired a new attitude toward love—more highly emotional than ever before—as his *Émile* (1762) changed educated views on how to bring up children. The romantic wave in Germany, with Goethe's *Sorrows of Werther* (1774) and the works of Jean-Paul Richter a generation later, similarly aroused modes of feeling that rejected the rational constraints of the 18th century. Nor can the influence of Sir Walter Scott's novels be neglected, both on Europe and on the American South (where Mark Twain thought it had had a deplorable effect). With Scott came new forms of regional sentiment, based on a romantic reading of history.

It is rarely, however, that a novelist makes a profound mark on a national language, as opposed to a regional dialect (to which, by using it for a literary end, he may impart a fresh dignity). It is conceivable that Alessandro Manzoni's *I promessi sposi* (1825–27; *The Betrothed*), often called the greatest modern Italian novel, gave 19th-century Italian intellectuals some notion of a viable modern prose style in an Italian that might be termed "national," but even this is a large claim. Günter Grass, in post-Hitler Germany, sought to revivify a language that had been corrupted by the Nazis; he threw whole dictionaries at his readers, in the hope that new freedom, fantasy, and exactness in the use of words might influence the publicists, politicians, and teachers in the direction of a new liberalism of thought and expression.

It is difficult to say whether the French Existentialists, such as Sartre and Albert Camus, have influenced their age primarily through their fiction or their philosophical writings. Certainly, Sartre's early novel *Nausea* (1938) established unforgettable images of the key terms of his philosophy, which has haunted a whole generation, as Camus's novel *The Stranger* (1942) created for all time the lineaments of "Existential man." In the same way, the English writer George Orwell's *Nineteen Eighty-four* (1949) incarnated brilliantly the nature of the political choices that are open to 20th-century humanity, and, with terms like "Big Brother" (*i.e.,* the leader of an authoritarian state) and "doublethink" (belief in contradictory ideas simultaneously), modified the political vocabulary. But no novelist's influence can compare to that of the poet's, who can give a language a soul and define, as Shakespeare and Dante did, the scope of a culture.

As an expression of the spirit of its age. The novelist, like the poet, can make the inchoate thoughts and feelings of a society come to articulation through the exact and imaginative use of language and symbol. In this sense, his work seems to precede the diffusion of new ideas and attitudes and to be the agent of change. But it is hard to draw a line between this function and that of expressing an existing climate of sensibility. Usually the nature of a historical period—that spirit known in German as the *Zeitgeist*—can be understood only in long retrospect, and it is then that the novelist can provide its best summation. The sickness of the Germany that produced Hitler had to wait some time for fictional diagnosis in such works as Thomas Mann's *Doctor Faustus* (1947) and, later, Günter Grass's *Tin Drum* (1959). Evelyn Waugh waited several years before beginning, in the trilogy *Sword of Honour,* to depict that moral decline of English society that started to manifest itself in World War II, the conduct of which was both a cause and a symptom of the decay of traditional notions of honour and justice.

The novel can certainly be used as a tool for the better understanding of a departed age. The period following World War I has been caught forever in Hemingway's *Sun Also Rises* (1926; called *Fiesta* in England), F. Scott Fitzgerald's novels and short stories about the so-called Jazz Age, the *Antic Hay* (1923) and *Point Counter Point* (1928) of Aldous Huxley, and D.H. Lawrence's *Aaron's Rod* (1922) and *Kangaroo* (1923). The spirit of the English 18th century, during which social, political, and religious ideas associated with rising middle classes conflicted with the old Anglican Tory rigidities, is better understood through reading Smollett and Fielding than by taking the cerebral elegance of Pope and his followers as the typical expression of the period.

Similarly, the unrest and bewilderment of the young in the period after World War II still speak in novels like J.D. Salinger's *Catcher in the Rye* (1951) and Kingsley Amis' *Lucky Jim* (1954). It is notable that with novels like these—and the beat-generation books of Jack Kerouac; the American-Jewish novels of Saul Bellow, Bernard Malamud, and Philip Roth; and the Negro novels of Ralph Ellison and James Baldwin—it is a segmented spirit that is expressed, the spirit of an age group, social group, or racial group, and not the spirit of an entire society in a particular phase of history. But probably a *Zeitgeist* has always been the emanation of a minority, the majority being generally silent. The 20th century seems, from this point of view, to be richer in vocal minorities than any other period in history.

As a creator of life styles and an arbiter of taste. Novels have been known to influence, though perhaps not very greatly, modes of social behaviour and even, among the very impressionable, conceptions of personal identity. But more young men have seen themselves as Hamlet or Childe Harold than as Julien Sorel, the protagonist of Stendhal's novel *The Red and the Black* (1830), or the sorrowing Werther. Richardson's novel may popularize Pamela, or Galsworthy's *Forsyte Saga* (1906–22) Jon, as a baptismal name, but it rarely makes a deeper impression on the mode of life of literate families. On the other hand, the capacity of Oscar Wilde's *Picture of Dorian Gray* (1891) to influence young men in the direction of sybaritic amorality, or of D.H. Lawrence's *Lady Chatterley's Lover* (1928) to engender a freer attitude to sex, has never been assessed adequately. With the lower middle class reading public, the effect of devouring *The Forsyte Saga* was to engender genteelisms —cucumber sandwiches for tea, supper renamed dinner—rather than to learn that book's sombre lesson about the decline of the old class structure. Similarly, the ladies who read Scott in the early 19th century were led to barbarous ornaments and tastefully arranged folk songs.

Fiction has to be translated into one of the dramatic media—stage, film, or television—before it can begin to exert a large influence. *Tom Jones* as a film in 1963 modified table manners and coiffures and gave American visitors to Great Britain a new (and probably false) set of expectations. The stoic heroes of Hemingway, given to drink, fights, boats, and monosyllables, became influential only when they were transferred to the screen. They engendered other, lesser heroes—incorruptible private detectives, partisans brave under interrogation—who in their turn have influenced the impressionable young when seeking an identity. Ian Fleming's James Bond led to a small revolution in martini ordering. But all these influences are a matter of minor poses, and such poses are most readily available in fiction easily adapted to the mass media—which means lesser fiction. Proust, though he recorded French patrician society with painful fidelity, had little influence on it, and it is hard to think of Henry James disturbing the universe even fractionally. Films and television programs dictate taste and behaviour more than the novel ever could.

G. K. CHESTERTON

ON

Charles Dickens

Gilbert Keith Chesterton (1874–1936) has, like his subject, added an adjective to the language. We all know what Chestertonian and Dickensian mean. Since Chesterton our knowledge of the life of Dickens has expanded phenomenally. Yes, we know more about him—but can we write about him any better than G. K. C. did? He wrote long before the Ellen Ternan revelations; he does not mention her. It doesn't seem to matter. What we have here is a love letter to what does matter: the novels themselves, and the volcanic genius that lay behind them. We reprint in its entirety the article that first appeared in the 14th edition (1929).

Dickens, Charles John Huffam (1812–1870), certainly the most popular and perhaps the greatest of the great English novelists, was born in Landport, a division of Portsea; in a house in Mile End terrace, Commercial road. The house can be identified and is in some sense a popular shrine or memorial, enabling the sightseer to link up in one journey two of the most romantic national names, associating Dickens with Portsea and Nelson with Portsmouth. But beyond this symbolic and almost legendary local interest, the actual address indicates little more than the drifting and often decaying fortunes of the class and family from which he came. It would be an exaggeration to compare it to Lant street, in the Borough, of which, it will be remembered, "the inhabitants were migratory, disappearing usually towards the verge of quarter-day." But there is the note of something nomadic about the social world to which he belonged. We talk of the solid middle class; he belonged, one might almost say, to the liquid middle class; certainly to the insecure middle class. His father, John Dickens, was a clerk in the Navy-Pay Office, and all through life a man of wavering and unstable status, partly by his misfortunes and partly by his fault. It is said that Dickens sketched him in a lighter spirit as Micawber and in a sadder and more realistic aspect as Dorrit. The contrast between the two men, as well as the two moods, should be a warning against the weakness of taking too literally the idea of Dickensian "originals." The habit has done grave injustice to many people, such as Leigh Hunt; and it may involve a grave injustice to John Dickens; and perhaps an even graver injustice to Mrs. John Dickens, née Elizabeth Barrow, whom a similar rumour reports as the real Mrs. Nickleby. Some may question, not without grief, whether there really could be a real Mrs. Nickleby. But in any case there certainly could not be a man who was both Dorrit and Micawber. The truth is that we shall misunderstand from the beginning the nature of the Dickensian imagination, if we suppose these things to be mechanical portraits in black and white, taken by "the profeel machine," as Mr. Weller said. It is the whole point of Dickens that he took hints from human beings; and turned them, one may say, into superhuman beings. But it is true that John Dickens was of the type that is often shifted from place to place; and this is the chief significance of Charles Dickens's connection with Portsea, or rather of his lack of connection with it. He can only have been two years old when the household moved for a short time to London and then for a longer time to Chatham. It was perhaps lucky that the formative period of his first childhood was also the most fortunate period of his not very fortunate family. The dockyard of Chatham, the towers of Rochester, the gardens and the great roads of Kent remained to him through life as the only normal memory of a nursery and a native soil; his house in later years looked down on the great road from Gads hill and the cathedral tower rose again in his last vision, in the opium dream called "Edwin Drood." Here he had leisure to learn a little from books, who was so soon to learn only from life; first in the stricter sense of school-books, from a Mr. Giles, a Baptist minister in Chatham; and second, and probably with greater profit, from a random heap of old novels that included much of the greatest English literature and even more of the type of literature from which he could learn most; *Roderick Random* and *Robinson Crusoe* and *Tom Jones* and *The Vicar of Wakefield.*

He can hardly have been ten years old when the household was once more upon the march. John Dickens had fallen heavily into debt; he continued the tendency to change his private address; and his next private address was the Debtors' Prison of the Marshalsea. His wife, the mother of eight children of whom Charles was the second, had to encamp desolately in Camden Town and open a dingy sort of "educational establishment." Meanwhile the unfortunate Charles was learning his lessons at a very different sort of educational establishment. After helping his mother in every sort of menial occupation, he was thrown forth to earn his own living by tying and labelling pots of blacking in a blacking warehouse at Old Hungerford Stairs. The blacking was symbolical enough; Dickens never doubted that this piece of his childhood was the darkest period of his life; and he seems indeed to have been in a mood to black himself all over, like the Othello of the Crummles Company. Of his pessimistic period, of the heartrending monotony and ignominy, he has given little more than a bitter abbreviation in *David Copperfield.* But he was storing up much more than bitterness; it is obvious that he had already developed an almost uncanny vigilance and alertness of attention. By the time his servitude came to an end, by his father falling into a legacy as he had fallen into a jail (there was really a touch of Micawber in the way in which things turned up and turned down for him) the boy was no longer a normal boy, let alone a child. He called his wandering parent "the Prodigal Father"; and there was something of the same fantastic family inversion in the very existence of so watchful and critical a son. We are struck at once with an almost malicious maturity of satire; some of the best passages of the prison life of the Pickwicks and the Dorrits occur in private letters about his own early life. He had shared, of course, the improvement in the family condition; which was represented in his case by a period of service as a clerk to a Mr. Blackmore, a Grays Inn solicitor, and afterwards in the equally successful, and much more congenial, occupation of a newspaper reporter and ultimately a Parliamentary reporter. His father had taken up the trade; but his son was already making a mark in it, as reporter to *The True Sun, The Mirror of Parliament* and *The Morning Chronicle.* In all these aspects and attitudes, at this time, he appears as alert, sharp-witted and detached; recalling that sort of metallic brightness which an observer at this period so often saw flash upon his face. It is worthy of note, because certain healthy social emotions which he always championed have somewhat falsified his personality in the eyes of the prigs whom he loved to rap over the head. He was a genuine champion of geniality; but he was not always genial; certainly not only genial. One of his earliest sketches, published not long after this time, was a defence of the Christian festivity of Christmas against the Puritans and the Utilitarians; it was called "Christmas Under Three Heads." All his life he defended valiantly the pleasures of the poor; and insisted that God had given ale and rum, as well as wine, to make glad the heart of man. But all this has clouded his character with fumes of mere conviviality and irresponsibility which were very far from being really characteristic. Even in youth, which is the period of irresponsibility, Dickens appears in some ways as highly responsible. He was in sharp reaction against the futility of his family; he was both ambitious and industrious; and there were some who even found him hard. In many moods he had as angry a dislike of the Skimpoles as of the Gradgrinds.

Indeed he had come in more ways than one to the high turning-point of his fortunes. His marriage and his first real literary work can be dated at about the same time. He had already begun to write sketches, chiefly in *The Old Monthly Magazine,* which were in the broadest sense caricatures, of the common objects of the street or the market-place. They were illustrated by Cruikshank; and in these early stages of the story the illustrator is often more important than the author. This was notoriously true of his next and perhaps his greatest experiment; but it is typical in any case of his time and his time of life. The prose sketches were signed "Boz" and the signature had become a recognized pseudonym when Messrs. Chapman and Hall, the publishers, approached him with the suggestion of a larger scheme. A well known humorous artist of that epoch, Seymour, was to produce a series of plates illustrating the adventures, or misadventures, of the Nimrod Club, a group of amateur sportsmen, destined to dwindle and yet to grow infinitely greater in the single figure of Mr. Nathaniel Winkle. Dickens consented to write the letter-press, which was little more than a running accompaniment like an ornamental border around the drawings; and in that strange fashion, secondary, subordinate and even trivial, first formed itself in the human fancy the epic and pantomime of *Pickwick* (1837). Dickens persuaded the publishers to let the Pickwick Club represent more varied interests or eccentricities, retained Mr. Winkle to represent or misrepresent the original notion of sport; and by that one stroke of independence cut himself free from a stale fashion and started a new artistic adventure and revolution. He gave as one of his reasons the fact that he had no special knowledge of sports or games, and proceeded to drive his argument home triumphantly by his description of the cricket-match at Dingley Dell. And yet that cricket-match alone might illustrate exactly the game which Dickens so gloriously won; and why that wild and ill-instructed batsman has had so many thousand runs and is not out. What did a few mistakes in the description of cricket, or even in the description of real life, matter in a man who could invent that orator at the cricket-dinner, who complimented the defeated eleven by saying, with the gesture of Alexander, "If I were not Dumkins, I would be Luffey; if I were not Podder, I would be Struggles"? Men do not read that sort of thing to learn about cricket, or even about life, but to find something more living than either. There had broken through the entanglements of that trumpery bargain a force of comic genius which swallowed up its own origin and excuses; a wild animal big enough to eat all its direction labels. People forgot about Seymour; forgot about sport; forgot about the Nimrod Club; soon forgot about the Pickwick Club. They forgot all that he forgot and followed whatever he followed; much bigger and wilder game than any aimed at by the mere gun of Mr. Winkle. The track of the story wandered; the tone of the story changed; a servant whom Pickwick found cleaning boots in an inn-yard took the centre of the stage and towered even over Pickwick; Pickwick from being a pompous buffoon became a generous and venerable old English gentleman; and the world still followed that incredible transformation-scene and wishes there were more of it to this day.

This was the emergence of Dickens into literature. It had, of course, many secondary effects in life. One was the first and almost the most bitter of his quarrels; Seymour may be excused for having been annoyed at the relations of artist and author being thus turned upside down in a whirlwind; but Seymour was not therefore necessarily justified in saying, as he did say and his widow long continued to say, that Dickens had gained glory from another man's ideas. Nobody, we may well imagine, believes that the oration of Sergeant Buzfuz or the poem of Mrs. Leo Hunter, were Mr. Seymour's ideas. Dickens had an inexhaustible torrent of such ideas; and no man on earth could pretend to have provided them. But it is true that in this quarrel, as in others, some found a touch of sharpness and acid self-defence in Dickens; and he was never without his enemies. His ideal was certainly the leisure and geniality of Pickwick; but he was fighting rather too hard for his own hand and had too much at stake and too pressing a knowledge of poverty to be anything but practical.

As Pickwick was the foundation of his public life, his marriage was naturally the foundation of his private life; and in this also he has been an object of criticism as he was certainly an object of sympathy. Very little good is done by making guesses about a story of which the spiritual balance and proportion were probably never known to more than three or four people. It is sufficiently significant that those who were nearest to it, and who survive to speak or rather to be silent, agree in laying no very heavy blame upon anyone involved. One of the principals of the *Morning Chronicle,* George Hogarth, had been so much struck by the "Boz" sketches as to insist on an improvement in the payment of the writer; he introduced Dickens to his family and especially (we may say) to his daughters, with all of whom the young journalist seems to have been on very friendly and even affectionate terms. One of them, Catherine, he married, and certainly married for love; but not perhaps with the sort of love which gives a man a full and serious realization of what he is doing. It is the pathos of the story that in a sense the friendship outlasted the love; for another sister, who understood him better, remained his friend long after his marriage had become a prolonged misunderstanding. All this, however, happened long afterwards; for the moment his marriage may be taken as marking his step into security and success; especially as he was probably stimulated and, as it were, intoxicated, by a romance that brought him into more refined social surroundings than his own. From that moment he was launched as a popular writer and a power in the world; and he never went back, until he died of popularity thirty years afterwards.

It is notable that his next work was *Oliver Twist* (1838); which might be meant for a contrast to *Pickwick*. If the first trick had succeeded, nobody could accuse the conjurer of trying the same trick twice. He was probably proud of proving his range; but he was certainly courageous in testing his popularity. It is true that Oliver Twist consists of a queer mixture of melodrama and realism; but both the realism and the melodrama are deliberately dark and grim. Nevertheless it is fortunate that with his second book he thus brought into play what may be called his second talent. It is too common to compare his humour with his pathos; for indeed there is no comparison. But there really is a comparison between his humour and his horror; and he really had a talent for a certain sort of horror, which is exactly rendered by the popular phrase of supping on horrors. For there is a sort of lurid conviviality that accompanies the panic; as if the nightmare could accompany and not follow the heavy meal. This suppressed vitality is due to his never for an instant losing the love of life; the love of death, which is despair and pessimism, was meaningless to him till he died. The sort of horror which afterwards conceived the death of Krook is already found in Oliver Twist; as in that intolerable repetition throbbing in the murderer's ears; "will wash out mud-stains, blood-stains" and so on. For the rest, the plot is preposterous and the flashes of fun excellent but few; yet there is another aspect of the book which makes it important in the story of Dickens. It is not only the first of his nightmare novels, but also the first of his social tracts. Something of social protest could be read between the lines of Pickwick in prison; but the prison of Pickwick was very mild compared with the charitable almshouse of Oliver. Dickens is witness, with Hood and Cobbett and many others, that the workhouse was felt by all generous people as something quite unnaturally new and hard and inhuman. It is sometimes said that he killed Bumble; it would be truer to say that, by making Bumble live, he created something by which it will always be possible to kill bureaucracies.

Whether we call the transition from *Pickwick* to *Oliver Twist* a change from comedy to tragedy, or merely a change from farce to melodrama, it is notable that the next act of Dickens is to mix the two in about equal proportions. Having shown how much he can vary, he tries to show how well he can combine. It is worth noting because it explains much of the failure as well as the success of his art as a whole. We may even say that, to the last, this sort of exhibition of power remained his principal weakness. When the critics, like those of *The Quarterly,* called him vulgar, it meant nothing except that the critics themselves were snobbish. There is nothing vulgar about drinking beer or describing the drinking of beer, or enjoying the humours of really humorous people who happen to black boots, like Sam Weller. But there is something just a little vulgar about professing to be a Universal Provider; a man who writes not only something that he wants to write, but anything that anybody wants to read. Anything in his work that can really be called failure is very largely due to this appetite for universal success. There is nothing wrong about the jester laughing at his own jokes; indeed they must be very poor jokes if even he cannot laugh at them. Dickens, in one of those endless private letters which are almost more entertaining than his published novels, describes himself as "a gentleman with rather long hair and no neckcloth, who writes and grins, as if he thought he was very funny indeed"; and so he was. But when he set out to prove that he was not only very funny, but very pathetic, very tragic, very powerful, he was not always enjoying the sense of power over his work, he was enjoying the sense of power over his audience. He was an admirable actor in private theatricals; and sometimes, unfortunately, they were public theatricals. And on this side of his character he had the proverbial itch of Toole to act Hamlet. When he was rendering the humours of the crowd, he was that rather rare thing, a real democrat. But when he was trying to command the tears and thrills of the crowd, he was something of a demagogue; that is, not one mingling with the crowd, but one trying to dazzle and to drive it. One of the ways in which he displayed this attribute, if not of vulgarity at least of vanity, was in his habit, from this time onwards, of running side by side in the same book about five different stories in about five different styles. It pleased the actor in him to show his versatility and his ease in turning from one to the other. He did not realize clearly enough that in some of the parts he was a first-rate actor and in some a second-rate and in some a fifth-rate actor. He did not remind himself that though he turned to each topic with equal ease, he did not turn to each with equal effect. But, whatever the disadvantages of the universal ambition, it definitely dates from the period of his next book. *Pickwick* has a prevailing tint of gaiety and *Oliver Twist* of gravity, not to say grimness; but with *Nicholas Nickleby* (1839) we have the new method, which is like a pattern of bright and dark stripes. The melodrama is if possible even more melodramatic than in *Oliver Twist;* but what there is of it is equally black and scowling. But the comedy or farce has already displayed the rapid ripening of his real genius in letters. There is no better company in all literature than the strolling company of Mr. Vincent Crummles; though it is to be hoped that in any convivial meeting of it, Miss Snevellicci will remember to invite her incomparable papa. Mr. Mantalini also is one of the great gifts of Dickens to the enduring happiness of humanity. For the rest, it is very difficult to take the serious part of the story seriously. There is precious little difference between the rant and claptrap of the Crummles plays, which Dickens makes fun of, and the rant and claptrap of Ralph Nickleby and Mulberry Hawke which Dickens gravely narrates to us. All that, however, was of little consequence either immediate or permanent. Dickens was not proving that he could write smooth and probable narratives, which many people could do. He was proving that he could create Mantalini and Snevellicci, which nobody could do.

Nevertheless, this pretence of providing for all tastes, which produced the serio-comic novel, is also the explanation of the next stage of his career. There runs or recurs throughout his whole life a certain ambition to preside over a more or less complex or many-sided publication: a large framework for many pictures; a system of tales within tales like the Arabian Nights or the tales of the Tabard. It is the ambition that he afterwards gratified by becoming the editor of two magazines, *Household Words* and *All the Year Round.*

But there is here something of a shadow of the original meaning of the word magazine, in the sense of a shop; and another hint of that excessive desire to keep a shop that sells everything. He had been for a time editor of something of the sort in *Bentley's Miscellany,* but the final form taken by this mild and genial megalomania (if we may so describe it) was the plan which Dickens formed immediately after the success of *Nicholas Nickleby*. The serial scheme was to be called, "Master Humphrey's Clock," and was to consist of different stories told by a group of friends. With the idea of making them the more friendly he turned some of them into old friends; reintroducing Mr. Pickwick and the two Wellers, though these characters were hardly at their best, the author's mind being already on other things. One of these things was a historical novel, perhaps conceived more in the romantic manner of Scott than the prosaic manner of Smollett, which Dickens generally followed. It was called *Barnaby Rudge* (1840) and the most interesting part of it perhaps is the business of the Gordon Riots; and the mob that has a madman for its mascot and a penny-dreadful prentice for its comic relief. But there is also a plot as complicated as, though rather clearer than, that of *Oliver Twist;* a plot that intensely interested the detective mind of Poe. *Barnaby Rudge,* however, is not so directly Dickensian as the romance that preceded or the romance that followed it. The second story, somewhat insecurely wedged into the framework of *Master Humphrey's Clock,* was *The Old Curiosity Shop* (1841), as the opening and some of the references in the story still vaguely attest. The public reception of this story very sharply illustrates what has been said about the double character of his success. On the one side was his true success as a craftsman carving figures of a certain type, generally gargoyles and grotesques. On the other side was his inferior success as a jack-of-all-trades tending only too much to be a cheapjack. As a matter of fact, *The Old Curiosity Shop* contains some of the most attractive and imaginative humour in all his humorous work; there is nothing better anywhere than Mr. Swiveller's imitation of the brigand or Mr. Brass's funeral oration over the dwarf. But in general gossip and association, everything else in the story is swallowed up in the lachrymose subject of Little Nell. There can be no doubt that this unfortunate female had a most unfortunate effect on Dickens's whole conception of his literary function. He was flattered because silly people wrote him letters imploring him not to let Little Nell die; and forgot how many sensible people there were, only hoping that the Marchioness would live for ever. Little Nell was better dead, but she was an unconscionable long time dying; and we cannot altogether acquit Dickens of keeping her lingering in agony as an exhibition of his power. It tended to fix him in that unfortunate attitude, of something between a showman and a magician, which explains almost all the real mistakes of his life.

About this time a very determining event interrupted his purely literary development, his first visit to America. It was destined to have, apart from any other results, a direct effect upon his next book, which was *Martin Chuzzlewit* (1844). There were, of course, many purely practical and personal elements in the criticism which he directed against the western democracy. An unjust copyright law, or one which he at any rate thought very unjust, had enabled Americans to pirate his most popular works; and it would seem that the people he met were, in their breezy way, but little inclined to apologize for the anomaly. But it would be very unjust to Dickens to deny that his sense and sensibility were alike irritated by some real divisions in the international relation. There were things in the American culture, or lack of culture, which he could not be expected to understand but which he might reasonably be expected to dislike. His English law-abiding liberalism would in any case have been startled by a certain streak of ferocity and persecution that there really is in the Americans; just as he might have recoiled from the same fierceness in the Irish or the Italians. But in the Americans it was also connected with something crude and incomplete in the society, and was not softened by tradition or romance. He was also both annoyed and amused at the American habit of uttering solemn idealistic soliloquies and of using rhetoric very rhetorically. But all these impressions are important chiefly as they changed the course of his next important narrative; and illustrated a certain condition or defect of his whole narrative method.

All these early books of Dickens, from Pickwick onward, appeared, it must always be remembered, serially and in separate parts. They were anticipated eagerly like bulletins; and they were often written up to time almost as hastily as newspaper reports. One effect of this method was that it encouraged the novelist in a sort of opportunism and something of a hand to mouth habit of work. And a character that always belonged, in varying degrees, to his novels is first and most sharply illustrated in *Martin Chuzzlewit*. The earlier numbers, though they contained the two superb caricatures called Pecksniff and Mrs. Gamp, had not for some reason been so popular as the caricatures called Pickwick and Miss Squeers. Dickens was already beginning to show something of that feverish fatigue which was the natural reaction of his fervid industry. He feared that the public was bored with the book; he became perhaps subconsciously a little bored with it himself. He conceived the bold idea of breaking the story in the middle and putting in a purple patch woven from his wild memories of the Yankees. It was completely successful, in the comedy sense; but it is worth noting that Dickens did something curiously Dickensian in thus suddenly sending Martin Chuzzlewit across the sea to America. It is not easy to imagine Thackeray suddenly hurling Pendennis from Mayfair into the middle of Australia; or George Eliot dislodging Felix Holt and flinging him as far as the North Pole. The difference was partly the result of the Dickensian temper and partly of the method of publication. But it will be well to remember it: for there is more than one example of what looks like a positive change of plan in the Dickens stories, made more possible by this early habit of not producing the work of art as a whole. Some have suggested that the degeneration of Boffin was originally meant to be real, and his rather clumsy plot an afterthought: and the same idea has figured in the reconstructions of *Edwin Drood*.

At this point there is a break in the life of Dickens, in more ways than one. It is represented by his decision to live abroad for a time, chiefly on grounds of economy; the last lingering results of the relative failure of *Martin Chuzzlewit*. He took a villa in the neighbourhood of Genoa in 1844; and he and his family, already a fairly large one, settled down there with a certain air of finality that deserved for a time the name of exile. But it is curious to note that the literary work done there has something of the character of an interlude, and indeed of a rather incongruous interlude. For it was in that Italian landscape that he concentrated on a study so very domestic, insular and even cockney as *The Chimes* (1845); and industriously continued the series of short Christmas stories which had recently begun in the very London fog of *A Christmas Carol* (1843). Whatever be the merits or demerits of the *Christmas Carol,* it really is a carol; in the sense of being short and direct and having the same chorus throughout. The same is true in another way of *The Chimes;* and of most things that occupied him in his Italian home. He had not settled down to another long and important book; and it soon became apparent that he had not settled down at all. He returned to London, the landscape which for him was really the most romantic and even historic; and did something so ominously typical of the place and time as almost to seem like tempting Providence. He became the first editor of the *Daily News,* a paper started to maintain those Liberal, if not Radical opinions of which he always shared the confident outlook and the humane simplicity. He did not long remain attached to the editorial chair or even to the metropolis, for this was the most restless period in all his restless life. He immediately went back to Lausanne and immediately wanted to go back to London. It seems probable that this break in his social life corresponded to a break in his artistic life: which was in a sense just about to begin all over again and begin at the other end. He did indeed write one more full-size novel of the earlier type, *Dombey and Son* (1846–48); but it has very much the character of the winding up of an old business, like the winding up of the Dombey firm at the end of it. It is comic as the earlier books were comic, and no praise can be higher; it is conventional as the earlier plots were conventional, and never really pretended to be anything else; it contains a dying child upon the pattern of Little Nell; it contains a very amusing major much improved from the pattern of Mr. Dowler. But underneath all this easy repetition of the old dexterity and the old clumsiness the mind of the conjurer is already elsewhere. *Dombey and Son* was more successful in a business sense than *Martin Chuzzlewit;* though really less successful in many others. Dickens settled again in England in a more prosperous style; sent his son to Eton and, what was more sensational, took a rest. It was after a long holiday at Broadstairs, in easier circumstances more favourable to imaginative growth and a general change of view, that there appeared in 1849 an entirely new novel in an entirely new style.

There is all the difference between the life and adventures of David Copperfield and the life and adventures of Nicholas Nickleby, that there is between the life of Charles Dickens and the life of Amadis of Gaul. The latter is a good or bad romance; the former is a romantic biography, only the more realistic for being romantic. For romance is a very real part of life and perhaps the most real part of youth. Dickens had turned the telescope round or was looking through the other end of it; looking perhaps into a mirror, looking in any case out of a new window. It was life as he saw it, which was somewhat fantastically; but it was his own life as he knew it, and even as he had lived it. In other words, it is fanciful but it is not fictitious; because not merely invented in the manner of fiction. In Pickwick or Nickleby he had in a sense breathed fresh imaginative life into stock characters, but they were still stage characters; in the new style he may be extravagant, but he is not stagey. That vague glow of exaggeration and glamour which lies over all the opening chapters of *David Copperfield,* which dilates some figures and distorts others, is the genuine sentimentalism and suppressed passion of youth; it is no longer a convention or tradition of caricature. There are men like Steerforth and girls like Dora; they are not as boys see them; but boys do see them so. This passionate autobiography, though it stiffens into greater conventionality at the real period of passion, is really, in the dismally battered phrase, a human document. But something of the new spirit, more subtle and sympathetic but perhaps less purely creative, belongs to all the books written after this date. The next of the novels in point of time was *Bleak House* (1853), a satire chiefly directed against Chancery and the law's delay, but containing some brilliant satire on other things, as on the philanthropic fool whose eyes are in the ends of the earth. But the description of the feverish idleness of Rick has the new note of one for whom a well-meaning young man is no longer merely a "first walking gentleman." After a still more severe phase in *Hard Times* (1854) (historically important as the revolt of a Radical against the economic individualism which was originally identified with Radicalism) he continued the same tendency in *Little Dorrit* (1857), the tone of which is perhaps as sad as anything illustrated by Dickensian humours can be; broke off into an equally serious and more sensational experiment in historical romance in *The Tale of Two Cities* (1859), largely an effect of the influence of Carlyle; and finally reached what was perhaps the height of his new artistic method in a purely artistic sense. He never wrote anything better, considered as literature, than the first chapters of *Great Expectations* (1861). But there is, after all, something about Dickens that prevents the critic from being ever quite content with criticizing his work as literature. Something larger seems involved, which is not literature, but life; and yet the very opposite of a mere recorded way of living. And he who remembers Pickwick and Pecksniff, creatures like Puck or Pan, may sometimes wonder whether the work had not most life when it was least lifelike.

The stretch of stories following on *David Copperfield,* from 1850 onwards, fall into the framework of another of Dickens's editorial schemes; and this time a much more successful one. He began to edit *Household Words,* in which some, though not all of his later tales appeared; and continued to do so until he exchanged it in 1859 for another and similar periodical called *All the Year Round.* Just as we find him about this time induced at last to settle down finally in a comparatively comfortable editorial chair, so we find him at last settled more comfortably in a domicile that could really be called a home, when, returning at last to his beloved Rochester district on the great road of Kent, he set up his house at Gads hill. It is sad to realize that this material domestic settlement had followed on a moral unsettlement; and the separation of Dickens and his wife, by agreement (of which the little that needs saying has already been said) had already taken place in 1856. But indeed, even apart from that tragedy, it is typical of Dickens that his repose could never be taken as final. His life was destined to end in a whirlwind of an entirely new type of activity; which none the less never interrupted that creative work which was the indwelling excitement of all his days. He wrote one more complete novel, *Our Mutual Friend* (1864–65), and it is more complete than most. Indeed it is one of the best though not one of the most Dickensian of the Dickens novels. He then turned his restless talent to something in the nature of a detective story, more in the manner of his friend Wilkie Collins; the sort of story which begins by asking a question; in this case a question about the secret and the sequel of the fate of the hero, Edwin Drood. The question will never be answered; for it was cut short by the only thing that could be more dramatic than the death of the hero; the death of the author. Charles Dickens was dead.

He died very suddenly, dropping from his chair at the dinner-table, in the year 1870 at the comparatively early age of fifty-eight. A death so abrupt, and essentially so premature, could not but raise doubts about the wisdom of his impetuous industry and debates almost as varied as those round the secret of Edwin Drood. But without exaggerating any one of the elements that contributed to it, we may note that the very last phase of his life was a new phase; and was almost entirely filled with his new activity in giving public readings from his works. He had gone to America once more in the November of 1867, with this particular purpose; and his campaign of public speaking in this style was truly American in its scope and scale. If he had indeed been unjust to America as a writer, it is curious that he should have reached his final popularity and perhaps his final collapse, in a character so supremely American. Differences exist about how far he exaggerated the function or how far his biographer exaggerated the danger; but his own letters, ragged with insomnia and impatience, full of desperate fatigue and more desperate courage, are alone enough to show that he was playing a very dangerous game for a man approaching sixty. But it is certainly true, as is alleged on the other side, that this was nothing new in the general conduct of Dickens; that he had long ago begun burning the candle at both ends; and there have been few men, in the matter of natural endowments, with so great and glorious a candle to burn.

He was buried in the Poet's Corner of Westminster Abbey; and new and vulgar as many critics had called his work, he was far more of a poet than many who were buried there as poets. He left a will commending his soul to God, and to the mercy of Jesus Christ, and leaving his works to the judgment of posterity; and in both respects the action was symbolic and will remain significant in history. Intellectually limited as he was by the rather cheap and cheery negations of an age of commercial rationalism, he had never been a bitter secularist or anti-clerical; he was at heart traditional and was drawn much more towards Anglican than Puritan Christianity; and his greatest work may yet prove to be the perpetuation of the joyful mystery of Christmas. On the other side, he has suffered and may suffer again the changes in the mere fashions of criticism; but his work was creative, it added something to life; and it is hard to believe that something so added will ever be entirely taken away. The defects of his work are glaring; they hardly need to be detected; they need the less to be emphasized because, unfortunately, he always emphasized them himself. It may be a fault, it is certainly a fact, that he enjoyed writing his worst work as much as his best.

The charge of exaggeration is itself exaggerated. It is also, which is much more important, merely repeated mechanically, without any consideration of its true meaning. Dickens did exaggerate; but his exaggeration was purely Dickensian. In this sense his very vulgarity had the quality of distinction. Mere overstatement, to say that a tall man is ten feet high, to say that a frosty morning froze Niagara; this is something relatively easy to do, though sometimes very cleverly done, especially by Americans. But the distinction of Dickens can be stated even in the common charge against him. He is said to have turned men into monsters of humour or horror, whereas the men were really commonplace and conventional persons in shops and offices. If any critic depreciates the Dickensian method as mere overstatement, the answer is obvious: let him take some of these commonplace people and overstate them. He will soon discover that he has not the vaguest notion of what to overstate. He will soon realise that it is not a simple matter of mere exaggeration, in the sense of mere extension. It is not a matter of making a man a little taller or a morning a little colder; the challenge to imagination is not whether he can exaggerate, but whether he can find anything worth exaggerating. Now the genius of Dickens consisted in seeing in somebody, whom others might call merely prosaic, the germ of a sort of prose poem. There was in this or that man's attitude, or affectation, or habit of thought, something which only needed a touch of exaggeration to be a charming fantasy or a dramatic contradiction. The books of Dickens are in fact full of bores; of bores who do not bore us, merely because they did not bore him. We have all of us heard a hundred times the tiresome trick of public speakers, of asking themselves rhetorical questions which they do not want answered. Any of us might have heard a fat Dissenting minister doing it at a tea-party and thankfully forgotten all about him. But Dickens seized on the fallacy and turned it into a fantasy; into Mr. Chadband's demands to know why he could not fly, or his wild and beautiful apologue about the elephant and the eel. We talk of the power of drawing people out; and that is the nearest parallel to the power of Dickens. He drew reels and reels of highly coloured caricature out of an ordinary person, as dazzlingly as a conjurer draws reels and reels of highly coloured paper out of an ordinary hat. But if anybody thinks the conjuring-trick is easy to perform, let him try it with the next ordinary person he sees. The exaggeration is always the logical extension of something that really exists; but genius appears, first in seeing that it exists, and second in seeing that it will bear to be thus exaggerated. That is something totally different from giving a man a long nose; it is the delicate surgical separation or extension of a living nerve. It is carrying a ludicrous train of thought further than the actual thinker carries it; but it requires a little thinking. It is making fools more gloriously foolish than they can be in this vale of tears; and it is not every fool who can do it.

There were other reasons for the injustice in the particular case of Dickens. Though his characters often were caricatures, they were not such wild caricatures as was supposed by those who had never met such characters. And the critics had never met the characters; because the critics did not live in the common life of the English people; and Dickens did. England was a much more amusing and horrible place than it appeared to the sort of man who wrote reviews in *The Quarterly;* and, in spite of all scientific progress or social reform, it is still. The poverty and anarchy of Dickens's early life had stuffed his memory with strange things and people never to be discovered in Tennysonian country houses or even Thackerayan drawing-rooms. Poverty makes strange bedfellows, the same sort of bedfellows whom Mr. Pickwick fought for the recovery of his nightcap. In the vivid phrase, he did indeed live in Queer street and was acquainted with very queer fish. And it is something of an irony that his tragedy was the justification of his farce. He not only learnt in suffering what he taught in song, but what he rendered, so to speak, in a comic song.

It is also true, however, that he caught many of these queer fish because he liked fishing in such troubled waters. A good example of this combination of opportunity and eccentricity is to be found in his affection for travelling showmen and vagabond entertainments of all sorts, especially those that exhibited giants and dwarfs and such monstrosities. Some might see in this truth a sort of travesty of all his travesties. It would be easy to suggest a psychological theory, by which all his art tended to the antics of the abnormal; it would also be entirely false. It would be much truer to say that Dickens created so many wild and fantastic caricatures because he was himself commonplace. He never identifies himself with anything abnormal, in the more modern manner. In his travelling show, the Giant always falls far short of being a Superman. And though he was tempted only too easily to an obvious pathos, there was never anything particularly pathetic about his dwarfs. His fun is more robust; and even, in that sense, more callous. The truth is that Dickens's attitude to the abnormal has been misunderstood owing to the modern misunderstanding of the idea of the normal. He was in many ways a wild satirist, but still a satirist; and satire is founded on sanity. He had his real Cockney limitations. But his moderation was not a limitation but a liberty; for it allowed him to hit out in all directions. It was precisely because he had an ordinary and sensible view of life that he could measure the full madness both of Gradgrind's greed or Micawber's improvidence. It was because he was what we call commonplace that Dombey appeared to him so stiff or Jellaby so slovenly. In a later generation a real person often assumed such an unreal pose and lost the power of merely laughing at it; as, for example, when Oscar Wilde said seriously all that Skimpole had said absurdly. The Victorian commonsense was not a complete commonsense; and Dickens did suffer from having a narrower culture than Swift or Rabelais. But he did not suffer from being sensible; it was even more from his sense than his sensibility, it was from a sort of inspired irritation and impatience of good sense, that he was able to give us so radiant a fairyland of fools.

His literary work produced of course much more than a literary effect. He was the last great poet, in the true sense of maker, who made something for the people and was in the highest sense popular. He still gives his name, not to a literary clique, but to a league or fellowship numbering thousands all over the world. In this connection it is often noted that he achieved many things even considered as a practical political and social reformer. He let light into dark corners, like the dens of dirt and brutality often called schools, especially in Yorkshire; he probably had much to do with making the professional nurse a duller but more reliable person than Mrs. Gamp; it is likely enough that his vivid descriptions, assisted by the whole trend of the time, hastened the extinction of ordinary imprisonment for debt and clarified much of the original chaos of Chancery. But precisely because this has often been said, it will be well not to say it too often. It has the effect of making his satire appear much more superficial and utilitarian than it really was; for the great satirist is concerned with things not so easily destroyed. We do more honour to Dickens in noting the evils he did not destroy than those he did. The eager worship of a man merely wealthy, however dull and trivial, which appears in the affair of Merdle, has by no means disappeared from our own more recent affairs. The pompous old Barnacle and the agreeable young Barnacle are still almost as much alive as in Dickens's day. The sweeping away of a genuine gentry, in the person of Mr. Twemlow, on the tide of a new plutocracy, represented by Mr. Veneering, has gone much further than in Dickens's day. But this makes Dickens's satire the more rather than the less valuable to posterity. The other mood, which pictures all such abuses as things of the past, tends not to reform but only too much to repose; and to the perpetuation of a rather snobbish and paltry version of the Dickensian tradition. In that spirit we may hear to this day a Stiltstalking telling the House of Commons that Stiltstalkings have perished before the march of progress; or in the law courts a Buzfuz quoting Buzfuz and jeering at himself as an instinct monster.

The future of the fame of Dickens is no part of the Dickens record and a very dubious part of the Dickens criticism. Some have suggested that his glory will fade as new fashions succeed those he satirized; others have said, at least equally reasonably, that the difference itself fades when all the fashions have grown old; and that Aristophanes and Cervantes have outlived their descendants as well as their contemporaries. But there can be no question of the importance of Dickens as a human event in history; a sort of conflagration and transfiguration in the very heart of what is called the conventional Victorian era; a naked flame of mere natural genius, breaking out in a man without culture, without tradition, without help from historic religions or philosophies or from the great foreign schools; and revealing a light that never was on sea or land, if only in the long fantastic shadows that it threw from common things.

MARIE CURIE

ON

Radium

Marie Skłowdowska Curie (1867–1934), the Polish-born chemist and physicist, working with her husband, Pierre, discovered polonium and radium, thus effectively raising the curtain on radiation. For their work they received the Nobel Prize for physics in 1903, and she alone won it again for chemistry in 1911. Modestly, and in the third person, she later described her momentous discovery in the Britannica, *13th edition (a Supplement to the 11th and 12th; 1926). (B.L.F.)*

In the year 1896 H. Becquerel discovered that uranium emits spontaneously a radiation that produces an impression on a photographic plate through a sheet of black paper, and ionises the air. Mme. P. Curie proved that this property, later called *radioactivity,* is characteristic of the atom of uranium and is possessed also by thorium. But she found that uranium minerals were much more active than could be predicted from their uranium content. By the hypothesis of the existence of a very radioactive unknown substance present in very small quantity, she undertook, with Pierre Curie, research for this substance in the uranium mineral called pitchblende.

The method they used in that work was entirely new; the result of the separations made by the ordinary process of chemical analysis was controlled by tests of the *activity* of every fraction; the activity was measured quantitatively by the current produced by the substance when placed in a special "ionisation chamber." Thus concentration of the radioactive property was traced in two fractions of the treatment, the fraction containing bismuth and the fraction containing barium.

In July 1898, P. Curie and Mme. Curie published the discovery of *polonium,* the element accompanying bismuth; in Dec. 1898, P. Curie, Mme. Curie and G. Bémont published the discovery of *radium.* Though the existence of these new substances was certain, they were present only in a very small proportion in the products obtained at that time; yet Demarçay was able to detect in the barium-radium mixture three new lines belonging to radium.

Only in 1902 did Mme. Curie succeed in preparing the first decigram of pure radium salt and made a determination of its atomic weight. The separation of barium was made by a process of fractional crystallisation. The work proved exceedingly difficult in practice on account of the great quantities of material that had to be treated. Later Mme. Curie made a new determination of its atomic weight and prepared metallic radium.

The new method used by P. Curie and Mme. Curie for the discovery of polonium and radium—chemical analysis controlled by measurements of radioactivity—has become fundamental for the chemistry of radioelements; it has served since for the discovery of many other radioactive substances. The discovery of radium and the preparation of the pure element has had very great importance in laying the basis of the new science of radioactivity. The identification of its spectrum and the determination of its atomic weight have been decisive facts for convincing chemists of the reality of the new elements.

CECIL B. DEMILLE

ON

The Movies

The 14th edition (1929) substantially enlarged the treatment given to the movies. In a new omnibus article, none other than Cecil B. DeMille wrote on acting and directing. Some extracts follow: (B.L.F.)

Acting. The element of acting is obviously of vital importance to the value of the photoplay, and it is an element which comes most closely under the director's control. He not only chooses his cast with great care that each part is suited to the actor, but he has much to do with the actor's performance. He controls his actors as the conductor controls the instruments of his orchestra. His function is not to teach acting any more than the conductor's is to teach his musicians how to play their instruments. But he must co-ordinate character conceptions so that each may stand in relation to the other as the story's true development demands. There is constant temptation to let an interesting character become too important for the proper story value of the moment, to over-emphasize a part in its relation to the whole. Careful contrasting of types, balancing a cast, harmonizing and moulding the conception of his characters until each is perfectly adjusted to the dramatic mechanism of which it is a part, are among his most delicate and most important duties. In his relation to the actor, the director must study the individual personality and method of each player and, if he is wise, he fits the part to the actor as much as he fits the actor to the part; he must, to some extent, vary his method to suit the need of each actor, if he is to attain the greatest result of which the actor is capable.

Technique. In general, the director faces this problem: to perfect each moment of the story separately and then to combine these bits into a smoothly flowing drama in which every moment will bear its proper relation to every other moment. In this connection, the question of *tempo* becomes most important, for the *crescendo* and *diminuendo* of drama are partly achieved through the varying *tempi* of successive scenes. Here again, the analogy of the motion picture to the symphony is close. But the director is powerless to control the speed at which the picture is projected in the theatre, and his carefully done work is frequently hurt by being run so fast as to lose all semblance of human life. . . .

As the picture progresses it is assembled in a rough cut which corresponds to the first draft of a play. Every scene and incident is in this first assembly, which almost invariably runs from twice to four times the length of the finished product. But in studying this rough assembly the director gets the "feel" of his picture; he senses its length and *tempo* and, frequently, changes his idea of its relative values. He guides himself accordingly in that part of the picture still to be made; he sees that certain incidents are less effective in their context than they felt when they were being made; that others are capable of further development than the first outline indicated; and so, sometimes groping his way, sometimes with true inspirational vision he finishes the "shooting" of the picture.

Then follows the task of editing the film; of reducing 30 reels to ten; of seeing the picture for the first time concretely, as a whole; of studying the new values which inevitably appear and, frequently, of compensating for values which seem to have disappeared. In the process of shortening the film captions must be rewritten, some left out as unnecessary, others put in where action has been so changed in the cutting that it is not sufficiently clear in pantomime alone. The importance of the cutting-room can hardly be overstated; it is here that the director selects and proportions the elements of his picture until its final form is achieved.

In the last analysis the director is a story-teller. His must be the art of combining the arts of others into one creation, and he must balance the values contributed by those other arts so that none of them is out of proportion to the true symmetry of the whole. He may not have conceived the story first, but he has to make it part of himself before he can put it on the screen; he may not have written it, but it is he who tells it; and upon the force, the clearness and the art of his telling depends the value of the work.

THOMAS DE QUINCEY

ON

Samuel Taylor Coleridge

Thomas De Quincey (1785–1859) wrote copiously for Britannica. *Indeed, some of his finest work may be found in that unlikely repository. In this article on Coleridge, the author of* Confessions of an English Opium-Eater *celebrates a writer close to the taste of his own romantic period. This terminal excerpt is from the 8th edition (1852–1860).*

The intellect of Coleridge is to be estimated rather by that of which it was capable, which it contemplated, and which it suggested, than by that which it achieved. Thrown upon life, poor and unsupported except by the benevolence of private friends, the inspired "charity boy," in his mission as the Apostle of Ideas, had a severe contest to fight. The friend of no party, he was obnoxious to all. Coleridge's bark sailed between the Scylla and Charybdis of the Edinburgh and Quarterly Reviews. It is to his credit, and to that of Southey and Wordsworth, that, in the face of a hostile age, they vindicated the freedom of poetical, political, and philosophical conscience; that, like the Scottish baron of old, they did "bide their time;" for all of them have left on the age that is succeeding an impress that will not soon be effaced. The literary fortitude of Coleridge under the continually-expressed conviction of the unpopularity of his writings is admirable. What would he not have achieved if this impassible fortitude had been animated by the aggressive vigour of industry and action so necessary in all who promulgate systems! The whole labours of Coleridge present the appearance of an unfinished city: the outline of the streets exhibits only how splendid they might have been; the basement of a pillar shows how gorgeous might have been its capital. A small, compact, complete beauty of poesy or of thought, pains us with the reflection that it stands surrounded by mere fragments of a similar promise. His works resemble a Californian valley, out of which may be dug in hundreds solid lumps of priceless gold from among materials useless or inappreciable. Besides the absence of a resolute will, another defect in the structure of Coleridge's mind was want of exactness. He had no capacity, he confesses himself, in the retention of facts: his mind was at home in the outline of generic ideas. Hence, while it could frequently chalk that outline with astonishing sagacity and philosophical accuracy, when it descended into the natural history of fact it frequently is found in "wandering mazes lost." This feature of the poet's intellect, in relation to theology; is illustrated with great clearness by the Rev. N. Porter in the American "Bibliotheca Sacra" (Vol. iv. No. 13). At an early period of his university career he lamented his distaste for the study of mathematics. Demonstrative and exact science lay beyond the dominion of his will; his was the logic of passion and imagination, as well as of the schools. His discussions often indicate this complexion of his reason. His own statement of his feelings in groping for religious truth through thorny regions of thought is, that "his head was with Spinosa and Leibnitz, while his heart was with Paul and John." The transcendental philosophy of Germany, acting on a mind of this semi-romantic temperament in inquiry, produced results resembling those of, as it were, metaphysical opium-eating. His metaphysical writings, encumbered with terminology, and algebraic symbols, stretching out into vast impalpable shadows, are frequently ungraspable as Ixion's cloud. And the haughty or embarrassed pretence (at the conclusion of vol. i. Biog. Lit., edit. 1817) that the age was unripe for the appreciation of his philosophical teachings, and his proud "Intelligibilia non intellectum adfero," are unworthy of a literary patriot, who should, for the objects of his mission, "make himself all things unto all men," and whose bread, if he had it to give, "cast upon the waters, would be found after many days." The bread he has left has been found, and to good purpose. His reputation has risen throughout Great Britain; and America, which is the empiric of all principles evolved by European physics or philosophy, has had her poetry, her philosophy, and even her theology, deeply tinctured by Coleridge.

With his ardent benevolence and desire for the moral and intellectual elevation of humanity, was mingled much of a species of academic contempt for the myriads of God's immortal and intelligent creatures, commonly characterized as "the masses." With the fear of the French revolution before him, he seems to have viewed them as "dogs of war," with innate tendencies to turn upon and rend society, especially when society deigned to cast before them her pearls of instruction and philosophy. He seems to have deemed that they should be nourished with food convenient not so much for themselves as for the peace and prosperity of the "clerisy" and "special state" whom he appoints their overseers; that an episcopal crook and an act of Parliament are the keys to the whole duty of man as a unit in the "masses;" that scholarship and philosophy walk in silver slippers in a higher sphere, and that learning is degraded when it is popularized. "From a philosophical populace, good Lord deliver us," is, if we remember rightly, one of his expressions of this contempt. If he wrote only for philosophers, who can wonder that he should complain of a somewhat unappreciating audience? . . .

Coleridge's whole mind was imbued with the love of truth and of beauty; for truth he wandered through the mazes of all philosophy, and wherever he found her, he grappled her to his soul with hooks of steel. When an extended horizon of Christianity enabled him to see the real position of his Socinian opinions, he embraced unchangeably with his whole heart "the truth as it is in Jesus." The very obscurities of Coleridge are "dark with excessive bright;" from his intense feeling of the beautiful, they are "golden mists" that rise from the morning of a pure heart; or they are lucid seas whose very depth prevents the eye from penetrating its extent. His prose style is disfigured by turgidity, and the affected use of words. His written humour is ponderous and unwieldy.

He was capable of immense services to poetry; but in this, as in other spheres of labour, he lived on the future; and Coleridge's future was a bad bank on which to draw; its bills were perpetually dishonoured. The conspicuous features of his poetry are its exquisite and original melody of versification, whose very sound chains the ear and soul; the harmonious grouping and skilful colouring of his pictures; statuesqueness and purity of taste in his living figures, and truth, in luxuriance or in simplicity, in majesty or in smallness, in his descriptions of nature. In sentiment, he opens with charming artlessness his own bosom in sorrow and in joy; this, it may be remarked, is a feature characteristic of the poetry of our own age above all that have preceded. There exists in general a decided contrast between the simplicity and lucidness of Coleridge's poetical style of expression, and the involved cloud-like fashion of his prose. Apart from his German translations and his dramas, there are few compositions of any extent complete in the works of Coleridge. "Christabel" is a fragment—a beauteous strain creeping in the ear, mysterious yet enrapturing as a celestial melody; but the import of whose language we scarcely comprehend, while we feel its sweetness. Capriciously it ceases in a moment, and leaves us in the position of Ariel's admirers in the tune played by the picture of nobody. The "Ancient Mariner" is, apart from certain defects in machinery, a composition the stature of whose idea "reaches the sky," and stretches its arms into other worlds; but it vanishes from the reader's grasp in a huddled conclusion—a moral utterly partial, like that of "Christabel," when viewed in reference to the piece as a whole. "Cain," the promise of a Titanic birth, and "Kubla Khan," a literal dream of oriental glory, withered in the blight of an unexecuting will. But how exquisite in their completeness are the "Hymn to Mont Blanc" (though, by the bye, this is one of the accused pieces), "Love," the "Odes," and many lesser jewels! He often expends his genius on trifles; and, even in his greater efforts, it is to be regretted that his idealism has placed much of his poetry beyond popular relish or sympathy. His dramatic pieces, like most modern efforts of this class, exhibit rather scenery, poetry, and sentiment, than character; but the surviving fragments of this dramatic criticism show that they need only completeness to be sufficient alone for his immortality. The best tribute to Coleridge's genius consists in its admiration—nay, imitation—by the highest minds among his contemporaries, Byron and Scott, while all must perceive that his melody and his phraseology still murmur in the finest strains that emanate from the present age.

W. E. B. Du BOIS

ON

Negro Literature

The 13th edition (1926) article on this subject, so titled in that period, was written by W. E. B. Du Bois (1868–1963). We publish his all-too-brief article in order to underline the enormous contribution made to American literature since Du Bois wrote the last two sentences of the subjoined.

The plight of the Africans brought to America during the slave trade and of their descendants is one of the most dramatic in human history. That there should arise a literature written by black Americans touching their own situation depended on many things—their education, their economic condition, their growth in group consciousness. Before 1910, the books written by American Negroes were with some exceptions either a part of the general American literature or individual voices of Americans of Negro descent.

There began, however, about 1910 something that can be called a renaissance. It came because of oppression, because the spread of education made self-expression possible, and because a larger number of these 10,000,000 people were raising themselves above the lowest poverty. The first sign of this renaissance was naturally a continuation of the self-revelations current during the abolition controversy in the slave narratives, of which Frederick Douglass's *Life and Times* (1892) was the most striking and Booker Washington's *Up from*

Slavery, published in 1901, the last great example. Since 1910, other autobiographies have followed. In these later stories there is, of course, less of the older spontaneity, little of adventure and more self-consciousness. John R. Lynch published his revealing *Facts of Reconstruction* in 1913. Alexander Walters (a black bishop), R. R. Moton (the successor of Booker Washington) and many others published autobiographies.

A more careful consideration of the Negro's social problems has characterised the period 1910–26. This is perhaps best illustrated by the three or four volumes of essays published by Kelley Miller, the trenchant work of William Pickens, W. E. B. DuBois's *Darkwater* (1920), and J. A. Rogers's *From Superman to Man* (1917), and especially by the files of the growing weekly Negro press. These general considerations have led to a number of scientific studies. Foremost among these are the series of Atlanta University studies covering 13 years and touching such matters as *Efforts for Social Betterment among Negro Americans* (1910); *The College-Bred Negro American* (1911); *The Common School and the Negro American* (1912); *The Negro American Artisan* (1913); *Morals and Manners among Negro Americans* (1915). There came also as a result of the Chicago riot the careful study of *The Negro in Chicago* (Illinois-Chicago Commission on Race Relations, 1922). The Tuskegee *Negro Year Book,* edited by M. N. Work annually since 1915, and the work of Dr. George E. Haynes have been along the same lines.

More striking work, however, begins with the rewriting of American history from the Negro point of view. The doyen of this effort since 1910 has been Carter G. Woodson, whose work has been prolific and painstaking. Beginning with 1916 he has published a considerable number of books, including the *Journal of Negro History,* 10 large volumes filled with documents, essays and research. Next comes Benjamin G. Brawley with his *Short History of the American Negro* (1913 and 1919), *Social History of the American Negro* (1921) and his study of *The Negro in Literature and Art in the United States* (1921). With these may be noted Steward's *The Haitian Revolution, 1791 to 1804* (1914), Emmett J. Scott's *The American Negro in the World War* (1919) and *The Gift of Black Folk: the Negroes in the Making of America* (1924), by W. E. B. DuBois, published by the Knights of Columbus.

But not in propaganda, science nor history has the essence of the renaissance shown itself. Rather the true renaissance has been a matter of the spirit and has shown itself among the poets as well as among the novelists and dramatists. In poetry, there are a dozen or more writers whose output has been small but significant. George McClellan, with his somewhat didactic and conventional verse, forms the link between past and present. Then comes James Weldon Johnson, Claude McKay, Leslie Hill, Joseph Cotter, Jr., Georgia Douglas Johnson, Countée Cullen and Langston Hughes, besides a half-dozen others. It is notable that already several critical anthologies (by James Weldon Johnson, Robert Kerlin, White and Jackson) have appeared. William Stanley Braithwaite has appeared as a widely read critic of poetry. The development in fiction is still newer and includes some earlier attempts like *The Quest of the Silver Fleece* by W. E. B. DuBois (1911) and James Weldon Johnson's *Autobiography of an Ex-Coloured Man* (1912), and newer and more significant work by Rudolph Fisher, Jessie Fauset, Walter White and Jean Toomer. In the drama, Willis Richardson and one or two others have been writing effectively, while in the explanation and collection of Negro music and folk-lore we have J. Rosamond Johnson, T. W. Talley and J. W. Cotter.

Perhaps the extent of this renaissance of Negro literature can be summed up in two works. One is the 15 volumes of *The Crisis* magazine, which began publication in Nov. 1910, and has since been a compendium of occurrences, thoughts and expression among American Negroes. Most of the newer Negro writers found first publication in its pages. The second is the book called *The New Negro,* published in 1925 and edited by Alain Locke, in which some 30 contemporary Negro writers express the spirit of their day. All these things are beginnings rather than fulfilments, but they are significant beginnings. They mean much for the future.

ALBERT EINSTEIN

ON

Space-Time

The article "Relativity" in the 13th edition (1926) was written by the British mathematician and physicist James (later Sir James) H. Jeans, well known for his ability to write about difficult scientific topics for the intelligent lay audience. Einstein's writing, however, was another matter, as this article on the basic logical and mathematical propositions underlying the theory of relativity clearly shows. (R. McH.)

This article, by our century's greatest name, Albert Einstein (1879–1955), also appeared in the 13th edition. Though parts of it will be transparent only to readers with considerable mathematical training, we are printing the whole. It is a landmark, a masterpiece of reflection on two of the most elusive and important concepts in the entire history of ideas. While we may not understand all of it, any intelligent reader willing to do a little work will come away with his or her mind enlarged and in motion. (It is not a sin to skip some of the equations.)

All our thoughts and concepts are called up by sense-experiences and have a meaning only in reference to these sense-experiences. On the other hand, however, they are products of the spontaneous activity of our minds; they are thus in no wise logical consequences of the contents of these sense-experiences. If, therefore, we wish to grasp the essence of a complex of abstract notions we must for the one part investigate the mutual relationships between the concepts and the assertions made about them; for the other, we must investigate how they are related to the experiences.

So far as the way is concerned in which concepts are connected with one another and with the experiences there is no difference of principle between the concept-systems of science and those of daily life. The concept-systems of science have grown out of those of daily life and have been modified and completed according to the objects and purposes of the science in question.

The more universal a concept is the more frequently it enters into our thinking; and the more indirect its relation to sense-experience, the more difficult it is for us to comprehend its meaning; this is particularly the case with pre-scientific concepts that we have been accustomed to use since childhood. Consider the concepts referred to in the words "where," "when," "why," "being," to the elucidation of which innumerable volumes of philosophy have been devoted. We fare no better in our speculations than a fish which should strive to become clear as to what is water.

Space

In the present article we are concerned with the meaning of "where," that is, of space. It appears that there is no quality contained in our individual primitive sense-experiences that may be designated as spatial. Rather, what is spatial appears to be a sort of order of the material objects of experience. The concept "material object" must therefore be available if concepts concerning space are to be possible. It is the logically primary concept. This is easily seen if we analyse the spatial concepts for example, "next to," "touch," and so forth, that is, if we strive to become aware of their equivalents in experience. The concept "object" is a means of taking into account the persistence in time or the continuity, respectively, of certain groups of experience-complexes. The existence of objects is thus of a conceptual nature, and the meaning of the concepts of objects depends wholly on their being connected (intuitively) with groups of elementary sense-experiences. This connection is the basis of the illusion which makes primitive experience appear to inform us directly about the relation of material bodies (which exist, after all, only in so far as they are thought).

In the sense thus indicated we have (the indirect) experience of the contact of two bodies. We need do no more than call attention to this, as we gain nothing for our present purpose by singling out the individual experiences to which this assertion alludes. Many bodies can be brought into permanent contact with one another in manifold ways. We speak in this sense of the position-relationships of bodies (*Lagenbeziehungen*). The general laws of such position-relationships are essentially the concern of geometry. This holds, at least, if we do not wish to restrict ourselves to regarding the propositions that occur in this branch of knowledge merely as relationships between empty words that have been set up according to certain principles.

Pre-scientific thought. Now, what is the meaning of the concept "space" which we also encounter in pre-scientific thought? The concept of space in pre-scientific thought is characterised by the sentence: "we can think away things but not the space which they occupy." It is as if, without having had experience of any sort, we had a concept, nay even a presentation, of space and as if we ordered our sense-experiences with the help of this concept, present *a priori*. On the other hand, space appears as a physical reality, as a thing which exists independently of our thought, like material objects. Under the influence of this view of space the fundamental concepts of geometry: the point, the straight line, the plane, were even regarded as having a self-evident character. The fundamental principles that deal with these configurations were regarded as being necessarily valid and as having at the same time an objective content. No scruples were felt about ascribing an objective meaning to such statements as "three empirically given bodies (practically infinitely small) lie on one straight line," without demanding a physical definition for such an assertion. This blind faith in evidence and in the immediately real meaning of the concepts and propositions of geometry became uncertain only after non-Euclidean geometry had been introduced.

Reference to the earth. If we start from the view that all spatial concepts are related to contact-experiences of solid bodies, it is easy to understand how the concept "space" originated, namely, how a thing independent of bodies and yet embodying their position-possibilities (*Lagerungsmöglichkeiten*) was posited. If we have a system of bodies in contact and at rest relatively to one another, some can be replaced by others. This property of allowing substitution is interpreted as "available space." Space denotes the property in virtue of which rigid bodies can occupy different positions. The view that space is something with a unity of its own is perhaps due to the circumstance that in pre-scientific thought all positions of bodies were referred to one body (reference body), namely the earth. In scientific thought the earth is represented by the co-ordinate system. The assertion that it would be possible to place an unlimited number of bodies next to one another denotes that space is infinite. In pre-scientific thought the concepts "space" and "time" and "body of reference" are scarcely differentiated at all. A place or point in space is always taken to mean a material point on a body of reference.

Euclidean geometry. If we consider Euclidean geometry we clearly discern that it refers to the laws regulating the positions of rigid bodies. It turns to account the ingenious thought of tracing back all relations concerning bodies and their relative positions to the very simple concept "distance" (*Strecke*). Distance denotes a rigid body on which two material points (marks) have been specified. The concept of the equality of distances (and angles) refers to experiments involving coincidences; the same remarks apply to the theorems on congruence. Now, Euclidean geometry, in the form in which it has been handed down to us from Euclid, uses the fundamental concepts "straight line" and "plane" which do not appear to correspond, or at any rate, not so directly, with experiences concerning the position of rigid bodies. On this it must be remarked that the concept of the straight line may be reduced to that of the distance.[1] Moreover, geometricians were less concerned with bringing out the

[1] A hint of this is contained in the theorem: "the straight line is the shortest connection between two points." This theorem served well as a definition of the straight line, although the definition played no part in the logical texture of the deductions.

relation of their fundamental concepts to experience than with deducing logically the geometrical propositions from a few axioms enunciated at the outset.

Let us outline briefly how perhaps the basis of Euclidean geometry may be gained from the concept of distance.

We start from the equality of distances (axiom of the equality of distances). Suppose that of two unequal distances one is always greater than the other. The same axioms are to hold for the inequality of distances as hold for the inequality of numbers.

Three distances $\overline{AB^1}$, $\overline{BC^1}$, $\overline{CA^1}$ may, if $\overline{CA^1}$ be suitably chosen, have their marks BB^1, CC^1, AA^1 superposed on one another in such a way that a triangle ABC results. The distance CA^1 has an upper limit for which this construction is still just possible. The points A, (BB′) and C then lie in a "straight line" (definition). This leads to the concepts: producing a distance by an amount equal to itself; dividing a distance into equal parts; expressing a distance in terms of a number by means of a measuring-rod (definition of the space-interval between two points).

When the concept of the interval between two points or the length of a distance has been gained in this way we require only the following axiom (Pythagoras' theorem) in order to arrive at Euclidean geometry analytically.

To every point of space (body of reference) three numbers (co-ordinates) x, y, z may be assigned—and conversely—in such a way that for each pair of points A $(x_1, y_1, z_1,)$ and B (x_2, y_2, z_2) the theorem holds:

$$\text{measure-number } \overline{AB} = \sqrt{(x_2 - x_1)^2 + (y_2 - y_1)^2 + (z_2 - z_1)^2}$$

All further concepts and propositions of Euclidean geometry can then be built up purely logically on this basis, in particular also the propositions about the straight line and the plane.

These remarks are not, of course, intended to replace the strictly axiomatic construction of Euclidean geometry. We merely wish to indicate plausibly how all conceptions of geometry may be traced back to that of distance. We might equally well have epitomised the whole basis of Euclidean geometry in the last theorem above. The relation to the foundations of experience would then be furnished by means of a supplementary theorem.

The co-ordinate may and *must* be chosen so that two pairs of points separated by equal intervals, as calculated by the help of Pythagoras' theorem,
369 may be made to coincide with one and the same suitably chosen distance (on a solid).

The concepts and propositions of Euclidean geometry may be derived from Pythagoras' proposition without the introduction of rigid bodies; but these concepts and propositions would not then have contents that could be tested. They are not "true" propositions but only logically correct propositions of purely formal content.

Difficulties. A serious difficulty is encountered in the above represented interpretation of geometry in that the rigid body of experience does not correspond *exactly* with the geometrical body. In stating this I am thinking less of the fact that there are no absolutely definite marks than that temperature, pressure and other circumstances modify the laws relating to position. It is also to be recollected that the structural constituents of matter (such as atom and electron, *q.v.*) assumed by physics are not in principle commensurate with rigid bodies, but that nevertheless the concepts of geometry are applied to them and to their parts. For this reason consistent thinkers have been disinclined to allow real contents of facts (*reale Tatsachenbestände*) to correspond to geometry alone. They considered it preferable to allow the content of experience (*Erfahrungsbestände*) to correspond to geometry and physics conjointly.

This view is certainly less open to attack than the one represented above; as opposed to the atomic theory it is the only one that can be consistently carried through. Nevertheless, in the opinion of the author it would not be advisable to give up the first view, from which geometry derives its origin. This connection is essentially founded on the belief that the ideal rigid body is an abstraction that is well rooted in the laws of nature.

Foundations of geometry. We come now to the question: what is *a priori* certain or necessary, respectively in geometry (doctrine of space) or its foundations? Formerly we thought everything—yes, everything; nowadays we think—nothing. Already the distance-concept is logically arbitrary; there need be no things that correspond to it, even approximately. Something similar may be said of the concepts straight line, plane, of three-dimensionality and of the validity of Pythagoras' theorem. Nay, even the continuum-doctrine is in no wise given with the nature of human thought, so that from the epistomological point of view no greater authority attaches to the purely topological relations than to the others.

Earlier physical concepts. We have yet to deal with those modifications in the space-concept, which have accompanied the advent of the theory of relativity. For this purpose we must consider the space-concept of the earlier physics from a point of view different from that above. If we apply the theorem of Pythagoras to infinitely near points, it reads

$$\bar{d}us^2 = dx^2 + dy^2 + dz^2$$

where $\bar{d}s$ denotes the measurable interval between them. For an empirically-given ds the co-ordinate system is not yet fully determined for every combination of points by this equation. Besides being translated, a co-ordinate system may also be rotated.[2] This signifies analytically: the relations of Euclidean geometry are covariant with respect to linear orthogonal transformations of the co-ordinates.

In applying Euclidean geometry to pre-relativistic mechanics a further indeterminateness enters through the choice of the co-ordinate system: the state of motion of the co-ordinate system is arbitrary to a certain degree, namely, in that substitutions of the co-ordinates of the form $x' = x - vt$

$$y' = y$$
$$z' = z$$

also appear possible. On the other hand, earlier mechanics did not allow co-ordinate systems to be applied of which the states of motion were different from those expressed in these equations. In this sense we speak of "inertial systems." In these favoured-inertial systems we are confronted with a new property of space so far as geometrical relations are concerned. Regarded more

[2] Change of direction of the co-ordinate axes while their orthogonality is preserved.

accurately, this is not a property of space alone but of the four-dimensional continuum consisting of time and space conjointly.

Appearance of time. At this point time enters explicitly into our discussion for the first time. In their applications space (place) and time always occur together. Every event that happens in the world is determined by the space-co-ordinates x, y, z, and the time-co-ordinate t. Thus the physical description was four-dimensional right from the beginning. But this four-dimensional continuum seemed to resolve itself into the three-dimensional continuum of space and the one-dimensional continuum of time. This apparent resolution owed its origin to the illusion that the meaning of the concept "simultaneity" is self-evident, and this illusion arises from the fact that we receive news of near events almost instantaneously owing to the agency of light.

This faith in the absolute significance of simultaneity was destroyed by the law regulating the propagation of light in empty space or, respectively, by the Maxwell-Lorentz electro-dynamics. Two infinitely near points can be connected by means of a light-signal if the relation

$$ds^2 = c^2dt^2 - dx^2 - dy^2 - dz^2 = 0$$

holds for them. It further follows that ds has a value which, for arbitrarily chosen infinitely near space-time points, is independent of the particular inertial system selected. In agreement with this we find that for passing from one inertial system to another, linear equations of transformation hold which do not in general leave the time-values of the events unchanged. It thus became manifest that the four-dimensional continuum of space cannot be split up into a time-continuum and a space-continuum except in an arbitrary way. This invariant quantity ds may be measured by means of measuring-rods and clocks.

Four dimensional geometry. On the invariant ds a four-dimensional geometry may be built up which is in a large measure analogous to Euclidean geometry in three dimensions. In this way physics becomes a sort of statics in a four-dimensional continuum. Apart from the difference in the number of dimensions the latter continuum is distinguished from that of Euclidean geometry in that ds^2 may be greater or less than zero. Corresponding to this we differentiate between time-like and space-like line-elements. The boundary between them is marked out by the element of the "light-cone" $ds^2 = 0$ which starts out from every point. If we consider only elements which belong to the same time-value, we have

$$-ds^2 = dx^2 + dy^2 + dz^2$$

These elements ds may have real counterparts in distances at rest and, as before, Euclidean geometry holds for these elements.

Effect of relativity, special and general. This is the modification which the doctrine of space and time has undergone through the restricted theory of relativity. The doctrine of space has been still further modified by the general theory of relativity, because this theory denies that the three-dimensional spatial section of the space-time continuum is Euclidean in character. Therefore it asserts that Euclidean geometry does not hold for the relative positions of bodies that are continuously in contact.

For the empirical law of the equality of inertial and gravitational mass led us to interpret the state of the continuum, in so far as it manifests itself with reference to a non-inertial system, as a gravitational field and to treat non-inertial systems as equivalent to inertial systems. Referred to such a system, which is connected with the inertial system by a non-linear transformation of the co-ordinates, the metrical invariant ds^2 assumes the general form:—

$$ds^2 = \sum_{\mu\nu} g_{\mu\nu} dx_\mu dx_\nu$$

where the $g_{\mu\nu}$'s are functions of the co-ordinates and where the sum is to be taken over the indices for all combinations 11, 12, . . . 44. The variability of the $g_{\mu\nu}$'s is equivalent to the existence of a gravitational field. If the gravitational field is sufficiently general it is not possible at all to find an inertial system, that is, a co-ordinate system with reference to which ds^2 may be expressed in the simple form given above:—

$$ds^2 = c^2dt^2 - dx^2 - dy^2 - dz^2$$

But in this case, too, there is in the infinitesimal neighbourhood of a space-time point a local system of reference for which the last-mentioned simple form for ds holds.

This state of the facts leads to a type of geometry which Riemann's genius created more than half a century before the advent of the general theory of relativity of which Riemann divined the high importance for physics.

Riemann's geometry. Riemann's geometry of an n-dimensional space bears the same relation to Euclidean geometry of an n-dimensional space as the general geometry of curved surfaces bears to the geometry of the plane. For the infinitesimal neighbourhood of a point on a curved surface there is a local co-ordinate system in which the distance ds between two infinitely near points is given by the equation

$$ds^2 = dx^2 + dy^2$$

For any arbitrary (Gaussian) co-ordinate system, however, an expression of the form

$$ds^2 = g_{11}dx^2 + 2g_{12}dx_1dx_2 + g_{22}dx_2{}^2$$

holds in a finite region of the curved surface. If the $g_{\mu\nu}$'s are given as functions .of x_1 and x_2 the surface is then fully determined geometrically. For from this formula we can calculate for every combination of two infinitely near points on the surface the length ds of the minute rod connecting them; and with the help of this formula all networks that can be constructed on the surface with these little rods can be calculated. In particular, the "curvature" at every point of the surface can be calculated; this is the quantity that expresses to what extent and in what way the laws regulating the positions of the minute rods in the immediate vicinity of the point under consideration deviate from those of the geometry of the plane.

This theory of surfaces by Gauss has been extended by Riemann to continua of any arbitrary number of dimensions and has thus paved the way for the general theory of relativity. For it was shown above that corresponding to two infinitely near space-time points there is a number ds which can be obtained by measurement with rigid measuring-rods and clocks (in the case of time-like elements, indeed, with a clock alone). This quantity occurs in the mathematical theory in place of the length of the minute rods in three-dimensional geometry. The curves for which $\int ds$ has stationary values determine the paths of material points and rays of light in the gravitational field, and the "curvature" of space is dependent on the matter distributed over space.

Just as in Euclidean geometry the space-concept refers to the position-possibilities of rigid bodies, so in the general theory of relativity the space-time-concept refers to the behaviour of rigid bodies and clocks. But the space-time-continuum differs from the space-continuum in that the laws regulating the behaviour of these objects (clocks and measuring-rods) depend on where they happen to be. The continuum (or the quantities that describe it) enters explicitly into the laws of nature, and conversely these properties of the continuum are determined by physical factors. The relations that connect space and time can no longer be kept distinct from physics proper.

Nothing certain is known of what the properties of the space-time-continuum may be as a whole. Through the general theory of relativity, however, the view that the continuum is infinite in its time-like extent but finite in its space-like extent has gained in probability.

Time

The physical time-concept answers to the time-concept of the extra-scientific mind. Now, the latter has its root in the time-order of the experiences of the individual, and this order we must accept as something primarily given.

I experience the moment "now," or, expressed more accurately, the present sense-experience (*Sinnen-Erlebnis*) combined with the recollection of (earlier) sense-experiences. That is why the sense-experiences seem to form a series, namely the time-series indicated by "earlier" and "later." The experience-series is thought of as a one-dimensional continuum. Experience-series can repeat themselves and can then be recognised. They can also be repeated inexactly, wherein some events are replaced by others without the character of the repetition becoming lost for us. In this way we form the time-concept as a one-dimensional frame which can be filled in by experiences in various ways. The same series of experiences answer to the same subjective time-intervals.

The transition from this "subjective" time (*Ich-Zeit*) to the time-concept of pre-scientific thought is connected with the formation of the idea that there is a real external world independent of the subject. In this sense the (objective) event is made to correspond with the subjective experience. In the same sense there is attributed to the "subjective" time of the experience a "time" of the corresponding "objective" event. In contrast with experiences external events and their order in time claim validity for all subjects.

This process of objectification would encounter no difficulties were the time-order of the experiences corresponding to a series of external events the same for all individuals. In the case of the immediate visual perceptions of our daily lives, this correspondence is exact. That is why the idea that there is an objective time-order became established to an extraordinary extent. In working out the idea of an objective world of external events in greater detail, it was found necessary to make events and experiences depend on each other in a more complicated way. This was at first done by means of rules and modes of thought instinctively gained, in which the conception of space plays a particularly prominent part. This process of refinement leads ultimately to natural science.

The measurement of time is effected by means of clocks. A clock is a thing which automatically passes in succession through a (practically) equal series of events (period). The number of periods (clock-time) elapsed serves as a measure of time. The meaning of this definition is at once clear if the event occurs in the immediate vicinity of the clock in space; for all observers then observe the same clock-time simultaneously with the event (by means of the eye) independently of their position. Until the theory of relativity was propounded it was assumed that the conception of simultaneity had an absolute objective meaning also for events separated in space.

This assumption was demolished by the discovery of the law of propagation of light. For if the velocity of light in empty space is to be a quantity that is independent of the choice (or, respectively, of the state of motion) of the inertial system to which it is referred, no absolute meaning can be assigned to the conception of the simultaneity of events that occur at points separated by a distance in space. Rather, a special time must be allocated to every inertial system. If no co-ordinate system (inertial system) is used as a basis of reference there is no sense in asserting that events at different points in space occur simultaneously. It is in consequence of this that space and time are welded together into a uniform four-dimensional continuum.

LOREN EISELEY

ON

Why We Are Here

Loren Eiseley (1907–1977), a well-known anthropologist, was a bit of an odd bird in the scientific community. He wrote poetry and, more to the point, was master of an eloquent, poetical prose style rather uncommon among the practitioners in his field. Two of his most moving books are The Immense Journey *(1957) and his autobiography,* All the Strange Hours *(1975). The following essay, titled "The Cosmic Orphan" and reprinted in its entirety, appears in the current 15th edition as the Introduction to Part Four: "Human Life."*

When I was a young lad of that indefinite but important age when one begins to ask, Who am I? Why am I here? What is the nature of my kind? What is growing up? What is the world? How long shall I live in it? Where shall I go? I found myself walking with a small companion over a high railroad trestle that spanned a stream, a country bridge, and a road. One could look fearfully down, between the ties, at the shallows and ripples in the shining water some 50 feet below. One was also doing a forbidden thing, against which our parents constantly warned. One must not be caught on the black bridge by a train. Something terrible might happen, a thing called death.

From the abutment of the bridge we gazed down upon the water and saw among the pebbles the shape of an animal we knew only from picture books—a turtle, a very large, dark mahogany-coloured turtle. We scrambled down the embankment to observe him more closely. From the little bridge a few feet above the stream, I saw that the turtle, whose beautiful markings shone in the afternoon sun, was not alive and that his flippers waved aimlessly in the rushing water. The reason for his death was plain. Not too long before we had come upon the trestle, someone engaged in idle practice with a repeating rifle had stitched a row of bullet holes across the turtle's carapace and sauntered on.

My father had once explained to me that it took a long time to make a big turtle, years really, in the sunlight and the water and the mud. I turned the ancient creature over and fingered the etched shell with its forlorn flippers flopping grotesquely. The question rose up unbidden. Why did the man have to kill something living that could never be replaced? I laid the turtle down in the water and gave it a little shove. It entered the current and began to drift away. "Let's go home," I said to my companion. From that moment I think I began to grow up.

"Papa," I said in the evening by the oil lamp in our kitchen. "Tell me how men got here." Papa paused. Like many fathers of that time, he was worn from long hours, he was not highly educated, but he had a beautiful resonant voice and he had been born on a frontier homestead. He knew the ritual way the Plains Indians opened a story.

"Son," he said, taking the pattern of another people for our own, "once there was a poor orphan." He said it in such a way that I sat down at his feet. "Once there was a poor orphan with no one to teach him either his way, or his manners. Sometimes animals helped him, sometimes supernatural beings. But above all, one thing was evident. Unlike other occupants of Earth he had to be helped. He did not know his place, he had to find it. Sometimes he was arrogant and had to learn humility, sometimes he was a coward and had to be taught bravery. Sometimes he did not understand his Mother Earth and suffered for it. The old ones who starved and sought visions on hilltops had known these things. They were all gone now and the magic had departed with them. The orphan was alone; he had to learn by himself; it was a hard school."

My father tousled my head; he gently touched my heart. "You will learn in time there is much pain here," he said. "Men will give it to you, time will give it to you, and you must learn to bear it all, not bear it alone, but be better for the wisdom that may come to you if you watch and listen and learn. Do not forget the turtle, nor the ways of men. They are all orphans and they go astray; they do wrong things. Try to see better."

"Yes, papa," I said, and that was how I believe I came to study men, not the men of written history but the ancestors beyond, beyond all writing, beyond time as we know it, beyond human form as it is known today. Papa was right when he told me men were orphans, eternal seekers. They had little in the way of instinct to instruct them, they had come a strange far road in the universe, passed more than one black, threatening bridge. There were even more to pass, and each one became more dangerous as our knowledge grew. Because man was truly an orphan and confined to no single way of life, he was, in essence, a prison breaker. But in ignorance his very knowledge sometimes led from one terrible prison to another. Was the final problem then, to escape himself, or, if not that, to reconcile his devastating intellect with his heart? All of the knowledge set down in great books directly or indirectly affects this problem. It is the problem of every man, for even the indifferent man is making, unknown to himself, his own callous judgment.

Long ago, however, in one of the Dead Sea Scrolls hidden in the Judaean Desert, an unknown scribe had written: "None there be, can rehearse the whole tale." That phrase, too, contains the warning that man is an orphan of uncertain beginnings and an indefinite ending. All that the archaeological and anthropological sciences can do is to place a somewhat flawed crystal before man and say: This is the way you came, these are your present dangers; somewhere, seen dimly beyond, lies your destiny. God help you, you are a cosmic orphan, a symbol-shifting magician, mostly immature and inattentive to your own dangers. Read, think, study, but do not expect this to save you without humility of heart. This the old ones knew long ago in the great deserts under the stars. This they sought to learn and pass on. It is the only hope of men.

What have we observed that might be buried as the Dead Sea Scrolls were buried for 2,000 years, and be broken out of a jar for human benefit, brief words that might be encompassed on a copper scroll or a ragged sheet of vellum? Only these thoughts, I think, we might reasonably set down as true, now and hereafter. For a long time, for many, many centuries, Western man believed in what we might call the existent world of nature; form as form was seen as constant in both animal and human guise. He believed in the instantaneous creation of his world by the Deity; he believed its duration to be very short, a stage upon which the short drama of a human fall from divine estate and a redemption was in progress.

Worldly time was a small parenthesis in eternity. Man lived with that belief, his cosmos small and man-centred. Then, beginning about 350 years ago, thoughts unventured upon since the time of the Greek philosophers began to enter the human consciousness. They may be summed up in Francis Bacon's dictum: "This is the foundation of all. We are not to imagine or suppose, but to *discover,* what nature does or may be made to do."

When in following years scientific experiment and observation became current, a vast change began to pass over Western thought. Man's conception of himself and his world began to alter beyond recall. " 'Tis all in pieces, all coherence gone," exclaimed the poet John Donne, Bacon's contemporary. The existing world was crumbling at the edges. It was cracking apart like an ill-nailed raft in a torrent—a torrent of incredible time. It was, in effect, a new nature comprising a past embedded in the present and a future yet to be.

First, Bacon discerned a *mundus alter,* another separate world that could be drawn out of nature by human intervention—the world that surrounds and troubles us today. Then, by degrees, time depths of tremendous magnitude began, in the late 18th century, to replace the Christian calendar. Space, from a surrounding candelabrum of stars, began to widen to infinity. The Earth was recognized as a mere speck drifting in the wake of a minor star, itself rotating around an immense galaxy composed of innumerable suns. Beyond and beyond, into billions of light years, other galaxies glowed through clouds of wandering gas and interstellar dust. Finally, and perhaps the most shocking blow of all, the natural world of the moment proved to be an illusion, a phantom of man's short lifetime. Organic novelty lay revealed in the strata of the Earth. Man had not always been here. He had been preceded, in the

4,000,000,000 years of the planet's history, by floating mollusks, strange fern forests, huge dinosaurs, flying lizards, giant mammals whose bones lay under the dropped boulders of vanished continental ice sheets.

The Orphan cried out in protest, as the cold of naked space entered his bones, "Who am I?" And once more science answered. "You are a changeling. You are linked by a genetic chain to all the vertebrates. The thing that is you bears the still aching wounds of evolution in body and in brain. Your hands are made-over fins, your lungs come from a creature gasping in a swamp, your femur has been twisted upright. Your foot is a reworked climbing pad. You are a rag doll resewn from the skins of extinct animals. Long ago, 2,000,000 years perhaps, you were smaller, your brain was not so large. We are not confident that you could speak. Seventy million years before that you were an even smaller climbing creature known as a tupaiid. You were the size of a rat. You ate insects. Now you fly to the Moon."

"This is a fairy tale," protested the Orphan. "I am here, I will look in the mirror."

"Of course it is a fairy tale," said the scientists, "but so is the world and so is life. That is what makes it true. Life is indefinite departure. That is why we are all orphans. That is why you must find your own way. Life is not stable. Everything alive is slipping through cracks and crevices in time, changing as it goes. Other creatures, however, have instincts that provide for them, holes in which to hide. They cannot ask questions. A fox is a fox, a wolf is a wolf, even if this, too, is illusion. You have learned to ask questions. That is why you are, an orphan. *You are the only creature in the universe who knows what it has been.* Now you must go on asking questions while all the time you are changing. You will ask what you are to become. The world will no longer satisfy you. You must find your way, your own true self."

"But how can I?" wept the Orphan, hiding his head. "This is magic. I do not know what I am. I have been too many things."

"You have indeed," said all the scientists together. "Your body and your nerves have been dragged about and twisted in the long effort of your ancestors to stay alive, but now, small orphan that you are, you must know a secret, a secret magic that nature has given to you. No other creature on the planet possesses it. You use language. You are a symbol-shifter. All this is hidden in your brain and transmitted from one generation to another. You are a time-binder, in your head the symbols that mean things in the world outside can fly about untrammeled. You can combine them differently into a new world of thought or you can also hold them tenaciously throughout a lifetime and pass them on to others."

Thus out of words, a puff of air, really, is made all that is uniquely human, all that is new from one human generation to another. But remember what was said of the wounds of evolution. The brain, parts of it at least, is very old, the parts laid down in sequence like geological strata. Buried deep beneath the brain with which we reason are ancient defense centres quick to anger, quick to aggression, quick to violence, over which the neocortex, the new brain, strives to exert control. Thus there are times when the Orphan is a divided being striving against himself. Evil men know this. Sometimes they can play upon it for their own political advantage. Men crowded together, subjected to the same stimuli, are quick to respond to emotion that in the quiet of their own homes they might analyze more cautiously.

Scientists have found that the very symbols which crowd our brains may possess their own dangers. It is convenient for the thinker to classify an idea with a word. This can sometimes lead to a process called hypostatization or reification. Take the word "Man," for example. There are times when it is useful to categorize the creature briefly, his history, his embracing characteristics. From this, if we are not careful of our meanings, it becomes easy to speak of all men as though they were one person. In reality men have been seeking this unreal man for thousands of years. They have found him bathed in blood, they have found him in the hermit's cell, he has been glimpsed among innumerable messiahs, or in meditation under the sacred bô tree; he has been found in the physician's study or lit by the satanic fires of the first atomic explosion.

In reality he has never been found at all. The reason is very simple: men have been seeking Man capitalized, an imaginary creature constructed out of disparate parts in the laboratory of the human imagination. Some men may thus perceive him and see him as either totally beneficent or wholly evil. They would be wrong. They are wrong so long as they have vitalized this creation and call it "Man." There is no Man; there are only men: good, evil, inconceivable mixtures marred by their genetic makeup, scarred or improved by their societal surroundings. So long as they live they are *men,* multitudinous and unspent potential for action. Men are great objects of study, but the moment we say "Man" we are in danger of wandering into a swamp of abstraction.

Surveying our fossil history perhaps we are not even justified as yet in calling ourselves true men. The word carries subtle implications that extend beyond us into the time stream. If a remote half-human ancestor, barely able to speak, had had a word for his kind, as very likely he did, and just supposing it had been "man," would we approve the usage, the shape-freezing quality of it, now? I think not. Perhaps no true orphan would wish to call himself anything but a traveler. Man in a cosmic timeless sense may not be here.

The point is particularly apparent in the light of a recent and portentous discovery. In 1953 James D. Watson and Francis H.C. Crick discovered the structure of the chemical alphabet out of which all that lives is constituted. It was a strange spiral ladder within the cell, far more organized and complicated than 19th-century biologists had imagined; the tiny building blocks constantly reshuffled in every mating had both an amazing stability and paradoxically, over long time periods, a power to alter the living structure of a species beyond recall. The thing called man had once been a tree shrew on a forest branch; now it manipulates abstract symbols in its brain from which skyscrapers rise, bridges span the horizon, disease is conquered, the Moon is visited.

Molecular biologists have begun to consider whether the marvelous living alphabet which lies at the root of evolution can be manipulated for human benefit. Already some varieties of domesticated plants and animals have been improved. Now at last man has begun to eye his own possible road into the future. By delicate excisions and intrusions could the mysterious alphabet we carry in our bodies be made to hasten our advancement into the future? Already our urban concentrations, with all their aberrations and faults, are future-oriented. Why not ourselves? It is in our power to perpetuate great minds *ad infinitum?* But who is to judge? Who is to select this future man? There is the problem. Which of us poor orphans by the roadside, even those peering learnedly through the electron microscope, can be confident of the way into the future? Could the fish unaided by nature have found the road to the reptile, the reptile to the mammal, the mammal to man? And how was man endowed with speech? *Could* men choose their way? Suddenly before us towers the blackest, most formidable bridge of our experience. Across what chasm does it run?

Biologists tell us that in the fullness of time more than ninety percent of the world's past species have perished. The mammalian ones in particular are not noted for longevity. If the scalpel, the excising laser ray in the laboratory, were placed in the hands of some one person, some one poor orphan, what would he do? If assured, would he reproduce himself alone? If cruel, would he by indirection succeed in abolishing the living world? If doubtful of the road, would he reproduce the doubt? "Nothing is more shameful than assertion without knowledge," the great Roman statesman and orator Cicero once pronounced as though he had foreseen this final bridge of human pride—the pride of a god without foresight.

After the disasters of the second World War when the dream of perpetual progress died from men's minds, an orphan of this violent century wrote a poem about the great extinctions revealed in the rocks of the planet. It concludes as follows:

> I am not sure I love
>   the cruelties found in our blood
>   from some lost evil tree in our beginnings.
> May the powers forgive and seal us deep
>   when we lie down,
> May harmless dormice creep and red leaves fall
>   over the prisons where we wreaked our will.
> Dachau, Auschwitz, those places everywhere.
> If I could pray, I would pray long for this.

One may conclude that the poet was a man of doubt. He did not regret man; he was confident that leaves, rabbits, and songbirds would continue life, as, long ago, a tree shrew had happily forgotten the ruling reptiles. The poet was an orphan in shabby circumstances pausing by the roadside to pray, for he did pray despite his denial; God forgive us all. He was a man in doubt upon the way. He was the eternal orphan of my father's story. Let us then, as similar orphans who have come this long way through time, be willing to assume the risks of the uncompleted journey. We must know, as that forlorn band of men in Judaea knew when they buried the jar, that man's road is to be sought beyond himself. *No man there is who can tell the whole tale.* After the small passage of 2,000 years who would deny this truth?

FERDINAND FOCH

ON

War

Ferdinand Foch (1851–1929), French marshal and commander in chief of Allied forces on the Western front in World War I, attempted in this article (13th edition, 1926) to sum up some of the morale implications of what is now known as "total war," of which World War I was the first full-fledged example. Despite the vagueness of much of Foch's prescription, it is obvious in the article that the numbing quality of trench warfare and the capacity for terror of modern armament had made deep impressions. (R. McH.)

Modern conditions of war are gradually extending the domain of *morale* and increasing its influence. For, among belligerent nations, war affects a greater number of people and does so with methods of increasing violence.

I. The Soldier in the Ranks

In battle, an enemy's long-range guns make their effects felt as far back as 5, 10 or 15 m., and, as they are capable of rapid firing, their effects become formidable to troops even at those distances. Difficulty in seeing their objective does not limit their powers, for they are aided by aeroplanes which inform them concerning the situation of their objective and the results of their fire.

At lesser distances they are supported by light artillery in large numbers, mobile, and capable of making the most advantageous use of chance features of the ground over the whole of the area at their command; and further support comes from machine-guns, which, of light weight and slender dimensions, can penetrate everywhere to equip in a short time the whole of the terrain.

Range of fire. It follows, then, that the soldier who approaches the battlefield and advances to carry the enemy position, finds that, at great range and over an extremely wide extent, that is to say during a long space of time, he is exposed to a heavy fire, the effects of which are multiplied in severity the further he advances to the position. Frequently, before being able to advance, he is forced to wait until, thanks to supplies of material, cannon, trench mortars and machine-guns, his army has gained a mastery of the fire, and the destructive capacity of the adversary has been thus reduced.

In this time of waiting hours succeed hours, nights follow days and weeks go by, always under the rain of steel from the enemy. It is under incessant bombardment that the march to victory has to be resumed and continued. Rarely is the battle decided in one day. And the nervous tension, the crisis imposed on the combatant, lasts the same time. During all this wearing period he must fulfil, automatically and often left to his own resources, his function as soldier, marksman, machine-gunner, pioneer, link in the chain of intelligence, carrier of supplies and so on. That is to say this function must be part of his own nature, and to fulfil it he must have received a serious training.

Interception of supplies. Furthermore, bombardment spreads its havoc no less widely on the rear of the battle-front, cuts communications, prevents the arrival of supplies. Not only has the combatant to show a bold face to the danger which threatens him, but he often finds himself reduced to a most precarious existence; along with the rigours of nights in the open, he has to put up with shortage of supplies. And thus physical exhaustion comes to be added to nervous shock, and the severity of the ordeal is heightened.

Tenacity and endurance. In the wars of the past, movement and enthusiasm, the qualities of dash and courage and personal pride, could suffice the soldier in a moment of intoxication to meet, with brilliance, the crisis of collision with the enemy. But to-day, if he is to traverse the long road of the hell which is the modern battle and reach a decision, he must possess an unbreakable tenacity and an energy ready for any sacrifice, and both must be unwavering for long days on end. To what greatness of soul must we not appeal, then, to see the emergence of virtues so solid, so tenacious, so generous? We must leave the answer to the soldiers of the Marne and Yser, Ypres and Verdun.

Further, who can forget the moving spectacle of the British leave-trains returning to the front during the War? The men were accompanied to the station by a silent throng composed for the most part of women and children. A few handkerchiefs furtively sought the eyes of those who were left behind, especially when the train began to move off. On board the vessel at Dover, the returning men donned their life-saving waistcoats, and stood closely crowded together on deck, imprisoned in their own thoughts. If, from a group here and there, came a song or a noisy demonstration, it was from young soldiers going out to the front for the first time. The others remained impassive, silent, gloomy, and their eyes gave token of the cold energy and the spirit of savage resolve on which they had fallen back. It was to the cry of "*Lusitania!*" that they would soon be marching to attack. Experience had taught them that mere knowledge of their duties and a fine, fleeting ardour would not suffice to bear the long and bitter ordeal of the modern battle. They required a spirit which must be imbued with the highest feelings, and, quickened with them, a spirit proved in the crucible of discipline.

The soldier of our national armies has drawn the spirit of sacrifice, the sentiment of discipline and duty, from love of his country, from attachment to the family as to the race, and from the indispensable military training, which left its strongest impression. Of this he gives proof in action by strict obedience to orders. But let there be no mistake; he conserves and maintains these virtues in lasting fashion only in proportion as the commanders have won his confidence by the care with which they surround his daily life; only in proportion as they know how to conserve that life by their vigilant economy of his blood.

As a whole, the war of the present day demands of the soldier a moral greatness, and a professional training, both developed in very high degree. The conservation of those forces, a conservation which alone can assure victory, is incumbent on the commanding officers. And in this way the rôle and responsibility of the officer expand in an exceptional degree, and grow sharply defined, especially in battle.

II. The Officer

In the course of any action of necessarily long duration, the officer can conserve the value of his unit, section, company or battalion, only by protecting it from the disasters which are continually menacing it, and by leading it step by step to the goal, to the final objective which has been assigned to it by the higher command, and the gaining of which constitutes for it the victory. He cannot confine himself to being a daring soldier, superior to his subordinates by his courage and personal example. He must show himself to be constantly dominated and impelled by a double preoccupation: to avoid the destruction of his unit and to bring it nearer its objective.

Avoidance of loss. To avoid its destruction, because he is in the presence of an armament capable, by suddenly inflicted losses, of destroying the unit, or at least of shattering its *morale* for a long time, if adequate precautions have not been taken in time. Hence springs the necessity that he should be familiar with the dispositions appropriate to this continual menace, and that he should be able to order and put readily into practice these dispositions, which by his selection of rendezvous, his tactical formations, by hastily constructed earthworks or by any other procedure, keep the troops halted under cover from the observation, projectiles or poison-gas of the enemy.

How many long hours will not troops have to pass in waiting, in preparation, before seeing the moment for action arrive? How often has not the officer to provide for these secure dispositions? Yet in this situation the slightest negligence is unpardonable. At that moment will appear all the vigilance and all the power of decision which the officer must bring to the field of action, in addition to the acquired knowledge and the experience, necessarily incomplete though this be, of manoeuvres. What is required of him, even at these moments, is the all-embracing eye, the sense of fitting opportunity and the gift of decision.

Precision in attack. Then, the moment of action having arrived, the operations of the unit must be carried out without hesitation or disturbance, in the presence of an adversary who, flinging all his resources again into action, may be able to regain some of his preponderance, to restore to his armament its formidable strength. That is to say, the operations must have been directed in all their details by a commanding officer who has previously assured himself of the participation of neighbouring troops, and has gauged as exactly as possible the position of the enemy which he is approaching.

To sum up, together with the feeling of readiness for action called up by the receipt of orders, but before the moment for action has come, it is by foresight and precision that an officer should be inspired and guided in his procedure. Without these he steps into imprudence, and he draws his troops along with him. They run the risk of not returning. He, and he alone, is to blame.

Value of experience. Without going into the increased need for technical knowledge resulting from the employment of material, at once more various and more potent and also more delicate, the art of bringing troops on to the battlefield has assumed in our day a capital importance. Every officer ought to concern himself with this, and shape himself for it in time of peace as fully as he devotes himself to the instruction of his men, so that he may be able when the great day comes, to present himself armed with a certain peace-time experience, and armed above all with faculties well maintained, developed, and turned ever on the alert in the direction of the march toward the objective. He must be ready on that day to resolve the difficulties of this march, difficulties which only the actual conditions will reveal to him, for peace gives no complete idea of the effects of modern weapons on a body of troops. War will bring him face to face with new problems, and will demand that he possess, over and above his professional knowledge, the habit of reflection and prompt decision on fresh circumstances. It is a habit which he will need to have acquired during peace-time.

It is needless to remark that these faculties of foresight, of adaptation to new problems, ought to be developed the more fully in an officer the higher his rank and the greater the instruments of control which are in his hands. For in this case his orders cover vast spaces, are laden with more far-reaching consequences, and are more difficult to modify in their execution. The moral forces and the capacities which the commander must bring to war, if he is to act in such a way that negligence or imprudence, both always disastrous, may be avoided, have increased in notable proportions, even for the lower ranks.

III. The Nation

But war, to pursue the theme further, does not confine its material and moral effects to the battlefields and the invaded regions. It extends them toward the rear, to populations which were formerly kept aloof from it by the barrier of distance. It spreads them overseas in every direction, even to non-belligerents, and produces the most complete upheaval.

The Non-combatants. In the rear, not to speak of refugee populations fleeing before the ravages of invasion, and terror systematically loosed in defiance of the laws of humanity, it is the women, the children and the aged who live in the emotions of the struggle, as a result of the facility and speed of communications; who undergo on occasion the stress of hostile bombardment from the air; who in any case suffer privations of every kind. This means that the field is open, in the heart of the country itself, to the most opposed sentiments and passions, as also to nervous shock and physical exhaustion. But, despite these difficulties, the interior of the country must hold firm to the end, and, what is more, must maintain in foodstuffs, arms, and munitions and support in energy of spirit, those who fight at the front. In its united aspects, the country becomes and must remain by its sentiments and its productive activity the source of the warring capacity of the armies.

Thus, in the old Europe, each country is perforce the near neighbour of powerful states, sees its warlike resistance measured by the degree of union between the interests and sentiments which it comprises, by its jealous watch over its independence, by its progress toward that moral unity which is the essence of a nation, and consequently by the depth of its national sentiment. Only in these moral factors is to be found the energy which will resist concussions of every kind, and will pursue, through ever-increasing sacrifices and through all the vicissitudes of the struggle, the success of the enterprise which will liberate it, once and for all, from all its anguish.

And if, among the states of the New World, where menace is less direct, the immediate danger does not demand the organisation of territorial defence, a blow struck against the principles whereby they live will awaken the apprehensions of the peoples and, in community of sentiments, will arm them for the safeguarding of their free civilisation. In short, a sturdy sentiment which binds the entire people as one, imposing itself upon them by the justice of their cause and the necessity for defending it, is indispensable to the success of a modern war, for that alone is capable of obliging them to the privations and sacrifices which war entails.

IV. The Government

To maintain and guide this sentiment during the days of the struggle, to exploit it and to extract victory from out of it—such is the task of the Government. In these days the Govt. must not be simply the representative of the interests of the country, but rather the expression of the passions which are animating it, and to that end, the organiser of defence, the creator of the material resources, the arms, munitions, foodstuffs essential to the struggle, and the motive and inspiring power of the forces assembled on the field of operations. It must show itself a "war government," with an active and effective policy, taking a wide view of the ends which it is possible to attain, bearing in mind the means at its disposal. And it must be animated by the will always to augment those means to hasten those ends, while still maintaining, in the interior of the country, the spirit which does not disarm.

It is obvious, then, that war calls for peculiar qualities in the statesmen who preside over it. Without these, it must inevitably end in impotence, or even defeat.

V. Conclusion

To sum up, whether we are dealing with the soldier, the high command, the nation or the Govt., in each of these divisions war demands an ever-increasing share of the moral forces whose close union and wise combination are alone capable of producing victory. It is to the insufficiency of certain of these forces, or to the lack of cohesion between them, that we must look to grasp and explain the collapse, in the course of the last war, of certain Great Powers, and likewise of armies of formidable repute, which in themselves certainly did not fall short of that repute.

HENRY FORD

ON

Mass Production

The appearance of this article in the 13th edition (Supplement to the 11th and 12th, 1926) epitomized one of the changes in editorial policy made at that time, the decision to do away with as much as possible of the ponderousness and abstruseness that, at least in the popular mind, characterized much of Britannica's *contents. Well intended and laudable as the new policy was, the choice of Ford as a contributor revealed one weakness: The article was doubtless written by Samuel Crowther, Ford's ghostwriter-in-residence. (R. McH.)*

Though Mr. McHenry's statement above is true, that does not lessen the importance of this article. It gives us a clear insight into the mind of one of the most influential Americans in our history. It's also interesting to see how the term "mass production," which we take for granted, affected people in Ford's time.

The term mass production is used to describe the modern method by which great quantities of a single standardised commodity are manufactured. As commonly employed it is made to refer to the quantity produced, but its primary reference is to method. In several particulars the term is unsatisfactory. Mass production is not merely quantity production, for this may be had with none of the requisites of mass production. Nor is it merely machine production, which also may exist without any resemblance to mass production. Mass production is the focussing upon a manufacturing project of the principles of power, accuracy, economy, system, continuity and speed. The interpretation of these principles, through studies of operation and machine development and their co-ordination, is the conspicuous task of management. And the normal result is a productive organisation that delivers in quantities a useful commodity of standard material, workmanship and design at minimum cost. The necessary, precedent condition of mass production is a capacity, latent or developed, of *mass consumption,* the ability to absorb large production. The two go together, and in the latter may be traced the reasons for the former. . . .

The motor industry leads the way. To the motor industry is given the credit of bringing mass production to experimental success, and by general consent the Ford Motor Co. is regarded as having pioneered in the largest development of the method under a single management and for a single purpose. It may, therefore, simplify the history of mass production and the description of its principles if the experience of this company is taken as a basis. It has been already suggested that mass production is possible only through the ability of the public to absorb large quantities of the commodity thus produced. These commodities are necessarily limited to necessities and conveniences. The greatest development of mass production methods has occurred in the production of conveniences. The automobile represents a basic and continuous convenience-transportation.

Mass production begins, then, in the conception of a public need of which the public may not as yet be conscious and proceeds on the principle that use-convenience must be matched by price-convenience. Under this principle the element of service remains uppermost; profit and expansion are trusted to emerge as consequences. As to which precedes the other, consumption or production, experiences will differ. But granted that the vision of the public need is correct, and the commodity adapted to meet it, the impulse to increased production may come in anticipation of demand, or in response to demand, but the resulting consumption is always utilised to obtain such increase of quality, or such decrease of cost, or both, as shall secure still greater use-convenience and price-convenience. As these increase, consumption increases, making possible still greater production advantages, and so on to a fulfilment that is not yet in view.

The commodities that conduce to civilised living are thus far enjoyed by only a small fraction of the world's inhabitants. The experience of the Ford Motor Co. has been that mass production precedes mass consumption and makes it possible, by reducing costs and thus permitting both greater use-convenience and price-convenience. If the production is increased, costs can be reduced. If production is increased 500%, costs may be cut 50%, and this decrease in cost, with its accompanying decrease in selling price, will probably multiply by 10 the number of people who can conveniently buy the product. This is a conservative illustration of production serving as the cause of demand instead of the effect. . . .

As to shop detail, the keyword to mass production is simplicity. Three plain principles underlie it: (*a*) the planned orderly progression of the commodity through the shop; (*b*) the delivery of work instead of leaving it to the workman's initiative to find it; (*c*) an analysis of operations into their constituent parts. These are distinct but not separate steps; all are involved in the first one. To plan the progress of material from the initial manufacturing operation until its emergence as a finished product involves shop planning on a large scale and the manufacture and delivery of material, tools and parts at various points along the line. To do this successfully with a progressing piece of work means a careful breaking up of the work into its "operations" in sequence. All three fundamentals are involved in the original act of planning a moving line of production.

This system is practised, not only on the final assembly line, but throughout the various arts and trades involved in the completed product. The automobile assembly line offers an impressive spectacle of hundreds of parts being quickly put together into a going vehicle, but flowing into that are other assembly lines on which each of the hundreds of parts have been fashioned. It may be far down the final assembly line that the springs, for example, appear, and they may seem to be a negligible part of the whole operation.

Formerly one artisan would cut, harden, bend and build a spring. To-day the making of one leaf of a spring is an operation of apparent complexity, yet is really the ultimate reduction to simplicity of operation. . . .

Some criticisms answered. Mass production has also been studied with reference to what has been called the monotony of repetitive work. This monotony does not exist as much in the shops as in the minds of theorists and bookish reformers. There is no form of work without its hardness; but needless hardship has no place in the modern industrial scheme. Mass production lightens work, but increases its repetitive quality. In this it is the opposite of the mediaeval ideal of craftsmanship where the artisan performed every operation, from the preparation of the material to its final form. It is doubtful, however, if the mass of mediaeval toil was as devoid of monotony as has sometimes been pictured, but it is absolutely certain that it was less satisfactory in its results to the worker. In well-managed modern factories the tendency to monotony is combatted by frequent changes of task.

The criticism of mass production as a means of reducing employment has long since been out of court. The experience of the Ford Motor Co. is that wherever the number of men has been reduced on manufacturing operations, more jobs have been created. A continuous programme of labour reduction has been paralleled by a continuous increase in employment. As to the effect of mass production on wages and the relations between managers and men, there is little need to speak. It is perhaps the most widely understood fact about mass production that it has resulted in higher wages than any other method of industry. The reason is at hand. The methods of mass production enable the worker to earn more and thus to have more. Moreover, the methods of mass production have thrown so much responsibility on the craftsmanship of management, that the old method of financial adjustment by reduction of wages has been abandoned by scientific manufacturers. A business that must finance by drafts out of the wage envelopes of its employees is not scientifically based. It is the problem of management so to organise production that it will pay the public, the workmen and the concern itself. Management that fails in any of these is poor management. Disturbed labour conditions, poor wages, uncertain profits indicate lapses in management. The craftsmanship of management absorbs the energies of many thousands of men who, without mass production methods, would have no creative opportunity. Here the modern method broadens instead of narrows individual opportunity.

JAMES FRAZER

ON

Totemism and Taboo

The Britannica*'s most famous, and perhaps most consequential, venture into the world of mythology stemmed from the commissioning of a young Cambridge don, James George Frazer (1854–1941), to write two articles for the 9th edition (1875–1889) on the insights offered by modern, late-nineteenth-century anthropology into the primitive practices of totem and taboo. The young Scottish scholar spent seven months researching the two articles. He was so intrigued that he focused his career on that field, developing into one of the world's most eminent and influential social anthropologists. His* Britannica *articles grew into the twelve volumes of* The Golden Bough *(1890; 1907–1915). A classic of anthropology, it made Frazer (later Sir George) famous to this day. The editor who prevailed on him to write the articles was William Robertson Smith. The article "Totemism," ten pages long with much fine print, is here represented by its opening passage. (B.L.F.)*

Of the remarkable books of which Britannica *was the* fons et origo, The Golden Bough *is perhaps the greatest. Though it ranges over every part of the known world, it was written by a scholar who rarely strayed from his desk. Selections from it will be found in Great Books of the Western World.*

The current Britannica *reminds us that Frazer's hypotheses with respect to totemism "are now out of date." It also warns us that the great French ethnologist Claude Lévi-Strauss even "denied the reality of totemism."*

Britannica*'s successive treatments of the subject suggest that its slogan, "Let Knowledge grow . . . ," expresses an ideal only. It gives the facts but can only hope to approximate the truth.*

A totem is a class of material objects which a savage regards with superstitious respect, believing that there exists between him and every member of the class an intimate and altogether special relation. The name is derived from an Ojibway (Chippeway) word which was first introduced into literature, so far as appears, by J. Long, an Indian interpreter of last century, who spelt it *totam*. The connexion between a man and his totem is mutually beneficent: the totem protects the man, and the man shows his respect for the totem in various ways, by not killing it if it be an animal, and not cutting or gathering it if it be a plant. As distinguished from a fetich, a totem is never an isolated individual, but always a class of objects, generally a species of animals or of plants, more rarely a class of inanimate natural objects, very rarely a class of artificial objects.

Considered in relation to men, totems are of at least three kinds:—(1) the clan totem, common to a whole clan, and passing by inheritance from generation to generation; (2) the sex totem, common either to all the males or to all the females of a tribe, to the exclusion in either case of the other sex; (3) the individual totem, belonging to a single individual and not passing to his descendants. Other kinds of totems exist and will be noticed, but they may perhaps be regarded as varieties of the clan totem. The latter is by far the most important of all; and where we speak of totems or totemism without qualification the reference is always to the clan totem.

The clan totem. The clan totem is reverenced by a body of men and women who call themselves by the name of the totem, believe themselves to be of one blood, descendants of a common ancestor, and are bound together by common obligations to each other and by a common faith in the totem. Totemism is thus both a religious and a social system. In its religious aspect it consists of the relations of mutual respect and protection between a man and his totem; in its social aspect it consists of the relations of the clansmen to each other and to men of other clans. In the later history of totemism these two sides, the religious and the social, tend to part company; the social system sometimes survives the religious; and, on the other hand, religion sometimes bears traces of totemism in countries where the social system based on totemism has disappeared. We begin with the religious side.

Totemism as a religion, or the relation between a man and his totem. The members of a totem clan call themselves by the name of their totem, and commonly believe themselves to be actually descended from it.

Thus the Turtle clan of the Iroquois are descended from a fat turtle, which, burdened by the weight of its shell in walking, contrived by great exertions to throw it off, and thereafter gradually developed into a man. The Cray-Fish clan of the Choctaws were originally cray-fish and lived underground, coming up occasionally through the mud to the surface. Once a party of Choctaws smoked them out, and, treating them kindly, taught them the Choctaw language, taught them to walk on two legs, made them cut off their toe nails and pluck the hair from their bodies, after which they adopted them into the tribe. But the rest of their kindred, the cray-fish, are still living underground. The Osages are descended from a male snail and a female beaver. The snail burst his shell, developed arms, feet, and legs, and became a fine tall man; afterwards he married the beaver maid. Some of the clans of western Australia are descended from ducks, swans, and other waterfowl. In Senegambia each family or clan is descended from an animal (hippopotamus, scorpion, &c.) with which it counts kindred.

Somewhat different are the myths in which a human ancestress is said to have given birth to an animal of the totem species. Thus the Snake clan among the Moquis of Arizona are descended from a woman who gave birth to snakes. The Bakalai in western equatorial Africa believe that their women once gave birth to the totem animals; one woman brought forth a calf, others a crocodile, hippopotamus, monkey, boa, and wild pig.

Believing himself to be descended from, and therefore akin to, his totem, the savage naturally treats it with respect. If it is an animal he will not, as a rule, kill nor eat it. In the Mount Gambier tribe (South Australia) "a man does not kill or use as food any of the animals of the same subdivision with himself, excepting when hunger compels; and then they express sorrow for having to eat their *wingong* (friends) or *tumanang* (their flesh). When using the last word they touch their breasts, to indicate the close relationship, meaning almost a part of themselves.

Shorter, but no less interesting and significant, was the article "Taboo." It, too, raised eyebrows and stirred controversy. (B.L.F.)

Taboo (also written Tabu and Tapu) is the name given to a system of religious prohibitions which attained its fullest development in Polynesia (from Hawaii to New Zealand), but of which under different names traces may be discovered in most parts of the world.

The word "taboo" is common to the different dialects of Polynesia, and is perhaps derived from *ta,* "to mark," and *pu,* an adverb of intensity. The compound word "taboo" (tapu) would thus originally mean "marked thoroughly." Its ordinary sense is "sacred." It does not, however, imply any moral quality, but only "a connexion with the gods or a separation from ordinary purposes and exclusive appropriation to persons or things considered sacred; sometimes it means devoted as by a vow." Chiefs who trace their lineage to the gods are called *arii tabu,* "chiefs sacred," and a temple is called a *uahi tabu,* "place sacred." The converse of taboo is *noa* (in Tonga *gnofoba*), which means "general" or "common." Thus the rule which forbade women to eat with men, as well as, except on special occasions, to eat any fruits or animals offered in sacrifice to the gods, was called *ai tabu,* "eating sacred"; while the present relaxation of the rule is called *ai noa,* eating generally, or having food in common. Although it was employed for civil as well as religious purposes, the taboo was essentially a religious observance. In Hawaii it could be imposed only by priests; but elsewhere in Polynesia kings and chiefs, and even to a certain extent ordinary individuals, exercised the same power. The strictness with which the taboo was observed depended largely on the influence of the person who imposed it: if he was a great chief it would not be broken; but a powerful man often set at nought the taboo of an inferior.

A taboo might be general or particular, permanent or temporary. A general taboo applied, *e.g.*, to a whole class of animals; a particular taboo was confined to one or more individuals of the class. Idols, temples, the persons and names of kings and of members of the royal family, the persons of chiefs and priests, and the property (canoes, houses, clothes, etc.) of all these classes of persons were always taboo or sacred. By a somewhat arbitrary extension of this principle a chief could render taboo to (*i.e.*, in favour of) himself anything which took his fancy by merely calling it by the name of a part of his person. Thus, if he said "That axe is my backbone," or "is my head," the axe was his; if he roared out "That canoe! my skull shall be the baler to bale it out," the canoe was his likewise. The names of chiefs and still more of kings were taboo, and could not be uttered. If the name of a king of Tahiti was a common word or even resembled a common word, that word dropped out of use and a new name was substituted for it. Thus in course of time most of the common words in the language underwent considerable modifications or were entirely changed.

Certain foods were permanently taboo to (*i.e.*, in favour of or for the use of) gods and men, but were forbidden to women. Thus in Hawaii the flesh of hogs, fowls, turtle, and several kinds of fish, cocoa-nuts, and nearly everything offered in sacrifice were reserved for gods and men, and could not, except in special cases, be consumed by women. In the Marquesas Islands human flesh was tabooed from women. Sometimes certain fruits, animals, and fish were taboo for months together from both men and women. In the Marquesas houses were tabooed against water: nothing was washed in them; no drop of water might be spilled in them. If an island or a district was tabooed, no canoe or person might approach it while the taboo lasted; if a path was tabooed, no one might walk on it. Seasons generally kept taboo were the approach of a great religious ceremony, the time of preparation for war, and the sickness of chiefs. The time during which they lasted varied from years to months or days. In Hawaii there was a tradition of one that lasted thirty years, during which men might not trim their beards, etc. A common period was forty days. A taboo was either common or strict. During a common taboo the men were only required to abstain from their ordinary occupations and to attend morning and evening prayers. But during a strict taboo every fire and light on the island or in the district was extinguished; no canoe was launched; no person bathed; no one, except those who had to attend at the temple, was allowed to be seen out of doors; no dog might bark, no pig grunt, no cock crow. Hence at these seasons they tied up the mouths of dogs and pigs, and put fowls under a calabash or bandaged their eyes. The taboo was imposed either by proclamation or by fixing certain marks (a pole with a bunch of bamboo leaves, a white cloth, etc.) on the places or things tabooed.

The penalty for the violation of a taboo was either religious or civil. The religious penalty inflicted by the offended *atuas* or spirits generally took the form of a disease: the offender swelled up and died, the notion being that the *atua* or his emissary (often an infant spirit) had entered into him and devoured his vitals. Cases are on record in which persons who had unwittingly broken a taboo actually died of terror on discovering their fatal error. Chiefs and priests, however, could in the case of involuntary transgressions perform certain mystical ceremonies which prevented this penalty from taking effect. The civil penalty for breaking a taboo varied in severity. In Hawaii there were police officers appointed by the king to see that the taboo was observed, and every breach of it was punished with death, unless the offender had powerful friends in the persons of priests or chiefs. Elsewhere the punishment was milder; in Fiji (which, however, is Melanesian) death was rarely inflicted, but the delinquent was robbed and his gardens despoiled. In New Zealand this judicial robbery was reduced to a system. No sooner was it known that a man had broken a taboo than all his friends and acquaintances swarmed down on him and carried off whatever they could lay hands on. Under this system (known as *muru*) property circulated with great rapidity. If, *e.g.*, a child fell into the fire, the father was robbed of nearly all he possessed.

SIGMUND FREUD

ON

Psychoanalysis

For a treatment of the Freudian school of psychoanalysis the editors of the 13th edition (1926) went directly to the fountainhead, as they did in the analogous case of Einstein. Freud's account is remarkable on several counts: its modesty, its concision, its clarity. It is fascinating to get this authoritative glimpse of the subject as it appeared to its master (1856–1939) almost three-quarters of a century ago. If we look up "Psychoanalysis" in the current edition, we now find dozens of references, all attesting to the subsequent influence of Freud's original doctrine on many areas of thought. His article is here reprinted in its entirety.

In the years 1880–2 a Viennese physician, Dr. Josef Breuer (1842–1925), discovered a new procedure by means of which he relieved a girl, who was suffering from severe hysteria, of her various symptoms. The idea occurred to him that the symptoms were connected with impressions which she had received during a period of excitement while she was nursing her sick father. He therefore induced her, while she was in a state of hypnotic somnambulism, to search for these connections in her memory and to live through the "pathogenic" scenes once again without inhibiting the affects that arose in the process. He found that when she had done this the symptom in question disappeared for good.

This was at a date before the investigations of Charcot and Pierre Janet into the origin of hysterical symptoms, and Breuer's discovery was thus entirely uninfluenced by them. But he did not pursue the matter any further at the time, and it was not until some 10 years later that he took it up again in collaboration with Sigmund Freud. In 1895 they published a book, *Studien über Hysterie,* in which Breuer's discoveries were described and an attempt was made to explain them by the theory of *Catharsis*. According to that hypothesis, hysterical symptoms originate through the energy of a mental process being withheld from conscious influence and being diverted into bodily innervation ("*Conversion*"). A hysterical symptom would thus be a substitute for an omitted mental act and a reminiscence of the occasion which should have given rise to that act. And, on this view, recovery would be a result of the liberation of the affect that had gone astray and of its discharge along a normal path ("*Abreaction*"). Cathartic treatment gave excellent therapeutic results, but it was found that they were not permanent and that they were dependent on the personal relation between the patient and the physician. Freud, who later proceeded with these investigations by himself, made an alteration in their technique, by replacing hypnosis by the method of free association. He invented the term "*psychoanalysis,*" which in the course of time came to have two meanings: (1) a particular method of treating nervous disorders and (2) the science of unconscious mental processes, which has also been appropriately described as "depth-psychology."

Subject matter of psychoanalysis. Psychoanalysis finds a constantly increasing amount of support as a therapeutic procedure, owing to the fact that it can do more for certain classes of patients than any other method of treatment. The principal field of its application is in the milder neuroses—hysteria, phobias and obsessional states, but in malformations of character and in sexual inhibitions or abnormalities it can also bring about marked improvements or even recoveries. Its influence upon dementia praecox and paranoia is doubtful; on the other hand, in favourable circumstances it can cope with depressive states, even if they are of a severe type.

In every instance the treatment makes heavy claims upon both the physician and the patient: the former requires a special training, and must devote a long period of time to exploring the mind of each patient, while the latter must make considerable sacrifices, both material and mental. Nevertheless, all the trouble involved is as a rule rewarded by the results. Psychoanalysis does not act as a convenient panacea ("*cito, tute, jucunde*") upon all psychological disorders. On the contrary, its application has been instrumental in making clear for the first time the difficulties and limitations in the treatment of such affections.

The therapeutic results of psychoanalysis depend upon the replacement of unconscious mental acts by conscious ones and are operative in so far as that process has significance in relation to the disorder under treatment. The replacement is effected by overcoming internal resistances in the patient's mind. The future will probably attribute far greater importance to psychoanalysis as the science of the unconscious than as a therapeutic procedure.

Depth-psychology. Psychoanalysis, in its character of depth-psychology, considers mental life from three points of view: the dynamic, the economic and the topographical.

From the first of these standpoints, the *dynamic* one, psychoanalysis derives all mental processes (apart from the reception of external stimuli) from the interplay of forces, which assist or inhibit one another, combine with one another, enter into compromises with one another, etc. All of these forces are originally in the nature of *instincts;* that is to say, they have an organic origin. They are characterised by possessing an immense (somatic) persistence and reserve of power ("*repetition-compulsion*"); and they are represented mentally as images or ideas with an affective charge ("*cathexis*"). In psychoanalysis, no less than in other sciences, the theory of instincts is an obscure subject. An empirical analysis leads to the formation of two groups of instincts: the so-called "ego-instincts," which are directed towards self-preservation and the "object-instincts," which are concerned with relations to an external object. The social instincts are not regarded as elementary or irreducible. Theoretical speculation leads to the suspicion that there are two fundamental instincts which lie concealed behind the manifest ego-instincts and object-instincts:

namely (*a*) Eros, the instinct which strives for ever closer union, and (*b*) the instinct of destruction, which leads toward the dissolution of what is living. In psychoanalysis the manifestation of the force of Eros is given the name "*libido*."

Pleasure-pain principle. From the *economic* standpoint psychoanalysis supposes that the mental representations of the instincts have a cathexis of definite quantities of energy, and that it is the purpose of the mental apparatus to hinder any damming-up of these energies and to keep as low as possible the total amount of the excitations to which it is subject. The course of mental processes is automatically regulated by the "*pleasure-pain principle*"; and pain is thus in some way related to an increase of excitation and pleasure to a decrease. In the course of development the original pleasure principle undergoes a modification with reference to the external world, giving place to the "*reality-principle,*" whereby the mental apparatus learns to postpone the pleasure of satisfaction and to tolerate temporarily feelings of pain.

Mental topography. *Topographically,* psychoanalysis regards the mental apparatus as a composite instrument, and endeavours to determine at what points in it the various mental processes take place. According to the most recent psychoanalytic views, the mental apparatus is composed of an "*id,*" which is the reservoir of the instinctive impulses, of an "*ego,*" which is the most superficial portion of the id and one which is modified by the influence of the external world, and of a "*super-ego,*" which develops out of the id, dominates the ego and represents the inhibitions of instinct characteristic of man. Further, the property of consciousness has a topographical reference; for processes in the id are entirely unconscious, while consciousness is the function of the ego's outermost layer, which is concerned with the perception of the external world.

At this point two observations may be in place. It must not be supposed that these very general ideas are presuppositions upon which the work of psychoanalysis depends. On the contrary, they are its latest conclusions and are in every respect open to revision. Psychoanalysis is founded securely upon the observation of the facts of mental life; and for that very reason its theoretical superstructure is still incomplete and subject to constant alteration. Secondly, there is no reason for astonishment that psychoanalysis, which was originally no more than an attempt at explaining pathological mental phenomena, should have developed into a psychology of normal mental life. The justification for this arose with the discovery that the dreams and mistakes ("*parapraxes,*" such as slips of the tongue, etc.) of normal men have the same mechanism as neurotic symptoms.

Theoretical basis. The first task of psychoanalysis was the elucidation of nervous disorders. The analytical theory of the neuroses is based upon three ground-pillars: the recognition of (1) "*repression,*" of (2) the importance of the sexual instincts and of (3) "*transference.*"

Censorship. There is a force in the mind which exercises the functions of a censorship, and which excludes from consciousness and from any influence upon action all tendencies which displease it. Such tendencies are described as "repressed." They remain unconscious; and if the physician attempts to bring them into the patient's consciousness he provokes a "*resistance.*" These repressed instinctual impulses, however, are not always made powerless by this process. In many cases they succeed in making their influence felt by circuitous paths, and the indirect or substitutive gratification of repressed impulses is what constitutes neurotic symptoms.

Sexual instincts. For cultural reasons the most intensive repression falls upon the sexual instincts; but it is precisely in connection with them that repression most easily miscarries, so that neurotic symptoms are found to be substitutive gratifications of repressed sexuality. The belief that in man sexual life begins only at puberty is incorrect. On the contrary, signs of it can be detected from the beginning of extra-uterine existence; it reaches a first culminating point at or before the fifth year ("early period"), after which it is inhibited or interrupted ("latency period") until the age of puberty, which is the second climax of its development. This double onset of sexual development seems to be distinctive of the genus Homo. All experiences during the first period of childhood are of the greatest importance to the individual, and in combination with his inherited sexual constitution, form the dispositions for the subsequent development of character or disease. It is a mistaken belief that sexuality coincides with "genitality." The sexual instincts pass through a complicated course of development, and it is only at the end of it that the "primacy of the genital zone" is attained. Before this there are a number of "pre-genital organisations" of the libido—points at which it may become "fixated" and to which, in the event of subsequent repression, it will return ("*regression*"). The infantile fixations of the libido are what determine the form of neurosis which sets in later. Thus the neuroses are to be regarded as inhibitions in the development of the libido.

The Oedipus complex. There are no specific causes of nervous disorders; the question whether a conflict finds a healthy solution or leads to a neurotic inhibition of function depends upon quantitative considerations, that is, upon the relative strength of the forces concerned. The most important conflict with which a small child is faced is his relation to his parents, the "*Oedipus complex*"; it is in attempting to grapple with this problem that persons destined to suffer from a neurosis habitually fail. The reactions against the instinctual demands of the Oedipus complex are the source of the most precious and socially important achievements of the human mind; and this probably holds true not only in the life of individuals but also in the history of the human species as a whole. The super-ego, the moral factor which dominates the ego, also has its origin in the process of overcoming the Oedipus complex.

Transference. By "*transference*" is meant a striking peculiarity of neurotics. They develop toward their physician emotional relations, both of an affectionate and hostile character, which are not based upon the actual situation but are derived from their relations toward their parents (the Oedipus complex). Transference is a proof of the fact that adults have not overcome their former childish dependence; it coincides with the force which has been named "suggestion"; and it is only by learning to make use of it that the physician is enabled to induce the patient to overcome his internal resistances and do away with his repressions. Thus psychoanalytic treatment acts as a second education of the adult, as a corrective to his education as a child.

Within this narrow compass it has not been possible to mention many matters of the greatest interest, such as the "*sublimation*" of instincts, the part played by symbolism, the problem of "*ambivalence,*" etc. Nor has there been space to allude to the applications of psychoanalysis, which originated, as we have seen, in the sphere of medicine, to other departments of knowledge (such as Anthropology, the Study of Religion, Literary History and Education) where its influence is constantly increasing. It is enough to say that psychoanalysis, in its character of the psychology of the deepest, unconscious mental acts, promises to become the link between Psychiatry and all of these other fields of study.

The psychoanalytic movement. The beginnings of psychoanalysis may be marked by two dates: 1895, which saw the publication of Breuer and Freud's *Studien über Hysterie,* and 1900, which saw that of Freud's *Traumdeutung.* At first the new discoveries aroused no interest either in the medical profession or among the general public. In 1907 the Swiss psychiatrists, under the leadership of E. Bleuler and C. G. Jung, began to concern themselves in the subject; and in 1908 there took place at Salzburg a first meeting of adherents from a number of different countries. In 1909 Freud and Jung were invited to America by G. Stanley Hall to deliver a series of lectures on psychoanalysis at Clark University, Worcester, Mass. From that time forward interest in Europe grew rapidly; it showed itself, however, in a forcible rejection of the new teachings, characterised by an emotional colouring which sometimes bordered upon the unscientific.

The reasons for this hostility are to be found, from the medical point of view, in the fact that psychoanalysis lays stress upon psychical factors, and from the philosophical point of view, in its assuming as an underlying postulate the concept of unconscious mental activity; but the strongest reason was undoubtedly the general disinclination of mankind to concede to the factor of sexuality such importance as is assigned to it by psychoanalysis. In spite of this widespread opposition, however, the movement in favour of psychoanalysis was not to be checked. Its adherents formed themselves into an International Association, which passed successfully through the ordeal of the World War, and at the present time comprises local groups in Vienna, Berlin, Budapest, London, Switzerland, Holland, Moscow and Calcutta, as well as two in the United States. There are three journals representing the views of these societies: the *Internationale Zeitschrift für Psychoanalyse, Imago* (which is concerned with the application of psychoanalysis to non-medical fields of knowledge), and the *International Journal of Psycho-Analysis.*

During the years 1911–3 two former adherents, Alfred Adler, of Vienna, and C. G. Jung, of Zürich, seceded from the psychoanalytic movement and founded schools of thought of their own. In 1921 Dr. M. Eitingon founded in Berlin the first public psychoanalytic clinic and training-school, and this was soon followed by a second in Vienna. For the moment these are the only institutions on the continent of Europe which make psychoanalytic treatment accessible to the wage-earning classes.

LILLIAN GISH

ON

The Silver Screen

Lillian Gish (1896–), with her sister Dorothy (1898–1968), starred in many early D. W. Griffith classics. Her work in his Birth of a Nation *(1915) established her as one of the cinema's greatest stars. She has also been a distinguished stage actress. Less well known is her expertise in many of the technical aspects of filmmaking. The following article appeared in the 14th edition (1929). Although "talkies" first appeared in 1927, Gish's theory of motion pictures as a kind of aesthetic Esperanto is based on silent films.*

The motion picture, by virtue of its intrinsic nature, is a species of amusing and informational Esperanto, and, potentially at least, a species of aesthetic Esperanto. Of all the arts, if it may be classified as one, the motion picture has in it, perhaps more than any other, the resources of universality. Even a simple waltz by Johann Strauss may remain alien and unassimilable to the musical ear of the Chinese; a Michelangelo fresco may fail to impress its significant beauty upon a Japanese or Hindu; a drama by Ibsen may remain completely unintelligible, even in competent translation, to a maharaja of India, just as Chinese music must ever remain strange, peculiar and incomprehensible to the Anglo-Saxon ear. But the motion picture art of Charlie Chaplin will inevitably make a Japanese laugh as heartily as a Dane.

The reason is simple. Pantomime is the aboriginal means of human communication and intercourse, and pictures bring to a child his first acquaintance with and understanding of the world about him. The motion picture, combining the two, is thus addressed to a common human understanding. It begins with the elementals of human perception and comprehension; it starts at the outset with the advantage of the fundamentals of human intercommunication and explicitness. It is for this reason that the moving picture has spread through the world and has been accepted far and wide in what has seemed an unbelievably short space of time.

The motion picture tells its stories directly, simply, quickly and elementally, not in words but in pictorial pantomime. To see is not only to believe; it is also in a measure to understand. In theatrical drama, seeing is closely allied with hearing, and hearing, in turn, with mental effort. In the motion picture, seeing is all—or at least nine-tenths of all.

This, of course, is the screen in its fundamental aspect. This is the motion picture simple and unsophisticated. This is the universal *engine* that is the cinema. The motion picture, plainly enough, in certain of its manifestations may remain largely vague and ambiguous to a people alien to the source of its imagination, preparation and making. But the motion picture in itself and in the aggregate is based upon materials of easy, common appreciation. Love, hate, desolation, despair, joy, ecstasy, defeat, triumph—these are universal emotions. Conveyed by words, as drama conveys them, they may offer difficulties to remote and various peoples. But conveyed by the movements of the human face and body, by smiles and tears, troubled brows and dejected shoulders, sparkling eyes and fluttering hands, they are immediately recognizable. A laugh or a sob is the same the world over. They need no words to explain them.

In another phase of the cinema, the so-called news-reel has already proved itself to be a form of journalistic Esperanto, just as the so-called educational moving picture has shown itself to be a form of informational Esperanto. The news-reel has brought to the far corners of the earth the life and daily activities of all nations and people. The educationals, as they are known, have acquainted the audiences of the world with various phenomena associated with invention, manufacture, discovery, ingenuity and enterprise peculiar to a certain country. The news-reel has informed every country of its neighbour, his leaders, his achievements, his troubles, his pleasures, his problems. It has spread a direct acquaintanceship with alien lands, peoples and customs to other lands. It has provided an international newspaper self-adapted to the understanding of all peoples, and a running commentary on contemporaneous history.

The motion picture is at once the common story-book, newspaper and text-book of the 20th century. In its loftier aspects, it may conceivably elude the comprehension of audiences remote from its birthplace. That is, when it abandons its more elemental nature and strives for isolation as an art form. But that is the fate of art, all art, wherever it be found. Art is for the few, unfortunately; the generality of people have difficulty in taking it into their understanding. Shakespeare and the Orient may remain strangers; Leonardo and Dostoievsky may find no sympathy and hospitality in the consciousness of half a dozen lands. But there is probably no land where the spectacle of soldiers marching off to war or a fat man being struck with a custard pie is not instantaneously hailed with understanding. It is in *elementary* excitements and humours such as these, together with the thousand and one others that they connote, that the motion picture, reaching constantly after higher things, finds the mainspring of its wide and comprehensive appeal. It deals for the most part with primitive instincts, primitive impulses, primitive human peace and alarm, happiness and ache, ambition and dream. These may be dressed in strange costumes and may be shown through strange peoples, but underneath they are the emotions and inspirations and trials of all the human race. The backgrounds may be unfamiliar, but the hearts that beat and struggle, triumph or fall, are the hearts of all mankind. And so the world laughs with Chaplin and Lloyd, cries with Seastrom and Murnau and Griffith, startles at the revelations of Eisenstein, gasps pleasurably at Fairbanks and Valentino, feels tenderness with Mary Pickford and warms to the homely lovableness of Wolheim and Beery.

WILLIAM HAZLITT
ON
The Fine Arts

One of the many ornaments of the illustrious Supplement to the 4th, 5th, and 6th editions (1815–1824) was the treatment of the fine arts—concentrating actually on the visual arts—by the brilliant essayist and critic William Hazlitt (1778–1830). Writing in about 1812, as his critical reputation was becoming solidly established, Hazlitt, then in his middle thirties, was tart in his assessment of the state of the visual arts in Britain. This article was criticized by some of his peers for omitting several important elements, which he was quick to acknowledge, promising to do better on his other work for the Supplement, which consisted mainly of biographies. (B.L.F.)

For at least two reasons Hazlitt on art remains interesting to us. First, he tells us how in his day people looked at pictures; their eyes, it sometimes seems, actually differed from ours. Second, his judgments, though we may disagree with some, are conveyed in a style of great clarity and energy. Art criticism today may be more profound, but all too often seems directed to sophisticated insiders. Hazlitt was addressing an emergent audience of the middle class. Britannica*'s eighteenth-century audience of learned amateurs and classically educated country gentlemen was receding in importance.*

These sample extracts will illustrate his style and stance. Almost eight columns devoted to a critical examination of Joshua Reynolds's ideas on art are omitted.

In the *Encyclopaedia* there is some account, under the head ARTS, of the general theory and history of the *Fine Arts,* including Poetry, Eloquence, Painting, Statuary, and Architecture. The term, in its widest application, would also embrace Music, Dancing, Theatrical Exhibition; and in general, all those arts, in which the powers of imitation or invention are exerted, chiefly with a view to the production of pleasure, by the immediate impression which they make on the mind. The phrase has of late, we think, been restricted to a narrower and more technical signification; namely, to Painting, Sculpture, Engraving, and Architecture, which appeal to the eye as the medium of pleasure; and by way of eminence, to the two first of these arts. In the present article, we shall adopt this limited sense of the term; and shall endeavour to develope the principles upon which the great Masters have proceeded, and also to inquire, in a more particular manner, into the present state and probable advancement of these arts in this Country.

The great works of art, at present extant, and which may be regarded as models of perfection in their several kinds, are the Greek statues—the pictures of the celebrated Italian Masters—those of the Dutch and Flemish schools—to which we may add the comic productions of our own countryman, Hogarth. These all stand unrivalled in the history of art; and they owe their pre-eminence and perfection to one and the same principle,—*the immediate imitation of nature.* This principle predominated equally in the classical forms of the antique, and in the grotesque figures of Hogarth; the perfection of art in each arose from the truth and identity of the imitation with the reality; the difference was in the subjects; there was none in the mode of imitation. Yet the advocates for the *ideal system of art* would persuade their disciples, that the difference between Hogarth and the antique does not consist in the different forms of nature which they imitated, but in this, that the one is like, and the other unlike nature. This is an error, the most detrimental, perhaps, of all others, both to the theory and practice of art. As, however, the prejudice is very strong and general, and supported by the highest authority, it will be necessary to go somewhat elaborately into the question, in order to produce an impression on the other side.

What has given rise to the common notion of the *ideal,* as something quite distinct from *actual* nature, is probably the perfection of the Greek statues. Not seeing among ourselves, anything to correspond in beauty and grandeur, either with the features or form of the limbs in these exquisite remains of antiquity, it was an obvious, but a superficial conclusion, that they must have been created from the idea existing in the artist's mind, and could not have been copied from anything existing in nature. The contrary, however, is the fact. . . .

In general, then, we would be understood to maintain, that the beauty and grandeur so much admired in the Greek statues were not a voluntary fiction of the brain of the artist, but existed substantially in the forms from which they were copied, and by which the artist was surrounded. A striking authority in support of these observations, which has in some measure been lately discovered, is to be found in the *Elgin marbles,* taken from the Acropolis at Athens, and supposed to be the works of the celebrated Phidias. The process of fastidious refinement and indefinite abstraction is certainly not visible there. The figures have all the ease, the simplicity, and variety, of individual nature. Even the details of the subordinate parts, the loose hanging folds in the skin, the veins under the belly, or on the sides of the horses, more or less swelled as the animal is more or less in action, are given with scrupulous exactness. This is true nature and true art. In a word, these invaluable remains of antiquity are precisely like casts taken from life. The *ideal* is not the preference of that which exists only in the mind, to that which exists in nature; but the preference of that which is fine in nature to that which is less so. There is nothing fine in art but what is taken almost immediately, and, as it were, in the mass, from what is finer in nature. Where there have been the finest models in nature, there have been the finest works of art.

As the Greek statues were copied from Greek forms, so Raphael's expressions were taken from Italian faces; and we have heard it remarked, that the women in the streets at Rome seem to have walked out of his pictures in the Vatican. . . .

Titian is at the head of the Venetian school. He is the first of all colourists. In delicacy and purity Correggio is equal to him, but his colouring has not the same warmth and gusto in it. Titian's flesh-colour partakes of the glowing nature of the climate, and of the luxuriousness of the manners of his country. He represents objects not through a merely lucid medium, but as if tinged with a golden light. Yet it is wonderful in how low a tone of local colouring his pictures are painted,—how rigidly his means are husbanded. . . .

Rubens is the Prince of the Flemish painters. Of all the great painters, he is perhaps the most artificial,—the one who painted most from his own imagination,—and, what was almost the inevitable consequence, the most of a mannerist. He had neither the Greek forms to study from, nor the Roman expression, nor the high character, picturesque costume, and sun-burnt hues which the Venetian painters had immediately before them. He took, however, what circumstances presented to him,—a fresher and more blooming tone of complexion, arising from moister air, and a colder climate. To this he added the congenial splendour of reflected lights and shadows cast from rich drapery; and he made what amends he could for the want of expression, by the richness of his compositions, and the fantastic variety of his allegorical groups. . . .

His drawing is often deficient in proportion, in knowledge, and in elegance, but it is always picturesque. The drawing of N. Poussin, on the contrary, which has been much cried up, is merely learned and anatomical: he has a knowledge of the structure and measurements of the human body, but very little feeling of the grand, or beautiful, or striking, in form. . . .

If ever there was a man of genius in the art, it was Rembrandt. He might be said to have created a medium of his own, through which he saw all objects. He was the grossest and the least vulgar, that is to say, the least commonplace in his grossness, of all men. He was the most downright, the least fastidious of the imitators of nature. He took any object, he cared not what, how mean soever in form, colour, and expression, and from the light and shade which he threw upon it, it came out gorgeous from his hands. As Vandyke made use of the smallest contrasts of light and shade, and painted as if in the open air, Rembrandt used the most violent and abrupt contrasts in this respect, and painted his objects as if in a dungeon. His pictures may be said to be "bright with excessive darkness." . . .

We come now to speak of the progress of art in our own Country,—of its present state,—and the means proposed for advancing it to still higher perfection.

We shall speak first of Hogarth, both as he is the first name in the order of time that we have to boast of, and as he is the greatest comic painter of any age or country. His pictures are not imitations of still life, or mere transcripts of incidental scenes or customs; but powerful moral satires, exposing vice and folly in their most ludicrous points of view, and with a profound insight into the weak sides of character and manners, in all their tendencies, combinations, and contrasts. There is not a single picture of his, containing a representation of merely natural or domestic scenery. His object is not so much "to hold the mirror up to nature," as "to show vice her own feature, scorn her own image." Folly is there seen at the height—the moon is at the full—it is the very error of the time. There is a perpetual collision of eccentricities, a tilt and tournament of absurdities, pampered into all sorts of affectation, airy, extravagant, and ostentatious! Yet he is as little a caricaturist as he is a painter of still life. Criticism has not done him justice, though public opinion has. His works have received a sanction which it would be vain to dispute, in the universal delight and admiration with which they have been regarded, from their first appearance, to the present moment. If the quantity of amusement, or of matter for reflection which they have afforded, is that by which we are to judge of precedence among the intellectual benefactors of mankind, there are perhaps few persons who can put in a stronger claim to our gratitude than Hogarth. The wonderful knowledge which he possessed of human life and manners, is only to be surpassed (if it can be) by the powers of invention with which he has arranged his materials, and by the mastery of execution with which he has embodied and made tangible the very thoughts and passing movements of the mind. Some persons object to the style of Hogarth's pictures, or the class to which they belong. First, Hogarth belongs to no class, or, if he belongs to any, it is to the same class as Fielding, Smollett, Vanbrugh, and Molière. Besides, the merit of his pictures does not depend on the nature of his subjects, but on the knowledge displayed of them, on the number of ideas, on the fund of observation and amusement contained in them. Make what deductions you please for the vulgarity of the subjects—yet in the research, the profundity, the absolute truth and precision of the delineation of character,—in the invention of incident, in wit and humour, in life and motion, in everlasting variety and originality,—they never have, and probably never will be surpassed. They stimulate the faculties, as well as amuse them. "Other pictures we see, Hogarth's we read!"

There is one error which has been frequently entertained on this subject, and which we wish to correct, namely, that Hogarth's genius was confined to the imitation of the coarse humours and broad farce of the lowest life. But he excelled quite as much in exhibiting the vices, the folly, and frivolity of the fashionable manners of his time. His fine ladies do not yield the palm of ridicule to his waiting-maids, and his lords and his porters are on a very respectable footing of equality. He is quite at home, either in St Giles's or St James's. There is no want, for example, in his *Marriage à la Mode,* or his *Taste in High Life,* of affectation verging into idiotcy, or of languid sensibility that might

"Die of a rose in aromatic pain." . . .

In general, Wilson's views of *English scenery* want almost every thing that ought to recommend them. The subjects he has chosen are not well fitted for the landscape-painter, and there is nothing in the execution to redeem them. Ill-shaped mountains, or great heaps of earth, trees that grow against them without character or elegance, motionless waterfalls, a want of relief, of transparency and distance, without the imposing grandeur of real magnitude (which it is scarcely within the province of art to give),—are the chief features and defects of this class of his pictures. . . .

Sir Joshua Reynolds owed his vast superiority over his contemporaries to incessant practice, and habitual attention to nature, to quick organic sensibility, to considerable power of observation, and still greater taste in perceiving and availing himself of those excellences of others, which lay within his own walk of art. We can by no means look upon Sir Joshua as having a claim to the first rank of genius. He would hardly have been a great painter, if other greater painters had not lived before him. He would not have given a first impulse to the art, nor did he advance any part of it beyond the point where he found it. He did not present any new view of nature, nor is he to be placed in the same class with those who did. Even in colour, his pallet was spread for him by the old Masters, and his eye imbibed its full perception of depth and harmony of tone, from the Dutch and Venetian schools, rather than from nature. His early pictures are poor and flimsy. He indeed learned to see the finer qualities of nature through the works of art, which he, perhaps, might never have discovered in nature itself. He became rich by the accumulation of borrowed wealth, and his genius was the offspring of taste. He combined and applied the materials of others to his own purpose, with admirable success; he was an industrious compiler, or skilful translator, not an original inventor in art. The art would remain, in all its essential elements, just where it is, if Sir Joshua had never lived. He has supplied the industry of future plagiarists with no new materials. But it has been well observed, that the value of every work of art, as well as the genius of the artist, depends, not more on the degree of excellence, than on the degree of originality displayed in it. Sir Joshua, however, was perhaps the most original imitator that ever appeared in the world: and the reason of this, in a great measure, was, that he was compelled to combine what he saw in art, with what he saw in nature, which was constantly before him. The portrait-painter is, in this respect, much less liable than the historical painter, to deviate into the extremes of manner and affectation; for he cannot discard nature altogether, under the excuse that *she only puts him out.* He must meet her, face to face; and if he is not incorrigible, he will see something there that cannot fail to be of service to him. Another circumstance which must have been favourable to Sir Joshua was, that though not the originator *in point of time,* he was the first Englishman who transplanted the higher excellences of his profession into his own country, and had the merit, if not of an inventor, of a reformer of the art. His mode of painting had the graces of novelty in the age and country in which he lived; and he had, therefore, all the stimulus to exertion, which arose from the enthusiastic applause of his contemporaries, and from a desire to expand and refine the taste of the public. . . .

With regard to the pecuniary advantages arising from the public patronage of the arts;—the plan unfortunately defeats itself; for it multiplies its objects faster than it can satisfy their claims; and raises up a swarm of competitors for the prize of genius from the dregs of idleness and dulness. . . . Offers of public and promiscuous patronage can in general be little better than a species of intellectual seduction, administering provocatives to vanity and avarice, and leading astray the youth of the nation by fallacious hopes, which can scarcely ever be realized. At the same time, the good that might be done by private taste and benevolence, is in a great measure defeated. . . .

By means of public institutions, the number of candidates for fame, and pretenders to criticism, is increased beyond all calculation, while the quantity of genius and feeling remain much the same as before; with these disadvantages, that the man of original genius is often lost among the crowd of competitors who would never have become such, but from encouragement and example, and that the voice of the few whom nature intended for judges, is apt to be drowned in the noisy and forward suffrages of shallow smatterers in Taste.

CHARLES EVANS HUGHES

ON

The Monroe Doctrine

For the 14th edition (1929), Britannica *had recourse to a great jurist and statesman, Charles Evans Hughes (1861–1948). He served as eleventh Chief Justice of the Supreme Court and was narrowly defeated by Wilson in the 1916 race for the Presidency. We present an excerpt from his article, of particular interest in these days of Latin American turmoil.*

There had long been a deep-seated conviction on the part of the people of the United States that the opportunities of a hard-won freedom would be threatened by the ambitions of European powers and that the aims of the new nation could be achieved only by keeping clear of the toils of European politics and strife. . . .

The people of the United States had watched with deep sympathy the long struggle of their southern neighbours for independence. While Spain maintained a doubtful contest, it was regarded as a civil war, but when that contest became so desperate that Spanish viceroys, governors, and captains-general concluded treaties with the insurgents virtually acknowledging their independence, the United States unreservedly recognized the facts. The republic of Colombia was recognized in 1822, the Government of Buenos Aires and the States of Mexico and Chile early in 1823. The United States was the first to recognize the independent empire of Brazil in May, 1824, not hesitating because of the political form of the Government, and this was followed by the recognition of the Federation of Central American States in August of the same year. Meanwhile, the Holy Alliance formed by the sovereigns of Austria, Russia and Prussia had sought to enforce the divine right of kings against the progress of liberal principles. Joined by France, they undertook "to put an end to the system of representative government" and after France had proceeded accordingly to restore the rule of Ferdinand VII. in Spain, it was proposed to direct their efforts to the overthrowing of the new Governments erected out of the old colonies of Spain in the western hemisphere.

Monroe's Message

This was the situation when, in Aug. 1823, George Canning, British foreign secretary, wrote to Richard Rush, American minister in London, suggesting a joint declaration in substance that the recovery of the colonies by Spain was hopeless; that neither Great Britain nor the United States was aiming at the possession of any portion of these colonies; and that they could not see with indifference any portion of them transferred to any other power. Great Britain, however, had not at that time recognized the new States in Spanish America. President Monroe sought the advice of Jefferson and Madison. Jefferson regarded the question as "the most momentous" which had arisen since that of Independence. "Our first and fundamental maxim," said he, "should be, never to entangle ourselves in the broils of Europe. Our second, never to suffer Europe to intermeddle with cis-Atlantic affairs." Jefferson favoured the acceptance of the British suggestion in some form and Madison took the same view. John Quincy Adams, Secretary of State, opposed a joint declaration. He wished to take the ground "of earnest remonstrance against the interference of the European powers by force with South America, but to disclaim all interference on our part with Europe; to make an American cause and adhere inflexibly to that." Upon the advice of Adams, and after mature deliberation by the president and his cabinet, it was decided to make a separate declaration on the sole responsibility of the United States, and this declaration was formulated in the president's message of Dec. 2, 1823.

Original statement of the doctrine. The doctrine is set forth in two paragraphs of this message. The first of these had a genesis distinct from the situation of the former colonies of Spain. It grew out of the question of Russian claims on the north-west coast of North America. . . . President Monroe . . . declared . . . "a principle in which the rights and interests of the United States are involved, that the American continents, by the free and independent condition which they have assumed and maintained, are henceforth not to be considered as subjects for future colonization by any European powers."

The other paragraph of President Monroe's message bore upon the situation of the nations to the south of the United States, as follows:

"In the wars of the European powers in matters relating to themselves we have never taken any part, nor does it comport with our policy so to do. It is only when our rights are invaded or seriously menaced that we resent injuries or make preparation for our defence. With the movements in this hemisphere we are, of necessity, more immediately connected, and by causes which must be obvious to all enlightened and impartial observers. The political system of the allied powers is essentially different in this respect from that of America. . . . We owe it, therefore, to candour, and to the amicable relations existing between the United States and those powers, to declare that we should consider any attempt on their part to extend their system to any portion of this hemisphere as dangerous to our peace and safety. With the existing colonies or dependencies of any European power we have not interfered and shall not interfere. But with the governments who have declared their independence and maintained it, and whose independence we have, on great consideration and on just principles, acknowledged, we could not view any interposition for the purpose of oppressing them, or controlling in any other manner their destiny, by any European power, in any other light than as the manifestation of an unfriendly disposition toward the United States. . . ."

T. H. HUXLEY

ON

Biology

Although his formal education occurred between the ages of eight and ten, plus four or five years at medical school, T. H. Huxley (Thomas Henry, 1825–1895) displayed outstanding scholarship and research abilities on a Royal Navy exploratory expedition to the South Seas in his early twenties and soon was recognized as one of the world's preeminent biologists. He was made a fellow of the Royal Society at the tender age of twenty-six. Upon publication of Darwin's On the Origin of Species *Huxley became perhaps the staunchest supporter of Darwin's theories of evolution. Among the many articles he wrote for the* Britannica's *famous 9th edition (1875–1889) was "Biology," which includes a discussion of evolution. (B.L.F.)*

The excerpts that follow are not only perfect examples of Huxley's calm, even staid, expository style but also illustrate how advanced thinkers viewed biology in the mid-Victorian period. The 9th edition was notable for its coverage of important contemporary issues.

Huxley's contribution ran to almost twenty columns. It is supplemented by a lengthy article (twelve columns) from another hand, headed "Limits and Classification of the Vegetable Kingdom." The greater part of it (not given here) deals in detail with biology as it was partitioned in Huxley's time. He considers the subject under four heads: morphology, distribution, physiology, aetiology.

Britannica*'s current edition reflects the broader perspectives that have opened up since Huxley. Now the subject occupies 114 columns. Called not "Biology" but "The*

Biological Sciences," it "deals with all the physicochemical aspects of life." It lays down basic principles toward which Huxley's period was advancing, offers a history of the subject, and connects biology concretely with chemistry and physics. In many of its themes and subdivisions it looks back to Huxley's penetrating formulations.

The Biological sciences are those which deal with the phenomena manifested by living matter; and though it is customary and convenient to group apart such of these phenomena as are termed mental, and such of them as are exhibited by men in society, under the heads of Psychology and Sociology, yet it must be allowed that no natural boundary separates the subject matter of the latter sciences from that of Biology. Psychology is inseparably linked with Physiology; and the phases of social life exhibited by animals other than man, which sometimes curiously foreshadow human policy, fall strictly within the province of the biologist.

On the other hand, the biological sciences are sharply marked off from the abiological, or those which treat of the phenomena manifested by not-living matter, in so far as the properties of living matter distinguish it absolutely from all other kinds of things, and as the present state of knowledge furnishes us with no link between the living and the not-living.

These distinctive properties of living matter are—

1. Its *chemical composition*—containing, as it invariably does, one or more forms of a complex compound of carbon, hydrogen, oxygen, and nitrogen, the so-called protein (which has never yet been obtained except as a product of living bodies) united with a large proportion of water, and forming the chief constituent of a substance which, in its primary unmodified state, is known as *protoplasm*.

2. Its *universal disintegration and waste by oxidation; and its concomitant reintegration by the intus-susception of new matter.*

A process of waste resulting from the decomposition of the molecules of the protoplasm, in virtue of which they break up into more highly oxidated products, which cease to form any part of the living body, is a constant concomitant of life. There is reason to believe that carbonic acid is always one of these waste products, while the others contain the remainder of the carbon, the nitrogen, the hydrogen, and the other elements which may enter into the composition of the protoplasm.

The new matter taken in to make good this constant loss is either a ready-formed protoplasmic material, supplied by some other living being, or it consists of the elements of protoplasm, united together in simpler combinations, which consequently have to be built up into protoplasm by the agency of the living matter itself. In either case, the addition of molecules to those which already existed takes place, not at the surface of the living mass, but by interposition between the existing molecules of the latter. If the processes of disintegration and of reconstruction which characterize life balance one another, the size of the mass of living matter remains stationary, while, if the reconstructive process is the more rapid, the living body *grows*. But the increase of size which constitutes growth is the result of a process of molecular intussusception, and therefore differs altogether from the process of growth by accretion, which may be observed in crystals and is effected purely by the external addition of new matter—so that, in the well-known aphorism of Linnaeus, the word "grow," as applied to stones, signifies a totally different process from what is called "growth" in plants and animals.

3. Its *tendency to undergo cyclical changes.*

In the ordinary course of nature, all living matter proceeds from pre-existing living matter, a portion of the latter being detached and acquiring an independent existence. The new form takes on the characters of that from which it arose; exhibits the same power of propagating itself by means of an offshoot; and, sooner or later, like its predecessor, ceases to live, and is resolved into more highly oxidated compounds of its elements.

Thus an individual living body is not only constantly changing its substance, but its size and form are undergoing continual modifications, the end of which is the death and decay of that individual; the continuation of the kind being secured by the detachment of portions which tend to run through the same cycle of forms as the parent. No forms of matter which are either not living, or have not been derived from living matter, exhibit these three properties, nor any approach to the remarkable phenomena defined under the second and third heads. But in addition to these distinctive characters, living matter has some other peculiarities, the chief of which are the dependence of all its activities upon moisture and upon heat, within a limited range of temperature, and the fact that it usually possesses a certain structure, or organization.

As has been said, a large proportion of water enters into the composition of all living matter; a certain amount of drying arrests vital activity, and the complete abstraction of this water is absolutely incompatible with either actual or potential life. But many of the simpler forms of life may undergo desiccation to such an extent as to arrest their vital manifestations and convert them into the semblance of not-living matter, and yet remain potentially alive. That is to say, on being duly moistened they return to life again. And this revivification may take place after months, or even years, of arrested life.

The properties of living matter are intimately related to temperature. Not only does exposure to heat sufficient to decompose protein matter destroy life, by demolishing the molecular structure upon which life depends; but all vital activity, all phenomena of nutritive growth, movement, and reproduction are possible only between certain limits of temperature. As the temperature approaches these limits the manifestations of life vanish, though they may be recovered by return to the normal conditions; but if it pass far beyond these limits, death takes place. . . .

Recent investigations point to the conclusion that the immediate cause of the arrest of vitality, in the first place, and of its destruction, in the second, is the coagulation of certain substances in the protoplasm, and that the latter contains various coagulable matters, which solidify at different temperatures. And it remains to be seen, how far the death of any form of living matter, at a given temperature, depends on the destruction of its fundamental substance at that heat, and how far death is brought about by the coagulation of merely accessory compounds.

It may be safely said of all those living things which are large enough to enable us to trust the evidence of microscopes, that they are heterogeneous optically, and that their different parts, and especially the surface layer, as contrasted with the interior, differ physically and chemically; while, in most living things, mere heterogeneity is exchanged for a definite structure, whereby the body is distinguished into visibly different parts, which possess different powers or functions. Living things which present this visible structure are said to be *organized;* and so widely does organization obtain among living beings, that *organized* and *living* are not unfrequently used as if they were terms of co-extensive applicability. This, however, is not exactly accurate, if it be thereby implied that all living things have a visible organization, as there are numerous forms of living matter of which it cannot properly be said that they possess either a definite structure or permanently specialized organs: though, doubtless, the simplest particle of living matter must possess a highly complex molecular structure, which is far beyond the reach of vision.

The broad distinctions which, as a matter of fact, exist between every known form of living substance and every other component of the material world, justify the separation of the biological sciences from all others. But it must not be supposed that the differences between living and not-living matter are such as to justify the assumption that the forces at work in the one are different from those which are to be met with in the other. Considered apart from the phenomena of consciousness, the phenomena of life are all dependent upon the working of the same physical and chemical forces as those which are active in the rest of the world. It may be convenient to use the terms "vitality" and "vital force" to denote the causes of certain great groups of natural operations, as we employ the names of "electricity" and "electrical force" to denote others; but it ceases to be proper to do so, if such a name implies the absurd assumption that "electricity" and "vitality" are entities playing the part of efficient causes of electrical or vital phenomena. A mass of living protoplasm is simply a molecular machine of great complexity, the total results of the working of which, or its vital phenomena, depend,—on the one hand, upon its construction, and, on the other, upon the energy supplied to it; and to speak of "vitality" as anything but the name of a series of operations is as if one should talk of the "horologity" of a clock. . . .

Of the causes which have led to the origination of living matter, then, it may be said that we know absolutely nothing. But postulating the existence of living matter endowed with that power of hereditary transmission, and with that tendency to vary which is found in all such matter, Mr Darwin has shown good reasons for believing that the interaction between living matter and surrounding conditions, which results in the survival of the fittest, is sufficient to account for the gradual evolution of plants and animals from their simplest to their most complicated forms, and for the known phenomena of Morphology, Physiology, and Distribution.

Mr Darwin has further endeavoured to give a physical explanation of hereditary transmission by his hypothesis of Pangenesis; while he seeks for the principal, if not the only, cause of variation in the influence of changing conditions.

It is on this point that the chief divergence exists among those who accept the doctrine of Evolution in its general outlines. Three views may be taken of the causes of variation:—

a. In virtue of its molecular structure, the organism may tend to vary. This variability may either be indefinite, or may be limited to certain directions by intrinsic conditions. In the former case, the result of the struggle for existence would be the survival of the fittest among an indefinite number of varieties; in the latter case, it would be the survival of the fittest among a certain set of varieties, the nature and number of which would be predetermined by the molecular structure of the organism.

b. The organism may have no intrinsic tendency to vary, but variation may be brought about by the influence of conditions external to it. And in this case also, the variability induced may be either indefinite or defined by intrinsic limitation.

c. The two former cases may be combined, and variation may to some extent depend upon intrinsic, and to some extent upon extrinsic, conditions.

At present it can hardly be said that such evidence as would justify the positive adoption of any one of these views exists.

If all living beings have come into existence by the gradual modification, through a long series of generations, of a primordial living matter, the phenomena of embryonic development ought to be explicable as particular cases of the general law of hereditary transmission. On this view, a tadpole is first a fish, and then a tailed amphibian, provided with both gills and lungs, before it becomes a frog, because the frog was the last term in a series of modifications whereby some ancient fish became an urodele amphibian; and the urodele amphibian became an anurous amphibian. In fact, the development of the embryo is a recapitulation of the ancestral history of the species.

If this be so, it follows that the development of any organism should furnish the key to its ancestral history; and the attempt to decipher the full pedigree of organisms from so much of the family history as is recorded in their development has given rise to a special branch of biological speculation, termed *phylogeny*.

In practice, however, the reconstruction of the pedigree of a group from the developmental history of its existing members is fraught with difficulties. It is highly probable that the series of developmental stages of the individual organism never presents more than an abbreviated and condensed summary of ancestral conditions; while this summary is often strangely modified by variation and adaptation to conditions; and it must be confessed that, in most cases, we can do little better than guess what is genuine recapitulation of ancestral forms, and what is the effect of comparatively late adaptation.

The only perfectly safe foundation for the doctrine of Evolution lies in the historical, or rather archaeological, evidence that particular organisms have arisen by the gradual modification of their predecessors, which is furnished by fossil remains. That evidence is daily increasing in amount and in weight; and it is to be hoped that the comparison of the actual pedigree of these organisms with the phenomena of their development may furnish some criterion by which the validity of phylogenetic conclusions, deduced from the facts of embryology alone, may be satisfactorily tested.

JULIAN HUXLEY
ON
Evolution

For the same 9th edition (1875–1889) T. H. Huxley also wrote a thirteen-column article on "Evolution." For him the period of controversy had ended; he could not foretell the Scopes trial and American Fundamentalism, so luxuriant today. Here is a paragraph from his masterly account:

> *Under these circumstances, only one alternative was left for those who denied the occurrence of evolution; namely, the supposition that the characteristic animals and plants of each great province were created, as such, within the limits in which we find them. And as the hypothesis of "specific centres," thus formulated, was heterodox from the theological point of view, and unintelligible under its scientific aspect, it may be passed over without further notice, as a phase of transition from the creational to the evolutional hypothesis.*

The family tradition was carried on by his famous grandson, Sir Julian Huxley (1887–1975), educator, biologist, and creative transformer of the zoo at Regent's Park, London. From his classic treatment of the subject in the 13th edition (1926) we have drawn the section dealing with the evidence for evolution. It is interesting to compare this 1926 handling with current post-Darwinian revisionism as discussed in the 15th edition under the heading "The Theory of Evolution." Since Sir Julian's time, of course, the scene has been enriched by the appearance of Watson, Crick, and Wilkins.

The topic of evolution is a very wide one. In its broadest sense it denotes little more than gradual change, as is indicated by the common French equivalent *transformisme.* In a somewhat more restricted sense it implies orderly change, while certain authors wish to combine it with orderly and progressive change. The two fields, however, in which it is most often applied are those of cosmic and of organic evolution, the former dealing with the development of stars and stellar systems, the latter with the changes undergone by life upon this planet. Here, only the topic of organic evolution will be discussed.

I. General Survey

Organic evolution. There are three quite distinct angles from which the subject can be treated. In the first place, there is the question of the *fact* of evolution: has organic evolution occurred or has it not occurred? Secondly, there is the *method* of evolution: by what mechanism has evolution been brought about? And thirdly, there is the *course* of evolution: granted that it has occurred, what were the main results of the process?

The evidence. The evidences on the first point are well known. They are chiefly drawn from the facts of comparative anatomy, of embryology, of geographical distribution and of palaeontology.

PALAEONTOLOGY. The last, or the history of life as revealed by actual fossil remains of organisms in the sedimentary rocks, affords the most direct evidence, since we find that many past organisms are now extinct, and that there are frequently to be traced long evolutionary chains, leading up from primitive extinct forms to specialised modern types.

EMBRYOLOGY. That of embryology is, however, equally important. The majority of animals run through, in the course of their development, stages which resemble other organisms. The fact that a fowl or a man passes through a stage in which its organisation is essentially like that of a fish is meaningless, save on the assumption that land vertebrates originally evolved from fish-like, aquatic ancestors.

DISTRIBUTION OF ANIMALS. The distribution of animals and plants over the earth's surface is, further, such that it cannot be explained except by assuming that evolution has occurred. If certain types have had their origins in certain areas, and have then spread thence, the facts are intelligible, but not otherwise. In the same way, the fact that oceanic islands contain but a very limited fauna and flora, and that, in oceanic archipelagoes, the types of animal life are often represented by different species on each different island, is readily explicable on the idea of chance spreading, followed by isolation and consequent evolutionary divergence.

COMPARATIVE ANATOMY. The evidence from comparative anatomy, though perhaps the most indirect, is equally strong, and was historically the first to attract attention. When we examine a series of, say, vertebrates, we soon perceive that a common general plan runs through them all, in spite of great differences in their various modes of life. The same is true for each particular organ. The hand and arm of man, the foreleg of a dog, the wing of a bird, the flipper of a whale—all these, and indeed the fore-limbs of all terrestrial vertebrates, show the same essential plan, though often much modified to suit the exigencies of the animal's particular mode of life. It must not be supposed that no other general ground-plan can exist: far from it. The insect or the crustacean is built on a wholly different general plan, and the special plan of its limbs is entirely different from that of the vertebrate limb. It is very difficult to explain these facts except on the theory of evolution.

VESTIGIAL ORGANS. The conclusion is strengthened by the existence of vestigial organs (often called rudimentary organs), which are useless to their possessor, although corresponding (homologous) organs in other species are of service. The vestigial hair on the surface of the human body affords one excellent example, while another is provided by the wholly useless remnants of limbs in various snakes. Often vestigial organs are recapitulatory as well, being better developed in the embryo or young than in the adult (hair and tail of man, teeth of certain whales, etc.).

NATURAL SELECTION. The evidences for evolution having taken place were first cogently marshalled by Charles Darwin in the *Origin of Species* (1859). No satisfactory alternative explanation of the data he adduced has ever been advanced, and the fact of evolution has passed beyond the realm of discussion. Darwin, however, accomplished much more than this. He also advanced a theory as to the method of evolution, and one so reasonable that it could be and is still widely held by scientific men. This was the theory of natural selection. He assumed as a fact the existence of variation, showed the universal presence of a struggle for existence due to the invariable birth of more young than can come to maturity, and then pointed out that this would inevitably lead on the average to the survival of those that were best fitted to survive and so to evolutionary change and progress. By so doing at one stroke he cut the ground from under the feet of those who, like Paley, argued that organic adaptations were evidences of conscious design.

SEXUAL SELECTION. He also advanced the subsidiary hypothesis of sexual selection to account for the development of special sexual adornments employed in courtship or display. . . . This theory has been much criticised, but has now, in somewhat modified form, been shown to rest on a firm basis.

Darwin also, in part, adopted the second main theory of the method of evolution, that of Lamarck, by assigning some weight to the direct effect of the environment and to the effects of use and disuse.

Three other main types of hypothesis to account for evolutionary change have also been advanced. The first has been styled Orthogenesis. It is frequently observed by palaeontologists that evolutionary trends in particular directions can be traced in series of fossils. The theory of orthogenesis assumes that the straight course pursued by such evolving types is due not to moulding, direct or indirect, from without, but to inner necessity, the hereditary constitution of the race unfolding and changing according to predetermined laws. Next, there is what may be called the crude theory of mutation, according to which species may enter upon a mutating period, and rapidly throw off a number of new and markedly distinct types, which may often be merely new without being better or worse suited to the environment. Finally, there is the view urged by Lotsy, that new types arise by recombination of characters after crossing. We know that when very distinct types are crossed and are fertile, there is (as demanded by the Mendelian theory) great diversity among their offspring from the second generation onward. Lotsy imagines that very wide crosses may occur, with enormous resultant variation, and that this variation is the sole raw material of evolutionary change. We may call this the recombination hypothesis, since it supposes that evolutionary novelty is due to new combinations of old characteristics. . . .

It cannot be said that the problem is yet by any means solved. In particular, the first origin of variations remains one of the great problems of biology. It would appear, however, that all theories can contribute something of value, although an adjustment of the theory of natural selection to a modified mutation theory will probably account for the majority of the facts.

JOHN F. KENNEDY

ON

Oliver Ellsworth

The following article is of special interest on only one count: It was written by John F. Kennedy.

Ellsworth, Oliver (1745–1807), U.S. statesman and jurist, chief author of the 1789 act establishing the U.S. federal court system and third chief justice of the United States, was born at Windsor, Conn., on April 29, 1745. He attended Yale and Princeton, from which he graduated in 1766. After pursuing theological and legal studies, he was admitted to the bar in Hartford, and represented Hartford in the Connecticut general assembly. He was subsequently state's attorney for Hartford county (1777), a member of the continental congress (1777–83), of the governor's council of Connecticut (1780–85) and a judge on the state superior court (1785–89).

In 1787 Ellsworth, together with Roger Sherman and William Samuel Johnson, represented Connecticut at the Constitutional Convention in Philadelphia, serving as a member of the important committee on detail. In the convention he proposed with Sherman the decisive "Connecticut compromise," by which the federal legislature was made to consist of two houses, the upper having equal representation from each state, the lower being chosen on the basis of population. This bargain, which insofar as it applies to the U.S. senate cannot be amended, is a keystone of the U.S. federal system. Ellsworth supported free international trade in slaves for as long as possible, insisting that moral responsibility for the trade must rest with the people of those states in which it was legally sanctioned. He vigorously defended the constitution in the Connecticut ratifying convention. His "Letters to a Landholder," printed in the *Connecticut Courant* and the *American Mercury,* had a broad influence during the ratification debates, much as the *Federalist* papers did in New York.

In 1789 Ellsworth became one of Connecticut's first United States senators and the acknowledged Federalist leader in the senate. He reported the first senate rules and suggested a plan for printing the journals, shaped the conference report on the Bill of Rights, framed the measure of admission for North Carolina, helped devise the government of the territory south of the Ohio and drafted the first bill regulating the consular service. He was chairman of the committee to establish the federal court system and the chief author of the Federal Judiciary act of 1789, the principal basis ever since of the U.S. court structure.

In 1796 Washington appointed him chief justice of the United States supreme court after John Rutledge had failed to receive senate confirmation and William Cushing, the senior associate justice, had declined. Ellsworth's service on the high court was cut short in 1800 by ill-health. His more important decisions were given on circuit such as his opinion in the Williams case (1799), which applied in the United States the common-law rule that the citizen may not expatriate himself without the consent of his government.

In 1799 he reluctantly accepted Pres. John Adams' request to join William Vans Murray and William R. Davie as commissioners to France to negotiate a new treaty. In Oct. 1800 Ellsworth persuaded Napoleon to accept a compromise convention which provided for freedom of commerce between the two nations and gave promise of preventing war between the United States and France.

From France he sent his resignation as chief justice. Until his death on Nov. 26, 1807, he lived a life of retirement in Windsor. Though his career included few acts of genius or public acclaim, Ellsworth's political skill, balanced judgment and clarity of purpose entitle him to recognition as a founding father of highest stature.

ARTHUR KOESTLER

ON

A Contraction of Fifteen Facial Muscles

Britannica's *motto is "Let Knowledge grow from more to more and thus be human life enriched." One cannot question the nobility of this sentiment, only its clarity. What is knowledge? As concerns the sciences, we think we know at least part of the answer. Similarly with respect to the* history *of almost anything. And so in these areas encyclopedists can in theory be "detached." But there are other areas, such as humor and wit, where subjectivity inevitably comes into play. The following treatment by Arthur Koestler is from the 15th edition. Although one does not automatically think of Koestler in connection with humor, he here proposes a particular and particularly engaging theory about a controversial aspect of human behavior.*

Arthur Koestler (1905–1983) was born in Hungary, wrote in English from 1940, and became a British citizen in 1948. His masterpiece, reflecting his disillusionment with Communism, is usually considered his novel Darkness at Noon. *Other influential books are* The Yogi and the Commissar and Other Essays *(1945) and* The Act of Creation *(1964). His latter years were in part occupied with a study of Eastern mysticism. A sufferer from leukemia and Parkinson's disease, he took his own life.*

Believing this article one of Britannica's *finest, we venture to print it in its entirety.*

In all its many-splendoured varieties, humour can be simply defined as a type of stimulation that tends to elicit the laughter reflex. Spontaneous laughter is a motor reflex produced by the coordinated contraction of 15 facial muscles in a stereotyped pattern and accompanied by altered breathing. Electrical stimulation of the main lifting muscle of the upper lip, the zygomatic major, with currents of varying intensity produces facial expressions ranging from the faint smile through the broad grin to the contortions typical of explosive laughter.

The laughter and smile of civilized man is, of course, often of a conventional kind, in which voluntary intent substitutes for, or interferes with, spontaneous reflex activity; this article is concerned, however, only with the latter. Once laughter is realized to be a humble reflex, several paradoxes must be faced. Motor reflexes, such as the contraction of the pupil of the eye in dazzling light, are simple responses to simple stimuli whose value to survival is obvious. But the involuntary contraction of 15 facial muscles, associated with certain irrepressible noises, strikes one as an activity without any utilitarian value, quite unrelated to the struggle for survival. Laughter is a reflex but unique in that it has no apparent biological purpose. One might call it a luxury reflex. Its only function seems to be to provide relief from tension.

The second related paradox is a striking discrepancy between the nature of the stimulus and that of the response in humorous transactions. When a blow beneath the kneecap causes an automatic upward kick, both "stimulus" and "response" function on the same primitive physiological level, without requiring the intervention of the higher mental functions. But that such a complex mental activity as reading a comic story should cause a specific reflex contraction of the facial muscles is a phenomenon that has puzzled philosophers since Plato. There is no clear-cut, predictable response that would tell a lecturer whether he has succeeded in convincing his listeners; but when he is telling a joke, laughter serves as an experimental test. *Humour is the only form of communication in which a stimulus on a high level of complexity produces a stereotyped, predictable response on the physiological reflex level.* Thus the response can be used as an indicator for the presence of the elusive quality that is called humour—

as the click of the Geiger counter is used to indicate the presence of radioactivity. Such a procedure is not possible in any other form of art; and since the step from the sublime to the ridiculous is reversible, the study of humour provides clues for the study of creativity in general.

This article deals with the changing concepts and practice of humour from the time of Aristotle to the influence of the mass media in the contemporary world.

The Logic of Laughter

The range of laughter-provoking experiences is enormous, from physical tickling to mental titillations of the most varied kinds. There is unity in this variety, however, a common denominator of a specific and specifiable pattern that reflects the "logic" or "grammar" of humour, as it were. A few examples will help to unravel that pattern.

1. A masochist is a person who likes a cold shower in the morning so he takes a hot one.

2. An English lady, on being asked by a friend what she thought of her departed husband's whereabouts: "Well, I suppose the poor soul is enjoying eternal bliss, but I wish you wouldn't talk about such unpleasant subjects."

3. A doctor comforts his patient: "You have a very serious disease. Of 10 persons who catch it, only one survives. It is lucky you came to me, for I have recently had nine patients with this disease and they all died of it."

4. Dialogue in a French film:

"Sir, I would like to ask for your daughter's hand."

"Why not? You have already had the rest."

5. A marquis of the court of Louis XV unexpectedly returned from a journey and, on entering his wife's boudoir, found her in the arms of a bishop. After a moment's hesitation, the marquis walked calmly to the window, leaned out, and began going through the motions of blessing the people in the street.

"What are you doing?" cried the anguished wife.

"Monseigneur is performing my functions, so I am performing his."

Is there a common pattern underlying these five stories? Starting with the last, a little reflection reveals that the marquis's behaviour is both unexpected and perfectly logical—but of a logic not usually applied to this type of situation. It is the logic of the division of labour, governed by rules as old as human civilization. But his reactions would have been expected to be governed by a different set of rules—the code of sexual morality. It is the sudden clash between these two mutually exclusive codes of rules—or associative contexts—that produces the comic effect. It compels the listener to perceive the situation in two self-consistent but incompatible frames of reference at the same time; his mind has to operate simultaneously on two different wavelengths. While this unusual condition lasts, the event is not only, as is normally the case, associated with a single frame of reference, but "bisociated" with two. The word bisociation was coined by the present writer to make a distinction between the routines of disciplined thinking within a single universe of discourse—on a single plane, as it were—and the creative types of mental activity that always operate on more than one plane. In humour, both the *creation* of a subtle joke and the *re-creative* act of perceiving the joke involve the delightful mental jolt of a sudden leap from one plane or associative context to another.

Turning to the other examples, in the French film dialogue, the daughter's "hand" is perceived first in a metaphorical frame of reference, then suddenly in a literal, bodily context. The doctor thinks in terms of abstract, statistical probabilities, the rules of which are inapplicable to individual cases; and there is an added twist because, in contrast to what common sense suggests, the patient's odds of survival are unaffected by whatever happened before; they are still one against 10. This is one of the profound paradoxes of the theory of probability, and the joke in fact implies a riddle; it pinpoints an absurdity that tends to be taken for granted. As for the lady who looks upon death as "eternal bliss" and at the same time "an unpleasant subject," she epitomizes the common human predicament of living in the divided house of faith and reason. Here again the simple joke carries unconscious overtones and undertones, audible to the inner ear alone.

The masochist who punishes himself by depriving himself of his daily punishment is governed by rules that are a *reversal* of those of normal logic. (A pattern can be constructed in which *both* frames of reference are reversed:

"A sadist is a person who is kind to a masochist.") But there is again an added twist. The joker does not really believe that the masochist takes his hot shower as a punishment; he only pretends to believe it. *Irony* is the satirist's most effective weapon; it pretends to adopt the opponent's ways of reasoning in order to expose their implicit absurdity or viciousness.

The common pattern underlying these stories is *the perceiving of a situation in two self-consistent but mutually incompatible frames of reference or associative contexts.* This formula can be shown to have a general validity for all forms of humour and wit, some of which will be discussed below. But it covers only one aspect of humour—its *intellectual structure.* Another fundamental aspect must be examined—the *emotional dynamics* that breathe life into that structure and make a person laugh, giggle, or smile.

Laughter and Emotion

When a comedian tells a story, he deliberately sets out to create a certain tension in his listeners, which mounts as the narrative progresses. But it never reaches its expected climax. The punch line, or point, acts as a verbal guillotine that cuts across the logical development of the story; it debunks the audience's dramatic expectations. The tension that was felt becomes suddenly redundant and is exploded in laughter. To put it differently, laughter disposes of emotive excitations that have become pointless and must somehow be worked off along physiological channels of least resistance; and the function of the "luxury reflex" is to provide these channels.

A glance at the caricatures of the 18th-century English artists William Hogarth or Thomas Rowlandson, showing the brutal merriment of people in a tavern, makes one realize at once that they are working off their surplus of adrenalin by contracting their face muscles into grimaces, slapping their thighs, and breathing in puffs through the half-closed glottis. Their flushed faces reveal that the emotions disposed of through these safety valves are brutality, envy, sexual gloating. In cartoons by the 20th-century American James Thurber, however, coarse laughter yields to an amused and rarefied smile: the flow of adrenalin has been distilled and crystallized into a grain of Attic salt—a sophisticated joke. The word witticism is derived from "wit" in its original sense of intelligence and acumen (as is *Witz* in German). The domains of humour and of ingenuity are continuous, without a sharp boundary: the jester is brother to the sage. Across the spectrum of humour, from its coarse to its subtle forms, from practical joke to brainteaser, from jibe to irony, from anecdote to epigram, the emotional climate shows a gradual transformation. The emotion discharged in coarse laughter is aggression robbed of its purpose. The jokes small children enjoy are mostly scatological; adolescents of all ages gloat on vicarious sex. The sick joke trades on repressed sadism, satire on righteous indignation. There is a bewildering variety of moods involved in different forms of humour, including mixed or contradictory feelings; but whatever the mixture, it must contain a basic ingredient that is indispensable: an impulse, however faint, of aggression or apprehension. It may appear in the guise of malice, contempt, the veiled cruelty of condescension, or merely an absence of sympathy with the victim of the joke—a momentary anesthesia of the heart, as the French philosopher Henri Bergson put it.

In the subtler types of humour, the aggressive tendency may be so faint that only careful analysis will detect it, like the presence of salt in a well-prepared dish—which, however, would be tasteless without it. Replace aggression by sympathy and the same situation—a drunk falling on his face, for example—will be no longer comic but pathetic and will evoke not laughter but pity. It is the aggressive element, the detached malice of the comic impersonator, that turns pathos into bathos, tragedy into travesty. Malice may be combined with affection in friendly teasing; and the aggressive component in civilized humour may be sublimated or no longer conscious. But in jokes that appeal to children and primitive people, cruelty and boastful self-assertiveness are much in evidence. In 1961 a survey carried out among American children aged eight to 15 made the researchers conclude that the mortification, discomfort, or hoaxing of others readily caused laughter, but witty or funny remarks often passed unnoticed.

Similar considerations apply to the historically earlier forms and theories of the comic. In Aristotle's view, laughter was intimately related to ugliness and debasement. Cicero held that the province of the ridiculous lay in a certain baseness and deformity. Descartes believed that laughter was a manifestation of joy mixed with surprise or hatred or both. In Francis Bacon's list of what causes laughter, the first place is again given to deformity. One of the most frequently quoted utterances on the subject is this definition in Thomas Hobbes's *Leviathan* (1651):

> The passion of laughter is nothing else but sudden glory arising from a sudden conception of some eminency in ourselves by comparison with the infirmity of others, or with our own formerly.

In the 19th century, Alexander Bain, an early experimental psychologist, thought along the same lines:

> Not in physical effects alone, but in everything where a man can achieve a stroke of superiority, in surpassing or discomforting a rival, is the disposition of laughter apparent.

In Bergson's view, laughter is the corrective punishment inflicted by society upon the unsocial individual: "In laughter we always find an unavowed intention to humiliate and consequently to correct our neighbour." Sir Max Beerbohm, the 20th-century English wit, found "two elements in the public's humour: delight in suffering, contempt for the unfamiliar." The American psychologist William McDougall believed that "laughter has been evolved in the human race as an antidote to sympathy, a protective reaction shielding us from the depressive influence of the shortcomings of our fellow men."

However much the opinions of the theorists differ, on this one point nearly all of them agree: that the emotions discharged in laughter always contain an element of aggressiveness. It must be borne in mind, however, that aggression and apprehension are twin phenomena, so much so that psychologists are used to talking of "aggressive-defensive impulses." Accordingly, one of the typical situations in which laughter occurs is the moment of sudden cessation of fear caused by some imaginary danger. Rarely is the nature of laughter as an overflow of redundant tensions more strikingly manifested than in the sudden change of expression on a small child's face from anxious apprehension to the happy laughter of relief. This seems to be unrelated to humour; yet a closer look reveals in it the same logical structure as in the joke: the wildly barking little dog was first perceived by the child in a context of danger, then discovered to be a harmless pup; the tension has suddenly become redundant and is spilled.

Immanuel Kant realized that what causes laughter is "the sudden transformation of a tense expectation into nothing." Herbert Spencer, the 19th-century English philosopher, took up the idea and attempted to formulate it in physiological terms: "Emotions and sensations tend to generate bodily movements. . . . When consciousness is unawares transferred from great things to small," the "liberated nerve force" will expend itself along channels of least resistance—the bodily movements of laughter. Freud incorporated Spencer's theory of humour into his own, with special emphasis on the release of repressed emotions in laughing; he also attempted to explain why the excess energy should be worked off in that particular way:

> According to the best of my knowledge, the grimaces and contortions of the corners of the mouth that characterise laughter appear first in the satisfied and over-satiated nursling when he drowsily quits the breast. . . . They are physical expressions of the determination to take no more nourishment, an "enough" so to speak, or rather a "more than enough" . . . This primal sense of pleasurable saturation may have provided the link between the smile—that basic phenomenon underlying laughter—and its subsequent connection with other pleasurable processes of detension.

In other words, the muscle contractions of the smile, as the earliest expressions of relief from tension, would thereafter serve as channels of least resistance. Similarly, the explosive exhalations of laughter seem designed to "puff away" surplus tension in a kind of respiratory gymnastics, and agitated gestures obviously serve the same function.

It may be objected that such massive reactions often seem quite out of proportion to the slight stimulations that provoke them. But it must be borne in mind that laughter is a phenomenon of the trigger-releaser type, where a sudden turn of the tap may release vast amounts of stored emotions, derived from various, often unconscious, sources: repressed sadism, sexual tumescence, unavowed fear, even boredom. The explosive laughter of a class of schoolboys at some trivial incident is a measure of their pent-up resentment during a boring lecture. Another factor that may amplify the reaction out of all proportion to the comic stimulus is the social infectiousness that laughter shares with other emotive manifestations of group behaviour.

Laughter or smiling may also be caused by stimulations that are not in themselves comic but signs or symbols deputizing for well-established comic patterns—such as Charlie Chaplin's oversized shoes or Groucho Marx's cigar—or catchphrases, or allusions to family jokes. To discover why people laugh requires, on some occasions, tracing back a long, involved thread of associations to its source. This task is further complicated by the fact that the effect of such comic symbols—in a cartoon or on the stage—appears to be instantaneous, without allowing time for the accumulation and subsequent discharge of "expectations" and "emotive tensions." But here memory comes into play, having already accumulated the required emotions in past experiences, acting as a storage battery whose charge can be sparked off at any time: the smile that greets Falstaff's appearance on the scene is derived from a mixture of memories and expectations. Besides, even if a reaction to a cartoon appears to be instantaneous, there is always a process in time until the reader "sees the joke"; the cartoon has to tell a story even if it is telescoped into a few seconds. All of this shows that to analyze humour is a task as delicate as analyzing the composition of a perfume with its multiple ingredients, some of which are never consciously perceived while others, when sniffed in isolation, would make one wince.

In this article there has been a discussion first of the logical structure of humour and then of its emotional dynamics. Putting the two together, the result may be summarized as follows: the "bisociation" of a situation or idea with two mutually incompatible contexts in a person's mind and the resulting abrupt transfer of his train of thought from one context to another put a sudden end to his "tense expectations"; the accumulated emotion, deprived of its object, is left hanging in the air and is discharged in laughter. Upon hearing that the marquis in the story told earlier walks to the window and starts blessing the people in the street, the intellect turns a somersault and enters with gusto into the new game. The malicious and erotic feelings aroused by the start of the story, however, cannot be fitted into the new context; deserted by the nimble intellect, these feelings gush out in laughter like air from a punctured tire.

To put it differently: people laugh because their emotions have a greater inertia and persistence than their thoughts. Affects are incapable of keeping step with reasoning; unlike reasoning, they cannot "change direction" at a moment's notice. To the physiologist, this is self-evident since emotions operate through the genetically old, massive sympathetic nervous system and its allied hormones, acting on the whole body, while the processes of conceptual thinking are confined to the neocortex at the roof of the brain. Common experience provides daily confirmation of this dichotomy. People are literally "poisoned" by their adrenal humours; it takes time to talk a person out of a mood; fear and anger show physical aftereffects long after their causes have been removed. If man were able to change his moods as quickly as his thoughts, he would be an acrobat of emotion; but since he is not, his thoughts and emotions frequently become dissociated. It is emotion deserted by thought that is discharged in laughter. For emotion, owing to its greater mass momentum, is, as has been shown, unable to follow the sudden switch of ideas to a different type of logic; it tends to persist in a straight line. Aldous Huxley once wrote:

> We carry around with us a glandular system which was admirably well adapted to life in the Paleolithic times but is not very well adapted to life now. Thus we tend to produce more adrenalin than is good for us, and we either suppress ourselves and turn destructive energies inwards or else we do not suppress ourselves and we start hitting people. (From *Man and Civilization: Control of the Mind,* ed. Seymour M. Farber and Roger H.L. Wilson. Copyright 1961. Used with permission of McGraw-Hill Book Company.)

A third alternative is to laugh at people. There are other outlets for tame aggression, such as competitive sports or literary criticism; but they are acquired skills, whereas laughter is a gift of nature, included in man's native equipment. The glands that control his emotions reflect conditions at a stage of evolution when the struggle for existence was more deadly than at present—and when the reaction to any strange sight or sound consisted in jumping, bristling, fighting, or running. As security and comfort increased in the species, new outlets were needed for emotions that could no longer be worked off through their original channels, and laughter is obviously one of them. But it could only emerge when reasoning had gained a degree of independence from the urges of emotion. Below the human level, thinking and feeling appear to form an indivisible unity. Not before thinking became gradually detached from feeling could man perceive his own emotion as redundant and make the smiling admission, "I have been fooled."

Verbal Humour

The foregoing discussion was intended to provide the tools for dissecting and analyzing any specimen of humour. The procedure is to determine the nature of the two (or more) frames of reference whose collision gives rise to the comic effect—to discover the type of logic or "rules of the game" that govern each. In the more sophisticated type of joke, the logic is implied and hidden, and the moment it is stated in explicit form, the joke is dead. Unavoidably, the section that follows will be strewn with cadavers.

Max Eastman, in *The Enjoyment of Laughter* (1936), remarked of a laboured pun by Ogden Nash: "It is not a pun but a punitive expedition." That applies to most puns, including Milton's famous lines about the Prophet Elijah's ravens, which were "though ravenous taught to abstain from what they brought," or the character mentioned by Freud, who calls the Christmas season the "alcoholidays." Most puns strike one as atrocious, perhaps because they represent the most primitive form of humour; two disparate strings of thought tied together by an acoustic knot. But the very primitiveness of such association based on pure sound ("hol") may account for the pun's immense popularity with children and its prevalence in certain types of mental disorder ("punning mania").

From the play on sounds—puns and Spoonerisms—an ascending series leads to the play on words and so to the play on ideas. When Groucho Marx says of a safari in Africa, "We shot two bucks, but that was all the money we had," the joke hinges on the two meanings of the word buck. It would be less funny without the reference to Groucho, which evokes a visual image instantly arousing high expectations. The story about the marquis above may be considered of a superior type of humour because it plays not on mere words but on ideas.

It would be quite easy—and equally boring—to draw up a list in which jokes and witticisms are classified according to the nature of the frames of reference whose collision creates the comic effect. A few have already been mentioned: metaphorical versus literal meaning (the daughter's "hand"); professional versus common sense logic (the doctor); incompatible codes of behaviour (the marquis); confrontations of the trivial and the exalted ("eternal bliss"); trains of reasoning travelling, happily joined together, in opposite directions (the sadist who is kind to the masochist). The list could be extended indefinitely; in fact *any* two frames of reference can be made to yield a comic effect of sorts by hooking them together and infusing a drop of malice into the concoction. The frames may even be defined by such abstract concepts as "time" and "weather": the absent-minded professor who tries to read the temperature from his watch or to tell the time from the thermometer is comic in the same way as a game of table tennis played with a soccer ball or a game of rugby played with a table tennis ball. The variations are infinite, the formula remains the same.

Jokes and anecdotes have a single point of culmination. The literary forms of *sustained humour,* such as the picaresque novel, do not rely on a single effect but on a series of minor climaxes. The narrative moves along the line of intersection of contrasted planes, such as the fantasy world of Don Quixote and the cunning horse sense of Sancho Panza, or is made to oscillate between them. As a result, tension is continuously generated and discharged in mild amusement.

Comic verse thrives on the melodious union of incongruities, such as the "cabbages and kings" in Lewis Carroll's "The Walrus and the Carpenter," and particularly on the contrast between lofty form and flat-footed content. Certain metric forms associated with heroic poetry, such as the hexameter or Alexandrine, arouse expectations of pathos, of the exalted; to pour into these epic molds some homely, trivial content—"beautiful soup, so rich and green/ waiting in a hot tureen"—is an almost infallible comic device. The rolling rhythms of the first lines of a limerick that carry, instead of a mythical hero such as Hector or Achilles, a young lady from Ohio for a ride make her ridiculous even before the expected calamities befall her. Instead of a heroic mold, a soft lyrical one may also pay off:

> . . . And what could be moister
> Than tears of an oyster?

Another type of incongruity between form and content yields the bogus proverb: "The rule is: jam tomorrow and jam yesterday—but never jam today." Two contradictory statements have been telescoped into a line whose homely, admonitory sound conveys the impression of a popular adage. In a similar way, nonsense verse achieves its effect by pretending to make sense, by forcing the reader to project meaning into the phonetic pattern of the jabberwocky, as one interprets the ink blots in a Rorschach test.

The *satire* is a verbal caricature that shows a deliberately distorted image of a person, institution, or society. The traditional method of the caricaturist is to exaggerate those features he considers to be characteristic of his victim's personality and to simplify by leaving out everything that is not relevant for his purpose. The satirist uses the same technique, and the features of society he selects for magnification are, of course, those of which he disapproves. The result is a juxtaposition, in the reader's mind, of his habitual image of the world in which he moves and its absurd reflection in the satirist's distorting mirror. He is made to recognize familiar features in the absurd and absurdity in the familiar. Without this double vision the satire would be humourless. If the human Yahoos were really such evil-smelling monsters as Gulliver's Houyhnhnm hosts claim, then Jonathan Swift's *Gulliver's Travels* (1726) would not be a satire but the statement of a deplorable truth. Straight invective is not satire; satire must deliberately overshoot its mark.

A similar effect is achieved if, instead of exaggerating the objectionable features, the satirist projects them by means of the *allegory* onto a different background, such as an animal society. A succession of writers, from the ancient Greek dramatist Aristophanes through Swift to such 20th-century satirists as Anatole France and George Orwell, have used this technique to focus attention on deformities of society that, blunted by habit, are taken for granted.

Situational Humour

The coarsest type of humour is the practical joke: pulling away the chair from under the dignitary's lowered bottom. The victim is perceived first as a person of consequence, then suddenly as an inert body subject to the laws of physics: authority is debunked by gravity, mind by matter; man is degraded to a mechanism. Goose-stepping soldiers acting like automatons, the pedant behaving like a mechanical robot, the Sergeant Major attacked by diarrhea, or Hamlet getting the hiccups—all show man's lofty aspirations deflated by his all-too-solid flesh. A similar effect is produced by artifacts that masquerade as humans: Punch and Judy, jack-in-the-box, gadgets playing tricks on their masters as if with calculated malice.

In Henri Bergson's theory of laughter, this dualism of subtle mind and inert matter—he calls it "the mechanical encrusted on the living"—is made to serve as an explanation of *all* varieties of the comic. In the light of what has been said, however, it would seem to apply only to *one* type of comic situation among many others.

From the "bisociation" of man and machine, there is only a step to the man-animal hybrid. Walt Disney's creations behave as if they were human without losing their animal appearance. The caricaturist follows the reverse procedure by discovering horsey, mousy, or piggish features in the human face.

This leads to the comic devices of imitation, impersonation, and disguise. The impersonator is perceived as himself and somebody else at the same time. If the result is slightly degrading—but only in that case—the spectator will laugh. The comedian impersonating a public personality, two pairs of trousers serving as the legs of the pantomime horse, men disguised as women and women as men—in each case the paired patterns reduce each other to absurdity.

The most aggressive form of impersonation is the *parody,* designed to deflate hollow pretense, to destroy illusion, and to undermine pathos by harping on the weaknesses of the victim. Wigs falling off, speakers forgetting their lines, gestures remaining suspended in the air: the parodist's favourite points of attack are again situated on the line of intersection between the sublime and the trivial.

Playful behaviour in young animals and children is amusing because it is an unintentional parody of adult behaviour, which it imitates or anticipates. Young puppies are droll because their helplessness, affection, and puzzled expression make them appear more "human" than full-grown dogs; because their growls strike one as impersonations of adult behaviour—like a child in a bowler hat; because the puppy's waddling, uncertain gait makes it a choice victim of nature's practical jokes; because its bodily disproportions—the huge padded paws, Falstaffian belly, and wrinkled brow—give it the appearance of a caricature; and lastly because the observer feels so superior to a puppy. A fleeting smile can contain many logical ingredients and emotional spices.

Both Cicero and Francis Bacon regarded *deformity* as the most frequent cause of laughter. Renaissance princes collected dwarfs and hunchbacks for their merriment. It obviously requires a certain amount of imagination and empathy to recognize in a midget a fellow human, who, though different in appearance, thinks and feels much as oneself does. In children, this projective faculty is still rudimentary: they tend to mock people with a stammer or a limp and laugh at the foreigner with an odd pronunciation. Similar attitudes are shown by tribal or parochial societies to any form of appearance or behaviour that deviates from their strict norms: the stranger is not really human; he only pretends to be "like us." The Greeks used the same word, barbarous, for the foreigner and the stutterer: the uncouth barking sounds the stranger uttered were considered a parody of human speech. Vestiges of this primitive attitude are still found in the curious fact that civilized people accept a foreign accent with tolerance, whereas imitation of a foreign accent strikes them as comic. The imitator's mispronunciations are recognized as mere pretense; this knowledge makes sympathy unnecessary and enables the audience to be childishly cruel with a clean conscience.

Other sources of innocent laughter are situations in which *the part and the whole* change roles, and attention becomes focussed on a detail torn out of the functional context on which its meaning depended. When the phonograph needle gets stuck, the soprano's voice keeps repeating the same word on the same quaver, which suddenly assumes a grotesquely independent life. The same happens when faulty orthography displaces attention from meaning to spelling, or whenever consciousness is directed at functions that otherwise are performed automatically. The latter situation is well illustrated by the story of the centipede who, when asked in which order he moved his hundred legs, became paralyzed and could walk no more. The self-conscious, awkward youth, who does not know what to do with his hands, is a victim of the paradox of the centipede.

Comedies have been classified according to their reliance on situations, manners, or characters. The logic of the last two needs no further discussion; in the first, comic effects are contrived by making a situation participate simultaneously in two independent chains of events with different associative contexts, which intersect through coincidence, mistaken identity, or confusions of time and occasion.

Why tickling should produce laughter remained an enigma in all earlier theories of the comic. As Darwin was the first to point out, the innate response to tickling is squirming and straining to withdraw the tickled part—a defense reaction designed to escape attacks on vulnerable areas such as the soles of the feet, armpits, belly, and flank. If a fly settles on the belly of a horse, it causes a ripple of muscle contractions across the skin—the equivalent of squirming in the tickled child. But the horse does not laugh when tickled, and the child not always. The child will laugh only—and this is the crux of the matter—when it perceives tickling as a *mock attack,* a caress in mildly aggressive disguise. For the same reason, people laugh only when tickled by others, not when they tickle themselves.

Experiments at Yale University on babies under one year revealed the not very surprising fact that they laughed 15 times more often when tickled by their mothers than by strangers; and when tickled by strangers, they mostly cried. For the mock attack must be recognized as being only pretense, and with strangers one cannot be sure. Even with its own mother, there is an ever-so-slight feeling of uncertainty and apprehension, the expression of which will alternate with laughter in the baby's behaviour. It is precisely this element of tension between the tickles that is relieved in the laughter accompanying the squirm. The rule of the game is "let me be just a little frightened so that I can enjoy the relief."

Thus the tickler is impersonating an aggressor but is simultaneously known not to be one. This is probably the first situation in life that makes the infant live on two planes at once, a delectable foretaste of being tickled by the horror comic.

Humour in the visual arts reflects the same logical structures as discussed before. Its most primitive form is the distorting mirror at the fun fair, which reflects the human frame elongated into a column or compressed into the shape of a toad. It plays a practical joke on the victim, who sees the image in the mirror both as his familiar self and as a lump of plasticine that can be stretched and squeezed into any absurd form. The mirror distorts mechanically while the caricaturist does so selectively, employing the same method as the satirist—exaggerating characteristic features and simplifying the rest. Like the satirist, the caricaturist reveals the absurd in the familiar; and, like the satirist, he must overshoot his mark. His malice is rendered harmless by the knowledge that the monstrous potbellies and bowlegs he draws are not real; real deformities are not comic but arouse pity.

The artist, painting a stylized portrait, also uses the technique of selection, exaggeration, and simplification; but his attitude toward the model is usually dominated by positive empathy instead of negative malice, and the features he selects for emphasis differ accordingly. In some character studies by Leonardo da Vinci, Hogarth, or Honoré Daumier, the passions reflected are so violent, the grimaces so ferocious, that it is impossible to tell whether the works were meant as portraits or caricatures. If one feels that such distortions of the human face are not really possible, that Daumier merely *pretended* that they exist, then one is absolved from horror and pity and can laugh at his grotesques. But if one feels that this is indeed what Daumier saw in those dehumanized faces, then they are not comic but tragic.

Humour in *music* is a subject to be approached with diffidence because the language of music ultimately eludes translation into verbal concepts. All one can do is to point out some analogies: a "rude" noise, such as the blast of a trumpet inserted into a passage where it does not belong, has the effect of a practical joke; a singer or an instrument out of tune produces a similar reaction; the imitation of animal sounds, vocally or instrumentally, exploits the technique of impersonation; a nocturne by Chopin transposed into hot jazz or a simple street song performed with Wagnerian pathos is a marriage of incompatibles. These are primitive devices corresponding to the lowest levels of humour; more sophisticated are the techniques employed by Maurice Ravel in *La Valse,* a parody of the sentimental Viennese waltz, or by Zoltán Kodály in the mock-heroics of his Hungarian folk opera, *Háry János.* But in comic operas it is almost impossible to sort out how much of the comic effect is derived from the book and how much from the music; and the highest forms of musical humour, the unexpected delights of a lighthearted scherzo by Mozart, defy verbal analysis, unless it is so specialized and technical as to defeat its purpose. Although a "witty" musical passage that springs a surprise on the audience and cheats it of its expectations certainly has the emotion-relieving effect that tends to produce laughter, a concert audience may occasionally smile but will hardly ever laugh: the emotions evoked by musical humour are of a subtler kind than those of the verbal and visual variety.

Styles and Techniques in Humour

The criteria that determine whether a humourous offering will be judged good, bad, or indifferent are partly a matter of period taste and personal preference and partly dependent on the style and technique of the humorist. It would seem that these criteria can be summed up under three main headings: originality, emphasis, and economy.

The merits of originality are self-evident; it provides the essential element of surprise, which cuts across our expectations. But true originality is not very often met either in humour or in other forms of art. One common substitute for it is to increase the tension of the audience by various techniques of suggestive emphasis. The clown's domain is the rich, coarse type of humour: he piles it on; he appeals to sadistic, sexual, scatological impulses. One of his favourite tricks is repetition of the same situation, the same key phrase. This diminishes the effect of surprise, but it has a tension-accumulating effect: emotion is easily drawn into the familiar channel—more and more liquid is being pumped into the punctured pipeline.

Emphasis on local colour and ethnic peculiarities, such as Scottish or Cockney stories, for example, is a further means to channel emotion into familiar tracks. The Scotsman or Cockney must, of course, be a caricature if the comic purpose is to be achieved. In other words, exaggeration and simplification once more appear as indispensable tools to provide emphasis.

In the higher forms of humour, however, emphasis tends to yield to the opposite kind of virtue—economy. Economy, in humour and art, does not mean mechanical brevity but implicit hints instead of explicit statements—the oblique allusion in lieu of the frontal attack. Old-fashioned cartoons, such as those featuring the British lion and the Russian bear, hammered their message in; the modern cartoon usually poses a riddle that the reader must solve by an imaginative effort in order to see the joke.

In humour, as in other forms of art, emphasis and economy are complementary techniques. The first forces the offering down the consumer's throat; the second tantalizes to whet his appetite.

Relations to Art and Science

Earlier theories of humour, including even those of Bergson and Freud, treated it as an isolated phenomenon, without attempting to throw light on the intimate connections between the comic and the tragic, between laughter and crying, between artistic inspiration, comic inventiveness, and scientific discovery. Yet these three domains of creative activity form a continuum with no sharp boundaries between wit and ingenuity, nor between discovery and art.

It has been said that scientific discovery consists in seeing an analogy where nobody has seen one before. When, in the Song of Solomon, Solomon compared the Shulamite's neck to a tower of ivory, he saw an analogy that nobody had seen before; when William Harvey compared the heart of a fish to a mechanical pump, he did the same; and when the caricaturist draws a nose like a cucumber, he again does just that. In fact, all the logical patterns discussed above, which constitute a "grammar" of humour, can also enter the service of art or discovery, as the case may be. The pun has structural equivalents in the rhyme and in word games, which range from crossword puzzles to the deciphering of the Rosetta Stone, the key to Egyptian hieroglyphic. The confrontation between diverse codes of behaviour may yield comedy, tragedy, or new psychological insights. The dualism of mind and inert matter is exploited by the practical joker but also provides one of the eternal themes of literature: man as a marionette on strings, manipulated by gods or chromosomes. The man-beast dichotomy is reflected by Walt Disney's cartoon character Donald Duck but also in Franz Kafka's macabre tale *The Metamorphosis* (1915) and in the psychologist's experiments with rats. The caricature corresponds not only to the artist's character portrait but also to the scientist's diagrams and charts, which emphasize the relevant features and leave out the rest.

Contemporary psychology regards the conscious and unconscious processes underlying creativity in all domains as an essentially combinative activity—the bringing together of previously separate areas of knowledge and experience. The scientist's purpose is to achieve *synthesis;* the artist aims at a *juxtaposition* of the familiar and the eternal; the humorist's game is to contrive a *collision.* And as their motivations differ, so do the emotional responses evoked by each type of creativity: discovery satisfies the exploratory drive; art induces emotional catharsis; humour arouses malice and provides a harmless outlet for it. Laughter has been described as the "Haha reaction"; the discoverer's Eureka cry as the "Aha! reaction"; and the delight of the aesthetic experience as the "Ah . . . reaction." But the transitions from one to the other are continuous: witticism blends into epigram, caricature into portrait; and whether one considers architecture, medicine, chess, or cookery, there is no clear frontier where the realm of science ends and that of art begins: the creative person is a citizen of both. Comedy and tragedy, laughter and weeping, mark the extremes of a continuous spectrum, and a comparison of the physiology of laughter and weeping yields further clues to this challenging problem. Such considerations, however, lie beyond the terms of reference of the present article.

The Humanization of Humour

The San (Bushmen) of the Kalahari desert of South West Africa/Namibia are among the oldest and most primitive inhabitants of the Earth. An anthropologist who made an exhaustive study of them provided a rare glimpse of prehistoric humour:

> On the way home we saw and shot a springbok, as there was no meat left in camp. The bullet hit the springbok in the stomach and partly eviscerated him, causing him to jump and kick before he finally died. The Bushmen thought that this was terribly funny and they laughed, slapping their thighs and kicking their heels to imitate the springbok, showing no pity at all, but then they regard animals with great detachment.

But the San remained "in good spirits, pleased with the amusement the springbok had given them." (From Elizabeth Marshall Thomas, *The Harmless People;* Alfred A. Knopf, New York, 1959.)

Obviously the San, like most primitive people, do not regard animals as sentient beings; the springbok's kicking in his agony appears to them funny because in their view the animal *pretends* to suffer pain like a human being, though it is incapable of such feelings. The ancient Greeks' attitude toward the stammering barbarian was similarly inspired by the conviction that he is not really human but only pretends to be. The ancient Hebrews' sense of humour seems to have been no less harsh: it has been pointed out that in the Old Testament there are 29 references to laughter, out of which 13 instances are linked with scorn, derision, mocking, and contempt and only two are born of joy.

As laughter emerged from antiquity, it was so aggressive that it has been likened to a dagger. It was in ancient Greece that the dagger was transformed into a quill, dripping with poison at first, then diluted and infused with delightfully lyrical and fanciful ingredients. The 5th century BC saw the first rise of humour into art, starting with parodies of Olympian heroics and soon reaching a peak, in some respects unsurpassed to this day, in the comedies of Aristophanes. From here onward, the evolution of humour in the Western world merges with the history of literature and art.

If the overall trend was toward the humanization of humour from primitive to sophisticated forms, there also have been ups and downs reflecting changes in political and cultural climate. George Orwell's satire of the 20th century, for example, is much more savage than that of Jonathan Swift in 18th-century England or of Voltaire in 18th-century France. If the Dark Ages produced works of humorous art, little of it has survived. And under the tyrannies of Hitler in Germany and of Stalin in the Soviet Union, humour was driven underground. Dictators fear laughter more than bombs.

Non-Western styles. About non-Western varieties of humour, the Westerner is tempted to repeat the middle-aged British matron's remark on watching Cleopatra rave and die on the stage: "How different, how very different from the home life of our dear Queen." Humour thrives only in its native climate, embedded in its native logic; when one does not know what to expect, one cannot be cheated of one's expectations. Hindu humour, for instance, as exemplified by the savage pranks played on humans by the monkey-god Hanuman, strikes the Westerner as particularly cruel, perhaps because the Hindu's approach to mythology is fundamentally alien to the Western mind. The humour of the Japanese, on the other hand, is, from the Western point of view, astonishingly mild and poetical, like weak, mint-flavoured tea:

> The boss of the monkeys ordered his thousands of henchmen to get the moon reflected in the water. They all tried various means but failed and were much troubled. One of the monkeys at last got the moon in the water and respectfully offered it to the boss, saying "This is what you

> asked for." The boss was delighted and praised him, saying, "What an exploit! You have distinguished yourself!" The monkey then asked, "By the way, master, what are you going to do with this?" "Well, yes . . . I didn't think of that." (From *Karukuchi Ukibyotan,* 1751; in R.H. Blyth, *Japanese Humour,* 1957.)

The following dates from about a century later:

> There was once a man who was always bewailing his lack of money to buy saké (rice wine) with. His wife, feeling sorry for him, dutifully cut off some of her hair and sold it to the hairdresser's for twenty-four mon, and bought her husband some saké. "Where on earth did you get this from?" "I sold my hair and bought it." "You did such a thing for me?" The wretched man shed tears, and fondling his wife's remaining hair said, "Yes, and there's another good half-bottle of saké here!" (From *Chanoko-mochi,* 1856; in Blyth.)

The combination of maudlin tears and brazen selfishness, and the crazy logic of equating the wife's coiffure with a liquid measure of saké, show the familiar Western pattern of the clash of incompatibles, even though transplanted into another culture.

Humour in the contemporary world. Humour today seems to be dominated by two main factors: the influence of the mass media and the crisis of values affecting a culture in rapid and violent transition. The former tends toward the commercialized manufacture of laughter by popular comedians and gags produced by conveyor-belt methods; the latter toward a sophisticated form of black humour larded with sick jokes, sadism, and sex.

Fashions, however, always run their course; perhaps the next one will delight in variations on the theme of the monkey boss who, having gained possession of the moon, does not know what to do with it. The only certainty regarding the humour of the future is contained in Dr. Samuel Johnson's dictum: "Sir, men have been wise in many different modes, but they have always laughed in the same way."

PYOTR KROPOTKIN

ON

Anarchism

Pyotr Kropotkin, (1842–1921), Russian prince, soldier, and geographer, gave up at the age of twenty-nine both his social position and a scientific career of exceptional promise to become an outcast in the name of social justice. As the principal theorist of "anarchist communism" Kropotkin was at the forefront of the broad social-political movement that kept the Europe of the latter part of the ninetheenth century and the early years of the twentieth in constant turmoil.

From the time of the 9th edition (1875–1889) Kropotkin contributed a great many articles to the Britannica, *mainly on topics of Asian geography and topography (some of the earliest were apparently sent in from his French prison). For the 11th edition (1910–1911) he wrote the article "Anarchism," outlining the political principles that had motivated his difficult career and tracing their history. (R.McH.)*

The extracts that follow are from the opening and closing passages of the article. The intervening section is mainly historical. The reader may wish to compare Kropotkin's essay with the excellent article "Anarchism" by George Woodcock in the 15th edition.

Anarchism (from the Gr. ἀν-, and ἀρχη, contrary to authority), the name given to a principle or theory of life and conduct under which society is conceived without government—Harmony in such a society being obtained, not by submission to law, or by obedience to any authority, but by free agreements concluded between the various groups, territorial and professional, freely constituted for the sake of production and consumption, as also for the satisfaction of the infinite variety of needs and aspirations of a civilized being. In a society developed on these lines, the voluntary associations which already now begin to cover all the fields of human activity would take a still greater extension so as to substitute themselves for the state in all its functions. They would represent an interwoven network, composed of an infinite variety of groups and federations of all sizes and degrees, local, regional, national and international—temporary or more or less permanent—for all possible purposes: production, consumption and exchange, communications, sanitary arrangements, education, mutual protection, defence of the territory, and so on; and, on the other side, for the satisfaction of an ever-increasing number of scientific, artistic, literary and sociable needs. Moreover, such a society would represent nothing immutable. On the contrary—as is seen in organic life at large—harmony would (it is contended) result from an ever-changing adjustment and readjustment of equilibrium between the multitudes of forces and influences, and this adjustment would be the easier to obtain as none of the forces would enjoy a special protection from the state.

If, it is contended, society were organized on these principles, man would not be limited in the free exercise of his powers in productive work by a capitalist monopoly, maintained by the state; nor would he be limited in the exercise of his will by a fear of punishment, or by obedience towards individuals or metaphysical entities, which both lead to depression of initiative and servility of mind. He would be guided in his actions by his own understanding, which necessarily would bear the impression of a free action and reaction between his own self and the ethical conceptions of his surroundings. Man would thus be enabled to obtain the full development of all his faculties, intellectual, artistic and moral, without being hampered by overwork for the monopolists, or by the servility and inertia of mind of the great number. He would thus be able to reach full *individualization,* which is not possible either under the present system of *individualism,* or under any system of state-socialism in the so-called *Volkstaat* (popular state).

The Anarchist writers consider, moreover, that their conception is not a Utopia, constructed on the *a priori* method, after a few desiderata have been taken as postulates. It is derived, they maintain, from an *analysis of tendencies* that are at work already, even though state socialism may find a temporary favour with the reformers. The progress of modern technics, which wonderfully simplifies the production of all the necessaries of life; the growing spirit of independence, and the rapid spread of free initiative and free understanding in all branches of activity—including those which formerly were considered as the proper attribution of church and state—are steadily reinforcing the no-government tendency.

As to their economical conceptions, the Anarchists, in common with all Socialists, of whom they constitute the left wing, maintain that the now prevailing system of private ownership in land, and our capitalist production for the sake of profits, represent a monopoly which runs against both the principles of justice and the dictates of utility. They are the main obstacle which prevents the successes of modern technics from being brought into the service of all, so as to produce general well-being. The Anarchists consider the wage-system and capitalist production altogether as an obstacle to progress. But they point out also that the state was, and continues to be, the chief instrument for permitting the few to monopolize the land, and the capitalists to appropriate for themselves a quite disproportionate share of the yearly accumulated surplus of production. Consequently, while combating the present monopolization of land, and capitalism altogether, the Anarchists combat with the same energy the state, as the main support of that system. Not this or that special form, but the state altogether, whether it be a monarchy or even a republic governed by means of the *referendum*.

The state organization, having always been, both in ancient and modern history (Macedonian empire, Roman empire, modern European states grown up on the ruins of the autonomous cities), the instrument for establishing monopolies in favour of the ruling minorities, cannot be made to work for the destruction of these monopolies. The Anarchists consider, therefore, that to hand over to the state all the main sources of economical life—the land, the mines, the railways, banking, insurance, and so on—as also the management of all the main branches of industry, in addition to all the functions already accumulated in its hands (education, state-supported religions, defence of the territory, &c.), would mean to create a new instrument of tyranny. State capitalism would only increase the powers of bureaucracy and capitalism. True progress lies in the direction of decentralization, both *territorial* and *functional,* in the development of the spirit of local and personal initiative, and of free federation from the simple to the compound, *in lieu* of the present hierarchy from the centre to the periphery.

In common with most Socialists, the Anarchists recognize that, like all evolution in nature, the slow evolution of society is followed from time to time by periods of accelerated evolution which are called revolutions; and they think that the era of revolutions is not yet closed. Periods of rapid changes will follow the periods of slow evolution, and these periods must be taken advantage of—not for increasing and widening the powers of the state, but for reducing them, through the organization in every township or commune of the local groups of producers and consumers, as also the regional, and eventually the international, federations of these groups.

In virtue of the above principles the Anarchists refuse to be party to the present state organization and to support it by infusing fresh blood into it. They do not seek to constitute, and invite the working men not to constitute, political parties in the parliaments. Accordingly, since the foundation of the International Working Men's Association in 1864–1866, they have endeavoured to promote their ideas directly amongst the labour organizations and to induce those unions to a direct struggle against capital, without placing their faith in parliamentary legislation. . . .

As one of the Anarchist-Communist direction, the present writer for many years endeavoured to develop the following ideas: to show the intimate, logical connexion which exists between the modern philosophy of natural sciences and Anarchism; to put Anarchism on a scientific basis by the study of the tendencies that are apparent now in society and may indicate its further evolution; and to work out the basis of Anarchist ethics. As regards the substance of Anarchism itself, it was Kropotkin's aim to prove that Communism—at least partial—has more chances of being established than Collectivism, especially in communes taking the lead, and that Free, or Anarchist-Communism is the only form of Communism that has any chance of being accepted in civilized societies; Communism and Anarchy are therefore two terms of evolution which complete each other, the one rendering the other possible and acceptable. He has tried, moreover, to indicate how, during a revolutionary period, a large city—if its inhabitants have accepted the idea—could organize itself on the lines of Free Communism; the city guaranteeing to every inhabitant dwelling, food and clothing to an extent corresponding to the comfort now available to the middle classes only, in exchange for a half-day's, or a five-hours' work; and how all those things which would be considered as luxuries might be obtained by every one if he joins for the other half of the day all sorts of free associations pursuing all possible aims—educational, literary, scientific, artistic, sports and so on. In order to prove the first of these assertions he has analysed the possibilities of agriculture and industrial work, both being combined with brain work. And in order to elucidate the main factors of human evolution, he has analysed the part played in history by the popular constructive agencies of mutual aid and the historical rôle of the state.

Without naming himself an Anarchist, Leo Tolstoy, like his predecessors in the popular religious movements of the 15th and 16th centuries, Chojecki, Denk and many others, took the Anarchist position as regards the state and property rights, deducing his conclusions from the general spirit of the teachings of the Christ and from the necessary dictates of reason. With all the might of his talent he made (especially in *The Kingdom of God in Yourselves*) a powerful criticism of the church, the state and law altogether, and especially of the present property laws. He describes the state as the domination of the wicked ones, supported by brutal force. Robbers, he says, are far less dangerous than a well-organized government. He makes a searching criticism of the prejudices which are current now concerning the benefits conferred upon men by the church, the state and the existing distribution of property, and from the teachings of the Christ he deduces the rule of non-resistance and the absolute condemnation of all wars. His religious arguments are, however, so well combined with arguments borrowed from a dispassionate observation of the present evils, that the anarchist portions of his works appeal to the religious and the non-religious reader alike.

T. E. LAWRENCE

ON

Guerrilla Warfare

For the editor of the 14th edition (1929) it must have been a small triumph to persuade Lawrence of Arabia (1888–1935) to write the article "Guerrilla Warfare." He was one of the few Britannica *writers who was also a legend. His contribution (given in full) is as dashing as he was. The current edition contains an excellent treatment by Stanley Weintraub of this bafflingly complex archaeologist-warrior-writer.*

This study of the science of guerrilla, or irregular, warfare is based on the concrete experience of the Arab Revolt against the Turks 1916–1918. But the historical example in turn gains value from the fact that its course was guided by the practical application of the theories here set forth.

The Arab Revolt began in June, 1916, with an attack by the half-armed and inexperienced tribesmen upon the Turkish garrisons in Medina and about Mecca. They met with no success, and after a few days' effort withdrew out of range and began a blockade. This method forced the early surrender of Mecca, the more remote of the two centres. Medina, however, was linked by railway to the Turkish main army in Syria, and the Turks were able to reinforce the garrison there. The Arab forces which had attacked it then fell back gradually and took up a position across the main road to Mecca.

At this point the campaign stood still for many weeks. The Turks prepared to send an expeditionary force to Mecca, to crush the revolt at its source, and accordingly moved an army corps to Medina by rail. Thence they began to advance down the main western road from Medina to Mecca, a distance of about 250 miles. The first 50 miles were easy, then came a belt of hills 20 miles wide, in which were Feisal's Arab tribesmen standing on the defensive: next a level stretch, for 70 miles along the coastal plain to Rabegh, rather more than half-way. Rabegh is a little port on the Red Sea, with good anchorage for ships, and because of its situation was regarded as the key to Mecca. Here lay Sherif Ali, Feisal's eldest brother, with more tribal forces, and the beginning of an Arab regular army, formed from officers and men of Arab blood who had served in the Turkish Army. As was almost inevitable in view of the general course of military thinking since Napoleon, the soldiers of all countries looked only to the regulars to win the war. Military opinion was obsessed by the dictum of Foch that the ethic of modern war is to seek for the enemy's army, his centre of power, and destroy it in battle. Irregulars would not attack positions and so they were regarded as incapable of forcing a decision.

While these Arab regulars were still being trained, the Turks suddenly began their advance on Mecca. They broke through the hills in 24 hours, and so proved the second theorem of irregular war—namely, that irregular troops are as unable to defend a point or line as they are to attack it. This lesson was received without gratitude, for the Turkish success put the Rabegh force in a critical position, and it was not capable of repelling the attack of a single battalion, much less of a corps.

In the emergency it occurred to the author that perhaps the virtue of irregulars lay in depth, not in face, and that it had been the threat of attack by them upon the Turkish northern flank which had made the enemy hesitate for so long. The actual Turkish flank ran from their front line to Medina, a distance of some 50 miles: but, if the Arab force moved towards the Hejaz railway behind Medina, it might stretch its threat (and, accordingly, the enemy's flank) as far, potentially, as Damascus, 800 miles away to the north. Such a move would force the Turks to the defensive, and the Arab force might regain the initiative. Anyhow, it seemed the only chance, and so, in Jan. 1917, Feisal's tribesmen turned their backs on Mecca, Rabegh and the Turks, and marched away north 200 miles to Wejh.

This eccentric movement acted like a charm. The Arabs did nothing concrete, but their march recalled the Turks (who were almost into Rabegh) all the way back to Medina. There, one half of the Turkish force took up the entrenched position about the city, which it held until after the Armistice. The other half was distributed along the railway to defend it against the Arab threat. For the rest of the war the Turks stood on the defensive and the Arab tribesmen won advantage over advantage till, when peace came, they had taken 35,000 prisoners, killed and wounded and worn out about as many, and occupied 100,000 square miles of the enemy's territory, at little loss to themselves. However, although Wejh was the turning point its significance was not yet realized. For the moment the move thither was regarded merely as a preliminary to cutting the railway in order to take Medina, the Turkish headquarters and main garrison.

Strategy and tactics. However, the author was unfortunately as much in charge of the campaign as he pleased, and lacking a training in command sought to find an immediate equation between past study of military theory and the present movements—as a guide to, and an intellectual basis for, future action. The text books gave the aim in war as "the destruction of the organized forces of the enemy" by "the one process battle." Victory could only be purchased by blood. This was a hard saying, as the Arabs had no organized forces, and so a Turkish Foch would have no aim: and the Arabs would not endure casualties, so that an Arab Clausewitz could not buy his victory. These wise men must be talking metaphors, for the Arabs were indubitably winning their war . . . and further reflection pointed to the deduction that they had actually won it. They were in occupation of 99% of the Hejaz. The Turks were welcome to the other fraction till peace or doomsday showed them the futility of clinging to the window pane. This part of the war was over, so why bother about Medina? The Turks sat in it on the defensive, immobile, eating for food the transport animals which were to have moved them to

Mecca, but for which there was no pasture in their now restricted lines. They were harmless sitting there; if taken prisoner, they would entail the cost of food and guards in Egypt: if driven out northward into Syria, they would join the main army blocking the British in Sinai. On all counts they were best where they were, and they valued Medina and wanted to keep it. Let them!

This seemed unlike the ritual of war of which Foch had been priest, and so it seemed that there was a difference of kind. Foch called his modern war "absolute." In it two nations professing incompatible philosophies set out to try them in the light of force. A struggle of two immaterial principles could only end when the supporters of one had no more means of resistance. An opinion can be argued with: a conviction is best shot. The logical end of a war of creeds is the final destruction of one, and Salammbo the classical textbook-instance. These were the lines of the struggle between France and Germany, but not, perhaps, between Germany and England, for all efforts to make the British soldier hate the enemy simply made him hate war. Thus the "absolute war" seemed only a variety of war; and beside it other sorts could be discerned, as Clausewitz had numbered them, personal wars for dynastic reasons, expulsive wars for party reasons, commercial wars for trading reasons.

Now the Arab aim was unmistakably geographical, to occupy all Arabic-speaking lands in Asia. In the doing of it Turks might be killed, yet "killing Turks" would never be an excuse or aim. If they would go quietly, the war would end. If not, they must be driven out: but at the cheapest possible price, since the Arabs were fighting for freedom, a pleasure only to be tasted by a man alive. The next task was to analyse the process, both from the point of view of strategy, the aim in war, the synoptic regard which sees everything by the standard of the whole, and from the point of view called tactics, the means towards the strategic end, the steps of its staircase. In each were found the same elements, one algebraical, one biological, a third psychological. The first seemed a pure science, subject to the laws of mathematics, without humanity. It dealt with known invariables, fixed conditions, space and time, inorganic things like hills and climates and railways, with mankind in type-masses too great for individual variety, with all artificial aids, and the extensions given our faculties by mechanical invention. It was essentially formulable.

In the Arab case the algebraic factor would take first account of the area to be conquered. A casual calculation indicated perhaps 140,000 square miles. How would the Turks defend all that—no doubt by a trench line across the bottom, if the Arabs were an army attacking with banners displayed . . . but suppose they were an influence, a thing invulnerable, intangible, without front or back, drifting about like a gas? Armies were like plants, immobile as a whole, firm-rooted, nourished through long stems to the head. The Arabs might be a vapour, blowing where they listed. It seemed that a regular soldier might be helpless without a target. He would own the ground he sat on, and what he could poke his rifle at. The next step was to estimate how many posts they would need to contain this attack in depth, sedition putting up her head in every unoccupied one of these 100,000 square miles. They would have need of a fortified post every four square miles, and a post could not be less than 20 men. The Turks would need 600,000 men to meet the combined ill wills of all the local Arab people. They had 100,000 men available. It seemed that the assets in this sphere were with the Arabs, and climate, railways, deserts, technical weapons could also be attached to their interests. The Turk was stupid and would believe that rebellion was absolute, like war, and deal with it on the analogy of absolute warfare.

Humanity in battle. So much for the mathematical element; the second factor was biological, the breaking-point, life and death, or better, wear and tear. Bionomics seemed a good name for it. The war-philosophers had properly made it an art, and had elevated one item in it, "effusion of blood," to the height of a principle. It became humanity in battle, an art touching every side of our corporal being. There was a line of variability (man) running through all its estimates. Its components were sensitive and illogical, and generals guarded themselves by the device of a reserve, the significant medium of their art. Goltz had said that when you know the enemy's strength, and he is fully deployed, then you know enough to dispense with a reserve. But this is never. There is always the possibility of accident, of some flaw in materials, present in the general's mind: and the reserve is unconsciously held to meet it. There is a "felt" element in troops, not expressible in figures, and the greatest commander is he whose intuitions most nearly happen. Nine-tenths of tactics are certain, and taught in books: but the irrational tenth is like the kingfisher flashing across the pool and that is the test of generals. It can only be ensued by instinct, sharpened by thought practising the stroke so often that at the crisis it is as natural as a reflex.

Yet to limit the art to humanity seemed an undue narrowing down. It must apply to materials as much as to organisms. In the Turkish Army materials were scarce and precious, men more plentiful than equipment. Consequently the cue should be to destroy not the army but the materials. The death of a Turkish bridge or rail, machine or gun, or high explosive was more profitable than the death of a Turk. The Arab army just then was equally chary of men and materials: of men because they being irregulars were not units, but individuals, and an individual casualty is like a pebble dropped in water: each may make only a brief hole, but rings of sorrow widen out from them. The Arab army could not afford casualties. Materials were easier to deal with. Hence its obvious duty to make itself superior in some one branch, guncotton or machine guns, or whatever could be most decisive. Foch had laid down the maxim, applying it to men, of being superior at the critical point and moment of attack. The Arab army might apply it to materials, and be superior in equipment in one dominant moment or respect.

For both men and things it might try to give Foch's doctrine a negative twisted side, for cheapness' sake, and be weaker than the enemy everywhere except in one point or matter. Most wars are wars of contact, both forces striving to keep in touch to avoid tactical surprise. The Arab war should be a war of detachment: to contain the enemy by the silent threat of a vast unknown desert, not disclosing themselves till the moment of attack. This attack need be only nominal, directed not against his men, but against his materials: so it should not seek for his main strength or his weaknesses, but for his most accessible material. In railway cutting this would be usually an empty stretch of rail. This was a tactical success. From this theory came to be developed ultimately an unconscious habit of never engaging the enemy at all. This chimed with the numerical plea of never giving the enemy's soldier a target. Many Turks on the Arab front had no chance all the war to fire a shot, and correspondingly the Arabs were never on the defensive, except by rare accident. The corollary of such a rule was perfect "intelligence," so that plans could be made in complete certainty. The chief agent had to be the general's head (de Feuquière said this first), and his knowledge had to be faultless, leaving no room for chance. The headquarters of the Arab army probably took more pains in this service than any other staff.

The crowd in action. The third factor in command seemed to be the psychological, that science (Xenophon called it diathetic) of which our propaganda is a stained and ignoble part. It concerns the crowd, the adjustment of spirit to the point where it becomes fit to exploit in action. It considers the capacity for mood of the men, their complexities and mutability, and the cultivation of what in them profits the intention. The command of the Arab army had to arrange their men's minds in order of battle, just as carefully and as formally as other officers arranged their bodies: and not only their own men's minds, though them first: the minds of the enemy, so far as it could reach them: and thirdly, the mind of the nation supporting it behind the firing-line, and the mind of the hostile nation waiting the verdict, and the neutrals looking on.

It was the ethical in war, and the process on which the command mainly depended for victory on the Arab front. The printing press is the greatest weapon in the armoury of the modern commander, and the commanders of the Arab army being amateurs in the art, began their war in the atmosphere of the 20th century, and thought of their weapons without prejudice, not distinguishing one from another socially. The regular officer has the tradition of 40 generations of serving soldiers behind him, and to him the old weapons are the most honoured. The Arab command had seldom to concern itself with what its men did, but much with what they thought, and to it the diathetic was more than half command. In Europe it was set a little aside and entrusted to men outside the General Staff. But the Arab army was so weak physically that it could not let the metaphysical weapon rust unused. It had won a province when the civilians in it had been taught to die for the ideal of freedom: the presence or absence of the enemy was a secondary matter.

These reasonings showed that the idea of assaulting Medina, or even of starving it quickly into surrender, was not in accord with the best strategy. Rather, let the enemy stay in Medina, and in every other harmless place, in the largest numbers. If he showed a disposition to evacuate too soon, as a step to concentrating in the small area which his numbers could dominate effectively, then the Arab army would have to try and restore his confidence, not harshly, but by reducing its enterprises against him. The ideal was to keep his railway just working, but only just, with the maximum of loss and discomfort to him.

The Turkish army was an accident, not a target. Our true strategic aim was to seek its weakest link, and bear only on that till time made the mass of it fall. The Arab army must impose the longest possible passive defence on the Turks (this being the most materially expensive form of war) by extending its own front to the maximum. Tactically it must develop a highly mobile, highly equipped type of force, of the smallest size, and use it successively at distributed points of the Turkish line, to make the Turks reinforce their occupying posts beyond the economic minimum of 20 men. The power of this striking force would not be reckoned merely by its strength. The ratio between number and area determined the character of the war, and by having five times the mobility of the Turks the Arabs could be on terms with them with one-fifth their number.

Range over force. Success was certain, to be proved by paper and pencil as soon as the proportion of space and number had been learned. The contest was not physical, but moral, and so battles were a mistake. All that could be won in a battle was the ammunition the enemy fired off. Napoleon had said it was rare to find generals willing to fight battles. The curse of this war was that so few could do anything else. Napoleon had spoken in angry reaction against the excessive finesse of the 18th century, when men almost forgot that war gave licence to murder. Military thought had been swinging out on his dictum for 100 years, and it was time to go back a bit again. Battles are impositions on the side which believes itself weaker, made unavoidable either by lack of land-room, or by the need to defend a material property dearer than the lives of soldiers. The Arabs had nothing material to lose, so they were to defend nothing and to shoot nothing. Their cards were speed and time, not hitting power, and these gave them strategical rather than tactical strength. Range is more to strategy than force. The invention of bully-beef had modified land-war more profoundly than the invention of gunpowder.

The British military authorities did not follow all these arguments, but gave leave for their practical application to be tried. Accordingly the Arab forces went off first to Akaba and took it easily. Then they took Tafileh and the Dead Sea; then Azrak and Deraa, and finally Damascus, all in successive stages worked out consciously on these theories. The process was to set up ladders of tribes, which should provide a safe and comfortable route from the sea-bases (Yenbo, Wejh or Akaba) to the advanced bases of operation. These were sometimes 300 miles away, a long distance in lands without railways or roads, but made short for the Arab Army by an assiduous cultivation of desert-power, control by camel parties of the desolate and unmapped wilderness which fills up all the centre of Arabia, from Mecca to Aleppo and Baghdad.

The desert and the sea. In character these operations were like naval warfare, in their mobility, their ubiquity, their independence of bases and communications, in their ignoring of ground features, of strategic areas, of fixed directions, of fixed points. "He who commands the sea is at great liberty, and may take as much or as little of the war as he will": he who commands the desert is equally fortunate. Camel raiding-parties, self-contained like ships, could cruise securely along the enemy's land-frontier, just out of sight of his posts along the edge of cultivation, and tap or raid into his lines where it seemed fittest or easiest or most profitable, with a sure retreat always behind them into an element which the Turks could not enter.

Discrimination of what point of the enemy organism to disarrange came with practice. The tactics were always tip and run; not pushes, but strokes. The Arab army never tried to maintain or improve an advantage, but to move off and strike again somewhere else. It used the smallest force in the quickest time at the farthest place. To continue the action till the enemy had changed his dispositions to resist it would have been to break the spirit of the fundamental rule of denying him targets.

The necessary speed and range were attained by the frugality of the desert men, and their efficiency on camels. In the heat of summer Arabian camels will do about 250 miles comfortably between drinks: and this represented three days' vigorous marching. This radius was always more than was needed, for wells are seldom more than 100 miles apart. The equipment of the raiding parties aimed at simplicity, with nevertheless a technical superiority over the Turks in the critical department. Quantities of light machine guns were obtained from Egypt for use not as machine guns, but as automatic rifles, snipers' tools, by men kept deliberately in ignorance of their mechanism, so that the speed of action would not be hampered by attempts at repair. Another special feature was high explosives, and nearly every one in the revolt was qualified by rule of thumb experience in demolition work.

Armoured cars. On some occasions tribal raids were strengthened by armoured cars, manned by Englishmen. Armoured cars, once they have found a possible track, can keep up with a camel party. On the march to Damascus, when nearly 400 miles off their base, they were first maintained by a baggage train of petrol-laden camels, and afterwards from the air. Cars are magnificent fighting machines, and decisive whenever they can come into action on their own conditions. But though each has for main principle that of "fire in movement," yet the tactical employments of cars and camel-corps are so different that their use in joint operations is difficult. It was found demoralizing to both to use armoured and unarmoured cavalry together.

The distribution of the raiding parties was unorthodox. It was impossible to mix or combine tribes, since they disliked or distrusted one another. Likewise the men of one tribe could not be used in the territory of another. In consequence, another canon of orthodox strategy was broken by following the principle of the widest distribution of force, in order to have the greatest number of raids on hand at once, and fluidity was added to speed by using one district on Monday, another on Tuesday, a third on Wednesday. This much reinforced the natural mobility of the Arab army, giving it priceless advantages in pursuit, for the force renewed itself with fresh men in every new tribal area, and so maintained its pristine energy. Maximum disorder was, in a real sense its equilibrium.

An undisciplined army. The internal economy of the raiding parties was equally curious. Maximum irregularity and articulation were the aims. Diversity threw the enemy intelligence off the track. By the regular organization in identical battalions and divisions information builds itself up, until the presence of a corps can be inferred on corpses from three companies. The Arabs, again, were serving a common ideal, without tribal emulation, and so could not hope for any *esprit de corps*. Soldiers are made a caste either by being given great pay and rewards in money, uniform or political privileges; or, as in England, by being made outcasts, cut off from the mass of their fellow-citizens. There have been many armies enlisted voluntarily: there have been few armies serving voluntarily under such trying conditions, for so long a war as the Arab revolt. Any of the Arabs could go home whenever the conviction failed him. Their only contract was honour.

Consequently the Arab army had no discipline, in the sense in which it is restrictive, submergent of individuality, the Lowest Common Denominator of men. In regular armies in peace it means the limit of energy attainable by everybody present: it is the hunt not of an average, but of an absolute, a 100-per-cent standard, in which the 99 stronger men are played down to the level of the worst. The aim is to render the unit a unit, and the man a type, in order that their effort shall be calculable, their collective output even in grain and in bulk. The deeper the discipline, the lower the individual efficiency, and the more sure the performance. It is a deliberate sacrifice of capacity in order to reduce the uncertain element, the bionomic factor, in enlisted humanity, and its accompaniment is *compound* or social war, that form in which the fighting man has to be the product of the multiplied exertions of long hierarchy, from workshop to supply unit, which maintains him in the field.

The Arab war, reacting against this, was *simple* and individual. Every enrolled man served in the line of battle, and was self-contained. There were no lines of communication or labour troops. It seemed that in this articulated warfare, the sum yielded by single men would be at least equal to the product of a compound system of the same strength, and it was certainly easier to adjust to tribal life and manners, given elasticity and understanding on the part of the commanding officers. Fortunately for its chances nearly every young Englishman has the roots of eccentricity in him. Only a sprinkling were employed, not more than one per 1,000 of the Arab troops. A larger proportion would have created friction, just because they were foreign bodies (pearls if you please) in the oyster: and those who were present controlled by influence and advice, by their superior knowledge, not by an extraneous authority.

The practice was, however, not to employ in the firing line the greater numbers which the adoption of a "simple" system made available theoretically. Instead, they were used in relay: otherwise the attack would have become too extended. Guerrillas must be allowed liberal work-room. In irregular war if two men are together one is being wasted. The moral strain of isolated action makes this simple form of war very hard on the individual soldier, and exacts from him special initiative, endurance and enthusiasm. Here the ideal was to make action a series of single combats to make the ranks a happy alliance of commanders-in-chief. The value of the Arab army depended entirely on quality, not on quantity. The members had to keep always cool, for the excitement of a blood-lust would impair their science, and their victory depended on a just use of speed, concealment, accuracy of fire. Guerrilla war is far more intellectual than a bayonet charge.

The exact science of guerrilla warfare. By careful persistence, kept strictly within its strength and following the spirit of these theories, the Arab army was able eventually to reduce the Turks to helplessness, and complete victory seemed to be almost within sight when General Allenby by his immense stroke in Palestine threw the enemy's main forces into hopeless confusion and put an immediate end to the Turkish war. His too-greatness deprived the Arab revolt of the opportunity of following to the end the dictum of Saxe that a war might be won without fighting battles. But it can at least be said that its leaders worked by his light for two years, and the work stood. This is a pragmatic argument that cannot be wholly derided. The experiment, although not complete, strengthened the belief that irregular war or rebellion could be proved to be an exact science, and an inevitable success, granted certain factors and if pursued along certain lines.

Here is the thesis: Rebellion must have an unassailable base, something guarded not merely from attack, but from the fear of it: such a base as the Arab revolt had in the Red Sea ports, the desert, or in the minds of men converted to its creed. It must have a sophisticated alien enemy, in the form of a disciplined army of occupation too small to fulfil the doctrine of acreage: too few to adjust number to space, in order to dominate the whole area effectively from fortified posts. It must have a friendly population, not actively friendly, but sympathetic to the point of not betraying rebel movements to the enemy. Rebellions can be made by 2% active in a striking force, and 98% passively sympathetic. The few active rebels must have the qualities of speed and endurance, ubiquity and independence of arteries of supply. They must have the technical equipment to destroy or paralyze the enemy's organized communications, for irregular war is fairly Willisen's definition of strategy, "the study of communication," in its extreme degree, of attack where the enemy is not. In 50 words: Granted mobility, security (in the form of denying targets to the enemy), time, and doctrine (the idea to convert every subject to friendliness), victory will rest with the insurgents, for the algebraical factors are in the end decisive, and against them perfections of means and spirit struggle quite in vain.

MAX LERNER
ON
Liberalism

Since liberalism is for many contemporary Americans merely a ten-letter word, it's interesting to see what it meant back in 1960 to one of its ablest exponents. Max Lerner (1902–1992) was a distinguished educator and political commentator. He was editor of The Nation *(1936–1938). At the age of eighty-eight he published* Wrestling with the Angel, *a moving account of his battle with illness. The following extract, the larger part of the article, is from the 1960 printing of the 14th edition.*

Liberalism is the creed, philosophy and movement which is committed to freedom as a method and policy in government, as an organizing principle in society and as a way of life for the individual and community. As a term it took its origins from the "Liberales," a Spanish political party in the early 19th century, but received its widest currency in the English language. As an idea and philosophy it predates its use as a term, and can be traced back to the Judaeo-Christian-Greek intellectual world, along with the idea of liberty itself with which it is closely linked.

Confusion of terms. Some of the confusions about liberalism arise from the various stages of meaning through which the term passed during a history of several centuries, and from the wide diversity of uses to which it has been put. There were in the second half of the 20th century a number of political parties, in Great Britain, Italy, Germany and elsewhere, called by the name of the "Liberal party" or some variant of it; there was a party of the same name active in the politics of New York state; and even a Liberal International which served as a clearinghouse for liberal political movements throughout the world. But while these parties expressed the liberal outlook, that outlook was not limited to them. Their emphasis was on an economic program and policy which minimized state intervention and control, and which sought to carry out the philosophy of economic freedom under the difficult conditions of modern industrial organization. They thus expressed the outlook of a liberal capitalism on the defensive against various forms of socialism and communism on one side, and against conservatism and the totalitarianisms of the right on the other. "Liberal" political parties tended thus in practice to be caught between the upper and nether millstones, and their appeal was for that reason constricted to a middle ground position.

Yet liberalism as a dynamic philosophy was not at the end of the road. Just as it had its modern origin in the revolutionary movements attending the emergence of the business class to power and enlisted the most radical energies of the 18th and 19th centuries, so it showed a capacity to absorb many of the ideas of the revolutionary movements which challenged that class. What gave it this resiliency was its master idea of freedom as a method and a credo, this master idea being one of the great seminal revolutionary ideas of world history, not limited to any one economic program nor to the social power of any one class.

Liberalism is thus a basic approach to individual and collective living in the modern world. Its locus has been largely the west, since it has come out of the intellectual and institutional history of the great western nations. Its golden age may be dated roughly between 1750 and 1914; *i.e.,* between the era of the French *philosophes* and the start of World War I. But there is nothing inherent in it to limit it thus either in time or place. It proved pervasive enough to penetrate to some degree into every 20th-century society and social climate. It was associated with revolutionary movements in England, France, Germany and Italy, but it was also an active force in tsarist Russia, opposing both tsarist reaction and communist totalitarianism. It became a force in political systems as diverse as post–World War II Japan, Israel, Turkey, Greece and a number of Latin-American nations. It was an ingredient (the extent of which was widely debated) in the democratic socialist movements of Great Britain, Germany, France, the Netherlands, Belgium, Austria and the Scandinavian countries, and of the "welfare state" in the U.S. The term has also been applied to certain "liberal" elements of conservatism (as in the phrases "liberal Republicanism" or "liberal Toryism"), and to the internal struggles within the U.S.S.R. and the communist bloc, as in the phrase "liberal Communist elements."

History. In its history as an idea liberalism is closely linked with the idea of liberty or of liberation, since the essence of the liberal idea is to aim at freeing—and thereby expressing and fulfilling—the human spirit in the individual. The idea can be pushed back to Socrates and his quiet insistence on holding to his truth even at the cost of his life. But it was the Stoics who, in an era of expanding world horizons, were able to break away from the idols of the organic tribe or city-state and universalize man as an individual, as something apart from his civic pattern. It was Christianity which, by giving a religious sanction to man's dignity as an individual, gave the movement to fulfill it a passionate quality.

In the early phases of modern Europe such 17th-century thinkers as Descartes, Milton and Spinoza served as the conduits through which the long-preparing stream of liberal thought came into European experience. Descartes shaped the instrument of rationalism; Spinoza forged the links between the life of reason and the values of an emerging liberal outlook; and Milton directed powerful assaults on the repressive engines of censorship, which kept men from access to what might be the liberating truth. Together they applied to everything, including the powerful institutions of state and religion, the shattering method of critical inquiry. The way had indeed been prepared for them by the Protestant Reformation, which stressed the role of individual private judgment even in religious concerns. But far more powerful was the scientific revolution, whose preparatory phase was the Renaissance, opening new vistas of time and place and turning men from the next world to the present one.

The grand centuries of this scientific revolution were the 16th and 17th, when man's growing knowledge and control of his environment and the rise of a new economic class to exploit it revolutionized the life claims and life prospects of the intellectuals in Europe and those in whose name they wrote and spoke.

All these streams of thought and tendency converged in the great explosive movement called variously the Enlightenment or the Age of Reason (in France the age of the *philosophes,* in Germany the *Aufklärung*), which spread throughout western Europe and even across the seas into the new world, and whose great voices were Voltaire, Locke, Goethe and Thomas Jefferson, Rousseau, Hume and Kant, Diderot, Lessing, Adam Smith and Giovanni Vico, Condorcet, Montesquieu and Benjamin Franklin. These were the miners and sappers of the intellectual and institutional life of a society of feudal ties, monarchical and church authority and aristocratic and clerical privilege. They also had the prevision of a new intellectual and cultural structure the outlines of which were still obscure because the political, economic and social cement necessary to build the structure and hold it together was still in formation. That cement was to come with the great political revolutions (the English, American and French, which took place within the century between 1688 and 1789) and with the rise to power of the new middle and business classes that used the revolutions to capture and consolidate their position. On their road to power they struck alliances—loose, often unconscious, but nonetheless real—with the intellectuals, each partner to the alliance using and being used by the other, and both of them helping to bring to fruition the master ideas of the liberal system of thought.

Leading concepts. To list some of these master ideas is an artificial process, since they were tied together in an ideological web, and each loses much of its meaning when torn from this web. Yet even a listing may suggest the richness of the intellectual armoury of liberalism.

Central to the whole is the idea of liberty itself—not absolute liberty ("No government allows absolute liberty," wrote Locke), but the maximizing of the individual's freedom to think, to believe, to express and discuss his views, to organize (associate) in parties, to find employment, to buy and sell commodities (including his own labour) freely and to keep the rewards, to choose his rulers as well as his form of government and to change both—by revolution, if necessary. So crucial is the idea of liberty that liberalism might be quite summarily defined as the effort to organize liberty socially and to follow out its implications.

As for where this right to maximal liberty comes from, liberalism's answer was nature. "The laws of Nature and of Nature's God," as Thomas Jefferson denominated them in the American Declaration of Independence, formed the true religion of liberalism, and on it they built what the 20th-century U.S. historian Carl Becker called "the heavenly city of the 18th-century philosophers." The 18th century carried on a love affair with nature, in religion, law, politics, metaphysics and landscape painting. Rousseau in France and Locke in England were the principal 17th- and 18th-century protagonists of the idea that men had rights rooted in nature, which governments must protect and which must be defended even against government.

Bills of rights, petitions of right, declarations of the rights of man and of the citizen—these became the watchwords of the era. Since they were based on nature and in natural law, they were universalized, abstracted and made absolute—"indubitable, inalienable, and indefeasible," as the Virginia constitution put it in describing the natural right of revolution. Actually this notion of natural law came less from theology than it did from Sir Isaac Newton and his colleagues in the scientific revolution, who showed that the operation of the universe could be explained rationally in terms of the laws of nature without bringing in any external divine intervention.

As a result even God became nature's God, and religion was universalized into a deism, thus diluting the rigours of revealed religious certitude and emphasizing tolerance toward the variety of forms in which nature's God might be worshipped. The Renaissance, the scientific revolutions, the march of technology, the rising living standards, all contributed to a growing rationalism in thinking and attitudes and to a secularism of belief. The axis of men's concerns shifted from the next world to this one, and from what had been laid down by tradition in the past to what men could achieve for themselves in the present and future. In place of the idea of sin men began to talk of the idea of progress, in place of predestination they caught a glimpse of the vision of men's perfectibility. Everything seemed possible in the "best of all possible worlds." The test of institutions became the question not of whether they were in the service of God but whether they ministered to the happiness of men.

Armed with these weapons of secularism, progress and happiness, liberalism was able to turn a withering fire on institutions. "Man is born free," wrote Rousseau in the *Contract sociale,* "yet he is everywhere in chains." And in *Émile:* "God makes all things good; man meddles with them and they become evil." It was a basic assumption of the liberal thinkers that man is endowed with reason and goodness, and that only the institutional frame into which he is born corrupts and enslaves him. The enemy was custom, tradition, institutions, social habit. The French *philosophes,* the English utilitarians, the philosophic radicals, the Italian patriot-intellectuals were the "angry young men" of their time, blasting away at the establishment of their day—the church, the feudal order, the aristocratic classes, the dynastic state, the educational system, the censorship. Always they sought to lift from men what Jefferson called the "dead hand of the past."

If it was man's meddling with the natural order that caused all the mischief, then it follows that the best human course is to leave things alone. This powerful nexus linked the liberal intellectuals with the emerging business class, who wanted free markets, the removal of crippling restrictions upon economic activity and the chance to amass wealth and property.

But *laissez faire* in itself was not the whole of the liberal program. To it was added republicanism, popular sovereignty and education—especially the last. The removal of governmental restrictions and the toppling of tyrannical institutions would provide the freedom for reason to function: but reason needed tools with which to function, and education would provide them. Since the liberals believed in man's goodness, they believed also in his perfectibility, and education was the instrument by which it could be furthered. Some of the more realistic liberal thinkers, however, saw the darker side of the moon as well: that if men were by nature good, they were also ruled by ambition, greed for power and the political passions. Hence it was necessary to curb the majority will by a concern for the protection of minorities. And it was especially necessary to provide in government for the separation of powers so that the legislative and executive powers would not be fused into a single tyranny, and the judiciary could remain independent of both.

Thus the liberal image of the state came to mirror the equilibrium physics that the scientific revolution had made familiar. And the liberal image of the human mind came to stress the primacy of self-interest as a drive (egoism), the primacy of reason as an instrument (intellectualism) and the ultimate value of individual efforts toward self-realization (progress, happiness) or of individual nonefforts (*laissez faire,* quietism) in a state of nature.

Men had by the mid-20th century become more aware of some of the weaknesses of this liberal outlook that characterized the vanguard thinking of liberalism's golden age. They knew about its oversimplifications, about its atomism, its primitivism, its utopianism, its naïve cults of nature, progress and happiness. But it is well to remember that in its emergence liberalism was an exciting new movement of thought that released the energies and enlisted the loyalties of men. For a historic moment they caught a vision of human possibility, and this vision armed them for their encounters with what they regarded as the powers and principalities of darkness.

THOMAS BABINGTON MACAULAY

ON

Samuel Johnson

One of the dominant names of eighteenth-century English letters was Samuel Johnson, and not alone for his creation of the dictionary that changed the nature of lexicography. The 8th edition (1852–1860) contained a biography of Johnson by one of the century's major literary figures, Thomas Babington Macaulay (1800–1859). That celebrated Whig statesman, essayist, poet, and historian was a close friend of Archibald Constable's successor as publisher of the Britannica, *and he readily agreed to contribute a number of biographical sketches to Adam Black's new edition. All were completed in the last few years of Macaulay's life, even as he was putting the finishing touches on his most famous work, the five-volume* History of England.

Lord Macaulay wrote the Johnson article, which remained a classic of short biography for a century and more, in 1857, the year he was elevated to the peerage as Baron Macaulay of Rothley, and two years before his death in 1859. It is agonizing and presumptuous—but necessary—to select excerpts from it, since it ran to some 17,000 words. (B.L.F.)

The current edition devotes eighteen columns to Johnson, of which almost two consist of bibliography, a necessary feature absent from earlier editions.

We might add that Macaulay refused to accept any pay for his Britannica *contributions, which included shorter accounts of Francis Atterbury, Oliver Goldsmith, William Pitt, and John Bunyan. This piece bears the distinguishing marks of his still underrated prose style.*

Johnson, Samuel, one of the most eminent English writers of the eighteenth century, was the son of Michael Johnson, who was, at the beginning of that century, a magistrate of Lichfield, and a bookseller of great note in the midland counties. . . . At his house, a house which is still pointed out to every traveller who visits Lichfield, Samuel was born on the 18th of September 1709. In the child the physical, intellectual, and moral peculiarities which afterwards distinguished the man were plainly discernible; great muscular strength accompanied by much awkwardness and many infirmities; great quickness of parts, with a morbid propensity to sloth and procrastination; a kind and generous heart, with a gloomy and irritable temper. He had inherited from his ancestors a scrofulous taint, which it was beyond the power of medicine to remove. His parents were weak enough to believe that the royal touch was a specific for this malady. In his third year he was taken up to London, inspected by the court surgeon, prayed over by the court chaplains, and stroked and presented with a piece of gold by Queen Anne. One of his earliest recollections was that of a stately lady in a diamond stomacher and a long black hood. Her hand was applied in vain. The boy's features, which were originally noble and not irregular, were distorted by his malady. His cheeks were deeply scarred. He lost for a time the sight of one eye; and he saw but very imperfectly with the other. But the force of his mind overcame every impediment. Indolent as he was, he acquired knowledge with such ease and rapidity, that at every school to which he was sent he was soon the best scholar. From sixteen to eighteen he resided at home, and was left to his own devices. He learned much at this time, though his studies were without guidance and without plan. He ransacked his father's shelves, dipped into a multitude of books, read what was interesting, and passed over what was dull. An ordinary lad would have acquired little or no useful knowledge in such a way: but much that was dull to ordinary lads was interesting to Samuel. He read little Greek; for his proficiency in that language was not such that he could take much pleasure in the masters of Attic poetry and eloquence. But he had left school a good Latinist, and he soon acquired, in the large and miscellaneous library of which he now had the command, an extensive knowledge of Latin literature. . . .

While he was thus irregularly educating himself, his family was sinking into hopeless poverty. Old Michael Johnson was much better qualified to pore upon books, and to talk about them, than to trade in them. His business declined: his debts increased: it was with difficulty that the daily expenses of his household were defrayed. It was out of his power to support his son at either university; but a wealthy neighbour offered assistance; and, in reliance on promises which proved to be of very little value, Samuel was entered at Pembroke College, Oxford. When the young scholar presented himself to the rulers of that society, they were amazed not more by his ungainly figure and eccentric manners than by the quantity of extensive and curious information which he had picked up during many months of desultory, but not unprofitable study. On the first day of his residence he surprised his teachers by quoting Macrobius; and one of the most learned among them declared, that he had never known a freshman of equal attainments.

At Oxford, Johnson resided during about three years. He was poor, even to raggedness; and his appearance excited a mirth and a pity, which were equally intolerable to his haughty spirit. He was driven from the quadrangle of Christ Church by the sneering looks which the members of that aristocratical society cast at the holes in his shoes. Some charitable person placed a new pair at his door; but he spurned them away in a fury. Distress made him, not servile, but reckless and ungovernable. No opulent gentleman commoner, panting for one-and-twenty, could have treated the academical authorities with more gross disrespect. The needy scholar was generally to be seen under the gate of Pembroke, a gate now adorned with his effigy, haranguing a circle of lads, over whom, in spite of his tattered gown and dirty linen, his wit and audacity gave him an undisputed ascendency. In every mutiny against the discipline of the college he was the ringleader. Much was pardoned, however, to a youth so highly distinguished by abilities and acquirements. He had early made himself known by turning Pope's Messiah into Latin verse. The style and rhythm, indeed, were not exactly Virgilian; but the translation found many admirers, and was read with pleasure by Pope himself.

The time drew near at which Johnson would, in the ordinary course of things, have become a Bachelor of Arts: but he was at the end of his resources. Those promises of support on which he had relied had not been kept. His family could do nothing for him. His debts to Oxford tradesmen were small indeed, yet larger than he could pay. In the autumn of 1731, he was under the necessity of quitting the university without a degree. In the following winter his father died. The old man left but a pittance; and of that pittance almost the whole was appropriated to the support of his widow. The property to which Samuel succeeded amounted to no more than twenty pounds.

His life, during the thirty years which followed, was one hard struggle with poverty. The misery of that struggle needed no aggravation, but was aggravated by the sufferings of an unsound body and an unsound mind. Before the young man left the university, his hereditary malady had broken forth in a singularly cruel form. He had become an incurable hypochondriac. He said long after that he had been mad all his life, or at least not perfectly sane; and, in truth, eccentricities less strange than his have often been thought grounds sufficient for absolving felons, and for setting aside wills. His grimaces, his gestures, his mutterings, sometimes diverted and sometimes terrified people who did not know him. At a dinner table he would, in a fit of absence, stoop down and twitch off a lady's shoe. He would amaze a drawing room by suddenly ejaculating a clause of the Lord's Prayer. He would conceive an unintelligible aversion to a particular alley, and perform a great circuit rather than see the hateful place. He would set his heart on touching every post in the streets through which he walked. If by any chance he missed a post, he would go back a hundred yards and repair the omission. Under the influence of his disease, his senses became morbidly torpid, and his imagination morbidly active. At one time he would stand poring on the town clock without being able to tell the hour. At another, he would distinctly hear his mother, who was many miles off, calling him by his name. But this was not the worst. A deep melancholy took possession of him, and gave a dark tinge to all his views of human nature and of human destiny. Such wretchedness as he endured has driven many men to shoot themselves or drown themselves. But he was under no temptation to commit suicide. He was sick of life; but he was afraid of death; and he shuddered at every sight or sound which reminded him of the inevitable hour. In religion he found but little comfort during his long and frequent fits of dejection; for his religion partook of his own character. The light from heaven shone on him indeed, but not in a direct line, or with its own pure splendour. The rays had to struggle through a disturbing medium: they reached him refracted, dulled and discoloured by the thick gloom which had settled on his soul; and, though they might be sufficiently clear to guide him, were too dim to cheer him.

With such infirmities of body and of mind, this celebrated man was left, at two-and-twenty, to fight his way through the world. . . .

While leading this vagrant and miserable life, Johnson fell in love. The object of his passion was Mrs Elizabeth Porter, a widow who had children as old as himself. To ordinary spectators, the lady appeared to be a short, fat, coarse woman, painted half an inch thick, dressed in gaudy colours, and fond of exhibiting provincial airs and graces which were not exactly those of the Queensberrys and Lepels. To Johnson, however, whose passions were strong, whose eyesight was too weak to distinguish ceruse from natural bloom, and who had seldom or never been in the same room with a woman of real fashion, his Titty, as he called her, was the most beautiful, graceful, and accomplished of her sex. That his admiration was unfeigned cannot be doubted; for she was as poor as himself. She accepted, with a readiness which did her little honour, the addresses of a suitor who might have been her son. The marriage, however, in spite of occasional wranglings, proved happier than might have been expected. The lover continued to be under the illusions of the wedding-day till the lady died in her sixty-fourth year. On her monument he placed an inscription extolling the charms of her person and of her manners; and when, long after her decease, he had occasion to mention her, he exclaimed, with a tenderness half ludicrous, half pathetic, "Pretty creature!"

His marriage made it necessary for him to exert himself more strenuously than he had hitherto done. He took a house in the neighbourhood of his native town, and advertised for pupils. But eighteen months passed away; and only three pupils came to his academy. Indeed, his appearance was so strange, and his temper so violent, that his schoolroom must have resembled an ogre's den. Nor was the tawdry painted grandmother whom he called his Titty well qualified to make provision for the comfort of young gentlemen. David Garrick, who was one of the pupils, used, many years later, to throw the best company of London into convulsions of laughter by mimicking the endearments of this extraordinary pair.

At length Johnson, in the twenty-eighth year of his age, determined to seek his fortune in the capital as a literary adventurer. He set out with a few guineas, three acts of the tragedy of Irene in manuscript, and two or three letters of introduction from his friend Walmesley. . . .

The effect of the privations and sufferings which he endured at this time was discernible to the last in his temper and his deportment. His manners had never been courtly. They now became almost savage. Being frequently under the necessity of wearing shabby coats and dirty shirts, he became a confirmed sloven. Being often very hungry when he sate down to his meals, he contracted a habit of eating with ravenous greediness. Even to the end of his life, and even at the tables of the great, the sight of food affected him as it affects wild beasts and birds of prey. His taste in cookery, formed in subterranean ordinaries and *Alamode* beefshops, was far from delicate. Whenever he was so fortunate as to have near him a hare that had been kept too long, or a meat pie made with rancid butter, he gorged himself with such violence that his veins swelled, and the moisture broke out on his forehead. The affronts which his poverty emboldened stupid and low-minded men to offer to him would have broken a mean spirit into sycophancy, but made him rude even to ferocity. Unhappily the insolence which, while it was defensive, was pardonable, and in some sense respectable, accompanied him into societies where he was treated with courtesy and kindness. He was repeatedly provoked into striking those who had taken liberties with him. All the sufferers, however, were wise enough to abstain from talking about their beatings, except Osborne, the most rapacious and brutal of booksellers, who proclaimed everywhere that he had been knocked down by the huge fellow whom he had hired to puff the Harleian Library. . . .

The last Rambler was written in a sad and gloomy hour. Mrs Johnson had been given over by the physicians. Three days later she died. She left her husband almost broken-hearted. Many people had been surprised to see a man of his genius and learning stooping to every drudgery, and denying himself almost every comfort, for the purpose of supplying a silly, affected old woman with superfluities, which she accepted with but little gratitude. But all his affection had been concentrated on her. He had neither brother nor sister, neither son nor daughter. To him she was beautiful as the Gunnings, and witty as Lady Mary. Her opinion of his writings was more important to him than the voice of the pit of Drury Lane Theatre, or the judgment of the Monthly Review. The chief support which had sustained him through the most arduous labour of his life was the hope that she would enjoy the fame and the profit which he anticipated from his Dictionary. She was gone; and, in that vast labyrinth of streets, peopled by eight hundred thousand human beings, he was alone. Yet it was necessary for him to set himself, as he expressed it, doggedly to work. After three more laborious years, the Dictionary was at length complete.

It had been generally supposed that this great work would be dedicated to the eloquent and accomplished nobleman to whom the Prospectus had been addressed. He well knew the value of such a compliment; and therefore, when the day of publication drew near, he exerted himself to sooth, by a show of zealous and at the same time of delicate and judicious kindness, the pride which he had so cruelly wounded. Since the Ramblers had ceased to appear, the town had been entertained by a journal called The World, to which many men of high rank and fashion contributed. In two successive numbers of the World, the Dictionary was, to use the modern phrase, puffed with wonderful skill. The writings of Johnson were warmly praised. It was proposed that he should be invested with the authority of a Dictator, nay, of a Pope, over our language, and that his decisions about the meaning and the spelling of words should be received as final. His two folios, it was said, would of course be bought by everybody who could afford to buy them. It was soon known that these papers were written by Chesterfield. But the just resentment of Johnson was not to be so appeased. In a letter written with singular energy and dignity of thought and language, he repelled the tardy advances of his patron. The Dictionary came forth without a dedication. In the preface the author truly declared that he owed nothing to the great, and described the difficulties with which he had been left to struggle so forcibly and pathetically that the ablest and most malevolent of all the enemies of his fame, Horne Tooke, never could read that passage without tears. . . .

He long continued to live upon the fame which he had already won. He was honoured by the University of Oxford with a Doctor's degree, by the Royal Academy with a professorship, and by the King with an interview, in which his Majesty most graciously expressed a hope that so excellent a writer would not cease to write. In the interval, however, between 1765 and 1775 Johnson published only two or three political tracts, the longest of which he could have produced in forty-eight hours, if he had worked as he worked on the Life of Savage and on Rasselas.

But, though his pen was now idle, his tongue was active. The influence exercised by his conversation, directly upon those with whom he lived, and indirectly on the whole literary world, was altogether without a parallel. His colloquial talents were indeed of the highest order. He had strong sense, quick discernment, wit, humour, immense knowledge of literature and of life, and an infinite store of curious anecdotes. As respected style, he spoke far better than he wrote. Every sentence which dropped from his lips was as correct in structure as the most nicely balanced period of the Rambler. But in his talk there were no pompous triads, and little more than a fair proportion of words in *osity* and *ation*. All was simplicity, ease, and vigour. He uttered his short, weighty, and pointed sentences with a power of voice, and a justness and energy of emphasis, of which the effect was rather increased than diminished by the rollings of his huge form, and by the asthmatic gaspings and puffings in which the peals of his eloquence generally ended. Nor did the laziness which made him unwilling to sit down to his desk prevent him from giving instruction or entertainment orally. To discuss questions of taste, of learning, of casuistry, in language so exact and so forcible that it might have been printed without the alteration of a word, was to him no exertion, but a pleasure. He loved, as he said, to fold his legs and have his talk out. He was ready to bestow the overflowings of his full mind on anybody who would start a subject, on a fellow-passenger in a stage coach, or on the person who sate at the same table with him in an eating-house. But his conversation was nowhere so brilliant and striking as when he was surrounded by a few friends, whose abilities and knowledge enabled them, as he once expressed it, to send him back every ball that he threw. Some of these, in 1764, formed themselves into a club, which gradually became a formidable power in the commonwealth of letters. The verdicts pronounced by this conclave on new books were speedily known over all London, and were sufficient to sell off a whole edition in a day, or to condemn the sheets to the service of the trunk-maker and the pastrycook. Nor shall we think this strange when we consider what great and various talents and acquirements met in the little fraternity. Goldsmith was the representative of poetry and light literature, Reynolds of the arts, Burke of political eloquence and political philosophy. There, too, were Gibbon, the greatest historian, and Jones the greatest linguist, of the age. Garrick brought to the meetings his inexhaustible pleasantry, his incomparable mimicry, and his consummate knowledge of stage effect. Among the most constant attendants were two high-born and high-bred gentlemen, closely bound together by friendship, but of widely different characters and habits; Bennet Langton, distinguished by his skill in Greek literature, by the orthodoxy of his opinions, and by the sanctity of his life; and Topham Beauclerk, renowned for his amours, his knowledge of the gay world, his fastidious taste, and his sarcastic wit. To predominate over such a society was not easy. Yet even over such a society Johnson predominated. Burke might indeed have disputed the supremacy to which others were under the necessity of submitting. But Burke, though not generally a very patient listener, was content to take the second part when Johnson was present; and the club itself, consisting of so many eminent men, is to this day popularly designated as Johnson's club.

Among the members of this celebrated body was one to whom it has owed the greater part of its celebrity, yet who was regarded with little respect by his brethren, and had not without difficulty obtained a seat among them. This was James Boswell, a young Scotch lawyer, heir to an honourable name and a fair estate. That he was a coxcomb and a bore, weak, vain, pushing, curious, garrulous, was obvious to all who were acquainted with him. That he could not reason, that he had no wit, no humour, no eloquence, is apparent from his writings. And yet his writings are read beyond the Mississippi, and under the Southern Cross, and are likely to be read as long as the English exists, either as a living or as a dead language. Nature had made him a slave and an idolater. His mind resembled those creepers which the botanists call parasites, and which can subsist only by clinging round the stems and imbibing the juices of stronger plants. He must have fastened himself on somebody. He might have fastened himself on Wilkes, and have become the fiercest patriot in the Bill of Rights Society. He might have fastened himself on Whitfield, and have become the loudest field preacher among the Calvinistic Methodists. In a happy hour he fastened himself on Johnson. The pair might seem ill matched. For Johnson had early been prejudiced against Boswell's country. To a man of Johnson's strong understanding and irritable temper, the silly egotism and adulation of Boswell must have been as teasing as the constant buzz of a fly. Johnson hated to be questioned; and Boswell was eternally catechizing him on all kinds of subjects, and sometimes propounded such questions as, "What would you do, sir, if you were locked up in a tower with a baby?" Johnson was a water drinker and Boswell was a winebibber, and indeed little better than a habitual sot. It was impossible that there should be perfect harmony between two such companions. Indeed, the great man was sometimes provoked into fits of passion, in which he said things which the small man, during a few hours, seriously resented. Every quarrel, however, was soon made up. During twenty years the disciple continued to worship the master: the master continued to scold the disciple, to sneer at him, and to love him. The two friends ordinarily resided at a great distance from each other. Boswell practised in the Parliament House of Edinburgh, and could pay only occasional visits to London. During those visits his chief business was to watch Johnson, to discover all Johnson's habits, to turn the conversation to subjects about which Johnson was likely to say something remarkable, and to fill quarto notebooks with minutes of what Johnson had said. In this way were gathered the materials, out of which was afterwards constructed the most interesting biographical work in the world.

Soon after the club began to exist, Johnson formed a connection less important indeed to his fame, but much more important to his happiness, than his connection with Boswell. Henry Thrale, one of the most opulent brewers in the kingdom, a man of sound and cultivated understanding, rigid principles, and liberal spirit, was married to one of those clever, kind-hearted, engaging, vain, pert, young women, who are perpetually doing or saying what is not exactly right, but who, do or say what they may, are always agreeable. In 1765 the Thrales became acquainted with Johnson, and the acquaintance ripened fast into friendship. They were astonished and delighted by the brilliancy of his conversation. They were flattered by finding that a man so widely celebrated preferred their house to any other in London. Even the peculiarities which seemed to unfit him for civilised society, his gesticulations, his rollings, his puffings, his mutterings, the strange way in which he put on his clothes, the ravenous eagerness with which he devoured his dinner, his fits of melancholy, his fits of anger, his frequent rudeness, his occasional ferocity, increased the interest which his new associates took in him. For these things were the cruel marks left behind by a life which had been one long conflict with disease and with adversity. In a vulgar hack writer, such oddities would have excited only disgust. But in a man of genius, learning, and virtue, their effect was to add pity to admiration and esteem. Johnson soon had an apartment at the brewery in Southwark, and a still more pleasant apartment at the villa of his friends on Streatham Common. A large part of every year he passed in those abodes, abodes which must have seemed magnificent and luxurious indeed, when compared with the dens in which he had generally been lodged. But his chief pleasures were derived from what the astronomer of his Abyssinian tale called "the endearing elegance of female friendship." Mrs Thrale rallied him, soothed him, coaxed him, and, if she sometimes provoked him by her flippancy, made ample amends by listening to his reproofs with angelic sweetness of temper. When he was diseased in body and in mind, she was the most tender of nurses. No comfort that wealth could purchase, no contrivance that womanly ingenuity, set to work by womanly compassion, could devise was wanting to his sick room. He requited her kindness by an affection pure as the affection of a father, yet delicately tinged with a gallantry, which, though awkward, must have been more flattering than the attentions of a crowd of the fools who gloried in the names, now obsolete, of Buck and Maccaroni. It should seem that a full half of Johnson's life, during about sixteen years, was passed under the roof of the Thrales. He accompanied the family sometimes to Bath, and sometimes to Brighton, once to Wales and once to Paris. But he had at the same time a house in one of the narrow and gloomy courts on the north of Fleet Street. In the garrets was his library, a large and miscellaneous collection of books, falling to pieces and begrimed with dust. On a lower floor he sometimes, but very rarely, regaled a friend with a plain dinner, a veal pie, or a leg of lamb and spinage, and a rice pudding. Nor was the dwelling uninhabited during his long absences. It was the home of the most extraordinary assemblage of inmates that ever was brought together. At the head of the establishment Johnson had placed an old lady named Williams, whose chief recommendations were her blindness and her poverty. But, in spite of her murmurs and reproaches, he gave an asylum to another lady who was as poor as herself, Mrs Desmoulins, whose family he had known many years before in Staffordshire. Room was found for the daughter of Mrs Desmoulins, and for another destitute damsel, who was generally addressed as Miss Carmichael, but whom her generous host called Polly. An old quack doctor named Levett, who bled and dosed coal-heavers and hackney coachmen, and received for fees crusts of bread, bits of bacon, glasses of gin, and sometimes a little copper, completed this strange menagerie. All these poor creatures were at constant war with each other, and with Johnson's negro servant Frank. Sometimes, indeed, they transferred their hostilities from the servant to the master, complained that a better table was not kept for them, and railed or maundered till their benefactor was glad to make his escape to Streatham, or to the Mitre Tavern. And yet he, who was generally the haughtiest and most irritable of mankind, who was but too prompt to resent anything which looked like a slight on the part of a purse-proud bookseller, or of a noble and powerful patron, bore patiently from mendicants, who, but for his bounty, must have gone to the workhouse, insults more provoking than those for which he had knocked down Osborne and bidden defiance to Chesterfield. Year after year Mrs Williams and Mrs Desmoulins, Polly and Levett, continued to torment him and to live upon him. . . .

Johnson was now in his seventy-second year. The infirmities of age were coming fast upon him. That inevitable event of which he never thought without horror was brought near to him; and his whole life was darkened by the shadow of death. He had often to pay the cruel price of longevity. Every year he lost what could never be replaced. The strange dependants to whom he had given shelter, and to whom, in spite of their faults, he was strongly attached by habit, dropped off one by one; and, in the silence of his home, he regretted even the noise of their scolding matches. The kind and generous Thrale was no more; and it would have been well if his wife had been laid beside him. But she survived to be the laughing-stock of those who had envied her, and to draw from the eyes of the old man who had loved her beyond any thing in the world, tears far more bitter than he would have shed over her grave. With some estimable, and many agreeable qualities, she was not made to be independent. The control of a mind more steadfast than her own was necessary to her respectability. While she was restrained by her husband, a man of sense and firmness, indulgent to her taste in trifles, but always the undisputed master of his house, her worst offences had been impertinent jokes, white lies, and short fits of pettishness ending in sunny good humour. But he was gone; and she was left an opulent widow of forty, with strong sensibility, volatile fancy, and slender judgment. She soon fell in love with a music-master from Brescia, in whom nobody but herself could discover anything to admire. Her pride, and perhaps some better feelings, struggled hard against this degrading passion. But the struggle irritated her nerves, soured her temper, and at length endangered her health. Conscious that her choice was one which Johnson could not approve, she became desirous to escape from his inspection. Her manner towards him changed. She was sometimes cold and sometimes petulant. She did not conceal her joy when he left Streatham: she never pressed him to return; and, if he came unbidden, she received him in a manner which convinced him that he was no longer a welcome guest. He took the very intelligible hints which she gave. He read, for the last time, a chapter of the Greek Testament in the library which had been formed by himself. In a solemn and tender prayer he commended the house and its inmates to the Divine protection, and, with emotions which choked his voice and convulsed his powerful frame, left for ever that beloved home for the gloomy and desolate house behind Fleet Street, where the few and evil days which still remained to him were to run out. Here, in June 1783, he had a paralytic stroke, from which, however, he recovered, and which does not appear to have at all impaired his intellectual faculties. But other maladies came thick upon him. His asthma tormented him day and night. Dropsical symptoms made their appearance. While sinking under a complication of diseases, he heard that the woman whose friendship had been the chief happiness of sixteen years of his life, had married an Italian fiddler; that all London was crying shame upon her; and that the newspapers and magazines were filled with allusions to the Ephesian matron and the two pictures in Hamlet. He vehemently said that he would try to forget her existence. He never uttered her name. Every memorial of her which met his eye he flung into the fire. She meanwhile fled from the laughter and hisses of her countrymen and countrywomen to a land where she was unknown, hastened across Mount Cenis, and learned, while passing a merry Christmas of concerts and lemonade parties at Milan, that the great man with whose name hers is inseparably associated, had ceased to exist.

He had, in spite of much mental and much bodily affliction, clung vehemently to life. The feeling described in that fine but gloomy paper which closes the series of his Idlers seemed to grow stronger in him as his last hour drew near. He fancied that he should be able to draw his breath more easily in a southern climate, and would probably have set out for Rome and Naples but for his fear of the expense of the journey. That expense, indeed, he had the means of defraying; for he had laid up about two thousand pounds, the fruit of labours which had made the fortune of several publishers. But he was unwilling to break in upon this hoard, and he seems to have wished even to keep its existence a secret. Some of his friends hoped that the government might be induced to increase his pension to six hundred pounds a-year, but this hope was disappointed, and he resolved to stand one English winter more. That winter was his last. His legs grew weaker; his breath grew shorter; the fatal water gathered fast, in spite of incisions which he, courageous against pain, but timid against death, urged his surgeons to make deeper and deeper. Though the tender care which had mitigated his sufferings during months of sickness at Streatham was withdrawn, he was not left desolate. The ablest physicians and surgeons attended him, and refused to accept fees from him. Burke parted from him with deep emotion. Windham sate much in the sick room, arranged the pillows, and sent his own servant to watch at night by the bed. Frances Burney, whom the old man had cherished with fatherly kindness, stood weeping at the door; while Langton, whose piety eminently qualified him to be an adviser and comforter at such a time, received the last pressure of his friend's hand within. When at length the moment, dreaded through so many years, came close, the dark cloud passed away from Johnson's mind. His temper became unusually patient and gentle; he ceased to think with terror of death, and of that which lies beyond death; and he spoke much of the mercy of God, and of the propitiation of Christ. In this serene frame of mind he died on the 13th of December 1784. He was laid, a week later, in Westminster Abbey, among the eminent men of whom he had been the historian,—Cowley and Denham, Dryden and Congreve, Gay, Prior, and Addison.

Since his death the popularity of his works—the Lives of the Poets, and, perhaps, the Vanity of Human Wishes, excepted—has greatly diminished. His Dictionary has been altered by editors till it can scarcely be called his. An allusion to his Rambler or his Idler is not readily apprehended in literary circles. The fame even of Rasselas has grown somewhat dim. But though the celebrity of the writings may have declined, the celebrity of the writer, strange to say, is as great as ever. Boswell's book has done for him more than the best of his own books could do. The memory of other authors is kept alive by their works. But the memory of Johnson keeps many of his works alive. The old philosopher is still among us in the brown coat with the metal buttons and the shirt which ought to be at wash, blinking, puffing, rolling his head, drumming with his fingers, tearing his meat like a tiger, and swallowing his tea in oceans. No human being who has been more than seventy years in the grave is so well known to us. And it is but just to say that our intimate acquaintance with what he would himself have called the anfractuosities of his intellect and of his temper, serves only to strengthen our conviction that he was both a great and a good man.

THOMAS MALTHUS

ON

Population Control

In the Rev. Thomas Robert Malthus (1766–1834) we meet a representative of that class of thinkers called seminal. By this term is usually meant a thinker who, by the novelty or force or outrageousness of his argument, arouses others for long afterwards to research, debate, and action. Malthus was reared on and according to the doctrines of Rousseau; and he demonstrated perfectly the propensity of each generation to overthrow the fondest schemes of the last, by publishing in 1798, when he was thirty-two years old, an Essay on the Principle of Population *in which he painted the gloomiest picture imaginable of the human prospect. His central thesis is well known: that population, tending to grow at a geometric rate, will ever press against the food supply, which at best increases only arithmetically, and thus poverty and misery are forever inescapable. This idea is altogether plausible, if simplistic, and its rapid adoption by theorists of the laissez-faire school is largely responsible for the designation of economics as the "dismal science." Malthus' argument had a profounder effect on, oddly, the science of biology, for it was the reading of his essay that sparked the idea of natural selection by survival of the fittest in the minds of both Charles Darwin and Alfred Wallace. By the time Malthus was asked to write an article on "Population" for the 1824 Supplement he had somewhat moderated the bleakness of his original essay, at least to the extent of adding to the "positive checks" on population—war, starvation, and so on—the idea of more benign "preventive checks," prudential acts like the purposeful delay of marriage and childbearing. Malthus and his wife, as it happens, had two children. (R. McH.)*

In the following extract we can observe the Britannica *enjoying a stroke of luck. Here, early in its career (in the Supplement to the 4th, 5th, and 6th editions, 1815–1824), it was able to offer its readers a unique spectacle: a powerful mind grappling with a powerful idea whose implications disturb us even more grievously today than they did in Malthus's time. The thoughtful reader may want to consult the many "Population" references in the current 15th edition, as well as the biography of Malthus in the* Micropaedia.

Consider . . . the nature of those checks which have been classed under the general heads of Preventive and Positive.

It will be found that they are all resolvable into *moral restraint, vice,* and *misery*. And if, from the laws of nature, some check to the increase of population be absolutely inevitable, and human institutions have any influence upon the extent to which each of these checks operates, a heavy responsibility will be incurred, if all that influence, whether direct or indirect, be not exerted to diminish the amount of vice and misery.

Moral restraint, in application to the present subject, may be defined to be, abstinence from marriage, either for a time or permanently, from prudential considerations, with a strictly moral conduct towards the sex in the interval. And this is the only mode of keeping population on a level with the means of subsistence, which is perfectly consistent with virtue and happiness. All other checks, whether of the preventive or the positive kind, though they may greatly vary in degree, resolve themselves into some form of vice or misery.

The remaining checks of the preventive kind, are the sort of intercourse which renders some of the women of large towns unprolific: a general corruption of morals with regard to the sex, which has a similar effect; unnatural passions and improper arts to prevent the consequences of irregular connections. These evidently come under the head of vice.

The positive checks to population include all the causes, which tend in any way prematurely to shorten the duration of human life; such as unwholesome occupations—severe labour and exposure to the seasons—bad and insufficient food and clothing arising from poverty—bad nursing of children—excesses of all kinds—great towns and manufactories—the whole train of common diseases and epidemics—wars, infanticide, plague, and famine. Of these positive checks, those which appear to arise from the laws of nature, may be called exclusively misery; and those which we bring upon ourselves, such as wars, excesses of all kinds, and many others, which it would be in our power to avoid, are of a mixed nature. They are brought upon us by vice, and their consequences are misery.

. . . Prudence cannot be enforced by laws, without a great violation of natural liberty, and a great risk of producing more evil than good. But still, the very great influence of a just and enlightened government, and the perfect security of property in creating habits of prudence, cannot for a moment be questioned. . . .

The existence of a tendency in mankind to increase, if unchecked, beyond the possibility of an adequate supply of food in a limited territory, must at once determine the question as to the natural right of the poor to full support in a state of society where the law of property is recognized. The question, therefore, resolves itself chiefly into a question relating to the necessity of those laws which establish and protect private property. It has been usual to consider the right of the strongest as the law of nature among mankind as well as among brutes; yet, in so doing, we at once give up the peculiar and distinctive superiority of man as a reasonable being, and class him with the beasts of the field. . . . If it be generally considered as so discreditable to receive parochial relief, that great exertions are made to avoid it, and few or none marry with a certain prospect of being obliged to have recourse to it, there is no doubt that those who were really in distress might be adequately assisted, with little danger of a constantly increasing proportion of paupers; and in that case a great good would be attained without any proportionate evil to counterbalance it.

ROY McMULLEN

ON

Style in the Arts

Roy McMullen (1911–1984) was an art historian, esthetician, and biographer of outstanding talent and originality. Unfortunately his gifts never coalesced in any single book, yet many good judges have felt that they were beautifully displayed in his subjoined article in the 15th edition.

It is improbable that early Britannica *editors would have considered "Style in the Arts" a proper encyclopedic subject. The thinking that produced the innovative 15th edition, however, was bound to come up with some such rubric, along with "Classification of the Arts," "Criticism of the Arts," and "Practice and Profession of the Arts." These latter three themes at once suggest concrete subject matter. But "style" is an elusive, protean concept. How to handle it? Mr. McMullen was not fazed by the challenge. He came up with an eleven-page essay, at once instructive and provocative, that should hold its own in the rather restricted literature of esthetics.*

From it we reprint almost the whole of his discussion of the nature of style and of its varieties. The original article continued with McMullen's reflections on what he called "the dynamics of style," by which he meant "the patterns of movement and change that are the concern of style-conscious historians and biographers."

Like much of the vocabulary of aesthetics, the word style resists straightforward definition. The word may point to little more than a mode or form of artistic production; or it can designate traits regarded simply as aids in the task of dating, grouping, and attributing works of art; it can imply skill, grace, or some other sort of excellence; it can mean a manner sanctioned by a standard; it refers to a mode, form, manner, tone, theme, subject, or quality—or a combination of such—that is felt to be characteristic enough to evoke a person, a group, a class, a nation, a place, a period, or a civilization; often also the reference is to features that are said to express an outlook, a doctrine, or a program. As a rule, even in the most carefully controlled context, several meanings will be present; and the tidy meanings will tend to bloom, or decay, into the untidy. Thus, although "sonata style," strictly constructed, should point only to a mode of musical production, in fact it will usually suggest a Classical outlook, the European 18th century, and perhaps the compositions of Haydn. Although to a field archaeologist "Late Helladic III" may designate merely a device for classifying pots of the ancient Greek city of Mycenae, in many imaginations the phrase is apt to inspire a vision of an entire culture, or perhaps of the legendary King Agamemnon bleeding in his bath after being murdered by his wife, as related in Aeschylus' tragedy.

The resulting confusion in thinking and talking about art is often deplored. One art historian likens style to a rainbow, a phenomenon of perception governed by the coincidence of certain physical conditions, which vanishes in the attempt to approach it. Another scholar takes the view that an adequate theory of style awaits a deeper knowledge of the principles of form construction and expression and a unified social theory comprising the practical means of life as well as emotional behaviour.

Such comments have not, however, had much effect; the majority of artists, critics, historians, and ordinary appreciators have continued to employ, loosely but confidently, the familiar term. And this persistence is not indefensible. Rainbows, after all, do exist; the chaser who fails to catch one demonstrates nothing except a mistake about their mode of existence. Also, in talking about art one can always cite the principle, first enunciated by Aristotle, that every study has its own degree of certainty and that a well-educated man will not ask for an unsuitable degree. . . .

The Nature of Style

It is easy to suppose that present notions about the nature of style are as old as the human ability to perceive differences, and a sampling of reasonably ancient cultural activity can seem to confirm the supposition. Much of the history of Chinese painting, for example, seems unthinkable without something like a modern critical apparatus for sorting out the dynastic periods, the local schools, and the copiers of venerated masters. Must not the ancient Greeks have been thinking of style when they noted the differences between Doric and Ionic orders in architecture? The way in which ancient Athenians contrasted the "rational" sound of the stringed cithara and the "irrational" reed-pipe wail of the aulos suggests the distinction between classical and romantic styles that was made in the 19th century, and the parodies of the tragic dramatist Euripides by the Athenian comic playwright Aristophanes imply modern conceptions of a personal style.

Much of what is now called stylistics seems to have existed already in the long succession of ancient Greek and Latin treatises that dealt with rhetoric. In sum, examples from both East and West can seem to support the assumption that there has always been something in the arts that may be called style.

Invention and discovery. That "seem," however, needs very heavy emphasis. Throughout the history of art some unexpected facts have resided below the surface of the sort of sampling that has just been cited—facts that are open to more than one interpretation, but certainly not wide open.

HISTORICAL BACKGROUND. The admirer of Chinese painting who consults the old texts on the subject will find illuminating accounts of brushwork and much wisdom about the creative process but practically no discussion of style in the full modern sense of the word. In Indian aesthetics since ancient times, the doctrine of *rasa* (Sanskrit: "essence") has been used in reference to the flavour or sentiment of works of art and to the modes of affective response to them, but not to what is properly called style. In the West, ancient writers on art exhibit a similar and finally rather enigmatic failure ever to focus squarely on the subject. Linguistic evidence, while inconclusive, suggests that in the

Greco-Roman world there was no word that meant quite what is now generally meant by "style."

Vitruvius, the Roman authority on architecture, writing sometime during the 1st century BC about the Doric, Ionic, Corinthian, and Tuscan orders, avoided even the Latin word *ordo* ("arrangement") and contented himself with *opus* ("work") and *genus* ("kind"). The Greek traveller Pausanias, writing about the visual arts in the 2nd century AD, used *kataskeuē* ("device" or "method of fitting out") and *ergasia* ("work"). Among writers on literature and rhetoric a parallel tendency is apparent. Speaking of the style of an author, Aristotle was likely to refer simply to *lexis* ("speech" or "word"), and he was also likely to be talking merely about lucidity. The unidentified Greek critic known as Demetrius, writing probably in the Hellenistic era, used *charaktēr* ("quality" or "mark"), but the noun carried overtones from the verb meaning merely to scratch or engrave. The anonymous Latin text called the *Ad Herennium,* dating from around 85 BC, used *figura* ("figure"). A generation later Cicero used an arsenal of terms that included, with greatly varying degrees of precision, *figura, color, habitus* ("condition," "character"), *dictio* ("diction"), *elocutio* ("elocution," in a very general sense), and *genus.*

Only in Late Latin does *stilus,* the word for the sharp-pointed instrument for writing, usually on wax, begin to mean also a manner of writing, as "pen" now does in such expressions as "a fluent pen" and "an acid pen"; and even here modern readers must be alert, for the derivation of English "style" from *stilus* does not prove that *stilus* always meant "style." The Latin term was reserved entirely for discussions of writing and speaking and usually for treatises on rhetoric; moreover, it seems to have implied little more than style in the sense of a skill or grace, and of a manner sanctioned by a standard. Apparently an author or orator in the closing years of the Roman Empire, in the 5th century AD, could have a periodic, loose, effective, ineffective, elevated, elegant, plain, high, middle, or low *stilus* but only very exceptionally, if ever, an idiosyncratic *stilus* that expressed a personality. And, again apparently, an architect, painter, sculptor, or musician could not have a *stilus* at all.

No important change in the usage thus established can be detected during the European Middle Ages. Words that suggest a kind, category, or mode of artistic production continued to be used in contexts in which a modern critic or historian might think in terms of a characteristic or expressive manner, or style. In architecture and the other visual arts, *opus* continued to be favoured; the French Gothic style of building was called Opus Francigenum, and English-style embroidery was known on the Continent simply as Opus Anglicanum. In music, the stylistic change apparent at the beginning of the 14th century, especially in France, was referred to as a new art: Ars Nova. The Latin *stilus*—and eventually its derivatives in other languages—was used only for talking about writing and speaking, and normally in the old rhetoricians' sense of a nonpersonal style sanctioned by a standard. When Dante (*Purgatorio,* xxiv) refers to the *dolce stil nuovo* ("sweet new style") that appeared in Italian poetry at the end of the 13th century, he stresses the importance not of the authors' personalities but of making the manner suit the matter and the occasion. The Host in Chaucer's *Canterbury Tales,* of the late 14th century, has this sense in mind when he addresses the Clerk of Oxford, in the prologue to the latter's tale:

> Your termes, your colours, and your figures,
> Kepe hem in stoor till so be ye endyte
> Heigh style, as whan that men to kinges wryte.
> Speketh so pleyn at this tyme, I yow preye,
> That we may understonde what ye seye.

In Renaissance Italy a shift in attitudes is apparent. Giorgio Vasari, for instance, in his widely influential *Lives of the Most Eminent Italian Painters, Sculptors and Architects . . .* (first edition in 1550, enlarged edition in 1568), built up a fairly consistent terminology on the basis of the word *maniera* ("manner"); his *maniera tedesca* ("German manner") refers to Gothic architecture, *buona maniera greca antica* ("good antique Greek manner") to ancient classical architecture, *maniera vecchia* ("old manner") to Byzantine or Byzantine-influenced painting, and *maniera moderna* to Renaissance architecture and painting. The *stilus* of the rhetoricians, *stile* in Italian, was still, however, reserved for literature. Not until around 1600 did musicians use such expressions as *stile moderno* and *stile rappresentativo,* and *stile* in criticism of the visual arts came still later.

In Britain, the equivalent extension of usage does not occur until the 18th century; the *Oxford English Dictionary* gives 1706 for the earliest reference to "style" in painting and 1728 for the earliest application of the term to music. Concerning the earliest English application to architecture there is some disagreement involving connotations, but a case has been made for a passage in Henry Fielding's novel *Tom Jones,* written in 1749: "The Gothic style of building could produce nothing nobler than Mr. Allworthy's house."

After that there was an era of the refinement of labels. A sharpened distinction between the art of ancient Greece and that of Rome began to be made in the 1760s. The division of British medieval architecture into Norman, Early English, Decorated, and Perpendicular styles dates from 1817. The term "roman" (Romanesque), referring to the architecture of western Europe before the Gothic, appeared in French criticism around 1820. Around 1850, "Rococo," after a career in slang, became a serious term for the style of the 18th century. The idea of the Renaissance as a cultural period, and not just an artistic movement, became fully-fledged around 1860. Definitions of the post-Renaissance styles of Mannerism and the Baroque were elaborated in the late 19th century. By the early 20th century, journalists were applying their own coinages to the styles discernible in modern painting and poetry.

CONTEMPORARY THOUGHT. The interpretation of the centuries-old mass of mostly semantic data on style is difficult and, for many people, exasperating. How is it possible to reconcile seemingly adequate perceptions of style throughout history with the long lack of adequate terms for it? How can the apparently adequate term, *stilus* or a derivative, be reconciled with inadequate perception of what it now connotes? Assuming that Chaucer's pilgrims reached their destination, what did the Host, familiar as he was with the figures and the high style of the rhetoricians, think when he was confronted by the Frenchness of Canterbury Cathedral?

Some historians have taken the easy course of assuming that when their ancestors used such words as "kind," or "work," or "speech" in certain contexts they somehow actually meant not what such words normally meant but what is now meant by "style." When *stilus* or a derivative was used, according to these historians, it somehow actually meant not what the rhetoricians meant but what is now meant in references to the composer Igor Stravinsky's or the novelist Ernest Hemingway's personal style. More rigorous minds have decided that style, viewed in the perspective of linguistic and general cultural history, is a will-o'-the-wisp. The majority of scholars, however, to judge from published essays, are reluctant to tamper with the evidence or to indulge themselves in a comfortable skepticism. They might therefore agree with the position that will be adopted in this article, which is that style in the arts is to a considerable extent a discovery, and to a large extent an invention, of a surprisingly late date.

Like many another cultural invention-discovery, style had a basis in human behaviour, but the distance between an ordinary ability to recognize things and what is meant by style in the arts is about as great as the distance between ordinary human memory and what is meant by history. Again like many another invention-discovery, style had a long phase during which some important levers and gears were already in place and more or less functioning. But the main job of assembling and powering the apparatus has been done since the end of the Middle Ages. Contributing to this development were Renaissance ideas of the importance of the individual personality, as opposed to medieval collectivism; 18th-century ideas of order and taxonomy in the natural sciences; and 19th-century ideas of biology, history, and, of course, aesthetics, all of which provided analogues for stylistic perceptions. The inventing and discovering are still going on, with much help from the experiments of artists and from such disciplines as archaeology, anthropology, psychology, sociology, and linguistics.

To talk of the nature of style in these terms is to raise some difficult philosophical questions, ranging from those posed by ancient thinkers down to those of recent logicians. For although in practical affairs it may be willingly granted that every invention is to some extent also a discovery and that every discovery involves some invention, the fact is that the word "invention" implies one sort of being and the word "discovery" quite another sort. Moreover, by a curious reversal of what happens in many inquiries, the philosophical questions that are thus raised for art critics, historians, and appreciators tend to be less pressing in regard to style as a concept or a collective noun than to style as it is actually experienced. People speculate calmly, if at all, about the nature of their comprehensive stylistic assumptions and become heated about the alleged reality or unreality of the style of the 19th-century French sculptor Rodin or of the *style galant* in 18th-century music or of the style of the Renaissance.

Can anything useful be said in this realm? Certainly any attempt to deal thoroughly with the issues would lead far beyond the scope of this article and deep into problems for which professional philosophers have not yet found accepted solutions. But it seems legitimate to confront antistyle "realists" with the suggestion that a style is no less real, or no more unreal, than a work of art, which is also a kind of invention-discovery, and to add that this degree of certainty is all that a well-tutored man should expect. Works of art can be, among other things, physical objects, imaginary objects, enduring possibilities, realized possibilities, sensible phenomena, insensible phenomena, sheer processes, and even, according to respectable opinion, transcendental entities. They can also have—and this is important to the argument—what has been called an emergent mode of existence and might be called a "do it yourself" mode; a picture, for instance, emerges from the blobs of pigment on a canvas when the viewer steps back and perhaps squints, and a symphony emerges from blobs of sound in the same way. All these modes of existence, and the emergent in particular, can be found among styles. Rodin's style emerges when a sufficient number of his works are contemplated from a certain psychic distance, and it is also a bronze entity in one of his statues of Balzac. The *style galant* emerges from compositions by Bach's sons, and it is also in a single Mozart serenade, which itself exists on paper, in performances, and, above all, as an enduring possibility. The Renaissance style, according to the scholar Arnold Hauser, "is at once more and less than what has actually been expressed in the works of the Renaissance masters. It is something like a musical theme of which only variations are known." In short, it is probably most usefully thought of as having an emergent mode of existence.

All this might be summarized by remarking that the process of invention and discovery that produced the general notion of style over a period of centuries is constantly being recapitulated by individuals, sometimes over a period very brief indeed, for particular styles. From this, one might hastily conclude that practically anyone can invent-discover what will pass unchallenged as a style; and anyone acquainted with modern art scholarship and art publicity must grant that there is a measure of truth in the conclusion. But in the long run, of course, there are certain limits to what can pass as style, just as there are certain limits to what can pass as a work of art; eventually opinion accumulates to the effect that the invention-discovery in question does not work well enough, or is simply not important enough, to qualify for the standard label. The annals of archaeology in Latin America and the eastern Mediterranean are strewn with styles that broke down, often after extensive repairs by their inventors. And, in fact, the world's major accepted styles turn out on examination to have more rigour and clarity in their nature than might be supposed. They have a number of recurring features that can be extracted and combined so as to constitute a working model of style, a sort of metastyle, that can be used for dealing critically with new labels.

Principal aspects of style. These recurring features can be grouped and considered under the headings of value aspects, poietic (or creative) aspects, morphological (or formal) aspects, metaphorical aspects, polar aspects, and measurable aspects. The word "aspect" is preferable to "feature" or "element" or some other possibility, for it must be kept in mind that a style is an invention-discovery with several modes of existence. Moreover, in each instance, what is being talked about is likely to be affected by the different viewpoints of producers, consumers, historians, critics, and other observers.

VALUE ASPECTS. The first group on the list is logically defective, since all the other aspects have value aspects, but it is important enough to merit some separate preliminary treatment. That styles are regarded as desirable is evident from common usage. Merely to say that an artist, a work, or a period has style is to judge him or it favourably; merely to use "style" in preference to such words as "manner" or "fashion" is to imply value; even to say that a thing is in a poor style is often to suggest that it does not have enough style. And that styles are actually worthwhile is difficult to doubt. They provide the art appreciator with the pleasure of recognizing somebody or something, a pleasure that is certainly among the basic ones of human existence: witness the popularity of handbooks that tell how to distinguish Tang from Sung styles in Chinese art or Louis Quinze from Louis Seize in French art. Styles provide the artist with the pleasure of being recognized, and they do so without the self-display of a signature. They are like codes; in the language of information theory, they help obtain an invariant output from a variable input, and nearly all art history, which is a comparatively recent phenomenon, and much criticism makes use of them. They also have many less evident sorts of value. They function as the signs and, to some extent, as the agents of integration in individual artists, groups of artists, and sometimes whole cultures; they are brakes on alienation. They are appetizing and preservative, like spices; they have saved from oblivion a number of great minds whose ideas have lost their fascination. To cite only a few examples from British critical and historical literature, it is hard to imagine anyone still reading much of Dr. Samuel Johnson, Edward Gibbon, Thomas Babington Macaulay, Thomas Carlyle, or John Ruskin for content alone.

These positive aspects are accompanied, of course, by some negative ones, and the latter have been worrying critics increasingly during recent decades. Since styles stress similarities and work partly as codes, they tend to blur differences and to simplify excessively; they encourage many viewers to see, for example, merely "a Picasso" or "Cubism" where one ought to see the rich uniqueness of a painting. The pleasure of being recognized, and the money that may come with it, can encourage some artists to develop a mere trademark. Successful period styles of the past may foster, as they did among 19th-century European architects, an absurd amount of eclecticism and fancy-dress historicism. Successful current styles can generate an equally absurd amount of imitation among artists. The difficulty of defining specific styles and style in general creates serious problems in art history, which will be discussed in the last section of this article.

Do these negative aspects outweigh the positive? The majority opinion is clearly that they do not, for there is no prospect of a return to the supposed innocence of the centuries before the massive, intricate, dangerous, useful invention-discovery got up steam.

CREATIVE ASPECTS. One of the complaints, however, is very legitimate: it is that people who talk about style do so too often from the viewpoint of an appreciator. The same complaint can be made about art discussions in general; a good deal is heard, for instance, about disinterested contemplation, which is fair enough from an appreciator's viewpoint but close to wild calumny from an artist's viewpoint. The hardworking men who built the Parthenon were certainly not disinterested in any usual way, nor were John Milton in writing *Paradise Lost,* Michelangelo in painting the frescoes for the Sistine Chapel, Richard Wagner in composing the opera *Tristan und Isolde,* and Leo Tolstoy in creating *War and Peace,* and what they were doing can scarcely be called contemplation. It was rather what the Greeks called *poiēsis* ("creation," or simply "making").

Style, then, has what can be called poietic aspects; the adjective brushes jargon but lacks the Romantic connotations of "creative" and the matter-of-factness of such an alternative as "productive." The existence of these aspects can be posited etymologically, with the risk inherent in arguing from dead metaphors; *stilus,* as has been noted, originally meant a writing instrument; and such near equivalents for "style" as "manner" (Latin *manuarius,* "of the hand") and "fashion" (Latin *facere,* "to make") also have clearly poietic pedigrees. Moreover, in some contexts "style" still means little more than a mode of artistic production.

But here an attempt to sharpen common usage seems to be called for, since a style in its poietic aspects is not the whole of an act of making. A style is only the part of the act that represents a deviation from a norm and that, as such, is apparent enough to offer the pleasure of recognition. The norm may be provided by a more inclusive style, by a tradition, by material conditions, or by some other frame of reference within which artists work. The norm may also be assumed, more or less arbitrarily, by observers. For example the personal style of the 17th-century Flemish painter Peter Paul Rubens is not, poietically speaking, the whole of his way of applying paint to canvas; his personal style is merely that part of his way that constitutes a recognizable deviation from a norm—the Baroque style—in which he worked. The Baroque, to continue the illustration, is not the whole of the Baroque painters' ways of applying paint to canvas; it refers to merely the part of their ways that constitutes a recognizable deviation from another norm, the general style that prevailed in European painting from roughly the middle of the 15th century to the end of the 19th, though in many histories of art the norm from which the Baroque deviated is instead assumed to be the High Renaissance style as exemplified by Raphael.

One can conclude that style is dependent on originality and the will to exercise it. But much depends also on the norm. In the first place, many norms are imposed, sometimes by accepted authority, sometimes by social pressure, and most often by unawareness of an alternative; the average Western composer, for instance, between Bach in the 18th century and Schoenberg in the 20th, seems to have regarded the tonal-style norm—the organization of tones and chords in a composition in relation to a keynote—as something like a law of nature. In the second place, certain norms contain fewer variables than others and therefore offer fewer opportunities for deviation; a Byzantine mosaicist had no possibility of developing a marked personal style. And, finally, there are the supernorms constituted by each art, by artistic materials, by languages, and by much else; at this level the number of variables may be decisive. Traditional sculpture offers fewer variables than painting and hence has yielded a much smaller number of styles. Granite offers fewer variables than bronze and hence has what might be called a lower yield in terms of style. Specialists in stylistics—the branch of linguistics that studies the variables in a language and their manipulation—have noted that one of the secrets of the 20th-century Welsh poet Dylan Thomas's strongly personal style was his discovery of unsuspected variables in English: thus where the norm had seemed to insist on nouns of temporal, or linear, measurement he could write "All the sun long," "A grief ago," and "farmyards away." In "Spelt from Sibyl's Leaves," the 19th-century English priest Gerard Manley Hopkins showed a comparable talent for finding possibilities of deviation:

Earnest, earthless, equal, attuneable, vaulty, voluminous. . . . stupendous
Evening strains to be time's vast, womb-of-all, home-of-all, hearse-of-all night.

FORMAL ASPECTS. Much of the above might have been put under the heading of the morphological—or "formal," if certain connotations are ignored—aspects of style, and much that is traditionally morphological is equally poietic. The form of a work of art can be regarded as the record left behind by the making process; this idea, implicit in ancient rhetoricians' descriptions of prose and poetry (*e.g.*, as laboured), has been prominent in modern criticism since the appearance in the 1950s of such process-emphasizing accomplishments as Action painting, in which the brush strokes and textures may be regarded as a record of the creation of the work; aleatoric music, in which the notes or sounds are selected by chance; and Brutalist architecture, the sort that leaves the concrete raw and plank marked.

The making process, however, involves the whole work, whereas form may be regarded as excluding content and including only shape, volume, space, structure, pattern, organization, texture, rhythm, imagery, emphasis, balance, and the like. This separation is often denounced by careful critics, and a successful work of art, when contemplated in a properly focussed and expanded state of awareness, does indeed present itself with form and content organically tangled. But there is little likelihood that art appreciation suffers when things are untangled for discussion, since most persons are quite capable of distinguishing between the critical analysis of a work and actual aesthetic experience. So it seems safe to accept common usage concerning "form" and then to agree with commentators who have been assuming for centuries that style has purely morphological aspects—without joining them in assuming that it has practically no other aspects.

Immediately an apparently drastic shift in emphasis occurs, from one of variables and deviations to one of repetitions and conformity. In fact, style can be reasonably, if incompletely, defined as constant formal elements and their combinations, with content excluded except in certain circumstances. But the shift in emphasis is obviously just a result of the play of aspects. A style is always generated by the manipulation of available variables in such a way as to yield a recognizable deviation from a given or an assumed norm. If, however, the deviation is to be recognized as something more than an accident or a solitary impulse, it must be repeated, either identically or in a recognizable variation. It must become understandable, which a unique event—an accident—cannot be.

Thus a style is always, when perceived from what can be called the poietic stance, rather surprising; the Baroque norm and the English-language norm do not lead to any expectation of Rubens' fleshly swirl and Thomas' "A grief ago." But thus also a style is always, when perceived from the morphological stance, rather familiar; what was unexpected in terms of the act of making becomes expected in terms of form. Again the illustration can be continued above the level of personal style: the energized masses found in Baroque painting of the 17th century are constant in their deviation from the balance of High Renaissance paintings of the 16th century. In sum, an artist, or a group of artists, is obliged by the nature of style to move freely into constraint, and heretically into orthodoxy.

METAPHORICAL ASPECTS. Hence certain styles are commonly said to be "characteristic," or "expressive." An aesthetic deviation, repeated sufficiently, may become converted into a form and yield recognition pleasure. The result may fairly be described as a manifestation of personality. The flame shapes in El Greco's paintings may be thought of as a handwriting, Bach's driving rhythms as a gait, Proust's long sentences as a voice; and usually no harm is done to understanding.

Such metaphors, however, along with the words "characteristic" and "expressive," can become whimsical or misleading in many situations. Moreover, the stylistic aspects in question are best perceived in depth and in the aggregate by noticing that nearly every style is itself a metaphor, functionally speaking. It implies, as Aristotle said a good metaphor does, an intuitive perception of the similarity in dissimilars. It works, as an ordinary simile does, by seizing striking likenesses and neglecting differences; to see that the 18th-century English poet William Cowper wrote in a Miltonic style resembles, as process, seeing that Robert Burns's sweetheart was "like a red red rose." There is a substitution of a part for a whole, as in synecdoche; in many eyes a pointed arch and a flying buttress are enough to evoke the Gothic style, and for many ears a single chord can summon up Beethoven.

Most importantly, in nearly every stylistic context, and not just in those involving personal and "characteristic" styles, there are two sections, like the two sections in the comparing process of metaphor; these can be thought of as the "window" and the "view." In the simplest situations the view through the window of the style is of an individual artist, or of a well-defined group; the 19th-century French poet Stéphane Mallarmé may be sensed through his repetition of the word *azur,* and the contemporaneous group of Impressionist painters that surrounded Claude Monet are recognizable through their deviant, flickering brushwork. The situation, however, is seldom quite that simple. Through Mallarmé's style as well as through Impressionism the view may be of a doctrine or a program; in other situations it may be of a class, a nation, a place, a period. There are styles that bear a functional resemblance to myths, if the latter are thought of as communal metaphors. The view that looms through the symmetrical frontality of the rigidly posed figures in ancient Egyptian sculpture is of an entire culture, a culture that is dramatically different from the one that looms through the asymmetrical twist, the contrapposto, of figures in Italian Renaissance statues.

These remarks have to be qualified, for if common usage is accepted there are styles that seem to have no metaphorical aspects, that are practically opaque. Possible examples are procedural styles in general: those described by the ancient rhetoricians, those associated with the fixed forms of music and poetry, those that are just simplifications, often geometrical, of natural forms.

POLAR ASPECTS. Common usage also provides evidence for the existence of certain structural or self-defining tendencies in style that can be grouped under a single heading as polar aspects. These have long been noticed; Hellenistic and Roman literary critics have a lot to say about the flowery, redundant oratorical prose known as Asiatic, which is presented as the diametrical opposite of the plain, economical Attic. The invention or discovery of such polarities did not get seriously under way, however, until the 18th century in western Europe; and most of it has been accomplished, mainly by German thinkers and largely in the visual arts, since the late 1800s.

Among the great number of such contrasting pairs that could be mentioned are haptic-optic (*i.e.,* oriented to the sense of touch as opposed to sight orientation), idealistic-naturalistic, multifarious-unitary, closed-open, linear-painterly, and many more. It will be noticed that the trend is toward all-inclusive world styles, or at least toward constantly recurring stylistic features, and that the emphasis is strongly on morphological aspects. This emphasis, although open to the usual objections to "formalism," has compensated handsomely, in terms of instrumental value, for the sometimes naïve scientism and general overconfidence implicit in the labelling. Indeed, it is not an exaggeration to say that the best visual-art criticism and history published since World War I could not have been written without the help of polar analysis of form.

But pairs like the rather abstruse ones mentioned are not the whole story. Any style, including the familiar established ones, may be polarized; the 19th-century French painter Delacroix's Romantic style may be paired with his older contemporary Ingres' Neoclassical style, the Gothic with the Renaissance, the French with the English, the Christian with the Islāmic, the Eastern with the Western. Each member of each pair is defined in terms of what the other member is not; each is at once the deviant from the other and the norm for the other. Often in such pairs the forms are not seriously analyzed; mere diametrical opposition, as in traditional political parties, is felt to be enough. This peculiarity may be especially evident in connection with a modern style, which is always polar to begin with and which may stay that way until in its turn it begins to cease to be modern. Only then may historians have a good chance to cut through the partisan propaganda, get at the constant forms, and decide if the style is internally consistent enough to merit a label of its own and a place in the parade that began some 40,000 years ago.

MEASURABLE ASPECTS. The historian who undertakes such a task is not likely to approach the constant forms with a yardstick, for in general the measurable aspects of style are not very highly considered by artists and art critics. But such aspects do exist.

The differences between Doric and Ionic orders in classical architecture are not only in the abacuses and volutes that decorate the columns and their capitals but also in proportions and in the number of flutes on a column. The 20th-century French architect Le Corbusier performed his subtle manipulation of architectural variables with the help of a system of proportion, which he called the *modulor,* based on the human figure. Sculpture styles were influenced for centuries by the canon (now lost) of Polyclitus, a Greek sculptor of the 5th century BC who believed that "the beautiful comes about little by little, through many numbers." In a portrait in the Mannerist style of mid-16th-century Italy, much of what makes it Mannerist may be a matter of how long the body is. Some of Hogarth's pictures can be analyzed in terms of what he called "the line of beauty," obtainable by winding a "precise serpentine line around the figure of a cone." Painters of the 20th century have revived the interest Renaissance artists had in the proportion (about 8:13) known as the golden section. An important part of the stylistic difference between a movie director of around 1930 and one of around 1970 may be discovered by simply noting the smaller number of camera shots and sequences used by the latter. Styles in poetry can be specified, often with surprising results, by counts of images, rhymes, run-on lines, and metrical variations; and such methods are accurate enough to help date Shakespeare's plays. Prose styles are, for certain modern linguists, a matter of the statistical averaging of the use of certain words, performed with the help of a computer. That musical styles have measurable aspects has been clear, of course, since at least the time of Pythagoras, who discovered in the 6th century BC the relationship of musical intervals to the lengths of strings; and the fact has become freshly clear under the impact of 20th-century science and technology. Computers have become standard equipment for many composers; synthesizers have become generators of styles translatable into mathematics; Beethoven's poietic deviations from a norm have turned out to be quantifiable in somewhat the same way as the unforeseeables studied by information theorists.

Some qualifications are in order. The analysis of a style is not the same as the experience of a style: the whole of a work of art is certainly not the sum of its measurable parts. While it may be true that under certain conditions quantity turns into quality, it does not follow that every quality can be quantified; and certain conditions—Beethoven's genius, for instance—remain to plague the quantifier. But all this does not alter the fact that styles do have certain measurable aspects. Nor does it excuse the neglect of these aspects by some art appreciators, critics, and historians. Perhaps the remedy both for the shortcomings of the quantity-minded and for the attitude of the quality-minded will eventually be found in interdisciplinary work on aesthetic problems.

The Varieties of Style

Since it is part of the nature of style to provide recognition pleasure, and since this pleasure is usually accompanied by an irrepressible impulse to name, one can suppose that unlabelled styles are rare. Would that they were not, an archaeologist may say; would that there were an opportunity to classify works of art scientifically and to substitute numbers or New Latin labels for such misnomers as "Gothic" (which is unrelated to the Goths) and "Cubist" (which has little to do with cubes). Actually, however, the downright mistaken or merely derisive labels are neither very numerous nor very misleading; to anybody who knows enough to be interested, "Gothic" is likely to mean something like "Medieval West European III," and "Cubist" something like "genus, partly abstract; species, Picasso-Braque 1907–14." And if the majority of style names are not scientifically descriptive, they do as a rule offer adequate clues not only to the thing being talked about but also to the class, or classes, to which the thing belongs. In other words, the familiar nomenclature, although accumulated apparently haphazardly through the centuries, has taxonomic—more precisely, typological—implications. To speak of Rembrandt's style is not only to refer to certain poietic deviations from a norm and to certain recurring formal elements; it is also to imply the existence of a personal variety of style plus a more general sort that includes the personal variety. To speak of a realistic style, or of one of its several polar opposites, is to imply a different variety and a correspondingly different general sort.

When such implications are grouped, they yield some 13 varieties of style in the arts. (The "some" is inserted here to allow for reasonable differences of opinion as to where the dividing lines should be drawn.) These 13 varieties are clearly of two general sorts, which emerge from two types of "view" beyond the metaphorical "windows" that styles create in a sufficiently knowledgeable imagination. The first general sort, to which Rembrandt's style belongs, affords views that focus on single cultures; the second sort, to which a realistic style may belong, affords views that cut across cultures. It will be noticed that a given style may move from one category to another; more will be said later about this mobility. But most styles are reasonably stable, and for the moment it is convenient to assume that the others have certain recognizable home categories. Even a slightly unstable classification can stiffen discussion.

Single-culture varieties. Single-culture styles are usually inhabited, so to speak. They usually evoke, more or less in the foreground of the contemplating imagination, either a person, a school, a social class, an ethnic division, a regional community, a nation, an ecological division, a religious community, or the generations that constitute a period. Rembrandt's style usually evokes the bulb-nosed, sad-eyed person known through dozens of remarkably self-searching self-portraits; the Venetian style usually evokes the 16th-century masters Giorgione, Titian, Tintoretto, and Veronese; each style in African sculpture usually evokes a tribe; and so on down the list. Single-culture styles are therefore frequently said to be "characteristic," or "expressive," of a particular people; and in this context these familiar terms of interpretative art criticism may seem to triumph over the mild objection raised earlier, in the discussion of the general metaphorical aspects of style. In fact, these adjectives, and also the noun "people," raise some awkward problems even here.

PERSONAL STYLES. No variety of style seems, at first thought, quite as vividly, specifically, indubitably inhabited as the personal variety. Quoting the celebrated and seldom-read *Discours sur le style* (1753), by the Comte de Buffon, and neglecting his qualifying remarks, many appreciators assume confidently that "the style is the man himself." In a somewhat modified form, the same assumption can be found as far back as the 1st century in the Stoic moralizing of the Roman philosopher Seneca. In a somewhat pseudoscientific form it has produced some disturbingly glib psychoanalysis of works of art. In its plebeian form it has led to such suppositions as that the flame shapes in El Greco's paintings are evidence of astigmatism, the long sentences in Proust's novels evidence of asthma, the rhetoric of Liszt's piano pieces evidence of Gypsy blood, and the right angles of Mies van der Rohe's architecture evidence of a subtle totalitarianism. The notion may be said to have reached one of the peaks of its career in 1935 in the earnest excogitation of the literary scholar

Caroline Spurgeon; after counting and sorting Shakespeare's images, she concluded that the poet was

> a compactly well-built man, probably on the slight side, extraordinarily well coordinated, lithe and nimble of body, quick and accurate of eye . . . probably fair-skinned and of a fresh color, which in youth came and went easily . . . very sensitive to dirt and evil smells . . . gentle, kindly, honest, brave and true.

She also saw, through the obviously wide-open window of the personal style, a man who at 35 had "probably experienced heartburn as a result of acidity."

It is easy to call this sort of interpretation wrong and not easy to explain exactly why it is wrong. After all, everyone indulges in it to a degree. Spurgeon, of course, went a bit too far; she was neglectful of complexity and of the possible differences between a dramatist and his personages. But her counting and sorting of images was a valuable and influential piece of research; it demonstrated, in an irrefutable way, the existence of some of the deviations and constants that make up Shakespeare's personal style. If the person who is certainly recognizable in this personal style is not quite the Stratford man himself, who is he?

When the question is asked about a large enough number of personal styles, a tentative answer may emerge. The style, it appears, is not the man himself but the artist himself—mostly, at least. Naturally, the artist is to a considerable extent the man; he has much of the latter's native capacities, acquired skills, secret drives, and painful defects. But the artist is a professional role, a programmatic personage, a cultural configuration, a persona; in sum, he is a remarkably, often deliberately, synthetic personality. Further, he is conditioned by much besides the man himself and notably by the work of other artists. To put all this another way, every personal style is in part sheer performance, and every artist as such is in a sense (not a pejorative one) a performer. Mies the man went on living in his relatively old-fashioned Chicago apartment, while Mies the artist was "performing" with gleaming right angles in the tall apartment buildings he designed for Chicago's fashionable Lake Shore Drive; Mozart the man disliked flute music, while Mozart the artist "performed" by composing flute music; Petrarch himself philandered, while Petrarch the poet "performed" as a faithful worshipper from afar of the idealized Laura.

Hence, in the opinion of many modern critics, the once-popular problem of personal stylistic sincerity is meaningless; to pose it is to mistake art for life. Hence also the distinction that is often made between creative personal styles and performing personal (or group) styles should not be too categorical. Although a dramatic text, a musical score, or a notated ballet may seem to constitute a norm that offers a very small number of variables, in practice a competent actor, musician, dancer, conductor, or director usually manages to produce enough deviations to have an easily recognizable personal style. No opera-record collector is likely to confuse an interpretation by the intensely dramatic soprano Maria Callas with one of the same role by the serenely lyrical soprano Renata Tebaldi; and ballet literature suggests that the ethereal 19th-century ballerina Marie Taglioni was as different from her rival the sensuous Fanny Elssler as the 19th-century Italian operas of Vincenzo Bellini were from those of his contemporary Gaetano Donizetti. Moreover, an interpreter has about the same choice as a creator among the more inclusive styles that can always be recognized simultaneously with a personal one; he can be modern, traditional, Classical, Romantic, Baroque, or whatever. And finally, if he tries to be as faithful as possible to his text, the result will approach another personal "performing" style, that of the artist who composed the work. To succeed in producing *Phèdre* exactly as it was conceived would be to play the player Jean Racine.

These remarks should not be interpreted as a complete denial of the presence of "the man himself" behind a personal style—into the polar opposite of Spurgeon's error. Since the artist is partly conditioned by the man, so, of course, is the style; and stylistic evidence can often be made to match biographical information in an enlightening way. Friends of Mies noticed in his manners and dress a certain fastidiousness and a love of good material that reminded them of his architecture. The reported simplicity, honesty, and modesty of Haydn are an agreeable match for qualities in his musical style. Most readers probably sense an authentic personality, a real voice, behind the sprung rhythm and breathless rush of the verse of Hopkins. Also, some quite successful methods of stylistic analysis apparently depend on a strict correspondence between the manner and the man himself; a fascinating example is the technique for attributing paintings, developed by the Italian art critic Giovanni Morelli in the 19th century, which assumes that the touch of a particular master can best be detected in unimportant details, such as the ears in a portrait, that were presumably painted without taking much thought.

None of the counter-evidence, however, seriously shakes the argument that the person in a personal style is mostly the artist as such, and some of it does not stand up very well under scrutiny. Fastidiousness, simplicity, and vehemence do not become meaningful in this context until they are given energy and focus by the artist; and the telltale details used for attributing paintings may have about as much aesthetic interest as fingerprints.

School Styles. When artists are considered as a stylistic group, or school, all the problems raised by personal styles reappear in new guises in the company of other problems; and one of the more nettling of the latter is the precise meaning of "school." For there is no denying that this part of the apparatus of criticism has got badly out of hand since its invention and discovery in the 18th century (largely by the pioneer Italian archaeologist Luigi Lanzi). Art critics, historians, and especially painting-museum curators have acquired the habit of using the term as an elegant variation for what usually turns out to be merely a country of residence; thus J.M.W. Turner is said to be a painter of the British school and Thomas Eakins of the American school. Sometimes the geographical designation is narrowed, with a commensurate gain in stylistic information; thus Mantegna is said to belong to the North Italian school and Perugino to the Umbrian school. The gain, however, may be in confusion; the division between the so-called Northern and Southern Sung schools of Chinese painting, for example, has been called the most misleading and arbitrary in art history. Sometimes geography is abandoned for a general stylistic designation; thus the 18th-century French painter Jean-Baptiste Chardin is said to belong to the Realist school. Sometimes the stylistic designation is narrowed drastically, and then a gallery visitor may be confronted by a brass plaque attributing a 15th-century Florentine painting to the school of Fra Angelico, for instance; this can mean that documents point to the studio or to a follower of Fra Angelico; or that the picture is an ancient, and therefore respectable, copy; or that it looks rather like a genuine Fra Angelico without his customary quality—the unstated premise being that all pictures by Fra Angelico are first class.

The situation is regrettable not only because one word is being forced to do things other words can do better but also because "school" has its own work to do. Musicologists can profitably use the term to talk about the centres of musical activity that existed in the 12th century at such places as Paris, Compostela, Padua, and Winchester; or about the late-16th-century amateur "academy" known as the Florentine Camerata, in which the monodic style that led to opera was fostered; or about the group of composers of atonal music that surrounded Arnold Schoenberg in 20th-century Vienna. Painting historians must refer to the Tours school of Carolingian miniaturists, the Shen Chou school of 15th-century Chinese ink artists, the Barbizon school of 19th-century French landscape painters. Literary historians must consider such schools of poetry as those of the 16th-century French Pléiade, the English Lake poets of around 1800, the Tokyo (then Edo) haiku masters of the 17th and 18th centuries, the American Imagists of around 1914. Even architectural historians, who tend to think in large units, have to take account of such phenomena as the Burlington group of Palladianists in 18th-century London, the Glasgow School in the 19th century, the slightly later Chicago School, and so on. Each of these examples, and of the hundreds of others that could be cited, involves a well-defined and usually not large geographical area, a relatively short time span, and a relatively small number of artists working in a describable shared style; here are the essential requirements for using the term "school" profitably. Of course, a curator, in announcing that Turner is of the British school, may really intend to commit his museum to the proposition that a nationally shared painting style has been perceptible in Great Britain down through the centuries. Such is not usually the intention, however, and when it is, it should be made explicit.

The confusion is worth dwelling on because in many works of art a school style, defined as the shared style of a relatively small number of artists, is as striking as a personal style. It is a "window" that affords a "view" inhabited by a synthetic personality, a programmatic personage, almost (but not quite) vivid enough to justify thinking in terms of something like an overartist, as some German philosophers have. Moreover, in the interaction between a personal style and a school style, there is a model, manageable for study, of the complex relations that emerge when several styles are found together in a given work. The personal style of John Donne, the 17th-century English poet of the Metaphysical school, is recognizable in the dense, macabre imagery, the sometimes violently wrenched metre, and the self-dramatizing switch of the following lines from his "Nocturnall upon St. Lucies Day, being the shortest day":

> The world's whole sap is sunke:
> The generalle balme th' hydroptique earth hath drunke,
> Whither, as to the beds-feet, life is shrunke,
> Dead and enterr'd; yet all these seeme to laugh,
> Compar'd with mee who am their epitaph.

At the same time, the style of the Metaphysical school is apparent in the rather conversational tone, the compact syntax, and the use of extravagant poetic conceits. Deviations and a norm solicit attention, and the solicitations will multiply if the recognition process is continued into the maze of styles—the Elizabethan, the Jacobean, the English, the religious, the aristocratic, the Mannerist, the formal, the haptic, etc.—which a sufficiently subtle and patient critic may discover in Donne's poetry. The common reader, in Dr. Johnson's sense, can be excusably irritated at a certain point by the game of hide-and-seek between the different and the same, the self and the other. But, in fact, such simultaneous recognitions are normal in the actual experience of art; and they are no more mysterious than recognizing, with confidence and usually without being able to say exactly why, that a given face is of an individual, a family, a region, a nation, and a race—is at once itself and not itself.

SOCIAL STYLES. On a scale of recognizability, many critics would probably put social styles—those associated with a particular class or section of society—directly after personal and school styles, at least when much of the art of the centuries before the Industrial Revolution is being considered. Even an untrained appreciator can sense courtly styles in the intricate fixed forms of troubadour verse, the stiff etiquette of a Louis XIV portrait, and the languors of medieval Japan's *Tale of Genji,* by Murasaki Shikibu; bourgeois styles in the solid forms of 17th-century Dutch still-lifes, the uncomplicated rhythm and harmony of a Protestant hymn, and the matter-of-fact, 18th-century English prose of Daniel Defoe; and peasant or proletarian styles—often more accurately described as traditions—in songs, carvings, and embroidery. In the 20th century such clear-cut social styles have become less and less noticeable, partly because class distinctions have become much less evident in the technologically more advanced nations. Also, artists have ceased to know for whom they work, the art market having replaced, except on special occasions that are most frequent for architects, the old system of direct commissioning by patrons. Nevertheless, a sophisticated, or merely mischievous, critic can point to contemporary social styles; some evoke the established families, others the new millionaires. A number are related to young people, who since the 1960s have exhibited many of the economic and cultural characteristics of a separate class. Politicians in all countries throughout the 20th century have occasionally attempted, sometimes on a totalitarian scale, to impose on artists one of the old courtly or bourgeois styles; and a few dictators, notably Hitler and Mussolini, have temporarily revived an imperial-court style with the parvenu touch, familiar to art historians in such outsized forms as those of Darius's palace at Persepolis in ancient Persia and Napoleon's church (originally temple) of the Madeleine in Paris.

Here two concessions seem called for. The first is that in talking about social styles it is often impossible, even for the purpose of cold analysis, to keep morphological aspects separate from content. The second is that throughout history the artist as such has been remarkably, sometimes depressingly, available for the "expression" or "characterization" of a social stratum other than that of the man himself. Perhaps the artist as such—shaman, bard, craftsman, entertainer, 19th-century demiurge, 20th-century iconoclast—has been rather more of a performer than has already been suggested.

ETHNIC STYLES. Like social styles, ethnic styles have become less noticeable in the modern era. Their formerly high level of recognizability, their complex morphological aspects, and their surprising persistence over long periods have made them, however, favourite subjects for study among both archaeologists and aestheticians. Good examples are plentiful in the Indian arts of North America; the sculpture, painting, and music of black Africa; the pottery of the ancient Middle East and east Asia; and the surviving decorated objects, mostly metalwork, of the so-called barbarian peoples who moved across Asia and Europe between roughly the 6th century BC and the time of Charlemagne, at the end of the 8th century AD. In some instances scholars have been able to trace the borrowing of motifs; the Germanic animal styles of the migration period, for example, show the influence of Roman figurative art and Mediterranean ribbon ornament. But the borrowed motif is invariably transformed by a repeated deviation into one of the morphological constants of the borrowing tribe, and the reasons for this enduring assimilative capacity are not well understood.

The notion of a physically inherited stylistic disposition has long since been discredited, and archetypes in a collective unconscious, as postulated by the 20th-century Swiss psychologist Carl Jung, have been dismissed by the majority of professional historians. Among the more attractive theories are some that point to analogies with the inertia and the assimilative capacity of a language; yet even these seem inadequate before such a fact as that the Eskimo ethnic style has lasted for about two millennia. Another attractive theory links the lack of stylistic change to a general lack of history—or at least to a general lack of awareness of history. But if this theory is plausible in a North American or an African context, it is much less so in the context of the Asian and European migrating peoples, who managed to pass through an immense amount of history without making important changes in the design of their crowns, buckles, and other useful objects.

Regional and National Styles. The problem of stylistic stability reappears in the consideration of regional and lagnational styles, which are partly just ethnic styles that have settled down. But they are always more than that. The high—and polar—recognizability of Oriental and Occidental styles cannot be satisfactorily accounted for by references to ancient tribes and by linguistic analogies; nor can the long preoccupation in the Mediterranean basin with human forms; the long preoccupation in northern Europe with animal, zoomorphic, fantastic, symbolic, and abstract forms; the rigidity of Egyptian pictorial and sculptural forms during some 3,000 years; the persistently emotional, romantic, and expressionist tendencies in German music, painting, and literature; the French emphasis on structure in architecture, painting, and poetry; the English linear and decorative tendency that runs through medieval miniature painting, Perpendicular Gothic architecture, the drawings of William Blake, and Art Nouveau. Common sense, of course, is needed in thinking about such styles; the theorizer who sets out to show that all French art is rational and all German art emotional will be in trouble immediately. Also, a certain vagueness is often suitable, for the distinctive features of a regional or national style may be of the sort better described as qualities than as morphological aspects. Recurring differences, however, finally add up to recognizability, and a quality hard to define can be strongly felt.

Climate and landscape were formerly popular as explanations for regional and national styles (for all styles, as a matter of fact); Gothic architecture was supposed to have emerged in northern Europe because of the many forests. Evocations of some kind of permanent national outlook were also frequent; Russian musical styles were thought to be inhabited by a Slav soul. Such ideas are now perhaps too much out of fashion; it is not quite unthinkable that an English stone carver's affection for linear pattern was encouraged by the frequent absence of bright, shadow-casting sunlight in England and that the symmetry of much French architecture and painting corresponds to the average Frenchman's enduring attachment to order. But eventually, of course, an explanation must include an entire regional or national culture and environment and at the same time take note of the fact that an art may have an existence of its own. To neglect this latter possibility would be to repeat on a large scale Spurgeon's confusion of men with writers.

Ecological Styles. A subvariety of the regional variety is perhaps distinct enough to be classed separately as the ecological: here, that is, the style in question evokes in fairly specific ways the relationship of human organisms to their environment. Here also there are likely to be strong polarities; typical contrasting pairs are urban-rural, mountain-plain, hunting-farming, inland-seaboard, nomadic-sedentary, capital-provincial (in some ways), and (at least in comic strips and science fiction) earth-space. Such styles are most recognizable in architecture, painting, and the making of such useful objects as furniture, tools, and weapons. But they may be recognized more distantly in the dance, in music, and in poetry: the imagery of the Parisian poet Charles Baudelaire is urban; that of the New England farmer-poet Robert Frost is rural; while Homer's is seaboard, at least in the *Odyssey*.

It is probable, too, that a well-defined ecological pattern affects in subtle respects the appreciation of foreign styles and hence the emergence of new local ones. Psychologists have found that the Zulus of South Africa, for instance, who live in a "circular culture" of windowless round huts and meandering paths, are relatively immune to visual illusions seen by people who have been conditioned by the right-angled, straight-perspective, so-called carpentered world of European and American cities.

RELIGIOUS STYLES. Conditioning also undoubtedly affects recognition of religious styles. The problem of hard-to-define "qualities" that contribute to recognizability, mentioned above in connection with regional and national styles, also returns here to vex a conscientious historian. So does the problem of the separation of form and content, plus the false problem of the sincerity of the artist as such—of the artist as mere "performer." Strictly speaking, in terms of forms and their combinations, one must grant that a vast number of profoundly moving works of religious art are not recognizably in religious styles. One can plausibly argue, for example, that there has been no religious style at all in Western painting since about the 15th century; later painters of religious subjects, such as Van Eyck, Raphael, Rubens, and their successors, painted the Virgin much as they painted their wives and mistresses. A similar point can be made about Western post-Renaissance music; Bach's sacred works sound much like his secular ones, and Giuseppe Verdi's magnificent *Requiem* (1874) has sounded to many ears like his operas. Even in the European Middle Ages and in the worlds of the great Eastern religions, the evidence is not always clear; the style that seems to yearn toward God in the 13th-century Gothic cathedral at Chartres, France, served also for town halls and ivory combs.

The point, of course, should not be exaggerated, partly because other styles often make use of borrowed forms and principally because many religious stylistic elements do exist in their own right, even though their secular ancestry can sometimes be traced. In architecture, examples of religious style can be seen in the basilican plan of Christian churches, the cosmic-mountain form of Hindu temples, the rectangular and cruciform plans of mosques, the needle shape of the minaret; in music, the single vocal line and free rhythm of Gregorian chant, the florid melody of Islāmic chant; in painting, the free brushwork of Zen Buddhists, the abstract arabesques of Islām, the nonillusionistic kinds of pictorial space favoured by medieval Christians. But when the list of such elements is completed, the fact still remains that the average appreciator recognizes a religious style primarily because it is tinged by long association with religious texts, ritual, and iconography. In brief, it has for him a quality that seems to emanate from content.

PERIOD STYLES. A style belonging to one of the single-culture varieties may be divided, conventionally or arbitrarily, into periods. Beethoven's personal style is usually split into early, middle, and late; the ethnic style of the migrating Germanic peoples may be referred to as Animal I, II, and III.

The adjective period is often reserved, however, for a distinct variety of style: the one in which the metaphorical "windows" afford "views" inhabited by generations whose cultural and other activities appear to constitute definable units of history. Familiar examples are the Gothic period style, the Renaissance, and, in general, all styles that bear the names of rulers or dynasties: the Victorian style, the Carolingian, the Sung. Frequently the period style is itself "periodized," the Gothic is Early and Late, the Renaissance is Early and High. . . . But period styles have their place in this part of the classification, for they are clearly, often emphatically, of the single-culture sort.

H. L. MENCKEN

ON

The American Language

The reputation of H. L. Mencken (1886–1956) as a debunker of hypocrisy and piety is so fearsome that it often obscures his immense contribution to philology. The American Language *(1919; frequent revision) remains a classic.*

Britannica*'s 13th edition (1926) engaged the authentic scholar that stood behind the journalist and hell-raiser. The title of his article seemed to leave a certain ambiguity because of his unsparing attacks on superpatriotism. His topic, however, was language. The title: "Americanism." The style: pungent, pulsing, pure Mencken. (B.L.F.)*

Although the volume you are reading celebrates the progress Britannica *has made, we must admit it is hard to find any really useful information in the current edition on the American language as Mencken conceived it. In fact, there is no entry for "Americanism." The* Propaedia *lists the biographies of twelve linguistic scholars, but our great Americanist is not among them. Sic transit gloria Mencken.*

Americanism, a term first used by John Witherspoon, president of Princeton University, in 1781, designates (*a*) any word or combination of words which taken into the English language in the United States, has not gained acceptance in England, or, if accepted, has retained its sense of foreignness; and (*b*) any word or combination of words which, becoming archaic in England, has continued in good usage in the United States. The first class is the larger and has the longer history. The earliest settlers in Virginia and New England, confronted by plants and animals that were unfamiliar to them, either borrowed the Indian names or invented names of their own.

Examples are afforded by *raccoon* (1608), *chinkapin* (1608), *opossum* (1610) and *squash* (1642) among Indian words and by *bull-frog, canvas-back, cat-bird* and *live-oak* among inventions. The former tended to take anglicised forms. Thus the Indian *isquontersquash* (at least, that is how the early chroniclers recorded it) became *squantersquash* and was then reduced to *squash,* and *otchock* became *woodchuck*. Many other words came in as the pioneers gained familiarity with the Indian life. Such words as *hominy, moccasin, pone, tapioca* and *succotash* remain everyday Americanisms.

The archaisms, of course, showed themselves more slowly. They had to go out of use in England before their survival in America was noticeable. But by the beginning of the 18th century there was already a considerable body of them, and all through that century they increased. The English language in Great Britain, chiefly under the influence of pedantry in the age of Anne, was changing rapidly, but in America it was holding to its old forms. There was very little fresh emigration to the colonies, and their own people seldom visited England. Thus by the end of the century "*I guess*" was already an Americanism, though it had been in almost universal use in England in Shakespeare's day. So, too, with many other verbs: *to wilt, to whittle, to fellowship* and *to approbate*. And with not a few adjectives: *burly, catty-cornered, likely* and *clever* (in the sense of amiable). And with multitudes of nouns: *cesspool, greenhorn, cordwood, jeans, flap-jack, bay-window, swingle-tree, muss* (in the sense of a row), *stock* (for cattle) and *fall* (for autumn).

Meanwhile, American English had begun to borrow words, chiefly nouns, from the non-English settlers, and to develop many new words of its own. To the former class the Dutch contributed *cruller, cold-slaw, cockey, scow, boss, smearcase* and *Santa Claus,* and the French contributed *gopher, prairie, chowder, carry-all* and *bureau* (a chest of drawers). Other contributions came from the Germans of Pennsylvania, the Spaniards of the southwest, and negro slaves.

The native coinages were large in number, and full of boldness and novelty. To this period belong, for example, *backwoods, hoe-cake, pop-corn, land-slide, shell-road, half-breed, hired-girl, spelling-bee, moss-back, crazy-quilt, stamping-ground* and *cat-boat*. These words were all made of the common materials of English, but there was something in them that was redolent of a pioneer people and a new world. In their coinage the elegances were disdained; the thing aimed at was simply vividness. At the same time, verbs were made out of nouns, nouns out of verbs and adjectives out of both.

In 1789 Benjamin Franklin, who had lived in England, denounced *to advocate, to progress* and *to oppose* as barbarisms, but all of them are good American to-day, and even good English. Noah Webster, the lexicographer, gave his imprimatur to *to appreciate* (in value); *to eventuate* was popularised by Gouverneur Morris; and no less a hero than Washington is said to have launched *to derange*. Many inventions of that daring era have succumbed to pedagogical criticism, *e.g., to happify, to compromit* and *to homologise*. But others equally harsh have gradually gained acceptance, *e.g., to placate* and *to deputise*. And with them have come in a vast number of characteristic American nouns, *e.g., breadstuffs, mileage, balance* (in the sense of remainder) and *elevator* (a place for storing grain).

Divergent meanings of words. It was during the same period that a number of important words, in daily use, began to show different meanings in England and America. Some familiar examples are *store, rock, lumber* and *corn*. What Englishmen call a *shop* was called a *store* by Americans as early as 1770, and long before that time *corn*, in American, had come to signify, not grains in general, but only maize. The use of *rock* to designate any stone, however small, goes back still further, and so does the use of *lumber* for *timber*. Many of these differences were produced by changes in English usage. Thus *cracker*, in England, once meant precisely what it now means in the United States. When the English abandoned it for *biscuit* the Americans stuck to *cracker*, and used *biscuit* to designate something else. How *shoe* came to be substituted in America for the English *boot* has yet to be determined. There is indeed much that remains obscure in the early history of such Americanisms. Until very lately, American philologians kept aloof from the subject, which they apparently regarded as low. Until George P. Krapp, of Columbia University, took it up, there was not even any serious investigation of the history of American pronunciation.

Thus the American dialect of English was firmly established by the time the Republic was well started, and in the half-century following it departed more and more from standard English. The settlement of the West, by taking large numbers of young men beyond the pale of urbane society, made for grotesque looseness in speech. Neologisms of the most extravagant sorts arose by the thousand, and many of them worked their way back to the East. During the two decades before the Civil War everyday American became almost unintelligible to an Englishman; every English visitor marked and denounced its vagaries. It was bold and lawless in its vocabulary, careless of grammatical niceties, and further disfigured by a drawling manner of speech. The congressional debates of the time were full of its phrases; soon they were to show themselves in the national literature.

Policing the language. After the Civil War there was an increase of national self-consciousness, and efforts were made to police the language. Free schools multiplied in the land, and the schoolmarm revealed all her immemorial preciosity. A clan of professional grammarians arose, led by Richard Grant White; it got help from certain of the literati, including Lowell. The campaign went to great lengths. "*It is me*" was banned as barbarous, though it is perfectly sound historically; *eye-ther* was substituted in polite usage for *ee-ther,* though the latter is correct and the former is on the part of an American an absurd affectation.

But the spirit of the language, and of the American people no less, was against such reforms. They were attacked on philological grounds by such iconoclasts as Thomas R. Lounsbury; they were reduced to vanity by the unconquerable speech habits of the folk. Under the very noses of the purists a new and vigorous American slang came into being, and simultaneously the common speech began to run amok. That common speech is to-day almost lawless. As Ring Lardner reports it—and he reports it very accurately—it seems destined in a few generations to dispose altogether of the few inflections that remain in English. "Me and her woulda went" will never, perhaps, force its way into the grammar-books, but it is used daily, or something like it, by a large part of the people of the United States, and the rest know precisely what it means.

On higher levels the language of the Americans is more decorous, but even there it is a genuinely living speech, taking in loan-words with vast hospitality and incessantly manufacturing neologisms of its own. The argot of sport enriches it almost daily. It runs to brilliantly vivid tropes. It is disdainful of grammatical pruderies. In the face of a new situation the American shows a far greater linguistic resourcefulness and daring than the Englishman. *Movie* is obviously better than *cinema,* just as *cow-catcher* is better than *plough* and *job-holder* is better than *public-servant.* The English seldom devise anything as pungent as *rubber-neck, ticket-scalper, lame-duck, pork-barrel, boot-legger* or *steam-roller* (in its political sense). Such exhilarating novelties are produced in the United States every day, and large numbers of them come into universal use, and gradually take on literary dignity. They are opposed violently, but they prevail. The visiting Englishman finds them very difficult. They puzzle him even more than do American peculiarities of pronunciation.

Of late the increase of travel and other inter-communication between England and America has tended to halt the differentiation of the two dialects. It was more marked, perhaps, before the World War than since. But if it ever vanishes altogether the fact will mark a victory for American. The American cinema floods England (and the rest of the English-speaking world) with American neologisms, but there is very little movement in the other direction. Thus the tail begins to wag the dog. How far the change has gone may be observed in Australia. There a cockneyfied pronunciation holds out, but the American vocabulary is increasingly triumphant. In Canada it long ago overcame the last vestiges of opposition.

JOHN MUIR

ON

Yosemite

John Muir (1838–1914)—"John of the Mountains"—a Scots-born, Wisconsin-reared, and entirely self-taught naturalist and conservationist, was almost singlehandedly responsible for the designation of the Yosemite Valley of California as a national park. Indeed, the park was not yet an established fact when Muir wrote this brief entry for the 10th edition (1902–1903), and he may have considered the writing of it as part of his remarkable campaign in the public prints for the preservation of Yosemite. His love of the place is strikingly evident in the article, and its survival today as a bit of nature at its most splendid is Muir's best memorial. (R. McH.)

A famous valley on the western slope of the Sierra Nevada of California, about 150 miles east of San Francisco and 4000 feet above the sea, [Yosemite] is 7 miles long, half a mile to a mile wide, and nearly a mile deep, eroded out of hard massive granite by glacial action. Its precipitous walls present a great variety of forms and sculpture, determined by the grain or cleavage of the rock—domes, gables, towers, battlements, and majestic mountain cliffs, partially separated and individualized by recesses and side cañons. The bottom, a filled-up lake basin, is level and park-like, diversified with groves of oak and pine, clumps of flowering shrubs, and spacious ferny meadows and wild gardens through which the river Merced meanders in tranquil beauty; while the whole valley resounds with the booming of its unrivalled waterfalls. The most notable of the wall rocks are: El Capitan, 3300 feet high, a sheer, plain mass of granite, the end of one of the most enduring of the mountain ridges, which stands forward beyond the general line of the north wall in imposing grandeur; the Three Brothers, North Dome, Glacier Point, the Sentinel, Cathedral, Sentinel Dome and Cloud's Rest, from 2800 to nearly 6000 feet high; and Half Dome, the noblest of all, which rises at the head of the valley from a broad, richly-sculptured base to the height of 4740 feet. These rocks are majestic glacial monuments, illustrating on a grand scale the action of ice in mountain sculpture. For here five large glaciers united to form the grand trunk glacier that eroded the valley and occupied it as its channel. Its moraines, though mostly obscured by vegetation and weathering, may still be traced; while on the snowy peaks at the headwaters of the Merced a considerable number of small glaciers, once tributary to the main Yosemite glacier, still exist. The Bridal Veil Fall, 900 feet high, is one of the most interesting features of the lower end of the valley. Towards the upper end the great Yosemite Fall pours its white floods from a height of 2600 feet, bathing the mighty cliffs with clouds of spray and making them tremble with its thunder-tones. The valley divides at the head into three branches, the Tenaya, Merced, and South Fork cañons. In the main (Merced) branch are the Vernal and Nevada Falls, 400 and 600 feet high, in the midst of most novel and sublime scenery. The Nevada is usually ranked next to the Yosemite among the five main falls of the valley. Its waters are chafed and dashed to foam in a rough channel before they arrive at the head of the fall, and are beaten yet finer by impinging on a sloping portion of the cliff about halfway down, thus making it the whitest of all the falls. The Vernal, about half a mile below the Nevada, famous for its afternoon rainbows, is staid and orderly, with scarce a hint of the passionate enthusiasm of its neighbour. Nevertheless it is a favourite with visitors, because it is better seen than any other. One may safely saunter along the edge of the river above it, and stand beside it at the top, as it calmly bends over the brow of the precipice. At flood time it is a nearly regular sheet about 80 feet wide, changing as it descends from green to purplish grey and white, and is dashed into clouds of irised foam on a rugged boulder talus that fills the gorge below. In the south branch, a mile from the head of the main valley, is the Illilouette Fall, 600 feet high, one of the most beautiful of the Yosemite choir. It is not nearly as grand a fall as the Yosemite, as symmetrical as the Vernal, or as airily graceful as the Bridal Veil; nor does it ever display as tremendous an outgush of snowy magnificence as the Nevada; but in fineness and beauty of colour and texture it surpasses them all.

Considering the great height of the snowy mountains about the valley, the climate of the Yosemite is remarkably mild. The vegetation is rich and luxuriant. The tallest pines are over 200 feet high; the trunks of some of the oaks are from 6 to 8 feet in diameter; violets, lilies, goldenrods, ceanothus, manzanita, wild rose, and azalea make broad beds and banks of bloom in the spring; and on the warmest parts of the walls flowers are in blossom every month of the year.

GEORGE JEAN NATHAN

ON

American Drama

In the America of the early twentieth century, the foremost, and most influential, theatre critic was surely George Jean Nathan (1882–1958), who contributed the American section of the article "Drama" in the 14th edition, 1929. It's interesting to note how the art of the American playwright appeared in those early days. (B.L.F.)

The first specimens of dramatic writing in the United States of America, reflecting the tastes and tendencies of colonial and revolutionary life, showed definite English, with now and then suggestions of Teutonic influences. They were all imitative and have no interest to-day except as curios. Only two plays written by Americans were actually presented on the stage before the Revolution: *The Prince of Parthia,* a blank-verse tragedy by Thomas Godfrey the younger, and *The Conquest of Canada, or the Siege of Quebec,* an attempt at historical drama by George Cocking. Neither contained a symptom of promise so far as native drama was concerned, nor was any discernible in the plays written by Americans in the period immediately after. . . .

The beginning of what, though still somewhat euphemistically, may be termed the real American drama was synchronous with the active appearance on the American scene of William Dunlap, in many respects the father of the American stage, and Royall Tyler. The latter's comedy *The Contrast* (the second play written by an American to be produced in America by a professional company of actors, *The Prince of Parthia* being the first) was acted in 1787 and was the first dramatic work to introduce the character that has since become known as the stage Yankee. Written under the inspiration of *The School for Scandal,* it was also the first American play to achieve a box-office success. Dunlap wrote or adapted some 60 plays, of which the best known is his blank-verse tragedy, *André,* produced in 1798. These two men seemed to give an impetus to dramatic writing and to theatrical interest in the new Republic.

Mrs. Mowatt's . . . *Fashion,* which enjoyed success in England as well, marks what is practically the birth of a native drama, however modest, worth critical consideration. In the years following its presentation there came into being *Uncle Tom's Cabin,* dramatized from Mrs. Harriet Beecher Stowe's novel by George L. Aiken . . . [and] the dramatization of Irving's *Rip Van Winkle,* made a theatrical classic by Joseph Jefferson. . . .

Gradually, now, the American drama began to move on feet of its own, instead of relying almost entirely upon foreign crutches. MacKaye revolutionized the mechanics of the American stage as he had found it and, with them, certain phases of dramaturgy, at least as it had been practised. A new order of playwrights grew up. Among these, the first was Bronson Howard, the dominant dramatist in the American theatre of his day. Howard is best known for his military melodrama, *Shenandoah,* based upon a work written 20 years before, subjected to several revisions and produced in the late '80s. . . . The last decade of the century witnessed the abandonment of the European crutches to an even greater degree. William Gillette with his melodramas, *Held by the Enemy* and *Secret Service,* established American drama as a thing of itself. . . .

One of the foremost figures in this present-day American drama is Eugene O'Neill, whose more notable works, such as *Strange Interlude, Marco's Millions, The Emperor Jones, The Great God Brown, Desire under the Elms, Beyond the Horizon* and *The Hairy Ape,* show genuine dramatic force and literary merit. Among his contemporaries are men and women who are raising American dramatic writing to a distinguished level. Maxwell Anderson and Laurence

Stallings in *What Price Glory?* contributed to the stage a war drama of sweeping eloquence and devastating irony. . . .

The American drama, whatever it may still lack in finish in the aggregate, has at least finally attained a flavour and character entirely its own. The native playwright, however unskilled he may be in the deeper delvings into human motives and in the capturing of dramatic-literary graces, has nevertheless achieved no mean measure of vitality and raciness, and has shaken off the last of the European shackles.

HOWARD NEMEROV
ON
Poetry

Howard Nemerov (1920–1991), one of our finest poets, was almost surely the wittiest. In 1978 he received the Pulitzer Prize in Arts and Letters and in 1977 the National Book Award for his Collected Poems. *He was a pilot in the Royal Canadian Air Force and the U.S. Army Air Force, novelist, critic, professor of English, consultant in poetry to the Library of Congress (1963–1964), and poet laureate of the United States (1988–1990).*

Encyclopaedia Britannica *is not in the business of publishing masterpieces. Every once in a while, however, one floats across the editor's desk and is greeted with both surprise and exultation. This editor believes Mr. Nemerov's discussion of poetry to be such a masterpiece. It forms part of the 15th edition* Macropaedia *article titled "The Art of Literature."*

Poetry is a vast subject, as old as history and older, present wherever religion is present, possibly—under some definitions—the primal and primary form of languages themselves. The present section means only to describe in as general a way as possible certain properties of poetry and of poetic thought regarded as in some sense independent modes of the mind. Naturally, not every tradition nor every local or individual variation can be—or need be—

included, but the article illustrates by examples of poetry ranging between nursery rhyme and epic.

Attempts to define poetry. Poetry is the other way of using language. Perhaps in some hypothetical beginning of things it was the only way of using language or simply was language *tout court,* prose being the derivative and younger rival. Both poetry and language are fashionably thought to have belonged to ritual in early agricultural societies; and poetry in particular, it has been claimed, arose at first in the form of magical spells recited to ensure a good harvest. Whatever the truth of this hypothesis, it blurs a useful distinction: by the time there begins to be a separate class of objects called poems, recognizable as such, these objects are no longer much regarded for their possible yam-growing properties, and such magic as they may be thought capable of has retired to do its business upon the human spirit and not directly upon the natural world outside.

Formally, poetry is recognizable by its greater dependence on at least one more parameter, the *line,* than appears in prose composition. This changes its appearance on the page; and it seems clear that people take their cue from this changed appearance, reading poetry aloud in a very different voice from their habitual voice, possibly because, as Ben Jonson said, poetry "speaketh somewhat above a mortal mouth." If, as a test of this description, people are shown poems printed as prose, it most often turns out that they will read the result as prose simply because it looks that way; which is to say that they are no longer guided in their reading by the balance and shift of the line in relation to the breadth as well as the syntax.

That is a minimal definition but perhaps not altogether uninformative. It may be all that ought to be attempted in the way of a definition: Poetry is the way it is because it looks that way, and it looks that way because it sounds that way and vice versa.

Poetry and prose. People's reason for wanting a definition is to take care of the borderline case, and this is what a definition, as if by definition, will not do. That is, if a man asks for a definition of poetry, it will most certainly not be the case that he has never seen one of the objects called poems that are said to embody poetry; on the contrary, he is already tolerably certain what poetry in the main is, and his reason for wanting a definition is either that his certainty has been challenged by someone else or that he wants to take care of a possible or seeming exception to it: hence the perennial squabble about distinguishing poetry from prose, which is rather like distinguishing rain from snow—everyone is reasonably capable of doing so, and yet there are some weathers that are either-neither.

Sensible things have been said on the question. The poet T.S. Eliot suggested that part of the difficulty lies in the fact that there is the technical term "verse" to go with the term "poetry," while there is no equivalent technical term to distinguish the mechanical part of prose and make the relation symmetrical. The French poet Paul Valéry said that prose was walking, poetry dancing. Indeed, the original two terms, *prosus* and *versus,* meant, respectively, "going straight forth" and "returning"; and that distinction does point up the tendency of poetry to incremental repetition, variation, and the treatment of many matters and different themes in a single recurrent form such as couplet or stanza.

Robert Frost said shrewdly that poetry was what got left behind in translation, which suggests a criterion of almost scientific refinement: when in doubt, translate; whatever comes through is prose, the remainder is poetry. And yet to even so acute a definition the obvious exception is a startling and a formidable one: some of the greatest poetry in the world is in the Authorized Version of the Bible, which is not only a translation but also, as to its appearance in print, identifiable neither with verse nor with prose in English but rather with a cadence owing something to both.

There may be a better way of putting the question by the simple test alluded to above. When people are presented with a series of passages drawn indifferently from poems and stories but all printed as prose, they will show a dominant inclination to identify everything they possibly can as prose. This will be true, surprisingly enough, even if the poem rhymes and will often be true even if the poem in its original typographical arrangement would have been familiar to them. The reason seems to be absurdly plain: the reader recognizes poems by their appearance on the page, and he responds to the convention whereby he recognizes them by reading them aloud in a quite different tone of voice from that which he applies to prose (which, indeed, he scarcely reads aloud at all). It should be added that he makes this distinction also without reading aloud; even in silence he confers upon a piece of poetry an attention that differs from what he gives to prose in two ways especially: in tone and in pace.

In place of further worrying over definitions, it may be both a relief and an illumination to exhibit certain plain and mighty differences between prose and poetry by a comparison. In the following passages a prose writer and a poet are talking about the same subject, growing older.

> Between the ages of 30 and 90, the weight of our muscles falls by 30 percent and the power we can exert likewise. . . . The number of nerve fibres in a nerve trunk falls by a quarter. The weight of our brains falls from an average of 3.03 lb. to 2.27 lb. as cells die and are not replaced. . . . (Gordon Rattray Taylor, *The Biological Time Bomb,* 1968.)

> Let me disclose the gifts reserved for age
> To set a crown upon your lifetime's effort.
> First, the cold friction of expiring sense
> Without enchantment, offering no promise
> But bitter tastelessness of shadow fruit
> As body and soul begin to fall asunder.
> Second, the conscious impotence of rage
> At human folly, and the laceration
> Of laughter at what ceases to amuse.
> And last, the rending pain of re-enactment
> Of all that you have done, and been. . . .
>
> (T.S. Eliot, *Four Quartets.*)

Before objecting that a simple comparison cannot possibly cover all the possible ranges of poetry and prose compared, the reader should consider for a moment what differences are exhibited. The passages are oddly parallel, hence comparable, even in a formal sense; for both consist of the several items of a catalog under the general title of growing old. The significant differences are of tone, pace, and object of attention. If the prose passage interests itself in the neutral, material, measurable properties of the process, while the poetry interests itself in what the process will signify to someone going through it, that is not accidental but of the essence; if one reads the prose passage with an interest in being informed, noting the parallel constructions without being affected by them either in tone or in pace, while reading the poetry with a sense of considerable gravity and solemnity, that too is of the essence. One might say as tersely as possible that the difference between prose and poetry is most strikingly shown in the two uses of the verb "to fall":

> The number of nerve fibres in a nerve trunk falls by a quarter
> As body and soul begin to fall asunder

It should be specified here that the important differences exhibited by the comparison belong to the present age. In each period, speaking for poetry in English at any rate, the dividing line will be seen to come at a different place. In Elizabethan times the diction of prose was much closer to that of poetry than it later became, and in the 18th century authors saw nothing strange about writing in couplets about subjects that later would automatically and compulsorily belong to prose—for example, horticulture, botany, even dentistry. Here is not the place for entering into a discussion of so rich a chapter in the history of ideas; but it should be remarked that the changes involved in the relation between poetry and prose are powerfully influenced by the immense growth of science, commerce, and number in man's ways of describing, even of viewing, the world.

Returning to the comparison, it is observable that though the diction of the poem is well within what could be commanded by a moderately well-educated speaker, it is at the same time well outside the range of terms in fact employed by such a speaker in his daily occasions; it is a diction very conscious, as it were, of its power of choosing terms with an effect of peculiar precision and of combining the terms into phrases with the same effect of peculiar precision and also of combining sounds with the same effect of peculiar precision. Doubtless the precision of the prose passage is greater in the more obvious property of dealing in the measurable; but the poet attempts a precision with respect to what is not in the same sense measurable nor even in the same sense accessible to observation; the distinction is perhaps just that made by the French scientist and philosopher Blaise Pascal in discriminating the spirits of geometry and finesse; and if one speaks of "effects of precision" rather than of precision itself, that serves to distinguish one's sense that the art work is always somewhat removed from what people are pleased to call the real world, operating instead, in Immanuel Kant's shrewd formula, by exhibiting "purposefulness without purpose." To much the same point is what Samuel Taylor Coleridge remembers having learned from his schoolmaster:

> I learnt from him, that Poetry, even that of the loftiest and, seemingly, that of the wildest odes, had a logic of its own, as severe as that of science; and more difficult, because more subtle, more complex, and dependent on more, and more fugitive causes. In the truly great poets, he would say, there is a reason assignable, not only for every word, but for the position of every word. (*Biographia Literaria,* ch. I)

Perhaps this is a somewhat exaggerated, as it is almost always an unprovable, claim, illustrating also a propensity for competing with the prestige of science on something like its own terms—but the last remark in particular illuminates the same author's terser formulation: "prose = words in the best order, poetry = the best words in the best order." This attempt at definition, impeccable because uninformative, was derived from Jonathan Swift, who had said, also impeccably and uninformatively, that style in writing was "the best words in the best order." Which may be much to the same effect as Louis Armstrong's saying, on being asked to define jazz, "Baby, if you got to ask the question, you're never going to know the answer." Or the painter Marcel Duchamp's elegant remark on what psychologists call "the problem of perception": "If no solution, then maybe no problem?" This species of gnomic, riddling remark may be determinate for the artistic attitude toward definition of every sort; and its skepticism is not confined to definitions of poetry but extends to definitions of anything whatever, directing one not to dictionaries but to experience and, above all, to use: "Anyone with a watch can tell you what time it is," said Valéry, "but who can tell you what is time?"

Happily, if poetry is almost impossible to define, it is extremely easy to recognize in experience; even untutored children are rarely in doubt about it when it appears:

> Little Jack Jingle,
> He used to live single,
> But when he got tired of this kind of life,
> He left off being single, and liv'd with his wife.

It might be objected that this little verse is not of sufficient import and weight to serve as an exemplar for poetry. It ought to be remembered, though, that it has given people pleasure so that they continued to say it until and after it was written down, nearly two centuries ago. The verse has survived, and its survival has something to do with pleasure, with delight; and while it still lives, how many more imposing works of language—epic poems, books of science, philosophy, theology—have gone down, deservedly or not, into dust and silence. It has, obviously, a form, an arrangement of sounds in relation to thoughts that somehow makes its agreeable nonsense closed, complete, and decisive. But this somewhat muddled matter of form deserves a heading and an instance all to itself.

Form in poetry. People nowadays who speak of form in poetry almost always mean such externals as regular measure and rhyme, and most often they mean to get rid of these in favour of the freedom they suppose must follow upon the absence of form in this limited sense. But in fact a poem having only one form would be of doubtful interest even if it could exist. In this connection, the poet J. V. Cunningham speaks of "a convergence of forms, and forms of disparate orders," adding: "It is the coincidence of forms that locks in the poem." For a poem is composed of internal and intellectual forms as well as forms externally imposed and preexisting any particular instance, and these may be sufficient without regular measure and rhyme; if the intellectual forms are absent, as in greeting-card verse and advertising jingles, no amount of thumping and banging will supply the want.

Form, in effect, is like the doughnut that may be said to be nothing in a circle of something or something around nothing; it is either the outside of an inside, as when people speak of "good form" or "bourgeois formalism," or the inside of an outside, as in the scholastic saying that "the soul is the form of the body." Taking this principle, together with what Cunningham says of the matter, one may now look at a very short and very powerful poem with a view to distinguishing the forms, or schemes, of which it is made. It was written by Rudyard Kipling—a great poet at present somewhat sunken in reputation, probably on account of misinterpretations having to do more with his imputed politics than with his poetry—and its subject, one of a series of epitaphs for the dead of World War I, is a soldier shot by his comrades for cowardice in battle.

> I could not look on Death, which being known,
> Men led me to him, blindfold and alone.

The aim of the following observations and reflections is to distinguish as clearly as possible—distinguish without dividing—the feelings evoked by the subject, so grim, horrifying, tending to helpless sorrow and despair, from the feelings, which might better be thought of as meanings, evoked by careful contemplation of the poem in its manifold and somewhat subtle ways of handling the subject, leading the reader on to a view of the strange delight intrinsic to art, whose mirroring and shielding power allows him to contemplate the world's horrible realities without being turned to stone.

There is, first, the obvious external form of a rhymed, closed couplet in iambic pentameter (that is, five poetic "feet," each consisting of an unstressed followed by a stressed syllable, per line). There is, second, the obvious external form of a single sentence balanced in four grammatical units with and in counterpoint with the metrical form. There is, third, the conventional form belonging to the epitaph and reflecting back to antiquity; it is terse enough to be cut in stone and tight-lipped also, perhaps for other reasons, such as the speaker's shame. There is, fourth, the fictional form belonging to the epitaph, according to which the dead man is supposed to be saying the words himself. There is, fifth, especially poignant in this instance, the real form behind or within the fictional one, for the reader is aware that in reality it is not the dead man speaking, nor are his feelings the only ones the reader is receiving, but that the comrades who were forced to execute him may themselves have made up these two lines with their incalculably complex and exquisite balance of scorn, awe, guilt, and consideration even to tenderness for the dead soldier. There is, sixth, the metaphorical form, with its many resonances ranging from the tragic through the pathetic to irony and apology: dying in battle is spoken of in language relating it to a social occasion in drawing room or court; the coward's fear is implicitly represented as merely the timorousness and embarassment one might feel about being introduced to a somewhat superior and majestic person, so that the soldiers responsible for killing him are seen as sympathetically helping him through a difficult moment in the realm of manners. In addition, there is, seventh, a linguistic or syntactical form, with at least a couple of tricks to it: the second clause, with its reminiscence of Latin construction, participates in the meaning by conferring a Roman stoicism and archaic gravity on the saying; remembering that the soldiers in the poem had been British schoolboys not long before, the reader might hear the remote resonance of a whole lost world built upon Greek and Roman models; and the last epithets, "blindfold and alone," while in the literal acceptation they clearly refer to the coward, show a distinct tendency to waver over and apply mysteriously to Death as well, sitting there waiting "blindfold and alone." One might add another form, the eighth, composed of the balance of sounds, from the obvious likeness in the rhyme down to subtleties and refinements beneath the ability of coarse analysis to discriminate. And even there one would not be quite at an end; an overall principle remains, the compression of what might have been epic or five-act tragedy into two lines, or the poet's precise election of a single instant to carry what the novelist, if he did his business properly, would have been hundreds of pages arriving at.

It is not at all to be inferred that the poet composed his poem in the manner of the above laborious analysis of its strands; the whole insistence, rather, is that he did not catalog eight or 10 forms and assemble them into a poem; more likely it "just came to him." But the example may serve to indicate how many modes of the mind go together in this articulation of an implied drama and the tension among many possible sentiments that might arise in response to it.

In this way, by the coincidence of forms that locks in the poem, one may see how to answer a question that often arises about poems: though their thoughts are commonplace, they themselves mysteriously are not. One may answer on the basis of the example and the inferences produced from it that a poem is not so much a thought as it is a mind: talk with it, and it will talk back, telling you many things that you might have thought for yourself but somehow didn't until it brought them together. Doubtless a poem is a much simplified model for the mind. But it might still be one of the best man has available. On this great theme, however, it will be best to proceed not by definition but by parable and interpretation.

Poetry as a mode of thought: the protean encounter. In the fourth book of the *Odyssey* Homer tells the following strange tale. After the war at Troy, Menelaus wanted very much to get home but was held up in Egypt for want of a wind because, as he later told Telemachus, he had not sacrificed enough to the gods. "Ever jealous the Gods are," he said, "that we men mind their dues." But because the gods work both ways, it was on the advice of a goddess, Eidothea, that Menelaus went to consult Proteus, the old one of the sea, as one might consult a travel agency.

Proteus was not easy to consult. He was herding seals, and the seals stank even through the ambrosia Eidothea had provided. And when Menelaus crept up close, disguised as a seal, and grabbed him, Proteus turned into a lion, a dragon, a leopard, a boar, a film of water, and a high-branched tree. But Menelaus managed to hang on until Proteus gave up and was himself again; whereupon Menelaus asked him the one great question: How do I get home? And Proteus told him: You had better go back to Egypt and sacrifice to the gods some more.

This story may be taken as a parable about poetry. A man has an urgent question about his way in the world. He already knows the answer, but it fails to satisfy him. So at great inconvenience, hardship, and even peril, he consults a powerful and refractory spirit who tries to evade his question by turning into anything in the world. Then, when the spirit sees he cannot get free of the man, and only then, he answers the man's question, not simply with a commonplace but with the same commonplace the man had been dissatisfied with before. Satisfied or not, however, the man now obeys the advice given him.

A foolish story? All the same, it is to be observed that Menelaus did get home. And it was a heroic thing to have hung onto Proteus through those terrifying changes and compelled him to be himself and answer up. Nor does it matter in the least to the story that Menelaus personally may have been a disagreeable old fool as well as a cuckold.

A poet also has one great and simple question, simple though it may take many forms indeed. Geoffrey Chaucer put it as well as anyone could, and in three lines at that:

> What is this world? what asketh men to have?
> Now with his love, now in his colde grave,
> Allone, with-outen any companye.
>
> ("The Knight's Tale")

And a poet gets the simple answer he might expect, the one the world grudgingly gives to anyone who asks such a question: The world is this way, not that way, and you ask for more than you will be given, which the poet, being scarcely more fool than his fellowmen, knew already. But on the path from question to answer, hanging onto the slippery disguiser and shape-shifter Proteus, he will see many marvels; he will follow the metamorphoses of things in the metamorphoses of their phrases, and he will be so elated and ecstatic in this realm of wonders that the voice in which he speaks these things, down even to the stupid, obvious, and commonplace answer, will be to his hearers a solace and a happiness in the midst of sorrows:

When I do count the clock that tells the time,
And see the brave day sunk in hideous night;
When I behold the violet past prime,
And sable curls, all silver'd o'er with white;
When lofty trees I see barren of leaves,
Which erst from heat did canopy the herd,
And summer's green all girded up in sheaves,
Borne on the bier with white and bristly beard,
Then of thy beauty do I question make,
That thou among the wastes of time must go,
Since sweets and beauties must themselves forsake
And die as fast as they see others grow;
    And nothing 'gainst Time's scythe can make defence
    Save breed, to brave him when he takes thee hence.

(Shakespeare, Sonnet 12.)

Like Menelaus, the poet asks a simple question, to which, moreover, he already knows the unsatisfying answer. Question and answer, one might say, have to be present, although of themselves they seem to do nothing much; but they assert the limits of a journey to be taken. They are the necessary but not sufficient conditions of what really seems to matter here, the Protean encounter itself, the grasping and hanging on to the powerful and refractory spirit in its slippery transformations of a single force flowing through clock, day, violet, graying hair, trees dropping their leaves, the harvest in which, by a peculiarly ceremonial transmutation, the grain man lives by is seen without contradiction as the corpse he comes to. As for the answer to the question, it is not surprising nor meant to be surprising; it is only just.

On this point—that the answer comes as no surprise—poets show an agreement that quite transcends the differences of periods and schools. Alexander Pope's formula, "What oft was thought, but ne'er so well expresst," sometimes considered as the epitome of a shallow and parochial decorum, is not in essence other than this offered by John Keats:

> I think Poetry should surprise by a fine excess, and not by Singularity —it should strike the Reader as a wording of his own highest thoughts, and appear almost a Remembrance. (Letter to John Taylor, 1818.)

In the present century, Robert Frost is strikingly in agreement:

> A word about recognition: In literature it is our business to give people the thing that will make them say, "Oh yes I know what you mean." It is never to tell them something they dont know, but something they know and hadn't thought of saying. It must be something they recognize.
> (Letter to John Bartlett, in *Modern Poetics,* ed. James Scully, 1965.)

And the poet and critic John Crowe Ransom gives the thought a cryptically and characteristically elegant variation: "Poetry is the kind of knowledge by which we must know that we have arranged that we shall not know otherwise." Perhaps this point about recognition might be carried further, to the extreme at which it would be seen to pose the problem of how poetry, which at its highest has always carried, at least implicitly, a kind of Platonism and claimed to give, if not knowledge itself, what was more important, a "form" to knowledge, can survive the triumph of scientific materialism and a positivism minded to skepticism about everything in the world except its own self (where it turns credulous, extremely). The poet's adjustment, over two or three centuries, to a Newtonian cosmos, Kantian criticism, the spectral universe portrayed by physics has conspicuously not been a happy one and has led alternately or simultaneously to the extremes of rejection of reason and speaking in tongues on the one hand and the hysterical claim that poetry will save the world on the other. But of this let the Protean parable speak as it will.

There is another part to the story of Menelaus and Proteus, for Menelaus asked another question: What happened to my friends who were with me at Troy? Proteus replies, "Son of Atreus, why enquire too closely of me on this? To know or learn what I know about it is not your need: I warn you that when you hear all the truth your tears will not be far behind. . . ." But he tells him all the same: "Of those others many went under; many came through. . . ." And Menelaus does indeed respond with tears of despair, until Proteus advises him to stop crying and get started on the journey home. So it sometimes happens in poetry, too: the sorrowful contemplation of what is, consoles, in the end, and heals, but only after the contemplative process has been gone through and articulated in the detail of its change:

> When to the sessions of sweet silent thought
> I summon up remembrance of things past,
> I sigh the lack of many a thing I sought,
> And with old woes new wail my dear time's waste;
> Then can I drown an eye, unused to flow,
> For precious friends hid in death's dateless night,
> And weep afresh love's long since cancell'd woe,
> And moan the expense of many a vanish'd sight.
> Then can I grieve at grievances foregone,
> And heavily from woe to woe tell o'er
> The sad account of fore-bemoaned moan,
> Which I new pay as if not paid before.
> But if the while I think on thee, dear friend,
> All losses are restor'd and sorrows end.
>
> (Shakespeare, Sonnet 30)

This poem, acknowledged to be a masterpiece by so many generations of readers, may stand as an epitome and emblem for the art altogether, about which it raises a question that must be put, although it cannot be satisfactorily and unequivocally answered: the question of whether poetry is a sacrament or a confidence game or both or neither. To reply firmly that poetry is not religion and must not promise what religion does is to preserve a useful distinction; nevertheless, the religions of the world, if they have nothing else in common, seem to be based on collections of sacred poems. Nor, at the other extreme, can any guarantee that poetry is not a confidence game be found in the often-heard appeal to the poet's "sincerity." One will never know whether

Shakespeare wept all over the page while writing the 30th sonnet, though one inclines to doubt it, nor would it be to his credit if he did, nor to the reader's that he should know it or care to know it.

For one thing, the sonnet is obviously artful—that is, full of artifice—and even the artifice degenerates here and there into being artsy. "Then can I drown an eye, unused to flow." Surely that is poesy itself, at or near its worst, where the literal and the conventional, whatever their relations may have been for Shakespeare and the first reader of these sugar'd sonnets among his friends, now live very uncomfortably together (Ben Jonson's "Drink to me only with thine eyes" is a like example of this bathetic crossing of levels), though perhaps it has merely become unattractive as a result of changing fashions in diction.

Moreover, while the whole poem is uniquely Shakespearean, the bits and pieces are many of them common property of the age, what one writer called "joint stock company poetry." And the tricks are terribly visible, too; art is not being used to conceal art in such goings-on as "grieve at grievances" and "fore-bemoaned moan." "He who thus grieves will excite no sympathy," as Samuel Johnson sternly wrote of John Milton's style in the elegy "Lycidas," "he who thus praises will confer no honour."

Nor is that the worst of it. This man who so powerfully works on the reader's sympathies by lamenting what is past contrives to do so by thinking obsessively about litigation and, of all things, money; his hand is ever at his wallet, bidding adieu. He cannot merely "think" sweet silent thoughts about the past; no, he has to turn them into a court in "session," whereto he "summons" the probable culprit "remembrance"; when he "grieves," it is at a "grievance"—in the hands of the law again; finally, as with the sinners in Dante's *Divine Comedy,* his avarice and prodigality occupy two halves of the one circle: he bemoans his expenses while paying double the asking price.

And still, for all that, the poem remains beautiful; it continues to move both the young who come to it still innocent of their dear time's waste and the old who have sorrows to match its sorrows. As between confidence game and sacrament there may be no need to decide, as well as no possibility of deciding: elements of play and artifice, elements of true feeling, elements of convention both in the writing and in one's response to it, all combine to veil the answer. But the poem remains.

If it could be plainly demonstrated by the partisans either of unaided reason or revealed religion that poetry was metaphorical, mythological, and a delusion, while science, say, or religion or politics were real and true, then one might throw poetry away and live honestly though poorly on what was left. But, for better or worse, that is not the condition of man's life in the world; and perhaps men care for poetry so much—if they care at all—because, at last, it is the only one of man's many mythologies to be aware, and to make him aware, that it, and the others, are indeed mythological. The literary critic I.A. Richards, in a deep and searching consideration of this matter, concludes: "It is the privilege of poetry to preserve us from mistaking our notions either for things or for ourselves. Poetry is the completest mode of utterance."

The last thing Proteus says to Menelaus is strange indeed:

> You are not to die in Argos of the fair horse-pastures, not there to encounter death: rather will the Deathless Ones carry you to the Elysian plain, the place beyond the world. . . . There you will have Helen to yourself and will be deemed of the household of Zeus.

So the greatest of our poets have said, or not so much said, perhaps, as indicated by their fables, though nowadays people mostly sing a different tune. To be as the gods, to be rejoined with the beloved, the world forgotten. . . . Sacrament or con game? Homer, of course, is only telling an old story and promises mankind nothing; that is left to the priests to do; and in that respect poetry, as one critic puts it, must always be "a ship that is wrecked on entering the harbor." And yet the greatest poetry sings always, at the end, of transcendence; while seeing clearly and saying plainly the wickedness and terror and beauty of the world, it is at the same time humming to itself, so that one overhears rather than hears: All will be well.

ROBERT REDFIELD

ON

Human Nature

Robert Redfield (1897–1958) was a cultural anthropologist associated for much of his working life with the University of Chicago. Much of his work centered on his observation of Mexican and Central American village life. For the 1961 printing of the 14th edition he wrote on the impossible topic of human nature. Much of the article deals—and very critically, too—with a review of Britannica's *articles on "Man." We reproduce, however, only the more general, introductory section. In all the thousands of the set's pages it would be hard to find more wisdom conveyed in fewer words.*

Man has a nature, widespread and persistent, that is obviously characteristic of his kind and notably different from the natures of other living things. Yet there is no generally acceptable account including all principal aspects of this nature as one whole. The nature of man is familiar, impressively unique and almost indescribable. Common experience meets it daily; every considered system of thought or action declares or implies some view of it; none of the scholarly or scientific disciplines presents it in terms of all that common sense recognizes in it.

Different meanings have been attached to the phrase "human nature." Most commonly it refers to an original, inborn nature characteristic of all men or of this particular man or these particular men. So understood, "human nature" is man's special form of that which is biologically inherited in any and all species. It is, of course, an abstraction or inference, for very early it combines with "environment," and from the effects of experience becomes something else. This original, inborn, never directly observed nature has been variously conceived: as composed of distinguishable dispositions to specific behaviour (reflex and instinct); as powers or faculties of the mind; as something greatly or even infinitely plastic, or empty and formless.

Of those who see man's inborn nature in this last way, some have come to identify "human natures"—now plural—with the particular unique manifestations of mankind in local groups; each traditional group, or culture, has its own human nature, and no nature true of all peoples in this view can be asserted.

Similar to this conception in its identification of "human nature" with what is acquired through experience is that conception which, in contrast to the foregoing, asserts the reality of an acquired nature that is widespread or even universal. "Human nature" is then taken to be a resultant of man's characteristic experiences in any and all societies so far. Everywhere he lives and has lived in groups with similar basic necessities and activities, has known intimate and personal relationships, has recognized differences between people close to him and of his own kind, and other people farther away and of another kind. And so on. Those who so think of man's nature attempt to describe the states of mind and feeling that underlie the great local differences and that are everywhere similar.

Of these three principal ways of conceiving man's nature—as defined or vague inborn potentiality or necessity; as knowable only in its locally developed special forms; as a nature universally acquired or developed and common to all—various combinations can and have been made. For example, the Freudian view of man combines the first and third.

The view adopted as to what man is, essentially and generally, is connected with the thinker's moral judgments and with his position as to the possibilities and the methods of action and reform. He who strongly believes in the power of education or of learning or of conditioned response conceives of original nature as very modifiable. He who takes a pessimistic view as to the elimination of such man-caused evils as war and crime is likely to think of these mischiefs as rooted in particularities of an unalterable inborn nature.

In the everyday experience of the ordinary person the nature of man presents itself as states of mind and feeling, and as characteristic action, in or by the people he meets and deals with. He comes to know human nature through the persons he knows, their characters and conduct. Behind what they do he comes to recognize qualities that often do not surprise him: they are what he comes to expect of other human beings and not of cows or horses. People are proud, sensitive, eager for recognition or admiration, often ambitious, hopeful or despondent, selfish or capable of sacrifice of self. They take satisfaction in their achievements, sometimes feel guilt or shame, have within them a something called a conscience, are loyal or disloyal. The common-sense view of human nature sees it not as innate and inferable from certain behaviour, but as present, however originating, in the conduct of grown people all the time. This is that kind of human nature from which Walt Whitman turned away when he said he would live with the animals because

> They do not sweat and whine about their condition;
> They do not lie awake at night and weep for their sins;
> They do not make me sick discussing their duty to God;
> Not one is dissatisfied—not one is demented with the
> mania of owning things;
> Not one kneels to another, nor to his kind that lived thousands of
> years ago. . . .

This is the common conception of human nature that has given rise to ideas—however differently defined—of the inhuman and the superhuman. It implies a probable range of conduct that is "just what you expect" of people; conduct beyond that range is held to violate or exceed the normal expectancy.

These common attributions of man's nature as human are variously made so as to include or exclude some people but not others. More remote and exotic peoples may be denied full inclusion: they are "really not quite human." On the whole, persons who have experience and acquaintance with man's nature as seen in customs and institutions very unlike their own tend to recognize in such alien peoples a humanity common with their own. On the whole, in the course of history, the popular category "human beings" has widened, including more and more people, and recognizing local variants as nevertheless only variants of common humanity.

This view of man's nature is that which is developed and deepened through experience with persons and their conduct. The acquaintance and understanding are gained in part through imaginative works of the mind: biography, letters, novels, drama. Literature is the great storehouse from which to draw experience of the human. It provides a variety and scope that direct experience cannot. In meeting human beings in literature the reader encounters that same question as to the local and special, and the widespread or universal, about which the systematic thinker, disciplined in a science or in philosophy, feels he must consider. Do the people presented in the Greek tragedies have the same human nature as those shown us by Shakespeare? In reading *War and Peace* and *The Tale of Genji,* we seem to see a human nature that is both different and the same. Though such impressions as to the universality and the variability of humanity do not submit to the procedures of a behavioural science, for those who think about them they seem to deepen and refine opinions, however imperfectly definable, as to the nature of man.

WILLIAM ROSSETTI

ON

Percy Bysshe Shelley

The romantic poet Percy Bysshe Shelley, whose enormous promise began to be realized in the last three or four years of his short life of thirty years, was the subject of a biography in the 9th edition (1875–1889) by the critic William Rossetti (1829–1919), brother of the painter and poet Dante Gabriel Rossetti and the poet Christina Rossetti. William Rossetti was the author of, among many other books, Lives of Some Famous Poets. *Some extracts from his article follow. (B.L.F.)*

In the character of Percy Bysshe Shelley three qualities become early manifest, and may be regarded as innate: impressionableness or extreme susceptibility to external and internal impulses of feeling; a lively imagination or erratic fancy, blurring a sound estimate of solid facts; and a resolute repudiation of outer authority or the despotism of custom. These qualities were highly developed in his earliest manhood. . . . Shelley was a shy, sensitive, mopish sort of boy from one point of view,—from another a very unruly one, having his own notions of justice, independence, and mental freedom; by nature gentle, kindly, and retiring,—under provocation dangerously violent. He resisted the odious fagging system, exerted himself little in the routine of school-learning, and was known both as "Mad Shelley" and as "Shelley the Atheist." . . . Shelley entered University College, Oxford, in April 1810, returned thence to Eton, and finally quitted the school at midsummer, and commenced residence in Oxford in October. Here he met a young Durham man, Thomas Jefferson Hogg, who had preceded him in the university by a couple of months; the two youths at once struck up a warm and intimate friendship. . . . In religious matters both were sceptics, or indeed decided anti-Christians; whether Hogg, as the senior and more informed disputant, pioneered Shelley into strict atheism, or whether Shelley, as the more impassioned and unflinching speculator, outran the easy-going jeering Hogg, is a moot point; we incline to the latter opinion. Certain it is that each egged on the other by perpetual disquisition on abstruse subjects, conducted partly for the sake of truth and partly for that of mental exercitation, without on either side any disposition to bow to authority or stop short of extreme conclusions. The upshot of this habit was that Shelley and Hogg, at the close of some five months of happy and uneventful academic life, got expelled from the university. . . .

Percy and his incensed father did not at once come to terms, and for a while he had no resource beyond pocket-money saved up by his sisters (four in number altogether) and sent round to him, sometimes by the hand of a singularly pretty school-fellow, Miss Harriet Westbrook, daughter of a retired and moderately opulent hotel-keeper. . . . Harriet not unnaturally fell in love with him; and he, though not it would seem at any time ardently in love with her, dallied along the flowery pathway which leads to sentiment and a definite courtship. . . . Shelley therefore returned to London, where he found Harriet agitated and wavering; finally they agreed to elope, travelled in haste to Edinburgh, and there, according to the law of Scotland, became husband and wife on 20th August. Shelley, it should be understood, had by this time openly broken, not only with the dogmas and conventions of Christian religion, but with many of the institutions of Christian polity, and in especial with such as enforce and regulate marriage; he held—with William Godwin and some other theorists—that marriage ought to be simply a voluntary relation between a man and a woman, to be assumed at joint option and terminated at the after-option of either party. . . .

Harriet Shelley was not only beautiful; she was amiable, accommodating, adequately well educated and well bred. She liked reading, and her reading was not strictly frivolous. But she could not (as Shelley said at a later date) "feel poetry and understand philosophy". . . .

At Tanyrallt Shelley was (to trust his own and Harriet's account, confirmed by the evidence of Miss Westbrook, the elder sister, who continued an inmate in most of their homes) attacked on the night of 26th February by an assassin who fired three pistol-shots. The motive of the attack was undefined; the fact of its occurrence was generally disbelieved; both at the time and by subsequent inquirers. To analyse the possibilities and probabilities of the case would lead us too far; we can only say that we rank with the decided sceptics. Shelley was full of wild unpractical notions; he dosed himself with laudanum as a palliative to spasmodic pains; he was given to strange assertions and romancing narratives (several of which might properly be specified here but for want of space), and was not incapable of conscious fibbing. His mind no doubt oscillated at times along the line which divides sanity from insane delusion. It is difficult to suppose that he simply invented such a monstrous story to serve a purpose. . . .

The Shelleys revisited Ireland, and then settled for a while in London. Here, in June 1813, Harriet gave birth to her daughter Ianthe Eliza (she married a Mr Esdaile, and died in 1876). Here also Shelley brought out his first poem of any importance, *Queen Mab;* it was privately printed, as its exceedingly aggressive tone in matters of religion and morals would not allow of publication.

The speculative sage whom Shelley especially reverenced was William Godwin, the author of *Political Justice* and of the romance *Caleb Williams;* in 1796 he had married Mary Wollstonecraft, authoress of *The Rights of Woman,* who died shortly after giving birth, on 30th August 1797, to a daughter Mary. With Godwin Shelley had opened a volunteered correspondence late in 1811, and he had known him personally since the winter which closed 1812. . . . It was towards May 1814 that Shelley first saw Mary Wollstonecraft Godwin as a grown-up girl (she was well on towards seventeen); he instantly fell in love with her, and she with him. Just before this, 24th March, Shelley had remarried Harriet in London, though with no obviously cogent motive for doing so; but, on becoming enamoured of Mary, he seems to have rapidly made up his mind that Harriet should not stand in the way. . . . The upshot came on 28th July, when Shelley aided Mary to elope from her father's house, Claire Clairmont deciding to accompany them. They crossed to Calais, and proceeded across France into Switzerland. Godwin and his wife were greatly incensed. Though he and Mary Wollstonecraft had entertained and avowed bold opinions regarding the marriage-bond, similar to Shelley's own, and had in their time acted upon these opinions, it is not clearly made out that Mary Godwin had ever been encouraged by paternal influence to think or do the like. Shelley and she chose to act upon their own likings and responsibility,—he disregarding any claim which Harriet had upon him, and Mary setting at nought her father's authority. Both were prepared to ignore the law of the land and the rules of society. . . . Shelley, and Mary as well, were on moderately good terms with Harriet, seeing her from time to time. His peculiar views as to the relations of the sexes appear markedly again in his having (so it is alleged) invited Harriet to return to his and Mary's house as a domicile; of course this curious arrangement did not take effect. Shelley and Mary (who was naturally always called Mrs Shelley) now settled at Bishopgate, near Windsor Forest; here he produced his first excellent poem, *Alastor, or the Spirit of Solitude,* which was published soon afterwards along with a few others. In May 1816 the pair left England for Switzerland, together with Miss Clairmont, and their own infant son William. They went straight to Sécheron, near Geneva; Lord Byron, whose separation from his wife had just then taken place, arrived there immediately afterwards. A great deal of controversy has lately arisen as to the motives and incidents of this foreign sojourn. The clear fact is that Miss Clairmont, who had a fine voice and some inclination for the stage, had seen Byron, as connected with the management of Drury Lane theatre, early in the year, and an amorous intrigue had begun between them in London. *Prima facie* it seems quite reasonable to suppose that she had explained the facts to Shelley or to Mary, or to both, and had induced them to convoy her to the society of Byron abroad. . . .

This was the time when Shelley began to see a great deal of Leigh Hunt, the poet and essayist, editor of *The Examiner;* they were close friends, and Hunt did something (hardly perhaps so much as might have been anticipated) to uphold the reputation of Shelley as a poet—which, we may here say once for all, scarcely obtained any public acceptance or solidity during his brief lifetime. . . . In Pisa Byron and Shelley were very constantly together, having in their company at one time or another Captain Medwin (cousin and school-fellow of Shelley, and one of his biographers), Lieutenant and Mrs Williams, to both of whom our poet was very warmly attached, and Captain Trelawny, the adventurous and romantic-natured seaman who has left important and interesting reminiscences of this period. Byron admired very highly the generous, unworldly, and enthusiastic character of Shelley, and set some value on his writings; Shelley half-worshipped Byron as a poet, and was anxious, but in some conjunctures by no means able, to respect him as a man. . . .

The last residence of Shelley was the Casa Magni, a bare and exposed dwelling on the Gulf of Spezia. He and his wife, with the Williamses, went there at the end of April 1822, to spend the summer, which proved an arid and scorching one. Shelley and Williams, both of them insatiably fond of boating, had a small schooner named the "Don Juan" built at Genoa after a design which Williams had procured from a naval friend, and which was the reverse of safe. They received her on 12th May, found her rapid and alert, and on 1st July started in her to Leghorn, to meet Leigh Hunt, whose arrival in Italy had just been notified. After doing his best to set things going comfortably between Byron and Hunt, Shelley returned on board with Williams on 8th July. It was a day of dark, louring, stifling heat. Trelawny took leave of his two friends, and about half-past six in the evening found himself startled from a doze by a frightful turmoil of storm. The "Don Juan" had by this time made Via Reggio; she was not to be seen, though other vessels which had sailed about the same time were still discernible. Shelley, Williams, and their only companion, a sailor-boy, perished in the squall. . . . The great poet's ashes were then collected, and buried in the new Protestant cemetery in Rome. He was, at the time of his untimely death, within a month of completing the thirtieth year of his age—a surprising example of rich poetic achievement for so young a man.

BERTRAND RUSSELL

ON

The Philosophical Consequences of Relativity

Not many scientists can write lucidly for the lay reader about such matters as the theory of relativity. One who could was the philosopher-logician-mathematician Bertrand Russell, 3rd Earl Russell. In his long and virtually hyperactive life Lord Russell spread scientific understanding as well as philosophical inquiry and reflection, atheism, pacifism, and left-wing socialist activism. His Britannica *article on the "Philosophical Consequences of Relativity" (13th edition, 1926) clarified the space-time concept. It was written while he was completing a popular book,* The ABC of Relativity. *(B.L.F.)*

Today we are all Einsteinians. Our view of the cosmos and to a degree man's place in it is as unconsciously colored and conditioned by relativity as that of our not-too-remote ancestors was by the Newtonian theory.

It's interesting therefore to note how a first-class mind viewed the philosophical rather than the scientific consequences of relativity almost three-quarters of a century ago. Particularly pertinent, in view of our era's love affair with technology, is the last paragraph.

In the current Britannica *the account of the mathematician, philosopher, and publicist Bertrand Russell extends over five columns, just as his life (1872–1970) extended over almost a century. The reader is referred to it. Among Russell's voluminous productions we call attention to what may oddly enough in the end turn out to be his masterpiece, his three-volume* Autobiography.

Of the consequences in philosophy which may be supposed to follow from the theory of relativity some are fairly certain, while others are open to question. There has been a tendency, not uncommon in the case of a new scientific theory, for every philosopher to interpret the work of Einstein in accordance with his own metaphysical system, and to suggest that the outcome is a great accession of strength to the views which the philosopher in question previously held. This cannot be true in all cases; and it may be hoped that it is true in none. It would be disappointing if so fundamental a change as Einstein has introduced involved no philosophical novelty.

Space-time. For philosophy, the most important novelty was present already in the special theory of relativity; that is, the substitution of space-time for space and time. In Newtonian dynamics, two events were separated by two kinds of interval, one being distance in space, the other lapse of time. As soon as it was realised that all motion is relative (which happened long before Einstein), distance in space became ambiguous except in the case of *simultaneous* events, but it was still thought that there was no ambiguity about simultaneity in different places. The special theory of relativity showed, by experimental arguments which were new, and by logical arguments which could have been discovered any time after it became known that light travels with a finite velocity, that simultaneity is only definite when it applies to events in the same place, and becomes more and more ambiguous as the events are more widely removed from each other in space.

This statement is not quite correct, since it still uses the notion of "space." The correct statement is this: Events have a four-dimensional order, by means of which we can say that an event A is nearer to an event B than to an event C; this is a purely ordinal matter, not involving anything quantitative. But, in addition, there is between neighbouring events a quantitative relation called "interval," which fulfils the functions both of distance in space and of lapse of time in the traditional dynamics, but fulfils them with a difference. If a body can move so as to be present at both events, the interval is time-like. If a ray of light can move so as to be present at both events, the interval is zero. If neither can happen, the interval is space-like. When we speak of a body being present "at" an event, we mean that the event occurs in the same place in space-time as one of the events which make up the history of the body; and when we say that two events occur at the same place in space-time, we mean that there is no event between them in the four-dimensional space-time order. All the events which happen to a man at a given moment (in his own time) are, in this sense, in one place; for example, if we hear a noise and see a colour simultaneously, our two perceptions are both in one place in space-time.

When one body can be present at two events which are not in one place in space-time, the time-order of the two events is not ambiguous, though the magnitude of the time-interval will be different in different systems of measurement. But whenever the interval between two events is space-like, their time-order will be different in different equally legitimate systems of measurement; in this case, therefore, the time-order does not represent a physical fact. It follows that, when two bodies are in relative motion, like the sun and a planet, there is no such physical fact as "the distance between the bodies at a given time"; this alone shows that Newton's law of gravitation is logically faulty. Fortunately, Einstein has not only pointed out the defect, but remedied it. His arguments against Newton, however, would have remained valid even if his own law of gravitation had not proved right.

Time not a single cosmic order. The fact that time is private to each body, not a single cosmic order, involves changes in the notions of substance and cause, and suggests the substitution of a series of events for a substance with changing states. The controversy about the aether thus becomes rather unreal. Undoubtedly, when light-waves travel, events occur, and it used to be thought that these events must be "in" something; the something in which they were was called the aether. But there seems no reason except a logical prejudice to suppose that the events are "in" anything. Matter, also, may be reduced to a law according to which events succeed each other and spread out from centres; but here we enter upon more speculative considerations.

Physical laws. Prof. Eddington has emphasised an aspect of relativity theory which is of great philosophical importance, but difficult to make clear without somewhat abstruse mathematics. The aspect in question is the reduction of what used to be regarded as physical laws to the status of truisms or definitions. Prof. Eddington, in a profoundly interesting essay on "The Domain of Physical Science,"[1] states the matter as follows:—

> In the present stage of science the laws of physics appear to be divisible into three classes—the identical, the statistical and the transcendental. The "identical laws" include the great field-laws which are commonly quoted as typical instances of natural law—the law of gravitation, the law of conservation of mass and energy, the laws of electric and magnetic force and the conservation of electric charge. These are seen to be identities, when we refer to the cycle so as to understand the constitution of the entities obeying them; and unless we have misunderstood this constitution, violation of these laws is inconceivable. They do not in any way limit the actual basal structure of the world, and are not laws of governance (*op. cit.*, pp. 214–5).

It is these identical laws that form the subject-matter of relativity theory; the other laws of physics, the statistical and transcendental, lie outside its scope. Thus the net result of relativity theory is to show that the traditional laws of physics, rightly understood, tell us almost nothing about the course of nature, being rather of the nature of logical truisms.

This surprising result is an outcome of increased mathematical skill. As the same author[2] says elsewhere:—

> In one sense deductive theory is the enemy of experimental physics. The latter is always striving to settle by crucial tests the nature of the fundamental things; the former strives to minimise the successes obtained by showing how wide a nature of things is compatible with all experimental results.

[1] In *Science, Religion and Reality*, ed. by Joseph Needham (1925).
[2] A. S. Eddington, *Mathematical Theory of Relativity*, p. 238 (Cambridge, 1924).

The suggestion is that, in almost any conceivable world, *something* will be conserved; mathematics gives us the means of constructing a variety of mathematical expressions having this property of conservation. It is natural to suppose that it is useful to have senses which notice these conserved entities; hence mass, energy, and so on *seem* to have a basis in our experience, but are in fact merely certain quantities which are conserved and which we are adapted for noticing. If this view is correct, physics tells us much less about the real world than was formerly supposed.

Force and gravitation. An important aspect of relativity is the elimination of "force." This is not new in idea; indeed, it was already accepted in rational dynamics. But there remained the outstanding difficulty of gravitation, which Einstein has overcome. The sun is, so to speak, at the summit of a hill, and the planets are on the slopes. They move as they do because of the slope where they are, not because of some mysterious influence emanating from the summit. Bodies move as they do because that is the easiest possible movement in the region of space-time in which they find themselves, not because "forces" operate upon them. The apparent need of forces to account for observed motions arises from mistaken insistence upon Euclidean geometry; when once we have overcome this prejudice, we find that observed motions, instead of showing the presence of forces, show the nature of the geometry applicable to the region concerned. Bodies thus become far more independent of each other than they were in Newtonian physics: there is an increase of individualism and a diminution of central government, if one may be permitted such metaphorical language. This may, in time, considerably modify the ordinary educated man's picture of the universe, possibly with far-reaching results.

Realism in relativity. It is a mistake to suppose that relativity adopts an idealistic picture of the world—using "idealism" in the technical sense, in which it implies that there can be nothing which is not experience. The "observer" who is often mentioned in expositions of relativity need not be a mind, but may be a photographic plate or any kind of recording instrument. The fundamental assumption of relativity is realistic, namely, that those respects in which all observers agree when they record a given phenomenon may be regarded as objective, and not as contributed by the observers. This assumption is made by common sense. The apparent sizes and shapes of objects differ according to the point of view, but common sense discounts these differences. Relativity theory merely extends this process. By taking into account not only human observers, who all share the motion of the earth, but also possible "observers" in very rapid motion relatively to the earth, it is found that much more depends upon the point of view of the observer than was formerly thought. But there is found to be a residue which is not so dependent; this is the part which can be expressed by the method of "tensors." The importance of this method can hardly be exaggerated; it is, however, quite impossible to explain it in non-mathematical terms.

Relativity physics. Relativity physics is, of course, concerned only with the quantitative aspects of the world. The picture which it suggests is somewhat as follows:—In the four-dimensional space-time frame there are events everywhere, usually many events in a single place in space-time. The abstract mathematical relations of these events proceed according to the laws of physics, but the intrinsic nature of the events is wholly and inevitably unknown except when they occur in a region where there is the sort of structure we call a brain. Then they become the familiar sights and sounds and so on of our daily life. We know what it is like to see a star, but we do not know the nature of the events which constitute the ray of light that travels from the star to our eye. And the space-time frame itself is known only in its abstract mathematical properties; there is no reason to suppose it similar in intrinsic character to the spatial and temporal relations of our perceptions as known in experience. There does not seem any possible way of overcoming this ignorance, since the very nature of physical reasoning allows only the most abstract inferences, and only the most abstract properties of our perceptions can be regarded as having objective validity. Whether any other science than physics can tell us more, does not fall within the scope of the present article.

Meanwhile, it is a curious fact that this meagre kind of knowledge is sufficient for the *practical* uses of physics. From a practical point of view, the physical world only matters in so far as it affects us, and the intrinsic nature of what goes on in our absence is irrelevant, provided we can predict the effects upon ourselves. This we can do, just as a person can use a telephone without understanding electricity. Only the most abstract knowledge is required for practical manipulation of matter. But there is a grave danger when this habit of manipulation based upon mathematical laws is carried over into our dealings with human beings, since they, unlike the telephone wire, are capable of happiness and misery, desire and aversion. It would therefore be unfortunate if the habits of mind which are appropriate and right in dealing with material mechanisms were allowed to dominate the administrator's attempts at social constructiveness.

CARL SAGAN

ON

Life, Terrestrial and Otherwise

Carl Sagan (1934–) is one of a small group of distinguished American scientists able to communicate with the general public. Some readers may recall with pleasure the remarkable television series "Cosmos" (1980) which he narrated and co-produced. His book of the same title is the best-selling science volume of all time. Since 1968 he has been Director of the Laboratory for Planetary Studies at Cornell University, where he is the David Duncan Professor of Astronomy. Among his main publications three have won wide popular audiences: The Dragons of Venice *(1977),* Broca's Brain *(1979), and* Contact *(1985). He is particularly interested in the possibilities of intelligent extraterrestrial life forms.*

His magisterial seventeen-page article on "Life" first appeared in the 1984 issue of the present 15th edition. From it we have excerpted the introduction and part of the concluding section, which deal respectively with definitions of life and with extraterrestrial life.

A great deal is known about life. Anatomists and taxonomists have studied the forms and relations of more than a million separate species of plants and animals. Physiologists have investigated the gross functioning of organisms. Biochemists have probed the biological interactions of the organic molecules that make up life on our planet. Molecular biologists have uncovered the very molecules responsible for reproduction and for the passage of hereditary information from generation to generation, a subject that geneticists had previously studied without going to the molecular level. Ecologists have inquired into the relations between organisms and their environments, ethologists the behaviour of animals and plants, embryologists the development of complex organisms from a single cell, evolutionary biologists the emergence of organisms from pre-existing forms over geological time. Yet despite the enormous fund of information that each of these biological specialties has provided, it is a remarkable fact that no general agreement exists on what it is that is being studied. There is no generally accepted definition of life. In fact, there is a certain clearly discernible tendency for each biological specialty to define life in its own terms. The average person also tends to think of life in his own terms. For example, the man in the street, if asked about life on other planets, will often picture life of a distinctly human sort. Many individuals believe that insects are not animals, because by "animals" they mean "mammals." Man tends to define in terms of the familiar. But the fundamental truths may not be familiar. Of the following definitions, the first two are in terms familiar in everyday life; the next three are based on more abstract concepts and theoretical frameworks.

Physiological. For many years a physiological definition of life was popular. Life was defined as any system capable of performing a number of such functions as eating, metabolizing, excreting, breathing, moving, growing, reproducing, and being responsive to external stimuli. But many such properties are either present in machines that nobody is willing to call alive, or absent from organisms that everybody is willing to call alive. An automobile, for example, can be said to eat, metabolize, excrete, breathe, move, and be responsive to external stimuli. And a visitor from another planet, judging from the enormous numbers of automobiles on the earth and the way in which cities and landscapes have been designed for the special benefit of motorcars, might well believe that automobiles are not only alive but are the dominant life form on the planet. Man, however, professes to know better.

On the other hand, some bacteria do not breathe at all but instead live out their days by altering the oxidation state of sulfur.

Metabolic. The metabolic definition is still popular with many biologists. It describes a living system as an object with a definite boundary, continually exchanging some of its materials with its surroundings, but without altering its general properties, at least over some period of time. But again there are exceptions. There are seeds and spores that remain, so far as is known, perfectly dormant and totally without metabolic activity at low temperatures for hundreds, perhaps thousands, of years but that can revive perfectly well upon being subjected to more clement conditions. A flame, such as that of a candle in a closed room, will have a perfectly defined shape with fixed boundary and will be maintained by the combination of its organic waxes with molecular oxygen, producing carbon dioxide and water. A similar chemical reaction, incidentally, is fundamental to most animal life on earth. Flames also have a well-known capacity for growth.

Biochemical. A biochemical or molecular biological definition sees living organisms as systems that contain reproducible hereditary information coded in nucleic acid molecules and that metabolize by controlling the rate of chemical reactions using proteinaceous catalysts known as enzymes. In many respects, this is more satisfying than the physiological or metabolic definitions of life. There are, however, even here, the hints of counterexamples. There seems to be some evidence that a virus-like agent called scrapie contains no nucleic acids at all, although it has been hypothesized that the nucleic acids of the host animal may nevertheless be involved in the reproduction of scrapie. Furthermore, a definition strictly in chemical terms seems peculiarly vulnerable. It implies that were man able to construct a system that had all the functional properties of life, it would still not be alive if it lacked the molecules that earthly biologists are fond of—and made of.

Genetic. All organisms on earth, from the simplest cell to man himself, are machines of extraordinary powers, effortlessly performing complex transformations of organic molecules, exhibiting elaborate behaviour patterns, and indefinitely constructing from raw materials in the environment more or less identical copies of themselves. How could machines of such staggering complexity and such stunning beauty ever arise? The answer, for which today there is excellent scientific evidence, was first discerned by the evolutionist Charles Darwin in the years before the publication in 1859 of his epoch-making work, the *Origin of Species*. A modern rephrasing of his theory of natural selection goes something like this: Hereditary information is carried by large molecules known as genes, comprised of nucleic acids. Different genes are responsible for the expression of different characteristics of the organism. During the reproduction of the organism the genes also reproduce, or replicate, passing the instructions for various characteristics on to the next generation. Occasionally, there are imperfections, called mutations, in gene replication. A mutation alters the instructions for a particular characteristic or characteristics. It also breeds true, in the sense that its capability for determining a given characteristic of the organism remains unimpaired for generations until the mutated gene is itself mutated. Some mutations, when expressed, will produce characteristics favourable for the organism; organisms with such favourable genes will reproduce preferentially over those without such genes. Most mutations, however, turn out to be deleterious and often lead to some impairment or to death of the organism. To illustrate, it is unlikely that one can improve the functioning of a finely crafted watch by dropping it from a tall building. The watch may run better, but this is highly improbable. Organisms are so much more finely crafted than the finest watch that any random change is even more likely to be deleterious. The accidental beneficial and inheritable change, however, does on occasion occur; it results in an organism better adapted to its environment. In this way organisms slowly evolve toward better adaptation, and, in most cases, toward greater complexity. This evolution occurs, however, only at enormous cost: man exists today, complex and reasonably well adapted, only because of billions of deaths of organisms slightly less adapted and somewhat less complex. In short, Darwin's theory of natural selection states that complex organisms developed, or evolved, through time because of replication, mutation, and replication of mutations. A genetic definition of life therefore would be: a system capable of evolution by natural selection.

This definition places great emphasis on the importance of replication. Indeed, in any organism enormous biological effort is directed toward replication, although it confers no obvious benefit on the replicating organism. Some organisms, many hybrids for example, do not replicate at all. But their individual cells do. It is also true that life defined in this way does not rule out synthetic duplication. It should be possible to construct a machine that is capable of producing identical copies of itself from preformed building blocks littering the landscape but that arranges its descendants in a slightly different manner if there is a random change in its instructions. Such a machine would, of course, replicate its instructions as well. But the fact that such a machine would satisfy the genetic definition of life is not an argument against such a definition; in fact, if the building blocks were simple enough, such a machine would have the capability of evolving into very complex systems that would probably have all the other properties attributed to living systems. The genetic definition has the additional advantage of being expressed purely in functional terms: it does not depend on any particular choice of constituent molecules. The improbability of contemporary organisms—dealt with more fully below—is so great that these organisms could not possibly have arisen by purely random processes and without historical continuity. Fundamental to the genetic definition of life then is the belief that a certain level of complexity cannot be achieved without natural selection.

Thermodynamic. Thermodynamics distinguishes between open and closed systems. A closed system is isolated from the rest of the environment and exchanges neither light, heat, nor matter with its surroundings. An open system is one in which such exchanges do occur. The second law of thermodynamics states that, in a closed system, no processes can occur that increase the net order (or decrease the net entropy) of the system. Thus the universe taken as a whole is steadily moving toward a state of complete randomness, lacking any order, pattern, or beauty. This fate has been known since the 19th century as the heat death of the universe. Yet living organisms are manifestly ordered and at first sight seem to represent a contradiction to the second law of thermodynamics. Living systems might then be defined as localized regions where there is a continuous increase in order. Living systems, however, are not really in contradiction to the second law. They increase their order at the expense of a larger decrease in order of the universe outside. Living systems are not closed but rather open. Most life on earth, for example, is dependent on the flow of sunlight, which is utilized by plants to construct complex molecules from simpler ones. But the order that results here on earth is more than compensated by the decrease in order on the sun, through the thermonuclear processes responsible for the sun's radiation.

Some scientists argue on grounds of quite general open-system thermodynamics that the order of a system increases as energy flows through it, and moreover that this occurs through the development of cycles. A simple biological cycle on the earth is the carbon cycle. Carbon from atmospheric carbon dioxide is incorporated by plants and converted into carbohydrates through the process of photosynthesis. These carbohydrates are ultimately oxidized by both plants and animals to extract useful energy locked in their chemical bonds. In the oxidation of carbohydrates, carbon dioxide is returned to the atmosphere, completing the cycle. It has been shown that similar cycles develop spontaneously and in the absence of life by the flow of energy through a chemical system. In this view, biological cycles are merely an exploitation by living systems of those thermodynamic cycles that pre-exist in the absence of life. It is not known whether open-system thermodynamic processes in the absence of replication are capable of leading to the sorts of complexity that characterize biological systems. It is clear, however, that the complexity of life on earth has arisen through replication, although thermodynamically favoured pathways have certainly been used.

The existence of diverse definitions of life surely means that life is something complicated. A fundamental understanding of biological systems has existed since the second half of the 19th century. But the number and diversity of definitions suggest something else as well. As detailed below, all the organisms on the earth are extremely closely related, despite superficial differences. The fundamental ground pattern, both in form and in matter, of all life on earth is essentially identical. As will emerge below, this identity probably implies that all organisms on earth are evolved from a single instance of the origin of life. It is difficult to generalize from a single example, and in this respect the biologist is fundamentally handicapped as compared, say, to the chemist or physicist or geologist or meteorologist, who now can study aspects of his discipline beyond the earth. If there is truly only one sort of life on earth, then perspective is lacking in the most fundamental way. . . .

Intelligent life beyond the solar system. For thousands of years man has wondered whether he is alone in the universe or whether there might be other worlds populated by creatures more or less like himself. The common view, both in early times and through the Middle Ages, was that the earth was the only "world" in the universe. Nevertheless, many mythologies populated the sky with divine beings, certainly a kind of extraterrestrial life. Many early philosophers held that life was not unique to the earth. Metrodorus, an Epicurean philosopher in the 3rd and 4th centuries BC, argued that "to consider the earth the only populated world in infinite space is as absurd as to assert that in an entire field sown with millet, only one grain will grow." Since the Renaissance there have been several fluctuations in the fashion of belief. In the late 18th century, for example, practically all informed opinion held that each of the planets was populated by more or less intelligent beings; in the early 20th century, by contrast, the prevailing informed opinion (except for the Lowellians) held that the chances for extraterrestrial intelligent life were insignificant. In fact the subject of intelligent extraterrestrial life is for many people a touchstone of their beliefs and desires, some individuals very urgently wanting there to be extraterrestrial intelligence, and others wanting equally fervently for there to be no such life. For this reason it is important to approach the subject in as unbiased a frame of mind as possible. A respectable modern scientific examination of extraterrestrial intelligence is no older than the 1950s. The probability of advanced technical civilizations in our galaxy depends on many controversial issues.

A simple way of approaching the problem, which illuminates the parameters and uncertainties involved, has been devised by a U.S. astrophysicist,

F.D. Drake. The number *N* of extant technical civilizations in the galaxy can be expressed by the following equation (the so-called Green Bank formula):

$$N = R_{\star} f_p n_e f_l f_i f_c L$$

where $R_{\star}$ is the average rate of star formation over the lifetime of the galaxy; f_p is the fraction of stars with planetary systems; n_e is the mean number of planets per star that are ecologically suitable for the origin and evolution of life; f_l is the fraction of such planets on which life in fact arises; f_i is the fraction of such planets on which intelligent life evolves; f_c is the fraction of such planets on which a technical civilization develops; and *L* is the mean lifetime of a technical civilization. What follows is a brief consideration of the factors involved in choosing numerical values for each of these parameters, and an indication of some currently popular choices. In several cases these estimates are no better than informed guesses and no very great reliability should be pretended for them.

There are about 2×10^{11} stars in the galaxy. The age of the galaxy is about 10^{10} years. A value of $R_{\star} = 10$ stars per year is probably fairly reliable. While most contemporary theories of star formation imply that the origin of planets is a usual accompaniment of the origin of stars, such theories are not well enough developed to merit much confidence. Through the painstaking measurement of slight gravitational perturbations in the proper motions of stars, it has been found that about half of the very nearest stars have dark companions with masses ranging from about the mass of Jupiter to about 30 times the mass of Jupiter. The nearest of these dark companions orbit Barnard's star, which is only six light years from the sun and is the second nearest star system. The most direct indication that planetary formation is a general process throughout the universe is the existence of satellite systems of the major planets of our own solar system. Jupiter, with 12 satellites, Saturn with 10, and Uranus with 5, each closely resemble miniature solar systems. It is not known what the distribution of distances of planets from their central star are in other solar systems and whether they tend to vary systematically with the luminosity of the parent star. But considering the wide range of temperatures that seem to be compatible with life, it can be tentatively concluded that $f_p n_e$ is about one.

Because of the apparent rapidity of the origin of life on earth, as implied by the fossil record, and because of the ease with which relevant organic molecules are produced in primitive earth simulation experiments, the likelihood of the origin of life over a period of billions of years seems high, and some scientists believe that the appropriate value of f_l is also about one. For the quantities of f_i and f_c the parameters are even more uncertain. The vagaries of the evolutionary path leading to the mammals, and the unlikelihood of such a path ever being repeated has already been mentioned. On the other hand, intelligence need not necessarily be restricted to the same evolutionary path that occurred on the earth; intelligence clearly has great selective advantage, both for predators and for prey.

Similar arguments can be made for the adaptive value of technical civilizations. Intelligence and technical civilization, however, are clearly not the same thing. For example, dolphins appear to be very intelligent, but the lack of manipulative organs on their bodies has apparently limited their technological advance. Both intelligence and technical civilization have evolved about halfway through the relevant lifetime of the earth and sun. Some, but by no means all, evolutionary biologists would conclude that the product $f_i f_c$ taken as 10^{-2} is a fairly conservative estimate.

Still more uncertain is the value of the final parameter, *L*, the lifetime of a technical civilization. Here, fortunately for man, but unfortunate for the discussion, there is not even one example. Contemporary world events do not provide a very convincing counterargument to the contention that technical civilizations tend, through the use of weapons of mass destruction, to destroy themselves shortly after they come into being. If we define a technical civilization as one capable of interstellar radio communication, our technical civilization is only a few decades old. If then *L* is about ten years, multiplication of all of the factors assumed above leads to the conclusion that there is in the second half of the 20th century only about one technical civilization in the galaxy—our own. But if technical civilizations tend to control the use of such weapons and avoid self-annihilation, then the lifetimes of technical civilizations may be very long, comparable to geological or stellar evolutionary time scales;

the number of technical civilizations in the galaxy would then be immense. If it is believed that about 1 percent of developing civilizations make peace with themselves in this way, then there are about 1,000,000 technical civilizations extant in the galaxy. If they are randomly distributed in space, the distance from the earth to the nearest such civilization will be several hundred light-years. These conclusions are, of course, very uncertain.

How is it possible to enter into communication with another technical civilization? Independent of the value of *L*, the above formulation implies that there is about one technical civilization arising every decade in the galaxy. Accordingly, it will be extraordinarily unlikely for man soon to find a technical civilization as backward as his. From the rate of technical advance that has occurred on the earth in the last few hundred years, it seems clear that man is in no position to project what future scientific and technical advances will be made even on earth in the next few hundred years. Very advanced civilizations will have techniques and sciences totally unknown to 20th-century man. Nevertheless man already has a technique capable of communication over large interstellar distances. This technique, already encountered in the discussion of life on earth, is radio transmission. Imagine that we employ the largest radio telescope available on earth, the 1,000-foot-diameter dish of Cornell University, the Arecibo Observatory in Puerto Rico, and existing receivers, and that the identical equipment is employed on some transmitting planet. How distant could the transmitting and receiving planets be for intelligible signals to be transmitted and received? The answer is a rather astonishing 1,000 light-years. Within a volume centred on the earth, with a radius of 1,000 light-years, there are over 10,000,000 stars.

There would of course be problems in establishing such radio communication. The choices of frequency, of target star, of time constant, and of the character of the message would all have to be selected by the transmitting planet so that the receiving planet would, without too much effort, be able to deduce the choices. But none of these problems seem insuperable. It has been suggested that there are certain natural radio frequencies (such as the 1420-megacycle line of neutral hydrogen) that might be tuned to; the first choice might be to listen to stars of approximately solar spectral type; in the absence of a common language there nevertheless are messages whose intelligent origin and intellectual content could be made very clear without making many anthropocentric assumptions.

Because of the expectation that the earth is relatively very backward, it does not make very much sense to transmit messages to hypothetical planets of other stars. But it may very well make sense to listen for radio transmissions from planets of other stars. Project Ozma, a very brief program of this sort, oriented to two nearby stars, Epsilon Eridani and Tau Ceti, was organized in 1960 by Drake. On the basis of the Green Bank formula, it would be very unlikely that success would greet an effort aimed at two stars only 12 light-years away, and Project Ozma was unsuccessful. It remains, however, the first pioneering attempt at interstellar communication. Related programs were organized on a larger scale and with great enthusiasm in the 1960s in the U.S.S.R., where a state scientific commission devoted to such an effort was organized. Other communication techniques including laser transmission and interstellar spaceflight have been discussed seriously and may not be infeasible, but if the measure of effectiveness is the amount of information communicated per unit cost, then radio is the method of choice.

The search for extraterrestrial intelligence is an extraordinary pursuit, in part because of the enormous significance of possible success, but in part because of the unity it brings to a wide range of disciplines: studies of the origins of stars, planets, and life; of the evolution of intelligence and of technical civilizations; and of the political problem of avoiding man's self-annihilation. But at least one point is clear. In the words of Loren Eiseley (from *The Immense Journey*),

> Lights come and go in the night sky. Men, troubled at last by the things they build, may toss in their sleep and dream bad dreams, or lie awake while the meteors whisper greenly overhead. But nowhere in all space or on a thousand worlds will there be men to share our loneliness. There may be wisdom; there may be power; somewhere across space great

instruments, handled by strange, manipulative organs, may stare vainly at our floating cloud wrack, their owners yearning as we yearn. Nevertheless, in the nature of life and in principles of evolution we have had our answer. Of men [as are known on earth] elsewhere, and beyond, there will be none forever.

WALTER SCOTT

ON

Chivalry

Britannica's *current edition devotes three scanty paragraphs to "Chivalry," supplemented by ten brief references. The Supplement to the 4th, 5th, and 6th editions (1815–1824) gave it thirty double-column pages—a simple but dramatic lesson in the mutability of ideas and institutions. However, that thirty-page article was written by Sir Walter Scott (1771–1832) and so retains its value.*

Sir Walter Scott assented to the request of the Britannica's *publisher, Archibald Constable, to write articles on "Chivalry," "Romance," and "Drama," which eventually ran to ninety-four printed pages. When the editor, Macvey Napier, proffered £100 in payment, Scott first assured himself that it would not come from the pocket of Napier, whom he considered "a literary brother," then took the money, observing that he had no conscience as to the purse of his "fat friend, to wit, Constable." (B.L.F.)*

The primitive sense of this well-known word, derived from the French *Chevalier,* signifies merely cavalry, or a body of soldiers serving on horseback; and has been used in that general acceptation by the best of our poets, ancient and modern, from Milton to Thomas Campbell.

But the present article respects the peculiar meaning given to the word in modern Europe, as applied to the order of knighthood, established in almost all her kingdoms during the middle ages, and the laws, rules, and customs, by which it was governed. Those laws and customs have long been antiquated, but their effects may still be traced in European manners; and, excepting only the change which flowed from the introduction of the Christian religion, we know no cause which has produced such general and permanent difference betwixt the ancients and moderns as that which has arisen out of the institution of chivalry. In attempting to treat this curious and important subject, rather as philosophers than as antiquaries, we cannot, however, avoid going at some length into the history and origin of the institution.

From the time that cavalry becomes used in war, the horseman who furnished and supported a charger arises, in all countries, into a person of superior importance to the mere foot soldier. The apparent difficulty of the art of training and managing in the field of battle an animal so spirited and active, gave the ιπποδομος Εχτοζ, or *Domitor equi,* in rude ages, a character of superior gallantry, while the necessary expence attending this mode of service attested his superior wealth. In various military nations, therefore, we find that horsemen are distinguished as an order in the state, and need only appeal to the *equites* of ancient Rome as a body interposed betwixt the senate and the people; or to the laws of the conquerors of New Spain, which assigned a double portion of spoil to the soldier who fought on horseback, in support of a proposition in itself very obvious. But, in the middle ages, the distinction ascribed to soldiers serving on horseback assumed a very peculiar and imposing character. They were not merely respected on account of their wealth or military skill, but were bound together by an union of a very peculiar character, which monarchs were ambitious to share with the poorest of their subjects, and governed by laws directed to enhance, into enthusiasm, the military spirit and the sense of personal honour associated with it. The aspirants to this dignity were not permitted to assume the sacred character of knighthood until after a long and severe probation, during which they practised, as acolytes, the virtues necessary to the order of chivalry. Knighthood was the goal to which the ambition of every noble youth turned, and to support its honours, which (in theory at least) could only be conferred on the gallant, the modest, and the virtuous, it was necessary he should spend a certain time in a subordinate situation, attendant upon some knight of eminence, observing the conduct of his master, as what must in future be the model of his own, and practising the virtues of humility, modesty, and temperance, until called upon to display those of an higher order.

The general practice of assigning some precise period when youths should be admitted into the society of the manhood of their tribe, and considered as entitled to use the privileges of that more mature class, is common to many primitive nations. The custom, also, of marking the transition from the one state to the other, by some peculiar formality and personal ceremonial, seems so very natural, that it is quite unnecessary to multiply instances, or crowd our pages with the barbarous names of the nations by whom it has been adopted. In the general and abstract definition of Chivalry, whether as comprising a body of men whose military service was on horseback, and who were invested with peculiar honours and privileges, or with reference to the mode and period in which these distinctions and privileges were conferred, there is nothing either original or exclusively proper to our Gothic ancestors. It was in the singular tenets of Chivalry,—in the exalted, enthusiastic, and almost sanctimonious ideas connected with its duties,—in the singular balance which its institutions offered against the evils of the rude ages in which it arose, that we are to seek those peculiarities which render it so worthy of our attention. . . .

In every age and country valour is held in esteem, and the more rude the period and the place, the greater respect is paid to boldness of enterprise and success in battle. But it was peculiar to the institution of Chivalry, to blend military valour with the strongest passions which actuate the human mind, the feelings of devotion and those of love. The Greeks and Romans fought for liberty or for conquest, and the knights of the middle ages for God and for their ladies. Loyalty to their sovereigns was a duty also incumbent upon these warriors, but although a powerful motive, and by which they often appear to have been strongly actuated, it entered less warmly into the composition of the chivalrous principle than the two preceding causes. Of patriotism, considered as a distinct predilection to the interests of one kingdom, we find comparatively few traces in the institutions of knighthood. But the love of personal freedom, and the obligation to maintain and defend it in the persons of others as in their own, was a duty particularly incumbent on those who attained the honour of chivalry. Generosity, gallantry, and an unblemished reputation, were no less necessary ingredients in the character of a perfect knight. He was not called upon simply to practise these virtues when opportunity offered, but to be sedulous and unwearied in searching for the means of exercising them, and to push them without hesitation to the brink of extravagance, or even beyond it. Founded on principles so pure, the order of chivalry could not, in the abstract at least, but occasion a pleasing, though a romantic developement of the energies of human nature. But as, in actual practice, every institution becomes deteriorated and degraded, we have too much occasion to remark, that the devotion of the knights often degenerated into superstition,—their love into licentiousness,—their spirit of loyalty or of freedom into tyranny and turmoil,—their generosity and gallantry into hairbrained madness and absurdity.

We have mentioned devotion as a principal feature in the character of chivalry. At what remote period the forms of chivalry were first blended with those of the Christian religion, would be a long and difficult inquiry. The religion which breathes nothing but love to our neighbour and forgiveness of injuries, was not, in its primitive purity, easily transferable into the warlike and military institutions of the Goths, the Franks, and the Saxons. At its first infusion, it appeared to soften the character of the people among whom it was introduced so much, as to render them less warlike than their heathen neighbours. Thus the pagan Danes ravaged England when inhabited by the Christian Saxons,—the heathen Normans conquered Neustria from the Franks,—the converted Goths were subdued by the sword of the heathen Huns,—the Visigoths of Spain fell before the Saracens. But the tide soon turned. As the necessity of military talent and courage became evident, the Christian religion was used by its ministers (justly and wisely so far as respected self-defence) as an additional spur to the temper of the valiant. Those books of the Old Testament which Ulphilas declined to translate, because they afforded too much fuel for the military zeal of the ancient Goths, were now commented upon to animate the sinking courage of their descendants. Victory and glory on earth, and a happy immortality after death, were promised to those champions who should distinguish themselves in battle against the infidels. And who shall blame the preachers who held such language, when it is remembered that the Saracens had at one time nearly possessed themselves of Aquitaine, and that but for the successful valour of Charles Martel, Pepin, and Charlemagne, the crescent might have dispossessed the cross of the fairest portion of Europe. The fervent sentiments of devotion which direct men's eyes toward heaven, were then justly invoked to unite with those which are most valuable on earth,—the love of our country and its liberties.

But the Romish clergy, who have in all ages possessed the wisdom of serpents, if they sometimes have fallen short of the simplicity of doves, saw the advantage of converting this temporary zeal, which animated the warriors of their creed against the invading infidels, into a permanent union of principles, which should blend the ceremonies of religious worship with the military establishment of the ancient Goths and Germans. The admission of the noble youth to the practice of arms was no longer a mere military ceremony, where the sword or javelin was delivered to him in presence of the prince or elders of his tribe; it became a religious rite, sanctified by the forms of the church which he was in future to defend. The novice had to watch his arms in a church or chapel, or at least on hallowed ground, the night before he had received the honour of knighthood. He was made to assume a white dress, in imitation of the Neophytes of the church. Fast and confession were added to vigils, and the purification of the bath was imposed on the military acolyte, in imitation of the initiatory rite of Christianity; and he was attended by godfathers, who became security for his performing his military vows, as sponsors had formerly appeared for him at baptism. In all points of ceremonial, the investiture of chivalry was brought to resemble, as nearly as possible, the administration of the sacraments of the church. The ceremony itself was performed, where circumstances would admit, in a church or cathedral, and the weapons with which the young warrior was invested were previously blessed by the priest. The oath of chivalry bound the knight to defend the rights of the holy church, to respect religious persons and institutions, and to obey the precepts of the gospel. Nay, more, so intimate was the union betwixt chivalry and religion supposed to be, that the several gradations of the former were seriously considered as parallel to those of the church, and the knight was supposed to resemble the bishop in rank, duties, and privileges. At what period this complete infusion of religious ceremonial into an order purely military first commenced, and when it became complete and perfect, would be a curious but a difficult subject of investigation. Down to the reign of Charlemagne, and somewhat lower, the investiture was of a nature purely civil; but long before the time of the crusades, it had assumed the religious character we have described. . . .

The next ingredient in the spirit of Chivalry, second in force only to the religious zeal of its professors, and frequently predominating over it, was a devotion to the female sex, and particularly to her whom each knight selected as the chief object of his affection, of a nature so extravagant and unbounded as to approach to a sort of idolatry.

The original source of this sentiment is to be found, like that of Chivalry itself, in the customs and habits of the northern tribes, who possessed, even in their rudest state, so many honourable and manly distinctions, over all the other nations in the same stage of society. The chaste and temperate habits of these youth, and the opinion that it was dishonourable to hold sexual intercourse until the twentieth year was attained, was in the highest degree favourable not only to the morals and health of the ancient Germans, but must have contributed greatly to place the females in that dignified and respectable rank which they held in society. Nothing tends so much to blunt the feelings, to harden the heart, and to destroy the imagination, as the worship of the Vaga Venus in early youth. Wherever women have been considered as the early, willing, and accommodating slaves of the voluptuousness of the other sex, their character has become degraded, and they have sunk into domestic drudges and bondswomen among the poor,—the slaves of a haram among the more wealthy. On the other hand, the men, easily and early sated with indulgences, which soon lose their poignancy when the senses only are interested, become first indifferent, then harsh and brutal to the unfortunate slaves of their pleasures. The sated lover,—and perhaps it is the most brutal part of humanity,—is soon converted into the capricious tyrant, like the successful seducer of the modern poet.

> "Hard! with their fears and terrors to behold
> The cause of all, the faithless lover cold,
> Impatient grown at every wish denied,
> And barely civil, soothed and gratified."
>
> Crabbe's *Borough,* p. 213. . . .

After the love of God and of his lady, the Preux Chevalier was to be guided by that of glory and renown. He was bound by his vow to seek out adventures of risk and peril, and never to abstain from the quest which he might undertake, for any unexpected odds of opposition which he might encounter. It was not indeed the sober and regulated exercise of valour, but its fanaticism, which the genius of chivalry demanded of its followers. Enterprizes the most extravagant in conception, the most difficult in execution, the most useless when achieved, were those by which an adventurous knight chose to distinguish himself. There were solemn occasions also, on which these displays of chivalrous enthusiasm were specially expected and called for. It is only sufficient to name the tournaments, single combats, and solemn banquets, at which vows of chivalry were usually formed and proclaimed. . . .

The third and highest rank of chivalry was that of Knighthood. In considering this last dignity, we shall first inquire, how it was conferred; secondly, the general privileges and duties of the order; thirdly, the peculiar ranks into which it was finally divided, and the difference betwixt them.

Knighthood was, in its origin, an order of a republican, or at least an oligarchic nature; arising, as has been shown, from the customs of the free tribes of Germany, and, in its essence, not requiring the sanction of a monarch. On the contrary, each knight could confer the order of knighthood upon whomsoever preparatory noviciate and probation had fitted to receive it. The highest potentates sought the *accolade,* or stroke which conferred the honour, at the hands of the worthiest knight whose achievements had dignified the period. Thus Francis I. requested the celebrated Bayard, the *Good Knight without reproach or fear,* to make him; an honour which Bayard valued so highly, that, on sheathing his sword, he vowed never more to use that blade, except against Turks, Moors, and Saracens. The same principle was carried to extravagance in a romance, where the hero is knighted by the hand of Sir Lancelot of the Lake, when dead. A sword was put into the hand of the skeleton, which was so guided as to let it drop on the neck of the aspirant. In the time of Francis I. it had already become customary to desire this honour at the hands of greatness rather than valour, so that the King's request was considered as an appeal to the first principles of chivalry. In theory, however, the power of creating knights was supposed to be inherent in every one who had reached that dignity. But it was natural that the soldier should desire to receive the highest military honour from the general under whose eye he was to combat, or from the prince or noble at whose court he passed as page and squire through the gradations of his noviciate. It was equally desirable, on the other hand, that the prince or noble should desire to be the immediate source of a privilege so important. And thus, though no positive regulation took place on the subject, ambition on the part of the aspirant, and pride and policy on that of the sovereign princes and nobles of high rank, gradually limited to the latter the power of conferring knighthood, or drew at least an unfavourable distinction between the knights dubbed by private individuals, and those who, with more state and solemnity, received the honoured title at the hand of one of high rank. Indeed, the change which took place respecting the character and consequences of the ceremony, naturally led to a limitation in the right of conferring it. While the order of knighthood merely implied a right to wear arms of a certain description, and to bear a certain title, there could be little harm in entrusting, to any one who had already received the honour, the power of conferring it on others. But when this highest order of chivalry conferred not only personal dignity, but the right of assembling under the banner, or pennon, a certain number of soldiers, when knighthood implied not merely personal privileges, but military rank, it was natural that sovereigns should use every effort to concentrate the right of conferring such distinction in themselves, or their immediate delegates. And latterly it was held, that the rank of knight only conferred those privileges on such as were dubbed by sovereign princes. . . .

The weapons of offence, however, most appropriate to knighthood were the lance and sword. They had frequently a battle axe or mace at their saddlebow, a formidable weapon even to men sheathed in iron like themselves. The knight had also a dagger which he used when at close quarters. It was called the dagger of mercy, probably because, when unsheathed, it behoved the antagonist to crave mercy or to die. The management of the lance and of the horse was the principal requisite of knighthood. To strike the foeman either on the helmet or full upon the breast with the point of the lance, and at full speed, was accounted perfect practice; to miss him, or to break a lance across, *i.e.* athwart the body of the antagonist, without striking him with the point, was accounted an awkward failure; to strike his horse, or to hurt his person under the girdle, was conceived a foul or felon action, and could only be excused by the hurry of a general encounter. When the knights, from the nature of the ground, or other circumstances, alighted to fight on foot, they used to cut some part from the length of their spears, in order to render them more manageable, like the pikes used by infantry. But their most formidable onset was when mounted and "in host." They seem then to have formed squadrons not unlike the present disposition of cavalry in the field,—their squires forming the rear-rank, and performing the part of serrefiles. As the horses were trained in the tourneys and exercises to run upon each other without flinching, the shock of two such bodies of heavy-armed cavalry was dreadful, and the event usually decided the battle; for, until the Swiss showed the superior steadiness which could be exhibited by infantry, all great actions were decided by the men at arms. The yeomanry of England, indeed, formed a singular exception; and, from the dexterous use of the long bow, to which they were trained from infancy, were capable of withstanding and destroying the mail-clad chivalry both of France and Scotland. Their shafts, according to the exaggerating eloquence of a monkish historian, Thomas of Walsingham, penetrated steel coats from side to side, transfixed helmets, and even splintered lances and pierced through swords! But, against every other pedestrian adversary, the knights, squires, and men-at-arms had the most decided advantage, from their impenetrable armour, the strength of their horses, and the fury of their onset. To render success yet more certain, and attack less hazardous, the horse, on the safety of which the riders so much depended, was armed en-barbe, as it was called, like himself. A masque made of iron covered the animal's face and ears; it had a breast-plate, and armour for the croupe. The strongest horses were selected for this service; they were generally stallions, and to ride a mare was reckoned base and unknightly. . . .

We are arrived at the third point proposed in our arrangement, the causes, namely, of the decay and extinction of Chivalry.

The spirit of chivalry sunk gradually under a combination of physical and moral causes; the first arising from the change gradually introduced into the art of war, and the last from the equally great alteration produced by time in the habits and modes of thinking in modern Europe. Chivalry began to dawn in the end of the tenth, and beginning of the eleventh century. It blazed forth with high vigour during the Crusades, which indeed may be considered as exploits of national knight-errantry, or general wars, undertaken on the very principles which actuated the conduct of individual knights adventurers. But its most brilliant period was during the wars between France and England, and it was unquestionably in those kingdoms, that the habit of constant and honourable opposition, unembittered by rancour or personal hatred, gave the fairest opportunity for the exercise of the virtues required from him whom Chaucer terms a very perfect gentle knight. Froissart frequently makes allusions to the generosity exercised by the French and English to their prisoners, and contrasts it with the dungeons to which captives taken in war were consigned, both in Spain and Germany. Yet both these countries, and indeed every kingdom in Europe, partook of the spirit of Chivalry in a greater or less degree; and even the Moors of Spain caught the emulation, and had their orders of knighthood as well as the Christians. But, even during this splendid period, various causes were silently operating the future extinction of the flame, which blazed thus wide and brightly.

An important discovery, the invention of gunpowder had taken place, and was beginning to be used in war, even when chivalry was in its highest glory. It is said Edward III. had field-pieces at the battle of Cressy, and the use of guns is mentioned even earlier. But the force of gunpowder was long known and used, ere it made any material change in the art of war. The long-bow continued to be the favourite, and it would seem the more formidable missile weapon, for well nigh two centuries after guns had been used in war. Still every successive improvement was gradually rendering the invention of fire arms more perfect, and their use more decisive of the fate of battle. In proportion as they came into general use, the suits of defensive armour began to be less generally worn. It was found, that these cumbrous defences, however efficient against lances, swords, and arrows, afforded no effectual protection against these more forcible missiles. The armour of the knight was gradually curtailed to a light head-piece, a cuirass, and the usual defences of men-at-arms. Complete harness was only worn by generals and persons of high rank, and that rather, it would seem, as a point of dignity than for real utility. The young nobility of France, especially, tired of the unwieldy steel coats in which their ancestors sheathed themselves, and adopted the slender and light armour of the German Reiters or mercenary cavalry. They also discontinued the use of the lance; in both cases, contrary to the injunctions of Henry IV. and the opinion of Sully. At length, the arms of the cavalry were changed almost in every particular from those which were proper to chivalry; and as, in such cases, much depends upon outward show and circumstance, the light armed cavalier, who did not carry the weapons, or practice the exercises of knighthood, laid aside, at the same time, the habits and sentiments peculiar to the order. . . .

The system, as we have seen, had its peculiar advantages during the middle ages. Its duties were not, and indeed could not always be performed in perfection, but they had a strong influence on public opinion; and we cannot doubt that its institutions, virtuous as they were in principle, and honourable and generous in their ends, must have done much good and prevented much evil. We can now only look back on it as a beautiful and fantastic piece of frostwork, which has dissolved in the beams of the sun! But though we look in vain for the pillars, the vaults, the cornices, and the fretted ornaments of the transitory fabric, we cannot but be sensible that its dissolution has left on the soil valuable tokens of its former existence. We do not mean, nor is it necessary to trace, the slight shades of chivalry, which are yet received in the law of England. An appeal to combat in a case of treason, was adjudged in the celebrated case of Ramsay and Lord Reay, in the time of Charles I. An appeal of murder seems to have been admitted as legal within the last year, and is perhaps still under decision. But it is not in such issues, rare as they must be, that we ought to trace the consequences of chivalry. We have already shown, that its effects are rather to be sought in the general feeling of respect to the female sex; in the rules of forbearance and decorum in society; in the duties of speaking truth and observing courtesy; and in the general conviction and assurance, that, as no man can encroach upon the property of another without accounting to the laws, so none can infringe on his personal honour, be the difference of rank what it may, without subjecting himself to personal responsibility.

GEORGE BERNARD SHAW

ON

Socialism

This forceful, almost hortatory essay appeared in the 13th edition (1926) and was so highly regarded that it was carried over into the 14th (1929). The article is nearly as interesting read between the lines, for there much is suggested about the general state of the world in the 1920s. Shaw, by the way, was proud to point out that in his youth he had read the 9th edition in its entirety, excepting only the scientific articles. (R. McH.)

We reproduce the whole of this piece by G. B. S. (1856–1950) for two reasons. First, it is a superb piece of writing. Second, in view of socialism's contemporary disarray, it is alive with an accidental irony Shaw could not possibly have foreseen.

Socialism, reduced to its simplest legal and practical expression, means the complete discarding of the institution of private property by transforming it into public property, and the division of the resultant public income equally and indiscriminately among the entire population. Thus it reverses the policy of Capitalism, which means establishing private or "real" property to the utmost physically possible extent, and then leaving distribution of income to take care of itself. The change involves a complete moral *volte-face*. In Socialism private property is anathema, and equal distribution of income the first consideration. In capitalism private property is cardinal, and distribution left to ensue from the play of free contract and selfish interest on that basis, no matter what anomalies it may present.

I. Socialism never arises in the earlier phases of capitalism, as, for instance, among the pioneers of civilisation in a country where there is plenty of land available for private appropriation by the last comer. The distribution which results under such circumstances presents no wider departures from a rough equality than those made morally plausible by their association with exceptional energy and ability at the one extreme, and with obvious defects of mind and character or accidental hard luck, at the other. This phase, however, does not last long under modern conditions. All the more favourable sites are soon privately appropriated; and the later comers (provided by immigration or the natural growth of the population), finding no eligible land to appropriate, are obliged to live by hiring it at a rent from its owners, transforming the latter into a *rentier* class enjoying unearned incomes which increase continually with the growth of the population until the landed class becomes a money-lending or capitalist class also, capital being the name given to spare money. The resource of hiring land and spare money is open to those only who are sufficiently educated to keep accounts and manage businesses, most of whom spring from the proprietary class as younger sons. The rest have to live by being hired as labourers and artisans at weekly or daily wages; so that a rough division of society into an upper or proprietary class, a middle or employing and managing class, and a wage proletariat is produced. In this division the proprietary class is purely parasitic, consuming without producing. As the inexorable operation of the economic law of rent makes this class richer and richer as the population increases, its demand for domestic servants and for luxuries of all kinds creates parasitic enterprise and employment for the middle class and the proletariat, not only withdrawing masses of them from productive industry, but also fortifying itself politically by a great body of workers and employers who vote with the owners because they are as dependent on the owners' unearned incomes as the owners themselves.

Meanwhile the competition of employers for custom, which leads to the production of a dozen articles to satisfy the demand for one, leads to disastrous crises of feverish overproduction alternated with periods of bad trade ("booms" and "slumps"), making continuous employment of the proletariat impossible. When wages fall to a point at which saving also is impossible, the unemployed have no means of subsistence except public relief during the slumps.

It is in this phase of capitalistic development, attained in Great Britain in the 19th century, that socialism arises as a revolt against a distribution of wealth that has lost all its moral plausibility. Colossal wealth is associated with unproductiveness, and sometimes with conspicuous worthlessness of character; and lifetimes of excessive toil beginning in early childhood leave the toiler so miserably poor that the only refuge left for old age is a general workhouse, purposely made repulsive to deter proletarians from resorting to it as long as they have strength enough left for the most poorly paid job in the labour market. The inequalities become monstrous: hardworking men get four or five shillings a day (post-War rates) in full view of persons who get several thousands a day without any obligation to work at all, and even consider industrial work degrading. Such variations in income defy all attempts to relate them to variations in personal merit. Governments are forced to intervene and readjust distribution to some extent by confiscating larger and larger percentages of incomes derived from property (income tax, supertax, and estate duties) and applying the proceeds to unemployment insurance and extensions of communal services, besides protecting the proletariat against the worst extremities of oppression by an elaborate factory code which takes the control of workshops and factories largely out of the hands of their proprietors, and makes it impossible for them to exact grossly excessive hours of labour from their employees or to neglect their health, physical safety, and moral welfare with complete selfishness.

This confiscation of private property incomes for public purposes without any pretence of compensation, which is now proceeding on a scale inconceivable by Victorian ministers, has destroyed the integrity of private property and inheritance; and the success with which the confiscated capital has been applied to communal industries by the municipalities and the central Government, contrasted with the many failures and comparative costliness of capitalist industrial adventure, has shaken superstition that private commercial management is always more effective and less corrupt than public management. In particular, the British attempt to depend on private industry for munitions during the War of 1914–8 nearly led to defeat; and the substitution of national factories was so sensationally successful, and the post-War resumption of private enterprise, after a brief burst of illusory prosperity, was followed by so distressing a slump, that the reversal of the relative efficiency prestige of socialism and capitalism was vigorously accelerated, leaving capitalism unpopular and on the defensive, whilst confiscation of private capital, communal enterprise, and nationalisation of the big industries, grew steadily in popularity in and out of Parliament.

This change in public opinion had already deeply penetrated the middle class, because of the change for the worse in the position of the ordinary employer. He, in the 19th century, was admittedly master of the industrial, and, after the Reform of 1832, of the political situation. He dealt directly and even domineeringly with the proprietary class, from which he hired his land and capital either directly or through agents who were his servants and not his masters. But the sums required to set on foot and develop modern industrial schemes grew until they were out of reach of ordinary employers. The collection of money to be used as capital became a special business, conducted by professional promoters and financiers. These experts, though they had no direct contact with industry, became so indispensable to it that they are now virtually the masters of the ordinary routine employers. Meanwhile the growth of joint-stock enterprise was substituting the employee-manager for the employer, and thus converting the old independent middle class into a proletariat, and pressing it politically to the left.

With every increase in the magnitude of the capital sums required for starting or extending large industrial concerns comes the need for an increase in the ability demanded by their management; and this the financiers cannot supply: indeed they bleed industry of middle class ability by attracting it into their own profession. Matters reach a point at which industrial management by the old-fashioned tradesman must be replaced by a professionally trained and educated bureaucracy; and as Capitalism does not provide such a bureaucracy, the industries tend to get into difficulties as they grow by combination (amalgamation), and thus outgrow the capacity of the managers who were able to handle them as separate units. This difficulty is increased by the hereditary element in business.

An employer may bequeath the control of an industry involving the subsistence of thousands of workers, and requiring from its chief either great natural ability and energy or considerable scientific and political culture, to his eldest son without being challenged to prove his son's qualifications, whilst if he proposes to make his second son a doctor or a naval officer he is peremptorily informed by the Government that only by undergoing an elaborate and prolonged training, and obtaining official certificates of qualification, can his son be permitted to assume such responsibilities. Under these circumstances, much of the management and control of industry gets divided between routine employers who do not really understand their own businesses, and financiers, who, having never entered a factory nor descended a mine shaft, do not understand any business except the business of collecting money to be used as capital, and forcing it into industrial adventures at all hazards, the result being too often reckless and senseless over-capitalisation, leading to bankruptcies (disguised as reconstructions) which reveal the most astonishing technical ignorance and economic blindness on the part of men in high repute as directors of huge industrial combinations, who draw large fees as the remuneration of a mystical ability which exists only in the imagination of the shareholders.

II. All this steadily saps the moral plausibility of capitalism. The loss of popular faith in it has gone much further than the gain of any widespread or intelligent faith in socialism. Consequently the end of the first quarter of the 20th century finds the political situation in Europe confused and threatening: all the political parties diagnosing dangerous social disease, and most of them proposing disastrous remedies. National governments, no matter what ancient party slogans they raise, find themselves controlled by financiers who follow the slot of gigantic international usuries without any public aims, and without any technical qualifications except their familiarity with a rule-of-thumb city routine quite inapplicable to public affairs, because it deals exclusively with stock exchange and banking categories of capital and credit. These, though valid in the money market when conducting exchanges of future incomes for spare ready money by the small minority of persons who have these luxuries to deal in, would vanish under pressure of any general political measure like —to take a perilously popular and plausible example—a levy on capital. Such a levy would produce a money market in which there were all sellers and no buyers, sending the Bank Rate up to infinity, breaking the banks, and bringing industry to a standstill by the transfer of all the cash available for wages to the national treasury. Unfortunately the parliamentary proletarian parties understand this as little as their capitalist opponents. They clamour for taxation of capital; and the capitalists, instead of frankly admitting that capital as they reckon it is a phantom, and that the assumption that a person with an income of £5 a year represents to the state an immediately available asset of £100 ready money, though it may work well enough as between a handful of investors and spendthrifts in a stockbroker's office, is pure fiction when applied to a whole nation, ignorantly defend their imaginary resources as if they really existed, and thus confirm the proletariat in its delusion instead of educating it.

The financiers have their own *ignis fatuus,* which is that they can double the capital of the country, and thus give an immense stimulus to industrial development and production, by inflating the currency until prices rise to a point at which goods formerly marked £50 are marked £100, a measure which does nothing nationally but enable every debtor to cheat his creditor, and every insurance company and pension fund to reduce by half the provision for which it has been paid. The history of inflation in Europe since the War of 1914–8, and the resultant impoverishment of pensioners and officials with small fixed incomes, forces the middle classes to realise the appalling consequences of abandoning finance and industry direction to the unskilled, politically ignorant, unpatriotic "practical business men."

Meanwhile, the nobility of capital leads to struggles for the possession of exploitable foreign territories ("places in the sun") produces war on a scale which threatens not only civilisation but human existence; for the old field combats between bodies of soldiers, from which women were shielded, are now replaced by attacks from the air on the civil population, in which women and men are slaughtered indiscriminately, making replacement of the killed impossible. The emotional reaction after such wars takes the form of acute disillusion, which further accelerates the moral revolt against capitalism, without unfortunately, producing any workable conception of an alternative. The proletarians are cynically sulky, no longer believing in the disinterestedness of those who appeal to them to make additional efforts and sacrifices to repair the waste of war. The moral mainspring of the private property system is broken; and it is the confiscations of unearned income, the extensions of municipal and national communism, above all, the new subsidies in aid of wages extorted from governments by threats of nationally disastrous lock-outs and strikes, which induce the proletariat to continue operating the capitalist system now that the old compulsion to work by imposing starvation as the alternative, fundamental in capitalism, has had to be discarded in its primitive ruthlessness. The worker who refuses to work can now quarter himself on public relief (which means finally on confiscated property income) to an extent formerly impossible.

Democracy, or votes for everybody, does not produce constructive solutions of social problems; nor does compulsory schooling help much. Unbounded hopes were based on each successive extension of the electoral franchise, culminating in the enfranchisement of women. These hopes have been disappointed, because the voters, male and female, being politically untrained and uneducated, have (*a*) no grasp of constructive measures, (*b*) loathe taxation as such, (*c*) dislike being governed at all, and (*d*) dread and resent any extension of official interference as an encroachment on their personal liberty. Compulsory schooling, far from enlightening them, inculcates the sacredness of private property, and stigmatises a distributive state as criminal and disastrous, thereby continually renewing the old public opinion against socialism, and making impossible a national education dogmatically inculcating as first principles the iniquity of private property, the paramount social importance of equality of income and the criminality of idleness.

Consequently, in spite of disillusion with capitalism, and the growing menace of failing trade and falling currencies, our democratic parliamentary Oppositions, faced with the fact that the only real remedy involves increased taxation, compulsory reorganisation or frank nationalisation of the bankrupt industries, and compulsory national service in civil as in military life for all classes, dare not confront their constituents with such proposals, knowing that on increased taxation alone they would lose their seats. To escape responsibility, they look to the suppression of parliamentary institutions by *coups d'état* and dictatorships, as in Italy, Spain and Russia. This despair of parliamentary institutions is a striking novelty in the present century; but it has failed to awaken the democratic electorates to the fact that, having after a long struggle gained the power to govern, they have neither the knowledge nor the will to exercise it, and are in fact using their votes to keep Government parochial when civilisation is bursting the dikes of nationality in all directions.

A more effective resistance to property arises from the organisation of the proletariat in trade unions to resist the effect of increase of population in cheapening labour and increasing its duration and severity. But trade unionism is itself a phase of capitalism, inasmuch as it applies to labour as a commodity that principle of selling in the dearest market, and giving as little as possible for the price, which was formerly applied only to land, capital and merchandise. Its method is that of a civil war between labour and capital in which the decisive battles are lock-outs and strikes, with intervals of minor adjustment by industrial diplomacy. Trade unionism now maintains a Labour party in the British Parliament. The most popular members and leaders are socialists in theory; so that there is always a paper programme of nationalisation of industries and of banking, taxation of unearned incomes to extinction, and other incidentals of a transition to socialism; but the trade union driving force aims at nothing more than capitalism with labour taking the lion's share, and energetically repudiates compulsory national service, which would deprive it of its power to strike. In this it is heartily seconded by the proprietary parties, which, though willing enough to make strikes illegal and proletarian labour compulsory, will not pay the price of surrendering its own power to idle. Compulsory national service being essential in socialism, it is thus deadlocked equally by organised labour and by capitalism.

It is a historic fact, recurrent enough to be called an economic law, that capitalism, which builds up great civilisations, also wrecks them if persisted in beyond a certain point. It is easy to demonstrate on paper that civilisation can be saved and immensely developed by, at the right moment, discarding capitalism and changing the private property profiteering state into the common property distributive state. But though the moment for the change has come again and again it has never been effected, because capitalism has never produced the necessary enlightenment among the masses, nor admitted to a controlling share in public affairs the order of intellect and character outside which Socialism, or indeed politics, as distinguished from mere party electioneering, is incomprehensible. Not until the two main tenets of socialism: abolition of private property (which must not be confused with personal property), and equality of income, have taken hold of the people as religious dogmas, as to which no controversy is regarded as sane, will a stable socialist state be possible. It should be observed, however, that of the two tenets, the need for equality of income is not the more difficult to demonstrate, because no other method of distribution is or ever has been possible. Omitting the few conspicuous instances in which actual earners of money make extraordinary fortunes by exceptional personal gifts or strokes of luck, the existing differences of income among workers are not individual but corporate differences. Within the corporation no discrimination between individuals is possible; all common labourers, like all upper division civil servants, are equally paid. The argument for equalising the class incomes are that unequal distribution of purchasing power upsets the proper order of economic production, causing luxuries to be produced on an extravagant scale whilst the primitive vital needs of the people are left unsatisfied; that its effect on marriage, by limiting and corrupting sexual selection, is highly dysgenic; that it reduces religion, legislation, education and the administration of justice to absurdity as between rich and poor; and that it creates an idolatry of riches and idleness which inverts all sane social morality.

Unfortunately, these are essentially public considerations. The private individual, with the odds overwhelmingly against him as a social climber, dreams even in the deepest poverty of some bequest or freak of fortune by which he may become a capitalist, and dreads that the little he has may be snatched from him by that terrible and unintelligible thing, state policy. Thus the private person's vote is the vote of Ananias and Sapphira; and democracy becomes a more effective bar to socialism than the pliant and bewildered conservatism of the plutocracy. Under such conditions the future is unpredictable. Empires end in ruins: commonwealths have hitherto been beyond the civic capacity of mankind. But there is always the possibility that mankind will this time weather the cape on which all the old civilisations have been wrecked. It is this possibility that gives intense interest to the present historic moment, and keeps the Socialist movement alive and militant.

ROBERT LOUIS STEVENSON

ON

Pierre Jean de Béranger

Robert Louis Stevenson (1850–1894) was a young Edinburgh writer of modest promise as publication of the 9th edition (1875–1889) was getting under way. He contributed a couple of biographies, one of which, on Robert Burns, was paid for but not used. The other dealt with Béranger. (B.L.F.)

Britannica*'s current edition accords four paragraphs to Béranger. They are clear, sensible, and adjusted to the modest proportions of their subject. They are properly encyclopedic. Stevenson is not properly encyclopedic. All he could do, poor man, was produce a minor and pleasing work of art. It is such simple juxtapositions that on occasion make one feel forcibly the difference between a good academic and a good writer.*

Béranger, Pierre Jean de, the national song-writer of France, was born at Paris on the 19th August 1780. The aristocratic particle before the name was a piece of groundless vanity on the part of his father, which the poet found useful as a distinction. He was descended, in truth, from a country innkeeper on the one side, and, on the other, from a tailor in the Rue Montorgueil. Of education, in the narrower sense, he had but little. From the roof of his first school he beheld the capture of the Bastille, and this stirring memory was all that he acquired. Later on he passed some time in a school at Péronne, founded by one Bellenglise on the principles of Rousseau, where the boys were formed into clubs and regiments, and taught to play solemnly at politics and war. Béranger was president of the club, made speeches before such members of Convention as passed through Péronne, and drew up addresses to Tallien or Robespierre at Paris. In the meanwhile he learned neither Greek nor Latin—not even French, it would appear; for it was after he left school, from the printer Laisney, that he acquired the elements of grammar. His true education was of another sort. In his childhood, shy, sickly, and skilful with his hands, as he sat at home alone to carve cherry stones, he was already forming for himself those habits of retirement and patient elaboration which influenced the whole tenor of his life and the character of all that he wrote. At Péronne he learned of his good aunt to be a stout republican; and from the doorstep of her inn, on quiet evenings, he would listen to the thunder of the guns before Valenciennes, and fortify himself in his passionate love of France and distaste for all things foreign. Although he could never read Horace save in a translation, he had been educated on *Telemaque,* Racine, and the dramas of Voltaire, and taught, from a child, in the tradition of all that is highest and most correct in French.

After serving his aunt for some time in the capacity of waiter, and passing some time also in the printing office of one Laisney, he was taken to Paris by his father. Here he saw much low speculation and many low royalist intrigues. In 1802, in consequence of a distressing quarrel, he left his father and began life for himself in the garret of his ever memorable song. For two years he did literary hackwork, when he could get it, and wrote pastorals, epics, and all manner of ambitious failures. At the end of that period (1804) he wrote to Lucien Bonaparte, enclosing some of these attempts. He was then in bad health, and in the last stage of misery. His watch was pledged. His wardrobe consisted of one pair of boots, one greatcoat, one pair of trousers with a hole in the knee, and "three bad shirts which a friendly hand wearied itself in endeavouring to mend." The friendly hand was that of Judith Frère, with whom he had been already more or less acquainted since 1796, and who continued to be his faithful companion until her death, three months before his own, in 1857. She must not be confounded with the Lisette of the songs; the pieces addressed to her (*La Bonne Vieille, Maudit Printemps,* etc.) are in a very different vein. Lucien Bonaparte interested himself in the young poet, transferred to him his own pension of 1000 francs from the Institute, and set him to work on a *Death of Nero*. Five years later, through the same patronage, although indirectly, Béranger became a clerk in the university at a salary of another thousand.

Meanwhile he had written many songs for convivial occasions, and "to console himself under all misfortunes;" some, according to M. Boiteau, had been already published by his father; but he set no great store on them himself; and it was only in 1812, while watching by the sick-bed of a friend, that it occurred to him to write down the best he could remember. Next year he was elected to the *Caveau Moderne,* and his reputation as a song-writer began to spread. Manuscript copies of *Les Gueux, Le Sénateur,* above all of *Le Roi d' Yvetot,* a satire against Napoleon, whom he was to magnify so much in the sequel, passed from hand to hand with acclamation. It was thus that all his best works went abroad; one man sang them to another over all the land of France. He was the only poet of modern times who could altogether have dispensed with printing.

His first collection escaped censure. "We must pardon many things to the author of the *Roi d' Yvetot,*" said Louis XVIII. The second (1821) was more daring. The apathy of the Liberal camp, he says, had convinced him of the need for some bugle call of awakening. This publication lost him his situation in the university, and subjected him to a trial, a fine of 500 francs, and an imprisonment of three months. Imprisonment was a small affair for Béranger. At Sainte Pélagie he occupied a room (it had just been quitted by Paul Louis Courier), warm, well-furnished, and preferable in every way to his own poor lodging, where the water froze on winter nights. He adds, on the occasion of his second imprisonment, that he found a certain charm in this quiet, claustral existence, with its regular hours and long evenings alone over the fire. This second imprisonment of nine months, together with a fine and expenses amounting to 1100 francs, followed on the appearance of his fourth collection. The Government proposed through Laffitte that, if he would submit to judgment without appearing or making defences, he should only be condemned in the smallest penalty. But his public spirit made him refuse the proposal; and he would not even ask permission to pass his term of imprisonment in a *Maison de Santé,* although his health was more than usually feeble at the time. "When you have taken your stand in a contest with Government, it seems to me," he wrote, "ridiculous to complain of the blows it inflicts on you, and impolitic to furnish it with any occasion of generosity." His first thought in La Force was to alleviate the condition of the other prisoners.

In the revolution of July he took no inconsiderable part. Copies of his song, *Le Vieux Drapeau,* were served out to the insurgent crowd. He had been for long the intimate friend and adviser of the leading men; and during the decisive week his counsels went a good way towards shaping the ultimate result. "As for the republic, that dream of my whole life," he wrote in 1831, "I did not wish it should be given to us a second time unripe." Louis Philippe, hearing how much the song-writer had done towards his elevation, expressed a wish to see and speak with him; but Béranger refused to present himself at court, and used his favour only to ask a place for a friend, and a pension for Rouget de l'Isle, author of the famous *Marseillaise,* who was now old and poor, and whom he had been already succouring for five years.

In 1848, in spite of every possible expression of his reluctance, he was elected to the assembly, and that by so large a number of votes (4471) that he felt himself obliged to accept the office. Not long afterwards, and with great difficulty, he obtained leave to resign. This was the last public event of Béranger's life. He continued to polish his songs in retirement, visited by nearly all the famous men of France. He numbered among his friends Chateaubriand, Thiers, Laffitte, Michelet, Lamennais, Mignet. Nothing could exceed the amiability of his private character; so poor a man has rarely been so rich in good actions; he was always ready to receive help from his friends when he was in need, and always forward to help others. His correspondence is full of wisdom and kindness, with a smack of Montaigne, and now and then a vein of pleasantry that will remind the English reader of Charles Lamb. He occupied some of his leisure in preparing his own memoirs, and a certain treatise on *Social and Political Morality,* intended for the people, a work he had much at heart, but judged at last to be beyond his strength. He died on the 16th July 1857. It was feared that his funeral would be the signal for some political disturbance; but the Government took immediate measures, and all went quietly. The streets of Paris were lined with soldiers and full of townsfolk, silent and uncovered. From time to time cries arose—*"Honneur, Honneur à Béranger!"*

LEE STRASBERG
ON
Acting

The Britannica *paid careful attention to what transpired on the other side of the footlights, securing, as was usual from the time of the Supplement, eminent authorities to do the writing. The distinguished actor and teacher of actors, Lee Strasberg (1901–1982), who became famous for his adoption of "the method" from the great founder of the Russian Art Theatre, Stanislavsky, wrote on acting and on the master's role. The subjoined is from the article "Acting, Directing and Production," 14th edition (1929; it first appeared in the 1959 printing). (B.L.F.)*

In this excerpt Strasberg seems somewhat doctrinaire. But he must not be held entirely responsible for the creative mutter of Marlon Brando. The whole article, much of it wisely retained in the 15th edition, bears witness to the breadth of his knowledge and the flexibility of his sympathies. It is a good example of the wisdom that impels Britannica*'s editors so frequently to seek writers outside academia, though the trained scholar must always remain the backbone of any responsible encyclopedia.*

Constantine Stanislavsky (1863–1938) set himself to fuse all the random thought and experiences into a form that could help the beginner and be of service to the experienced actor. His aim was to find a "grammar of acting," to achieve that level of inspiration, or of living on stage, which great actors had found accidentally and sporadically. Without minimizing the value of voice, speech and body training, which are the actor's tools, Stanislavsky tried to find means to stimulate and develop the actor's essential requirements: his concentration, his belief and his imagination. He did not seek to fabricate inspiration, but to create the proper foundation for its appearance.

The actor, according to Stanislavsky, should come on the stage not to play-act but to perform the activities required of the character, to act. His appearance on the stage is not the beginning, but is a continuation of the given circumstances that have previously taken place. The actor trains his concentration so that he is able to create the impression of being private in public. He trains his senses so that he is able to see, hear, touch, taste, smell and relate to the many objects which compose his imaginary situation. He learns to use not only intellectual knowledge but emotional experience by means of affective memory. Wordsworth has defined poetry as originating in "emotion recollected in tranquillity." Shaw emphasized that "vital art work comes from a cross between art and life." Thomas Wolfe in one of his short stories and Proust in a passage in *Swann's Way* have brilliantly described the workings of affective memory. It is not limited to the ability to recreate one's previously experienced real emotions, but also to learn to repeat previously experienced stage emotions. The actor's training of himself goes hand in hand with the actor's work on a role. The actor learns to delve beneath the lines to find the meaning or subtext of a play. He learns to find the "kernel" or core of a part, to find the actions of the character that define the important sections, to set smaller tasks or problems for his concentration throughout each section. In later years Stanislavsky tried to correct the overly intellectual approach of this part of the work by simplifying the action work in terms of physical or psychophysical actions. Some have interpreted this as a reversal of his previous methods. Actually, it was intended not to rule out or contrast with, but to serve as a life belt by means of which the previous preparation and work on a role could be securely held onto, like the notes of a melody.

ALGERNON CHARLES SWINBURNE

ON

Mary Queen of Scots

In the "scholars' edition," the famous 9th (1875–1889), the poet Algernon Charles Swinburne (1837–1909) wrote a passionate encomium in his biography of Mary Queen of Scots. Near the end he touched on Elizabeth's conduct in the execution of Mary and the latter's gallant comportment in facing her death.

Swinburne's devotion to the Scottish queen, so evident in this nine-page biography, was also reflected in his dramatic trilogy on her life, which he was about to complete with the play Mary Stuart *(1881) as he submitted the* Britannica *biography. An incidental stylistic note: The Mary Stuart biography in the 9th was written in enormous paragraphs, several of them three thousand or more words in length, i.e., occupying more than two two-column pages. (B.L.F.)*

Swinburne was given to what he called "the noble pleasure of praising." It is not a pleasure modern encyclopedia writers often indulge in, and so it is all the more interesting to observe it being exercised by a devotee like Swinburne. Some readers may well feel that he was a better poet than biographer.

As time passes, editorial policy changes. Today's Britannica *editors would be astonished by the very idea of sacrificing nine precious pages to Mary. But they were perhaps less judicious in the 1800s, and Swinburne's logorrhea might have intimidated them, and so they left the article uncut. The current edition devotes not quite three judicious and beautifully written columns to Mary, written by the acknowledged au-*

thority Antonia Fraser. Like Swinburne, she bears witness to her judgment that "public interest in this 16th century femme fatale remains unabated."

Here are Swinburne's terminal paragraphs:

Elizabeth, fearless almost to a fault in face of physical danger, constant in her confidence even after discovery of her narrow escape from the poisoned bullets of household conspirators, was cowardly even to a crime in face of subtler and more complicated peril. She rejected with resolute dignity the intercession of French envoys for the life of the queen-dowager of France; she allowed the sentence of death to be proclaimed, and welcomed with bonfires and bell-ringing throughout the length of England; she yielded a respite of twelve days to the pleading of the French ambassador, and had a charge trumped up against him of participation in a conspiracy against her life; at length, on the 1st of February 1587, she signed the death-warrant, and then made her secretaries write word to Paulet of her displeasure that in all this time he should not of himself have found out some way to shorten the life of his prisoner, as in duty bound by his oath, and thus relieve her singularly tender conscience from the guilt of bloodshed. Paulet, with loyal and regretful indignation, declined the disgrace proposed to him in a suggestion "to shed blood without law or warrant"; and on the 7th of February the earls of Shrewsbury and Kent arrived at Fotheringay with the commission of the council for execution of the sentence given against his prisoner. Mary received the announcement with majestic tranquillity, expressing in dignified terms her readiness to die, her consciousness that she was a martyr for her religion, and her total ignorance of any conspiracy against the life of Elizabeth. At night she took a graceful and affectionate leave of her attendants, distributed among them her money and jewels, wrote out in full the various legacies to be conveyed by her will, and charged her apothecary Gorion with her last messages for the king of Spain. In these messages the whole nature of the woman was revealed. Not a single friend, not a single enemy, was forgotten; the slightest service, the slightest wrong, had its place assigned in her faithful and implacable memory for retribution or reward. Forgiveness of injuries was as alien from her fierce and loyal spirit as forgetfulness of benefits; the destruction of England and its liberties by Spanish invasion and conquest was the strongest aspiration of her parting soul. At eight next morning she entered the hall of execution, having taken leave of the weeping envoy from Scotland, to whom she gave a brief message for her son; took her seat on the scaffold, listened with an air of even cheerful unconcern to the reading of her sentence, solemnly declared her innocence of the charge conveyed in it and her consolation in the prospect of ultimate justice, rejected the professional services of Richard Fletcher, dean of Peterborough, lifted up her voice in Latin against his in English prayer, and when he and his fellow-worshippers had fallen duly silent prayed aloud for the prosperity of her own church, for Elizabeth, for her son, and for all the enemies whom she had commended overnight to the notice of the Spanish invader; then, with no less courage than had marked every hour and every action of her life, received the stroke of death from the wavering hand of the headsman.

Mary Stuart was in many respects the creature of her age, of her creed, and of her station; but the noblest and most noteworthy qualities of her nature were independent of rank, opinion, or time. Even the detractors who defend her conduct on the plea that she was a dastard and a dupe are compelled in the same breath to retract this implied reproach, and to admit, with illogical acclamation and incongruous applause, that the world never saw more splendid courage at the service of more brilliant intelligence, that a braver if not "a rarer spirit never did steer humanity." A kinder or more faithful friend, a deadlier or more dangerous enemy, it would be impossible to dread or to desire. Passion alone could shake the double fortress of her impregnable heart and ever active brain. The passion of love, after very sufficient experience, she apparently and naturally outlived; the passion of hatred and revenge was as inextinguishable in her inmost nature as the emotion of loyalty and gratitude. Of repentance it would seem that she knew as little as of fear, having been trained from her infancy in a religion where the Decalogue was supplanted by the Creed. Adept as she was in the most exquisite delicacy of dissimulation, the most salient note of her original disposition was daring rather than subtlety.

Beside or behind the voluptuous or intellectual attractions of beauty and culture, she had about her the fresher charm of a fearless and frank simplicity, a genuine and enduring pleasure in small and harmless things no less than in such as were neither. In 1562 she amused herself for some days by living "with her little troop" in the house of a burgess of St Andrews "like a burgess's wife," assuring the English ambassador that he should not find the queen there,—"nor I know not myself where she is become." From Sheffield Lodge, twelve years later, she applied to the archbishop of Glasgow and the cardinal of Guise for some pretty little dogs, to be sent her in baskets very warmly packed,—"for besides reading and working, I take pleasure only in all the little animals that I can get." No lapse of reconciling time, no extent of comparative indulgence, could break her in to resignation, submission, or toleration of even partial restraint. Three months after the massacre of St Bartholomew had caused some additional restrictions to be placed upon her freedom of action, Shrewsbury writes to Burghley that "rather than continue this imprisonment she sticks not to say she will give her body, her son, and country for liberty"; nor did she ever show any excess of regard for any of the three. For her own freedom of will and of way, of passion and of action, she cared much; for her creed she cared something; for her country she cared less than nothing. She would have flung Scotland with England into the hellfire of Spanish Catholicism rather than forego the faintest chance of personal revenge. Her profession of a desire to be instructed in the doctrines of Anglican Protestantism was so transparently a pious fraud as rather to afford confirmation than to arouse suspicion of her fidelity to the teaching of her church. Elizabeth, so shamefully her inferior in personal loyalty, fidelity, and gratitude, was as clearly her superior on the one all-important point of patriotism. The saving salt of Elizabeth's character, with all its wellnigh incredible mixture of heroism and egotism, meanness and magnificence, was simply this, that, overmuch as she loved herself, she did yet love England better. Her best though not her only fine qualities were national and political, the high public virtues of a good public servant; in the private and personal qualities which attract and attach a friend to his friend and a follower to his leader, no man or woman was ever more constant and more eminent than Mary Queen of Scots.

ARNOLD TOYNBEE

ON

The Cycle of Time

In the current edition the Macropaedia *devotes almost twenty columns to "Time." Several writers contribute to the subject, but perhaps the most brilliant section is that by Arnold Toynbee, classicist and historian (1889–1975), on prescientific conceptions of time. Toynbee is best known for his twelve-volume* A Study of History *(1934–1961). This vast work, as impressive as it is controversial, examines the rise, flourishing, and (not inevitable) decline of twenty civilizations. Like the Huxleys, who appear elsewhere in this volume, the Toynbees are a distinguished family. Arnold was the nephew of the identically named nineteenth-century economist and social reformer, as well as the father of the experimental novelist Philip Toynbee. Arnold Toynbee's article is reproduced in its entirety from the current 15th edition.*

One facet of human consciousness is the awareness of time. Men feel the passage of time in their personal experience, both psychic and physical, and observe it in their environment, both human (social) and nonhuman (animate and inanimate). Time, as experienced, is a one-way flow at a pace that is slow enough to be perceptible. (Actually, only material fluids flow; but, like psychic experiences in general, that of time can be described only in the language of material phenomena.) Men feel and think in the time flow. They also act in it, either seizing opportunities or missing them.

The individual's experience and observation of time. The irreversibility and inexorability of the passage of time is borne in on a human being by the fact of death. Unlike other living creatures, he knows that his life may be cut short at any moment and that, even if he attains the full expectation of a human life, his growth is bound to be followed by eventual decay and, in due time, death.

Although there is no generally accepted evidence that death is not the conclusive end of life, it is a tenet of some religions (*e.g.*, of Zoroastrianism, Judaism, Christianity, and Islām) that death is followed by everlasting life elsewhere—in *sheol,* hell, or heaven—and that eventually there will be a universal physical resurrection. Others (*e.g.*, Buddhists, Orphics, Pythagoreans, and Plato) have held that people are reborn in the time flow of life on Earth and that the notion that a man has only one life on Earth is the illusion of a lost memory. It is said that the Buddha recollected all of his previous lives. The Greek philosophers Pythagoras and Empedocles, of the 6th and early 5th centuries BC, whose lives probably overlapped that of the Buddha, are likewise said to have recollected some of their previous lives. Such rebirths, they held, would continue to recur any number of times unless a person should succeed in breaking the vicious circle (releasing himself from the "sorrowful wheel") by strenuous ascetic performances.

The belief that a man's life in time on Earth is repetitive may have been an inference from the observed repetitiveness of phenomena in his environment. The day-and-night cycle and the annual cycle of the seasons dominated the conduct of human life until the recent harnessing of inanimate physical forces in the Industrial Revolution made it possible for work to be carried on for 24 hours a day throughout the year—under cover, by artificial light, and at an artificial temperature. There is also the generation cycle, which the Industrial Revolution has not suppressed: the generations still replace each other, in spite of the lengthening of life expectancies. In some societies it has been customary to give a man's son a different name but to give his grandson the same name. To name father and son differently is an admission that generations change; but to name grandfather and grandson the same is perhaps an intimation that the grandson is the grandfather reincarnate.

Thus, though every human being has the experience of irreversible change in his own life, he also observes cyclic change in his environment; hence the adherents of some religions and philosophies have inferred that, despite appearances, time flows cyclically for the individual human being, too.

The human experience and observation of time has been variously interpreted. Parmenides, an Italiote Greek (Eleatic) philosopher (6th–5th century BC) and Zeno, his fellow townsman and disciple, found that change is logically inconceivable and that logic is a surer indicator of reality than experience; thus, despite appearances, reality is unitary and motionless. In this view, time is an illusion. The illusoriness of the world that "flows" in time is also to be found in some Indian philosophy. The Buddha and, among the Greeks, Plato and Plotinus, all held that life in the time flow, though not wholly illusory, is at best a low-grade condition by comparison, respectively, with the Buddhist Nirvāṇa (in which desires are extinguished) and with the Platonic world of Ideas; *i.e.,* of incorporeal timeless exemplars, of which phenomena in the time flow are imperfect and ephemeral copies.

It has been held, however—*e.g.,* by disciples of the Greek philosopher Heracleitus—that the time flow is of the essence of reality. Others have held that life in the time flow, though it may be wretched, is nevertheless momentous; for it is here that a man decides his destiny. In the Buddhist view, a person's conduct in any one of his successive lives on Earth will increase or diminish his prospects of eventually breaking out of the cycle of recurrent births. For those who believe in only one earthly life, however, the momentousness of life in the time flow is still greater because this life will be followed by an everlasting life at a destination decided by conduct in this brief and painful testing time. The view that life in time on Earth is a probation for weal or woe in an everlasting future has often been associated—as it was by the Iranian prophet Zoroaster (*c.* 600 BC)—with a belief in a general judgment of all who have ever lived to be held on a common judgment day, which will be the end of time. The belief in an immediate individual judgment was also held in pharaonic Egypt. Both of these beliefs have been adopted by Jews, Christians, and Muslims.

Cyclic view of time in the philosophy of history. The foregoing diverse interpretations of the nature and significance of the individual human being's experience and observation of time differ sharply from each other, and they have led to equally sharp differences in views of human history and of ultimate reality and in prescriptions for the conduct, both collective and individual, of human life. Thinkers have been divided between holders of the cyclic view and holders of the one-way view of time and between believers in the different prescriptions for the conduct of life that these differing views have suggested. Variations in the two basic views of time and in the corresponding codes of conduct have been among the salient characteristics distinguishing the principal civilizations and philosophies and higher religions that have appeared in history to date.

Environmental Recurrences and Religion. The cyclic theory of time has been held in regard to the three fields of religion, of history (both human and cosmic), and of personal life. That this view arose from the observation of recurrences in man's environment is most conspicuously seen in the field of religion. The observation of the generation cycle has been reflected in the cult of ancestors, important in Chinese religion and also in older civilizations and in precivilizational societies. The observation of the annual cycle of the seasons and its crucial effect on agriculture is reflected in a ceremony in which the emperor of China used to plow the first furrow of the current year; in the ceremonial opening of a breach in the dike of the Nile to let the annual floodwaters irrigate the land; and in the annual "sacred marriage," performed by a priest and priestess representing a god and goddess, which was deemed to ensure the continuing fertility of Babylonia. A cycle longer than that of the seasons is represented by the recurrent *avatāras* (epiphanies, incarnate, on Earth) of the Hindu god Viṣṇu (Vishnu) and in the corresponding series of buddhas and *bodhisattvas* (potential buddhas). Although the only historical Buddha was Siddhārtha Gautama (6th–5th century BC), in the mythology of the northern school of Buddhism (the Mahāyāna), the identity of the historical Buddha has been almost effaced by a long vista of putative buddhas extending through previous and future times.

In contrast to northern Buddhism and to Vaiṣṇava Hinduism, Christianity holds that the incarnation of God in Jesus was a unique event; yet the rite of the Eucharist, in which Christ's self-sacrifice is held by Catholic and Eastern Orthodox Christians to be reperformed, is celebrated every day by thousands of priests and the nature of this rite has suggested to some scholars that it originated in an annual festival at the culmination of the agricultural year. In this interpretation, the bread that is Christ's body and the wine that is his blood associate him with the annually dying gods Adonis, Osiris, and Attis —the divinities, inherent in the vital and vitalizing power of man's crops, who die in order that men may eat and drink and live. "Unless a grain of wheat falls into the earth and dies, it remains alone; but, if it dies, it bears much fruit" (John 12:24).

THE CYCLIC VIEW IN VARIOUS CULTURES. The cyclic view of history, both cosmic and human, has been prevalent among the Hindus and the pre-Christian Greeks, the Chinese, and the pre-Columbian peoples of Central America; and it has reappeared in the modern West, although this civilization was originally Christian—that is, was nurtured on a religion that sees time as a one-way flow and not as a cyclic one.

The Chinese, Hindus, and Greeks saw cosmic time as moving in an alternating rhythm, classically expressed in the Chinese concept of the alternation between Yin, the passive female principle, and Yang, the dynamic male principle. When either Yin or Yang goes to extremes, it lops over into the other principle, which is its correlative and complement in consequence of being its opposite. In the philosophy of Empedocles, an early Greek pluralist, the equivalents of Yin and Yang were Love and Strife. Empedocles revolted against the denial of the reality of motion and plurality that was made by his Eleatic predecessors on the strength of mere logic. He broke up the Eleatics' motionless, and therefore timeless, unitary reality into a movement of four elements that alternately were harmonized by Love and set at variance by Strife. Empedocles' Love and Strife, like Yin and Yang, each lopped over into the other when they had gone to extremes.

Plato translated Empedocles' concept from psychological into theistic terms. At the outset, in his view, the gods guide the cosmos, and they then leave it to its own devices. But when the cosmos, thus left to itself, has brought itself to the brink of disaster, the gods resume control at the eleventh hour—and these two phases of its condition alternate with each other endlessly. The recurrence of alternating phases in which, at the darkest hour, catastrophe is averted by divine intervention is similarly an article of Vaiṣṇava Hindu faith. In guessing the lengths of the recurrent eons (kalpas), the Hindus arrived, intuitively, at figures of the magnitude of those reached by modern astronomers through meticulous observations and calculations. Similarly, the pre-Columbian Mayas rivalled the modern Westerners and the Hindus in the scale on which they envisaged the flow of time, and they kept an astonishingly accurate time count by inventing a set of interlocking cycles of different wavelengths.

Plato and Aristotle took it for granted that human society, as well as the cosmos, has been, and will continue to be, wrecked and rehabilitated any number of times. This rhythm can be discerned, as a matter of historical fact, in the histories of the pharaonic Egyptian and of the Chinese civilizations during the three millennia that elapsed, in each of them, between its first political unification and its final disintegration. The prosperity that had been conferred on a peasant society by political unity and peace turned into adversity when the cost of large-scale administration and defense became too heavy for an unmechanized economy to bear. In each instance, the unified state then broke up—only to be reunited for the starting of another similar cycle. The Muslim historian Ibn Khaldūn, writing in the 14th century AD, observed the same cyclic rhythm in the histories of the successive conquests of sedentary populations by pastoral nomads.

In the modern West, an Italian philosopher of history, Giambattista Vico, observed that the phases through which Western civilization had passed had counterparts in the history of the antecedent Greco-Roman civilization. Thanks to a subsequent increase in the number of civilizations known to Western students of cultural morphology, Oswald Spengler, a German philosopher of history, was able, in the early 20th century, to make a comparative study of civilizations over a much broader spectrum than that of Vico. The comparison of different civilizations or of successive periods of order and disorder in Chinese or in pharaonic Egyptian history implied, of course, that, in human affairs, recurrence is a reality.

The application of the cyclic view to the life of a human being in the hypothesis of rebirth was mentioned earlier. This hypothesis relaxes man's anxiety about being annihilated through death by replacing it with a no less agonizing anxiety about being condemned to a potentially endless series of rebirths. The strength of the reincarnationist's anxiety can be gauged by the severity of the self-mortification to which he resorts to liberate himself from the "sorrowful wheel." Among the peoples who have not believed in rebirth, the pharaonic Egyptians have taken the offensive against death and decay with the greatest determination: they embalmed corpses; they built colossal tombs; and, in the Book of the Dead, they provided instructions and spells for ensuring for that portion of the soul that did not hover around the sarcophagus an acquittal in the post mortem judgment and an entry into a blissful life in another world. No other human society has succeeded in achieving this degree of indestructibility despite the ravages of time.

One-way view of time in the philosophy of history. When the flow of time is held to be not recurrent but one-way, it can be conceived of as having a beginning and perhaps an end. Some thinkers have felt that such limits can be imagined only if there is some timeless power that has set time going and intends or is set to stop it. A god who creates and then annihilates time, if he is held to be omnipotent, is often credited with having done this with a benevolent purpose that he is carrying out according to plan. The omnipotent god's plan, in this view, governs the time flow and is made manifest to man in progressive revelations through the prophets—from Abraham, by way of Moses, Isaiah, and Jesus, to the prophet Muḥammad (as Muslims believe).

This belief in *Heilsgeschichte* (salvational history) has been derived by Islām and Christianity from Judaism and Zoroastrianism. Late in the 12th century, the Christian seer Joachim of Fiore saw this divinely ordained spiritual progress in the time flow as unfolding in a series of three ages—those of the Father, the Son, and the Spirit. Karl Jaspers, a 20th-century Western philosopher, has discerned an "axis age"—*i.e.,* a turning point in human history—in the 6th century BC, when Confucius, the Buddha, Zoroaster, Deutero-Isaiah, and Pythagoras were alive contemporaneously. If the "axis age" is extended backward in time to the original Isaiah's generation and forward to Muḥammad's, it may perhaps be recognized as the age in which men first sought to make direct contact with the ultimate spiritual reality behind phenomena instead of making such communication only indirectly through their nonhuman and social environments.

The belief in an omnipotent creator god, however, has been challenged. The creation of time, or of anything else, out of nothing is difficult to imagine; and, if God is not a creator but is merely a shaper, his power is limited by the intractability of the independent material with which he has had to work. Plato, in the *Timaeus,* conceived of God as being a nonomnipotent shaper and thus accounted for the manifest element of evil in phenomena. Marcion, a 2nd-century Christian heretic, inferred from the evil in phenomena that the creator was bad and held that a "stranger god" had come to redeem the bad creator's work at the benevolent stranger's cost. Zoroaster saw the phenomenal world as a battlefield between a bad god and a good one and saw time as the duration of this battle. Though he held that the good god was destined to be the victor, a god who needs to fight and win is not omnipotent. In an attenuated form, this evil adversary appears in the three Judaic religions as Satan.

Observation of historical phenomena suggests that, in spite of the manifestness of evil, there has in truth been progress in the history of life on this planet, culminating in the emergence of man, who knows himself to be a sinner yet feels himself to be something better than inanimate matter. Charles Darwin, in his theory of the selection of mutations by the environment, sought to vindicate apparent progress in the organic realm without recourse to an extraneous god. In the history of Greek thought, the counterpart of such mutations was the swerving of atoms. After Empedocles had broken up the indivisible, motionless, and timeless reality of Parmenides and Zeno into four elements played upon alternately by Love and Strife, it was a short step for the Atomists of the 5th century BC Leucippus and Democritus to break up reality still further into an innumerable host of minute atoms moving in time through a vacuum. Granting that one single atom had once made a single slight swerve, the build-up of observed phenomena could be accounted for on Darwinian lines. Democritus' account of evolution survives in the fifth book of *De rerum natura,* written by a 1st-century-BC Roman poet, Lucretius. The credibility of both Democritus' and Darwin's accounts of evolution depends on the assumption that time is real and that its flow has been extraordinarily long.

Heracleitus had seen in phenomena a harmony of opposites in tension with each other and had concluded that War (*i.e.,* Empedocles' Strife and the Chinese Yang) "is father of all and king of all." This vision of Strife as being the dominant and creative force is grimmer than that of Strife alternating on equal terms with Love and Yang with Yin. In the 19th-century West, Heracleitus' vision has been revived in the view of G.W.F. Hegel, a German Idealist, that progress occurs through a synthesis resulting from an encounter between a thesis and an antithesis. In political terms, Heracleitus' vision has reappeared in Karl Marx's concept of an encounter between the bourgeoisie and the proletariat and the emergence of a classless society without a government.

In the Zoroastrian and Jewish-Christian-Islāmic vision of the time flow, time is destined to be consummated—as depicted luridly in the Revelation to John—in a terrifying climax. Present-day man has recently become aware that history has been accelerating—and this at an accelerating rate. The present generation has been conscious of this increase of acceleration in its own lifetime; and the advance in man's knowledge of his past has revealed, in retrospect, that the acceleration began about 30,000 years ago, with the transition from the Lower to the Upper Paleolithic Period, and that it has taken successive "great leaps forward" with the invention of agriculture, with the dawn of civilization, and with the progressive harnessing—within the last two centuries—of the titanic physical forces of inanimate nature. The approach of the climax foreseen intuitively by the prophets is being felt, and feared, as a coming event. Its imminence is, today, not an article of faith; it is a datum of observation and experience.

LEON TROTSKY

ON

Vladimir Ilyich Lenin

We reprint this article almost in its entirety not because it is trustworthy in its judgments but because it is unique. Here is one giant figure writing about another (who happened to have been his boss) at a time when both had been—until Lenin's death in 1924—engaged in making history. The article has added fascination for us who know that the flawed system Lenin and Trotsky (1879–1940) helped to create has lasted less than three-quarters of a century. Trotsky's prose, however, military in its energy, reaching its peak in his History of the Russian Revolution, *may last longer.*

For this article, printed in the 13th edition (1926), Trotsky received $106. He completed it just months before Stalin banished him. He had no premonition that he would eventually be murdered by an agent of the dictator.

Lenin, Vladimir Ilyich Ulyanov (1870–1924), founder and guiding spirit of the Soviet Republics and the Communist International, the disciple of Marx both in theory and in practice, the leader of the Bolshevik party and the organiser of the Oct. revolution in Russia, was born on April 9 (22) 1870 in the town of Simbirsk, now Ulyanovsk. His father, Ilya Nicolaevitch, was a schoolmaster. His mother, Maria Alexandrovna, whose maiden name was Berg, was the daughter of a doctor. His eldest brother (b. 1866) joined the "Narodovoltze" (Freedom of the People movement), and took part in the unsuccessful attempt on the life of Alexander III. For this he was executed in his 22nd year. Lenin, the third of a family of six, completed his course at the Simbirsk gymnasium in 1887, winning the gold medal. His brother's execution, indelibly stamped on his consciousness, helped to determine his later life.

In the summer of 1887 Lenin entered the Kazan University to study law, but was sent down in Dec. of the same year for taking part in a gathering of students and was banished to the countryside. His repeated petitions in 1888–9 for permission to re-enter the University of Kazan or to be allowed to go abroad to continue his studies met with refusal. In the autumn, however, he was allowed to return to Kazan, where he began the systematic study of Marx and first entered into relations with the members of the local Marxist circle. In 1891 Lenin passed the law examinations of the St. Petersburg University, and in 1892 he began to practise as a barrister at Samara. During this year and the next he appeared for the defence in several trials. His life, however, was chiefly filled by the study of Marxism and its application to the investigation of the course of the economic and political development of Russia and subsequently of the whole world.

In 1894 he moved to St. Petersburg, where he came into touch with the workers and began his propaganda work. To this period belong Lenin's first polemical writings directed against the popular party, who taught that Russia would know neither capitalism nor the proletariat. These were passed from hand to hand in manuscript form. Soon after, Lenin started a theoretical struggle against the falsifiers of Marx, in the legal Press. In April 1895 Lenin first went abroad with the intention of entering into relations with the Marxist group abroad known as the "Osvobozhdenie Truda," "Deliverance of Labour" (Plekhanov, Zasulich, Axelrod). On his return to St. Petersburg, he organised the illegal "Union for the struggle for the liberation of the Working Class," which rapidly became an important organisation, carrying on propaganda and agitation among the workers and getting into touch with the provinces. In Dec. 1895 Lenin and his closest collaborators were arrested. He spent the year 1896 in prison, where he studied the lines of Russia's economic development. In Feb. 1897 he was sent into exile for three years to the Yenisei province in eastern Siberia. At this time, 1898, he married N. K. Krupskaya, his comrade in the work of the St. Petersburg Union and his faithful companion during the remaining 26 years of his life and revolutionary struggle. During his exile he finished his most important economic work, *The Development of Capitalism in Russia,* based on a comprehensive and systematic study of an enormous mass of statistical material (1899). In 1900 Lenin went abroad to Switzerland with the intention of organising, with the "Deliverance of Labour" group, the publication of a revolutionary paper intended for Russia. At the end of the year the first number of the paper *Iskra* (The Spark) appeared in Munich, with the motto "From the Spark to the Flame." The aim of the paper was to give a Marxian interpretation of the problems facing the revolution, to give the political watchwords of the struggle, and to organise on this basis a centralised "underground" revolutionary party of Social Democrats, which, standing at the head of the proletariat, should open the struggle against Tsarism, rousing the oppressed masses, and, above all, the many millions of peasants. . . .

In Oct. 1905 the All-Russian strike began. On the 17th of the month the Tsar issued his manifesto about the "Constitution." In the beginning of Nov. Lenin returned to Russia from Geneva, and already, in his first article, appealed to the Bolsheviks, in view of the new situation, to increase the scope of their organisation and to bring into the party wider circles of workers, but to preserve their illegal apparatus in anticipation of the counter-revolutionary blows which were inevitable. In Dec. Tsarism began to counter-attack. The rising in Moscow at the end of Dec., lacking as it did the support of the army, without simultaneous risings in other towns and sufficient response in the country districts, was quickly suppressed.

In the events of 1905 Lenin distinguished three main features—(1) the temporary seizure by the people of real political freedom, real in the sense of not being limited by their class enemies, apart from and in spite of all existing laws and institutions; (2) the creation of new and as yet only potential organs of revolutionary power in the shape of soviets of workers', soldiers' and peasants' deputies; (3) the use of force by the people against those who had employed it against them. Those conclusions, from the events of 1905, became the guiding principles of Lenin's policy in 1917 and led to the dictatorship of the proletariat in the form of the Soviet State.

The suppression of the Dec. rising in Moscow threw the masses into the background. The Liberal bourgeoisie came to the front. The epoch of the first two Dumas began. At this time, Lenin formulated the principles of the revolutionary exploitation of parliamentary methods in immediate connection with the struggle of the masses and as a means of preparation for a fresh attack.

In Dec. 1907 Lenin left Russia, to return only in 1917. Now (in 1907) began the epoch of victorious counter-revolution, prosecutions, exile, executions and emigration. Lenin led the struggle against all decadent tendencies among the revolutionaries; against the Mensheviks, the advocates of the liquidation of the "underground" party—hence those known as "liquidators"—and of the change of their methods of work into purely legal ones within the framework of the pseudo-constitutional régime; against the "conciliators" who failed to grasp the complete antagonism between Bolshevism and Menshevism and tried to take up an intermediate position—against the adventurist policy of the Socialist revolutionaries who tried to make up for the inertia of the masses by personal terrorism; finally, against the narrow partisanship of a part of the Bolsheviks, the so-called "callers-off," who demanded the recall of the Social Democratic deputies from the Duma in the name of immediate revolutionary activity, though conditions at that moment offered no opportunity for this. In this dim epoch Lenin showed very vividly a combination of his two fundamental qualities—that of being an implacable revolutionary at bottom, while yet remaining a realist who made no mistakes in the choice of methods and means.

At the same time, Lenin carried on an extensive campaign against the attempt to revise the theoretic basis of Marxism on which his whole policy was founded. In 1908 he wrote a major treatise dealing with the fundamental questions of knowledge and directed against the essentially idealistic philosophy of Mach, Avenarius and their Russian followers, who tried to unite empiric criticism with Marxism. On the basis of a deep and comprehensive study of science Lenin proved that the methods of dialectical materialism as formulated by Marx and Engels were entirely confirmed by the development of scientific thought in general and natural science in particular. Thus Lenin's constant revolutionary struggle, in which he never lost sight of the smallest practical details, went hand in hand with his equally constant theoretical controversies, in which he attained to the greatest heights of comprehensive generalisations. . . .

Lenin was prepared for his struggle on an international scale not only by his profound knowledge of Marxism and his experience of the revolutionary struggle and party organisation in Russia, but also by his intimate acquaintance with the workers' movement throughout the world. For many years he had followed closely the internal affairs of the most important capitalist States. He was a thorough master of the English, German and French languages, and could read Italian, Swedish and Polish. His realistic imagination and political intuition often enabled him to reconstruct a complete picture from isolated phenomena. Lenin was always firmly opposed to the mechanical application of the methods of one country to another, and he investigated and decided questions concerning revolutionary movements, not only in their international interreactions, but also in their concrete national form.

The revolution of Feb. 1917 found Lenin in Switzerland. His attempts to reach Russia met with the decided opposition of the British Government. He accordingly decided to exploit the antagonism of the belligerent countries and to reach Russia through Germany. The success of this plan gave occasion to Lenin's enemies for a fierce campaign of slander, which, however, was powerless to prevent him from assuming the leadership of his party and shortly afterwards of the revolution.

On the night of April 4, on leaving the train, Lenin made a speech in the Finlyandsky station in Petrograd. He repeated and developed the leading ideas it contained in the days which followed. The overthrow of Tsarism, he said, was only the first stage in the revolution. The bourgeois revolution could no longer satisfy the masses. The task of the proletariat was to arm, to strengthen the power of the Soviets, to rouse the country districts and to prepare for the conquest of supreme power in the name of the reconstruction of society on a Socialist basis.

This far-reaching programme was not only unwelcome to those engaged in propagating patriotic Socialism, but even roused opposition among the Bolsheviks themselves. Plekhanov called Lenin's programme "crazy." Lenin, however, built up his policy not on the inclinations and views of the temporary leaders of the revolution, but on the interrelations of the classes and the logic of mass movements. He foresaw that the distrust of the bourgeoisie and of the Provisional Government would grow stronger daily, that the Bolshevik party would obtain a majority in the Soviets and that the supreme power would pass into their hands. The small daily *Pravda* became at once in his hands a powerful instrument for the overthrow of bourgeois society.

The policy of coalition with the bourgeoisie pursued by the patriotic Socialists, and the hopeless attack which the Allies forced the Russian Army to assume at the front—both these roused the masses and led to armed demonstrations in Petrograd in the first days of July. The struggle against Bolshevism became most intense. On July 5th grossly forged "documents" were published by the counter-revolutionary secret service. These purported to prove that Lenin was acting under the orders of the German general staff. In the evening "reliable" detachments summoned from the front by Kerensky and Cadet officers from the districts round Petrograd occupied the city. The popular movement was crushed. The hounding of Lenin reached its height. He now began to work "underground," hiding first in Petrograd with a worker's family and then in Finland; he managed, however, to keep in touch with the leaders of the party.

The July days and the retributions which followed aroused a burst of energy in the masses—Lenin's forecast proved right in every particular. The Bolsheviks obtained a majority in the Soviets of Petrograd and Moscow. Lenin demanded decisive action to seize the supreme power, and on his side began an unremitting fight against the hesitations of the leaders of the party. He wrote articles and pamphlets, letters, both official and private, examining the question of the seizure of supreme power from every angle, refuting objections and dispelling doubts. He drew a picture of Russia's conversion into a foreign colony if the policy of Miliukov and Kerensky continued, and he predicted that they would consciously hand over Petrograd to the Germans in order to destroy the proletariat. "Now or never!" he repeated in passionate articles, letters and interviews.

The rising against the Provisional Government coincided with the opening of the second Congress of the Soviets on Oct. 25. On that day, Lenin, after being in hiding for three and a half months, appeared in the Smolny and from there personally directed the fight. In the night sitting of Oct. 27 he proposed, at the session of the Congress of the Soviets, a draft decree about peace which was passed unanimously and another about the land, which was passed with one dissentient and eight abstentions. The Bolshevik majority, supported by the left wing of the Socialist revolutionaries, declared that supreme power was now vested in the Soviets. The Soviet of People's Commissaries was appointed, with Lenin at their head. Thus Lenin passed straight from the log cabin where he had been hiding from persecution to the place of highest authority.

The proletarian revolution spread quickly. Having obtained the land of the landed estate owners, the peasants forsook the Socialist revolutionaries and supported the Bolsheviks. The Soviets became masters of the situation both in the towns and the country districts. In such circumstances the constituent assembly which was elected in Nov. and met on Jan. 5 appeared a patent anachronism. The conflict between the two stages of the revolution was now at hand. Lenin did not hesitate for an instant. On the night of Jan. 7 the All-Russian Central Executive Committee, on Lenin's motion, passed a decree dissolving the constituent assembly. The dictatorship of the proletariat, said Lenin, meant the greatest possible degree of actual and not merely formal democracy for the toiling majority of the people. For it guaranteed to them the real possibility of utilising their abilities, putting as it did in the hands of labour all those material goods (buildings for meetings, printing presses and so on) lacking which "liberty" remains an empty word and an illusion. The dictatorship of the proletariat in Lenin's view is a necessary stage in the abolition of class divisions in society. . . .

The exhaustion brought on by excessive hard work over a number of years ruined Lenin's health. Sclerosis attacked his cerebral arteries. At the beginning of 1922 his doctors forbade him daily work. From June to Aug. the disease made rapid progress, and for the first time he began to lose, although transiently, the power of speech. At the beginning of Oct. his health had so much improved that he once again returned to work, but not for long. His last public utterance ends with the expression of his conviction that "from Russia under N.E.P. will come Socialist Russia."

On Dec. 16 he became paralysed in the right arm and leg. However, during Jan. and Feb. he still dictated a number of articles of great importance for the policy of the party on the struggle against bureaucracy in the Soviet and party organisation; on the importance of co-operation in gradually bringing the peasants into the Socialist organisation; on the struggle against illiteracy; and finally on the policy in regard to nationalities oppressed under Tsarism.

The disease progressed and he lost completely the power of speech. His work for the party came to an end, and very soon his life also. Lenin died on Jan. 21, 1924, at 6:30 P.M., at Gorky, near Moscow. His funeral was the occasion for an unexampled manifestation of love and grief on the part of millions.

The main work of Lenin's life was the organisation of a party capable of carrying through the Oct. revolution and of directing the construction of Socialism. The theory of the proletarian revolution—the methods and tactics to be pursued—constitutes the fundamental content of Leninism which as an international system forms the culminating point of Marxism. Lenin's single aim filled his life from his school days onwards. He never knew hesitation in the fight against those he considered the enemies of the working class. In his passionate struggle there was never any personal element. He fulfilled what he considered to be the demands of an inevitable historical process. Lenin combined the ability to use the materialistic dialectic as a method of scientific orientation in social developments with the deep intuition of the true leader.

Lenin's outward appearance was distinguished by simplicity and strength. He was of middle or rather below the middle height, with the plebeian features of the Slavonic type of face, brightened, however, by piercing eyes; and his powerful forehead and his still more powerful head gave him a marked distinction. He was tireless in work to an unparalleled degree. His thoughts were equally concentrated whether in his Siberian exile, the British Museum or at a sitting of the People's Commissaries. He put the same exemplary conscientiousness into reading lectures in a small workmen's club in Zurich and in organising the first Socialist State in the world. He appreciated and loved to the full science, art and culture, but he never forgot that as yet these things are the property of a small minority. The simplicity of his literary and oratorical style expressed the extreme concentration of his spiritual forces bent on a single aim. In personal intercourse Lenin was even-tempered, courteous and attentive, especially to the weak and oppressed and to children. His way of life in the Kremlin was little different from his life as an emigré abroad. The simplicity of his daily habits, his asceticism in regard to food, drink, clothes and the "good things" of life in general in his case did not spring from so called moral principles, but came about because intellectual work and intense struggle not only absorbed his interests and passions but also gave him such intense satisfaction as to leave no room for subsidiary enjoyments. His thoughts never ceased to labour at the task of freeing the workers till the moment of its final extinction.

GENE TUNNEY

ON

Boxing

The five crowded columns headed "Boxing" to be found in the Micropaedia *of the current edition are lucid and comprehensive. But they lack the verve and intimate authority of the article "Boxing in America" in the 14th edition (1929). That article was written by the man who knocked out Jack Dempsey and held the world's heavyweight championship belt 1926–1928. There is probably no boxer alive today who could write an article about his profession approaching Tunney's in style or insight.*

Boxing, pugilism, prize-fighting and ruffianism were synonymous in the public mind from the earliest days of prize-fighting in the United States down to the World War, when boxing was prescribed as a means of quickly fitting untrained men for action at the front. Boxing up to this time had a most dreadful inheritance in the way of reputation, due to the practices of the persons connected with prize-fighting in its early stages in America, and to the type of men who took active part in these prize-fights. As a rule, they were, both fighters and associates, sinister people with few scruples, vulgar and brutal to a marked degree. The populace realized this and branded as outcasts all persons who were in any way connected with this "sport." Almost every State in the Union passed laws prohibiting prize-fights. Occasionally, however, in spite of the laws, important contests would be held secretly in out of the way places. But they usually were terminated by the police, who would get the information that such a fight was being held and after stopping the match would place the principals under arrest. This kind of contest attracted few people, first because they were slow, uninteresting mauling affairs in which one man was trying to outlast his opponent, and, therefore, making few efforts to end matters for fear he would over-exert himself and be at the mercy of the other; and secondly the fear of being arrested, or possibly injured, in the free-for-all that usually accompanied the termination of these, made attendance at them quite a risky matter. The possibilities of arrest or injury naturally kept the self-respecting and prudent people away.

Despite the old laws prohibiting fighting having been modified, and new laws called Boxing laws permitting boxing contests in certain States, boxing was still regarded as an outlaw "sport," and a brutalizing and degrading form of amusement, until the government, in 1917, through its directors of training camp activities, adopted it as an important means for quickly fitting untrained men for rigorous soldier-life. It was then that modern boxing was brought to the attention of its greatest calumniators, viz., the ministers of the gospel, religious and lay woman organizations and societies and those who did not know the difference between brutal prize-fighting and legalized, regulated, modern boxing. This was the moment of rebirth for boxing. The interest in boxing has grown rapidly and steadily ever since. As a sport for young boys during their impressionable and developing years, there is no equal to it; it develops self-reliance, self-control, self-confidence, individual and quick thinking, physical courage and sportsmanship. There is no other game or sport that can boast of these attributes.

That fighting or boxing has an appeal to the elemental and primitive in man boxing's bitterest foes cannot deny. There is something terrifically fascinating about it to both man and woman. Its grip on man is probably due to his fundamental urge—self-preservation. In boxing contests the spectators' imagination sees a test for physical supremacy, a struggle to preserve oneself; and for the right to live. There is no other source of amusement or entertainment, sport or game, that contains quite as much real drama as can be found in a contest between two evenly matched, well trained boxers.

After the World War as boxing gained the recognition and interest of the general public; and those who took it up as a profession, just as a young man does law or medicine, were no longer looked upon as pariahs; many serious-minded and ambitious young men adopted it as a means of livelihood and profession. This brought an altogether new element into the sport, a thinking element; men who believed mental preparedness as important as physical preparedness; men who studied their game just as a surgeon does his anatomy. Naturally, this made for a marked increase in the knowledge of the "science" and raised the standard of the boxer proportionately, so that boxing methods must have improved just as sprinting and other athletic performances have bettered all records during the past decade. We have advanced in every other branch of athletic endeavour, so it seems only logical to assume that boxing has kept pace with the progress of its sister sports. Styles in boxing have variegated and changed considerably. New methods of attack and defence have been introduced and improved upon. Foot-work takes an important place in the repertoire of the modern boxer. The Classic style; i.e., the upright stance, with the left hand and left foot extended, and the right arm crooked across the chest ready to parry an opponent's lead to the head or body, has been almost entirely discarded as obsolete. It has been found more efficient to learn to avoid leads by either slipping the head to one side or the other, depending on how you expect to counter, or, by ducking, pulling away or slipping inside the lead. This gives a boxer the free use of his two hands for hitting, being a great improvement over the older style of using one or both arms to parry, which effectually warded off the blows, but by doing so prevented the use of the hands to counter. It has been discovered it is tremendously more effective to use the hands to strike the opponent than to keep them busy parrying and blocking blows. So that now we have the "bobbing and weaving" style of attack with the hands poised in a hitting position ready to strike out at the first opening as the advance toward the opponent is made. Jack Dempsey, heavyweight champion 1919–26, has been the greatest exponent of this style up to date. Benny Leonard, lightweight champion 1916–25, was one of the greatest exponents of the splendid combination of rhythmic foot work and hard, accurate, straight hitting. Jack Britton, welterweight champion 1919–

1922, though lacking a heavy blow, was, undoubtedly, the greatest exponent of pure boxing skill of his time. The three men mentioned were the outstanding boxing figures of their time, and while their "styles" differed somewhat outwardly, basically they were the same, in that they learnt to avoid blows by slipping and ducking the head so that they would at all times have the free use of both hands. This factor is, undoubtedly, the mainspring in the improvement of the modern boxer.

Mental fitness has as much to do with success as has physical. This is true not only in boxing but in every endeavour of life. The modern boxer realizes that unless he is mentally equipped his chances for success are very slim. He therefore cuts himself free from all other business interests, believing he cannot have diversified interests and find success as a professional boxer. Boxing being a highly specialized sport, none can remain successfully in it unless he becomes a specialist. All successful boxers have done this, and it is not until they acquire money and make investments, in which they are compelled to take an active interest, that they meet reverses in the ring. This has been the case in four out of every five of the great champions, and goes to prove the point in question. Freedom from all outside interest, and worry of every nature; with a complete knowledge of the "science" of the game; a quick, active brain, with perfect co-ordination; and sound physical condition are necessary qualifications for a successful boxer of to-day.

E. B. WHITE
ON
Harold Ross

E. B. White (1899–1985) will in future years quietly take his proper place among the finest essayists in the language.

A mainstay of The New Yorker *for fifty-six years, he was well qualified to write about his boss, Harold Ross. No one but he could, with a handful of tiny touches, impart such warmth to the mini-article that appeared in the 14th edition (1929 and revised with periodic updates).*

Ross, Harold Wallace (1892–1951), a revolutionary figure in U.S. journalism, founder and first editor of *The New Yorker,* was born in Aspen, Colo., Nov. 6, 1892. He quit high school to become a reporter, and in World War I edited *Stars and Stripes,* the serviceman's newspaper, in France. When he launched *The New Yorker* in 1925 he quickly toppled many conventional literary forms in his quest for ways to capture the contemporary scene in the magazine's pages.

Young new writers and artists, attracted by the rich odour of innovation, were drawn to the magazine. Under Ross's guidance, satire and parody flourished, reporting became lighthearted and searching, humour was allowed to infect everything, biography achieved bold strokes in the "Profiles," the short story enjoyed a reprieve from the heavy burden of plot, and social cartooning became less diagrammatic and more vigorous. In *The New Yorker,* the unknown writer was on equal footing with the established one; the editor sought good writing, not great names. Restless, noisy, consumed by curiosity, driven by a passion for clarity and perfection, Ross spent himself recklessly on each succeeding issue, and with unabating discontent.

Ross died in Boston on Dec. 6, 1951, having to a notable extent changed the face of journalism in his time.

ALFRED NORTH WHITEHEAD

ON

Mathematics

Alfred North Whitehead (1861–1947), the great British mathematician who was Bertrand Russell's teacher, friend, and collaborator, was, like Russell, a lucid expositor of math for the lay reader. He reviewed the subject, with a substantial focus on applied mathematics, in the Britannica's *famous 11th edition (1910–1911). Some excerpts follow. (B.L.F.)*

Mathematics (Gr. μαθηματική, *sc.* τέχνη or ἐπιστμ́Μη; from μάθημα, "learning" or "science"), the general term for the various applications of mathematical thought, the traditional field of which is number and quantity. It has been usual to define mathematics as "the science of discrete and continuous magnitude." Even Leibnitz, who initiated a more modern point of view, follows the tradition in thus confining the scope of mathematics properly so called, while apparently conceiving it as a department of a yet wider science of reasoning. A short consideration of some leading topics of the science will exemplify both the plausibility and inadequacy of the above definition. Arithmetic, algebra, and the infinitesimal calculus, are sciences directly concerned with integral numbers, rational (or fractional) numbers, and real numbers generally, which include incommensurable numbers. It would seem that "the general theory of discrete and continuous quantity" is the exact description of the topics of these sciences. Furthermore, can we not complete the circle of the mathematical sciences by adding geometry? Now geometry deals with points, lines, planes and cubic contents. Of these all except points are quantities: lines involve lengths, planes involve areas, and cubic contents involve volumes. Also, as the Cartesian geometry shows, all the relations between points are expressible in terms of geometric quantities. Accordingly, at first sight it seems reasonable to define geometry in some such way as "the science of dimensional quantity." Thus every subdivision of mathematical science would appear to deal with quantity, and the definition of mathematics as "the science of quantity" would appear to be justified. We have now to consider the reasons for rejecting this definition as inadequate.

Types of critical questions. What are numbers? We can talk of five apples and ten pears. But what are "five" and "ten" apart from the apples and pears? Also in addition to the cardinal numbers there are the ordinal numbers: the fifth apple and the tenth pear claim thought. What is the relation of "the fifth" and "the tenth" to "five" and "ten"? "The first rose of summer" and "the last rose of summer" are parallel phrases, yet one explicitly introduces an ordinal number and the other does not. Again, "half a foot" and "half a pound" are easily defined. But in what sense is there "a half," which is the same for "half a foot" as "half a pound"? Furthermore, incommensurable numbers are defined as the limits arrived at as the result of certain procedures with rational numbers. But how do we know that there is anything to reach? We must know that $\sqrt{2}$ exists before we can prove that any procedure will reach it. An expedition to the North Pole has nothing to reach unless the earth rotates.

Also in geometry, what is a point? The straightness of a straight line and the planeness of a plane require consideration. Furthermore, "congruence" is a difficulty. For when a triangle "moves," the points do not move with it. So what is it that keeps unaltered in the moving triangle? Thus the whole method of measurement in geometry as described in the elementary textbooks and the older treatises is obscure to the last degree. Lastly, what are "dimensions"? All these topics require thorough discussion before we can rest content with the definition of mathematics as the general science of magnitude; and by the time they are discussed the definition has evaporated. . . .

Definition of mathematics. It has now become apparent that the traditional field of mathematics in the province of discrete and continuous number can only be separated from the general abstract theory of classes and relations by a wavering and indeterminate line. Of course a discussion as to the mere application of a word easily degenerates into the most fruitless logomachy. It is open to any one to use any word in any sense. But on the assumption that "mathematics" is to denote a science well marked out by its subject matter and its methods from other topics of thought, and that at least it is to include all topics habitually assigned to it, there is now no option but to employ "mathematics" in the general sense of the "science concerned with the logical deduction of consequences from the general premisses of all reasoning."

Geometry. The typical mathematical proposition is: "If x, y, z . . . satisfy such and such conditions, then such and such other conditions hold with respect to them." By taking fixed conditions for the hypothesis of such a proposition a definite department of mathematics is marked out. For example, geometry is such a department. The "axioms" of geometry are the fixed conditions which occur in the hypotheses of the geometrical propositions. . . . It is sufficient to observe here that they are concerned with special types of classes of classes and of classes of relations, and that the connexion of geometry with number and magnitude is in no way an essential part of the foundation of the science. In fact, the whole theory of measurement in geometry arises at a comparatively late stage as the result of a variety of complicated considerations. . . .

Applied mathematics. The selection of the topics of mathematical inquiry among the infinite variety open to it has been guided by the useful applications, and indeed the abstract theory has only recently been disentangled from the empirical elements connected with these applications. For example, the application of the theory of cardinal numbers to classes of physical entities involves in practice some process of counting. It is only recently that the *succession* of processes which is involved in any act of counting has been seen to be irrelevant to the idea of number. Indeed, it is only by experience that we can know that any definite process of counting will give the true cardinal number of some class of entities. It is perfectly possible to imagine a universe in which any act of counting by a being in it annihilated some members of the class counted during the time and only during the time of its continuance. A legend of the Council of Nicea illustrates this point: "When the Bishops took their places on their thrones, they were 318; when they rose up to be called over, it appeared that they were 319; so that they never could make the number come right, and whenever they approached the last of the series, he immediately turned into the likeness of his next neighbour." Whatever be the historical worth of this story, it may safely be said that it cannot be disproved by deductive reasoning from the premisses of abstract logic. The most we can do is to assert that a universe in which such things are liable to happen on a large scale is unfitted for the practical application of the theory of cardinal numbers. The application of the theory of real numbers to physical quantities involves analogous considerations. In the first place, some physical process of addition is presupposed, involving some inductively inferred law of permanence during that process. Thus in the theory of masses we must know that two pounds of lead when put together will counterbalance in the scales two pounds of sugar, or a pound of lead and a pound of sugar. Furthermore, the sort of continuity of the series (in order of magnitude) of rational numbers is known to be different from that of the series of real numbers. Indeed, mathematicians now reserve "continuity" as the term for the latter kind of continuity; the mere property of having an infinite number of terms between any two terms is called "compactness." The compactness of the series of rational numbers is consistent with quasi-gaps in it—that is, with the possible absence of limits to classes in it. Thus the class of rational numbers whose squares are less than 2 has no upper limit among the rational numbers. But among the real numbers all classes have limits. Now, owing to the necessary inexactness of measurement, it is impossible to discriminate directly whether any kind of continuous physical quantity possesses the compactness of the series of rationals or the continuity of the series of real numbers. In calculations the latter hypothesis is made because of its mathematical simplicity. But, the assumption has certainly no a priori grounds in its favour, and it is not very easy to see how to base it upon experience. For example, if it should turn out that the mass of a body is to be estimated by counting the number of corpuscles (whatever they may be) which go to form it, then a body with an irrational measure of mass is intrinsically impossible. Similarly, the continuity of space apparently rests upon sheer assumption unsupported by any a priori or experimental grounds. Thus the current applications of mathematics to the analysis of phenomena can be justified by no a priori necessity.

In one sense there is no science of applied mathematics. When once the fixed conditions which any hypothetical group of entities are to satisfy have been precisely formulated, the deduction of the further propositions, which also will hold respecting them, can proceed in complete independence of the question as to whether or no any such group of entities can be found in the world of phenomena. Thus rational mechanics, based on the Newtonian Laws, viewed as mathematics is independent of its supposed application, and hydrodynamics remains a coherent and respected science though it is extremely improbable that any perfect fluid exists in the physical world. But this unbendingly logical point of view cannot be the last word upon the matter. For no one can doubt the essential difference between characteristic treatises upon "pure" and "applied" mathematics. The difference is a difference in method. In pure mathematics the hypotheses which a set of entities are to satisfy are given, and a group of interesting deductions are sought. In "applied mathematics" the "deductions" are given in the shape of the experimental evidence of natural science, and the hypotheses from which the "deductions" can be deduced are sought. Accordingly, every treatise on applied mathematics, properly so-called, is directed to the criticism of the "laws" from which the reasoning starts, or to a suggestion of results which experiment may hope to find. Thus if it calculates the result of some experiment, it is not the experimentalist's well-attested results which are on their trial, but the basis of the calculation. Newton's *Hypotheses non fingo* was a proud boast, but it rests upon an entire misconception of the capacities of the mind of man in dealing with external nature.

RALPH VAUGHAN WILLIAMS

ON

Folk-Song

For the article "Folk-Song," which first appeared in the 1963 printing of the 14th edition (1929) no more distinguished name could have been secured than that of Ralph Vaughan Williams (1872–1958). This composer-scholar did for the nationalist movement in English music what Moussorgsky, Smetana, and de Falla did for the nationalist musical movements in their countries. Extracts from his article follow.

Any art if it is to have life must be able to trace its origin to a fundamental human need. Such needs find prompt expression among people even in their most primitive and uncultivated state. To this rule the art of music is no exception. Parry has pointed out that the universal law of evolution demands that we should be able to trace even the most elaborate compositions of Beethoven or Wagner back to some primitive germ. This primitive, spontaneous music has been called "Folk-song," a rather awkward translation of the German word "Volkslied," but nevertheless a word which stands for a very definite fact in the realm of music.

It has been said that if we did not know by experience of the existence of folk-song we should have to presuppose it theoretically to account for the art of music. . . .

It is sometimes held that the word "folk-song" should be used in what is called a "broad" sense so as to include not only genuinely traditional music, but all those songs of a popular character which are habitually sung by the people of a country. But, in fact, the difference between these two classes of music is a real and scientific one, which is properly recognized by the Germans in their distinction between a "Volkslied" and a "Volksthümlicheslied." What common denominator can be found which will cover, on the one hand, such a song as "Tom Bowling" and, on the other, the "Lazarus" tune in *English County Songs?* In the one case we can judge the date and even guess at the composer; but who can date a folk-song? Indeed, a folk-song is neither new nor old; it is like a forest tree with its roots deeply buried in the past but which continually puts forth new branches, new leaves, new fruit.

Collectors are often asked by would-be intelligent enquirers as to the age of some folk-song, as if the question of age were either important or relevant. Others (sceptics) suggest that the traditional singer "made it up himself." The answer to this, of course, is that quite possibly he did to some extent "make it up himself," although this in no way adds to, or takes away from, its scientific or artistic value. It is not the question of age or authorship that is important in a folk-song but that of spontaneity and beauty. When a collector nowadays hears a song sung by a traditional singer he may be pretty sure that, if the singer is a true artist, he will have unconsciously added something of his own to what he sings. A folk-song then is always grafting the new on to the old. This is the answer to the question: "How old is that folk-song?" A folk-song is neither new nor old because it is continually taking on new life; it is an individual flowering on a common stem.

This brings us to the vexed question of the "communal growth" of folk-song; and here it may be pointed out that much useless derision has been wasted over a supposed theory of "communal origin." No one has ever laid it down as an indisputable proposition that folk-song has a communal origin, though even this is not so impossible an idea as some people suppose. No one insists that some individual must have invented every word of our language. Who invented "father" or "plough" or "sun" or any other of the words that belong to primitive life? If we admit communal authorship in our language, is it not even more probable in such an intangible matter as music?

However, it is not necessary to prove the communal origin of folk-song in order to argue in favour of its communal growth. It is well known that when a rumoured fact or story becomes spread about it soon is circulated in various altered forms and this in spite of the fact that everyone who repeats the story is anxious to repeat it correctly. How much more then will a song become altered by oral repetition when each new singer is bound only by his artistic predilections? If he thinks he can improve the song, why should he not do so? If he finds it too difficult why should he not simplify it? Thus a folk-song evolves gradually as it passes through the minds of different men and different generations.

Nor will this gradual change ever be a process of deterioration, because those versions of the tune which are distasteful to others will die a natural death. Here then is a clear case of the survival of the fittest. A tune which has been handed down from father to son through many generations will represent the united imaginations of thousands of men and women through hundreds of years of evolution.

This then is the much discussed "communal growth" theory, and it is borne out by the facts. Collectors know well that numerous variants of the same tune have been found in different parts of the country and, conversely, that tunes have been found which are quite distinct from each other, but at the same time have features that point to a common stock. Thus Grimm's famous apophthegm "a folk-song composes itself" is not, after all, a piece of misty emotionalism but represents the hard common-sense facts of the case.

ORVILLE WRIGHT
ON
Wilbur Wright

Britannica biography ran the gamut from the earliest scientists to modern figures who harnessed the discoveries of science through technology. For instance, that twentieth-century Daedalus, Wilbur Wright. This sketch, written with charming modesty by "his brother," Orville Wright (1871–1948), is from the 14th edition (1929). It is a unique example of fraternal biography. (B.L.F./C.F.)

Wright, Wilbur (1867–1912), American inventor, son of Milton and Susan Catharine (Koerner) Wright, was born near Millville, Ind., on April 16, 1867. When Wilbur Wright was one month old his father was elected editor of the official organ of the Church of the United Brethren in Christ, necessitating moving his family to Dayton, O.; and eight years later he was elected a bishop of that denomination requiring other changes of residence. As a result Wilbur Wright received his education in the public schools of Dayton, Ohio, Richmond, Indiana, and Cedar Rapids, Iowa. Just when he was expecting to enter college, an accident, while playing in a game of ice hockey, disabled him for some six or eight years for active work. These years of poor health he devoted to the care of his invalid mother and to assisting his father in legal matters connected with the church. In 1890 he joined his brother, Orville, who was publishing a small weekly newspaper.

Experiments in gliding. Reading of the experiments of Otto Lilienthal in Germany, Wilbur and his brother became intensely interested in gliding as a sport. Lilienthal's experiments were suddenly ended in 1896 by his death, resulting from an accident due to insufficient control of the equilibrium of his glider. Lilienthal had balanced his machine by shifting the weight of his body. The brothers, believing this method incapable of expansion to meet the requirements of flight, set about to develop a more effective system. They developed a system in which the centre of gravity remained constant and the equilibrium was maintained by varying the air pressures on different parts of the machine through adjustments of the angles of the wings and auxiliary surfaces. This system, patented by them, is now generally known as aileron control.

Although Wilbur and his brother had taken up aeronautics merely as a sport, their chief interest soon turned to its more scientific aspects. Having found in their experiments that the existing scientific data was almost altogether untrustworthy, they cast it all aside and began investigations of their own, using methods which avoided many of the errors in the work of their predecessors. In 1901 they set up a small wind tunnel in their work-shop at Dayton in which they made measurements of the lift and drag of a great number of different-shaped aerofoils at angles from zero to 45 degrees. The results derived from this tunnel so stimulated their interest that often they worked into the early hours of the morning. Measurements also were made to determine the position of the centre of pressure on cambered surfaces and to determine the effect on the lift and drag when one surface was placed above another or when one surface followed another.

The first motor-driven aeroplane. With this mass of data in their possession they thought it now possible to predict from calculation the performance of a flying machine; they thought they could design a machine which would require not over one-half to one-fourth of the power that would have been necessary for any of the earlier proposed machines. Accordingly in Oct. 1902, they began the design of a motor-driven aeroplane. When completed the machine including the pilot weighed 750 lb. and was propelled by a four cylinder petrol motor of 12 horse power. Tested at Kitty Hawk, N.C., on Dec. 17, 1903, the machine carrying a man made four sustained free flights. The longest of these had a duration of 59 seconds and a speed of 30 m. an hour. This machine is now exhibited in the Science museum at South Kensington, London.

THOMAS YOUNG

ON

The Rosetta Stone

Thomas Young (1773–1829) was an English polymath who as a physician discovered the cause of astigmatism, as a physicist formulated the wave theory of light, and as an Egyptologist and linguist first deciphered the Rosetta Stone after it was dug up in 1799. That his translation contained some errors is unimportant; independent efforts by Young and, later, the French Egyptologist Jean-François Champollion decisively unlocked Egyptian hieroglyphics to modern interpretation. He wrote the article "Egypt" for the famous Supplement of 1815–1824—along with more than sixty other articles, most of them biographies. Half or more of his forty-two-page Egypt article told readers the story of his momentous decipherment of the Rosetta Stone. It was the first publication anywhere in the world of news of that remarkable event. A brief extract follows. (B.L.F.)

The block or pillar of black basalt, found by the French in digging up some ground at Rosetta, and now placed in the British Museum, exhibits the remains of three distinct inscriptions: and the last, which is in Greek, ends with the information, that the decrees, which it contains, was ordered to be engraved in three different characters, the sacred letters, the letters of the country, and the Greek. Unfortunately a considerable part of the first inscription is wanting: the beginning of the second, and the end of the third, are also mutilated; so that we have no precise points of coincidence from which we can set out, in our attempts to decipher the unknown characters. The second inscription, which it will be safest to distinguish by the Greek name *enchorial,* signifying merely the characters "of the country," notwithstanding its deficiencies near the beginning, is still sufficiently perfect to allow us to compare its different parts with each other, and with the Greek, by the same method that we should employ if it were entire. Thus, if we examine the parts corresponding, in their relative situation, to two passages of the Greek inscription in which *Alexander* and *Alexandria* occur, we soon recognize two well marked groups of characters resembling each other, which we may therefore consider as representing these names: a remark which was first made by Mr. de Sacy, in his Letter relating to this inscription. A small group of characters, occurring very often in almost every line, might be either some termination, or some very common particle: it must, therefore, be reserved till it is found in some decisive situation, after some other words have been identified, and it will then easily be shown to mean *and.* The next remarkable collection of characters is repeated twenty nine or thirty times in the enchorial inscription; and we find nothing that occurs so often in the Greek, except the word *king,* with its compounds, which is found about thirty seven times. A fourth assemblage of characters is found fourteen times in the enchorial inscription, agreeing sufficiently well in frequency with the name of *Ptolemy,* which occurs eleven times in the Greek, and generally in passages corresponding to those of the enchorial text in their relative situation: and, by a similar comparison, the name of Egypt is identified, although it occurs much more frequently in the enchorial inscription than in the Greek, which often substitutes for it country only, or omits it entirely. Having thus obtained a sufficient number of common points of subdivision, we may next proceed to write the Greek text over the enchorial, in such a manner that the passages ascertained may all coincide as nearly as possible; and it is obvious that the intermediate parts of each inscription will then stand very near to the corresponding passages of the other.

In this process, it will be necessary to observe that the lines of the enchorial inscription are written from right to left, as, Herodotus tells us, was the custom of the Egyptians; the division of several words and phrases plainly indicating the direction in which they are to be read. It is well known that the distinct hieroglyphical inscriptions, engraved on different monuments, differ in the direction of the corresponding characters: they always face the right or the left of the spectator according as the principal personages of the tablets, to which they belong, are looking in the one or the other direction; where, however, there are no tablets, they almost always look towards the right; and it is easily demonstrable that they must always have been read beginning from the front, and proceeding to the rear of each rank. But the Egyptians seem never to have written alternately backwards and forwards, as the most ancient Greeks occasionally did. In both cases, however, the whole of the characters thus employed were completely reversed in the two different modes of using them, as if they were seen in a glass, or printed off like the impression of a seal.

By pursuing the comparison of the inscriptions, thus arranged, we ultimately discover the signification of the greater part of the individual enchorial words. . . .

It might naturally have been expected that the final characters of the enchorial inscription, of which the sense is thus determined with tolerable certainty, although the corresponding part of the Greek is wanting, would have immediately led us to a knowledge of the concluding phrase of the distinct hieroglyphical characters, which remains unimpaired. But the agreement between the two conclusions is by no means precise; and the difficulty can only be removed by supposing the king to be expressly named in the one, while he is only designated by his titles in the other. With this slight variation, and with the knowledge of the singular accident, that the name of Ptolemy occurs three times in a passage of the enchorial inscription, where the Greek has it but twice, we proceed to identify this name among the sacred characters, in a form sufficiently conspicuous, to have been recognised upon the most superficial examination of the inscriptions, if this total disagreement of the frequency of occurrence had not imposed the condition of a long and laborious investigation, as an indispensable requisite for the solution of so much of the enigma: this step, however, being made good, we obtain from it a tolerably correct scale for the comparative extent of the sacred characters, of which it now appears that almost half of the lines are entirely wanting, those which remain being also much mutilated. Such a scale may also be obtained, in a different manner, by marking, on a straight ruler, the places in which the most characteristic words, such as *god, king, priest,* and *shrine* occur, in the latter parts of the other inscriptions, at distances proportional to the actual distances from the end; and then trying to find corresponding characters among the hieroglyphics of the first inscription, by varying the obliquity of the ruler, so as to correspond to all possible lengths which that inscription can be supposed to have occupied, allowing always a certain latitude for the variations of the comparative lengths of the different phrases and expressions. By these steps it is not very difficult to assure ourselves, that a *shrine* and a *priest* are denoted by representations which must have been intended for pictures of objects denoted by them; and this appears to be the precise point of the investigation at which it becomes completely demonstrative, and promises a substantial foundation for further inferences. The other terms, *god* and *king,* are still more easily ascertained, from their situation near the name of Ptolemy.

Appendix

Encyclopedias

Anyone reading this book probably likes encyclopedias. To learn all about them, consult the current edition under "Encyclopaedias" and "Dictionaries." The first section on encyclopedias alone comprises twenty pages and is the work of Robert L. Collison and Warren E. Preece. Mr. Collison (1914–1989) was Emeritus Professor of Library Sciences and Information Studies, University of California, Los Angeles. Mr. Preece (1921–) is a member of the Britannica*'s Board of Editors and was its vice-chairman, 1975–1979, serving as editor 1964–1975.*

The following excerpt is taken from the first section, and deals with the nature of encyclopedias and with encyclopedias in general. The full article continues with a discussion of the various types of encyclopedias and their history in the West and East.

For more than 2,000 years encyclopaedias have existed as summaries of scholarship in forms comprehensible to their readers. The word encyclopaedia, of Greek origin (*enkyklopaideia*), at first meant a circle or a complete system of learning; that is, an all-round education. When Rabelais used the term in French for the first time in *Pantagruel* (chapter 20), he was still talking of education. Paul Scalich, a German writer and compiler, was the first to use the word to describe a book in the title of his *Encyclopaedia; seu, orbis disciplinarum, tam sacrarum quam prophanum epistemon . . .* ("Encyclopaedia; or Knowledge of the World of Disciplines, Not Only Sacred but Profane . . ."), issued at Basel in 1559. The many encyclopaedias that had been published prior to this time had either been given fanciful titles (*Hortus deliciarum*, "Garden of Delights") or had been simply called "dictionary." The word dictionary has been widely used as a name for encyclopaedias, and Scalich's pioneer use of "encyclopaedia" did not find general acceptance until Denis Diderot made it fashionable with his historic French encyclopaedia, although "cyclopaedia" was then becoming fairly popular as an alternative term.

The meaning of the word encyclopaedia has changed considerably during its long history. Today most people think of an encyclopaedia as a multivolume compendium of all available knowledge, complete with maps and a very detailed index, as well as numerous adjuncts such as bibliographies, illustrations, lists of abbreviations and foreign expressions, gazetteers, and so on. They expect it to include biographies of the great men and women of the present as well as those of the past, and they take it for granted that the alphabetically arranged contents will have been written in their own language by many people and will have been edited by a highly skilled and scholarly staff. Yet not one of these ingredients has remained the same throughout the ages. Encyclopaedias have come in all sizes from a single 200-page volume written by one man to giant sets of 100 volumes or more. The degree of coverage of knowledge has varied according to the time and country of publication. Illustrations, atlases, and bibliographies have been omitted from many encyclopaedias, and for a long time it was not thought fitting to include biographies of living persons. Indexes are a late addition, and most of the early ones were useless. Alphabetical arrangement was as strongly opposed as the use of any language but Latin, at least in the first 1,000 years of publication in the West, and skilled group editorship has a history of scarcely 200 years.

In this article the word encyclopaedia has been taken to include not only the great general encyclopaedias of the past and the present but all types of works that claim to provide in an orderly arrangement the essence of "all that is known" on a subject or a group of subjects. This includes dictionaries of philosophy and of American history as well as volumes such as *The World*

Almanac and Book of Facts, which is really a kind of encyclopaedia of current information.

An outline of the scope and history of encyclopaedias is essentially a guide to the story of the development of scholarship, for encyclopaedias stand out as landmarks throughout the centuries, recording much of what was known at the time of publication. Many homes have no encyclopaedia at all, very few have more than one, yet in the past 2,000 years at least 2,000 encyclopaedias have been issued in various parts of the world, and some of these have had many editions. No library has copies of them all; if it were possible to collect them they would occupy some two miles of shelf space. But they are worth preserving—even those that appear to be hopelessly out-of-date—for they contain many contributions by a large number of the world's leaders and scholars.

The Nature of Encyclopaedias

In the *Speculum majus* ("The Greater Mirror"; completed 1244), one of the most important of all encyclopaedias, the French medieval scholar Vincent of Beauvais maintained not only that his work should be perused but that the ideas it recorded should be taken to heart and imitated. Alluding to a secondary sense of the word *speculum* ("mirror"), he implied that his book showed the world what it is and what it should become. This theme, that encyclopaedias can contribute significantly to the improvement of mankind, recurs constantly throughout their long history. A Catalan ecclesiastic and scholastic philosopher, Ramon Llull, regarded the 13th-century encyclopaedias, together with language and grammar, as instruments for the pursuit of truth. Domenico Bandini, an Italian humanist, planned his *Fons memorabilium universi* ("The Source of Noteworthy Facts of the Universe") at the beginning of the 15th century to provide accurate information on any subject to educated men who lacked books and to give edifying lessons to guide them in their lives. Francis Bacon believed that the intellect of the 17th-century individual could be refined by contact with the intellect of the ideal man. Another Englishman, the poet and critic Samuel Taylor Coleridge, was well aware of this point of view and said in his "Preliminary Treatise on Method" (1817) that in the *Encyclopaedia Metropolitana,* which he was proposing to create, "our great objects are to exhibit the Arts and Sciences in their Philosophical harmony; to teach Philosophy in union with Morals; and to sustain Morality by Revealed Religion." He added that he intended to convey methodically "the pure and unsophisticated knowledge of the past . . . to aid the progress of the future." The Society for the Diffusion of Useful Knowledge declared in *The Penny Cyclopaedia* (1833–43) that, although most encyclopaedias attempted to form systems of knowledge, their own would in addition endeavour to "give such general views of all great branches of knowledge, as may help to the formation of just ideas on their extent and relative importance, and to point out the best sources of complete information."

In *De disciplinis* ("On the Disciplines"; 1531) the Spanish humanist Juan Luis Vives emphasized the encyclopaedia's role in the pursuit of truth. In Germany of the early 19th century the encyclopaedia was expected to provide the right or necessary knowledge for good society. Probably the boldest claim was that of Alexander Aitchison, that his new *Encyclopaedia Perthensis* (1796–1806) was intended to supersede the use of all other English books of reference.

All these ideas were a far cry from the Greek concept, deriving from Plato, that in order to think better it is necessary to know all, and from the Roman attitude of the advisability of acquiring all useful knowledge in order to carry out one's tasks in life competently. The present concept of the encyclopaedia as an essential starting point from which one can embark on a voyage of discovery, or as a point of basic reference on which one can always rely, is little more than two centuries old.

The alphabetically arranged encyclopaedia has a history of less than 1,000 years, most of the encyclopaedias issued before the introduction of printing into Europe having been arranged in a methodical or classified form. The early compilers of encyclopaedias held, as Coleridge was to hold, that "To call a huge unconnected miscellany of the *omne scibile,* in an arrangement determined by the accident of initial letters, an encyclopaedia, is the impudent ignorance of your Presbyterian bookmakers!" Today several encyclopaedias still retain the classified form of arrangement.

There has never been any general agreement on the way in which the contents of an encyclopaedia should be arranged. In Roman times the approach was usually practical, with everyday topics such as astronomy and geography coming first, while the fine arts were relegated to the end of the work. The Roman statesman and writer Cassiodorus, however, in his 6th-century *Institutiones,* began with the Scriptures and the church and gave only brief attention to such subjects as arithmetic and geometry. St. Isidore of Seville, educated in the classical tradition, redressed the balance in the next century in his *Etymologiarum sive originum libri XX* ("Twenty Books on Origins, or Etymologies"), commonly called *Etymologiae,* giving pride of place to the liberal arts and medicine, the Bible and the church coming later, but still preceding such subjects as agriculture and warfare, shipping and furniture. The earliest recorded Arabic encyclopaedia, compiled by the Arab philologist and historian Ibn Qutayba, had a completely different approach, beginning with power, war, and nobility, and ending with food and women. A later Persian encyclopaedia, compiled in 975–997 by the Persian scholar and statesman al-Khwārizmī, started with jurisprudence and scholastic philosophy, the more practical matters of medicine, geometry, and mechanics being relegated to a second group labelled "foreign knowledge." The general trend in classification in the Middle Ages is exemplified by Vincent of Beauvais's *Speculum majus,* which was arranged in three sections: "Naturale"—God, the creation, man; "Doctrinale"—language, ethics, crafts, medicine; "Historiale"—world history. The encyclopaedists were, however, still uncertain of the logical sequence of subjects, and although there were many who started with theological matters, there were just as many who preferred to put practical topics first.

A turning point came with Francis Bacon's plan for his uncompleted *Instauratio magna* ("Great Instauration"; 1620) in which he eschewed the endless controversies in favour of a three-section structure, including "External Nature" (covering such topics as astronomy, meteorology, geography, and species of minerals, vegetables, and animals), "Man" (covering anatomy, physiology, structure and powers, and actions), and "Man's Action on Nature" (including medicine, chemistry, the visual arts, the senses, the emotions, the intellectual faculties, architecture, transport, printing, agriculture, navigation, arithmetic, and numerous other subjects).

In his plan Bacon had achieved more than a thoroughly scientific and acceptable arrangement of the contents of an encyclopaedia; he had ensured that the encyclopaedists would have a comprehensive outline of the scope of human knowledge that would operate as a checklist to prevent the omission of whole fields of human thought and endeavour. Bacon so profoundly altered the editorial policy of encyclopaedists that even 130 years later Diderot gratefully acknowledged his debt in the prospectus (1750) of the *Encyclopédie*. Because every later encyclopaedia was influenced by Diderot's work, the guidance of Bacon still plays its part today.

Coleridge, who was very much impressed by Bacon's scheme, in 1817 drew up a rather different table of arrangement for the *Encyclopaedia Metropolitana*. It comprised five main classes: Pure Sciences—Formal (philology, logic, mathematics) and Real (metaphysics, morals, theology); Mixed and Applied Sciences—Mixed (mechanics, hydrostatics, pneumatics, optics, astronomy) and Applied (experimental philosophy, the fine arts, the useful arts, natural history, application of natural history); Biographical and Historical, chronologically arranged; Miscellaneous and Lexicographical, a gazetteer, and a philosophical and etymological lexicon. The fifth class was to be an analytical index.

Although Coleridge's classification was altered by the publisher, and although the *Metropolitana* was an impressive failure, the ideas for it had a lasting influence. Even though nearly all encyclopaedias today are arranged alphabetically, the classifications of Bacon and Coleridge still enable editors to plan their work with regard to an assumed hierarchy of the various branches of human knowledge.

The concept of alphabetical order was well known to both the Greeks and Romans, but the latter made little use of it. Neither the Greeks nor the Romans employed it for encyclopaedia arrangement, with the exception of Sextus Pompeius Festus in his 2nd-century *De verborum significatu* ("On the

Meaning of Words"). St. Isidore's encyclopaedia was classified, but it included an alphabetically arranged etymological dictionary. The 10th- or 11th-century encyclopaedic dictionary known as *Suidas* was the first such work to be completely arranged alphabetically, but it had no influence on succeeding encyclopaedias, although glossaries, when included, were so arranged. Bandini's *Fons memorabilium universi* ("The Source of Noteworthy Facts of the Universe"), though classified, used separate alphabetical orders for more than a quarter of its sections, and the Italian Domenico Nani Mirabelli's *Polyanthea nova* ("The New Polyanthea"; 1503) was arranged in one alphabetical sequence. These were rare exceptions, however; the real breakthrough came only with the considerable number of encyclopaedic Latin-language dictionaries that appeared in the early 16th century, the best known of which is a series of publications by the French printer Charles Estienne. The last of the great Latin-language encyclopaedias arranged in alphabetical order was *Encyclopaedia* (1630) by the German Protestant theologian and philosopher Johann Heinrich Alsted. The publication of *Le Grand Dictionnaire historique* ("The Great Historical Dictionary"; 1674) of Louis Moréri, a French Roman Catholic priest and scholar, confirmed public preference both for the vernacular and the alphabetically arranged encyclopaedia; this choice was emphasized by the success of the posthumous *Dictionnaire universel* (1690) by the French lexicographer Antoine Furetière.

From time to time important attempts have been made to reestablish the idea of the superiority of the classified encyclopaedia. Coleridge saw the encyclopaedia as a vehicle for enabling man to think methodically. He felt that his philosophical arrangement would "present the circle of knowledge in its harmony" and give a "unity of design and of elucidation." He did agree that his appended gazetteer and English dictionary would best be arranged alphabetically for ease of reference. By then, however, alphabetical arrangement had too strong a hold, and it was not until 1935 that a new major classified encyclopaedia began to appear—the *Encyclopédie française* ("French Encyclopaedia"), founded by Anatole de Monzie. The Dutch *Eerste nederlandse systematisch ingerichte encyclopaedie* ("First Dutch Systematic and Comprehensive Encyclopaedia"; 1946–52) has a classification that is in almost reverse order of that of the *Encyclopédie française,* but it is clear that behind both works lies a philosophical concept of the order and main divisions of knowledge that is influenced by both Bacon and Coleridge. The Spanish *Enciclopedia labor* (1955–60) and the *Oxford Junior Encyclopaedia* (1948–56) follow systems of arrangement that are closer to the French than to the Dutch example.

From earliest times it had been held that the trivium (grammar, logic, rhetoric) and the quadrivium (geometry, arithmetic, astronomy, music) were essential ingredients in any encyclopaedia. Even as late as 1435 Alfonso de la Torre began his *Visiõ delectable* in almost that exact order, and only when he had laid these foundations did he proceed to the problems of science, philosophy, theology, law, and politics. Thus the seven liberal arts were regarded by the early encyclopaedists as the very mathematics of human knowledge, without a knowledge of which it would be foolish to proceed. This idea survived to a certain extent in Coleridge's classification; he stated that grammar and logic provide the rules of speech and reasoning, while mathematics opens mankind to truths that are applicable to external existence.

When Louis Shores became editor in chief of *Collier's Encyclopedia* in 1962, he said that he considered the encyclopaedia to be "one of the few generalizing influences in a world of overspecialization. It serves to recall that knowledge has unity." This echoes the view of the English novelist H.G. Wells, that the encyclopaedia should not be "a miscellany, but a concentration, a clarification and a synthesis." The Austrian sociologist Otto Neurath in the same year suggested that a proposed new international encyclopaedia of unified science should be constructed like an onion, the different layers enclosing the "heart"—comprising in this case the foundations of the unity of science.

Even a brief survey of contemporary encyclopaedia publishing is enough to make clear that, as the trivium and quadrivium and the topically classified encyclopaedias that they influenced receded further and further into history, there arose a number of modern encyclopaedists concerned with the importance of making a restatement of the unity of knowledge and of the consequent interdependence of its parts. Though most encyclopaedists were willing to accept the essential reference-book function of encyclopaedias and the role of an alphabetical organization in carrying out that function, they became increasingly disturbed about the emphasis on the fragmentation of knowledge that such a function and such an organization encouraged. A number looked for ways of enhancing the educational function of encyclopaedias by reclaiming for them some of the values of the classified or topical organizations of earlier history.

Notable among the results of such activities was the 15th edition of *Encyclopaedia Britannica* (1974), which was designed in large part to enhance the role of an encyclopaedia in education and understanding without detracting from its role as a reference book. Its three parts (*Propaedia,* or *Outline of Knowledge; Micropaedia,* or *Ready Reference and Index;* and *Macropaedia,* or *Knowledge in Depth*) represented an effort to design an entire set on the understanding that there is a circle of learning and that an encyclopaedia's short informational articles on the details of matter within that circle as well as its long articles on general topics must all be planned and prepared in such a way as to reflect their relation to one another and to the whole of knowledge. The *Propaedia* specifically was a reader's version of the circle of learning on which the set had been based and was organized in such a way that a reader might reassemble in meaningful ways material that the accident of alphabetization had dispersed.

Encyclopaedias in General

The Role of Encyclopaedias. Of the various types of reference works —who's whos, dictionaries, atlases, gazetteers, directories, and so forth—the encyclopaedia is the only one that can be termed self-contained. Each of the others conveys some information concerning every item it deals with; only the encyclopaedia attempts to provide coverage over the whole range of knowledge, and only the encyclopaedia attempts to offer a comprehensive summary of what is known of each topic considered. To this end it employs many features that can help in its task, including pictures, maps, diagrams, charts, and statistical tables. It also frequently incorporates other types of reference works. Several modern encyclopaedias, from the time of Abraham Rees's *New*

Cyclopaedia (1802–20) and the *Encyclopédie méthodique* ("Systematic Encyclopaedia"; 1782–1832) onward, have included a world atlas and a gazetteer, and language dictionaries have been an intermittent feature of encyclopaedias for most of their history.

Most modern encyclopaedias since the *Universal-Lexicon* (1732–50) of the Leipzig bookseller Johann Heinrich Zedler have included biographical material concerning living persons, though the first edition of *Encyclopaedia Britannica* (1768–71) had no biographical material at all. In their treatment of this kind of information they differ, however, from the form of reference work that limits itself to the provision of salient facts without comment. Similarly, with dictionary material, some encyclopaedias—such as the great Spanish "Espasa" (1905 to date)—provide foreign-language equivalents as well.

An English lexicographer, Henry Watson Fowler, wrote in the preface to the first edition (1911) of *The Concise Oxford Dictionary of Current English* that a dictionary is concerned with the uses of words and phrases and with giving information about the things for which they stand only so far as current use of the words depends upon knowledge of those things. The emphasis in an encyclopaedia is much more on the nature of the things for which the words and phrases stand. Thus the encyclopaedic dictionary, whose history extends as far back as the 10th- or 11th-century *Suidas,* forms a convenient bridge between the dictionary and the encyclopaedia, in that it combines the essential features of both, embellishing them where necessary with pictures or diagrams, at the same time that it reduces most entries to a few lines that can provide a rapid but accurate introduction to the subject.

INTERRELATIONS. An encyclopaedia does not come into being by itself. Each new work builds on the experience and contents of its predecessors. In many cases the debt is acknowledged: the German publisher Friedrich Arnold Brockhaus bought up the bankrupt encyclopaedia of Gotthelf Renatus Löbel in 1808 and converted it into his famous *Conversations-Lexikon;* but Jesuits adapted Antoine Furetière's *Dictionnaire universel* without acknowledgment in their *Dictionnaire de Trévoux* (1704). Classical writers made many references to their predecessors' efforts and often incorporated whole passages from other encyclopaedias. Of all the many examples, the *Cyclopaedia* (1728) of the English encyclopaedist Ephraim Chambers has been outstanding in its influence, for Diderot's and Rees's encyclopaedias would have been very different if Chambers had not demonstrated what a modern encyclopaedia could be. In turn, the publication of *Encyclopaedia Britannica* was stimulated by the issue of the *Encyclopédie.* Almost every subsequent move in encyclopaedia making is thus directly traceable to Chambers' pioneer work.

Readership. Encyclopaedia makers have usually envisaged the particular public they addressed. Cassiodorus wrote for the "instruction of simple and unpolished brothers"; the Roman statesman Cato wrote for the guidance of his son; Gregor Reisch, prior of the Carthusian monastery of Freiburg, addressed himself to "Ingenuous Youth"; the Franciscan encyclopaedist Bartholomaeus Anglicus wrote for *ordinary* people; the German professor Johann Christoph Wagenseil wrote for children; and Herrad of Landsberg, abbess of Hohenburg, wrote for her nuns. *Encyclopaedia Britannica* is designed for the use of the curious and intelligent layman. The editor of *The Columbia Encyclopedia* in 1935 tried to provide a work compact enough and simply enough written to serve as a guide to the "young Abraham Lincoln." The Jesuit Michael Pexenfelder (1670) made his intended audience clear enough by writing his *Apparatus Eruditionis* ("Apparatus of Learning") in the form of a series of conversations between teacher and pupil. St. Isidore addressed himself to the needs not only of his former pupils in the episcopal school but also to all the priests and monks for whom he was responsible. At the same time, he tried to provide the newly converted population of Spain with a national culture that would enable it to hold its own in the Byzantine world.

Contributors. In sympathy with many of their various ends, many scholars have contributed to encyclopaedias. Not all their contributions are known because, until recently, it was not the custom to sign articles. Even today there is what amounts to partial concealment in that articles are often initialled only, and, although a key is provided, few readers look up the writer's identity. It is known, however, that the English encyclopaedist John Harris enlisted the help of such scientists as John Ray and Sir Isaac Newton for his *Lexicon Technicum* (1704) and that Rees's *New Cyclopaedia* (1802–20) included articles on music by the English organist and music historian Charles Burney and on botany by the English botanist Sir J.E. Smith. Illustrious Frenchmen such as Voltaire, Rousseau, Condorcet, Montesquieu, and Georges Boulanger contributed to the *Encyclopédie;* the writer and statesman Thomas Macaulay, the Russian-born jurist and medieval historian Sir Paul Vinogradoff, and the Czech statesman Tomáš Masaryk to the *Britannica;* the Scottish physicist Sir David Brewster and the Danish physicist Hans Christian Ørsted to *The Edinburgh Encyclopaedia* (1808–30); the English astronomer Sir William Herschel and the English mathematician and mechanical genius Charles Babbage to the *Metropolitana;* the Russian Communist leader Lenin to the "Granat" encyclopaedia; and the dictator Benito Mussolini to the *Enciclopedia italiana.*

LANGUAGE. The language of Western encyclopaedias was almost exclusively Latin up to the time of the first printed works. As with most scholarly writings, the use of Latin was advantageous because it made works available internationally on a wide scale and thus promoted unlimited sharing of information. On the other hand, it made the contents of encyclopaedias inaccessible to the great majority of people. Consequently, there was from the early days on a movement to translate the more important encyclopaedias into various vernaculars. Honorius Inclusus' *Imago mundi* ("Image of the World"; *c.* 1122) was rendered into French, Italian, and Spanish; Bartholomaeus Anglicus' *De proprietatibus rerum* ("On the Characteristics of Things"; 1220–40) into English; the Dominican friar Thomas de Cantimpré's *De natura rerum* ("On the Nature of Things"; *c.* 1228–44) into Flemish and German; and Vincent of Beauvais's *Speculum majus* ("The Greater Mirror") into French, Spanish, German, Dutch, and Catalan. In later years the more successful encyclopaedias were translated from one vernacular into another. Moréri's encyclopaedia, *Le Grand Dictionnaire historique,* was translated into both English and German. The German *Brockhaus* appeared in a Russian translation (1890–1907), and the French *Petit Larousse* had several foreign-language editions. Nevertheless, an encyclopaedia, however successful in its own country, may find acceptance in another country far from easy, because each nation appears to have its own very individual concept of what an encyclopaedia should comprise.

THE CONTEMPORARY WORLD. Encyclopaedias have often reflected fairly accurately the civilization in which they appeared; that this was deliberate is shown by the frequency with which the earlier compilers included such words as *speculum* ("mirror"), *imago* ("image"), and so forth in their titles. Thus as early as the 2nd century the Greek sophist Julius Pollux was already defining current technical terms in his *Onomastikon*. In the 13th century Vincent of Beauvais quoted the ideas of both pagan and Christian philosophers freely and without differentiation, for their statements often agreed on questions of morals. In doing so, he reflected the rapidly widening horizons of a period that saw the founding of so many universities. Bartholomaeus Anglicus devoted a considerable part of his work to psychology and medicine. "Theophilus" (thought to be Roger of Helmarshausen, a Benedictine monk) as early as the 12th century gave a clear and practical account in his *De diversis artibus* ("On Diverse Arts") of contemporary processes used in painting, glassmaking and decoration, metalworking, bone carving, and the working of precious stones, even listing the necessary tools and conditions for successful operations. Pierre Bayle, a French philosopher and critic, showed in his *Dictionnaire historique et critique* ("Historical and Critical Dictionary"; 1697) how the scientific renaissance of the previous 40 years had revolutionized contemporary thought. To every detail he applied a mercilessly scientific and inquiring mind that challenged the assumptions and blind reverence for authority that had characterized most of his predecessors.

At that point in history, much attention was being paid to practical matters: the statesman Jean-Baptiste Colbert himself directed the French Académie des Sciences (1675) to produce a work that eventually appeared as the *Description et perfection des arts et métiers* ("Description and Perfection of the Arts and Crafts"; 1761). The German Meyer's *Grosses Conversations-Lexicon* from the first edition (1840–55) onward paid particular attention to scientific and technical developments, and the *Encyclopedia Americana,* aided by the *Scientific American,* strengthened its coverage in this area from 1911 onward. In its very first edition the *Encyclopaedia Britannica* included lengthy articles containing detailed instructions on such topics as surgery, bookkeeping, and many aspects of farming. Similarly, Abraham Rees had been including articles on subjects such as candle making and coachbuilding earlier in the century. The outstanding example of a completely contemporary encyclopaedia was, of course, the

Encyclopédie, in which the philosopher Denis Diderot and the mathematician and philosopher Jean Le Rond d'Alembert and their friends set out to reject much of the heritage of the past in favour of the scientific discoveries and the more advanced thought of their own age. Their decision in this respect was both intellectually and commercially successful; since that time every edition of any good encyclopaedia has the additional merit of being a valuable source for the thought and attitudes of the world for which it was published.

ENCYCLOPAEDIAS AND POLITICS. All great encyclopaedia makers have tried to be truthful and to present a balanced picture of civilization as they knew it, although it is probable that no encyclopaedia is totally unbiassed. A great encyclopaedia is inevitably a sign of national maturity and, as such, will pay tribute to the ideals of its country and its times. The first Hungarian encyclopaedia, János Apáczai Csere's *Magyar encyclopaedia* (1653–55), was mostly a summary of what was available in foreign works, but the *Révai nagy lexikona* ("Révai's Great Lexicon"; 1911–35) was a handsome tribute to Hungary's emergence as a country in its own right, just as the *Enciklopedija Jugoslavije* (1955–) is a prestige work that does full justice to the advances made by Yugoslavia in the mid-20th century. The supreme example of an encyclopaedia that set out to present the best possible image of its people and the wealth and stature of their culture is undoubtedly the *Enciclopedia italiana* (1929–36). Mussolini's contribution of an article on Fascism indicates the extent to which the work might be regarded as an ideological tool, but, in fact, the bulk of its contents is admirably international and objective in approach. The various Soviet encyclopaedias already occupy many feet of shelf space, and the later editions each devote one complete volume to the Soviet Union in all its aspects. Though successive editions have been notable for the obvious political factors that have been responsible for the inclusion and exclusion of entries for famous nationals according to the current state of their acceptance or condemnation by the existing regime, many critics have felt that the newest edition, the first volume of which was issued in 1970, is maturer than any of the others in this regard.

Diderot, the editor, and André-François Le Breton, the publisher, faced such opposition from both church and state in their publication of the *Ency-*

clopédie (1751–65) that many of the volumes were secretly printed, and the last 10 were issued with a false imprint. In the early part of the 19th century, *Brockhaus* was condemned by the Austrian censor, and in 1950 its 11th edition was branded as reactionary by the East German government. Nor was political censorship the only form of oppression in the world of encyclopaedias. Antoine Furetière, on issuing his prospectus (1675) for his *Dictionnaire universel,* found his privilege to publish cancelled by the French government at the request of the Académie Française, which accused him of plagiarizing its own dictionary. The Leipzig book trade, fearing that publication of Johann Heinrich Zedler's huge *Universal-Lexikon* (1732–50) might put them out of business, made such difficulties that Zedler thought it best to issue his work in Halle.

THE READER'S NEEDS. People look to encyclopaedias to give them an adequate introduction to a topic that interests them. Many expect the encyclopaedia to omit nothing and to include consideration of all controversial aspects of a subject. Encyclopaedia makers of the past assumed that there was a large public willing to read through an entire encyclopaedia if it was not too large. In the 18th century, for example, there was a good market for pocket-size compendia for the traveller, or for the courtier to browse in as he waited for an audience. Thus, although most encyclopaedias are multivolume works, there are many small works ranging from the *Didascalion* of the scholastic philosopher and mystic theologian Hugh of Saint-Victor (*c.* 1128), through Gregor Reisch's *Margarita philosophica* (1496) and the French writer Pons-Augustin Alletz' *Petite Encyclopédie* (1766), to C.T. Watkins' *Portable Cyclopaedia* (1817). The last was issued by a remarkable publisher, Sir Richard Phillips, who realized the great demand for pocket-size compendia and drove a thriving trade in issuing a number of these; he is thought to have written large sections of these himself.

ROYALTY AND ENCYCLOPAEDIAS. Most of the classic Chinese encyclopaedias owe their existence to the patronage of emperors. In the West, the Roman scholar Pliny dedicated his *Historia naturalis* ("Natural History") to the emperor Titus; Julius Pollux dedicated his *Onomastikon* to his former pupil, the Roman emperor Commodus, while the Byzantine philosopher and politician Michael Psellus dedicated his *De omnifaria doctrina* ("On All Sorts of Teaching") to his former pupil the emperor Michael VII Ducas, ruler of the Eastern Roman Empire. Gervase of Tilbury, an English ecclesiastic, compiled his *Otia imperialia* ("Imperial Pastimes") for the Holy Roman emperor Otto IV, and Alfonso de la Torre prepared his *Visiõ delectable* for Prince Carlos of Viana. St. Isidore dedicated his encyclopaedia to the Visigothic king Sisebut, and the French king Louis IX patronized Vincent of Beauvais's *Speculum majus*. Nor did kings eschew the work of compiling encyclopaedias. The emperor Constantine VII of the Eastern Roman Empire was responsible for a series of encyclopaedias, and Alfonso X of Spain organized the making of the *Grande e general estoria* ("Great and General History").

CONTENTS AND AUTHORITY. The extent to which readers have been dependent on editorial decisions concerning not only what to include but also what to exclude has yet to be explored in detail. For example, Vincent of Beauvais rarely mentioned the pagan and Christian legends that were so popular in his day. The anonymous compiler of the scholarly *Compendium philosophiae* ("Compendium of Philosophy"; *c.* 1316) was careful to omit the credulous tales that appeared in contemporary bestiaries. For many centuries it was not considered right to include biographies of men and women who were still alive. And the early Romans, such as Cato the Censor, rejected much of Greek theoretical knowledge, regarding it as a dangerous foreign influence and believing with the Stoics that wisdom consisted in living according to nature's precepts.

Whatever the compiler did decide to include had a far-reaching influence. Pliny's vast *Historia naturalis* has survived intact because for so many centuries it symbolized human knowledge, and even the "old wives' tales" it injudiciously included were unquestioningly copied into many later encyclopaedias. The influence of St. Isidore's work can be traced in writings as late as Sir John Mandeville's travels (published in French between 1357 and 1371) and the English poet John Gower's 14th-century *Confessio amantis* ("A Lover's Confession"). Honorius' *Imago mundi* is known to have influenced some of the German medieval chronicles and the Norse saga of Olaf Tryggvason. The main source of classics such as the *Roman de la rose,* the Alexander romances, Archbishop Giovanni da Colonna's *Liber de viris illustribus* ("Book Concerning Illustrious Men"), and the recorded lives of the saints can be traced to the *Speculum majus.* The direct and indirect influence of the critical encyclopaedias of Pierre Bayle and Denis Diderot is, of course, incalculable.

The Cyclopeedy

Havin' lived next door to the Hobart place f'r goin' on thirty years, I calc'late that I know jest about ez much about the case ez anybody else now on airth, exceptin' perhaps it's ol' Jedge Baker, and he's so plaguy old 'nd so powerful feeble that *he* don't know nothin'.

It seems that in the spring uv '47—the year that Cy Watson's oldest boy wuz drownded in West River—there come along a book-agent sellin' volyumes 'nd tracks f'r the diffusion uv knowledge, 'nd havin' got the recommend of the minister 'nd uv the selectmen, he done an all-fired big business in our part uv the county. His name wuz Lemuel Higgins, 'nd he wuz ez likely a talker ez I ever heerd, barrin' Lawyer Conkey, 'nd everybody allowed that when Conkey wuz round he talked so fast that the town pump 'u'd have to be greased every twenty minutes.

One of the first uv our folks that this Lemuel Higgins struck wuz Leander Hobart. Leander had jest marr'd one uv the Peasley girls, 'nd had moved into the old homestead on the Plainville road,—old Deacon Hobart havin' give up the place to him, the other boys havin' moved out West (like a lot o' darned fools that they wuz!). Leander wuz feelin' his oats jest about this time, 'nd nuthin' wuz too good f'r him.

"Hattie," sez he, "I guess I 'll have to lay in a few books f'r readin' in the winter time, 'nd I 've half a notion to subscribe f'r a cyclopeedy. Mr.

Higgins here says they're invalerable in a family, and that we orter have 'em, bein' as how we 're likely to have the fam'ly bime by."

"Lor's sakes, Leander, how you talk!" sez Hattie, blushin' all over, ez brides allers does to heern tell uv sich things.

Waal, to make a long story short, Leander bargained with Mr. Higgins for a set uv them cylopeedies, 'nd he signed his name to a long printed paper that showed how he agreed to take a cyclopeedy oncet in so often, which wuz to be ez often ez a new one uv the volyumes wuz printed. A cyclopeedy is n't printed all at oncet, because that would make it cost too much; consekently the man that gets it up has it strung along fur apart, so as to hit folks oncet every year or two, and gin'rally about harvest time. So Leander kind uv liked the idee, and he signed the printed paper 'nd made his affidavit to it afore Jedge Warner.

The fust volyume of the cyclopeedy stood on a shelf in the old seckertary in the settin'-room about four months before they had any use f'r it. One night 'Squire Turner's son come over to visit Leander 'nd Hattie, and they got to talkin' about apples, 'nd the sort uv apples that wuz the best. Leander allowed that the Rhode Island greenin' wuz the best, but Hattie and the Turner boy stuck up f'r the Roxbury russet, until at last a happy idee struck Leander, and sez he: "We'll leave it to the cyclopeedy, b'gosh! Whichever one the cyclopeedy sez is the best will settle it."

"But you can't find out nothin' 'bout Roxbury russets nor Rhode Island greenin's in *our* cyclopeedy," sez Hattie.

"Why not, I 'd like to know?" sez Leander, kind uv indignant like.

" 'Cause ours hain't got down to the R yet," sez Hattie. "All ours tells about is things beginnin' with A."

"Well, ain't we talkin' about Apples?" sez Leander. "You aggervate me terrible, Hattie, by insistin' on knowin' what you don't know nothin' 'bout."

Leander went to the seckertary 'nd took down the cyclopeedy 'nd hunted all through it f'r Apples, but all he could find wuz "Apple—See Pomology."

"How in thunder kin I see Pomology," sez Leander, "when there ain't no Pomology to see? Gol durn a cyclopeedy, anyhow!"

And he put the volyume back onto the shelf 'nd never sot eyes into it ag'in.

That 's the way the thing run f'r years 'nd years. Leander would 've gin up the plaguy bargain, but he could n't; he had signed a printed paper 'nd had swore to it afore a justice of the peace. Higgins would have the law on him if he had throwed up the trade.

The most aggervatin' feature uv it all wuz that a new one uv them cussid cyclopeedies wuz allus sure to show up at the wrong time,—when Leander wuz hard up or had jest been afflicted some way or other. His barn burnt down two nights afore the volyume containin' the letter B arrived, and Leander needed all his chink to pay f'r lumber, but Higgins sot back on that affidavit and defied the life out uv him.

"Never mind, Leander," sez his wife, soothin' like, "it's a good book to have in the house, anyhow, now that we've got a baby."

"That's so," sez Leander, "babies does begin with B, don't it?"

You see their fust baby had been born; they named him Peasley,—Peasley Hobart,—after Hattie's folks. So, seein' as how it wuz payin' f'r a book that told about babies, Leander did n't begredge that five dollars so very much after all.

"Leander," sez Hattie one forenoon, "that B cyclopeedy ain't no account. There ain't nothin' in it about babies except 'See Maternity'!"

"Waal, I 'll be gosh durned!" sez Leander. That wuz all he said, and he could n't do nothin' at all, f'r that book-agent, Lemuel Higgins, had the dead wood on him,—the mean, sneakin' critter!

So the years passed on, one of them cyclopeedies showin' up now 'nd then,—sometimes every two years 'nd sometimes every four, but allus at a time when Leander found it pesky hard to give up a fiver. It war n't no use cussin' Higgins; Higgins just laffed when Leander allowed that the cyclopeedy was no good 'nd that he wuz bein' robbed. Meantime Leander's family wuz increasin' and growin'. Little Sarey had the hoopin' cough dreadful one winter, but the cyclopeedy did n't help out at all, 'cause all it said wuz: "Hoopin' Cough—See Whoopin' Cough"—and uv course there war n't no Whoopin' Cough to see, bein' as how the W had n't come yet!

Oncet when Hiram wanted to dreen the home pasture, he went to the cyclopeedy to find out about it, but all he diskivered wuz: "Drain—See Tile." This wuz in 1859, and the cyclopeedy had only got down to G.

The cow wuz sick with lung fever one spell, and Leander laid her dyin' to that cussid cyclopeedy, 'cause when he went to readin' 'bout cows it told him to "See Zoology."

But what's the use uv harrowin' up one's feelin's talkin' 'nd thinkin' about these things? Leander got so after a while that the cyclopeedy did n't worry him at all: he grew to look at it ez one uv the crosses that human critters has to bear without complainin' through this vale uv tears. The only thing that bothered him wuz the fear that mebbe he would n't live to see the last volyume,—to tell the truth, this kind uv got to be his hobby, and I 've heern him talk 'bout it many a time settin' round the stove at the tarvern 'nd squirtin' tobacco juice at the sawdust box. His wife, Hattie, passed away with the yaller janders the winter W come, and all that seemed to reconcile Leander to survivin' her wuz the prospect uv seein' the last volyume of that cyclopeedy. Lemuel Higgins, the book-agent, had gone to his everlastin' punishment; but his son, Hiram, had succeeded to his father's business 'nd continued to visit the folks his old man had roped in. By this time Leander's children had growed up; all on 'em wuz marr'd, and there wuz numeris grandchildren to amuse the ol' gentleman. But Leander wuz n't to be satisfied with the common things uv airth; he did n't seem to take no pleasure in his grandchildren like most men do; his mind wuz allers sot on somethin' else,—for hours 'nd hours, yes, all day long, he'd set out on the front stoop lookin' wistfully up the road for that book-agent to come along with a cyclopeedy. He did n't want to die till he 'd got all the cyclopeedies his contract called for; he wanted to have everything straightened out before he passed away.

When—oh, how well I recollect it—when Y come along he wuz so overcome that he fell over in a fit uv paralysis, 'nd the old gentleman never got over it. For the next three years he drooped 'nd pined, and seemed like he could n't hold out much longer. Finally he had to take to his bed,—he was so old 'nd feeble,—but he made 'em move the bed up ag'inst the winder so he could watch for that last volyume of the cyclopeedy.

The end come one balmy day in the spring uv '87. His life wuz a-ebbin' powerful fast; the minister wuz there, 'nd me, 'nd Dock Wilson, 'nd Jedge Baker, 'nd most uv the fam'ly. Lovin' hands smoothed the wrinkled forehead 'nd breshed back the long, scant, white hair, but the eyes of the dyin' man wuz sot upon that piece uv road down which the cyclopeedy man allus come.

All to oncet a bright 'nd joyful look come into them eyes, 'nd ol' Leander riz up in bed 'nd sez, "It 's come!"

"What is it, Father?" asked his daughter Sarey, sobbin' like.

"Hush," says the minister, solemnly; "he sees the shinin' gates uv the Noo Jerusalum."

"No, no," cried the aged man; "it is the cyclopeedy—the letter Z—it 's comin'!"

And, sure enough! the door opened, and in walked Higgins. He tottered rather than walked, f'r he had growed old 'nd feeble in his wicked perfession.

"Here's the Z cyclopeedy, Mr. Hobart," sez Higgins.

Leander clutched it; he hugged it to his pantin' bosom; then stealin' one pale hand under the piller he drew out a faded banknote 'nd gave it to Higgins.

"I thank Thee for this boon," sez Leander, rollin' his eyes up devoutly; then he gave a deep sigh.

"Hold on," cried Higgins, excitedly, "you 've made a mistake—it is n't the last—"

But Leander did n't hear him—his soul hed fled from its mortal tenement 'nd hed soared rejoicin' to realms uv everlastin' bliss.

"He is no more," sez Dock Wilson, metaphorically.

"Then who are his heirs?" asked that mean critter Higgins.

"We be," sez the family.

"Do you conjointly and severally acknowledge and assume the obligation of deceased to me?" he asked 'em.

"What obligation?" asked Peasley Hobart, stern like.

"Deceased died owin' me f'r a cyclopeedy!" sez Higgins.

"That 's a lie!" sez Peasley. "We all seen him pay you for the Z!"

"But there 's another one to come," sez Higgins.

"Another?" they all asked.

"Yes, the index!" sez he.

So there wuz, and I 'll be eternally gol durned if he ain't a-suin' the estate in the probate court now f'r the price uv it!

—Eugene Field

INDEX

PHYSICAL

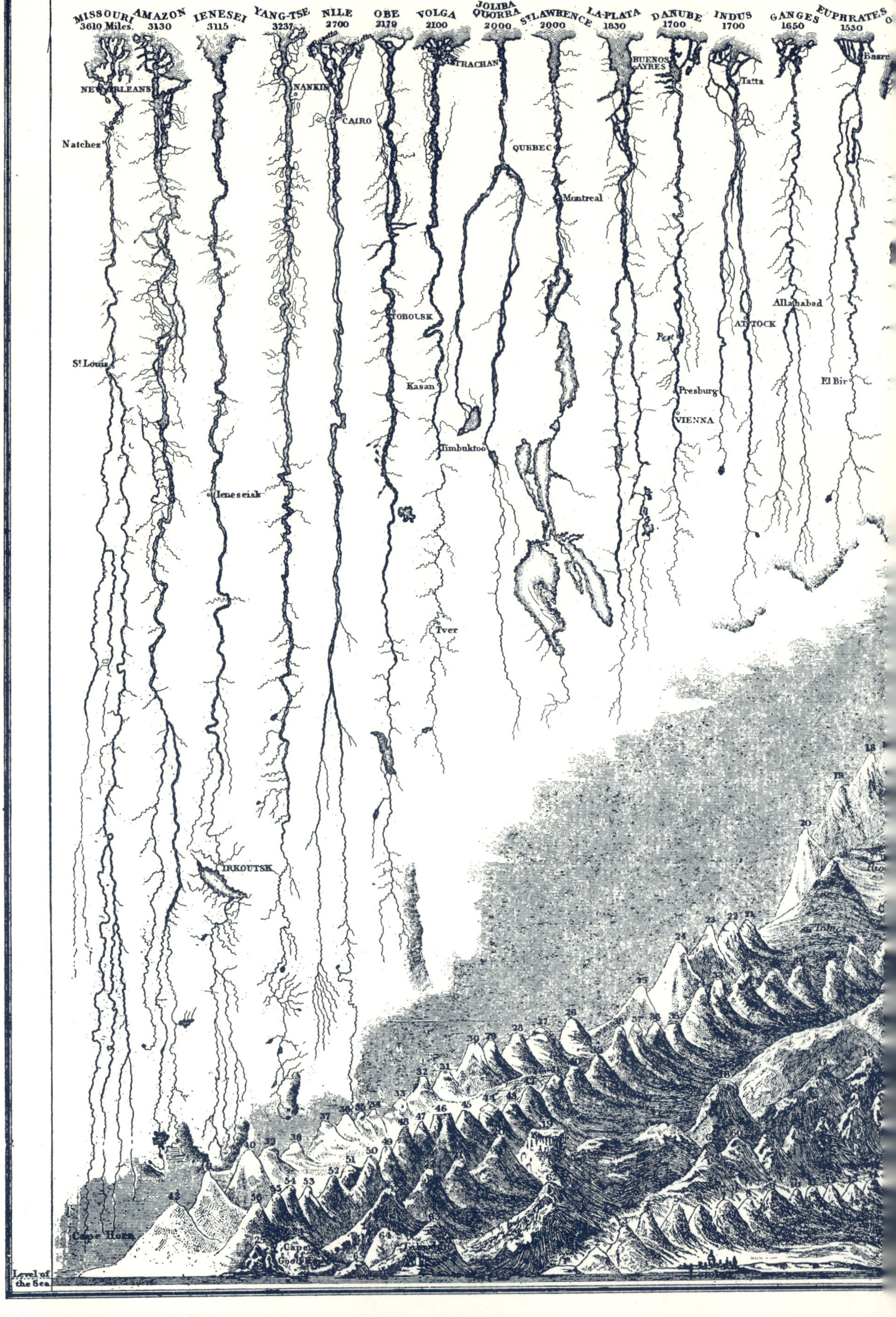
MISSOURI
3610 Miles.
AMAZON
3130
IENESEI
3115
YANG-TSE
3237
NILE
2700
OBE
2179
VOLGA
2100
JOLIBA
QUORRA
2000
St. LAWRENCE
2000
LA-PLATA
1830
DANUBE
1700
INDUS
1700
GANGES
1650
EUPHRATES
1530
NEW ORLEANS
Natchez
St. Louis
NANKIN
CAIRO
ASTRACHAN
QUEBEC
Montreal
BUENOS AYRES
Tatta
TOBOLSK
Kasan
Timbuktoo
Tver
Ieneseiak
IRKOUTSK
Pest
Presburg
VIENNA
ATTOCK
Allahabad
El Bir
Cape Horn
Level of the Sea